W9-AUI-475

Fodor's

FLORENCE
AND TUSCANY

11th Edition

Fodor's Travel Publications   New York, Toronto, London, Sydney, Auckland
www.fodors.com

FODOR'S FLORENCE AND TUSCANY

Writers: Peter Blackman, Patricia Rucidlo, Jonathan Willcocks

Editors: Amanda Theunissen (lead editor), Maria Hart

Production Editor: Carolyn Roth
Maps & Illustrations: Henry Colomb and Mark Stroud, Moon Street Cartography,
David Lindroth, Inc., *cartographers;* Rebecca Baer, *map editor;* William Wu,
information graphics
Design: Fabrizio La Rocca, *creative director*; Tina Malaney, Chie Ushio,
Jessica Walsh, *designers*; Melanie Marin, *associate director of photography;*
Jennifer Romains, *photo research*
Cover Photo: (Replica of "David" by Michelangelo in the Piazza del Signoria, Florence)
Masterfile
Production Manager: Angela L. McLean

11th Edition

ISBN 978-0-307-92925-9

ISSN 1533–1628

SPECIAL SALES

This book is available at special discounts for bulk purchases for sales promotions or
premiums. Special editions, including personalized covers, excerpts of existing books,
and corporate imprints, can be created in large quantities for special needs. For more
information, write to Special Markets/Premium Sales, 1745 Broadway, MD 3-1, New
York, NY 10019, or e-mail specialmarkets@randomhouse.com.

AN IMPORTANT TIP & AN INVITATION

Although all prices, opening times, and other details in this book are based on information supplied to us at press time, changes occur all the time in the travel world, and
Fodor's cannot accept responsibility for facts that become outdated or for inadvertent
errors or omissions. So **always confirm information when it matters,** especially if you're
making a detour to visit a specific place. Your experiences—positive and negative—
matter to us. If we have missed or misstated something, **please write to us.** Share your
opinion instantly through our online feedback center at fodors.com/contact-us.

PRINTED IN SINGAPORE

10 9 8 7 6 5 4 3 2 1

CONTENTS

MAPS

ABOUT THIS BOOK

Our Ratings

At Fodor's, we spend considerable time choosing the best places in a destination so you don't have to. By default, anything we recommend in this book is worth visiting. But some sights, properties, and experiences are so great that we've recognized them with additional accolades. Orange **Fodor's Choice** stars indicate our top recommendations; black stars highlight places we deem **Highly Recommended;** and **Best Bets** call attention to top properties in various categories. Disagree with any of our choices? Care to nominate a new place? Visit our feedback center at www.fodors.com/feedback.

Hotels

Hotels have private bath, phone, TV, and air-conditioning, and do not offer meals unless we specify that in the review. We always list facilities but not whether you'll be charged an extra fee to use them.

> For expanded hotel reviews, visit **Fodors.com**

Restaurants

Unless we state otherwise, restaurants are open for lunch and dinner daily. We mention dress only when there's a specific requirement and reservations only when they're essential or not accepted—it's always best to book ahead.

Credit Cards

We assume that restaurants and hotels accept credit cards. If not, we'll note it in the review.

Budget Well

Hotel and restaurant price categories from ¢ to $$$$ are defined in the opening pages of the respective chapters. For attractions, we always give standard adult admission fees; reductions are usually available for children, students, and senior citizens.

Listings		Hotels & Restaurants	Outdoors
★ Fodor's Choice	✉ E-mail	**Hotels & Restaurants**	**Outdoors**
★ Highly recommended	✆ Admission fee	☒ Hotel	⚐ Golf
⊠ Physical address	⊙ Open/closed times	⤴ Number of rooms	⚊ Camping
✛ Directions or Map coordinates	Ⓜ Metro stations	⚲ Facilities	**Other**
⌖ Mailing address	⊟ No credit cards	ⓘⓞⓘ Meal plans	☺ Family-friendly
☎ Telephone		✕ Restaurant	⇨ See also
🖷 Fax		⚑ Reservations	⊠ Branch address
⊕ On the Web		⚮ Dress code	☞ Take note
		⚊ Smoking	

Experience Florence and Tuscany

WHAT'S NEW

Painting the Town Green

Mayor Matteo Renzi continues on his mission to make Florence "green." In November 2009, he closed the Piazza del Duomo to all vehicular traffic. In summer 2011, he closed additional streets, including the bustling via Tornabuoni and parts of Piazza Pitti. What's resulted is often lovely, pedestrian-only piazze, as well as confusing new traffic patterns and bus routes. Under Renzi's administration, the city has also offered a major water fountain that provides an alternative to bottled water: it's just behind the Neptune Fountain in Piazza della Signoria. Bring your own bottle and fill it up for free.

Controversial Trams

Controversy still swirls around a three-line tram system designed to crisscross Florence. Work started in 2005 and remains unfinished. The only operative line runs entirely aboveground and connects the central Santa Maria Novella train station with Scandicci, a commuter suburb to the southwest. Initially, the tram thoroughly divided Florentines: politically, those opposed were usually center to center right; those for, on the left. Now that one line is operational, Florentines, regardless of political affiliation, have taken to this way of getting from the suburbs to the city with great aplomb. The ticket price is the same as that of the bus.

Florence's New Museum Pass

Serious museumgoers might want to invest €50 in the new Firenze Card (www. firenzecard.it). This allows entrance to most major museums (including the Uffizi and the Accademia), and allows you to skip the lines. It's good for 72 hours once it's activated, and also includes free bus and tram transportation.

Art Closings and Controversy in Florence

In 2011, the Museo Firenze com'Era closed; it will be reborn (at a yet-to-be-determined date) as the Museo Civico.

At press time, a somewhat controversial project to uncover a possible lost fresco by Leonardo da Vinci in the Salone del Cinquecento in Palazzo Vecchio was in the works. Dr. Maurizio Seracini has insisted for many years that this fresco exists under a large painting by Vasari. He has many adherents, and many detractors. Sophisticated imaging began in summer 2011, but work proceeds slowly.

Another artistic controversy is brewing thanks to Mayor Matteo Renzi's suggestion that the long-unfinished facade of the basilica of San Lorenzo be completed according to Michelangelo's early-16th-century design. This would involve a lot of money, as Michelangelo envisioned an all-marble facade.

A major new opera house in Florence was scheduled to be completed by the end of 2012. Unfortunately, funds have run dry. If and when funding is reestablished and the project is completed, Maggio Musicale will abandon Teatro Comunale, where it has staged operas, classical concerts, recitals, and the like for many years, and relocate to the new structure in Piazza Leopoldo—practically a stone's throw away.

FAQS

How likely am I to find English-speaking locals? English is widely spoken, especially in the cities. Odds are if the person you want to speak to doesn't know English, there will be someone within earshot who can translate. Nonetheless, if you pick up a few common phrases in Italian, your effort will be appreciated.

Are Italian drivers as crazy as I've heard? Yes—at least many of them are. When you hit the road, don't be surprised to encounter tailgating and high-risk passing. Your best response is to take the same safety-first approach you use at home; on the road is one place where you don't want to be mistaken for a local. On the plus side, Italy's roads are usually well maintained (though *strade regionali*—local roads—often are not). Note that wearing a seat belt and having your lights on at all times are required by law.

Is it okay to drink cappuccino after 11 am? For most Italians, a frothy cappuccino is a morning thing: drinking milk later in the day is thought to be bad for the stomach. Unless you're trying to pass as a local, there's no reason not to order whatever suits your fancy.

What's the best thing to do with the kids? One tried-and-true way of keeping kids entertained while giving then some exercise is to have them climb a tower. There are plenty of medieval towers to choose from, including the Torre del Mangia in Siena, the Torre Grossa in San Gimignano, the Torre Guigini in Lucca, and the Campanile in Florence—not to mention Brunelleschi's Duomo. Note that the Leaning Tower in Pisa doesn't permit climbers under the age of eight.

Are the Cinque Terre a viable day trip from Florence? Technically it's doable, but we don't recommend it. You'll spend about five hours on the train round-trip, or something close to that if you go by car. And if it's summer and you want to hike the trails (which most people do), you're better off getting started early in the morning so you can beat the heat. The Cinque Terre is a beautiful, one-of-a-kind destination, and it deserves an overnight—but if you're set on a day trip, you're better off starting from Pisa or Lucca.

What's crime like in Florence and the other cities of Tuscany and Umbria? By and large, the cities of the region are remarkably crime-free. The exceptions, unfortunately, are tourist-focused crimes of purse snatching and pickpocketing. It would be an overstatement to say these crimes are rampant, but they do happen somewhat regularly, particularly around train stations, on crowded buses, and at major tourist attractions. They're commonly perpetrated by groups of street kids and by well-dressed professionals looking for easy targets. A little common sense goes a long way toward keeping you safe: if children approach you, don't be reluctant to shoo them away firmly; don't keep your wallet in your back pocket; carry a purse with a shoulder strap, and wear it across your chest, so it can't be separated from you with a simple tug.

WHAT'S WHERE

Numbers refer to chapters.

2 Florence. In the 15th century Florence was at the center of the artistic revolution that would later be known as the Renaissance. Today the Renaissance remains the main reason people come here—the abundance of art treasures is mind-boggling.

3 Northwest Tuscany. West of Florence the main attractions are **Pisa,** home of the Leaning Tower, and **Lucca,** a town with a charming historic center. Farther north and west are snowcapped peaks, thermal waters, and miles of Mediterranean coast, including, across the regional border in Liguria, the **Cinque Terre**—five fishing villages that have become a major destination.

4 Central Tuscany. The hills spreading south from Florence to Siena make up **Chianti,** a region of sublime wine and marvelous views. **Siena,** once Florence's main rival, remains one of Italy's most appealing medieval towns. To its northwest, little **San Gimignano** is famous for its 13th- and 14th-century towers. Farther west still is **Volterra,** a town dating back to the Etruscans.

5 Eastern Tuscany. Arezzo, Tuscany's third-largest city (after Florence and Pisa), has a car-free historic center and a basilica containing beautiful frescoes. **Cortona,** perched on a steep hill with sweeping views, exemplifies an alluringly old-fashioned way of life.

6 Southern Tuscany. In the **Val d'Orcia** the towns of **Montalcino** and **Montepulciano** are surrounded by some of Italy's finest vineyards, and **Pienza** is a unique example of Renaissance urban planning. Farther south is the **Maremma,** Tuscany's cattle-ranching country. Off the coast, the lush island of **Elba** is a popular resort destination.

7 Umbria. Like Tuscany, Umbria has beautiful rolling hills topped by attractive old towns. **Perugia** is Umbria's largest city, but it's far from overwhelming, and it has a well-preserved medieval core. In **Assisi,** birthplace of Saint Francis, the grand basilica draws millions of pilgrims annually. Spoleto is a quiet, elegant hill town, but each summer it brims with activity during the Festival dei Due Mondi. To the east in the Marches region, **Urbino** is famed for its splendid Renaissance palace.

FLORENCE AND TUSCANY PLANNER

Getting Here

Most flights to Tuscany originating in the United States stop either in Rome, London, Paris, or Frankfurt, and then connect to Florence's small **Aeroporto A. Vespucci** (commonly called **Peretola**), or to Pisa's **Aeroporto Galileo Galilei**. The only exception at this writing is Delta's seasonal New York/JFK direct flight to Pisa.

There are several other alternatives for getting to the region. If you want to start your trip in Umbria, it makes sense to fly into Rome's Aeroporto Leonardo da Vinci (commonly called Fiumicino) and rent a car or take the train from Rome's Termini station. The drive to the Umbrian hill town of Orvieto takes an hour and a half, and the train ride is an hour. Another option is to fly to Milan and pick up a connecting Alitalia flight to Pisa, Florence, or Perugia.

What to Pack

In summer, stick with light clothing, as things get steamy in June, July, and August, but throw in a sweater in case of cool evenings, especially if you're headed for the mountains and/or islands. Sunglasses, a hat, and sunblock are essential. In winter, bring a coat, gloves, hats, scarves, and boots. Winter weather is generally milder than in the northern and central United States, but central heating may not be up to your standards, and interiors can be cold and damp; take wools or flannel rather than sheer fabrics. Bring sturdy shoes for winter and comfortable walking shoes in any season.

As a rule, Italians are more particular about dress than Americans are. To their minds, shorts are for the beach or for hiking, not for urban settings. Men aren't required to wear ties or jackets in most places other than some of the grander hotel dining rooms and top-level restaurants, but they are expected to look reasonably sharp—and they do. Formal wear is the exception rather than the rule at the opera nowadays, though people in expensive seats usually do get dressed up.

Modesty of dress (no bare shoulders or knees) is expected of both men and women in all churches, and is strictly enforced in many.

For sightseeing, **pack a pair of binoculars**; they will help you get a good look at poorly lighted ceilings and domes. Best to bring your own soap if you plan to stay in budget hotels.

1

Restaurants: The Basics

A meal in Tuscany and Umbria (and elsewhere in Italy) has traditionally consisted of five courses, and every menu you encounter will still be organized along this five-course plan:

First up is the *antipasto* (appetizer), often consisting of cured meats or marinated vegetables. Next to appear is the *primo*, usually pasta or soup, and after that the *secondo*, a meat or fish course with, perhaps, a *contorno* (vegetable dish) on the side. A simple *dolce* (dessert) rounds out the meal.

This, you've probably noticed, is a lot of food. Italians have noticed as well—a full, five-course meal is an indulgence usually reserved for special occasions. Instead, restaurant meals are a mix-and-match affair: you might order a primo and a secondo, or an antipasto and a primo, or a secondo and a contorno.

The crucial rule of restaurant dining is that you should **order at least two courses.** It's a common mistake for tourists to order only a secondo, thinking they're getting a "main course" complete with side dishes. What they usually wind up with is one lonely piece of meat.

Hotels: The Basics

Hotels in these regions are usually well maintained (especially if they've earned our recommendation in this book), but in some respects they won't match what you find at comparably priced U.S. lodgings. Keep the following points in mind as you set your expectations, and you're likely to have a good experience:

■ First and foremost, rooms are usually smaller, particularly in cities. If you're truly cramped, ask for another room, but don't expect things to be spacious.

■ A "double bed" is usually two singles pushed together.

■ In the bathroom, tubs are not a given—request one if it's essential. In budget places, showers sometimes use a drain in the middle of the bathroom floor.

■ Most hotels have satellite TV, but there are fewer channels than in the United States, and only one or two will be in English.

■ Wall-to-wall carpet is uncommon. Terra-cotta or tiled floors are the norm.

How's the Weather?

Throughout Tuscany and Umbria the best times to visit are spring and fall. Days are warm, nights are cool, and though there are still tourists, the crowds are smaller. In the countryside the scenery is gorgeous, with abundant greenery and flowers in spring, and burnished leaves in autumn.

July and August are the most popular times to visit. Note, though, that the heat is often oppressive and mosquitoes are prevalent. Try to start your days early and visit major sights first to beat the crowds and the midday sun. For relief from the heat, head to the mountains of the Garfagnana, where hiking is spectacular, or hit the beach at resort towns such as Forte dei Marmi and Viareggio, along the Maremma coast, or on the island of Elba.

November through March, you might wonder who invented the term "sunny Italy." The panoramas are still beautiful, even with overcast skies, frequent rain, and occasional snow. In winter, Florence benefits from shorter museum lines and less competition for restaurant tables. Outside the cities, though, many hotels and restaurants close for the season.

FLORENCE AND TUSCANY TODAY

The People

"And what greater fortune, if in Italy there were more Tuscans and fewer Italians," writes Curzio Malaparte (Prato, 1898– Rome, 1957) in his celebrated novel *Maledetti Toscani* (*Accursed Tuscans*). He's being provocative and arrogant, qualities of which his fellow Tuscans, especially the Florentines, are often accused.

The Florentines, for their own part, acknowledge all this with evident pride, even using the term *toscanaccio* (nasty Tuscan) to describe themselves. Many attempts have been made to identify Italy's regional differences. In the "you are what you eat" category is Marcella Hazan's description (in the introduction to *The Classic Italian Cookbook*) of the "careful and calculating" Florentine, "a man who knows the measure of all things," whose "cooking is an austerely composed play upon essential and unadorned themes." Historical reasons and age-old disputes underlie city rivalries. The Sienese, called "genteel" by Malaparte, are the first to say, "it's an ill-wind that blows from the direction of Arezzo!" *Meglio un morto in casa, che un Pisano all'uscio* (Better a death in the house than a Pisan at the door), states a Florentine proverb.

In recent years (since the formation of the European Union), there has been a rapid growth of the immigrant populations in both Tuscany and Umbria—predominantly Romanians and Albanians (roughly 20% each of the regions' immigrants), and Chinese and Moroccans (each under 10%), but also Ukranians, Filipinos, Egyptians, and sub-Saharan Africans in growing numbers. These groups are having a profound impact, but their presence is felt primarily in the day-to-day Italian life that goes on outside the centers of tourism. On the other hand, you can hardly help noticing the more marginalized recent arrivals hawking cheap goods and sometimes panhandling on the sidewalks of the tourist centers.

Culture and Tradition

In the 1950s, when Italy's largely agrarian population began to move to the cities, large numbers of farmhouses in Tuscany and Umbria were abandoned. The essentially feudal system of land usage, called *mezzadria* (sharecropping), also disappeared, taking with it a long and very rich tradition of *contadino* (peasant) culture. The abandoned farmhouses have since been restored as summer homes or permanent residences by numerous English, Germans, and Americans, among others.

In the 1970s and '80s a sort of "folk revival" began, with interest developing in the festivals, food, popular theater, songs, and local religious events that were once a vital part of local tradition. Today the calendar overflows with resurrected *sagre* (festivals or fairs) that derive from contadino practice.

You'll find them all through Tuscany and Umbria, in towns large and small, January through December, with names like Sagra del Cinghiale (Wild Boar Festival), Sagra della Castagna (Chestnut Festival), and Festa del Fungo (Mushroom Festival). There's the Befana (celebrating Italy's witchlike Santa equivalent) in Grossetto during Epiphany, the Teatro Povero (a folk theater production) in the village of Monticchiello (near Pienza) in July, and throughout the Maremma on the night of April 30 they perform the Cantano il Maggio (literally, "They Sing the May").

The events are fun, and there's often delicious traditionally prepared food to be had. You can check with the local or regional tourist information offices for the dates and times of any sagre that happen to coincide with your visit.

Politics

Along with the Marches and the Emilia-Romagna regions, Tuscany and Umbria once formed the so-called red quadrilateral of central Italy, with strong left-wing political inclinations dating back to World War II.

Today, little remains of the cold-war rivalry between right and left. The collapse of the Soviet Union brought about an identity crisis in the 1990s among the Communists, who started the now widespread practice of periodically changing the name of their party. Meanwhile, in 1992 a nation-wide kickback crackdown labeled *mani pulite* (clean hands) brought down the ruling coalition partners—the Christian-Democrat and Socialist parties—leaving room in Italy's political midfield for media mogul Silvio Berlusconi. He adroitly maneuvered his party, originally named *Forza Italia* (Go Italy, a soccer cheer), into a position of leadership that would go largely unchecked for the better part of two decades. His government was finally forced to resign in the fall of 2011 and replaced by an interim government, which was still in place at press time.

The Economy

Italy's economy has been largely stagnant since the late 1990s. The adoption of the euro in 2002 resulted in surreptitious price increases, while the average wage remained level, meaning that for much of the decade many Tuscans and Umbrians were finding it hard to make ends meet. Long-time employment was difficult to come by for those entering the job market, replaced by serial short-term project-based contracts.

The 2008–09 recession brought an almost 10% national unemployment rate. Tuscany and Umbria have both fared better than Italy as a whole, but not by much. In the first part of 2011, Tuscany's unemployment rate was 8.3%, and Umbria's 7%. The hardest hit is the younger generation, which accounts for the incredible rise of horrible graffiti (no Keith Harings among this bunch) and a brain drain, as those with university degrees seek employment outside the country.

The tourism industry, which generates around 10% of each region's economy, has also suffered from the recession both as a result of a reduction in travelers from abroad and the shortening of vacations by Italians.

FLORENCE, TUSCANY, AND UMBRIA TOP ATTRACTIONS

Galleria degli Uffizi, Florence

(A) Florence has many museums, but the Uffizi is king. Walking its halls is like stepping into an art-history textbook, except here you're looking at the genuine articles—masterpieces by Leonardo, Michelangelo, Raphael, Botticelli, Caravaggio, and dozens of other luminaries. When planning your visit, make a point to reserve a ticket in advance. (⇨ *Chapter 2*)

Duomo, Florence

(B) The Cathedral of Santa Maria del Fiore, Florence's Duomo, is the city's most distinctive landmark, sitting at the very heart of the city and towering over the neighboring rooftops. Its massive dome is one of the world's great engineering masterpieces. For an up-close look, you can climb the 463 steps to the top—then gaze out at the city beneath you. (⇨ *Chapter 2*)

Leaning Tower, Pisa

(C) This tower may be too famous for its own good (it's one of Italy's most popular tourist attractions), but there's something undeniably appealing about its perilous tilt, and climbing to the top is a kick. The square on which it sits, known as the Campo dei Miracoli, has a majestic beauty that no quantity of tourists can diminish. (⇨ *Chapter 3*)

Piazza del Campo, Siena

(D) The sloping, fan-shape square in the heart of Siena is one of the best places in Italy to engage in the distinctly Italian activity of hanging out and people-watching. The flanking Palazzo Pubblico and Torre del Mangia are first-rate sights. (⇨ *Chapter 4*)

San Gimignano, Central Tuscany

(E) This classic Tuscan hill town has been dubbed a "medieval Manhattan" because of its numerous towers, built by noble families of the time, each striving to outdo its neighbors. The streets fill with tour groups during the day, but if you stick around until sunset the crowds diminish and you see the town at its most beautiful. (⇨ *Chapter 4*)

Abbazia di Sant'Antimo, Southern Tuscany

In a peaceful valley, surrounded by gently rolling hills, olive trees, and thick oak woods, Sant'Antimo is one of Italy's most beautifully situated abbeys—and a great "off the beaten path" destination. Stick around for mass and you'll hear the halls resound with Gregorian chants. (⇨ *Chapter 6*)

Palazzo Ducale, Urbino, the Marches

(F) East of Umbria in the Marches region, Urbino is a university town in the Italian style—meaning its small but prestigious university dates to the 15th century. The highlight here is the Palazzo Ducale, a palace that exemplifies the Renaissance ideals of grace and harmony. (⇨ *Chapter 7*)

Basilica di San Francesco, Assisi

(G) The basilica, built to honor Saint Francis, consists of two great churches—one Romanesque, fittingly solemn with its low ceilings and deep shadows; the other Gothic, with soaring arches and stained-glass windows (possibly the first in Italy). They're both filled with some of Europe's finest frescoes. (⇨ *Chapter 7*)

Duomo, Orvieto

(H) The facade of Orvieto's monumental Duomo contains a bas-relief masterpiece depicting the stories of the Creation and the Last Judgment (with the horrors of hell shown in striking detail). Inside, there's more glorious gore in the right transept, frescoed with Luca Signorelli's *Stories of the Antichrist and the Last Judgment*. (⇨ *Chapter 7*)

TOP EXPERIENCES

The View from Florence's Piazzale Michelangelo

One of the best ways to introduce yourself to Florence is by walking up to this square on the hill south of the Arno. From here you can take in the whole city, and much of the surrounding countryside, in one spectacular vista. To extend the experience, linger at one of the outdoor cafés, and for the finest view of all, time your visit to correspond with sunset.

Strolling the Ramparts of Lucca

Lucca, 80 km (50 miles) west of Florence, isn't situated on a hilltop in the way commonly associated with Tuscan towns, and it doesn't have quite the abundance of art treasures that you find in Siena or Pisa (to say nothing of Florence). Yet for many visitors, Lucca is a favorite Tuscan destination, and the source of its appeal has everything to do with its ramparts. These hulking barricades, built around the city between 1544 and 1645, were a source of security; now they are an elevated, oval park, complete with walkways, picnic areas, grass, and trees. The citizens of Lucca spend much of their spare time here, strolling, biking, and lounging.

Taking the Waters at a Tuscan Spa

Tuscany is dotted throughout with small *terme* (thermal baths), where hot water flows from natural springs deep beneath the earth's surface. It's been believed for millennia that these waters have the power to cure whatever ails you; although their medicinal power may be questionable, that doesn't keep a dip from being an extremely pleasant way to spend an afternoon. In northwest Tuscany you can take the waters at Montecatini Terme (made famous as a setting for Fellini's *8½* and seemingly little changed since then) or Bagni di Lucca (which had its heyday in the era of the 19th-century Romantic poets). To the south, Saturnia is the biggest draw, along with the more humble Chianciano Terme and Bagno Vignoni.

Discovering the Cinque Terre

A short trip west across the Tuscan border, along the Ligurian coast, are five tiny, remote fishing villages known collectively as the Cinque Terre. Tourism here was once limited to backpackers, but the beauty of the landscape—with steep, vine-covered hills pushing smack-dab against an azure sea—and the charm of the villages have turned the area into one of Italy's top destinations. The number-one activity is hiking the trails that run between the villages—the views are once-in-a-lifetime gorgeous—but if hiking isn't your thing, you can still have fun lounging about in cafés, admiring the water, and perhaps sticking a toe in it.

In October 2011, a disastrous mud slide, caused by torrential rains, killed several people in Liguria, including two hikers on one of the Cinque Terre trails who were swept out to sea. Monterosso al Mare and Vernazza, the two northernmost towns, were leveled by mud. At press time, locals were optimistic that both towns would be up and running and open for business by March 2012.

Wine-Tasting in Chianti

The gorgeous hills of the Chianti region, between Florence and Siena, produce exceptional wines, and they never taste better than when sampled on their home turf. Many Chianti vineyards are visitor-friendly, but the logistics of a visit are different from what you may have experienced in other wine regions. If you just drop in, you're likely to get a tasting, but for a tour you usually need to make an appointment several days ahead of time.

The upside is that your tour may end up being a half day of full immersion—including extended conversation with the winemakers and even a meal.

Passeggiata along Corso Vanucci, Perugia

The *passeggiata*—the evening stroll—is a ritual practiced in towns throughout Italy. One of its most pleasant manifestations is along Perugia's Corso Vanucci, a wide, pedestrians-only boulevard through the heart of the city, lined with elegant palaces—and many bars where you can stop for a predinner *aperitivo* and watch the world go by.

Sampling Umbrian Truffles

The truffle (*tartufo* in Italian) is a peculiar delicacy; a gnarly clump of fungus that grows wild in the forest a few inches underground, is hunted down by specially trained truffle-sniffing dogs (or sometimes pigs), and can sell for a small fortune. The payoff is a powerful, aromatic flavor that makes food lovers swoon. Umbria is one of Italy's richest black truffle–hunting grounds, and in many of the region's restaurants you'll encounter truffle-infused dishes or be offered a shaving of truffle over your pasta. Indulge yourself at least once—it's an experience you won't forget.

Hiking in the Footsteps of Saint Francis

Umbria, which bills itself as "Italy's Green Heart," is fantastic hiking country. Among the many options are two with a Franciscan twist: from the town of Cannara, 16 km (10 miles) south of Assisi, an easy half-hour walk leads to the fields of Pian d'Arca, where Saint Francis delivered his sermon to the birds. For slightly more demanding walks, you can follow the saint's path from Assisi to the Ermeo delle Carceri (Hermitage of Prisons), where Francis and his followers went to "imprison" themselves in prayer, and from here continue along the trails that crisscross Monte Subasio.

Spoleto's Festival dei Due Mondi

For two weeks in late June–early July the Umbrian town of Spoleto is entirely given over to the Festival dei Due Mondi (Festival of Two Worlds), one of Europe's great performing-arts events. Classical music, opera, dance, and theater fill every conceivable venue with performances mixing old with new and tradition with innovation. In many cases it's the opportunity to see world-renowned talent in one-of-a-kind, intimate settings. Attending the festival takes planning months in advance—most events sell out, and hotel rooms are at a premium—but for a dedicated arts lover, it's an effort that's richly rewarded.

Il Dolce Far Niente

"The sweetness of doing nothing" has long been an art form in Italy. This is a country in which life's pleasures are warmly celebrated, not guiltily indulged. Of course, doing "nothing" doesn't really mean nothing. It means doing things differently. It means lingering over a glass of wine or two for the better part of an evening just to watch the sun slowly set. It means savoring a slow and flirtatious evening passeggiata along the main street of a little town, a procession with no destination other than the town and its streets. And it means making a commitment—however temporary—to thinking, feeling, and believing that there is nowhere that you have to be next, that there is no other time but the magical present.

QUINTESSENTIAL FLORENCE AND TUSCANY

Il Caffè (Coffee)

The Italian day begins and ends with coffee, and more cups of coffee punctuate the time in between. To live like the Italians do, drink as they drink, standing at the counter or sitting at an outdoor table of the corner bar. (In Italy a "bar" is a coffee bar.) A primer: *caffè* means coffee, and Italian standard issue is what Americans call espresso—short and strong. *Cappuccino* is a foamy half-and-half of espresso and steamed milk; cocoa powder *(cacao)* on top is acceptable, cinnamon is not. If you're thinking of having a cappuccino for dessert, you'll get it, but realize that most Italians drink only caffè or caffè *macchiato* (with a spot of steamed milk) after lunchtime. Confused? Homesick? Order caffè *americano* for a reasonable facsimile of good-old filtered joe.

Il Calcio (Soccer)

Imagine the most rabid American football fans—the ones who paint their faces on game day and sleep in pajamas emblazoned with the logo of their favorite team. Throw in a dose of melodrama along the lines of a sentimental Puccini opera. Ratchet up the intensity by a factor of 10, and you'll start to get a sense of how Italians feel about their national game, soccer—known in the mother tongue as *calcio*. On Sunday afternoons throughout the long September-to-May season, stadiums are packed throughout Italy. Those who don't get to games in person tend to congregate around television sets in restaurants and bars, rooting for the home team with a passion that feels like a last vestige of the days when the country was a series of warring medieval city-states. How calcio mania affects your stay in Italy depends on how eager you are to get involved. At the very least, you may notice

If you want to get a sense of contemporary Italian culture and indulge in some of its pleasures, start by familiarizing yourself with the rituals of daily life. These are a few highlights—things you can take part in with relative ease.

an eerie Sunday-afternoon silence on the city streets, or erratic restaurant service around the same time, accompanied by cheers and groans from a neighboring room. If you want a memorable, truly Italian experience, attend a game yourself. Availability of tickets may depend on the current fortunes of the team in the town where you're staying, but they often can be acquired with help from your hotel concierge.

Il Gelato (Ice Cream)
During warmer months *gelato*—the Italian equivalent of ice cream—is a national obsession. It's considered a snack more than a dessert, bought at stands and shops in piazzas and on street corners, and consumed on foot, usually at a leisurely stroll *(see La Passeggiata, following)*. Gelato is softer, less creamy, and more intensely flavored than its American counterpart. It comes in simple flavors that capture the essence of the main ingredient. (You

won't find Chunky Monkey or Cookies 'n' Cream.) At most gelaterias choices include pistachio, *nocciola* (hazelnut), caffè, and numerous fruit varieties. Look for signs boasting *produzione propria* for gelato made in-house. Quality varies; the surest sign that you've hit on a good spot is a line at the counter.

La Passeggiata (Strolling)
A favorite Italian pastime is the passeggiata (literally, the promenade). In the late afternoon and early evening, especially on weekends, couples, families, and packs of teenagers stroll the main streets and piazzas of Italy's towns. It's a ritual of exchanged news and gossip, window-shopping, flirting, seeing and being seen, that adds up to a uniquely Italian experience. To join in, simply hit the streets for a bit of wandering. You may feel more like an observer than a participant, until you realize that observing is what la passeggiata is all about.

IF YOU LIKE

Renaissance Art

Travel veterans will tell you that the seemingly countless masterpieces of Italian art can cause first-time visitors—eyes glazed over from a heavy downpour of images, dates, and names—to lean, Pisa-like, on their companions for support. After a surfeit of Michelangelos and Raphaels, even the miracle of the High Renaissance may begin to pall. The secret is to act like a tortoise, not a hare, and take your sweet time.

Allow the splendors of the age to unfold slowly. Don't stop at the museums; get out and explore the chapels, palaces, and town squares for which Italy's marvelous art was conceived centuries ago and where much of it remains. Take in Michelangelo's *David* in Florence's Accademia, but don't miss his other gems in the Bargello and the Cappelle Medicee. Those caveats aside, here are the places to go when you're ready for an art feast:

Galleria degli Uffizi, Florence. Allow at least several hours to explore the world's greatest collection of Italian Renaissance art.

Basilica di San Francesco, Arezzo, Eastern Tuscany. Piero della Francesca's *Legend of the True Cross* merits a pilgrimage to this Tuscan town.

Galleria Nazionale dell Umbria, Perugia. At one of Italy's finest small museums the art is the star, but the first-class presentation adds to the appeal.

Palazzo Ducale, Urbino, the Marches. Head off the beaten path to visit a palace that perfectly displays the values of the Renaissance.

Monumental Churches

Few images are more identifiable with Italy than the country's great churches, stunning works of architecture that often took one or more centuries to build.

The name *duomo* (derived from the Latin for "house," *domus,* and the root of the English "dome") is used to refer to the cathedral (the bishop's see) of a town or city.

Generally speaking, the bigger the city, the more splendid its duomo. Still, some impressive churches inhabit some surprisingly small locales—the Umbrian hill towns of Assisi and Orvieto, for example.

Duomo, Florence. Brunelleschi's beautiful dome, the most recognizable in Italy, is an unequaled feat of 15th-century engineering.

Santa Croce, Florence. The resting place of Michelangelo, Galileo, and Machiavelli (among others) also contains the most important art of any church in Florence.

Cripta, Siena, Central Tuscany. Siena's Duomo is large and lush with art, but the vivid frescoes in its crypt merit special mention.

Basilica di San Francesco, Assisi. The fresco cycle here illustrating the life of Saint Francis is counted among the masterpieces of the Renaissance; the massive double basilica is a striking contrast of darkness and light.

Duomo, Orvieto, Southern Umbria. Few cathedrals can claim masterpieces inside and out, but here you'll find Italy's most perfect Gothic facade matched with Luca Signorelli's phenomenal frescoes in the Cappella di San Brizio.

Traditional Cooking

Italian cuisine all comes back to *la cucina di casalinga* (home cooking). From *ribollita* (bread soup) to a simply grilled whole fish from along the Ligurian coastline, the finest plates are often the simplest. Emphasis is on exceptionally good *materie prime* (primary ingredients) handled with skill and with respect for the foods themselves and for the traditional methods of preparing them.

Within Tuscany and Umbria, towns and regions have their own time-tested specialties that are a source of local pride, and even sophisticated restaurants often maintain an orthodox focus on generations-old recipes. Chefs revere the most humble ingredients, devoting the same attention to day-old bread that they do to costly truffles. Here are a few places where the simplest food will take your breath away:

Antico Noe, Florence. If Florence had diners, this unpretentious restaurant would be the best diner in town. Stick to the antipasti and primi, which really shine. What's on the menu depends on what's best that day at the market.

Buca di Sant'Antonio, Lucca, Northwest Tuscany. Simple, traditional Tuscan cuisine is created here with exceptional grace.

Osteria Il Grattacielo, Siena, Central Tuscany. It has all the charm of a 1950s diner, but locals flock here to enjoy savory regional specialties at their very few tables.

La Pallotta, Assisi, Northern Umbria. It's a family affair at this homey trattoria, which is a true gem among Assisi's hit-or-miss dining options.

Shopping

"Made in Italy" is synonymous with style, quality, and craftsmanship, whether it refers to high fashion or Maserati automobiles.

The best buys include leather goods of all kinds (from gloves to bags to jackets); silk goods; knitwear; ceramics; and, of course, the country's world-famous food products, from artisanal pasta sauces to world-class wine to extra-virgin olive oil.

Every region has its specialties. Florence is known for straw goods, gold jewelry, leather, and paper products (including beautiful handmade notebooks); Siena and Assisi for embroidery; and much of Umbria for ceramics.

And almost every town in Tuscany and Umbria has its own candidate for Italy's best olive oil.

And in Florence, as well as the other mid-size cities, Italy's famous fashion names are never hard to find.

Via Tornabuoni, Florence. Whether you're looking to splurge or just browse, Florence's chicest shopping street is the place to find Italian high style.

Via Tiberina Nord, Deruta, Northern Umbria. Deruta is the top spot for Umbrian ceramics; along this road you'll find one factory after another selling first-class wares.

Enoteca Italia, Siena, Central Tuscany. Italy's only state-sponsored wineshop is like a library of wine (with a vast collection).

A GREAT ITINERARY

Day 1: Florence

If you're coming in on an international flight, you'll probably settle in Florence in time for an afternoon stroll or siesta (depending on your jet-lag strategy) before dinner.

Logistics: On your flight in, read through the restaurant listings in this guide and begin anticipating the first dinner of your trip. Look for a place near your hotel, and when you arrive, reserve a table (or have your concierge do it for you). Making a meal the focus of your first day is a great way to ease into Italian life.

Day 2: Florence

Begin your morning at the **Uffizi Gallery** (reserve your ticket in advance). The extensive collection will occupy much of your morning. Next, take in the neighboring **Piazza della Signoria**, one of Florence's impressive squares, then head a few blocks north to the **Duomo**. There, check out Ghiberti's famous bronze doors on the **Battistero** (they're high-quality copies; the originals are normally in the Museo dell'Opera del Duomo but, at press time, were in restoration), and work up an appetite by climbing the 463 steps to the cupola of Brunelleschi's splendid cathedral dome, atop which you'll experience a memorable view. Spend the afternoon relaxing, shopping, and wandering Florence's medieval streets; or, if you're up for a more involved journey, head out to **Fiesole** to experience the ancient amphitheater and beautiful views of the Tuscan countryside.

Day 3: Florence

Keep the energy level up for your second full day in Florence, sticking with art and architecture for the morning, trying to see most of the following: Michelangelo's *David* at the **Galleria dell'Accademia**, the Medici Chapels, the **Palazzo Pitti** and **Boboli Gardens**, and the churches of **Santa Maria Novella** and **Santa Croce**. If it's a clear day, spend the afternoon on a trip to **Piazzale Michelangelo**, high on a hill, for sweeping views of idyllic Florentine countryside. Given all the walking you've been doing, tonight would be a good night to recharge by trying the famed *bistecca alla fiorentina* (a grilled, very rare T-bone steak).

Logistics: You can get up to the Piazzale Michelangelo by taxi or by taking Bus 12 or 13 from the Lungarno. Otherwise, do your best to get around on foot; Florence is a brilliant city for walking.

Day 4: San Gimignano

Now that you've been appropriately introduced to the bewildering splendor of Renaissance Italy, it's time for a change of pace—and time for a rental car, which will enable you to see the back roads of Tuscany and Umbria. After breakfast, pick up your car, stop back at your hotel for your luggage, and head on out. On a good day the lazy drive from Florence to **San Gimignano**, past vineyards and typical Tuscan landscapes, is truly spectacular. The first thing that will hit you when you arrive at the hill town of San Gimignano will be its multiple towers. The medieval skyscrapers of Italy, they also once occupied the role now played by Ferraris or Hummers: they were public displays of wealth and family power—and they provided sanctuary and security during times of civic strife, which was often. After finding your way to a hotel in the old town, set out on foot and check out the city's turrets and alleyways, doing your best to get away from the trinket shops, and later enjoying a leisurely dinner with the light but delicious local white wine, Vernaccia di San Gimignano.

Logistics: Some hotels might be able to coordinate with some rental-car agencies so that your car can be brought to your hotel for you. Once you navigate your way out of Florence (no easy task), San Gimignano is only 57 km (35 miles) to the southwest, so it's an easy drive; you could even take a detour on the SS222 (Strada Chiantigiana), stop at one of the Chianti wine towns, and visit a winery along the way.

Day 5: Siena

In the morning, set out for nearby **Siena,** which is known worldwide for its Palio, a festival that culminates in an elaborate horse-race competition among the 17 *contrade* (medieval neighborhoods) of the city. Siena is one of Tuscany's most impressive sights; however many tourists you have to bump elbows with, it's hard not to be blown away by the city's precious medieval streets and memorable fan-shape **Piazza del Campo.** Not to be missed while in town are the spectacular **Duomo,** the **Battistero,** and the **Spedale di Santa Maria della Scala,** an old hospital and hostel that now contains an underground archaeological museum.

Logistics: It's a short and pretty drive from San Gimignano to Siena, but once there, parking can be a challenge. Look for the *stadio* (soccer stadium), where there's a parking lot that often has space.

Day 6: Arezzo/Cortona

Get an early start, because there's a lot to see today. From Siena you'll first head to **Arezzo,** home to the **Basilica di San Francesco,** which contains important frescoes by Piero della Francesca. Check out the **Piazza Grande** along with its beautiful Romanesque church of **Pieve di Santa Maria.** Try to do all of this before lunch, after which you'll head straight to **Cortona.** If Arezzo didn't capture your imagination, Cortona, whose origins date to the 5th century BC, will. Olive trees and vineyards give way to a medieval hill town with views over idyllic Tuscan countryside and Lake Trasimeno. Cortona is a town for walking and relaxing, not sightseeing, so enjoy yourself, wandering through the **Piazza della Repubblica** and **Piazza Signorelli,** perhaps doing a bit of shopping.

Logistics: Siena to Arezzo is 63 km (39 miles) on the E78. From Arezzo to Cortona, it's just 30 km (18 miles)—take S71.

Day 7: Assisi

Today you'll cross over into Umbria, a region just as beautiful as Tuscany but still less trodden. Yet another impossibly beautiful hill town, **Assisi,** is the home of Saint Francis and host to the many religious pilgrims who come to celebrate his legacy. Visiting here is the most treasured memory of many a traveler's visit to Italy. Upon arriving and checking into your lodging, head straight for the **Basilica di San Francesco,** which displays the tomb of Saint Francis and unbelievable frescoes. From here take Via San Francesco to **Piazza del Commune** and see the **Tempio di Minerva** before a break for lunch. After lunch, see **San Rufino,** the town cathedral, and then go back through the piazza to Corso Mazzini and see **Santa Chiara.** If you're a true fan of the Franciscans, you could instead devote the afternoon to heading out 16 km (10 miles) to **Cannara,** where Saint Francis delivered his sermon to the birds.

Logistics: From Cortona, take the S71 to the A1 autostrada toward Perugia. After about 40 km (24 miles), take the Assisi exit (E45), and it's another 14 km (8 miles) to Assisi.

Day 8: Spoleto

This morning will take you from a small Umbrian hill town to a slightly bigger one: **Spoleto,** a walled city that's home to a world-renowned arts festival each summer. But Spoleto needs no festival to be celebrated. Its **Duomo** is wonderful. Its fortress, **La Rocca,** is impressive. And the **Ponte delle Torri,** a 14th-century bridge that separates Spoleto from Monteluco, is a marvelous sight, traversing a gorge 260 feet below and built upon the foundations of a Roman aqueduct. See all these during the day, stopping for a light lunch of a *panino* (sandwich) or salad, saving your appetite for a serious last dinner in Italy: Umbrian cuisine is excellent everywhere, but Spoleto is a memorable culinary destination. Do your best to sample black

AN ITINERARY TIP

Because of spotty train service to Tuscan hill towns, this itinerary is extremely difficult to complete without a car. Driving is easy and relaxing in the region, whose roads can be winding but are generally wide, well kept, well marked, and not too crowded. If you absolutely don't want to drive, buses are the best way to go, but you'll often have to change buses in hubs like Florence, and it would be best to cut out some of the smaller Tuscan hill towns and spend extra time in Siena and Spoleto.

truffles, a proud product of the region; they're delicious on pasta or meat.

Logistics: One school of thought would be to time your visit to Spoleto's world-renowned arts festival that runs from mid-June through mid-July. Another would be to do anything you can to avoid it. It all depends on your taste for big festivals and big crowds. The trip from Assisi to Spoleto is a pretty 47-km (29-mile) drive (S75 to the S3) that should take you less than an hour.

Day 9: Spoleto/Departure

It's a fair distance from Spoleto to the Florence airport, your point of departure. Depending on your comfort level with Italian driving, allow at least 2½ hours to reach Florence's airport.

Logistics: An alternative possibility would be to try to get a flight out of Perugia's tiny airport, which is a lot closer to Spoleto than Florence. It offers connections to Milan and Rome (Ciampino)—but not many. Otherwise, just get an early start and drive to Florence along the A1 autostrada.

WHO'S WHO in RENAISSANCE ART

Michelangelo. Leonardo da Vinci. Raphael. This heady triumvirate of the Italian Renaissance is synonymous with artistic genius. Yet they are only three of the remarkable cast of characters whose work defines the Renaissance, that extraordinary flourishing of art and culture in Italy, especially in Florence, as the Middle Ages drew to a close. The artists were visionaries, who redefined painting, sculpture, architecture, and even what it means to be an artist.

THE PIONEER. In the mid-14th century, a few artists began to move away the flat, two-dimensional painting of the Middle Ages. **Giotto**, who painted seemingly three-dimensional figures who show emotion, had a major impact on the artists of the next century.

THE GROUNDBREAKERS. The generations of **Brunelleschi** and **Botticelli** took center stage in the 15th century. **Ghiberti, Masaccio, Donatello, Uccello, Fra Angelico**, and **Filippo Lippi** were other major players. Part of the Renaissance (or "re-birth") was a renewed interest in classical sources—the texts, monuments, and sculpture of Ancient Greece and Rome. Perspective and the illusion of three-dimensional space in painting was another discovery of this era, known as the Early Renaissance. Suddenly the art appearing on the walls looked real, or more realistic than it used to.

Roman ruins were not the only thing to inspire these artists. There was an incredible exchange of ideas going on. In Santa Maria del Carmine, Filippo Lippi was inspired by the work of Masaccio, who in turn was a friend of Brunelleschi. Young artists also learned from the masters via the apprentice system. Ghiberti's workshop (*bottega* in Italian) included, at one time or another, Donatello, Masaccio, and Uccello. Botticelli was apprenticed to Filippo Lippi.

THE BIG THREE. The mathematical rationality and precision of 15th-century art gave way to what is known as the High Renaissance. **Leonardo, Michelangelo**, and **Raphael** were much more concerned with portraying the body in all its glory and with achieving harmony and grandeur in their work. Oil paint, used infrequently up until this time, became more widely employed: as a result, Leonardo's colors are deeper, more sensual, more alive. For one brief period, all three were in Florence at the same time. Michelangelo and Leonardo surely knew one another, as they were simultaneously working on frescoes (never completed) inside Palazzo Vecchio.

When Michelangelo left Florence for Rome in 1508, he began the slow drain of artistic exodus from Florence, which never really recovered her previous glory.

A RENAISSANCE TIMELINE

IN THE WORLD

Black Death in Europe kills one third of the population, 1347-50.

Joan of Arc burned at the stake, 1431.

IN FLORENCE

Founding of the Medici bank, 1397.

Medici family made official papal bankers.

1434, Cosimo il Vecchio becomes de facto ruler of Florence. The Medici family will dominate the city until 1494.

Dante, a native of Florence, writes *The Divine Comedy*, 1302-21.

1300

1400

IN ART

EARLY RENAISSANCE

Masaccio and Masolino fresco Santa Maria del Carmine, 1424-28.

GIOTTO (ca. 1267-1337)

Giotto fresoes in Santa Croce, 1320-25.

BRUNELLESCHI (1377-1446)

LORENZO GHIBERTI (ca. 1381-1455)

DONATELLO (ca. 1386-1466)

PAOLO UCCELLO (1397-1475)

FRA ANGELICO (ca. 1400-1455)

MASACCIO (1401-1428)

FILIPPO LIPPI (ca. 1406-1469)

1334, 67-year-old Giotto is appointed chief architect of Santa Maria del Fiore, Florence's Duomo (below). He begins to work on the Campanile, which will be completed in 1359, after his death.

Donatello sculpts his bronze *David*, ca. 1440.

Fra Angelico frescoes friars' cells in San Marco, c 1438-45.

Uccello's *Sir John Hawkwood*, ca. 1436.

Ghiberti wins the competition for the Baptistery doors (above) in Florence, 1401.

Brunelleschi wins the competition for the Duomo's cupola (right), 1418.

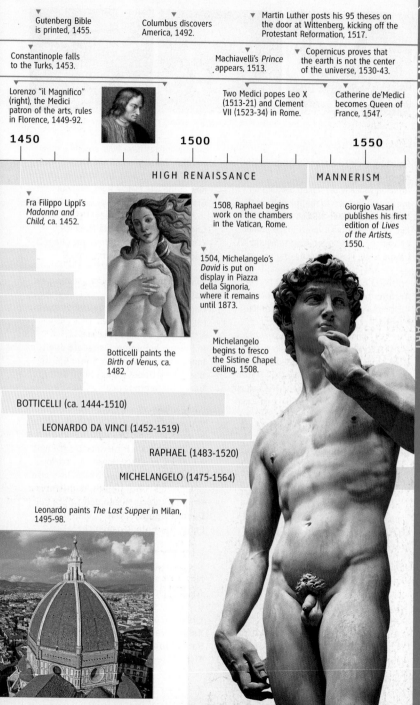

Gutenberg Bible is printed, 1455.

Columbus discovers America, 1492.

Martin Luther posts his 95 theses on the door at Wittenberg, kicking off the Protestant Reformation, 1517.

Constantinople falls to the Turks, 1453.

Machiavelli's *Prince* appears, 1513.

Copernicus proves that the earth is not the center of the universe, 1530-43.

Lorenzo "il Magnifico" (right), the Medici patron of the arts, rules in Florence, 1449-92.

Two Medici popes Leo X (1513-21) and Clement VII (1523-34) in Rome.

Catherine de'Medici becomes Queen of France, 1547.

1450　　　　　**1500**　　　　　**1550**

HIGH RENAISSANCE　　　　MANNERISM

Fra Filippo Lippi's *Madonna and Child*, ca. 1452.

1508, Raphael begins work on the chambers in the Vatican, Rome.

Giorgio Vasari publishes his first edition of *Lives of the Artists*, 1550.

1504, Michelangelo's *David* is put on display in Piazza della Signoria, where it remains until 1873.

Botticelli paints the *Birth of Venus*, ca. 1482.

Michelangelo begins to fresco the Sistine Chapel ceiling, 1508.

BOTTICELLI (ca. 1444-1510)

LEONARDO DA VINCI (1452-1519)

RAPHAEL (1483-1520)

MICHELANGELO (1475-1564)

Leonardo paints *The Last Supper* in Milan, 1495-98.

Giotto's *Nativity*

Donatello's *St. John the Baptist*

Ghiberti's *Gates of Paradise*

GIOTTO (CA. 1267-1337)
Painter/architect from a small town north of Florence.
He unequivocally set Italian painting on the course that led to the triumphs of the Renaissance masters. Unlike the rather flat, two-dimensional forms found in then prevailing Byzantine art, Giotto's figures have a fresh, life-like quality. The people in his paintings have bulk, and they show emotion, which you can see on their faces and in their gestures. This was something new in the late Middle Ages. Without Giotto, there wouldn't have been a Raphael.
In Florence: **Santa Croce; Uffizi; Campanile; Santa Maria Novella**
Elsewhere in Italy: **Scrovegni Chapel, Padua; Vatican Museums, Rome**

FILIPPO BRUNELLESCHI (1377-1446)
Architect/engineer from Florence.
If Brunelleschi had beaten Ghiberti in the Baptistery doors competition in Florence, the city's Duomo most likely would not have the striking appearance and authority that it has today. After his loss, he sulked off to Rome, where he studied the ancient Roman structures first-hand. Brunelleschi figured out how to vault the Duomo's dome, a structure unprecedented in its colossal size and great height. His Ospedale degli Innocenti employs classical elements in the creation of a stunning, new architectural statement; it is the first truly Renaissance structure.
In Florence: **Duomo; Ospedale degli Innocenti; San Lorenzo; Santo Spirito; Baptistery Doors Competition Entry, Bargello; Santa Croce**

LORENZO GHIBERTI (CA. 1381-1455)
Sculptor from Florence.
Ghiberti won a competition—besting his chief rival, Brunelleschi—to cast the gilded bronze North Doors of the Baptistery in Florence. These doors, and the East Doors that he subsequently executed, took up the next 50 years of his life. He created intricately worked figures that are more true-to-life than any since antiquity, and he was one of the first Renaissance sculptors to work in bronze. Ghiberti taught the next generation of artists; Donatello, Uccello, and Masaccio all passed through his studio.
In Florence: **Door Copies, Baptistery; Original Doors, Museo dell'Opera del Duomo; Baptistry Door Competition Entry, Bargello; Orsanmichele**

DONATELLO (CA. 1386-1466)
Sculptor from Florence.
Donatello was an innovator who, like his good friend Brunelleschi, spent most of his long life in Florence. Consumed with the science of optics, he used light and shadow to create the effects of nearness and distance. He made an essentially flat slab look like a three- dimensional scene. His bronze *David* is probably the first free-standing male nude since antiquity. Not only technically brilliant, his work is also emotionally resonant; few sculptors are as expressive.
In Florence: **David, Bargello; St. Mark, Orsanmichele; Palazzo Vecchio; Museo dell'Opera del Duomo; San Lorenzo; Santa Croce**
Elsewhere in Italy: **Padua; Prato; Venice**

Fra Angelico's *The Deposition*   Masaccio's *Trinity*   Filippo Lippi's *Madonna and Child*

PAOLO UCCELLO (1397-1475)
Painter from Florence.
Renaissance chronicler Vasari once observed that had Uccello not been so obsessed with the mathematical problems posed by perspective, he would have been a very good painter. The struggle to master single-point perspective and to render motion in two dimensions is nowhere more apparent than in his battle scenes. His first major commission in Florence was the gargantuan fresco of the English mercenary Sir John Hawkwood (the Italians called him Giovanni Acuto) in Florence's Duomo.
In Florence: *Sir John Hawkwood*, Duomo; *Battle of San Romano*, Uffizi; Santa Maria Novella
Elsewhere in Italy: Urbino, Prato

FRA ANGELICO (CA. 1400-1455)
Painter from a small town north of Florence.
A Dominican friar, who eventually made his way to the convent of San Marco, Fra Angelico and his assistants painted frescoes for aid in prayer and meditation. He was known for his piety; Vasari wrote that Fra Angelico could never paint a crucifix without a tear running down his face. Perhaps no other painter so successfully translated the mysteries of faith and the sacred into painting. And yet his figures emote, his command of perspective is superb, and his use of color startles even today.
In Florence: Museo di San Marco; Uffizi
Elsewhere in Italy: Vatican Museums, Rome; Fiesole; Cortona; Perugia; Orvieto

MASACCIO (1401-1428)
Painter from San Giovanni Valdarno, southeast of Florence.
Masaccio and Masolino, a frequent collaborator, worked most famously together at Santa Maria del Carmine. Their frescoes of the life of St. Peter use light to mold figures in the painting by imitating the way light falls on figures in real life. Masaccio also pioneered the use of single-point perspective, masterfully rendered in his *Trinity*. His friend Brunelleschi probably introduced him to the technique, yet another step forward in rendering things the way the eye sees them. Masaccio died young and under mysterious circumstances.
In Florence: Santa Maria del Carmine; *Trinity*, Santa Maria Novella

FILIPPO LIPPI (CA. 1406-1469)
Painter from Prato.
At a young age, Filippo Lippi entered the friary of Santa Maria del Carmine, where he was highly influenced by Masaccio and Masolino's frescoes. His religious vows appear to have made less of an impact; his affair with a young nun produced a son, Filippino (Little Philip, who later apprenticed with Botticelli), and a daughter. His religious paintings often have a playful, humorous note; some of his angels are downright impish and look directly out at the viewer. Lippi links the earlier painters of the 15th century with those who follow; Botticelli apprenticed with him.
In Florence: Uffizi; Palazzo Medici Riccardi; San Lorenzo; Palazzo Pitti
Elsewhere in Italy: Prato

Botticelli's *Primavera*

Leonardo's *Portrait of a Young Woman*

Raphael's *Madonna on the Meadow*

BOTTICELLI (CA. 1444-1510)
Painter from Florence.

Botticelli's work is characterized by stunning, elongated blondes, cherubic angels (something he undoubtedly learned from his time with Filippo Lippi), and tender Christs. Though he did many religious paintings, he also painted monumental, nonreligious panels—his *Birth of Venus* and *Primavera* being the two most famous of these. A brief sojourn took him to Rome, where he and a number of other artists frescoed the Sistine Chapel walls.

In Florence: ***Birth of Venus*, *Primavera*, Uffizi; Palazzo Pitti**
Elsewhere in Italy: **Vatican Museums, Rome**

LEONARDO DA VINCI (1452-1519)
Painter/sculptor/engineer from Anchiano, a small town outside Vinci.

Leonardo never lingered long in any place; his restless nature and his international reputation led to commissions throughout Italy, and took him to Milan, Vigevano, Pavia, Rome, and, ultimately, France. Though he is most famous for his mysterious *Mona Lisa* (at the Louvre in Paris), he painted other penetrating, psychological portraits in addition to his scientific experiments: his design for a flying machine (never built) predates Kitty Hawk by nearly 500 years. The greatest collection of Leonardo's work in Italy can be seen on one wall in the Uffizi.

In Florence: ***Adoration of the Magi*, Uffizi**
Elsewhere in Italy: ***Last Supper*, Santa Maria delle Grazie, Milan**

RAPHAEL (1483-1520)
Painter/architect from Urbino.

Raphael spent only four highly productive years of his short life in Florence, where he turned out made-to-order panel paintings of the Madonna and Child for a hungry public; he also executed a number of portraits of Florentine aristocrats. Perhaps no other artist had such a fine command of line and color, and could render it, seemingly effortlessly, in paint. His painting acquired new authority after he came up against Michelangelo toiling away on the Sistine ceiling. Raphael worked nearly next door in the Vatican, where his figures take on an epic, Michelangelesque scale.

In Florence: **Uffizi; Palazzo Pitti**
Elsewhere in Italy: **Vatican Museums, Rome**

MICHELANGELO (1475-1564)
Painter/sculptor/architect from Caprese.

Although Florentine and proud of it (he famously signed his St. Peter's *Pietà* to avoid confusion about where he was from), he spent most of his 89 years outside his native city. He painted and sculpted the male body on an epic scale and glorified it while doing so. Though he complained throughout the proceedings that he was really a sculptor, Michelangelo's Sistine Chapel ceiling is arguably the greatest fresco cycle ever painted (and the massive figures owe no small debt to Giotto).

In Florence: ***David*, Galleria dell'Accademia; Uffizi; Casa Buonarroti; Bargello**
Elsewhere in Italy: **St. Peter's Basilica, Vatican Museums, and Piazza del Campidoglio in Rome**

Florence

WORD OF MOUTH

"Follow your nose to the many bakeries and cafés open early in the mornings. I always . . . enjoy a stop at a coffee bar where I have a cappuccino or two at the bar. Then it's a stop at a bakery to pick up still warm breads to bring back and enjoy."   —kfusto

WELCOME TO FLORENCE

TOP REASONS TO GO

★ **Galleria degli Uffizi:** Italian Renaissance art doesn't get much better than this vast collection bequeathed to the city by the last Medici, Anna Maria Luisa.

★ **The dome of the Duomo:** Brunelleschi's work of engineering genius is the city's undisputed centerpiece.

★ **Michelangelo's *David*:** One look and you'll know why this is one of the Western world's most famous sculptures.

★ **The view from Piazzale Michelangelo:** From this perch the city is laid out before you. The colors at sunset heighten the experience.

★ **Piazza Santa Croce:** After you've had your fill of Renaissance masterpieces, hang out here and watch the world go by.

1 **The Duomo to the Ponte Vecchio.** You're in the heart of Florence here. Among the numerous highlights are the city's greatest museum (the Uffizi) and its most impressive square (Piazza della Signoria).

2 **San Lorenzo to the Accademia.** The blocks from the church of San Lorenzo to the Accademia museum bear the imprints of the Medici and of Michelangelo, culminating in his masterful *David*. Just to the north, the former convent of San Marco is an oasis decorated with ethereal frescoes.

3 **Santa Maria Novella to the Arno.** This part of town includes the train station, 16th-century palaces, and the city's chicest shopping street, Via Tornabuoni.

4 **Santa Croce.** The district centers on its namesake basilica, which is filled with the tombs of Renaissance (and other) luminaries. The area is also known for its leather shops.

5 **The Oltrarno.** Across the Arno you encounter the massive Palazzo Pitti and the narrow streets of the Santo Spirito neighborhood, which is filled with artisans' workshops and antiques stores. A climb to Piazzale Michelangelo gives you a spectacular view of the city.

2

GETTING ORIENTED

The historic center of Florence is flat and compact—you could walk from one end to the other in half an hour. In the middle of everything is the Duomo, with its huge dome towering over the city's terra-cotta rooftops. Radiating from the Duomo are Renaissance-era neighborhoods identified by their central churches and piazzas. Though the majority of sights are north of the Arno River, the area to the south, known as the Oltrarno, has its charms as well.

EATING AND DRINKING WELL IN FLORENCE

In Florence simply prepared meats, grilled or roasted, are the culinary stars, usually paired with seasonal vegetables like artichokes or porcini. Bistecca's big here, but there's plenty more that tastes great on the grill, too.

Traditionalists (and many Florentines are) go for their gustatory pleasures in trattorie and osterie, places where decor is unimportant, place mats are mere paper, and service is often perfunctory. Culinary innovation comes slowly in this town, though some cutting-edge restaurants have been appearing, usually with young chefs who've traveled and worked outside Italy. Some of these places lack charm (many have an international you-could-be-anywhere feel), but their menus offer exciting, updated versions of Tuscan standards.

By American standards, Florentines eat late: 1:30 or 2 is typical for lunch and 9 for dinner. Consuming a primo, secondo, and dolce is largely a thing of the past, and no one looks askance if you don't order the whole nine yards. For lunch, many Florentines simply grab a panino and a glass of wine at a bar. Those opting for a simple trattoria lunch often order a plate of pasta and dessert.

STALE AND STELLAR

Florence lacks signature pasta and rice dishes, perhaps because it has raised frugality with bread to culinary craft. Stale bread is the basis for three classic Florentine primi: *pappa al pomodoro, ribollita,* and *panzanella.* "Pappa" is made with either fresh or canned tomatoes and that stale bread. Ribollita is a vegetable soup fortified with *cavolo nero* (sometimes called Tuscan kale), cannellini beans, and thickened with bread. Panzanella, a summertime dish, is reconstituted Tuscan bread combined with tomatoes, cucumber, and basil. They all are greatly enhanced with a generous application of fragrant Tuscan olive oil.

A CLASSIC ANTIPASTO: *CROSTINI DI FEGATINI*

This beloved dish consists of a chicken-liver spread, served warm or at room temperature, on toasted, garlic-rubbed bread. It can be served smooth, like a pâté, or in a chunkier, more rustic spread. It's made by sautéeing chicken livers with finely diced carrot and onion, enlivened with the addition of wine, broth, or Marsala reductions, and mashed anchovies and capers.

A CLASSIC SECONDO: *BISTECCA FIORENTINA*

The town's culinary pride and joy is a thick slab of beef, resembling a T-bone steak, from large white oxen called Chianina. The meat's slapped on the grill and served rare, sometimes with a pinch of salt.

It's always seared on both sides, and just barely cooked inside (experts say 5 minutes per side, and then 15 minutes with the bone sitting perpendicularly on the grill). To ask for it more well-done is to incur disdain; some restaurants simply won't serve it any other way than rare.

A CLASSIC CONTORNO: CANNELLINI BEANS

Simply boiled, they provide the perfect accompaniment to bistecca. The small white beans are best when they go straight from the garden into the pot. They should be anointed with a

generous dose of Tuscan olive oil; the combination is oddly felicitous, and it goes a long way toward explaining why Tuscans are referred to as *mangiafagioli* (bean eaters) by other Italians.

A CLASSIC DOLCE: *BISCOTTI DI PRATO*

These are sometimes the only dessert on offer (if you find yourself in such a restaurant, you'll know you're in a really, truly Tuscan eatery) and are more or less an afterthought to the glories that have preceded them. "Biscotti" means twice-cooked (or, in this case, twice baked). They are hard almond cookies that soften considerably when dipped languidly into *vin santo* ("holy wine"), a sweet dessert wine, or into a simple *caffè*.

A CLASSIC WINE: CHIANTI CLASSICO

This blend from the region just south of Florence relies mainly on the local, hardy Sangiovese grape; it's aged for at least one year before hitting the market. (*Riserve*—reserves—are aged at least an additional six months.)

Chianti is usually the libation of choice for Florentines, and it pairs magnificently with grilled foods and seasonal vegetables. Traditionalists opt for the younger, fruitier (and usually less expensive) versions often served in straw flasks. You can sample *Chianti classico* all over town, and buy it in local *salumerie, enoteche*, and supermarkets.

Updated
by Patricia
Rucidlo

FLORENCE, THE CITY OF THE LILY, gave birth to the Renaissance and changed the way we see the world. For centuries it has captured the imaginations of travelers, who have come seeking rooms with views and phenomenal art. Florence's is a subtle beauty—its staid, unprepossessing palaces built in local stone are not showy. They take on a certain magnificence when day breaks and when the sun sets; their muted colors glow in this light. A walk along the Arno offers views that don't quit and haven't much changed in 700 years; navigating Piazza della Signoria, almost always packed with tourists and locals alike, requires patience. There's a reason why everyone seems to be here, however. It's the heart of the city, and home to the Uffizi—arguably the world's finest repository of Italian (and other) Renaissance art.

Florence was "discovered" in the 1700s by upper-class northerners making the grand tour. It became a mecca for travelers, particularly the Romantics, who were inspired by the elegance of its palazzi and its artistic wealth. Today millions of modern visitors follow in their footsteps. When the sun sets over the Arno and, as Mark Twain described it, "overwhelms Florence with tides of color that make all the sharp lines dim and faint and turn the solid city to a city of dreams," it's hard not to fall under the city's spell.

PLANNING

MAKING THE MOST OF YOUR TIME

With some planning, you can see Florence's most famous sights in a couple of days. Start off at the city's most awe-inspiring work of architecture, the **Duomo**, climbing to the top of the dome if you have the stamina (and are not claustrophobic: it gets a little tight going up and coming back down). On the same piazza, check out Ghiberti's bronze doors at the **Battistero.** (They're actually high-quality copies; the Museo dell'Opera del Duomo has the originals though, at press time, they were in restoration.) Set aside the afternoon for the **Galleria degli Uffizi**, making sure to reserve tickets in advance.

On Day 2, visit Michelangelo's *David* in the **Galleria dell'Accademia**—reserve tickets here, too. Linger in **Piazza della Signoria,** Florence's central square, where a copy of *David* stands in the spot the original occupied for centuries, then head east a couple of blocks to **Santa Croce**, the city's most artistically rich church. Double back and walk across Florence's landmark bridge, the **Ponte Vecchio.**

Do all that, and you'll have seen some great art, but you've just scratched the surface. If you have more time, put the **Bargello**, the **Museo di San Marco**, and the **Cappelle Medicee** at the top of your list. When you're ready for an art break, stroll through the **Boboli Gardens** or explore Florence's lively shopping scene, from the food stalls of the **Mercato Centrale** to the chic boutiques of the **Via Tornabuoni.**

FLORENTINE HOURS

Florence's sights keep tricky hours. Some are closed Wednesday, some Monday, some every other Monday. Quite a few shut their doors each day (or on most days) by 2 in the afternoon. Things get even more confusing on weekends. Make it a general rule to check the hours closely for any place you're planning to visit; if it's someplace you have your heart set on seeing, it's worthwhile to call to confirm.

Here's a selection of major sights that might not be open when you'd expect—*consult the sight listings within this chapter for the full details*. And be aware that, as always, hours can and do change.

The **Uffizi** and the **Accademia** are both closed Monday. All but a few of the galleries at Palazzo Pitti are closed Monday as well.

The **Duomo** closes at 3:30 Thursday (as opposed to 5:30 other weekdays, 4:45 weekends). The dome of the Duomo is closed Sunday.

The **Battistero** is open from noon until 7, Monday through Saturday, and Sunday from 8:30 to 2.

The **Bargello** closes at 1:50 pm, and is closed entirely on alternating Sundays and Mondays. However, it's often open much later during high season and when there's a special exhibition on.

The **Cappelle Medicee** are closed alternating Sundays and Mondays.

Museo di San Marco closes at 1:50 weekdays but stays open until 7 weekends—except for alternating Sundays and Mondays, when it's closed entirely.

Palazzo Medici-Riccardi is closed Wednesday.

UFFIZI RESERVATIONS

At most times of day you'll see a line of people snaking around the Uffizi. They're waiting to buy tickets, and you don't want to be one of them. Instead, call ahead for a reservation (☎ *055/294883*; reservationists speak English). You'll be given a reservation number and a time of admission—the further in advance you call, the more time slots you'll have to choose from. Go to the museum's reservation door at the appointed hour, give the clerk your number, pick up your ticket, and go inside. You'll pay €4 for this privilege, but it's money well spent. You can also book tickets online through the website ⊕ *www.polomuseale. firenze.it*; the booking process takes some patience, but it works.

Use the same reservation service to book tickets for the Galleria dell'Accademia, where lines rival those of the Uffizi. (Reservations can also be made for the Palazzo Pitti, the Bargello, and several other sights, but they usually aren't needed.) An alternative strategy is to check with your hotel—many will handle reservations.

PACING YOUR ART INTAKE

Even for the most dedicated art enthusiast, trying to take in Florence's abundance of masterpieces can turn into a headache—there's just too much to see. Especially if you don't count yourself as an art lover, remember to pace yourself. Allow time to wander and follow your whims, and ignore any pangs of guilt if you'd rather relax in a café and watch the world go by than trudge on sore feet through another breathtaking palace or church.

Florence isn't a city that can be "done." It's a place you can return to again and again, confident there will always be more treasures to discover.

GETTING HERE AND AROUND
AIR TRAVEL
Aeroporto A. Vespucci. Florence's small Aeroporto A. Vespucci, commonly called **Peretola**, is just outside town, and receives flights from Milan, Rome, London, and Paris. ✉ *10 km [6 miles] northwest of Florence* ☎ *055/30615* ⊕ *www.aeroporto.firenze.it.*

To get into the city center from the airport by car, take the autostrada A11. A Sita bus will take you directly from the airport to the center of town. Tickets may be purchased on the bus.

Aeroporto Galileo Galilei. Pisa's Aeroporto Galileo Galilei is the closest landing point with significant international service, including a few direct flights from New York each week on Delta. Sadly, the flight is seasonal and shuts down when it's cold outside. It's a straight shot down the SS67 to Florence. A train service connects Pisa's airport station with Santa Maria Novella, roughly a one- hour trip. Trains start running about 7 am from the airport, 6 am from Florence, and continue service every hour until about 11 pm from the airport, 10 pm from Florence. ✉ *12 km [7 miles] south of Pisa and 80 km [50 miles] west of Florence* ☎ *050/849300* ⊕ *www.pisa-airport.com.*

Florence Air Terminal. For flight information, call the airport or Florence Air Terminal, which—despite the misleading name—is simply an office at the Santa Maria Novella train station, around the corner from train tracks 1 and 2. ✉ *Stazione Centrale di Santa Maria Novella* ☎ *055/216073.*

BIKE AND MOPED TRAVEL
Brave souls (cycling in Florence is difficult at best) may rent bicycles at easy-to-spot locations at Fortezza da Basso, the Stazione Centrale di Santa Maria Novella, and Piazza Pitti. Otherwise, try **Alinari** (✉ *Via San Zanobi 38/r, San Marco* ☎ *055/280500* ⊕ *www.alinarirental. com*). You'll be up against hordes of tourists and those pesky *motorini* (mopeds). (For a safer ride, try Le Cascine, a former Medici hunting ground turned into a large public park with paved pathways.) The historic center can be circumnavigated via bike paths lining the *viali*, the ring road surrounding the area. If you want to go native and rent a noisy Vespa (Italian for "wasp") or other make of motorcycle or *motorino*, you may do so at **Massimo** (✉ *Via Campo d'Arrigo 16/r* ☎ *055/573689*).

BUS TRAVEL
Florence's flat, compact city center is made for walking, but when your feet get weary you can use the efficient bus system, which includes small electric buses making the rounds in the center. Buses also climb to Piazzale Michelangelo and San Miniato south of the Arno.

Maps and timetables for local bus service are available for a small fee at the ATAF (Azienda Trasporti Area Fiorentina) booth next to the train station, or for free at visitor information offices. Tickets must be bought in advance from tobacco shops, newsstands, automatic ticket machines near main stops, or ATAF booths. The ticket must be canceled in the small validation machine immediately upon boarding.

2

You have several ticket options, all valid for one or more rides on all lines. A €1.20 ticket is good for one hour from the time it is first canceled. A multiple ticket—four tickets, each valid for 70 minutes—costs €4.50. A 24-hour tourist ticket costs €5. Two-, three-, and seven-day passes are also available.

Long-distance buses provide inexpensive service between Florence and other cities in Italy and Europe. **Lazzi Eurolines** (⊠ *Via Mercadante 2* ☎ *055/363041* ⊕ *www.lazzi.it*) and **SITA** (⊠ *Via Santa Caterina da Siena 17/r* ☎ *055/47821* ⊕ *www.sita-on-line.it*) are the major lines.

CAR TRAVEL

Florence is connected to the north and south of Italy by the Autostrada del Sole (A1). It takes about 1½ hours of driving on scenic roads to get to Bologna (although heavy truck traffic over the Apennines often makes for slower going), about 3 hours to Rome, and 3 to 3½ hours to Milan. The Tyrrhenian Coast is an hour west on the A11.

An automobile in Florence is a major liability. If your itinerary includes parts of Italy where you'll want a car (such as Tuscany), pick the vehicle up on your way out of town.

TAXI TRAVEL

Taxis usually wait at stands throughout the city (in front of the train station and in Piazza della Repubblica, for example), or you can call for one (☎ *055/4390 or 055/4798*). The meter starts at €3.20, with extra charges at night, on Sunday, for radio dispatch, and for luggage. Women out on the town after midnight seeking taxis are entitled to a 10% discount on the fare; you must, however, request it.

TRAIN TRAVEL

Florence is on the principal Italian train route between most European capitals and Rome, and within Italy it is served frequently from Milan, Venice, and Rome by Intercity (IC) and nonstop Eurostar trains. Avoid trains that stop only at the Campo di Marte or Rifredi station, which are not convenient to the city center.

Stazione Centrale di Santa Maria Novella. Florence's main train station is in the center of town. ☎ *892021* ⊕ *www.trenitalia.com*.

VISITOR INFORMATION

The Florence tourist office, known as the APT (☎ *055/290832* ⊕ *www. firenze.turismo.it*), has branches next to the Palazzo Medici-Riccardi, across the street from Stazione di Santa Maria Novella (the main train station), and around the corner from the Basilica di Santa Croce. The offices are generally open from 9 in the morning until 7 in the evening. The multilingual staff will give you directions (but usually not free maps) and the latest on happenings in the city. It's particularly worth a stop if you're interested in finding out about performing-arts events. The APT website provides information in both Italian and English.

THE DUOMO TO THE PONTE VECCHIO

The heart of Florence, stretching from the Piazza del Duomo south to the Arno, is as dense with artistic treasures as anyplace in the world. Its churches, medieval towers, Renaissance palaces, and world-class museums and galleries contain some of the most outstanding achievements of Western art history.

Much of the *centro storico* (historic center) is closed to automobile traffic, but you still must dodge mopeds, cyclists, and masses of fellow tourists as you walk the narrow streets, especially in the area bounded by the Duomo, Piazza della Signoria, Galleria degli Uffizi, and Ponte Vecchio. Via dei Calzaiuoli, between Piazza del Duomo and Piazza della Signoria, is the city's favorite *passeggiata,* where Florentines come out for an evening stroll.

TOP ATTRACTIONS

★ **Bargello.** This building started out as the headquarters for the Capitano del Popolo (captain of the people) during the Middle Ages, and was later used as a prison. The exterior served as a "most wanted" billboard: effigies of notorious criminals and Medici enemies were painted on its walls. Today it houses the **Museo Nazionale,** home to what is probably the finest collection of Renaissance sculpture in Italy. The concentration of masterworks by Michelangelo (1475–1564), Donatello (circa 1386–1466), and Benvenuto Cellini (1500–71) is remarkable; the works are distributed among an eclectic collection of arms, ceramics, and miniature bronzes, among other things. For Renaissance art lovers, the Bargello is to sculpture what the Uffizi is to painting.

In 1401 Filippo Brunelleschi (1377–1446) and Lorenzo Ghiberti (circa 1378–1455) competed to earn the most prestigious commission of the day: the decoration of the north doors of the Baptistery in Piazza del Duomo. For the contest, each designed a bronze bas-relief panel depicting the sacrifice of Isaac; the panels are displayed together in the room devoted to the sculpture of Donatello, on the upper floor. The judges chose Ghiberti for the commission; see if you agree with their choice. ⊠ *Via del Proconsolo 4, Bargello* ☎ *055/294883* ⊕ *www.polomuseale. firenze.it* ☑ *€4* ⊘ *Daily 8:15–1:50; closed 2nd and 4th Mon. of month and 1st, 3rd, and 5th Sun. of month.*

Battistero (*Baptistery*). The octagonal Baptistery is one of the supreme monuments of the Italian Romanesque style and one of Florence's oldest structures. Local legend has it that it was once a Roman temple dedicated to Mars; modern excavations, however, suggest that its foundations date from the 1st century AD. The round Romanesque arches on the exterior date from the 11th century. The interior dome mosaics from the beginning of the 14th century are justly renowned, but—glittering beauties though they are—they could never outshine the building's famed bronze Renaissance doors decorated with panels crafted by Lorenzo Ghiberti. The doors—or at least copies of them—on which Ghiberti worked most of his adult life (1403–52) are on the north and east sides of the Baptistery, and the Gothic panels on the south door were designed by Andrea Pisano (circa 1290–1348) in 1330.

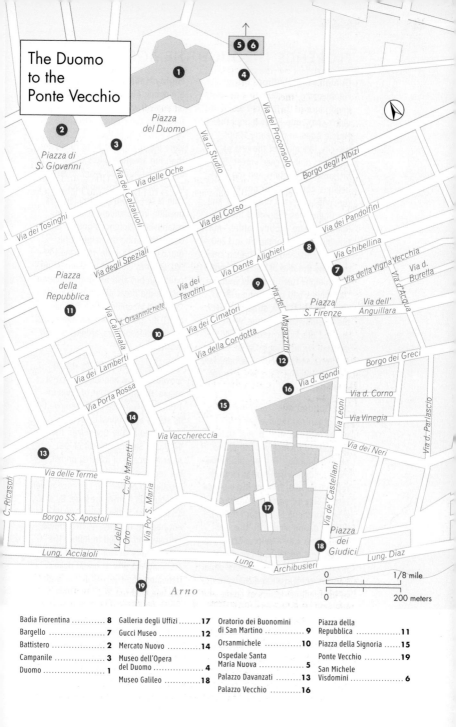

The Duomo to the Ponte Vecchio

Piazza del Duomo

Piazza di S. Giovanni

Piazza della Repubblica

Via dei Tosinghi

Via delle Oche

Via del Calzaiuoli

Via del Corso

Via d. Studio

Via del Proconsolo

Borgo degli Albizi

Via dei Pandolfini

Via Ghibellina

Via della Vigna Vecchia

Via d. Burella

Via Dante Alighieri

Via degli Speziali

Via dei Tavolini

Via V. Orsanmichele

Via dei Cimatori

Via della Condotta

Via Calimala

Via dei Lamberti

Via Porta Rossa

Via dei Magazzini

Piazza S. Firenze

Via dell' Anguillara

Borgo dei Greci

Via d. Gondi

Via d. Corno

Via Vinegia

Via d. Parlascio

Via Leoni

Via Vacchereccia

C. de Manetti

Via Por S. Maria

Via dei Neri

Via de' Castellani

Via delle Terme

Borgo SS. Apostoli

V. dell' Oro

Piazza dei Giudici

Lung. Acciaioli

Lung. Archibusieri

Lung. Diaz

C. Ricasoli

Arno

0   1/8 mile

0   200 meters

FLORENCE THROUGH THE AGES

Guelph vs. Ghibelline. Though Florence can lay claim to a modest importance in the ancient world, it didn't come into its own until the Middle Ages. In the early 1200s the city, like most of the rest of Italy, was rent by civic unrest. Two factions, the Guelphs and the Ghibellines, competed for power. The Guelphs supported the papacy, and the Ghibellines supported the Holy Roman Empire. Bloody battles—most notably one at Montaperti in 1260—tore Florence and other Italian cities apart. By the end of the 13th century the Guelphs ruled securely, and the Ghibellines had been vanquished. This didn't end civic strife, however: the Guelphs split into the Whites and the Blacks for reasons still debated by historians. Dante, author of The *Divine Comedy,* was banished from Florence in 1301 because he was a White.

The Guilded Age. Local merchants had organized themselves into guilds by 1250. In that year they proclaimed themselves the *primo popolo* (literally, "first people"), making a landmark attempt at elective, republican rule. Though the episode lasted only 10 years, it constituted a breakthrough in Western history. Such a daring stance by the merchant class was a by-product of Florence's emergence as an economic powerhouse. Florentines were papal bankers; they instituted the system of international letters of credit; and the gold florin became the international standard of currency. With this economic strength came a building boom. Sculptors such as Donatello and Ghiberti decorated them; painters such as Giotto and Botticelli frescoed their walls.

Mighty Medici. Though ostensibly a republic, Florence was blessed (or cursed) with one very powerful family, the Medici, who came to prominence in the 1430s and were initially the de facto rulers and then the absolute rulers of Florence for several hundred years. It was under patriarch Cosimo il Vecchio (1389–1464) that the Medici's position in Florence was securely established. Florence's golden age occurred during the reign of his grandson Lorenzo de' Medici (1449–92). Lorenzo was not only an astute politician but also a highly educated man and a great patron of the arts. Called "Il Magnifico" (the Magnificent), he gathered around him poets, artists, philosophers, architects, and musicians.

Lorenzo's son Piero (1471–1503) proved inept at handling the city's affairs. He was run out of town in 1494, and Florence briefly enjoyed its status as a republic while dominated by the Dominican friar Girolamo Savonarola (1452–98). After a decade of internal unrest, the republic fell and the Medici were recalled to power, but Florence never regained its former prestige. By the 1530s most of the major artistic talent had left the city—Michelangelo, for one, had settled in Rome. The now-ineffectual Medici, eventually attaining the title of grand dukes, remained nominally in power until the line died out in 1737, after which time Florence passed from the Austrians to the French and back again until the unification of Italy (1865–70), when it briefly became the capital under King Vittorio Emanuele II.

The original Ghiberti doors were removed to protect them from the effects of pollution and acid rain and have been beautifully restored; they are now on display in the Museo dell'Opera del Duomo. At press time, they were in restoration.

Ghiberti's north doors depict scenes from the life of Christ; his later east doors (dating from 1425–52), facing the Duomo facade, render scenes from the Old Testament.

Both merit close examination, for they are very different in style and illustrate the artistic changes that marked the beginning of the Renaissance. Look at the far right panel of the middle row on the earlier (1403–24) north doors (*Jesus Calming the Waters*). Ghiberti here captured the chaos of a storm at sea with great skill and economy, but the artistic conventions he used are basically pre-Renaissance: Jesus is the most important figure, so he is the largest; the disciples are next in size, being next in importance; the ship on which they founder looks like a mere toy.

The exquisitely rendered panels on the east doors are larger, more expansive, more sweeping—and more convincing. The middle panel on the left-hand door tells the story of Jacob and Esau, and the various episodes of the story—the selling of the birthright, Isaac ordering Esau to go hunting, the blessing of Jacob, and so forth—have been merged into a single beautifully realized street scene. Ghiberti's use of perspective suggests depth: the background architecture looks far more credible than on the north-door panels, the figures in the foreground are grouped realistically, and the naturalism and grace of the poses (look at Esau's left leg and the dog next to him) have nothing to do with the sacred message being conveyed. Although the religious content remains, the figures and their place in the natural world are given new prominence, and are portrayed with a realism not seen in art since the fall of the Roman Empire nearly a thousand years before.

As a footnote to Ghiberti's panels, one small detail of the east doors is worth a special look. To the lower left of the Jacob and Esau panel, Ghiberti placed a tiny self-portrait bust. From either side, the portrait is extremely appealing—Ghiberti looks like everyone's favorite uncle—but the bust is carefully placed so that you can make direct eye contact with the tiny head from a single spot. When that contact is made, the impression of intelligent life—of *modern* intelligent life—is astonishing. It's no wonder that these doors received one of the most famous compliments in the history of art from an artist known to be notoriously stingy with praise: Michelangelo declared them so beautiful that they could serve as the Gates of Paradise. ✉ *Piazza del Duomo* ☎ *055/2302885* ⊕ *www. operaduomo.firenze.it* 🎟 *€4* ⊙ *Mon.–Sat. 12:15–7, Sun. 8:30–2, 1st Sat. of month 8:30–2.*

Terrace

TO
PALAZZO
VECCHIO

ENTRANCE

1

Vestibolo
d'entrata
◆

3   4

**Giotto &
13th Century**

2   5-6

**International
Gothic**

7

Early Renaissance
● Uccello's Battle of
San Romano
[in restoration]

8

45

44

43

42

41

Filippo Lippi
● Madonna & Child
with Two Angels

9

Piero della Francesca
● The Portraits of the
Duke Federico da Montefeltro
& his wife, Battista Sforza

10-14

Sandro Botticelli
● Birth of Venus;
Primavera

15   16

17

18

Leonardo Da Vinci
● Adoration of
the Magi
● Annunciation

**GALLERIA DEGLI UFFIZI
SECOND FLOOR**

**Titian & Sebastiano
Del Piombo**
● Venus of Urbino

35

**Michelangelo
& The Florentines**
● Doni Tondo

19

**The Tribune
[in restoration]**

20

21

22

23

24

31   32   33   34

29   28   27   26   25

30

Raphael & Andrea Del Sarto
● Madonna of the Goldfinch

Fodor's Choice
★

Galleria degli Uffizi. The venerable Uffizi Gallery occupies the top floor of the U-shaped **Palazzo degli Uffizi,** designed by Giorgio Vasari (1511–74) in 1560 to hold the *uffizi* (administrative offices) of the Medici grand duke Cosimo I (1519–74). Later, the Medici installed their art collections here, creating what was Europe's first modern museum, open to the public (at first only by request) since 1591.

Among the highlights are Paolo Uccello's *Battle of San Romano,* its brutal chaos of lances one of the finest visual metaphors for warfare ever captured in paint (at press time, it was in restoration); the *Madonna and Child with Two Angels,* by Fra Filippo Lippi (1406–69), in which the impudent eye contact established by the angel would have been unthinkable prior to the Renaissance; the *Birth of Venus* and *Primavera* by Sandro Botticelli (1445–1510), the goddess of the former seeming to float on air and the fairy-tale charm of the latter exhibiting the painter's idiosyncratic genius at its zenith; the portraits of the Renaissance duke Federico da Montefeltro and his wife Battista Sforza, by Piero della Francesca (circa 1420–92); the *Madonna of the Goldfinch* by Raphael (1483–1520), which underwent a stunning years-long restoration, completed in 2009 (check out the brilliant blues that decorate the sky, as well as the eye contact between mother and child, both clearly anticipating the painful future; Michelangelo's *Doni Tondo*; the *Venus of Urbino* by Titian (circa 1488/90–1576); and the splendid *Bacchus* by Caravaggio (circa 1571/72–1610). In the last two works, the approaches to myth and sexuality are diametrically opposed, to put it mildly. Don't forget to see the Caravaggios, which are in an easily missable room during the exiting process.

Late in the afternoon is the least crowded time to visit. For a €4 fee, advance tickets can be reserved by phone, online, or, once in Florence, at the Uffizi reservation booth (*advance tickets* ⊠ *Consorzio ITA, Piazza Pitti 1* ☎ *055/294883)* at least one day in advance of your visit. Keep the confirmation number and take it with you to the door at the museum marked "Reservations." Usually you're ushered in almost immediately. Come with cash, because credit cards are not accepted (though you can use a credit card when booking online). When there's a special exhibit on, which is often, the base ticket price goes up to €11. ⊠ *Piazzale degli Uffizi 6, Piazza della Signoria* ☎ *055/23885* ⊕ *www. uffizi.firenze.it; reservations www.polomuseale.firenze.it* 🖼 *€10, €11 during special exhibitions; reservation fee €4* ⊙ *Tues.–Sun. 8:15–6:50.*

★ **Piazza della Signoria.** This is by far the most striking square in Florence. It was here, in 1497, that the famous "bonfire of the vanities" took place, when the fanatical friar Savonarola induced his followers to hurl their worldly goods into the flames; it was also here, a year later, that he was hanged as a heretic and, ironically, burned. A bronze plaque in the piazza pavement marks the exact spot of his execution.

The statues in the square and in the 14th-century **Loggia dei Lanzi** on the south side vary in quality. Cellini's famous bronze *Perseus* holding the severed head of Medusa is certainly the most important sculpture in the loggia. Other works here include *The Rape of the Sabine* and *Hercules and the Centaur,* both late-16th-century works by Giambologna

(1529–1608), and in the back, a row of sober matrons dating from Roman times.

In the square, the Neptune Fountain, created between 1550 and 1575, takes something of a booby prize. It was created by Bartolomeo Ammannati, who considered it a failure himself. The Florentines call it il Biancone, which may be translated as "the big white man" or "the big white lump." Giambologna's equestrian statue, to the left of the fountain, portrays Grand Duke Cosimo I. Occupying the steps of the Palazzo Vecchio are a copy of Donatello's proud heraldic lion of Florence, the *Marzocco* (the original is now in the Bargello); a copy of Donatello's *Judith and Holofernes* (the original is in the Palazzo Vecchio); a copy of Michelangelo's *David* (the original is in the Galleria dell'Accademia); and Baccio Bandinelli's *Hercules* (1534). The Marzocco, the Judith, and the David were symbols of Florentine civic pride—the latter two subjects had stood up to their oppressors. They provided apt metaphors for the republic-loving Florentines, who often chafed at Medici hegemony.

★ **Ponte Vecchio** (*Old Bridge*). This charmingly simple bridge was built in 1345 to replace an earlier bridge swept away by flood. Its shops first housed butchers, then grocers, blacksmiths, and other merchants. But in 1593 the Medici grand duke Ferdinand I (1549–1609), whose private corridor linking the Medici palace (Palazzo Pitti) with the Medici offices (the Uffizi) crossed the bridge atop the shops, decided that all this plebeian commerce under his feet was unseemly. So he threw out the butchers and blacksmiths and installed 41 goldsmiths and eight jewelers. The bridge has been devoted solely to these two trades ever since.

The **Corridoio Vasariano** (✉ *Piazzale degli Uffizi 6, Piazza della Signoria* ☎ *055/23885 or 055/294883*), the private Medici corridor, was built by Vasari in 1565. Though the ostensible reason for its construction was one of security, it was more likely designed so that the Medici family wouldn't have to walk amid the commoners. The corridor is notoriously fickle with its operating hours; at this writing, it is temporarily open but only to groups. It can sometimes be visited by prior special arrangement. Call for the most up-to-date details. Take a moment to study the Ponte Santa Trinita, the next bridge downriver, from either the bridge or the corridor. It was designed by Bartolomeo Ammannati in 1567 (probably from sketches by Michelangelo), blown up by the retreating Germans during World War II, and painstakingly reconstructed after the war. The view from the Ponte Santa Trinita is beautiful, which might explain why so many young lovers seem to hang out there.

WORTH NOTING

Badia Fiorentina. Originally endowed by Willa, Marquess of Tuscany, in 978, this ancient church is an interesting mélange of 13th-century, Renaissance, baroque, and 18th-century architectural refurbishing. Its graceful bell tower, best seen from the interior courtyard, is beautiful for its unusual construction—a hexagonal tower built on a quadrangular base. The interior of the church (open Monday afternoon only) was halfheartedly remodeled in the baroque style during the 17th century. Three tombs by Mino da Fiesole (circa 1430–84) line the walls, including the *monumento funebre di Conte Ugo* (tomb sculpture of Count

Continued on page 55

THE DUOMO
FLORENCE'S BIGGEST MASTERPIECE

For all its monumental art and architecture, Florence has one undisputed centerpiece: the Cathedral of Santa Maria del Fiore, better known as the Duomo. Its cupola dominates the skyline, presiding over the city's rooftops like a red hen over her brood. Little wonder that when Florentines feel homesick, they say they have *"nostalgia del cupolone."*

The Duomo's construction began in 1296, following the design of Arnolfo da Cambio, Florence's greatest architect of the time. By modern standards, construction was slow and haphazard—it continued through the 14th and into the 15th century, with some dozen architects having a hand in the project.

In 1366 Neri di Fioravante created a model for the hugely ambitious cupola: it was to be the largest dome in the world, surpassing Rome's Pantheon. But when the time finally came to build the dome in 1418, no one was sure how—or even if—it could be done. Florence was faced with a 143-ft hole in the roof of its cathedral, and one of the greatest challenges in the history of architecture.

Fortunately, local genius Filippo Brunelleschi was just the man for the job. Brunelleschi won the 1418 competition to design the dome, and for the next 18 years he oversaw its construction. The enormity of his achievement can hardly be overstated. Working on such a large scale (the dome weighs 37,000 tons and uses 4 million bricks) required him to invent hoists and cranes that were engineering marvels. A "dome within a dome" design and a novel herringbone bricklaying pattern were just two of the innovations used to establish structural integrity. Perhaps most remarkably, he executed the construction without a supporting wooden framework, which had previously been thought indispensable.

Brunelleschi designed the lantern atop the dome, but he died soon after its first stone was laid in 1446; it wouldn't be completed until 1461. Another 400 years passed before the Duomo received its façade, a 19th-century neo-Gothic creation.

DUOMO TIMELINE

1296 Work begins, following design by Arnolfo di Cambio.

1302 Arnolfo dies; work continues, with sporadic interruptions.

1331 Management of construction taken over by the Wool Merchants guild.

1334 Giotto appointed project overseer, designs campanile.

1337 Giotto dies; Andrea Pisano takes leadership role.

1348 The Black Plague; all work ceases.

1366 Vaulting on nave completed; Neri di Fioravante makes model for dome.

1417 Drum for dome completed.

1418 Competition is held to design the dome.

1420 Brunelleschi begins work on the dome.

1436 Dome completed.

1446 Construction of lantern begins; Brunelleschi dies.

1461 Antonio Manetti, a student of Brunelleschi, completes lantern.

1469 Gilt copper ball and cross added by Verrocchio.

1587 Original façade is torn down by Medici court.

1871 Emilio de Fabris wins competition to design new façade.

1887 Façade completed.

WHAT TO LOOK FOR INSIDE THE DUOMO

The interior of the Duomo is a fine example of Florentine Gothic with a beautiful marble floor, but the space feels strangely barren—a result of its great size and the fact that some of the best art has been moved to the nearby **Museo dell'Opera del Duomo**.

Notable among the works that remain are two towering equestrian frescoes of famous mercenaries: *Niccolò da Tolentino* (1456), by Andrea del Castagno, and *Sir John Hawkwood* (1436), by Paolo Uccello. There's also fine terra-cotta work by Luca della Robbia. Ghiberti,

Brunelleschi's great rival, is responsible for much of the stained glass, as well as a reliquary urn with gorgeous reliefs. A vast fresco of the Last Judgment, painted by Vasari and Zuccari, covers the dome's interior. Brunelleschi had wanted mosaics to go there; it's a pity he didn't get his wish.

In the crypt beneath the cathedral, you can explore excavations of a Roman wall and mosaic fragments from the late sixth century; entry is near the first pier on the right. On the way down you pass Brunelleschi's modest tomb.

1. Entrance; stained glass by Ghiberti
2. Fresco of Niccolò da Tolentino by Andrea del Castagno
3. Fresco of John Hawkwood by Paolo Uccello
4. *Dante and the Divine Comedy* by Domenico di Michelino
5. Lunette: *Ascension* by Luca della Robbia
6. Above altar: two angels by Luca della Robbia. Below the altar: reliquary of St. Zenobius by Ghiberti.
7. Lunette: *Resurrection* by Luca della Robbia
8. Entrance to dome
9. Bust of Brunelleschi by Buggiano
10. Stairs to crypt
11. Campanile

500 Feet

300 Feet

MAKING THE CLIMB

Climbing the 463 steps to the top of the dome is not for the faint of heart—or for the claustrophobic—but those who do it will be awarded a smashing view of Florence ❶. Keep in mind that the way up is also the way down, which means that while you're huffing and puffing in the ascent, people very close to you in a narrow staircase are making their way down ❷.

300 Feet

75 Feet

DUOMO BASICS

• Even first thing in the morning during high season (May through September), a line is likely to have formed to climb the dome. Expect an hour wait.

• For an alternative to the dome, consider climbing the less trafficked campanile, which gives you a view from on high of the dome itself.

• Dress code essentials: covered shoulders, no short shorts, and hats off upon entering.

✉ Piazza del Duomo

☎ 055/2302885

🌐 www.operaduomo.firenze.it

🎟 Free, crypt €3, cupola €8

🕐 Crypt: Mon.–Wed., Fri., Sun. 10–5; Thurs. 10–4:30; Sat. 10–5:45; first Sat. of month 10–3:30. Cupola: Weekdays 8:30–7, Sat. 8:30–5:40, 1st Sat. of month 8:30–4. Duomo: Mon.–Wed. and Fri. 10–5, Thurs. 10–4:30, Sat., 10–4:45, Sun 1:30–4:45, 1st Sat. of month 10–3:30.

BRUNELLESCHI vs. GHIBERTI
The Rivalry of Two Renaissance Geniuses

In Renaissance Florence, painters, sculptors, and architects competed for major commissions, with the winner earning the right to undertake a project that might occupy him (and keep him paid) for a decade or more. Stakes were high, and the resulting rivalries fierce—none more so than that between Filippo Brunelleschi and Lorenzo Ghiberti.

The two first clashed in 1401, for the commission to create the bronze doors of the Baptistery. When Ghiberti won, Brunelleschi took it hard, fleeing to Rome, where he would remain for 15 years. Their rematch came in 1418, over the design of the Duomo's cupola, with Brunelleschi triumphant. For the remainder of their lives, the two would miss no opportunity to belittle each other's work.

FILIPPO BRUNELLESCHI (1377–1446)

MASTERPIECE: The dome of Santa Maria del Fiore.

BEST FRIENDS: Donatello, whom he stayed with in Rome after losing the Baptistery doors competition; the Medici family, who rescued him from bankruptcy.

SIGNATURE TRAITS: Paranoid, secretive, bad tempered, practical joker, inept businessman.

SAVVIEST POLITICAL MOVE: Feigned sickness and left for Rome after his dome plans were publicly criticized by Ghiberti, who was second-in-command. The project proved too much for Ghiberti to manage on his own, and Brunelleschi returned triumphant.

MOST EMBARRASSING MOMENT: In 1434 he was imprisoned for two weeks for failure to pay a small guild fee. The humiliation might have been orchestrated by Ghiberti.

OTHER CAREER: Shipbuilder. He built a huge vessel, *Il Badalone*, to transport marble for the dome up the Arno. It sank on its first voyage.

INSPIRED: The dome of St. Peter's in Rome.

LORENZO GHIBERTI (1378–1455)

MASTERPIECE: *The Gates of Paradise*, the ten-paneled east doors of the Baptistery.

BEST FRIEND: Giovanni da Prato, an underling who wrote diatribes attacking the dome's design and Brunelleschi's character.

SIGNATURE TRAITS: Instigator, egoist, know-it-all, shrewd businessman.

SAVVIEST POLITICAL MOVE: During the Baptistery doors competition, he had an open studio and welcomed opinions on his work, while Brunelleschi labored behind closed doors.

OTHER CAREER: Collector of classical artifacts, historian.

INSPIRED: *The Gates of Hell* by Auguste Rodin.

The Gates of Paradise detail

Ugo), widely regarded as Mino's masterpiece. Executed in 1469–81, it shows Mino at his most lyrical: the faces seem to be lighted from within—no small feat in marble. The best-known work of art here is the delicate *Vision of St. Bernard*, by Filippino Lippi (circa 1457–1504), on the left as you enter. The painting—one of Filippino's finest—is in superb condition; note the Virgin Mary's hands, perhaps the most beautifully rendered in the city. On the right side of the church, above the **cappella di San Mauro**, is a monumental organ dating from

1558. Constructed by Onofrio Zeffirini da Cortona (1510–86), it's largely intact but is missing its 16th-century keyboard. ⊠ *Via Dante Alighieri 1, Bargello* ☎ *055/264402* ☉ *Mon. 3–6.*

Campanile. The Gothic bell tower designed by Giotto (circa 1266–1337) is a soaring structure of multicolor marble originally decorated with sculptures by Donatello and reliefs by Giotto, Andrea Pisano, and others (which are now in the Museo dell'Opera del Duomo). A climb of 414 steps rewards you with a close-up of Brunelleschi's cupola on the Duomo next door and a sweeping view of the city. ⊠ *Piazza del Duomo* ☎ *055/2302885* ⊕ *www.operaduomo.firenze.it* 🎟 *€6* ☉ *Daily 8:30–7:30.*

Gucci Museo. Open since September 2011, this museum has all the class and elegance associated with the Gucci name. Tasteful displays of their famous luggage, shoes, and sporting goods (including snorkels and flippers) fill this 14th-century building called the Palazzo del Tribunale di Mercatanzia. Centuries ago, the place heard and tried cases by disgruntled guildsmen, and it's an odd juxtaposition to see an early 15th-century fresco of Christ crucified in a room filled with 20th-century jewelry. You can also see Hillary Swank's 2011 Academy Awards dress, as well as several others in a dramatically lightedt room. Also on hand are rooms for temporary exhibitions, a bookstore devoted mostly to things fashionista, and a café serving light lunches and other, more substantial fare. ⊠ *Piazza Signoria, Duomo* ☎ *055/75923300* ⊕ *www. gucci.com* 🎟 *€6* ☉ *Museum: Daily 10–8. Café/restaurant and bookstore: Daily 10 am–11 pm.*

☺ **Mercato Nuovo** (*New Market*). The open-air loggia, built in 1551, teems with souvenir stands, but the real attraction is a copy of Pietro Tacca's bronze *Porcellino* (which translates as "little pig" despite the fact the animal is, in fact, a wild boar). The *Porcellino* is Florence's equivalent of the Trevi Fountain: put a coin in his mouth, and if it falls through the grate below (according to one interpretation), it means you'll return to Florence someday. What you're seeing is a copy of a copy: Tacca's original version, in the Museo Bardini, is actually a copy of an ancient

Greek work. ⊠ *Corner of Via Por Santa Maria and Via Porta Rossa, Piazza della Repubblica* ⊙ *Market: Tues.–Sat. 8–7, Mon. 1–7.*

Museo dei Ragazzi. Florence's "Children's Museum" may be the best-kept public access secret in Florence. A series of interactive tours includes "Encounters with History," during which participants meet and talk with Giorgio Vasari or Galileo Galilei and explore secret passageways. Events occur at different venues (Palazzo Vecchio, Museo Stibbert, Cappella Brancacci, and the Museo Galileo). Tours are in English and must be booked in advance. Though most of the tours are geared for the three-to eight-year-old crowd, adults will find it lots of fun, too. ⊠ *Piazza della Signoria 1* ☎ *055/2768224* ⊕ *www.palazzovecchio-museoragazzi.it* ⊠ €6 ⊙ *By reservation only.*

Museo dell'Opera del Duomo (*Cathedral Museum*). Ghiberti's original Baptistery door panels (in restoration at press time) and the *cantorie* (choir loft) reliefs by Donatello and Luca della Robbia (1400–82) keep company with Donatello's *Mary Magdalene* and Michelangelo's *Pietà* (not to be confused with his more famous *Pietà* in St. Peter's in Rome). Renaissance sculpture is in part defined by its revolutionary realism, but in its palpable suffering Donatello's *Magdalene* goes beyond realism. Michelangelo's heart-wrenching *Pietà* was unfinished at his death; the female figure supporting the body of Christ on the left was added by Tiberio Calcagni (1532–65), and never has the difference between competence and genius been manifested so clearly. ⊠ *Piazza del Duomo 9* ☎ *055/2302885* ⊕ *www.operaduomo.firenze.it* ⊠ €6 ⊙ *Mon.–Sat. 9–7:30, Sun. 9–1:45.*

Museo Galileo. Although it tends to be obscured by the glamour of the neighboring Uffizi, this science museum has much to commend it: Galileo's own instruments, antique armillary spheres—some of them real works of art—and other reminders that the Renaissance made not only artistic but also scientific history. ⊠ *Piazza dei Giudici 1, Piazza della Signoria* ☎ *055/265311* ⊕ *www.museogalileo.it* ⊠ €8 ⊙ *Mon., Wed., Fri., and Sat. 9:30–6; Thurs. 9:30–1.*

NEED A BREAK?

La Canova di GustaVino. Calling itself a "zupperia," La Canova di Gusta-Vino keeps several hearty, restorative soups on hand. Solid fare includes mixed cheese plates (both French and Italian), as well as *tomino con prosciutto* (mild cow's cheese topped with thin slices of prosciutto) run under the broiler. ⊠ *Via della Condotta 29/r, Piazza della Signoria* ☎ *055/2399806.*

Oratorio dei Buonomini di San Martino. Founded in 1441 by Antoninus, Bishop of Florence, to offer alms to the *poveri vergognosi* (the ashamed poor), this one-room oratory is decorated with 15th-century frescoes by the school of Ghirlandaio that vividly depict the confraternity's activities. More than 500 years later, the Compagnia dei Buonomini, or Confraternity of the Good Men, continues to perform charitable works, linking Renaissance notions of charity to the 21st century. ⊠ *Piazza San Martino, Bargello* ☎ *No phone* ⊠ *Free* ⊙ *Mon.–Thurs. and Sat. 10–noon and 3–5, Fri. 10–noon.*

Orsanmichele. This multipurpose structure began as an 8th-century oratory and then in 1290 was turned into an open-air loggia for selling grain. Destroyed by fire in 1304, it was rebuilt as a loggia-market. Between 1367 and 1380 the arcades were closed and two stories were added above; finally,

at century's end it was turned into a church. Inside is a beautifully detailed 14th-century Gothic tabernacle by Andrea Orcagna (1308–68). The exterior niches contain sculptures (all copies) dating from the early 1400s to the early 1600s by Donatello and Verrocchio (1435–88), among others, which were paid for by the guilds. Although it is a copy, Verrocchio's *Doubting Thomas* (circa 1470) is particularly deserving of attention. Here you see Christ, like the building's other figures, entirely framed within the niche, and St. Thomas standing on its bottom ledge, with his right foot outside the niche frame. This one detail, the position-ing of a single foot, brings the whole composition to life. It's possible to see the original sculptures at the **Museo di Orsanmichele,** which is open Monday. ⊠ *Via dei Calzaiuoli, Piazza della Repubblica* ☎ *055/284944* ⊘ *Museum: Mon. 10–5.*

Ospedale Santa Maria Nuova. Folco Portinari, the father of Dante's Bea-trice, founded this sprawling complex in 1288. It was originally a hos-tel for visiting pilgrims and travelers. During the Black Death of 1348 it served as a hospice for those afflicted. At another point it served as an office where money could be exchanged and deposited and letters could be received; Michelangelo did his banking here. It had been lav-ishly decorated by the top Florentine artists of the day, but most of the works, such as the frescoes by Domenico Veneziano and Piero della Francesca, have disappeared or been moved to the Uffizi for safekeep-ing. Today it functions as a hospital in the modern sense of the word, but you can visit the single-nave church of **Sant'Egidio,** in the middle of the complex, where the frescoes would have stood. Imagine, too, Hugo van der Goes's (1435–82) magnificent *Portinari Altarpiece,* which once crowned the high altar; it's now in the Uffizi. Commissioned by Tommaso Portinari, a descendent of Folco's, it arrived from Bruges in 1483 and created quite a stir. Bernardo Rossellino's immense marble tabernacle (1450), still in the church, is worth a look. ⊠ *Via Sant'Egidio and Piazza di Santa Maria Nuova, San Lorenzo.*

Palazzo Davanzati. The prestigious Davanzati family owned this 14th-century palace in one of Florence's swankiest medieval neighborhoods. The place is a delight, as you can wander through the surprisingly light-filled courtyard, and climb the steep stairs to the *piano nobile,* where the family did most of its living. The beautiful *Sala dei Pappagalli* (Par-rot Room) is adorned with trompe-l'oeil tapestries and gaily painted birds. Though some claim that these date from the 14th century, many art historians are much less sure. ⊠ *Piazza Davanzati 13, Piazza della Repubblica* ☎ *055/2388610* 🎟 *€2* ⊘ *Daily 8:15–1:50. Closed 1st, 3rd, and 5th Sun. of month; closed 2nd and 4th Mon. of month.*

Palazzo Vecchio (*Old Palace*). Florence's forbidding, fortresslike city hall was begun in 1299, presumably designed by Arnolfo di Cambio, and its massive bulk and towering campanile dominate Piazza della Signoria. It was built as a meeting place for the guildsmen governing the city at the time; today it is still City Hall. The interior courtyard is a good deal less severe, having been remodeled by Michelozzo (1396–1472) in 1453; a copy of Verrocchio's bronze *puttino* (cherub), topping the central fountain, softens the space. (The original is upstairs.)

The main attraction is on the second floor: two adjoining rooms that supply one of the most startling contrasts in Florence. The first is the opulently vast **Sala dei Cinquecento** (Room of the Five Hundred), named for the 500-member Great Council, the people's assembly established after the death of Lorenzo the Magnificent, that met here. Giorgio Vasari and others decorated the room, around 1563–65, with gargantuan frescoes celebrating Florentine history; depictions of battles with nearby cities predominate. Continuing the martial theme, the room also contains Michelangelo's *Victory*, intended for the never-completed tomb of Pope Julius II (1443–1513), plus other sculptures of decidedly lesser quality.

In comparison, the little **Studiolo,** just off the Sala dei Cinquecento's entrance, was a private room meant for the duke and those whom he invited in. Here's where the melancholy Francesco I (1541–87), son of Cosimo I, stored his priceless treasures and conducted scientific experiments. Designed by Vasari, it was decorated by him, Giambologna, and many others. ⊠ *Piazza della Signoria* ☎ *055/2768465* ☞ *€6* ☉ *Mon.– Wed. and Fri.–Sun. 9–7, Thurs. 9–2.*

Piazza della Repubblica. The square marks the site of the ancient forum that was the core of the original Roman settlement. The street plan around the piazza still reflects the carefully plotted Roman military encampment. The Mercato Vecchio (Old Market), which had been here since the Middle Ages, was demolished and the current piazza was constructed between 1885 and 1895 as a neoclassical showpiece. The piazza is lined with outdoor cafés, affording an excellent opportunity for people-watching.

San Michele Visdomini. Aficionados of 16th-century mannerism should stop in this church, which has a *Sacra Conversazione* by Jacopo Pontormo (1494–1556). The early work, said by Vasari to have been executed on paper, is in dire need of a cleaning. Its palette is somewhat bereft of the lively colors typically associated with Pontormo. ⊠ *Via dei Servi at Via Bufalini, Duomo* ☎ *No phone* ☉ *Daily 7–noon and 3–6.*

SAN LORENZO TO THE ACCADEMIA

A sculptor, painter, architect, and even a poet, Florentine native son Michelangelo was a consummate genius, and some of his finest creations remain in his hometown. The Biblioteca Medicea Laurenziana is perhaps his most fanciful work of architecture. A key to understanding Michelangelo's genius can be found in the magnificent Cappelle Medicee, where both his sculptural and architectural prowess can be clearly seen. Planned frescoes were never completed, sadly, for they would have shown in one space the artistic triple threat that he certainly was. The towering yet graceful *David*, perhaps his most famous work, resides in the Galleria dell'Accademia.

After visiting San Lorenzo, resist the temptation to explore the market that surrounds the church: the market is open until 7 pm, while the churches and museums you may want to visit are not. Come back to the market later, after other sites have closed. Note that the Museo di San Marco closes at 1:50 on weekdays.

TOP ATTRACTIONS

★ **Cappelle Medicee** (*Medici Chapels*). This magnificent complex includes the **Cappella dei Principi,** the Medici chapel and mausoleum that was begun in 1605 and kept marble workers busy for several hundred years, and the **Sagrestia Nuova** (New Sacristy), designed by Michelangelo and so called to distinguish it from Brunelleschi's Sagrestia Vecchia (Old Sacristy) in San Lorenzo.

Michelangelo received the commission for the New Sacristy in 1520 from Cardinal Giulio de' Medici (1478–1534), who later became Pope Clement VII. The cardinal wanted a new burial chapel for his cousins Giuliano, Duke of Nemours (1478–1534), and Lorenzo, Duke of Urbino (1492–1519), and he also wanted to honor his father, also named Giuliano, and his uncle, Lorenzo il Magnifico. The result was a tour de force of architecture and sculpture. Architecturally, Michelangelo was as original and inventive here as ever, but it is, quite properly, the powerfully sculpted tombs that dominate the room. The scheme is allegorical: on the tomb on the right are figures representing Day and Night, and on the tomb to the left are figures representing Dawn and Dusk; above them are idealized sculptures of the two men, usually interpreted to represent the active life and the contemplative life. But the allegorical meanings are secondary; what is most important is the intense presence of the sculptural figures and the force with which they hit the viewer. Ticket prices jump to €9 when special exhibitions are on—which is frequently. ⊠ *Piazza di Madonna degli Aldobrandini, San Lorenzo* ☎ *055/294883 reservations* ☐€6; €9 during special exhibits ☉ *Mar.–Nov., daily 8:15–3:50; Dec.–Feb., daily 8:15–1:50. Closed 1st, 3rd, and 5th Mon. and 2nd and 4th Sun. of month.*

★ **Galleria dell'Accademia** (*Accademia Gallery*). The collection of Florentine paintings, dating from the 13th to the 18th century, is largely unremarkable, but the sculptures by Michelangelo are worth the price of admission. The unfinished *Slaves*, fighting their way out of their marble prisons, were meant for the tomb of Michelangelo's overly demanding patron Pope Julius II (1443–1513). But the focal point is the original *David*, moved here from Piazza della Signoria in 1873. *David* was commissioned in 1501 by the Opera del Duomo (Cathedral Works Committee), which gave the 26-year-old sculptor a leftover block of marble that had been ruined 40 years earlier by two other sculptors. Michelangelo's success with the block was so dramatic that the city showered him with honors, and the Opera del Duomo voted to build him a house and a studio in which to live and work.

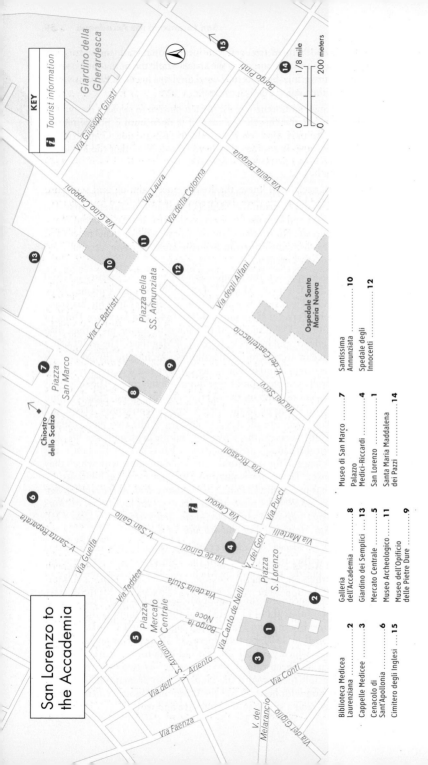

San Lorenzo to the Accademia

KEY

🛈 Tourist Information

Giardino della Gherardesca

Giardino dei Semplici

Piazza San Marco

Chiostro dello Scalzo

Piazza Mercato Centrale

Piazza S. Lorenzo

Piazza della SS. Annunziata

Ospedale Santa Maria Nuova

0 ———— 1/8 mile
0 ———— 200 meters

Today *David* is beset not by Goliath but by tourists, and seeing the statue at all—much less really studying it—can be a trial. Save yourself a long wait in line by reserving tickets in advance. A Plexiglas barrier surrounds the sculpture, following a 1991 attack on it by a self-proclaimed hammer-wielding art anarchist who, luckily, inflicted only a few minor nicks on the toes. The statue is not quite what it seems. It is so poised and graceful and alert—so miraculously alive—that it is often considered the definitive sculptural embodiment of the High Renaissance perfection. But its true place in the history of art is a bit more complicated.

As Michelangelo well knew, the Renaissance painting and sculpture that preceded his work were deeply concerned with ideal form. Perfection of proportion was the ever-sought Holy Grail; during the Renaissance, ideal proportion was equated with ideal beauty, and ideal beauty was equated with spiritual perfection. But *David*, despite its supremely calm and dignified pose, departs from these ideals. Michelangelo didn't give the statue perfect proportions. The head is slightly too large for the body, the arms are too large for the torso, and the hands are dramatically large for the arms. The work was originally commissioned to adorn the exterior of the Duomo and was intended to be seen from a distance and on high. Michelangelo knew exactly what he was doing, calculating that the perspective of the viewer would be such that, in order for the statue to appear proportioned, the upper body, head, and arms would have to be bigger, as they are farther away from the viewer. But he also did it to express and embody, as powerfully as possible in a single figure, an entire biblical story. David's hands *are* big, but so was Goliath, and these are the hands that slew him. Music lovers might want to check out the Museo degli Instrumenti Musicali contained within the Accademia; its Stradivarius is the main attraction. ⊠ *Via Ricasoli 60, San Marco* ☎ *055/294883 reservations, 055/2388609 gallery* 🎫*€11, reservation fee €4* ☉ *Tues.–Sun. 8:15–6:50.*

Museo di San Marco. A Dominican convent adjacent to the church of San Marco now houses this museum, which contains many stunning works by Fra Angelico (circa 1400–55), the Dominican friar famous for his piety as well as for his painting. When the friars' cells were restructured between 1439 and 1444, he decorated many of them with frescoes meant to spur religious contemplation. His unostentatious and direct paintings exalt the simple beauties of the contemplative life. Fra Angelico's works are everywhere, from the friars' cells to the superb panel paintings on view in the museum. Don't miss the famous *Annunciation*, on the upper floor, and the works in the gallery off the cloister as you enter. Here you can see his beautiful *Last Judgment*; as usual, the tortures of the damned are far more inventive and interesting than the pleasures of the redeemed. ⊠ *Piazza San Marco 1* ☎ *055/2388608* 🎫 *€4.50* ☉ *Weekdays 8:15–1:50, weekends 8:15–4:50. Closed 1st, 3rd, and 5th Sun., and 2nd and 4th Mon. of month.*

San Lorenzo. Filippo Brunelleschi designed this basilica, as well as that of Santo Spirito in the Oltrarno, in the 15th century. He never lived to see either finished. The two interiors are similar in design and effect. San Lorenzo, however, has a grid of dark, inlaid marble lines on the floor,

Florence's Trial by Fire

One of the most striking figures of Renaissance Florence was Girolamo Savonarola, a Dominican friar who, for a moment, captured the conscience of the city. In 1491 he became prior of the convent of San Marco, where he adopted a life of austerity and delivered sermons condemning Florence's excesses and the immorality of his fellow clergy. Following the death of Lorenzo de' Medici in 1492, Savonarola was instrumental in the formation of the republic of Florence, ruled by a representative council with Christ enthroned as monarch. In one of his most memorable acts he urged Florentines to toss worldly possessions—from sumptuous dresses to Botticelli paintings—onto a "bonfire of the vanities" in Piazza della Signoria. Savonarola's antagonism toward church hierarchy led to his undoing: he was excommunicated in 1497, and the following year was hanged and burned on charges of heresy. Today, at the Museo di San Marco, you can visit Savonarola's cell.

which considerably heightens the dramatic effect. The grid makes the rigorous geometry of the interior immediately visible, and is an illuminating lesson on the laws of perspective. If you stand in the middle of the nave at the church entrance, on the line that stretches to the high altar, every element in the church—the grid, the nave columns, the side aisles, the coffered nave ceiling—seems to march inexorably toward a hypothetical vanishing point beyond the high altar, exactly as in a single-point-perspective painting. Brunelleschi's **Sagrestia Vecchia** (Old Sacristy) has stucco decorations by Donatello; it's at the end of the left transept. ⊠ *Piazza San Lorenzo* 🕾 *055/2645144* 🖃 *€2.50* ☾ *Mon.–Sat. 10–5 year round; Mar.–Oct., Sun. 1:30–5. Closed Sun. Nov.–Feb.*

WORTH NOTING

Biblioteca Medicea Laurenziana (*Laurentian Library*). Michelangelo the architect was every bit as original as Michelangelo the sculptor. Unlike Brunelleschi (the architect of the Spedale degli Innocenti), however, he wasn't obsessed with proportion and perfect geometry. He was interested in experimentation and invention and in the expression of a personal vision at times highly idiosyncratic.

It was never more idiosyncratic than in the Laurentian Library, begun in 1524 and finished in 1568 by Bartolomeo Ammannati. Its famous **vestibolo,** a strangely shaped anteroom, has had scholars scratching their heads for centuries. In a space more than two stories high, why did Michelangelo limit his use of columns and pilasters to the upper two-thirds of the wall? Why didn't he rest them on strong pedestals instead of on huge, decorative curlicue scrolls, which rob them of all visual support? Why did he recess them into the wall, which makes them look weaker still? The architectural elements here do not stand firm and strong and tall, as inside San Lorenzo, next door; instead, they seem to be pressed into the wall as if into putty, giving the room a soft, rubbery look that is one of the strangest effects ever achieved by 16th-century architecture. It's almost as if Michelangelo intentionally flouted the conventions of the High Renaissance to see what kind of bizarre, mannered effect might result. His innovations were tremendously influential, and produced a period of architectural experimentation. As his contemporary Giorgio Vasari put it, "Artisans have been infinitely and perpetually indebted to him because he broke the bonds and chains of a way of working that had become habitual by common usage."

WORD OF MOUTH

"For a different experience, go to the Mercado Centrale (Central Market) which is full of specialty food stalls that will just amaze you! This is only a few blocks from the Accademia where the Michelangelo *David* is." —Charnees

The anteroom's staircase (best viewed straight-on), which emerges from the library with the visual force of an unstoppable lava flow, has been exempted from the criticism, however. In its highly sculptural conception and execution, it is quite simply one of the most original and fluid staircases in the world. ⊠ *Piazza San Lorenzo 9, entrance to left of San Lorenzo* ☎ *055/210760* ⊕ *www.bml.firenze.sbn.it* ✉ *Special exhibitions €5, museum €3* ⊘ *Sun.–Fri. 9–1.*

Cenacolo di Sant'Apollonia. The frescoes of the refectory of a former Benedictine nunnery were painted in sinewy style by Andrea del Castagno, a follower of Masaccio (1401–28). The *Last Supper* is a powerful version of this typical refectory theme. From the entrance, walk around the corner to Via San Gallo 25 and take a peek at the lovely 15th-century cloister that belonged to the same monastery but is now part of the University of Florence. ⊠ *Via XXVII Aprile 1, San Marco* ☎ *055/2388607* ⊘ *Daily 8:15–1:50. Closed 1st, 3rd, and 5th Sun. of month, and 2nd and 4th Mon. of month.*

Cimitero degli Inglesi. Familiarly known as the English Cemetery, this is the final resting place for some 1,400 souls. It was designed in 1828 by Carlo Reishammer and originally intended for the Swiss community in Florence. Just outside Florence's 14th-century walls (no longer visible), the cemetery grew to accommodate other foreigners living here, and thus earned another of its names, the Protestant Cemetery. Perhaps its most famous resident is Elizabeth Barrett Browning (1809–61), who spent the last 15 years of her life in the city. Other expats, including Arthur Clough, Walter Savage Landor, Frances Trollope (mother of Anthony), and the American preacher Theodore Parker, are buried in this cemetery, which is also referred to as the "Island of the Dead." (Swiss painter Arnold Böcklin [1827–1901] used the cemetery as inspiration for his haunting painting of that name.) ⊠ *Piazzale Donatello 38, Santa Croce* ☎ *055/582608* ✉ *Free; suggested €3 per person for large groups* ⊘ *Nov.–Mar., Mon. 9–noon, Tues.–Fri. 2–5; Apr.–Oct., Mon. 9–noon, Tues.–Fri. 3–6.*

Giardino dei Semplici. Created by Cosimo I in 1550, this delightful garden was designed by favorite Medici architect Niccolò Tribolo. Many of the plants here have been grown since the 16th century. Springtime, especially May, is a particularly beautiful time to visit, as multitudes of azaleas create a riot of color. ⊠ *Via Pier Micheli 3, San Marco* ☎ *055/2757402* ⊕ *www.unifi.it* 🎫 *€6* ⊙ *Thurs.–Tues. 9–1.*

Mercato Centrale. Some of the food at this huge, two-story market hall is remarkably exotic. The ground floor contains meat and cheese stalls, as well as some very good bars that have *panini* (sandwiches), and the second floor teems with vegetable stands. At press time, the second floor was closed for renovations. ⊠ *Piazza del Mercato Centrale, San Lorenzo* ☎ *No phone* ⊙ *Mon.–Sat. 7–2.*

Museo Archeologico (*Archaeological Museum*). Of the Etruscan, Egyptian, and Greco-Roman antiquities here, the Etruscan collection is particularly notable—one of the most important in Italy (the other being in Turin). The famous bronze *Chimera* was discovered (without the tail, which is a 16th-century reconstruction by Cellini). If you're traveling with kids, they might particularly enjoy the small mummy collection. Those with a fondness for gardens should visit on Saturday morning, when the tiny but eminently pleasurable garden is open for tours. ⊠ *Piazza Santissima Annunziata 9/b, Santissima Annunziata* ☎ *055/23575* ⊕ *www.archeotoscana.beniculturali.it* 🎫 *€4* ⊙ *Tues.–Fri. 8:30–7, weekends 8:30–2.*

Museo dell'Opificio delle Pietre Dure. Adjacent to this fascinating small museum is an *opificio,* or workshop, that Ferdinand I established in 1588 to train craftsmen in the art of working with precious and semiprecious stones and marble (*pietre dure* means "hard stones"). Four hundred–plus years later, the workshop is renowned as a center for the restoration of mosaics and inlays in semiprecious stones. The museum is highly informative, and includes some magnificent late Renaissance examples of this highly specialized and beautiful craft. ⊠ *Via degli Alfani 78, San Marco* ☎ *055/26511* 🎫 *€2* ⊙ *Mon.–Wed., Fri., and Sat. 8:15–2; Thurs. 8:15–7.*

Palazzo Medici-Riccardi. The main attraction of this palace, begun in 1444 by Michelozzo for Cosimo de' Medici, is the interior chapel, the so-called **Cappella dei Magi** on the piano nobile (second) floor. Painted on its walls is Benozzo Gozzoli's famous *Procession of the Magi,* finished in 1460 and celebrating both the birth of Christ and the greatness of the Medici family. Gozzoli wasn't a revolutionary painter, and today is considered by some not quite first-rate because of his technique, which was old-fashioned even for his day. Gozzoli's gift, however, was for entrancing the eye, not challenging the mind, and on those terms his success here is beyond question. Entering the chapel is like walking into the middle of a magnificently illustrated children's storybook, and this beauty makes it one of the most enjoyable rooms in the city. Do note that officially only eight visitors are allowed in at a time for a maximum of seven minutes; sometimes, however, there are lenient guards. ⊠ *Via Cavour 1, San Lorenzo* ☎ *055/2760340* 🎫 *€7* ⊙ *Thurs.–Tues. 9–7.*

Santa Maria Maddalena dei Pazzi. One of Florence's hidden treasures, a cool and composed *Crucifixion* by Perugino (circa 1445/50–1523), is in the chapter house of the monastery below this church. Here you can see the Virgin Mary and St. John the Evangelist with Mary Magdalene and Sts. Benedict and Bernard of Clairvaux posed against a simple but haunting landscape. The figure of Christ crucified occupies the center of this brilliantly hued fresco. Perugino's colors radiate—note the juxtaposition of the yellow-green cuff against the orange tones of Magdalene's robe. Entrance to this beauteous fresco is through the Liceo Michelangelo (a high school). ⊠ *Via della Colonna 9, Santa Croce* ☎ *055/2478420* 🎫 *Suggested €1* ☉ *Tues. and Thurs. 2:30–5:30.*

Santissima Annunziata. Dating from the mid-13th century, this church was restructured in 1447 by Michelozzo, who gave it an uncommon (and lovely) entrance cloister with frescoes by Andrea del Sarto (1486–1530), Pontormo (1494–1556), and Rosso Fiorentino (1494–1540). The interior is a rarity for Florence: an overwhelming example of the baroque. But it's not really a fair example, because it's merely 17th-century baroque decoration applied willy-nilly to an earlier structure—exactly the sort of violent remodeling exercise that has given baroque a bad name. The **Cappella dell'Annunziata,** immediately inside the entrance to the left, illustrates the point. The lower half, with its stately Corinthian columns and carved frieze bearing the Medici arms, was commissioned by Piero de' Medici in 1447; the upper half, with its erupting curves and impish sculpted cherubs, was added 200 years later. Fifteenth-century-fresco enthusiasts should also note the very fine *Holy Trinity with St. Jerome* in the second chapel on the left. Done by Andrea del Castagno (circa 1421–57), it shows a wiry and emaciated St. Jerome with Paula and Eustochium, two of his closest followers. ⊠ *Piazza di Santissima Annunziata* ☎ *055/266186* ☉ *Daily 7–12:30 and 4–6:30.*

Spedale degli Innocenti. Built by Brunelleschi in 1419 to serve as an orphanage, this structure takes the historical prize as the very first Renaissance building. Brunelleschi designed its portico with his usual rigor, constructing it from the two shapes he considered mathematically (and therefore philosophically and aesthetically) perfect: the square and the circle. Below the level of the arches, the portico encloses a row of perfect cubes; above the level of the arches, the portico encloses a row of intersecting hemispheres. The entire geometric scheme is articulated with Corinthian columns, capitals, and arches borrowed directly from antiquity. At the time he designed the portico, Brunelleschi was also designing the interior of San Lorenzo, using the same basic ideas. But because the portico was finished before San Lorenzo, the Spedale degli Innocenti can claim the honor of ushering in Renaissance architecture. The 10 ceramic medallions depicting swaddled infants that decorate the portico are by Andrea della Robbia (1435–1525/28), done in about 1487.

Within the Spedale degli Innocenti is a small museum, or **Pinacoteca** (🎫 *€5* ☉ *Thurs.–Tues. 9–7*). Most of the objects are minor works by major artists, but well worth a look is Domenico Ghirlandaio's (1449–94) *Adorazione dei Magi (Adoration of the Magi),* executed in 1488. His use of color, and his eye for flora and fauna, shows that art from north of the Alps made a great impression on him. ⊠ *Piazza di Santissima Annunziata 12* ☎ *055/20371* 🎫 *€4* ☉ *Mon.–Sat. 8:30–7, Sun. 8:30–2.*

Chiostro dello Scalzo. Often overlooked, this small, peaceful 16th-century cloister was frescoed in grisaille by Andrea del Sarto (1486–1530) and Franciabigio with scenes from the life of St. John the Baptist, Florence's patron saint. ⊠ *Via Cavour 69, San Marco* ☎ *055/2388604* ◷ *Mon., Thurs., and Sat. 8:30–1:50.*

SANTA MARIA NOVELLA TO THE ARNO

Piazza Santa Maria Novella, near the train station, suffered from a degree of squalor until a restoration several years in the making and completed in spring 2009, gave it a boost. It's now a gorgeous, pedestrian-only square, with grass and plenty of places to sit and rest your feet. The streets in and around the piazza have their share of architectural treasures, including some of Florence's most tasteful palaces. Between Santa Maria Novella and the Arno is Via Tornabuoni, Florence's finest shopping street.

TOP ATTRACTIONS

Santa Maria Novella. The facade of this church looks distinctly clumsy by later Renaissance standards, and with good reason: it is an architectural hybrid. The lower half was completed mostly in the 14th century; its pointed-arch niches and decorative marble patterns reflect the Gothic style of the day. About 100 years later (around 1456), architect Leon Battista Alberti was called in to complete the job. The marble decoration of his upper story clearly defers to the already existing work below, but the architectural motifs he added evince an entirely different style. The central doorway, the four ground-floor half-columns with Corinthian capitals, the triangular pediment atop the second story, the inscribed frieze immediately below the pediment—these are borrowings from antiquity, and they reflect the new Renaissance style in architecture, born some 35 years earlier at the Spedale degli Innocenti. Alberti's most important addition—the S-curve scrolls (called volutes) surmounting the decorative circles on either side of the upper story—had no precedent whatsoever in antiquity. The problem was to soften the abrupt transition between wide ground floor and narrow upper story. Alberti's solution turned out to be definitive. Once you start to look for them, you will find scrolls such as these (or sculptural variations of them) on churches all over Italy, and every one of them derives from Alberti's example here.

The architecture of the interior is, like that of the Duomo, a dignified but somber example of Florentine Gothic. Exploration is essential, however, because the church's store of art treasures is remarkable. Highlights include the 14th-century stained-glass rose window depicting the *Coronation of the Virgin* (above the central entrance); the Cappella Filippo Strozzi (to the right of the altar), containing late-15th-century frescoes and stained glass by Filippino Lippi; the *cappella maggiore* (the area around the high altar), displaying frescoes by Ghirlandaio; and the Cappella Gondi (to the left of the altar), containing Filippo Brunelleschi's famous wood crucifix, carved around 1410 and said to have so stunned the great Donatello when he first saw it that he dropped a basket of eggs.

Of special interest for its great historical importance and beauty is Masaccio's *Trinity,* on the left-hand wall, almost halfway down the nave. Painted around 1426–27 (at the same time he was working on his frescoes in Santa Maria del Carmine), it unequivocally announced the arrival of the Renaissance. The realism of the figure of Christ was revolutionary in itself, but what was probably even more startling to contemporary Florentines was the barrel vault in the background. The mathematical rules for employing single-point perspective in painting had just been discovered (probably by Brunelleschi), and this was one of the first works of art to employ them with utterly convincing success.

In the cloisters of the **Museo di Santa Maria Novella,** to the left of Santa Maria Novella, is a faded fresco cycle by Paolo Uccello depicting tales from Genesis, with a dramatic vision of the Deluge. Earlier and better-preserved frescoes painted in 1348–55 by Andrea da Firenze are in the chapter house, or the **Cappellone degli Spagnoli** (Spanish Chapel), off the cloister. ⊠ *Piazza Santa Maria Novella 19* ☎ *055/210113, 055/282187 museo* ⊕ *www.museicivicifiorentini.it* ◈ *Church €3.50, museum and chapel €2.70* ⊗ *Museum: Fri.–Mon. 10–4. Church: Mon.–Thurs. 9–5:30, Fri. 11–5:30, Sat. 9–5, Sun. noon–5.*

Santa Trinita. Started in the 11th century by Vallombrosian monks and originally Romanesque in style, the church underwent a Gothic remodeling during the 14th century. (Remains of the Romanesque construction are visible on the interior front wall.) Its major works are the fresco cycle and altarpiece in the Cappella Sassetti, the second to the high altar's right, painted by Ghirlandaio between 1480 and 1485. His work here possesses such graceful decorative appeal as well as a proud depiction of his native city (most of the cityscapes show 15th-century Florence in all her glory). The wall frescoes illustrate scenes from the life of St. Francis, and the altarpiece, depicting the *Adoration of the Shepherds,* veritably glows. ⊠ *Piazza Santa Trinita, Santa Maria Novella* ☎ *055/216912* ⊗ *Mon.–Sat. 8–noon and 4–6.*

WORTH NOTING

Colonna della Giustizia. In the center of **Piazza Santa Trinita** is this column from Rome's Terme di Caracalla, given to the Medici grand duke Cosimo I by Pope Pius IV in 1560. Typical of Medici self-assurance, the name translates as the Column of Justice. The column was raised here by Cosimo in 1565 to mark the spot where he heard the news that Florentine ducal forces had prevailed over a ragtag army composed of Florentine republican exiles and their French allies at the 1554 battle of Marciano near Prato; the victory made his power in Florence all but absolute. ⊠ *Piazza Santa Trinita, Santa Maria Novella.*

Croce al Trebbio. In 1338 the Dominican friars (the Dominican church of Santa Maria Novella is down the street) erected this little granite column near Piazza Santa Maria Novella to commemorate a famous local victory: it was here in 1244 that they defeated their avowed enemies, the Patarene heretics, in a bloody street brawl. ⊠ *Via del Trebbio, Santa Maria Novella.*

Le Cascine. In the 16th century this vast park belonged to the Medici, who used it for hunting, one of their favorite pastimes. It was opened

Santa Maria Novella to the Arno

0 — 1/8 mile
0 — 200 meters

Cenacolo del Foligno

Via San Zanobi
Via Guelfa
Via Taddea
Via Paniale
Via Faenza
Mercato Centrale
Piazza Mercato Centrale
Via dell' Ariento
Borgo la Noce
Via della Stufa
Via de' Ginori
Via Cavour
Via Fiume
Piazza Adua
Via Vallonda
Via Nazionale
Via Canto de Nelli
V. dei Gori
Via Faenza
Via Conti
Via S. Antonio
2
Via del Melarancio
Via del Giglio
Via dell'Alloro
Via Cerretani
Stazione Maria Novella
Piazza dell' Unità Italiana
3
Via dei Panzani
Piazza S. Maria Maggiore
Via Pecori
V. S. Caterina da Siena
Via dei Banchi
Via dei Rondinelli
Via Vecchietti
V. d. Belle Donne
V. del Trebbio
5
Via della Scala
Piazza S. Maria Novella
V. dei Cenacci
V. Benedetta
V. d. Corsi
Via dei Pescioni
Via dell'Albero
4
Via del Sole
Via Strozzi
Pza. Strozzi
V. del Sassetti
Via Palazzuolo
Piazza San Pancrazio
Via Spada
6
V. Maso Finiguerra
7
Via Tornabuoni
V. del Purgatorio
Via d. Porcellana
8
V. d. Vigna Nuova
9
Piazza Santa Trinita
Borgo Ognissanti
12
Piazza Ognissanti
V. dei Fossi
V. del Moro
Via Federighi
Via del Parione
10
C. Ricasoli
Via Montebello
13
V. Parioncino
11
Piazza Goldoni
Lung. Amerigo Vespucci
Lung. Corsini

CLOSE UP

Meet the Medici

The Medici were the dominant family of Renaissance Florence, wielding political power and financing some of the world's greatest art. You'll see their names at every turn around the city. These are some of the clan's more notable members:

Cosimo il Vecchio (1389–1464), incredibly wealthy banker to the popes, was the first in the family line to act as de facto ruler of Florence. He was a great patron of the arts and architecture; he was the moving force behind the family palace and the Dominican complex of San Marco.

Lorenzo il Magnifico (1449–92), grandson of Cosimo il Vecchio, presided over a Florence largely at peace with her neighbors. A collector of cameos, a writer of sonnets, and lover of ancient texts, he was the preeminent Renaissance man.

Leo X (1475–1521), also known as Giovanni de' Medici, became the first Medici pope, helping extend the family power base to include Rome and the Papal States. His reign was characterized by a host of problems, the biggest one being a former friar named Martin Luther.

Catherine de' Medici (1519–89) was married by her great uncle Pope Clement VII to Henry of Valois, who later became Henry II of France. Wife of one king and mother of three, she was the first Medici to marry into European royalty. Lorenzo il Magnifico, her great-grandfather, would have been thrilled.

Cosimo I (1537–74), the first grand duke of Tuscany, should not be confused with his ancestor Cosimo il Vecchio.

to the public in the 19th century. The park runs for nearly 3 km (2 miles) along the Arno and has roughly 291 acres. It's ideal for strolling on sunny days, and there are paths for jogging, allées perfect for biking, grassy fields for picnicking, and lots of space for rollerblading (as well as a place to rent skates). At the northern tip of the park is the **Piazzaletto dell'Indiano,** an oddly moving monument dedicated to Rajaram Cuttraputti, Marajah of Kolepoor, who died in Florence in 1870. The park hosts sports enthusiasts, a weekly open-air market, and discotheques. But be warned: at night there's a booming sex-for-sale trade. ✉ *Main entrance: Piazza Vittorio Veneto, Viale Fratelli Roselli (at Ponte della Vittoria).*

Museo di Casa Martelli. The wealthy Martelli family, long associated with the all-powerful Medici, lived, from the 16th century, in this palace on a quiet street near the basilica of San Lorenzo. The last Martelli died in 1986, and in October 2009 the casa-museo (house-museum) opened to the public. It's the only non-reconstructed example of such a house in all of Florence, and for that reason alone it's worth a visit. The family collected art, and while most of the stuff is B-list, a couple of gems by Beccafumi, Salvatore Rosa, and Piero di Cosimo adorn the walls. Reservations are essential, and you will be shown the glories of this place by well-informed, English-speaking guides. ✉ *Via Zanetti 8, San*

Lorenzo ☎ *055/294883* ⊕ *www.uffizi.firenze.it* 🎟 *€3* ⊘ *Guided tours Thurs. 2, 3:30, and 5; Sat. 9, 10:30, and noon.*

Museo Marino Marini. A 21-foot-tall bronze horse and rider, one of the major works by artist Marini (1901–80), dominates the space of the main gallery here. The museum itself is an eruption of contemporary space in a deconsecrated 9th-century church, designed with a series of open stairways, walkways, and balconies that allow you to peer at Marini's work from all angles. In addition to his Etruscanesque sculpture, the museum houses Marini's paintings, drawings, and engravings. ⊠ *Piazza San Pancrazio, Santa Maria Novella* ☎ *055/219432* ⊕ *www.museomarinomarini.it* 🎟 *€4* ⊘ *Mon. and Wed.–Sat. 10–5.*

Museo Nazionale Alinari della Fotografia. Housed in part of what was once an ancient hospice across the piazza from the church of Santa Maria Novella, this museum hosts temporary photography exhibitions in its two largest rooms. The rest of the ground floor and the long narrow hall upstairs hold part of the museum's vast permanent collection devoted to the history of photography. There are many old cameras of all sizes dating as far back as 1820, and special niches dedicated to specific camera models. ⊠ *Piazza Santa Maria Novella 14/a* ☎ *055/216310* ⊕ *www.alinarifondazione.it* 🎟 *€9* ⊘ *Thurs.–Tues. 10:30–7:30.*

Museo Salvatore Ferragamo. If there's such a thing as a temple for footwear, this is it. The shoes in this dramatically displayed collection were designed by Salvatore Ferragamo (1898–1960) beginning in the early 20th century. Born in southern Italy, the late master jump-started his career in Hollywood by creating shoes for the likes of Mary Pickford and Rudolph Valentino. He then returned to Florence and set up shop in the 13th-century Palazzo Spini Ferroni. The collection includes about 16,000 shoes, and those on exhibition are frequently rotated. ⊠ *Via dei Tornabuoni 2, Santa Maria Novella* ☎ *055/3561* 🎟 *€5* ⊘ *Wed.–Mon. 10–6.*

Museo Stibbert. Federico Stibbert (1838–1906), born in Florence to an Italian mother and an English father, liked to collect things. Over a lifetime of doing so, he amassed some 50,000 objects. This museum, which was also his home, displays many of them. He had a fascination with medieval armor and also collected costumes, particularly Uzbek costumes, which are exhibited in a room called the Moresque Hall. These are mingled with an extensive collection of swords, guns, and other devices whose sole function was to kill people. The paintings, most of which date from the 15th century, are largely second-rate. The house itself is an interesting amalgam of neo-Gothic, Renaissance, and English eccentric. To get here, take Bus 4 (across the street from the station at Santa Maria Novella) and get off at the stop marked "Fabbroni 4." Then follow signs to the museum. ⊠ *Via Federico Stibbert 26* ☎ *055/475520* ⊕ *www.museostibbert.it* 🎟 *€5* ⊘ *Mon.–Wed. 10–2, Fri.–Sun. 10–6. Tours every half hr.*

Ognissanti. The Umiliati owned this architectural hodgepodge of a church before the Franciscans took it over in the mid-16th century. (They were ousted in 2001, and replaced by the Benedictines, who moved out in 2003, only to be replaced, once again, by the Franciscans.)

Beyond the fanciful baroque facade by Matteo Nigetti (1560–1649) are a couple of wonderful 15th-century gems. On the right in the nave is the *Madonna della Misericordia* by Ghirlandaio; a little farther down is Botticelli's *St. Augustine in His Study.* A companion piece, directly across the way, is Ghirlandaio's *St. Jerome.* Also check out the recently restored (as of 2011) wooden crucifix by Giotto: the colors dazzle. Pass through the rather dreadfully frescoed cloister to view Ghirlandaio's superb *Last Supper*—which proves definitively that Leonardo da Vinci was not the only Tuscan painter who could do them well. ⊠ *Piazza Ognissanti, Santa Maria Novella* ☎ *055/2398700* 🎫 *Free* ☉ *Church: daily 7–noon and 3–6; Last Supper: Mon., Tues., and Sat. 9–noon.*

Palazzo Rucellai. Architect Leon Battista Alberti (1404–72) designed perhaps the very first private residence inspired by antique models—which goes a step further than the Palazzo Strozzi. A comparison between the two is illuminating. Evident on the facade of the Palazzo Rucellai, dating between 1455 and 1470, is the ordered arrangement of windows and rusticated stonework seen on the Palazzo Strozzi, but Alberti's facade is far less forbidding. Alberti devoted a far larger proportion of his wall space to windows, which lighten the facade's appearance, and filled in the remainder with rigorously ordered classical elements borrowed from antiquity. The result, though still severe, is less fortress-like, and Alberti strove for this effect purposely (he is on record as saying that only tyrants need fortresses). Ironically, the Palazzo Rucellai was built some 30 years *before* the Palazzo Strozzi. Alberti's civilizing ideas here, it turned out, had little influence on the Florentine palazzi that followed. To Renaissance Florentines power—in architecture, as in life—was equally as impressive as beauty. While you are admiring the facade (the palazzo isn't open to the public), turn around and look at the Loggia dei Rucellai across the street. Built in 1463–66, it was the private "terrace" of the Rucellai family, in-laws to the Medici. Its soaring heights and grand arches are a firm testament to the family's status and wealth. ⊠ *Via della Vigna Nuova, Santa Maria Novella.*

Palazzo Strozzi. The Strozzi family built this imposing palazzo in an attempt to outshine the nearby Palazzo Medici. Based on a model by Giuliano da Sangallo (circa 1452–1516) dating from around 1489 and executed between 1489 and 1504 under il Cronaca (1457–1508) and Benedetto da Maiaino (1442–97), it was inspired by Michelozzo's earlier Palazzo Medici-Riccardi. The palazzo's exterior is simple, severe, and massive: it's a testament to the wealth of a patrician, 15th-century Florentine family. The interior courtyard, entered from the rear of the palazzo, is another matter altogether. It is here that the classical vocabulary—columns, capitals, pilasters, arches, and cornices—is given uninhibited and powerful expression. Blockbuster art shows frequently occur here. ⊠ *Via Tornabuoni, Piazza della Repubblica* ☎ *055/2776461* ⊕ *www.palazzostrozzi.org* 🎫 *Free, except during exhibitions* ☉ *Daily 10–7.*

OFF THE BEATEN PATH

Cenacolo del Foligno. This delightful *Last Supper,* executed sometime in the 1470s, has been variously attributed to Perugino or to one of his followers. Its placement, at the end of a long room—the former refectory for a group of nuns—is simply breathtaking; because the white walls are otherwise unadorned, the fresco packs quite a visual punch. In the middle of the lunette in the upper center, Christ appears in the Garden of Gethsemane with the sleeping apostles. The delicate brushstrokes of the leaves in the trees are exquisite. Judas, as is typical of so many representations of the Last Supper, is shown seated at the other side of the table, quite apart from the other 11 apostles. Note how the artist has carefully labeled each apostle except for Judas. The tondi surrounding the fresco show portraits of prominent Franciscans such as St. Anthony of Padua, Francis of Assisi, St. Bernardino of Siena, and St. Louis of Toulouse. ⊠ *Via Faenza 42, Santa Maria Novella* ☎ *055/286982* 🎫 *Free* 🕓 *Mon., Tues., and Sat. 9–noon.*

SANTA CROCE

The Santa Croce quarter, on the southeast fringe of the historic center, was built up in the Middle Ages outside the second set of medieval city walls. The centerpiece of the neighborhood was (and is) the basilica of Santa Croce, which could hold great numbers of worshippers; the vast piazza could accommodate any overflow and also served as a fairground and, allegedly since the middle of the 16th century, as a playing field for no-holds-barred soccer games. A center of leatherworking since the Middle Ages, the neighborhood is still packed with leatherworkers and leather shops.

TOP ATTRACTIONS

Piazza Santa Croce. Originally outside the city's 12th-century walls, this piazza grew with the Franciscans, who used the large square for public preaching. During the Renaissance it was used for *giostre* (jousts), including one sponsored by Lorenzo de' Medici. "Bonfires of the vanities" occurred here, as well as soccer matches in the 16th century. Lined with many palazzi dating from the 15th century, it remains one of Florence's loveliest piazzas and is a great place to people-watch.

Sinagoga. Jews were well settled in Florence by the end of the 14th century, but by 1570 they were required to live within the large "ghetto," at the north side of today's Piazza della Repubblica, by decree of Cosimo I, who had cut a deal with Pope Pius V (1504–72): in exchange for ghettoizing the Jews, he would receive the title Grand Duke of Tuscany.

Construction of the modern Moorish-style synagogue began in 1874 as a bequest of David Levi, who wished to endow a synagogue "worthy of the city." Falcini, Micheli, and Treves designed the building on a domed Greek cross plan with galleries in the transept and a roofline bearing three distinctive copper cupolas visible from all over Florence. The exterior has alternating bands of tan travertine and pink granite, reflecting an Islamic style repeated in Giovanni Panti's ornate interior. Of particular interest are the cast-iron gates by Pasquale Franci, the eternal light by Francesco Morini, and the Murano glass mosaics by Giacomo dal Medico. The gilded doors of the Moorish ark, which fronts the pulpit and is flanked by extravagant candelabra, are decorated with symbols of the ancient Temple of Jerusalem and bear bayonet marks from vandals. The synagogue was used as a garage by the Nazis, who

Santa Croce

0		1/8 mile
0		200 meters

V. Luigi Carlo Farini

Via dei Pilastri

Via di Mezzo

Via dei Pepi

Borgo Pinti

Via Fiesolana

Via Pietrapiana

Via Martiri d. Popolo

Via S. Egidio

Piazza Salvemini

Via M. Buonarroti

Piazza San Pier Maggiore

V. San Pier Maggiore

Via dell' Ulivo

Via dell' Agnolo

V. dei Pandolfini

Via Ghibellina

Via Matteo Palmieri

Via delle Pinzochere

Via San Cristofano

Borgo Allegri

V. Ghibellina

Via della Vigna Vecchia

Via Giuseppi Verdi

Via Verrazzano

V. di S. Giuseppe

Via d. Buretta

Via d. Torta

Via dell' Anguillara

Borgo dei Greci

Via de' Benci

Borgo S. Croce

Via Antonio Magliabechi

Santa Croce

Via d. Parlascio

Via d. Magalotti

Via d. Rustici

V. dei Neri

Corso Tintori

Via d. Vagelli

Via V. Malenchini

Lung. d. Grazie

Arno

KEY	
i	Tourist information

failed to inflict much damage in spite of an attempt to blow up the place with dynamite. Only the columns on the left side were destroyed, and even then, the Women's Balcony above did not collapse. Note the Star of David in black and yellow marble inlay on the floor. The original capitals can be seen in the garden.

Some of the oldest and most beautiful Jewish ritual artifacts in all of Europe are displayed upstairs in the small **Museo Ebraico.** Exhibits document the Florentine Jewish community and the building of the synagogue. The donated objects all belonged to local families and date from as early as the late 16th century. Take special note of the exquisite needlework and silver pieces. A small but well-stocked gift shop is downstairs. ⊠ *Via Farini 4, Santa Croce* ☎ *055/2346654* 🖃 *Synagogue and museum €5* 🕙 *Apr.– Sept., Sun.–Thurs. 10–6, Fri. 10–2; Oct.–Mar., Sun.–Thurs. 10–3, Fri. 10–2. English guided tours: 10, 11, noon, 1, 2 (no tour at 2 on Fri.).*

Ruth's. The only kosher–vegetarian restaurant in Tuscany (at this writing) is Ruth's, adjacent to Florence's synagogue. On the menu: inexpensive vegetarian and Mediterranean dishes and a large selection of kosher wines. It's closed for Friday dinner and Saturday lunch. ⊠ *Via Farini 2/a, Santa Croce* ☎ *055/2480888* ⊕ *www.kosheruth.com.*

WORTH NOTING

Casa Buonarroti. If you are really enjoying walking in the footsteps of the great genius, you may want to complete the picture by visiting the Buonarroti family home. Michelangelo lived here from 1516 to 1525, and later gave it to his nephew, whose son, called Michelangelo il Giovane (Michelangelo the Younger) turned it into a gallery dedicated to his great-uncle. The artist's descendants filled it with art treasures, some by Michelangelo himself. Two early marble works—the *Madonna of the Steps* and the *Battle of the Centaurs*—hint at the marvels to come. ⊠ *Via Ghibellina 70, Santa Croce* ☎ *055/241752* ⊕ *www.casabuonarroti.it* 🖃 *€6.50* 🕙 *Fri.–Wed. 9:30–2.*

Museo Horne. Englishman Herbert P. Horne (1864–1916), architect, art historian, and collector, spent much of his life in his 15th-century palazzo surrounded by carefully culled paintings, sculptures, and other decorative arts mostly from the 14th to 16th century. His home has since been turned into a museum, and the jewel of the collection is Giotto's *St. Stephen.* The rest of the collection is decidedly B-list (he owned plenty of minor works by major artists such as Masaccio and Bernini), but it's still worth a visit to see how a gentleman lived in the 19th century. Many of the furnishings, such as the 15th-century *lettuccio* (divan), are exemplary. ⊠ *Via dei Benci 6, Santa Croce* ☎ *055/244661* ⊕ *www. stanzedeitesori.it* 🖃 *€5* 🕙 *Mon.–Sat. 9–1.*

Piazza dei Ciompi. Now the site of a daily flea market, this piazza was a working-class neighborhood of primarily wool- and silk-trade workers in the 14th century. The disenfranchised wool workers, forbidden entry to the Arte della Lana (the Wool Guild, whose members included those who traded in wool), briefly seized control of the government. It was a

Continued on page 80

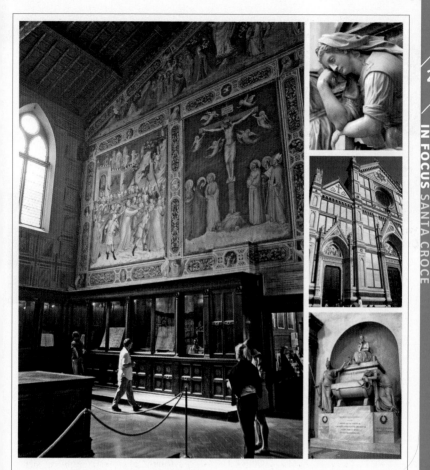

SANTA CROCE

The Duomo may catch your eye first, but to discover Florence's most impressive tombs and finest church art, cross town to this Gothic masterpiece.

Construction of Santa Croce was initiated in 1294 by Florence's Franciscan friars, who were aiming to outdo Santa Maria Novella, the church of their Dominican rivals. In the centuries that followed, Santa Croce would fulfill this goal in ways the Franciscans never could have imagined: it became the resting place of Italian geniuses—a sort of Florentine Westminister Abbey—and the site of revolutionary frescoes that helped change the course of Western art.

Clockwise from left: Sacristy inside Santa Croce; detail from Michelangelo's tomb; exterior of Sante Croce; Dante Alighieri monument.

WHAT TO LOOK FOR INSIDE SANTA CROCE

THE ART WITHIN SANTA CROCE is the most impressive of any church in Florence. Historically, the most significant works are the Giotto frescoes. Time hasn't been kind to them; over the centuries, they've been whitewashed, plastered over, and clumsily restored. But you can still sense the realism and drama of Giotto's work—it may look primitive, but in the 14th century it sparked a revolution. Before Giotto, the role of painting was to symbolize the attributes of God; after him, it was to imitate life.

Giotto fresco, Capella Bardi

Donatello's Crucifixion

ENTRANCE

BASILICA

CLOISTER 1

Pazzi Chapel

Sacristy

Museum

CLOISTER 2

Cimabue's Triumphal Cross

Donatello's Annunciation

6 Donatello's **Annunciation** (c. 1435) exquisitely renders the surprise of the Virgin as Gabriel announces that the Lord is with her.

9 Donatello's **Crucifixion** (1425) annoyed his friend Brunelleschi, who complained that it made Christ look like a peasant. It's located in the Cappella Bardi di Vernio, the chapel at the end of the left transept.

10 Giotto's **Cappella Bardi frescoes** (1320–25), in the first chapel to the right of the main altar, show scenes from the life of St. Francis.

11 Giotto's **Cappella Peruzzi frescoes** (1320–25), in the second chapel to the right of the main altar, depict scenes from the lives of John the Evangelist and Baptist.

12 Brunelleschi's **Cappella Pazzi** (begun 1429) shows the master architect in an intimate light; Brunelleschi did not live to see it completed.

13 Cimabue's **Triumphal Cross** (1287–88) in the attached Museo dell'Opera di Santa Croce, heartbreakingly shows what damage the flood of 1966 did to some very important works of art.

TOMBS & MONUMENTS OF GREAT MEN

1 Galileo Galilei (1564–1642). Galileo's tomb wasn't given prominence until 100 years after his death, as his evidence that the earth was not the center of the universe was highly displeasing to the Church.

2 Lorenzo Ghiberti (1378–1455). The tomb slab of sculptor Lorenzo Ghiberti, who created the Baptistery doors, is on the floor near Galileo's tomb.

3 Michelangelo (1475–1564; tomb shown above). The great master supposedly picked this spot so he'd see Brunelleschi's dome on Judgment Day.

4 Dante Alighieri (1265–1321). A memorial to Dante was built in 1829 to honor the poet, who was banished from Florence and buried in Ravenna.

5 Niccolò Machiavelli (1469–1527). The Renaissance political theoretician has the quote *Tanto nomini nullum par elogium* ("For so great a name, no praise is adequate") on his tomb, built in 1787.

7 Leonardo Bruni (1370–1444). Bernardo Rossellino's *Tomb of Leonardo Bruni* (1444–45), one of Santa Croce's finest works, depicts the humanist chancellor of Florence, the first *uomo illustre* (illustrious man) to be buried in the church.

8 Gioacchino Rossini (1792–1868). The great Italian composer wrote more than 30 operas; his most famous was *Il barbiere di Siviglia* (The Barber of Seville).

Santa Croce Basics

Like the Duomo, Santa Croce is Gothic in design, and in all likelihood the two churches had the same initial architect, Arnolfo di Cambio. In the typical fashion of the Middle Ages, construction continued for decades— the church was finally consecrated by Pope Eugene IV in 1442. And, also like the Duomo, Santa Croce's neo-Gothic façade is a 19th-century addition.

✉ Piazza Santa Croce 16
☎ 055/2466105
🎫 €5 Basilica and museum (combined ticket)
🕑 Mon.–Sat. 9:30–5:30, Sun. 1–5:30.

short-lived exercise in rule by the nonrepresented and was eventually overpowered by the ruling upper class. The loggia, executed in 1567, is by Giorgio Vasari.

Sant'Ambrogio. Named for the Bishop of Milan, this 10th-century church once belonged to an order of Benedictine nuns. Just this side of austere, the church is one of the oldest in Florence. Though its facade is 19th-century, inside are 15th-century panel paintings and a lovely but rather damaged 1486 fresco by Cosimo Roselli, in the chapel to the left of the high altar. The tabernacle of the Blessed Sacrament was carved by Mino da Fiesole, who, like Verrocchio, il Cronaca, and Francesco Granacci (1469/77–1543), is buried here. ⊠ *Piazza Sant'Ambrogio, Santa Croce* 🕾 *No phone* 🖾 *Free* ☉ *Daily 8–noon and 3–6.*

OFF THE BEATEN PATH

American Military Cemetery. About 8 km (5 miles) south of Florence on the road to Siena is one of two American cemeteries in Italy (the other is in Nettuno). It contains 4,402 bodies of Americans who died in Italy during World War II. Spread across a gently rolling hill, the simple crosses and Stars of David bearing only name, date of death, and state seem to stretch endlessly. At the top of the hill is a place for reflection and large mosaic maps depicting the Allied assault in 1943. The two fronts—called the Gothic Line and the Gustav Line—are vividly rendered. So, too, is the list containing 1,409 names of those missing in action. ⊠ *From Florence, take Via Cassia south to Località Scopeti* 🕾 *055/2020020* 🖾 *Free* ☉ *Daily 9–5.*

Museo del Cenacolo. This way-off-the-beaten-path museum (the name translates as the Museum of the Last Supper) has a stunning fresco by Andrea del Sarto. Begun sometime around 1511 and finished in 1526–27, the fresco depicts the moment when Christ announced that one of his apostles would betray him. Andrea has rendered the scene in subtle yet still brilliant colors. Also on display are a couple of lesser-known works by Pontormo and copies of other 16th-century works. (Down the street is the church of San Salvi, founded by John Gualbert and begun in 1048. Though it suffered damage during the siege of 1529–30, the interior has a modest but lovely *Madonna and Child* by Lorenzo di Bicci as well as a 16th-century wood cross on the altar.) To get here, take Bus 6 from Piazza San Marco and get off at the Lungo L'Affrico stop—it's the first stop after crossing the railroad tracks. ⊠ *Via San Salvi 16* 🕾 *055/2388603* 🖾 *Free* ☉ *Tues.–Sun. 8:15–1:50.*

THE OLTRARNO

A walk through the Oltrarno (literally "the other side of the Arno") takes in two very different aspects of Florence: the splendor of the Medici, manifest in the riches of the mammoth Palazzo Pitti and the gracious Giardino di Boboli; and the charm of the Oltrarno, a slightly gentrified but still fiercely proud working-class neighborhood with artisans' and antiques shops.

Farther east across the Arno, a series of ramps and stairs climbs to Piazzale Michelangelo, where the city lies before you in all its glory (skip this trip if it's a hazy day). More stairs (behind La Loggia restaurant) lead to the church of San Miniato al Monte. You can avoid the long walk by taking Bus 12 or 13 at the west end of Ponte alle Grazie and getting off at Piazzale Michelangelo; you still have to climb the monumental stairs to and from San Miniato, but you can then take the bus from Piazzale Michelangelo back to the center of town. If you decide to take a bus, remember to buy your ticket before you board.

TOP ATTRACTIONS

Giardino di Boboli (*Boboli Gardens*). The main entrance to these land-scaped gardens is from the right side of the courtyard of **Palazzo Pitti.** The gardens began to take shape in 1549, when the Pitti family sold the palazzo to Eleanor of Toledo, wife of the Medici grand duke Cosimo I. The initial landscaping plans were laid out by Niccolò Tribolo (1500–50). After his death, work was continued by Ammannati, Giambologna, Bernardo Buontalenti (circa 1536–1608), and Giulio (1571–1635) and Alfonso Parigi (1606–56), among others. Italian land-scaping is less formal than French, but still full of sweeping drama. A copy of the famous *Morgante*, Cosimo I's favorite dwarf astride a particularly unhappy tortoise, is near the exit. Sculpted by Valerio Cioli (circa 1529–99), the work seems to illustrate the perils of culi-nary overindulgence. A visit here can be disappointing, because the gardens are somewhat underplanted and under-cared for, but it's still a great walk with some terrific views. ✉ *Enter through Palazzo Pitti* ☎ *055/294883* ⊕ *www.polomuseale.firenze.it* 🎫 *€10, combined ticket with Museo degli Argenti, Museo delle Porcellane, Villa Bardini, and Giardino Bardini* ⊙ *Jan., Feb., Nov., and Dec., daily 8:15–4:30; Mar., daily 8:15–5:30; Apr., May, Sept., and Oct., daily 8:15–6:30; June–Aug., daily 8:15–7:30. Closed 1st and last Mon. of month.*

Piazzale Michelangelo. From this lookout you have a marvelous view of Florence and the hills around it, rivaling the vista from the Forte di Belvedere. It has a copy of Michelangelo's *David* and outdoor cafés packed with tourists during the day and with Florentines in the evening. In May the **Giardino dell'Iris** (Iris Garden) off the piazza is abloom with more than 2,500 varieties of the flower. The **Giardino delle Rose** (Rose Garden) on the terraces below the piazza is also in full bloom in May and June.

Palazzo Pitti. This enormous palace is one of Florence's largest architec-tural set pieces. The original palazzo, built for the Pitti family around 1460, comprised only the main entrance and the three windows on either side. In 1549 the property was sold to the Medici, and Bartolo-meo Ammannati was called in to make substantial additions. Although he apparently operated on the principle that more is better, he succeeded only in producing proof that more is just that: more.

Today the palace houses several museums: The **Museo degli Argenti** dis-plays a vast collection of Medici treasures, including exquisite antique vases belonging to Lorenzo the Magnificent. The **Galleria del Costume** showcases fashions from the past 300 years. The **Galleria d'Arte Mod-erna** holds a collection of 19th- and 20th-century paintings, mostly Tuscan. Most famous of the Pitti galleries is the **Galleria Palatina,** which contains a broad collection of paintings from the 15th to 17th century.

A GOOD WALK: FLORENTINE PIAZZAS

You may come to Florence for the art, but once here you're likely to be won over by the vibrant, pedestrian-friendly street life played out on its numerous and wonderfully varied piazzas—which are often works of art themselves. This walk, designed for a beautiful day, takes you through many of them (but bypasses some of the most prominent ones you'll inevitably encounter while sightseeing).

Start off in **Piazza Santa Maria Novella**, by the train station; note the glorious facade by Leon Battista Alberti decorating the square's church. Take Via delle Belle Donne, a narrow street running southeast from the piazza, and go left heading toward Via del Trebbio. Here you'll see a cross marking the site of a 13th-century street scuffle between Dominican friars and Patarene heretics. (The Dominicans won.) A right on Via Tornabuoni takes you to tiny **Piazza Antinori**; the 15th-century Antinori palace has been in the hands of its wine-producing namesake family for generations.

Continue south on Via Tornabuoni, stopping in **Piazza Strozzi** to admire (or recoil at) the gargantuan Palazzo Strozzi, a 15th-century family palace designed specifically to dwarf the Palazzo Medici. Step into the courtyard, which is as graceful and delicate as the facade is not. Next stop on Via Tornabuoni is the lovely little **Piazza Santa Trinita**. Take a quick look into the church of Santa Trinita; in its Sassetti Chapel in the right transept, Ghirlandaio's 15th-century frescoes neatly depict the square in which you were just standing.

Continue south to the Arno and cross it via the Ponte Trinita. Go south on Via Maggio, then make a right on Via Michelozzi, which leads to **Piazza Santo Spirito**, one of the loveliest—and liveliest—squares in Florence. Walking away from the piazza's church (heading south), make a left on Via Sant'Agostino, which quickly turns into Via Mazzetta. Stop briefly in **Piazza San Felice** and note No. 8, home of the English poets Elizabeth Barrett Browning and Robert Browning from 1849 to 1861.

From here Via Guicciardini takes you to the massive **Piazza dei Pitti**. Palazzo Pitti was intended to outstrip Palazzo Strozzi in size and ostentation, and it certainly succeeds. Behind the palazzo is the Giardino di Boboli. Walking the straight axis to its top, you'll pass man-made lakes, waterfalls, and grottoes. Head for the 18th-century Giardino dei Cavalieri; when you arrive, pause and admire the view. It's hard to believe the pastoral scene in front of you, complete with olive groves, is in the city center.

If you still have stamina, head back toward the Arno along Via Guicciardini. Just before the Ponte Vecchio, turn right onto Via de' Bardi. Stop for a moment in **Piazza Maria Sopr'Arno** and check out the eerie 20th-century sculpture of John the Baptist, patron saint of Florence. Continue along Via de' Bardi until it becomes Via San Niccolò. Make a right on Via San Miniato, passing through the city walls at Porta San Niccolò. Head up, steeply, on Via Monte alle Croci, and veer left, taking the steps of Via di San Salvatore al Monte. At the top is **Piazzale Michelangelo**, where your effort is rewarded with a breathtaking view of Florence below.

2

The Oltrarno

0 ——— 1/4 mile
0 ——— 400 meters

Forte di Belvedere

Certosa **2**
Giardino Bardini **7**
Giardino di Boboli **6**
Museo Bardini **8**
Palazzo Pitti **5**

Piazzale
Michelangelo **9**
San Miniato al Monte **10**
Santa Felicita **4**
Santa Maria del Carmine ... **1**
Santo Spirito **3**

The rooms of the Galleria Palatina remain much as the Lorena, the rulers who took over after the last Medici died in 1737, left them. Their floor-to-ceiling paintings are considered by some to be Italy's most egregious exercise in conspicuous consumption, aesthetic overkill, and trumpery. Still, the collection possesses high points, including a number of portraits by Titian and an unparalleled collection of paintings by Raphael, notably the double portraits of Angelo Doni and his wife, the sullen Maddalena Strozzi. The price of admission to the Galleria Palatina also allows you to explore the former **Appartamenti Reali,** containing furnishings from a remodeling done in the 19th century. ⊠ *Piazza Pitti* ☎ *055/210323* 🖃 *Galleria Palatina and Galleria d'Arte Moderna, combined ticket €13; Galleria del Costume, Giardino Bardini, Giardino di Boboli, Museo degli Argenti, and Museo Porcelleane, combined ticket €10* 🕙 *Tues.–Sun. 8:15–6:50.*

San Miniato al Monte. This church, like the Baptistery, is a fine example of Romanesque architecture and is one of the oldest churches in Florence, dating from the 11th century. A 12th-century mosaic topped by a gilt bronze eagle, emblem of San Miniato's sponsors, the Calimala (cloth merchants' guild) crowns the lovely green-and-white marble facade. Inside are a 13th-century inlaid-marble floor and apse mosaic. Artist Spinello Aretino (1350–1410) covered the walls of the **Sagrestia** with frescoes depicting scenes from the life of St. Benedict. The **Cappella del Cardinale del Portogallo** (Chapel of the Portuguese Cardinal) is one of the richest 15th-century Renaissance works in Florence. It contains the tomb of a young Portuguese cardinal, Prince James of Lusitania, who died in Florence in 1459. Its glorious ceiling is by Luca della Robbia, and the sculpted tomb by Antonio Rossellino (1427–79). ⊠ *Viale Galileo Galilei, Piazzale Michelangelo, Lungarno Sud* ☎ *055/2342731* 🕙 *Daily 8–12:30 and 3–5:15.*

Santa Maria del Carmine. The **Cappella Brancacci,** at the end of the right transept of this church, houses a masterpiece of Renaissance painting: a fresco cycle that changed the course of Western art. Fire almost destroyed the church in the 18th century; miraculously, the Brancacci Chapel survived almost intact. The cycle is the work of three artists: Masaccio and Masolino (1383–circa 1447), who began it around 1424, and Filippino Lippi, who finished it some 50 years later, after a long interruption during which the sponsoring Brancacci family was exiled. It was Masaccio's work that opened a new frontier for painting, as he was among the first artists to employ single-point perspective; tragically, he died in 1428 at the age of 27, so he didn't live to experience the revolution his innovations caused.

Masaccio collaborated with Masolino on several of the frescoes, but his style predominates in the *Tribute Money,* on the upper-left wall; *St. Peter Baptizing,* on the upper altar wall; the *Distribution of Goods,* on the lower altar wall; and the *Expulsion of Adam and Eve,* on the chapel's upper-left entrance pier. If you look closely at the last painting and compare it with some of the chapel's other works, you should see a pronounced difference. The figures of Adam and Eve possess a startling presence primarily thanks to the dramatic way in which their bodies seem to reflect light. Masaccio here shaded his figures consistently, so as to suggest a single, strong source of light within the world of the painting but outside its frame. In so doing, he succeeded in imitating with paint the real-world effect of light on mass, and he thereby imparted to his figures a sculptural reality unprecedented in his day.

These matters have to do with technique, but with the *Expulsion of Adam and Eve* his skill went beyond mere technical innovation. In the faces of Adam and Eve, you see more than finely modeled figures; you see terrible shame and suffering depicted with a humanity rarely achieved in art. Reservations to see the chapel are mandatory, but can be booked on the same day. Your time inside is limited to 15 minutes—a frustration that's only partly mitigated by a highly informative 40-minute DVD about the history of the chapel you can watch either before or after your visit. ⊠ *Piazza del Carmine, Santo Spirito* ☎ *055/2768224 reservations* ⊒ *€4* ⊗ *Mon. and Wed.–Sat. 10–5, Sun. 1–5.*

Santo Spirito. The plain, unfinished facade gives nothing away, but the interior, although it appears chilly compared with later churches, is one of the most important examples of Renaissance architecture in Italy.

The interior is one of a pair designed in Florence by Filippo Brunelleschi in the early decades of the 15th century (the other is San Lorenzo). It was here that Brunelleschi supplied definitive solutions to the two major problems of interior Renaissance church design: how to build a cross-shaped interior using classical architectural elements borrowed from antiquity and how to reflect in that interior the order and regularity that Renaissance scientists (among them Brunelleschi himself) were at the time discovering in the natural world around them.

Brunelleschi's solution to the first problem was brilliantly simple: turn a Greek temple inside out. While ancient Greek temples were walled buildings surrounded by classical colonnades, Brunelleschi's churches were classical arcades surrounded by walled buildings. This brilliant architectural idea overthrew the previous era's religious taboo against pagan architecture once and for all, triumphantly claiming that architecture for Christian use.

Brunelleschi's solution to the second problem—making the entire interior orderly and regular—was mathematically precise: he designed the ground plan of the church so that all its parts were proportionally related. The transepts and nave have exactly the same width; the side aisles are precisely half as wide as the nave; the little chapels off the side aisles are exactly half as deep as the side.aisles; the chancel and transepts are exactly one-eighth the depth of the nave; and so on, with dizzying exactitude. For Brunelleschi, such a design technique was a matter of passionate conviction. Like most theoreticians of his day, he believed that mathematical regularity and aesthetic beauty were flip sides of the same coin, that one was not possible without the other.

Santo Spirito refectory. In the Santo Spirito refectory (✉ *Piazza Santo Spirito 29* ☎ *055/287043*), adjacent to the church, you can see Andrea Orcagna's highly damaged fresco of the Crucifixion. ✉ *Piazza Santo Spirito* ☎ *055/210030* 🎫 *Church free, refectory €2.20* ⊘ *Mon., Tues., and Thurs.–Sat. 10–12:30 and 4–5:30; Sun. 4–5:30.*

WORTH NOTING

Certosa. The incredible Carthusian complex was largely funded in 1342 by the wealthy Florentine banker Niccolò Acciaiuoli, whose guilt at having amassed so much money must have been at least temporarily assuaged with the creation of such a structure to honor God. In the grand cloister are stunning (but faded) frescoes of *Christ's Passion* by Pontormo. Though much of the paint is missing, their power is still unmistakable. Also of great interest are the monks' cells; the monks could spend most of their lives tending their own private gardens without dealing with any other monks. To get here, you must either take Bus 37 and get off at the stop marked "Certosa" or have a car. Tours, which are mandatory, are given only in Italian, but even if you can't understand what's being said, you can still take in the sights. ✉ *From Florence, take Viale Petrarca to Via Senese and follow it for about 10 mins; the Certosa is on the right, Via di Colleramole 11, Galluzzo* ☎ *055/2049226* 🎫 *Suggested €3–€4* ⊘ *Tues.–Sat. guided visits at 9, 10, 11, 3, 4, and 5; Sun. guided visits at 3, 4, and 5.*

Giardino Bardini. Garden lovers, those who crave a view, and those who enjoy a nice hike should visit this lovely villa and garden, whose history spans centuries. The villa had a walled garden as early as the 14th century; the "Grand Stairs"—a zigzag ascent well worth scaling—has been around since the 16th. The garden is filled with irises, roses, and heirloom flowers, and includes a Japanese garden and statuary. A very pretty walk (all for the same admission ticket) takes you through the Giardino di Boboli and past the Forte Belvedere to the upper entrance to the giardino. ✉ *Via de'Bardini, San Niccolò* ☎ *005/294883* 🎫 *€10, combined ticket with Galleria Costume, Giardino di Boboli, Museo Argenti, Museo Porcellane* ⊘ *Jan., Feb., Nov., and Dec., daily 8:15– 4:30; Mar., daily 8:15–5:30; Apr., May, Sept., and Oct., daily 8:15– 6:30; June–Aug., daily 8:15–7:30. Closed 1st and last Mon. of month.*

Museo Bardini. The 19th-century collector and antiquarian Stefano Bardini turned his palace into his own private museum. Upon his death, the collection was turned over to the state. It includes an interesting assortment of Etruscan pieces, sculpture, paintings, and furniture that dates mostly from the Renaissance and the baroque. ✉ *Piazza de' Mozzi 1* ☎ *055/2342427* ⊕ *www.museifiorentini.it* 🎫 *€5* ⊘ *Thurs.–Mon. 11–5.*

Santa Felicita. This late-baroque church (its facade was remodeled between 1736 and 1739) contains the mannerist Jacopo Pontormo's *Deposition,* the centerpiece of the Cappella Capponi (executed 1525–28) and a masterpiece of 16th-century Florentine art. The remote figures, which transcend the realm of Renaissance classical form, are portrayed in tangled shapes and intense pastel colors (well preserved because of the low lights in the church), in a space and depth that defy reality. Note, too, the exquisitely frescoed *Annunciation,* also by Pontormo, at a right angle to the *Deposition.* The granite column in the piazza was erected in 1381 and marks a Christian cemetery. ⊠ *Piazza Santa Felicita, Via Guicciardini, Palazzo Pitti* ☯ *Mon.–Sat. 9–noon and 3–6, Sun. 9–1.*

NEED A BREAK? **Cabiria.** Across the piazza from the church of Santo Spirito, this welcoming spot draws funky locals and visitors in search of a cappuccino, a quenching ade, or an expertly mixed drink. When it's warm, sit outside on the terrace. ⊠ *Piazza Santo Spirito 4/r* ☎ *055/215732.*

WHERE TO EAT

Florence's popularity with tourists means that, unfortunately, there's a higher percentage of mediocre restaurants here than you'll find in most Italian towns (Venice, perhaps, might win the prize). Some restaurant owners cut corners and let standards slip, knowing that a customer today is unlikely to return tomorrow, regardless of the quality of the meal. So, if you're looking to eat well, it pays to do some research, starting with the recommendations here. Dining hours start at around 1 for lunch and 8 for dinner. Many of Florence's restaurants are small, so reservations are a must. You can sample such specialties as creamy *fegatini* (a chicken-liver spread) and *ribollita* (minestrone thickened with bread and beans and swirled with extra-virgin olive oil) in a bustling, convivial trattoria, where you share long wooden tables set with paper place mats, or in an upscale *ristorante* with linen tablecloths and napkins.

Those with a sense of culinary adventure should not miss the tripe sandwich, served from stands throughout town. This Florentine favorite comes with a fragrant *salsa verde* (green sauce) or a piquant red hot sauce—or both. Follow the Florentines' lead and take a break at an *enoteca* (wine bar) during the day and discover some excellent Chiantis and Super Tuscans from small producers who rarely export.

Eating ethnic in Florence is a hit-or-miss affair. Although numerous Asian restaurants have sprung up since the 1990s, most are nothing to write home about. Still, if you need a break from Italian, some relief is available.

Pizzas in Florence can't compete with their counterparts in Rome or Naples, but you can sample a few good approximations.

Cafés in Italy serve not only coffee concoctions and pastries but also sweets, drinks, and panini, and some have hot pasta and lunch dishes. They are usually open from early in the morning to late at night, and are often closed Sunday.

WHAT IT COSTS IN EUROS					
	¢	$	$$	$$$	$$$$
Restaurants	under €20	€20–€30	€30–€45	€45–€65	over €65

Prices are for a first course *(primo)*, second course *(secondo)*, and dessert *(dolce)*.

THE DUOMO TO THE PONTE VECCHIO

Use the coordinate (✛ A1) at the end of each listing to locate a site on the corresponding map.

$
ECLECTIC

✕ **Birreria Centrale.** The feel here is more Munich beer hall than Florentine trattoria; indeed, although the menu lists plenty of Italian dishes, it also emphasizes sausages and sauerkraut. The *würstel rossi con crauti, speck, e patate alla tedesca* (a large and quite plump hotdog with sauerkraut, cured beef, potatoes, and pickles), for instance, comes with a dollop of spicy mustard. Heavy wooden tables are set closely together, and copies of 19th-century paintings adorn the intensely yellow walls, along with two frescoed Michelangelesque nudes that cavort over a brick arch. There's outside seating in warm weather—a great place to enjoy a beer. ⊠ *Piazza Cimatori 1/r, Duomo* ☎ *055/211915* ◯ *Closed Sun.* ✛ *F3.*

¢
ITALIAN
★

✕ **Coquinarius.** This rustically elegant space, which has served many purposes over the past 600 years, offers some of the tastiest food in town at great prices. It's the perfect place to come if you aren't sure what you're hungry for, as they offer a little bit of everything: salad-lovers will have a hard time choosing from among the lengthy list (the Scozzese, with poached chicken, avocado, and bacon, is a winner); those with a yen for pasta will face agonizing choices (the ravioli with pecorino and pears is particularly good). A revolving list of *piatti unici* (single dishes that can be ordered on their own, usually served only at lunch) can also whet the whistle, as well as terrific cheese and cured-meat plates. The well-culled wine list has lots of great wines by the glass, and even more by the bottle. ⊠ *Via delle Oche 15/r, Piazza della Signoria* ☎ *055/2302153* ⊕ *www.coquinarius.it* ⌁ *Reservations essential* ✛ *F3.*

$$
WINE BAR

✕ **Frescobaldi Wine Bar.** The Frescobaldi family has run a vineyard for more than 700 years, and this swanky establishment offers tasty and sumptuous fare to accompany the seriously fine wines. Warm terracotta-color walls with trompe-l'oeil tapestries provide a soothing atmosphere. The menu is typically Tuscan, but turned up a notch or two: the *faraona in umido con l'uva* (stewed guinea fowl with grapes) comes with a side of feather-light mashed potatoes. Save room for dessert, as well as one of the dessert wines. A separate, lovely little wine bar called Frescobaldino has a shorter—but equally good—menu and a delightful, multilingual barman called Primo. ⊠ *Via de' Magazzini 2–4/r, Piazza della Signoria* ☎ *055/284724* ◯ *Closed Sun. No lunch Mon.* ✛ *E4.*

¢
ITALIAN

✕ **Giuliano Centro.** Near the Uffizi is Giuliano Centro, with a mouthwatering assortment of food including crisp *pollo fritto* (fried chicken). If you want to mingle with locals, grab a sandwich and an inexpensive glass of wine at their enoteca directly across the street. ⊠ *Via de' Neri 74/r, Piazza della Signoria* ☎ *055/2382723* ▭ *No credit cards* ✛ *F4.*

BEST BETS FOR
FOR FLORENCE DINING

With hundreds of restaurants to choose from, how will you decide where to eat? Fodor's writers and editors have selected their favorite restaurants by price, cuisine, and experience in the Best Bets lists below. In the first column, Fodor's Choice properties represent the "best of the best."

2

WINE LIST

Cantinetta Antinori, $$$, p. 95
Enoteca Pinchiorri, $$$$, p. 99
Fuori Porta, ¢, p. 101
La Giostra, $$, p. 99
Taverna del Bronzino, $$, p. 91

Fodor'sChoice ★

Cibrèo, $$$$, p. 98
Mario, ¢, p. 91
Ora d'Aria, $$$, p. 90
Taverna del Bronzino, $$, p. 91

Best by Price

¢

All'Antico Vinaio, p. 96
da Nerbone, p. 90
da Rocco, p. 98
La Casalinga, p. 101
La Mescita, p. 91
Mario, p. 91
Osteria Antica Mescita San Niccolò, p. 101

$

Baldovino, p. 98
Cibrèo Trattoria, p. 98
Il Santo Bevitore, p. 101

$$

Frescobaldi Wine Bar, p. 88
Il Latini, p. 95

La Giostra, p. 99
Simon Boccanegra, p. 100
Taverna del Bronzino, p. 91

$$$

Ora d'Aria, $$$, p. 90

$$$$

Cibrèo, p. 98

Best Experiences

FOR KIDS

Baldovino, $, p. 98
Danny Rock, $, p. 98
Il Latini, $$, p. 95

ROMANTIC

Enoteca Pinchiorri, $$$$, p. 99

BISTECCA FIORENTINA (TUSCAN STEAK)

Il Latini, $$, p. 95
La Giostra, $$, p. 99
Osteria de'Benci, $$, p. 99

OUTDOOR DINING

Fuori Porta, ¢, p. 101
Osteria de'Benci, $$, p. 99

WINE BARS

Casa del Vino, $, p. 102
Il Santino, ¢, p. 102
Le Volpi e l'Uva, $, p. 102

ALTA CUCINA (SOPHISTICATED CUISINE)

Enoteca Pinchiorri, $$$$, p. 99
Taverna del Bronzino, $$, p. 91

CASALINGA (HOME COOKING)

La Casalinga, ¢, p. 101
Mario, ¢, p. 91

LUNCH SPOTS

Antico Noe, $$, p. 97
Cantinetta Antinori, $$$, p. 95
Coquinarius, ¢, p. 88
Frescobaldi Wine Bar, $$, p. 88

$ ✕ **Le Mosacce.** Come to this tiny, cramped, and boisterous place for a
TUSCAN quick bite to eat. The menu, written in three languages, includes hearty,
stick-to-the-ribs Florentine food such as ribollita. Seating is communal,
and fellow diners share the big, straw-covered flask of wine. Service is
prompt and efficient; two nimble cooks with impeccable timing staff
the small kitchen. ⊠ *Via del Proconsolo 55/r, Duomo* ☎ *055/294361*
⌁ *Reservations not accepted* ⊘ *Closed weekends* ✛ *F3.*

$$$ ✕ **Ora d'Aria.** The name means "Hour of Air" and refers to the time
MODERN ITALIAN of day when prisoners were let outside for fresh air—alluding to the
Fodor's Choice fact that this gem was originally located across the street from what
★ was once the old prison. In the kitchen, gifted young chef Marco Sta-
bile turns out exquisite Tuscan classics as well as more fanciful dishes,
which are as beautiful as they are delicious; intrepid diners will be
vastly rewarded for ordering the tortellini *farciti con piccione* (stuffed
with pigeon) if it's on the day's menu. Two tasting menus give Stabile
even greater opportunity to shine, and the carefully culled wine list has
something to please every palate. Do not miss his tiramisu espresso—
something halfway between a dessert and a coffee. In fact, if you're a
serious gourmand, do not miss this place. ⊠ *Via Georgofili 79/r, Piazza
della Signoria* ☎ *055/2001699* ⌁ *Reservations essential* ⊘ *Closed Sun.
No lunch* ✛ *H4.*

¢ ✕ **Rivoire.** One of the best spots in Florence for people-watching is Riv-
CAFÉ oire. Stellar service, light snacks, and terrific aperitivi are the norm. It's
been around since the 1860s, and has been famous for its hot and cold
chocolate (with or without cream) for over a century. ⊠ *Via Vaccherec-
cia 4/r, Piazza della Signoria* ☎ *055/214412* ✛ *E4.*

SAN LORENZO AND BEYOND

¢ ✕ **Alfio e Beppe.** Watch chickens roast over high flames as you decide
ITALIAN which of the other delightful things you're going to eat with it. The
beauty of this place is that it's closed Saturday (when most things are
open), and open Sunday (when most things are not). ⊠ *Via Cavour
118–120/r, San Marco* ☎ *055/214108* ▬ *No credit cards* ✛ *F1.*

¢ ✕ **da Nerbone.** This *tavola calda* in the middle of the covered Mer-
TUSCAN cato Centrale has been serving up food to Florentines who like their
tripe since 1872. Tasty primi and secondi are available every day, but
cognoscenti come for the *panino con il lampredotto* (tripe sandwich).
Less adventurous sorts might want to sample the *panino con il bollito*
(boiled beef sandwich). Ask that the bread be *bagnato* (briefly dipped
in the tripe cooking liquid), and have both the salsa verde and *salsa pic-
cante* (a spicy cayenne sauce) slathered on top. ⊠ *Mercato San Lorenzo*
☎ *055/219949* ▬ *No credit cards* ⊘ *Closed Sun. No dinner* ✛ *D1.*

¢ ✕ **da Sergio.** In 2015, this little eatery will celebrate its centenary, and
TUSCAN with good reason. It's been in the capable hands of the Gozzi family,
who have ensured continuity and stuck to Tuscan tradition. The food's
terrific, eminently affordable, and just across the way from the basilica
of San Lorenzo, which means that you can imbibe well-prepared food
while marveling at the Brunelleschi and Michelangelo you've just seen.
The menu is short, and changes daily. Their *lombatina alla griglia* (a

grilled veal T-bone steak) is almost always on, and meat-eaters should not miss it. Pastas are equally terrific. Dessert, in true Florentine fashion, is limited to biscotti with vin Santo (twice-cooked biscuits with sweet wine). ⊠ *Piazza San Lorenzo 8/r, San Lorenzo* ☎ *055/281941* ⊙ *Closed Sun. No dinner* ✛ *E2.*

¢ ✕ **Dioniso.** Located in the midst of university buildings, Dioniso draws a
GREEK mostly student crowd who come to enjoy tasty kebab and other tasty, inexpensive Greek fare. ⊠ *Via San Gallo 16/r, San Lorenzo* ☎ *055/217882* ✛ *E1.*

¢ ✕ **Gran Caffè.** Down the street from the Accademia, Gran Caffè is a per-
CAFÉ fect stop for a marvelous panino or sweet while raving about the majesty of Michelangelo's *David.* Do be aware that sitting at a table is more expensive at most cafés, and this place is particularly notorious in trying to get you to sit down. ⊠ *Piazza San Marco 11/r* ☎ *055/215833* ✛ *F1.*

¢ ✕ **La Mescita.** Come early (or late) to grab a seat at this tiny spot fre-
TUSCAN quented by Florentine university students and businesspeople. You can get a sandwich to go or sit and enjoy the day's *primi* (such as a terrific *lasagne*) and follow it with their *polpettona* (meat loaf) and tomato sauce. Though seats are cramped and the wine is no great shakes, the service is friendly and the food hits the spot. Groups of 15 or more can reserve in the evening for special meals. ⊠ *Via degli Alfani 70/r, San Lorenzo* ☎ *No phone* ▭ *No credit cards* ⊙ *Closed Sun. No dinner* ✛ *G1.*

¢ ✕ **Mario.** Florentines flock to this narrow family-run trattoria near San
TUSCAN Lorenzo to feast on Tuscan favorites served at simple tables under a
Fodor'sChoice wooden ceiling dating from 1536. A distinct cafeteria feel and genuine
★ Florentine hospitality prevail: you'll be seated wherever there's room, which often means with strangers. Yes, there's a bit of extra oil in most dishes, which imparts calories as well as taste, but aren't you on vacation in Italy? Worth the splurge is *riso al ragù* (rice with ground beef and tomatoes). ⊠ *Via Rosina 2/r, corner of Piazza del Mercato Centrale, San Lorenzo* ☎ *055/218550* ⚌ *Reservations not accepted* ⊙ *Closed Sun. and Aug. No dinner* ✛ *E1.*

¢ ✕ **Oliandolo.** Just down the street from the Accademia, Oliandolo is a
CAFÉ perfect place to have a light lunch. ⊠ *Via Ricasoli 38–40/r, Santissima Annunziata* ☎ *055/211296* ✛ *F1.*

¢ ✕ **Pugi.** Handily across the street from San Marco, Pugi sells the popular
PIZZA *pizza a taglio* (pizza by the slice); their *focaccie* and other breads are equally good. It's a great place to grab a quick lunch or snack. ⊠ *Piazza San Marco 9/b, San Marco* ☎ *055/280981* ▭ *No credit cards* ✛ *F1.*

$$ ✕ **Taverna del Bronzino.** Want to have a sophisticated meal in a 16th-
TUSCAN century Renaissance artist's studio? The former studio of Santi di Tito,
Fodor'sChoice a student of Bronzino's, has a simple, formal decor, with white table-
★ cloths and place settings. The classic, elegantly presented Tuscan food is superb, and the solid, afforable wine list rounds out the menu— especially because Stefano, the sommelier, really knows his stuff. The service is outstanding. Reservations are advised, especially for eating at the wine cellar's only table. ⊠ *Via delle Ruote 25/r, San Marco* ☎ *055/495220* ⊙ *Closed Sun. and 3 wks in Aug.* ✛ *G1.*

Sweets for the Sweet

Sweet-lovers have a bounty of gelato and pastry shops to choose from in Florence.

Caffè delle Carrozze. A convenient café, around the corner from the Uffizi and practically at the foot of the Ponte Vecchio, this spot has many terrific flavors, especially the chocolate-chip-laced coffee. ⊠ *Piazza del Pesce 3–5/r, Piazza della Signoria* ☎ *055/2396810* ⊟ *No credit cards.*

Dolci e Dolcezze. This *pasticceria* (bakery), just off colorful Borgo La Croce, has the prettiest and tastiest cakes, sweets, and tarts in town. It's closed Monday. ⊠ *Piazza C. Beccaria 8/r, Sant'Ambrogio* ☎ *055/2345458* ⊟ *No credit cards.*

★ **Gelaterie Carabe.** Specializing in things Sicilian (including cannoli), this shop is known for its tart and flavorful *granità* (granular flavored ices), made only in summer, which are great thirst-quenchers. ⊠ *Via Ricasoli 60/r, San Marco* ☎ *055/289476* ⊟ *No credit cards.*

I Dolci di Patrizio Corsi. Florentines with serious sweet tooths come here for a deliciously bewildering selection of chocolate- and cream-filled pastries. It's closed Sunday afternoon. ⊠ *Borgo Albizi 15/r, Santa Croce* ☎ *055/2480367.*

Fodor's Choice ★ **Grom.** A stone's throw from the Duomo, this is one of the best gelaterias in town. Flavors change frequently according to the season, so expect a fragrant gelato *di cannella* (cinnamon ice cream) in winter and lively fresh fruit flavors in summer. Though the original Grom hails from Turin (and there's a Grom in New York City), this is still probably the best gelato in town. ⊠ *Via del Campanile, Duomo* ☎ *055/216158* ⊟ *No credit cards.*

Vestri. This shop is devoted to chocolate in all its guises. The small but sublime selection of chocolate-based gelati includes one with hot peppers. ⊠ *Borgo Albizi 11/r, Santa Croce* ☎ *055/2340374* ⊟ *No credit cards.*

Vivoli. The reputation of Vivoli as the best gelateria in town is somewhat dated, but it's still worth visiting this Florentine institution. ⊠ *Via Isola delle Stinche 7/r, Santa Croce* ☎ *055/292334* ⊟ *No credit cards.*

¢ ✕**Turkuaz.** Döner kebabs at Turkuaz have a killer hot sauce; you can
TURKISH order hot rice and meat dishes to eat in or take out. It's generally agreed by aficionados that this is the best kebab in town. ⊠ *Via de'Servi 65/r, Santissima Annunziata* ☎ *055/2399959* ✛ *F1.*

SANTA MARIA NOVELLA TO THE ARNO

¢ ✕**Amon.** This standing-only spot serves Egyptian and other Middle
MIDDLE EASTERN Eastern fare at rock-bottom prices. ⊠ *Via Palazzuolo 26/28r, Santa Maria Novella* ☎ *No phone* ⊟ *No credit cards* ✛ *B2.*

$$ ✕**Buca Lapi.** The Antinori family started selling wine from their palace's
ITALIAN basement in the 15th century. Six hundred years later, this *buca* (hole) is a lively, subterranean restaurant filled with Florentine aristocrats chowing down on what might be the best (and most expensive) *bistecca fiorentina* in town. The classical Tuscan menu has the usual suspects:

2

crostino di cavolo nero (black cabbage on toasted garlic bread), along with ribollita and *pappa al pomodoro* (two bread-based soups). You might want to cut directly to the chase, however, and order the bistecca, an immense slab of Chianina beef impeccably grilled on the outside, just barely warmed on the inside. (If you're not into rare meat, order something else from the grill.) Roast potatoes and cannellini beans make perfect accompaniments. ☒ *Via del Trebbio 1, Santa Maria Novella* ☎ *055/213768* ⊕ *www.bucalapi.com* ⌕ *Reservations essential* ✛ *B2.*

¢ ✕ **Buddakan.** Come here for a pan-Asian experience, with Thai, Korean, ASIAN FUSION and Chinese dishes. It's popular with young Florentines looking for tasty non-Italian food in a somewhat swank setting. ☒ *Largo Bargellini 2, Santa Maria Novella* ☎ *055/2346123* ✛ *H4.*

¢ ✕ **Caffè Giacosa.** This café opens early in the morning for coffee, serves CAFÉ tasty light lunches, and makes excellent cocktails in the evening. ☒ *Via della Spada 10/r, Santa Maria Novella* ☎ *055/2776328* ⊕ *www. caffegiacosa.it* ✛ *B2.*

$$$ ✕ **Cantinetta Antinori.** After a morning of shopping on Via Tornabuoni, ITALIAN stop for lunch in this 15th-century palazzo in the company of Florentine ladies (and men) who come to see and be seen over lunch. The panache of the food matches its clientele: expect treats such as *tramezzino con pane di campagna al tartufo* (country pâté with truffles served on bread) and the *insalata di gamberoni e gamberetti con carciofi freschi* (crayfish and prawn salad with shaved raw artichokes). ☒ *Piazza Antinori 3, Santa Maria Novella* ☎ *055/292234* ✚ *Closed weekends, 20 days in Aug., and Dec. 25–Jan. 6* ✛ *D3.*

¢ ✕ **i 5 Tavoli.** Around the corner from the church of Santa Maria Novella, CAFÉ i 5 Tavoli has only five tables (as its name implies), many fine sand- ☺ wiches, hot pasta specials, and a very good (and inexpensive) cheeseburger. ☒ *Via del Sole 26/r, Santa Maria Novella* ☎ *055/294438* ✛ *C3.*

$$ ✕ **Il Latini.** It may be the noisiest, most crowded trattoria in Florence, TUSCAN but it's also one of the most fun. The genial host, Torello ("little bull") Latini, presides over his four big dining rooms, and somehow it feels as if you're dining in his home. Ample portions of ribollita prepare the palate for the hearty meat dishes that follow. Both Florentines and tourists alike tuck into the *agnello fritto* (fried lamb) with aplomb. There's almost always a wait, even with a reservation. ☒ *Via dei Palchetti 6/r, Santa Maria Novella* ☎ *055/210916* ✚ *Closed Mon. and 15 days at Christmas* ✛ *C3.*

¢ ✕ **La Spada.** Near Santa Maria Novella is La Spada. Walk in and inhale ITALIAN the fragrant aromas of meats cooking in the wood-burning oven. La Spada also has a complete line of takeout. ☒ *Via del Moro 66/r, Santa Maria Novella* ☎ *055/218757* ▭ *No credit cards* ✛ *C2.*

¢ ✕ **Noir.** At night Noir is often a chaotic scene (especially on hot sum- CAFÉ mer nights), but in the daytime it's significantly calmer. Light lunches and a good list of panini are on the menu, and you can nosh at an outdoor table with a view of the Arno. For those craving Sunday brunch, Noir has that, too. ☒ *Lungarno Corsini 12/14r, Lungarno Sud* ☎ *055/210751* ✛ *C3.*

$ ✕ **Obika.** Mozzarella takes center stage at this sleek eatery on Florence's ITALIAN swankiest street. The cheese, along with its culinary cousin *burrata* (a soft cheese filled with butter), arrives daily from southern Italy to become the centerpiece for various salads and pastas. Four different kinds of *rotoli* (rolled, stuffed mozzarella) are available; the one with smoked salmon and arugula is particularly tasty. You can pair your cheese with a number of accompaniments, including *caponata* (a Sicilian eggplant mélange) and mortadella from nearby Prato. Efficient service (in a 16th century-palazzo courtyard when the weather's nice) and a well-priced wine list add to the pleasure of a meal here. Nightly happy hour, with an extensive selection of snacks, is fun and a bargain. ⊠ *Via Tornabuoni 16, Santa Maria Novella* ☎ *055/2773526* ✛ *D3.*

$ ╳ **Osteria delle Belle Donne.** Down the street from the church of Santa
TUSCAN Maria Novella, this gaily decorated spot, festooned with ropes of garlic and other vegetables, has an ever-changing menu and stellar service led by the irrepressible Giacinto who, after a brief sabbatical, has returned to oversee tasty-again food emerging from the kitchen. The menu offers Tuscan standards, but shakes things up with alternatives such as *sedani con bacon, verza, e uova* (thick noodles sauced with bacon, cabbage, and egg); when avocados are ripe, they're on the menu, too (either with cold boiled shrimp or expertly grilled chicken breast). If you want to eat alfresco, request a table outside when booking—and remember to save room for dessert. ⊠ *Via delle Belle Donne 16/r, Santa Maria Novella* ☎ *055/2382609* ✛ *D3.*

¢ ╳ **Procacci.** Classy Procacci is a Florentine institution dating to 1885; try
CAFÉ one of the panini tartufati and swish it down with a glass of Prosecco. It's closed Sunday. ⊠ *Via Tornabuoni 64/r, Santa Maria Novella* ☎ *055/ 211656* ✛ *D3.*

$ ╳ **Trattoria Sostanza (il Troia).** Since opening its doors in 1869, this trat-
ITALIAN toria has been serving top-notch, unpretentious food to Florentines who
★ like their *bistecca fiorentina* very large and very rare. A single room with white tiles on the wall and paper mats on the tables provides the setting for delicious meals. Along with fine Tuscan classics, they have two signature dishes: the *tortino di carciofi* (artichoke tart) and the *pollo al burro* (chicken with butter). The latter is an amazing surprise, a succulent chicken breast cooked very quickly and served as soon as it leaves the grill. Leave room for dessert, as their *torta alla Meringa* (a semifrozen dessert flecked with chocolate and topped with meringue) is scrumptious. ⊠ *Via della Porcellana 25, Santa Maria Novella* ☎ *055/212691* ╚ *Reservations essential* ▭ *No credit cards* ✛ *B3.*

SANTA CROCE

¢ ╳ **All'Antico Vinaio.** Florentines like to grab a quick bite to eat at this
DELI narrow little sandwich shop near the Uffizi. A handful of stools offer places to perch while devouring one of their very fine sandwiches; most folks, however, simply grab a sandwich, pour themselves a glass of inexpensive wine in a paper cup (more serious wines can be poured into glasses), and mingle on the pedestrians-only street in front. If *porchetta* (a very rich, deliciously fatty roasted pork) is on offer, don't miss it. They also offer first-rate primi, which change daily. ⊠ *Via de' Neri 65, Santa Croce* ☎ *No phone* ▭ *No credit cards* ⊗ *Closed Sun.* ✛ *F4.*

CLOSE UP

Salumerie

2

Salumerie, specialty food shops similar to delis, are strong on fine fresh ingredients such as meats and cheeses. They're great places to assemble a picnic lunch.

Antico Salumificio Anzuini-Massi. This salumeria shrink-wraps their own pork products, making it a snap to take home some *salame di cinghiale* (wild boar salami). ⊠ *Via de' Neri 84/r, Santa Croce* ☎ *055/294901* ▭ No credit cards.

Baroni. The cheese collection at Baroni may be the most comprehensive in Florence. They also have high-quality truffle products, vinegars, and other delicacies. ⊠ *Mercato Central, enter at Via Signa, San Lorenzo* ☎ *055/289576* ⊕ *www. baronialimentari.it.*

Conti. Stop here for top-quality wines, olive oils, and dried fruits; they'll shrink-wrap the highest-quality dried porcini for traveling. Closed Sunday. ⊠ *Mercato Centrale, enter at Via Signa, San Lorenzo* ☎ *055/2398501* ⊕ *www.tuscanyflavours.com.*

Fodor's Choice ★ **'ino.** Serving arguably the best *panini* (sandwiches) in town, proprietor Alessandro sources only the very best ingredients. Located right behind the Uffizi, 'ino is a perfect place to grab a tasty sandwich and glass of wine before forging on to the next museum. ⊠ *Via dei Georgofili 3/r–7/r* ☎ *055/219208.*

Pegna. Looking for some cheddar cheese to pile in your panino? Pegna has been selling both Italian and non-Italian food since 1860. It's closed Saturday afternoon in July and August, Wednesday afternoon September through June, and Sunday year-round. ⊠ *Via dello Studio 8, Duomo* ☎ *055/282701.*

★ **Perini.** Closed Sunday, Perini sells prosciutto, mixed meats, sauces for pasta, and a wide assortment of antipasti. They're generous with their free samples. ⊠ *Mercato Centrale, enter at Via dell'Aretino, San Lorenzo* ☎ *055/2398306.*

$$
TUSCAN

✕**Antico Noe.** If Florence had diners (it doesn't), this would be the best diner in town. The short menu at the one-room eatery relies heavily on seasonal ingredients picked up daily at the market. Though the secondi are good, it's the antipasti and primi that really shine. The menu comes alive particularly during truffle and artichoke season (don't miss the grilled artichokes if they're on the menu). Locals rave about the tagliatelle *ai porcini* (with mushrooms); the fried eggs liberally laced with truffle might be the greatest truffle bargain in town. Ask for the menu in Italian, as the English version is much more limited. The short wine list has some great bargains. ⊠ *Volta di San Piero 6/r, Santa Croce* ☎ *055/2340838* ♁ *Closed Sun. and 2 wks in Aug.* ✛ *G3.*

¢
CAFÉ

✕**Baldobar.** This tiny space next to the basilica of Santa Croce offers a perfect spot for a light lunch or snack. It opens at 8 in the morning, and closes at 8 at night. In between, you could have breakfast, a cup of tea, or a glass of non-Italian wine (a rarity in this town). Tasty baguette sandwiches and soups of the day make for a nice, light lunch. ⊠ *Via San Giuseppe 20/r, Santa Croce* ☎ *055/2260107* ✛ *H4.*

$
ITALIAN
✕ **Baldovino.** David and Catherine Gardner, expat Scots, have created this lively, brightly colored restaurant down the street from the church of Santa Croce. From its humble beginnings as a pizzeria, it has evolved into something more. It's a happy thing that pizza is still on the menu, but now it shares billing with sophisticated primi and secondi. The menu changes monthly, and has such treats as *filetto di manzo alla Bernaise* (filet mignon with light béarnaise sauce). Baldovino also serves pasta dishes and grilled meat until the wee hours. ⊠ *Via San Giuseppe 22/r, Santa Croce* ☎ *055/241773* ✛ *H4.*

$$$$
TUSCAN
Fodor's Choice
★
✕ **Cibrèo.** The food at this upscale trattoria is fantastic, from the creamy crostini *di fegatini* (a savory chicken-liver spread) to the melt-in-your-mouth desserts. Many Florentines hail this as the city's best restaurant, and Fodor's readers tend to agree—though some take issue with the prices and complain of long waits for a table (even with a reservation). If you thought you'd never try tripe—let alone like it—this is the place to lay any doubts to rest: the *trippa in insalata* (cold tripe salad) with parsley and garlic is an epiphany. The food is traditionally Tuscan, impeccably served by a staff that's multilingual—which is a good thing, because there are no written menus. ⊠ *Via A. del Verrocchio 8/r, Santa Croce* ☎ *055/2341100* ⌂ *Reservations essential* ⊗ *Closed Sun. and Mon. and July 25–Sept. 5* ✛ *H3.*

$
TUSCAN
✕ **Cibrèo Trattoria.** This intimate little trattoria, known to locals as Cibreino, shares its kitchen with the famed Florentine culinary institution from which it gets its name. They share the same menu, too, though Cibreino's is much shorter. Start with *il gelatina di pomodoro* (tomato gelatin) liberally laced with basil, garlic, and a pinch of hot pepper, and then sample the justifiably renowned *passato in zucca gialla* (pureed yellow-pepper soup) before moving on to any of the succulent second courses. Save room for dessert, as the pastry chef has a deft hand with chocolate tarts. To avoid sometimes agonizingly long waits, come early (7 pm) or late (after 9:30). ⊠ *Via dei Macci 118, Santa Croce* ☎ *055/2341100* ⌂ *Reservations not accepted* ▭ *No credit cards* ⊗ *Closed Sun. and Mon. and July 25–Sept. 5* ✛ *H3.*

$
AMERICAN
☺
✕ **Danny Rock.** There's a bit of everything at this restaurant, which is always hopping with Italians eager to eat well-made cheeseburgers and fries or one of the many tasty crepes (served both sweet and savory). You can also find a basic plate of spaghetti as well as a respectable pizza here. Interior decor isn't high on the list: you dine at a green metal table with matching chairs. The young-at-heart feel might explain why the main dining room has a big screen showing *Looney Tunes.* ⊠ *Via Pandolfini 13/r, Santa Croce* ☎ *055/2340307* ✛ *G3.*

¢
TUSCAN
✕ **da Rocco.** At one of Florence's biggest markets you can grab lunch to go, or you could cram yourself into one of the booths and pour from the straw-cloaked flask (wine here is *da consumo,* which means they charge you for how much you drink). Food is abundant, Tuscan, and fast; locals pack in. The menu changes daily, and the prices are great. ⊠ *In Mercato Sant'Ambrogio, Piazza Ghiberti, Santa Croce* ☎ *No phone* ⌂ *Reservations not accepted* ▭ *No credit cards* ⊗ *Closed Sun. No dinner* ✛ *H2.*

2

$$$$ ✕**Enoteca Pinchiorri.** A sumptuous Renaissance palace with high frescoed
ITALIAN ceilings and bouquets in silver vases provides the backdrop for this
restaurant, one of the most expensive in Italy. Some consider it one of
the best, and others consider it a non-Italian rip-off, as the kitchen is
presided over by a Frenchwoman with sophisticated, yet international-
ist, leanings. Prices are high (think $100 for a plate of spaghetti) and
portions are small; the vast holdings of the wine cellar (undoubtedly the
best in Florence), as well as stellar service, dull the pain, however, when
the bill is presented. ✉ *Via Ghibellina 87, Santa Croce* ☎ *055/242777*
⌨ *Reservations essential. Jacket required* ☉ *Closed Sun., Mon., and
Aug. No lunch.* ✛ *G4.*

$ ✕**Kome.** If you're looking for a break from the ubiquitous ribollita, stop
JAPANESE in at this eatery, which may be the only Japanese restaurant in the world
to be housed in a 15th-century Renaissance palazzo. High, vaulted
arches frame the Kaiten sushi conveyor belt. It's Japanese food, cafeteria
style: selections, priced according to the color of the plate, make their
way around a bar, where diners pick whatever they find appealing.
Those seeking a more substantial meal head to the second floor, where
Japanese barbecue is prepared at your table. The minimalist basement
provides a subtle but dramatic backdrop for a well-prepared cocktail.
✉ *Via de' Benci 41/r, Santa Croce* ☎ *055/2008009* ✛ *G4.*

¢ ✕**La Ghiotta.** This shop sells whole and half chickens, grilled or roasted,
ITALIAN among other things. The baked fennel is also a treat. ✉ *Via Pietrapiana
7/r, Santa Croce* ☎ *055/241237* ▭ *No credit cards* ✛ *H3.*

$$ ✕**La Giostra.** This clubby spot, whose name means "carousel" in Italian,
ITALIAN was created by the late Prince Dimitri Kunz d'Asburgo Lorena, and is
★ now expertly run by his handsome twin sons. In perfect English they
will describe favorite dishes, such as the *taglierini con tartufo bianco,*
a decadently rich pasta with white truffles. The constantly changing
menu has terrific vegetarian and vegan options. For dessert, this might
be the only show in town with a sublime tiramisu *and* a wonderfully
gooey Sacher torte. ✉ *Borgo Pinti 12/r, Santa Croce* ☎ *055/241341*
⌨ *Reservations essential* ✛ *H3.*

¢ ✕**Le Campane.** The *pizziauoli* (pizza-makers) successfully merge Roman
PIZZA (thin) crust with Neapolitan (thick) crust at Le Campane. ✉ *Borgo
La Croce 85–87/r, Santa Croce* ☎ *055/2341101* ⊕ *www.lecampane.it*
▭ *No credit cards* ✛ *H3.*

$$ ✕**Osteria de'Benci.** A few minutes from Santa Croce, this charming oste-
ITALIAN ria serves some of the most eclectic food in Florence. Try the spaghetti
degli eretici (in tomato sauce with fresh herbs). The grilled meats are justifiably famous; the *carbonata* is a succulent piece of grilled beef served
rare. Weekly specials complement what's happening in the market, and
all of the food pairs beautifully with their wine list, which is heavy on
things Tuscan. When it's warm, you can dine outside with a view of the
13th-century tower belonging to the prestigious Alberti family. ✉ *Via
de' Benci 11–13/r, Santa Croce* ☎ *055/2344923* ⌨ *Reservations essential* ☉ *Closed Sun. and 2 wks in Aug.* ✛ *F5.*

¢ ✕**Pizzeria Caffè Italiano.** This small pizzeria is favored by locals. Come
PIZZA early to grab one of the few tables, and don't mind the fact that service

What Tripe!

While in Florence, those with a sense of culinary adventure should seek out a tripe sandwich, which is just about as revered by local gourmands as the *bistecca alla fiorentina*. In this case, however, the treasure comes on the cheap—sandwiches are sold from small stands found in the city center, topped with a fragrant green sauce or a piquant red hot sauce, or both. *Bagnato* means that the hard, crusty roll is first dipped in the tripe's cooking liquid; it's advisable to say "*sì*" when asked if that's how you like it. Sandwiches are usually taken with a glass of red wine poured from the tripe seller's *fiasco* (flask). If you find the tripe to your liking, you might also enjoy *lampredotto*, another (some say better) cut of stomach. For an exalted, high-end tripe treat, try Fabio Picchi's cold tripe salad, served gratis

as an *amuse-bouche* at the restaurant Cibrèo. It could make a convert of even the staunchest "I'd never try *that*" kind of eater.

Tripe carts are lunchtime favorites of Florentine working men—it's uncommon, but not unheard of, to see a woman at a tripe stand. Aficionados will argue which sandwich purveyor is best; here are three that frequently get mentioned:

La Trippaia ⊠ *Via dell'Ariento, Santa Maria Novella* 🕾 *No phone* ☾ *Closed Sun.*

Il Trippaio ⊠ *Via de' Macci at Borgo La Croce, Santa Croce* 🕾 *No phone* ☾ *Closed Sun.*

Nerbone ⊠ *Inside the Mercato Centrale, Santa Maria Novella* 🕾 *No phone* ☾ *Closed Sun.*

here is intentionally rushed: turning tables is paramount. ⊠ *Via Isole delle Stinche 11/r, Santa Croce* 🕾 *055/289368* ▭ *No credit cards* ✛ *G4.*

$$
ITALIAN ✕ **Simon Boccanegra.** Florentine epicures flock to this place named for a *condottiere* (mercenary) hero in a Verdi opera. Under high ceilings, candles on every table cast a rosy glow; the fine wine list and superb service make a meal here a true pleasure. The chef has a deft hand with fish dishes, as well as an inventiveness when it comes to reinterpreting such classics as risotto with chicken liver—he adds leek and saffron to give it a lift. A less expensive, less formal wine bar serving a basic Tuscan menu is also on the premises. ⊠ *Via Ghibellina 124/r, Santa Croce* 🕾 *055/2001098* ⌖ *Reservations essential* ☾ *Closed Sun. No lunch* ✛ *G4.*

¢
MEXICAN ✕ **Tijuana.** Open only at night, Tijuana is frequented by young Florentines and U.S. junior-year-abroad students craving enchiladas and fajitas. ⊠ *Via Ghibellina 156–158/r, Santa Croce* 🕾 *055/2341330* ☾ *No lunch* ✛ *G3.*

¢
LEBANESE ✕ **Valle dei Cedri.** For delicious Lebanese fare at more than reasonable prices, head here. Florentines pack this place for both lunch and dinner; reservations are essential, especially at night. ⊠ *Borgo Santa Croce 11/r, Santa Croce* 🕾 *055/2346340* ✛ *G4.*

THE OLTRARNO

¢ ✗**Borgo Antico.** In the Oltrarno, try this spot for pizza and other trattoria
PIZZA fare. ✉ *Piazza Santo Spirito 6/r, Santo Spirito* ☎ *055/210437* ✛ *C5.*

¢ ✗**Fuori Porta.** One of the oldest and best wine bars in Florence, this place
WINE BAR serves cured meats and cheeses, as well as daily specials such as the
sublime spaghetti *al curry. Crostini* and *crostoni*—grilled breads topped
with a mélange of cheeses and meats—are the house specialty; the *verdure sott'olio* (vegetables with oil) are divine. All this can be enjoyed at
rustic wooden tables, and outdoors when weather allows. One short-
coming is the staff, some of whom can be disinclined to explain the
absolutely wonderful wine list. ✉ *Via Monte alle Croci 10/r, San Niccolò* ☎ *055/2342483* ✛ *G6.*

$ ✗**Il Santo Bevitore.** Florentines and other lovers of good food flock to
TUSCAN "The Holy Drinker" for tasty, well-priced dishes. Unpretentious white
★ walls, dark wood furniture, and paper place mats provide the simple
decor; start with the exceptional vegetables *sott'olio* (marinated in olive
oil) or the *terrina di fegatini* (a creamy chicken-liver spread) before
sampling any of the divine pastas, such as the fragrant spaghetti with
shrimp sauce. Count yourself lucky if the extraordinary potato gratin,
served in compact triangular wedges, is on the menu. The extensive
wine list is well priced, and the well-informed staff is happy to explain
it. ✉ *Via Santo Spirito 64/66r, Santo Spirito* ☎ *055/211264* ☾ *No lunch
Sun.* ✛ *B4.*

¢ ✗**La Casalinga.** *Casalinga* means "housewife," and this place has the
TUSCAN nostalgic charm of a 1950s kitchen with Tuscan comfort food to match.
If you eat ribollita anywhere in Florence, eat it here—it couldn't be more
authentic. Mediocre paintings clutter the semipaneled walls, tables are
set close together, and the place is usually jammed. The menu is long,
portions are plentiful, and service is prompt and friendly. For dessert,
the lemon sorbet perfectly caps off the meal. ✉ *Via Michelozzi 9/r,
Santo Spirito* ☎ *055/218624* ☾ *Closed Sun., 1 wk at Christmas, and
3 wks in Aug.* ✛ *C5.*

$$ ✗**La Vecchia Bettola.** The name doesn't exactly mean "old dive," but
TUSCAN it comes pretty close. This lively trattoria has been around only since
1979, but it feels as if it's been a whole lot longer. Tile floors and simple
wood tables and chairs provide the interior decoration, such as it is. The
recipes come from "wise grandmothers" and celebrate Tuscan food in
its glorious simplicity. Here prosciutto is sliced with a knife, portions
of grilled meat are tender and ample, service is friendly, and the wine
list is well priced and good. This place is worth a taxi ride, even though
it's just outside the centro storico. ✉ *Viale Vasco Pratolini, Oltrarno*
☎ *055/224158* 🖃 *No credit cards* ✛ *A6.*

¢ ✗**Osteria Antica Mescita San Niccolò.** It's always crowded, always good,
TUSCAN and always inexpensive. The osteria is next to the church of San Nic-
colò, and if you sit in the lower part you'll find yourself in what was
once a chapel dating from the 11th century. The subtle but dramatic
background is a nice complement to the food, which is simple Tuscan
at its best. The *pollo con limone* is tasty pieces of chicken in a lemon-
scented broth. In winter, try the *spezzatino di cinghiale con aromi* (wild

Florence's Wine Bars

Wine bars are found all over Florence, and most of them have light fare as well as lengthy wine lists—perfect places for lunch or dinner. Many are closed Sunday.

Cantinetta dei Verrazzano. In the heart of the centro storico is Cantinetta dei Verrazzano, where serious wines may be had as well as tasty baked treats in the morning and light lunches. ⊠ *Via dei Tavolini 18/20/r, Piazza della Signoria* ☎ *055/268590.*

★ **Casa del Vino.** Come here for creative *panini*, such as *sgrombri e carciofini sott'olio* (mackerel and marinated baby artichokes), and an ever-changing list of significant wines by the glass. They also have a well-stocked collection of bottles to go, at more than fair prices. ⊠ *Via dell'Ariento 16/r, San Lorenzo* ☎ *055/215609.*

I Fratellini. A hop, skip, and a jump from Orsanmichele in the centro storico is I Fratellini, in existence since 1875. It sells wines by the glass and has a lengthy list of panini, including pecorino with sun-dried tomatoes and spicy wild-boar salami with goat cheese. There are no seats, so perch on the curb and make like a local. ⊠ *Via dei Cimatori 38/r, Piazza della Signoria* ☎ *055/2396096* ⊕ *www.iduefratellini.com.*

★ **Il Santino.** Though it has only four tables and four small stools at an equally small bar, Il Santino is blessed with a big wine list and superior cheeses, cured meats, and other delicacies to match. ⊠ *Via Santo Spirito 60/r, Santo Spirito* ☎ *055/2302820.*

La Botte. You can conduct your very own, custom-designed wine tasting at this little joint just across the street from the basilica of Santa Croce. Buy a card, then plug it into any of the dispensers which emit top-quality wine from all over Italy. ⊠ *Via San Giuseppe 18/r, Santa Croce* ☎ *055/2476420.*

Le Volpi e l'Uva. Situated off Piazza Santa Trinita, Le Volpi e l'Uva is an oenophile's dream: the waiters pour significant wines by the glass and serve equally impressive cheeses and little sandwiches to go with them. ⊠ *Piazza de' Rossi 1, Palazzo Pitti* ☎ *055/2398132.*

Olio & Convivium. Here, you'll find a great selection of cheeses and cured meats, wines by the glass, food products to take home (like powdered porcini mushrooms), and daily specials. ⊠ *Via Santo Spirito 4, Santo Spirito* ☎ *055/2658198.*

---

boar stew with herbs). Reservations are advised. ⊠ *Via San Niccolò 60/r, San Niccolò* ☎ *055/2342836* ☉ *Closed Sun. and Aug.* ✛ *G6.*

¢ ✕ **Zeb.** The food is incredibly tasty at this well-priced *alimentari* (deli-

TUSCAN   catessen). Zeb stands for *zuppa e bollito* (soup and boiled things), and nothing here disappoints. Here's home-style Tuscan cuisine at its very best, served in unpretentious, intimate surroundings: there's only room for about 15 guests. In the kitchen is Giuseppina, who staunchly insists on cooking what's best that day; which means the menu changes daily, reflecting the season's best offerings. ⊠ *Via San Miniato 2, Oltrarno* ☎ *055/2342864* ✛ *G6.*

BEYOND THE CITY CENTER

¢ ✕ **l'Giuggiolo.** They call themselves an osteria-pizzeria, and certainly
TUSCAN many Florentines come here to indulge in the sinfully rich, thin-crust
pizzas turned out by a skilled *pizzaiuolo* (pizza-maker). However, the
real thrills come from the fantastic osteria part of the menu. Start with
the *bavarese di pomodoro fresco su salsa al basilico* (a chilled tomato
concoction spiked with garlic and sauced with basil), sample one of the
divine pastas, and then move on to any of the meats, like the *millefoglie
di manza con pomodori secchi e parmigiano* (thinly sliced rare roast
beef with sun-dried tomatoes and Parmesan). ⊠ *Viale Righi 3, northeast
of city center* ☎ *055/606240* ♨ *Reservations essential* ✢ *H1.*

$$ ✕ **Targa.** It looks and feels like California on the Arno at this sleek, airy
ECLECTIC restaurant a short ride from the city center. Owner-chef Gabriele Tarchi-
ani has spent time in the United States, which shows in the plants that
fill the interior as well as the creative touches on the frequently changing
menu. Somewhat unusual combinations such as the *fusilli al ragù di
anatra e finferli* (fusilli with a minced duck and wild mushroom sauce)
provide the perfect prelude for the exquisitely prepared secondi that
follow. Leave room for dessert—they're culinary masterpieces. No won-
der Florentines come here to celebrate special occasions. ⊠ *Lungarno
Colombo 7, east of city center* ☎ *055/677377* ⊕ *www.targabistrot.net*
♨ *Reservations essential* ⊘ *Closed Sun.* ✢ *B1.*

$$ ✕ **Zibibbo.** Benedetta Vitali, formerly of Florence's famed Cibrèo, has a
TUSCAN restaurant of her very own. It's a welcome addition to the sometimes
claustrophobic Florentine dining scene—particularly as you have to
drive a few minutes out of town to get here. Off a quiet piazza, it
has two intimate rooms with rustic, maroon-painted wood floors and
a sloped ceiling. The *tagliatelle al sugo d'anatra* (wide pasta ribbons
with duck sauce) are aromatic and flavorful, and *crocchette di fave con
salsa di yogurt* (fava-bean croquettes with a lively yogurt sauce) are
innovative and tasty. ⊠ *Via di Terzollina 3/r, northwest of city center*
☎ *055/433383* ⊘ *Closed Sun.* ✢ *B1.*

WHERE TO STAY

For expanded hotel reviews, visit Fodors.com.

Florence is equipped with hotels for all budgets; for instance, you can
find both budget and luxury hotels in the *centro storico* (historic center)
and along the Arno. Florence has so many famous landmarks that it's
not hard to find lodging with a panoramic vista. The equivalent of the
genteel *pensioni* of yesteryear can still be found, though they are now
officially classified as hotels. Generally small and intimate, they often
have a quaint appeal that usually doesn't preclude modern plumbing.

Florence's importance not only as a tourist city but as a convention
center and the site of the Pitti fashion collections guarantees a variety of
accommodations. The high demand also means that, except in winter,
reservations are a must.

If you find yourself in Florence with no reservations, go to **Consorzio ITA** (⊠ *Stazione Centrale, Santa Maria Novella* ☎ *055/282893*). You must go there in person to make a booking.

WHAT IT COSTS IN EUROS					
	¢	$	$$	$$$	$$$$
Hotels	under €75	€75–€125	€125–€200	€200–€300	over €300

Prices are for a standard double room in high season, including tax and service.

THE DUOMO TO THE ARNO

Use the coordinate (✛ A1) at the end of each listing to locate a site on the corresponding map.

$ 🏨 **Albergo Firenze.** A block from the Duomo, this hotel is on one of the oldest piazzas in Florence. **Pros:** for the location, a great bargain. **Cons:** no-frills public areas. ⊠ *Piazza Donati 4, Duomo* ☎ *055/214203* ⊕ *www.hotelfirenze-fi.it* ⤳ *58 rooms* ⚬ *In-room: Wi-Fi. In-hotel: business center, parking* ⦿ *Breakfast* ✛ *E3.*

$ 🏨 **Cristina.** A friendly and enthusiastic staff runs this tiny hotel one block from the Uffizi and the Bargello. **Pros:** great deal for families. **Cons:** steep flight of stairs; some rooms share bath. ⊠ *Via della Condotta 4, Duomo* ☎ *055/214484* ⊕ *www.hotelcristina-florence.com* ⤳ *9 rooms, 5 with bath* ⚬ *In-room: no a/c, no TV. In-hotel: parking, some pets allowed* ⦿ *No meals* ✛ *F4.*

$$ 🏨 **Hermitage.** A stone's throw from the Ponte Vecchio, this is a fine little hotel with an enviable location. **Pros:** views; friendly, English-speaking staff. **Cons:** short flight of stairs to reach elevator. ⊠ *Vicolo Marzio 1, Piazza della Signoria* ☎ *055/287216* ⊕ *www.hermitagehotel.com* ⤳ *27 rooms, 1 suite* ⚬ *In-room: safe. In-hotel: parking, some pets allowed* ⦿ *Breakfast* ✛ *E4.*

$$$ 🏨 **Hotel Benivieni.** This tranquil, former 15th-century palace is one block from the Duomo. **Pros:** location. **Cons:** smallish bathrooms; some Fodor's readers detect street noise, despite triple-glazed windows. ⊠ *Via delle Oche 5, Duomo* ☎ *055/2382133* ⊕ *www.hotelbenivieni.it* ⤳ *15 rooms* ⚬ *In-room: safe, Wi-Fi. In-hotel: parking, some pets allowed* ⦿ *Breakfast* ✛ *E3.*

$$$$ 🏨 **Hotel degli Orafi.** A key scene in *A Room with a View* was shot in this pensione, which is today a luxury hotel adorned with chintz and marble. **Pros:** stellar Arno views, welcome drink upon arrival. **Cons:** extra charge for Internet use. ⊠ *Lungarno Archibusieri 4, Piazza della Signoria* ☎ *055/26622* ⊕ *www.hoteldegliorafi.it* ⤳ *42 rooms* ⚬ *In-room: safe, Wi-Fi. In-hotel: business center, parking* ⦿ *Breakfast* ✛ *E5.*

$$$$ 🏨 **Hotel Helvetia and Bristol.** Painstaking care has gone into making this
★ hotel one of the prettiest and most intimate in town. **Pros:** central location; superb staff. **Cons:** rooms facing the street get some noise. ⊠ *Via dei Pescioni 2, Piazza della Repubblica* ☎ *055/26651* ⊕ *www.hbf. royaldemeure.com* ⤳ *54 rooms, 13 suites* ⚬ *In-room: safe, Wi-Fi. In-hotel: restaurant, bar, parking, some pets allowed* ⦿ *No meals* ✛ *D3.*

$$ 🏨 **In Piazza della Signoria.** Proprietors Alessandro and Sonia Pini want
Fodor's Choice you to use their house—in this case, part of a 15th-century palazzo—as
★ if it were your own. **Pros:** marvelous staff; tasty breakfast with a view

of Piazza della Signoria. **Cons:** short flight of stairs to reach elevator. ⊠ *Via dei Magazzini 2, near Piazza della Signoria* ☎ *055/2399546* ⊕ *www.inpiazzadellasignoria.com* ⚲ *10 rooms, 3 apartments* ⚘ *In-room: safe, kitchen, Wi-Fi. In-hotel: business center, parking* ﴾◯﴿ *Breakfast* ✛ *E4.*

2

$$$ ﷽ **Palazzo Niccolini al Duomo.** The graceful Marchesa Ginevra Niccolini di Camugliano refers to her lovingly restored hotel as her third child. **Pros:** steps away from the Duomo. **Cons:** street noise sometimes a problem. ⊠ *Via dei Servi 2, San Marco* ☎ *055/282412* ⊕ *www. niccolinidomepalace.com* ⚲ *5 rooms, 5 suites* ⚘ *In-room: safe, Wi-Fi. In-hotel: business center, parking* ✛ *F2.*

$ ﷽ **Sani Tourist House.** Hosts Elizabeth and Remi have taken their former no-frills accommodation and spruced it up a bit, adding such amenities as air-conditioning and the occasional private bath to make a stay here more pleasant. **Pros:** good deals for single travelers, even lower rates off-season. **Cons:** no reception. ⊠ *Piazza dei Giuochi 1, Duomo* ☎ *335/82244133* ⊕ *www.sanibnb.it* ⚲ *6 rooms, 4 with bath* ⚘ *In-room: safe. In-hotel: parking* ﴾◯﴿ *No meals* ✛ *F3.*

SAN LORENZO AND BEYOND

$ ﷽ **Antica Dimora Firenze.** Each room in the intimate *residenza* is painted a different pastel color—peach, rose, powder-blue. **Pros:** ample DVD library; honor bar with Antinori wines. **Cons:** staff goes home at 8; no credit cards accepted. ⊠ *Via San Gallo 72, San Marco* ☎ *055/4627296* ⊕ *www.anticadimorafirenze.it* ⚲ *6 rooms* ⚘ *In-room: safe, Internet, Wi-Fi* ▬ *No credit cards* ﴾◯﴿ *Breakfast* ✛ *E1.*

$ Fodor'sChoice ★ ﷽ **Antica Dimora Johlea.** Lively color runs rampant at this small, cheerful hotel just minutes from San Marco. **Pros:** great staff; cheerful rooms; honor bar. **Cons:** staff goes home at 7; narrow staircase to get to roof terrace. ⊠ *Via San Gallo 80, San Marco* ☎ *055/4633292* ⊕ *www. johanna.it* ⚲ *6 rooms* ⚘ *In-room: safe, Internet, Wi-Fi. In-hotel: business center, parking* ▬ *No credit cards* ﴾◯﴿ *Breakfast* ✛ *E1.*

$$$ ﷽ **Arti & Hotel.** If Florence had town houses, this would be one: the entrance to the public room downstairs feels as if you're in someone's living room. **Pros:** down the street from the Duomo. **Cons:** staff goes home at 11. ⊠ *Via dei Servi 38/a, Santissima Annunziata* ☎ *055/2645307* ⊕ *www.hoteldellearti.it* ⚲ *9 rooms* ⚘ *In-room: Wi-Fi. In-hotel: some pets allowed* ﴾◯﴿ *Breakfast* ✛ *G1.*

$$ ﷽ **Hotel Casci.** In this refurbished 14th-century palace, the home of Giacchino Rossini in 1851–55, the friendly Lombardi family runs a hotel with spotless rooms. **Pros:** helpful staff; good option for families; English-language DVD collection with good selections for kids. **Cons:** bit of a college-dorm atmosphere; small elevator ⊠ *Via Cavour 13, San Marco* ☎ *055/211686* ⊕ *www.hotelcasci.com* ⚲ *25 rooms*

Where to Stay in Florence

A   **B**   **C**   **D**

Plus Florence

STAZIONE CENTRALE

Residenza Johanna I

V. Vallonda

V. Fiume

V. Nazionale

Nuova Italia

V. Panicale

V. dell' Ariento

V. S. Antonino

V. S. Faenza

V.

Piazza dell'Unità Italiana

V. del Melarancio

V. del Giglio

V. dell'Alloro

V. d. Conti

V. Rucellai

V. Palazzuolo

V. dell' Albero

V. dei Canaci

V. Benedetta

V. della Scala

S. MARIA NOVELLA

Piazza S. Maria Novella

V. dei Panzani

V. Maso Finiguerra

Borgo Ognissanti

V. dei Banchi

JK Place

V. d. Belle Donne

V. del Trebbio

V. Rondinelli

V. dei Pecori

V. dei Pesciani

V. Vecchietti

Piazza Ognissanti

V. d. Porcellana

Via dei Fossi

V. del Moro

V. Spada

V. del Sole

Hotel Helvetia and Bristol

Via Strozzi

V. dei Sassetti

V. Anselmi

Lung. A. Vespucci

V. dei Federighi

V. dei Palchetti

Vigna Nuova

V. d.

V. del Purgatorio

V. del Parione

V. Tornabuoni

Pza. Strozzi

Piazza Goldoni

Piazza di Cestello

SAN FREDIANO IN CESTELLO

Lung. Soderini

Lung. Corsini

Beacci Tornabuoni

V. Porta Rossa

Piazza Santa Trinita

Antica Torre di Via Tornabuoni

V. delle Terme

Ponte alla Carraia

Ponte S. Trinita

Lung. Acciaioli

Borgo SS. Apostoli

Torre Guelfa

Borgo S. Frediano

Piazza N. Sauro

Lung. Guicciardini

Palazzo Magnani Feroni

Piazza del Carmine

Via Santo Spirito

Alessandra

Gallery Hotel Art

Ponte Vecchio

V. S. Monaca

V. dell' Ardiglione

V. dei Serragli

V. Maffia

V. Sant' Agostino

Borgo Sant'Jacopo

Lungarno

S. MARIA DEL CARMINE

Borgo Tegolaio

V. Michelozzi

V. Maggio

V. Sguazza

V. dello Sprone

V. del Ramaglianta

Piazza S. Maria Sopr'Arno

Piazza S. Spirito

Sdrucciolo dei Pitti

Albergo La Scaletta

V. della Chiesa

V. della Caldaie

V. Guicciardini

V. del Campuccio

Giardino Torrigiani

Annalena

Torre di Bellosguardo

V. Santa Maria

Piazza S. Felice

Piazza dei Pitti

PALAZZO PITTI

Via Romana

Boboli Gardens

KEY

☐ Hotels

🛈 Tourist Information

↔ following lodging reviews indicates a map-grid coordinate

🛏 *In-room: safe, Wi-Fi. In-hotel: business center, parking, some pets allowed* 🎽 *Breakfast* ✚ *E1.*

$$$ 🏨 **Il Guelfo Bianco.** The 15th-century building has all modern conveniences, but its Renaissance charm still shines. **Pros:** stellar multilingual staff. **Cons:** rooms facing the street can be noisy. ✉ *Via Cavour 29, San Marco* ☎ *055/288330* ⊕ *www.ilguelfobianco.it* 📞 *40 rooms* 🛏 *In-room: safe. In-hotel: business center, parking, some pets allowed* 🎽 *Breakfast* ✚ *F1.*

¢ 🏨 **Plus Florence.** The name is the only odd thing about this hostel, which has been in operation since 2008. **Pros:** bargain price; multiligual staff. **Cons:** feels like a college dorm; somewhat removed from the action. ✉ *Via Santa Caterina d'Alessandria 15, San Marco* ☎ *055/4628934* ⊕ *www.plusflorence.com* 📞 *4 rooms, 9 dorm rooms* 🛏 *In-room: Wi-Fi. In-hotel: restaurant, bar, pool, spa, laundry facilities, business center, parking* 🎽 *No meals* ✚ *B1.*

¢ 🏨 **Residenza Johanna I.** Savvy travelers and those on a budget should look no further, as this *residenza* is a tremendous value for quality and location. **Pros:** great value. **Cons:** staff goes home at 7; no credit cards. ✉ *Via Bonifacio Lupi 14, San Marco* ☎ *055/481896* ⊕ *www.johanna.it* 📞 *11 rooms* 🛏 *In-room: no a/c, no TV. In-hotel: parking* ❒ *No credit cards* 🎽 *No meals* ✚ *D1.*

SANTA MARIA NOVELLA TO THE ARNO

$ 🏨 **Alessandra.** The location, a block from the Ponte Vecchio, and the clean, ample rooms make this a good choice. **Pros:** several rooms have views of the Arno; the spacious suite is a bargain. **Cons:** stairs to elevator; some rooms share bath. ✉ *Borgo Santi Apostoli 17, Santa Maria Novella* ☎ *055/283438* ⊕ *www.hotelalessandra.com* 📞 *26 rooms, 19 with bath; 1 suite; 1 apartment* 🛏 *In-room: safe, Internet, Wi-Fi. In-hotel: parking* ◔ *Closed Dec. 10–26* 🎽 *Breakfast* ✚ *D4.*

$$$ 🏨 **Antica Torre di Via Tornabuoni.** If you're looking for a room with a view, stop here, where just about every one has a window that frames the awe-inspiring Duomo or the Arno (some even have small terraces). **Pros:** views and terraces. **Cons:** no staff after 7; seemingly ongoing remodeling. ✉ *Via Tornabuoni 1, Santa Maria Novella* ☎ *055/2658161* ⊕ *www.tornabuoni1.com* 📞 *11 rooms, 1 suite* 🛏 *In-room: safe, Wi-Fi. In-hotel: bar, parking, some pets allowed* 🎽 *Breakfast* ✚ *D4.*

$$ 🏨 **Beacci Tornabuoni.** Florentine pensioni don't get any classier than this. **Pros:** multilingual staff; flower-filled terrace. **Cons:** hall noise can sometimes be a problem. ✉ *Via Tornabuoni 3, Santa Maria Novella* ☎ *055/212645* ⊕ *www.tornabuonihotels.com* 📞 *37 rooms, 16 suites* 🛏 *In-hotel: restaurant, bar, business center, parking, some pets allowed* 🎽 *Breakfast* ✚ *D4.*

$$$ 🏨 **Gallery Hotel Art.** High design resides at this art showcase near the Ponte Vecchio. **Pros:** cool atmosphere; beautiful people; miso soup on the breakfast menu. **Cons:** sometimes elevator is slow. ✉ *Vicolo dell'Oro 5, Santa Maria Novella* ☎ *055/27263* ⊕ *www.lungarnohotels.com* 📞 *65 rooms, 9 suites* 🛏 *In-room: safe, Wi-Fi. In-hotel: restaurant, bar, parking* 🎽 *Breakfast* ✚ *D4.*

$$$$ 🏨 **JK Place.** This sumptuously appointed boutique hotel has all the
Fodor's Choice comforts of a luxe home away from home. **Pros:** intimate feel; stellar
★ staff; free minibar; linen sheets; organic meals on room-service menu;
Wi-Fi. **Cons:** breakfast at a shared table. ☒ *Piazza Santa Maria Novella
7* ☎ *055/2645181* ⊕ *www.jkplace.com* ⤴ *14 doubles, 6 suites* ⏃ *In-
room: safe, Wi-Fi. In-hotel: bar, parking, some pets allowed* ¶❍¶ *Breakfast* ✚ *C3.*

$$ 🏨 **Nuova Italia.** The genial English-speaking Viti family runs this hotel
near the train station and well within walking distance of the sights.
Pros: reasonable rates. **Cons:** no elevator. ☒ *Via Faenza 26, Santa Maria
Novella* ☎ *055/268430* ⊕ *www.hote-nuovaitalia.com* ⤴ *20 rooms*
⏃ *In-room: Wi-Fi. In-hotel: parking, some pets allowed* ⊗ *Closed Dec.
8–Dec. 26* ¶❍¶ *Breakfast* ✚ *D1.*

$$ 🏨 **Torre Guelfa.** If you want a taste of medieval Florence, try this hotel
hidden within a 13th-century tower. **Pros:** rooftop terrace with tremen-
dous views; wonderful staff; some family-friendly triple rooms. **Cons:**
72 steps to get to terrace; continental breakfast is available only at
8 am. ☒ *Borgo Santi Apostoli 8, Santa Maria Novella* ☎ *055/2396338*
⊕ *www.hoteltorreguelfa.com* ⤴ *24 rooms, 2 suites* ⏃ *In-room: safe,
no TV, Wi-Fi. In-hotel: business center, parking, some pets allowed*
¶❍¶ *Breakfast* ✚ *D4.*

THE OLTRARNO AND BEYOND

$ 🏨 **Albergo La Scaletta.** For a tremendous view of the Boboli Gardens,
look no further than this exquisite pensione near the Ponte Vecchio and
Palazzo Pitti. **Pros:** fantastic terrace. **Cons:** small elevator, many steps.
☒ *Via Guicciardini 13, Palazzo Pitti* ☎ *055/283028* ⊕ *www.lascaletta.
com* ⤴ *13 rooms* ⏃ *In-room: Wi-Fi. In-hotel: restaurant, bar, parking,
some pets allowed* ¶❍¶ *Breakfast* ✚ *D5.*

$ 🏨 **Annalena.** The story goes that Annalena, a 15th-century maiden, mar-
ried a Medici; another man, smitten with her and angry at her refusal to
capitulate, murdered her husband and her young son. **Pros:** the triples
and quads are great for families. **Cons:** a hefty flight of stairs to get to
reception. ☒ *Via Romana 34, Santo Spirito/San Frediano* ☎ *055/222402*
⊕ *www.hotelannalena.it* ⤴ *20 rooms* ⏃ *In-hotel: parking, some pets
allowed* ¶❍¶ *Breakfast* ✚ *B6.*

$$$ 🏨 **Hotel Silla.** The entrance to this slightly off-the-beaten-path hotel
is through a 15th-century courtyard lined with potted plants and
sculpture-filled niches. **Pros:** a Fodor's reader raves, "It's in the mid-
dle of everything except the crowds." **Cons:** some readers complain
of street noise and too-small rooms. ☒ *Via de' Renai 5, San Niccolò*
☎ *055/2342888* ⊕ *www.hotelsilla.it* ⤴ *35 rooms* ⏃ *In-room: safe,
Wi-Fi. In-hotel: bar, parking, some pets allowed* ¶❍¶ *Breakfast* ✚ *G6.*

$$$$ 🏨 **Lungarno.** Many rooms and suites here have private terraces that jut
out right over the Arno, granting stunning views of the Palazzo Vec-
chio and the Lungarno. **Pros:** upscale without being stuffy. **Cons:** rooms
without Arno views feel less special. ☒ *Borgo San Jacopo 14, Lungarno
Sud* ☎ *055/27261* ⊕ *www.lungarnohotels.com* ⤴ *59 rooms, 14 suites*
⏃ *In-room: Wi-Fi. In-hotel: restaurant, bar, parking* ¶❍¶ *Breakfast* ✚ *D5.*

$$$$ 🖥 **Palazzo Magnani Feroni.** The perfect place to play the part of a Florentine aristocrat is here at this 16th-century palazzo, which despite its massive halls and sweeping staircase could almost feel like home. **Pros:** 24-hour room service; billiard room; Bulgari bath products; generous buffet breakfast; terrific staff. **Cons:** a few steps up to the elevator; many steps to the rooftop terrace; Wi-Fi's not free. ⊠ *Borgo San Frediano 5, Santo Spirito* ☎ *055/2399544* ⊕ *www.florencepalace.it* ⤵ *12 suites* ♻ *In-room: safe, Wi-Fi. In-hotel: bar, parking* ⓔ *Breakfast* ✢ *B4.*

SANTA CROCE

$$$$ 🖥 **The Four Seasons.** Seven years of restoration have turned this 15th-century palazzo in Florence's center into a luxury hotel unlike any other in town. **Pros:** a unique "city meets country" experience; the marvelous garden. **Cons:** for this price, breakfast really ought to be included; some feel it's a little too removed from the historic center. ⊠ *Borgo Pinti 99e, Santa Croce* ☎ *055/26261* ⊕ *www.fourseasons.com/florence* ⤵ *117 rooms* ♻ *In-room: safe, Internet. In-hotel: restaurant, bar, pool, gym, spa, business center, parking* ⓔ *No meals* ✢ *H1.*

$$$$ 🖥 **Hotel Regency.** The noise and crowds of Florence seem far from this stylish hotel in a residential district near the Sinagoga, though you're not more than 10 minutes from the Accademia and Michelangelo's *David.* **Pros:** faces one of the few green parks in the center of Florence. **Cons:** a small flight of stairs takes you to reception. ⊠ *Piazza d'Azeglio 3, Santa Croce* ☎ *055/245247* ⊕ *www.regency-hotel.com* ⤵ *30 rooms, 4 suites* ♻ *In-room: safe, Wi-Fi. In-hotel: restaurant, bar, parking, some pets allowed* ⓔ *Breakfast* ✢ *H1.*

$$$ 🖥 **Hotel Villa Liana.** In this hotel it's possible to experience palazzo life without breaking the bank. **Pros:** good for kids—playground around the corner. **Cons:** rooms facing street are noisy. ⊠ *Via V. Alfieri 18, Santa Croce* ☎ *055/245303 or 055/245304* ⊕ *www.hotelliana.com* ⤵ *24 rooms* ♻ *In-room: safe, Wi-Fi. In-hotel: bar, business center, parking, some pets allowed* ⓔ *Breakfast* ✢ *H1.*

$ 🖥 **Istituto Oblate dell'Assunzione.** Twelve nuns run this convent, which is minutes from the Duomo. **Pros:** bargain price; great location; quiet rooms; garden. **Cons:** curfew; no credit cards. ⊠ *Borgo Pinti 15, Santa Croce* ☎ *055/2480582* ⤵ *28 rooms, 22 with bath* ♻ *In-room: no TV. In-hotel: parking* ▬ *No credit cards* ⓔ *No meals* ✢ *G3.*

$$$ 🖥 **J&J.** On a quiet street within walking distance of the sights sits this unusual hotel, a converted 16th-century convent. **Pros:** large rooms. **Cons:** one flight of steep stairs to get to rooms; Wi-Fi in public areas only, for an hourly fee. ⊠ *Via di Mezzo 20, Santa Croce* ☎ *055/26312* ⊕ *www.jandjhotel.net* ⤵ *19 rooms, 7 suites* ♻ *In-room: Internet. In-hotel: bar, parking* ⓔ *Breakfast* ✢ *H3.*

$$$$ 🖥 **Monna Lisa.** Housed in a 15th-century palazzo, this hotel retains some
★ of its wood-coffered ceilings from the 1500s, as well as its original staircase. **Pros:** lavish buffet breakfast; cheerful staff; garden. **Cons:** rooms in annex are less charming than those in palazzo. ⊠ *Borgo Pinti 27, Santa Croce* ☎ *055/2479751* ⊕ *www.monnalisa.it* ⤵ *45 rooms* ♻ *In-room: safe, Wi-Fi. In-hotel: bar, business center, parking, some pets allowed* ⓔ *Breakfast* ✢ *G3.*

$$ ★ 🏠 **Morandi alla Crocetta.** You're made to feel like privileged friends of the family at this charming and distinguished residence near Piazza Santissima Annunziata. **Pros:** interesting, offbeat location; terrific staff. **Cons:** two flights of stairs to reach reception and rooms. ⊠ *Via Laura 50, Santissima Annunziata* ☎ *055/2344747* ⊕ *www.hotelmorandi.it* ↙ *10 rooms* ⚿ *In-room: safe, Wi-Fi. In-hotel: parking, some pets allowed* ✛ *H1.*

OUTSIDE THE CITY

$$$$ 🏠 **Il Salviatino.** A winding drive up a cypress-studded lane brings you to this jewel of a hotel just outside Florence. **Pros:** great views; attentive staff. **Cons:** no reception area; some hall noise. ⊠ *Via del Salviatino 21* ☎ *055/904111* ⊕ *www.salviatino.com* ↙ *23 rooms, 22 suites* ⚿ *In-room: a/c, Wi-Fi. In-hotel: restaurant, bar, pool, gym, spa, parking, some pets allowed* ❛◯❜ *Breakfast* ✛ *H5.*

$$ 🏠 **Relais Villa l'Olmo.** Alberto and Claudia Giannotti have turned a former 16th-century country villa into an elegantly comfortable agriturismo 20 minutes south of the center of Florence. **Pros:** good for families and groups; golf privileges. **Cons:** you need a car if you don't want to depend on the city bus; breakfast must be ordered in advance; concierge goes home at 7:30. ⊠ *Via Imprunetana per Tavarnuzze 19, Impruneta* ☎ *055/2311311* ⊕ *www.relaisfarmholiday.it* ↙ *8 apartments, 2 cottages, 1 farmhouse* ⚿ *In-room: safe, kitchen, Wi-Fi. In-hotel: pool, laundry facilities, business center, parking, some pets allowed* ❛◯❜ *Breakfast* ✛ *H6.*

$$$ 🏠 **Torre di Bellosguardo.** *Bellosguardo* means "beautiful view"; given the view of Florence you get here, the name is fitting. **Pros:** great for escaping heat of the city in summer; a villa experience with the city just minutes away. **Cons:** a car is a necessity. ⊠ *Via Roti Michelozzi 2* ☎ *055/2298145* ⊕ *www.torrebellosguardo.com* ↙ *9 rooms, 7 suites* ⚿ *In-room: no a/c, Internet. In-hotel: bar, pool, parking, some pets allowed* ✛ *B6.*

$$$$ 🏠 **Villa La Massa.** You approach this tall and imposing villa, 15 minutes out of town, via a gravel drive lined with flowers. **Pros:** pleasing mix of city and country life; sumptuous buffet breakfast; views of the Tuscan hills; phenomenal staff. **Cons:** even with shuttle, a car is a necessity; not open year-round. ⊠ *Via della Massa 24, Candeli* ☎ *055/62611* ⊕ *www.villalamassa.com* ↙ *19 rooms, 18 suites* ⚿ *In-room: safe, Internet. In-hotel: restaurant, bar, pool, business center, parking, some pets allowed* ◑ *Closed Dec.–Mar.* ❛◯❜ *Breakfast* ✛ *H5.*

NIGHTLIFE AND THE ARTS

THE ARTS

Florence has a lively classical music scene. The internationally famous annual Maggio Musicale lights up the musical calendar in early spring. Fans of rock, pop, and hip-hop might be somewhat surprised by the absence of live acts that make it to town (for such offerings, travel to

Rome or Milan is often a necessity). What it lacks in contemporary music, however, is more than made up for with its many theatrical offerings.

FESTIVALS AND SPECIAL EVENTS

Festa di San Giovanni (*Feast of St. John the Baptist*). On June 24 Florence grinds to a halt to celebrate the Festa di San Giovanni in honor of its patron saint. Many shops and bars close, and at night a fireworks display lights up the Arno and attracts thousands.

Holy Thursday. At the Duomo on Holy Thursday, a centuries-old ritual is reenacted with members of the Compagnia della Misericordia, a lay association that during the Renaissance comforted those condemned to death and provided dowries for poor girls as well as other services for its members. (Today the confraternity runs an efficient ambulance service.) A solemn procession of priests and confraternity members wends its way into the Duomo, then the priests wash the feet of the confraternity members.

Scoppio del Carro (*Explosion of the Cart*). On Easter Sunday Florentines and foreigners alike flock to the Piazza del Duomo to watch as the Scoppio del Carro, a monstrosity of a carriage, pulled by two huge oxen decorated for the occasion, makes its way through the city center and ends up in the piazza. Through an elaborate wiring system, an object representing a "dove" is sent from inside the cathedral to the Baptistery across the way. The dove sets off an explosion of fireworks that come streaming from the carriage. You have to see it to believe it. If you don't like crowds, don't worry: video replays figure prominently on the nightly newscasts afterward.

FILM

La Nazione. The daily Florentine newspaper *La Nazione* has movie listings. Note that most American films are dubbed into Italian rather than subtitled. ⊕ *www.lanazione.it.*

British Institute of Florence. Several English-language film series take place here throughout the year; the programmer has a penchant for classic movies. Also on offer are weekly lectures, courses mostly related to things Florentine or Italian, and a most wonderful library. ⊠ *Palazzo Lanfredini, Lungarno Guicciardini 9* ☎ *055/26778270* ⊕ *www.britishinstitute.it.*

Festival dei Popoli. This weeklong documentary film festival happens in November or December with screenings at various venues around town. ⊠ *Borgo Pinti 82/r* ☎ *055/244778* ⊕ *www.festivaldeipopoli.org.*

Odeon. This magnificent Art Deco theater shows first-run English-language films on Monday, Tuesday, and Thursday. ⊠ *Piazza Strozzi 2* ☎ *055/295051* ⊕ *www.cinehall.it.*

MUSIC

Accademia Bartolomeo Cristofori. Also known as the Amici del Fortepiano (Friends of the Fortepiano), the Accademia Bartolomeo Cristofori sponsors fortepiano concerts throughout the year. ⊠ *Via di Camaldoli 7/r* ☎ *055/221646* ⊕ *www.accademiacristofori.it.*

Amici della Musica. This organization sponsors classical and contemporary concerts at the **Teatro della Pergola** (*Box office* ✉ *Via Alamanni 39* ☎ *055/210804* ⊕ *www.teatrodellapergola.comt*). ⊕ *www. amicimusica.fi.it.*

Maggio Musicale Fiorentino. At press time, construction had been halted due to lack of funds on the **Parco della Musica** (Music Park) designed by Paolo Desideri and associates. Three concert halls (two indoor, one outdoor) are planned, and only one has been completed. Maggio Musicale plans to relocate once construction is finished. In the meantime, it continues to be held at the **Teatro Comunale** (✉ *Corso Italia 16* ☎ *055/287222* ⊕ *www.maggiofiorentino.com*). Within Italy you can purchase tickets from late April through July directly at the box office or by phone at 055/2779350. You can also buy them online. Call ahead to confirm if performances are taking place in this venue or have switched over to the new space. ✉ *Via Alamanni 39* ☎ *055/210804.*

OBIHALL. This large exhibition space, formerly Teatro Saschall, hosts many events throughout the year, including a large Christmas bazaar run by the Red Cross, visiting rock stars, and trendy bands from all over Europe. ✉ *Lungarno Aldo Moro 3* ☎ *055/6503068* ⊕ *www.obihall.it.*

Orchestra da Camera Fiorentina. This orchestra performs various concerts of classical music throughout the year at Orsanmichele, the grain market–turned–church. ✉ *Via Monferrato 2* ☎ *055/783374* ⊕ *www. orcafi.it.*

Orchestra della Toscana. The concert season of the Orchestra della Toscana runs from November to June. ✉ *Via Ghibellina 101* ☎ *055/2340710* ⊕ *www.orchestradellatoscana.it.*

THEATER

Teatro della Pergola. Theater lovers might want to try an evening at Teatro della Pergola. The season runs from mid-October to mid-April. If the idea of hearing a play in Italian is too forbidding, visit the lovely theater. Built in 1656 by Ferdinando Tacca, and once the private theater of the grand dukes, it was opened to the public in 1755. The theater has undergone several metamorphoses; its present incarnation dates to 1828, and the atrium was constructed nine years later. ✉ *Via della Pergola 12/r* ☎ *055/2264353* ⊕ *www.teatrodellapergola.com.*

NIGHTLIFE

Florentines are rather proud of their nightlife options. Most bars now have some sort of happy hour, which usually lasts for many hours and often has snacks that can substitute for a light dinner. (Check, though, that the buffet is free or comes with the price of a drink.) Clubs typically don't open until very late in the evening, and don't get crowded until 1 or 2 in the morning.

DUOMO

il bar de l'O. This swanky, American-style bar is attached to the Hotel l'Orologio. It's a good spot for a well-executed cocktail with tasty snacks; when it's warm, you can sit outside and gaze at the beautiful facade of Santa Maria Novella. ⊠ *Via delle Belle Donne 34/r* ☎ *055/ 277380* ⊕ *www.ilbardelo.com.*

LUNGARNO NORTH

Harry's Bar. For a posh evening, lubricated with trademark Bellinis and the best martinis in Florence, head to Harry's Bar. ⊠ *Lungarno Vespucci 22/r* ☎ *055/2396700* ⊕ *www.harrysbarfirenze.it.*

LUNGARNO SUD

Noir. Noir makes great Bloody Marys, and it's *the* place to be at cocktail time when young Florentines crowd the doors and spill out into the street. ⊠ *Lungarno Corsini 12/14r* ☎ *055/210751.*

SAN MARCO

Kitsch. Choose from indoor or outdoor seating and take advantage of the great list of wines by the glass. At aperitivo time €8 will buy you a truly tasty cocktail and give you access to the tremendous buffet— it's so good, you won't need dinner afterward. ⊠ *Via San Gallo 22/r* ☎ *055/4620016.*

SAN NICCOLÒ

Montecarla. People sip cocktails against a backdrop of exotic flowers, leopard-print chairs and chintz, and red walls on the two crowded floors at Montecarla. ⊠ *Via de' Bardi 2* ☎ *055/2340259.*

Negroni. Well-dressed young Florentines flock to Negroni at happy hour. ⊠ *Via de' Renai 17/r* ☎ *055/243647* ⊕ *www.negronibar.it.*

Zoe. Though it's called a "caffetteria," and coffee is served (as well as terrific salads and burgers at lunchtime), Zoe's fine cocktails are the real draw for elegant youngish Florentines who come here to see and be seen. Here's people-watching at its very best, done while listening to the latest CDs imported from England. ⊠ *Via de' Renai 13/r* ☎ *055/243111.*

SANTA CROCE

Jazz Club. Enjoy live music in this small basement club. ⊠ *Via Nuova de' Caccini 3, corner of Borgo Pinti* ☎ *055/2479700* ⊕ *www. jazzclubfirenze.it.*

Rex. A trendy, artsy clientele frequents this bar at aperitivo time; around 10 o'clock, the place is packed with mostly young folks sipping artfully made cocktails. ⊠ *Via Fiesolana 23–25/r* ☎ *055/2480331.*

Sant'Ambrogio Caffè. Come here in summer for outdoor seating with a view of an 11th-century church (Sant'Ambrogio) directly across the street. ⊠ *Piazza Sant'Ambrogio 7–8/r* ☎ *055/2477277.*

PIAZZA DELLA REPUBBLICA

Hard Rock Cafe. Opened to great fanfare in June 2011, Hard Rock packs in young Florentines and travelers eager to sample the iconic chain's take on classic American grub. ⊠ *Piazza della Repubblica* ☎ *055/2670499* ⊕ *www.hardrock.com.*

Yab. Having celebrated its 25th anniversary in 2004, Yab never seems to go out of style, though it increasingly becomes the haunt of Florentine high schoolers and university students intent on dancing and doing vodka shots. ⊠ *Via Sassetti 5/r* ☎ *055/215160* ⊕ *www.yab.it.*

BEYOND THE CITY CENTER

Central. This is a great spot for those who want to put on their dancing shoes for some house and hip-hop music. ⊠ *Via Fosso Macinante 2* ☎ *055/353505* ⊕ *www.centralfirenze.it.*

Meccanò. This is a multimedia experience in a high-tech disco with a late-night restaurant. ⊠ *Le Cascine, Viale degli Olmi 1* ☎ *No phone.*

SHOPPING

Window-shopping in Florence is like visiting an enormous contemporary-art gallery. Many of today's greatest Italian artists are fashion designers, and most keep shops in Florence. Discerning shoppers may find bargains in the street markets. ⚠ Do not buy any knockoff goods from any of the hawkers plying their fake Prada (or any other high-end designer) on the streets. It's illegal, and fines are astronomical if the police happen to catch you. (You pay the fine, not the vendor.)

Shops are generally open 9 to 1 and 3:30 to 7:30, and are closed Sunday and Monday mornings most of the year. Summer (June to September) hours are usually 9 to 1 and 4 to 8, and some shops close Saturday afternoon instead of Monday morning. When looking for addresses, you'll see two color-coded numbering systems on each street. The red numbers are commercial addresses and are indicated, for example, as 31/r. The blue or black numbers are residential addresses. Most shops take major credit cards and ship purchases, but because of possible delays it's wise to take your purchases with you.

The usual fashion suspects—Prada, Gucci, Versace, to name but a few—all have shops in Florence. But if you want to buy Florentine in Florence, stick to Gucci, Pucci, Ferragamo, and Roberto Cavalli—they're either all native sons or adopted native sons (Salvatore Ferragamo).

The intrepid shopper might want to check out some other, lesser-known shops. For bargains on Italian designer clothing, you need to leave the city.

SHOPPING DISTRICTS

Florence's most fashionable shops are concentrated in the center of town. The fanciest designer shops are mainly on **Via Tornabuoni** and **Via della Vigna Nuova.** The city's largest concentrations of antiques shops are on **Borgo Ognissanti** and the Oltrarno's **Via Maggio.** The **Ponte Vecchio** houses reputable but very expensive jewelry shops, as it has since the 16th century. The area near **Santa Croce** is the heart of the leather merchants' district.

PIAZZA DELLA REPUBBLICA

Bernardo. Come here for men's trousers, cashmere sweaters, and shirts with details like mother-of-pearl buttons. ⊠ *Via Porta Rossa 87/r* ☎ *055/283333.*

Cabó. Missoni knitwear is the main draw at Cabó. ⊠ *Via Porta Rossa 77–79/r* ☎ *055/215774.*

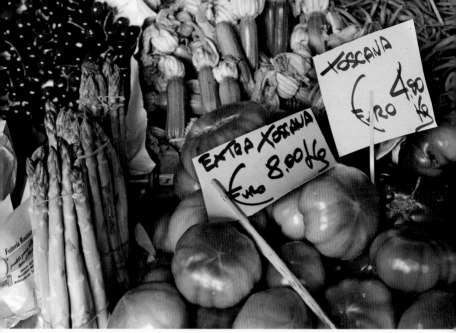
The bounty at Florence's Mercato Centrale

Furla. Internationally renowned, Furla makes beautiful leather bags, shoes, and wallets in up-to-the-minute designs. ✉ *Via Calzaiuoli 47/r* ☎ *055/2382883.*

Liu-Jo. If you're looking for something hot to wear to the clubs, check out Liu-Jo. ✉ *Via Calimala 14/r* ☎ *055/216164.*

Mercato dei Fiori (*flower market*). Every Thursday morning from September through June the covered loggia in Piazza della Repubblica hosts a Mercato dei Fiori; it's awash in a lively riot of plants, flowers, and difficult-to-find herbs. ✉ *Piazza della Repubblica.*

Mercato del Porcellino. If you're looking for cheery, inexpensive trinkets to take home, you might want to stop and roam through the stalls under the loggia of the Mercato del Porcellino. ✉ *Via Por Santa Maria at Via Porta Rossa.*

My Walit. Brightly colored wallets, purses, and other lovely leather accessories are on offer here at affordable prices. ✉ *Via della Condotta 30/r* ⊕ *www.mywalit.com.*

Spazio A. For cutting-edge fashion, the fun and funky window displays at Spazio A merit a stop. The shop carries such well-known designers as Alberta Ferretti and Moschino, as well as lesser-known Italian, English, and French designers. ✉ *Via Porta Rossa 109–115/r* ☎ *055/212995* ⊕ *www.aeffe.com.*

SAN LORENZO

Mercato Centrale. This huge indoor food market offers a staggering selection of all things edible. ✉ *Piazza del Mercato Centrale.*

Mercato di San Lorenzo. The clothing and leather-goods stalls of the Mercato di San Lorenzo in the streets next to the church of San Lorenzo have bargains for shoppers on a budget.

SANTA CROCE

Antica Officina del Farmacista Dr. Vranjes. Aromatherapy has been elevated to an art form at Antica Officina del Farmacista Dr. Vranjes. Dr. Vranjes makes scents for the body and for the house. ⊠ *Borgo La Croce 44/r* ☎ *055/241748* ⊕ *www.drvranjes.it* ⊠ *Via San Gallo 63/r* ☎ *055/494537* ⊠ *Via della Spada 9* ☎ *055/288796.*

♺ **La Tartaruga.** This innovative shop sells brightly colored, recycled paper in lots of guises (such as calendars and stationery), as well as toys for children. ⊠ *Borgo Albizzi 60/r* ☎ *055/2340845.*

Libreria Salimbeni. Long one of Florence's best art-book shops, Libreria Salimbeni has an outstanding selection. ⊠ *Via Matteo Palmieri 14–16/r* ☎ *055/2340905* ⊕ *www.liberiasalimbeni.com.*

Mercato di Sant'Ambrogio. It's possible to strike gold at the Mercato di Sant'Ambrogio, where clothing stalls abut the fruit and vegetables. ⊠ *Piazza Ghiberti, off Via dei Macci.*

Oreria. The two women who run Oreria create divine designs using silver and semiprecious stones. Send suitors to purchase significant gifts here. ⊠ *Borgo Pinti 87/a* ☎ *055/244708.*

Paolo Carandini. Stop in here for exquisite leather objects such as picture frames, jewelry boxes, and desk accessories. ⊠ *Borgo Allegri 17/r* ☎ *055/245397.*

Piazza dei Ciompi flea market. You can find bargains at the Piazza dei Ciompi flea market Monday through Saturday and on the last Sunday of the month. ⊠ *Sant'Ambrogio.*

Piccolo Slam. Members of the junior set desiring to look well-clad, Florentine style, should consider stopping at Piccolo Slam. ⊠ *Via dei Neri 9–11/r* ☎ *055/214504.*

Sbigoli Terrecotte. Traditional Tuscan terra-cotta and ceramic vases, pots, and cups and saucers are on offer at this shop in the Santa Croce neighborhood. ⊠ *Via Sant'Egidio 4/r* ☎ *055/2479713.*

★ **Scuola del Cuoio.** A consortium of leatherworkers plies its trade at La Scuola del Cuoio (Leather School), in the former dormitory of the convent of Santa Croce; high-quality, fairly priced jackets, belts, and purses are sold here. ⊠ *Piazza Santa Croce 16* ☎ *055/244533* ⊕ *www. scuoladelcuoio.com.*

LUNGARNO SUD

Galleria Luigi Bellini. This gallery claims to be Italy's oldest antiques dealer, which may be true, since father Mario Bellini was responsible for instituting Florence's international antiques biennial. ⊠ *Lungarno Soderini 5* ☎ *055/214031.*

Giulio Giannini e Figlio. One of Florence's oldest paper-goods stores, Giulio Giannini e Figlio is *the* place to buy the marbleized stock, which comes in many shapes and sizes, from flat sheets to boxes and even pencils. ⊠ *Piazza Pitti 37/r* ☎ *055/212621* ⊕ *www.giuliogiannini.it.*

Lorenzo Villoresi. Proprietor Lorenzo Villoresi makes one-of-a-kind fragrances, which he develops after meeting with you. Such personalized attention does not come cheap. ⊠ *Via de'Bardi 14* ☎ *055/2341187* ⊕ *www.lorenzovilloresi.com.*

PALAZZO PITTI

Geraldine Tayar. Eclectic fabric combinations are the focal point of Geraldine Tayar's unique clothing and accessories. ⊠ *Sdrucciolo de' Pitti 6/r* ☎ *055/290405.*

Maçel. Browse collections by lesser-known Italian designers, many of whom use the same factories as the A-list, at this women's clothing shop. ⊠ *Via Guicciardini 128/r* ☎ *055/287355.*

Madova. Complete your winter wardrobe with a pair of high-quality leather gloves, available in a rainbow of colors and a choice of linings (silk, cashmere, and unlined), from Madova. ⊠ *Via Guicciardini 1/r* ☎ *055/2396526.*

Paolo Paoletti. Look for Florentine antiques with an emphasis on Medici-era objects from the 15th and 16th centuries at Paolo Paoletti. ⊠ *Via Maggio 30/r* ☎ *055/214728.*

Pitti Mosaici. Stones are worked into exquisite tables, pictures, and jewelry at Pitti Mosaici, which continues the pietre dure tradition that was all the rage of 16th-century Florence. ⊠ *Piazza dei Pitti 23/r* ☎ *055/282127.*

SANTO SPIRITO

Marino. This shop has been in the antiques business for three generations: brothers Luca and Fabio continue the family trade. There's a little of everything here, but they're particularly strong on objects from the 19th century. ⊠ *Via Santo Spirito 8* ☎ *055/213184* ⊕ *www. marinoantichita.com.*

Santo Spirito flea market. The second Sunday of every month brings the Santo Spirito flea market. On the third Sunday of the month, vendors at the Fierucola organic fest sell such delectables as honeys, jams, spice mixes, and fresh vegetables.

PIAZZA DELLA SIGNORIA

Carlo Piccini. Still in operation after several generations, Carlo Piccini sells antique jewelry and makes pieces to order; you can also get old jewelry reset here. ⊠ *Ponte Vecchio 31/r* ☎ *055/292030* ⊕ *www. carlopiccini.com.*

Cassetti. This jeweler combines precious and semiprecious stones and metals in contemporary settings. ⊠ *Ponte Vecchio 54/r* ☎ *055/2396028.*

Diesel. Trendy Diesel started in Vicenza; its gear is on the "must-have" list of many self-respecting Italian teens. ⊠ *Via dei Lamberti 13/r* ☎ *055/2399963* ⊕ *www.diesel.com.*

Gherardi. Florence's king of coral, Gherardi has the city's largest selection of finely crafted pieces, as well as cultured pearls, jade, and turquoise. ⊠ *Ponte Vecchio 5/r* ☎ *055/211809.*

Oro Due. Gold jewelry and other beauteous objects are priced according to the level of craftsmanship and the price of gold bullion that day at Oro Due. ⊠ *Via Lambertesca 12/r* ☎ *055/292143.*

Pineider. Though it has shops throughout the world, Pineider started out in Florence and still does all its printing here. Stationery and business cards are the mainstay, but the stores also sell fine leather desk accessories as well as a less stuffy, more lighthearted line of products. ⊠ *Piazza della Signoria 13/r* ☎ *055/284655.*

SAN NICCOLÒ

★ **Il Torchio.** Photograph albums, frames, diaries, and other objects dressed in handmade paper can be purchased at Il Torchio. The products are high-quality, and the prices lower than usual. ⊠ *Via dei Bardi 17* ☎ *055/2342862.*

SANTA MARIA NOVELLA

Alberto Cozzi. You'll find an extensive line of Florentine papers and paper products at Alberto Cozzi. The artisans in the shop rebind and restore books and works on paper. Their hours are tricky, so it's best to call first before stopping by. ⊠ *Via del Parione 35/r* ☎ *055/294968.*

Angela Caputi. Angela Caputi wows Florentine cognoscenti with her highly creative, often outsized plastic jewelry. A small, but equally creative, collection of women's clothing made of fine fabrics is also on offer. ⊠ *Borgo Santi Apostoli 44/46* ☎ *055/292993.*

Blue Home. This home goods store sells sumptuous fabrics that can be rendered into sofas, rugs, and other home furnishings to create divinely inspired interiors. Antique and contemporary rugs are also on hand. ⊠ *Borgo Santi Apostoli 58/r* ☎ *055/2658262.*

Casadei. The ultimate fine leathers are crafted into classic shapes at Casadei, winding up as women's shoes and bags. ⊠ *Via Tornabuoni 33/r* ☎ *055/287240* ⊕ *www.casadei.com.*

Cellerini. In a city where it seems just about everybody wears an expensive leather jacket, Cellerini is an institution. ⊠ *Via del Sole 37/r* ☎ *055/282533* ⊕ *www.cellerini.it.*

Emilio Pucci. The aristocratic Marchese di Barsento, Emilio Pucci, became an international name in the late 1950s when the stretch ski clothes he designed for himself caught on with the dolce vita crowd—his pseudo-psychedelic prints and "palazzo pajamas" became all the rage. ⊠ *Via Tornabuoni 20–22/r* ☎ *055/2658082.*

Emporio Armani. The sister store of the Giorgio Armani boutique has slightly more affordable nightclub- and office-friendly garb. ⊠ *Piazza Strozzi 16/r* ☏ *055/284315.*

Ferragamo. The classy Ferragamo, in a 13th-century palazzo, displays designer clothing and accessories, though elegant footwear still underlies the Ferragamo success. ⊠ *Via Tornabuoni 2/r* ☏ *055/292123.*

Gatto Bianco. This contemporary jeweler has breathtakingly beautiful pieces worked in semiprecious and precious stones. ⊠ *Borgo Santi Apostoli 12/r* ☏ *055/282989.*

G.B. Frugone 1885. If you're looking for elegant cashmere, look no further. This Genoese-based company has been making scarves, dresses, and sweaters (among other things) for men and women since 1885. ⊠ *Via delle Belle Donne 35/r* ☏ *055/287820.*

Giorgio Armani. The sleek, classic boutique Giorgio Armani is a centerpiece of the dazzling high-end shops clustered in this part of town. ⊠ *Via Tornabuoni 48/r* ☏ *055/219041.*

Giorgio Vannini. You can take home a custom-made suit or dress from Giorgio Vannini, who has a showroom for his prêt-à-porter designs. ⊠ *Borgo Santi Apostoli 43/r* ☏ *055/293037.*

Gucci. Florentine perennial Gucci puts its famous initials on just about everything it sells. ⊠ *Via Tornabuoni 73/r* ☏ *055/2645432.*

La Bottega dell'Olio. Experience olive oil in all its permutations at La Bottega dell'Olio. The shop, which is tucked into a small piazza, has a great collection of fine olive oils, as well as bath products made from olive oil. ⊠ *Piazza del Limbo 2/r* ☏ *055/2670468.*

Loretta Caponi. Synonymous with Florentine embroidery, Loretta Caponi's luxury lace, linens, and lingerie have earned the eponymous signora worldwide renown. ⊠ *Piazza Antinori 4/r* ☏ *055/213668.*

Officina Profumo Farmaceutica di Santa Maria Novella. The essence of a Florentine holiday is captured in the sachets of the Officina Profumo Farmaceutica di Santa Maria Novella, an art nouveau emporium of herbal cosmetics and soaps that are made following centuries-old recipes created by friars. It celebrated its 400th birthday in 2012. ⊠ *Via della Scala 16* ☏ *055/216276* ⊕ *www.smnovella.it.*

Prada. Known to mix schoolmarmish sensibility with sexy cuts and funky fabrics, Prada appeals to an exclusive clientele. ⊠ *Via Tornabuoni 67/r* ☏ *055/267471.*

Principe. This Florentine institution sells casual clothes for men, women, and children at far-from-casual prices. It also has a great housewares department. ⊠ *Via del Sole 2* ☏ *055/292764.*

Roberto Cavalli. The outlandish designs of native son Roberto Cavalli appeal to Hollywood celebrities and to those who want a little bit of rock star in their wardrobe. ⊠ *Via Tornabuoni 83/r* ☏ *055/2396226.*

Tiffany. One of Florence's oldest jewelers, Tiffany has supplied Italian (and other) royalty with finely crafted gems for centuries. Its selection of antique-looking classics has been updated with a selection of contemporary silver. ⊠ *Via Tornabuoni 25/r* ☏ *055/215506.*

Valli. Gifted seamstresses (and seamsters) should look no further than this place, which sells sumptuous silks, beaded fabrics, lace, wool, and tweeds by the meter. ⊠ *Via della Vigna Nuova 81/r* ☎ *055/282485* ⊕ *www.tessutialtamodavalli.it.*

DUOMO

Luisa Via Roma. The surreal window displays at Luisa Via Roma hint at the trendy yet tasteful clothing inside this fascinating, *alta moda* (high-style) boutique, which stocks the world's top designers as well as Luisa's own line. ⊠ *Via Roma 19–21/r* ☎ *055/217826.*

Mandragora Art Store. This is one of the first attempts in Florence to cash in on the museum-store craze. It's a lovely store with reproductions of valued works of art and jewelry. ⊠ *Piazza del Duomo 50/r* ☎ *055/292559.*

Patrizia Pepe. Florentine designer Patrizia Pepe has body-conscious clothes perfect for all ages, especially for women with a tiny streak of rebelliousness. Women who are not size zero—or close to it—need not apply. ⊠ *Via Strozzi 11/19r* ☎ *055/2302518.*

Penko. Renaissance goldsmiths provide the inspiration for this dazzling jewelry with a contemporary feel. ⊠ *Via F. Zannetti 14/16r* ☎ *055/211661.*

LUNGARNO NORD

Bracciolini. Florentine women with a sense of whimsical style adore the purses at Bracciolini. Each season, the animal theme changes, and the selected animal will adorn any number of beautiful objects. ⊠ *Via delle Vigna Nuova 30/r* ☎ *No phone.*

Giotti. You'll find a full line of leather goods, including clothing at Giotti. ⊠ *Piazza Ognissanti 3–4/r* ☎ *055/294265.*

Rampini Ceramiche. Exquisitely crafted, and expensive, ceramics fill the shelves at Rampini Ceramiche. ⊠ *Borgo Ognissanti 32/34* ☎ *055/219720* ⊕ *www.rampiniceramics.com.*

BEYOND THE CITY CENTER

Barberino Designer Outlet. Prada, Pollini, Missoni, and Bruno Magli, among others, are all found at Barberino Designer Outlet. To get here, take the A1 to the Barberino di Mugello exit, and follow signs to the mall. ⊠ *Via Meucci snc* ☎ *055/842161* ⊕ *www.mercatoglenn.it.*

Le Cascine's open-air market. Held every Tuesday morning, this market includes stalls selling food, bargain clothing, and gadgets.

Mall. One-stop bargain shopping awaits at the Mall, where the stores sell goods by such names as Bottega Veneta, Giorgio Armani, Loro Piana, Sergio Rossi, and Yves St. Laurent. ⊠ *Via Europa 8, Leccio Reggello* ☎ *055/8657775* ⊕ *www.themall.it.*

Prada Outlet. Cognoscenti drive 45 minutes (or take the train to Montevarchi, and then a taxi) to the Prada Outlet. ✉ *Levanella Spacceo, Estrada Statale 69* ☎ *055/91911.*

SIDE TRIPS FROM FLORENCE

FIESOLE

A half-day excursion to Fiesole, in the hills 8 km (5 miles) above Florence, gives you a pleasant respite from museums and a wonderful view of the city. From here the view of the Duomo gives you a new appreciation for what the Renaissance accomplished. Fiesole began life as an ancient Etruscan and later Roman village that held some power until it succumbed to barbarian invasions. Eventually it gave up its independence in exchange for Florence's protection. The medieval cathedral, ancient Roman amphitheater, and lovely old villas behind garden walls are clustered on a series of hilltops. A walk around Fiesole can take from one to two or three hours, depending on how far you stroll from the main piazza.

GETTING HERE AND AROUND

The trip from Florence by car takes 20–30 minutes. Drive to Piazza Liberta and cross the Ponte Rosso heading in the direction of the SS65/SR65. Turn right on to Via Salviati and continue on to Via Roccettini. Make a left turn to Via Vecchia Fiesolana, which will take you directly to the center of town. There are several possible routes for the two-hour walk from central Florence to Fiesole. One route begins in a residential area of Florence called Salviatino (Via Barbacane, near Piazza Edison, on the Bus 7 route), and after a short time, offers peeks over garden walls of beautiful villas, as well as the view over your shoulder at the panorama of Florence in the valley.

VISITOR INFORMATION

Fiesole tourism office ✉ *Via Portigiani 3* ☎ *055/5961323* ⊕ *www.comune. fiesole.fi.it.*

EXPLORING

Duomo. The Duomo presents a stark medieval interior. In the raised presbytery, the **Cappella Salutati** was frescoed by 15th-century artist Cosimo Rosselli, but it was his contemporary, sculptor Mino da Fiesole (1430–84), who put the town on the artistic map. The Madonna on the altarpiece and the tomb of Bishop Salutati are fine examples of the artist's work. ✉ *Piazza Mino da Fiesole* ☎ *055/59400* ☉ *Nov.–Mar., daily 7:30–noon and 2–5; Apr.–Oct., daily 7:30–noon and 3–6.*

Anfiteatro Romano (*Roman Amphitheater*). The beautifully preserved 2,000-seat Anfiteatro Romano, near the Duomo, dates from the 1st century BC and is still used for summer concerts. To the right of the amphitheater are the remains of the **Terme Romani** (Roman Baths), where you can see the gymnasium, hot and cold baths, and rectangular chamber where the water was heated. A beautifully designed **Museo Archeologico**, its facade evoking an ancient Roman temple, is built amid the ruins and contains objects dating from as early as 2000 BC. The nearby **Museo Bandini** is filled with the private collection of Canon Angelo Maria Bandini (1726–1803); he fancied 13th- to 15th-century Florentine paintings, terra-cotta pieces, and wood sculpture, which he later bequeathed to the Diocese of Fiesole. ⊠ *Via Portigiani 1* ☎ *055/5961293* 🖃 *€12, includes access to the archaeological park and museums* ⊙ *Apr.–Sept., daily 9:30–7; Oct.–Mar., Wed.–Mon. 10–4:30.*

San Francesco. The hilltop church of San Francesco has a good view of Florence and the plain below from its terrace and benches. Off the little cloister is a small, eclectic museum containing, among other things, two Egyptian mummies. Halfway up the hill you'll see sloping steps to the right; they lead to a lovely wooded park with trails that loop out and back to the church.

San Domenico. If you really want to stretch your legs, walk 4 km (2½ miles) toward the center of Florence along Via Vecchia Fiesolana, a narrow lane in use since Etruscan times, to the church of San Domenico. Sheltered in the church is the *Madonna and Child with Saints* by Fra Angelico, who was a Dominican friar here. ⊠ *Piazza San Domenico, off Via Giuseppe Mantellini* ☎ *055/59230* ⊙ *Mon.–Sat. 9–noon.*

Badia Fiesolana. From the church of San Domenico it's a five-minute walk northwest to the Badia Fiesolana, which was Fiesole's original cathedral. Dating to the 11th century, it was first the home of the Camaldolese monks. Thanks to Cosimo il Vecchio, the complex was substantially restructured. The facade, never completed owing to Cosimo's death, contains elements of its original Romanesque decoration. The attached convent once housed Cosimo's valued manuscripts. Its mid-15th-century cloister is well worth a look. ⊠ *Via della Badia dei Roccettini 11* ☎ *055/46851* ⊙ *Weekdays 9–6, Sat. 9:30–12:30.*

WHERE TO EAT AND STAY
For expanded hotel reviews, visit Fodors.com.

$$
ITALIAN
✕ **La Reggia degli Etruschi.** If you want a breath of fresh air—literally—this lovely little eatery is worth a detour. Stamina is necessary to get here, as it's on a steep hill on the way up to the church of San Francesco. The rewards upon arrival, in the form of inventive reworkings of Tuscan classics, are well worth it. The *mezzaluna di pera a pecorino* (little half moon pasta stuffed with pear and pecorino) is sauced with Roquefort and poppy seeds. Slivers of papaya—a rare commodity on restaurant menus in these parts—anoints the tasty *carpaccio di tonno affumicato* (smoked tuna carpaccio). The wine list and the attentive service help make this a terrific place to have a meal. When it's warm, you can sit on the little terrace outside. ⊠ *Via San Francesco* ☎ *055/59385* ⊕ *www.lareggiadeglietruschi.com.*

$$
TUSCAN
✕ **Le Cave di Maiano.** If you're looking to get out of town, hop in your car (or take a taxi) to this simple trattoria in the hills just outside Florence. Italians flock here for the *buon rapporto fra qualità e prezzo* (the good rapport between quality and price). Tuscan staples are on hand, as is a fine plate of spaghetti with truffled asparagus. They grill well here, so consider something from the grill to follow. By all means leave room for dessert. Though the food is typical, they do it exceedingly

well: the *zuppa cotta* should not be missed. ⊠ *Via Cave di Maiano 16* ☎ *055/59133.*

$$ 🏨 **Villa Aurora.** The attractive hotel on the main piazza takes advantage of its hilltop spot, with beautiful views in many of the rooms, some of which are on two levels with beamed ceilings and balconies. **Pros:** some rooms have pretty views; air quality better than in Florence. **Cons:** a little worn at the edges. ⊠ *Piazza Mino da Fiesole 39* ☎ *055/59363* ⊕ *www.villaaurora.net* ⟿ *23 rooms, 2 suites* ♿ *In-room: Wi-Fi. In-hotel: restaurant, bar, business center, some pets allowed* ⑩ *Breakfast.*

$$$$ 🏨 **Villa San Michele.** The cypress-lined driveway provides an elegant preamble to this incredibly gorgeous (and very expensive) hotel nestled in the hills of Fiesole. **Pros:** exceptional convent conversion. **Cons:** money must be no object. ⊠ *Via Doccia 4* ☎ *055/5678200* ⊕ *www.villasanmichele.com* ⟿ *21 rooms, 24 suites* ♿ *In-room: safe, Wi-Fi. In-hotel: restaurant, bar, pool, gym, business center, parking, some pets allowed* ☉ *Closed Nov.–Easter.*

NIGHTLIFE AND THE ARTS

Estate Fiesolana. From June through August, Estate Fiesolana, a festival of theater, music, dance, and film, takes place in Fiesole's churches and in the Roman amphitheater—demonstrating that the ancient Romans knew a thing or two about acoustics. ⊠ *Teatro Romano* ☎ *055/5961323* ⊕ *www.comune.fiesole.fi.it.*

SETTIGNANO

When Florence is overcrowded and hot—that is, for most of the summer—this village, a 20-minute car or bus trip east of Florence, is particularly appealing. It was the birthplace of many artists, including the sculptors Desiderio di Settignano (circa 1428–64), Antonio (1427–79) and Bernardo (1409–64) Rossellino, and Bartolomeo Ammannati (1511–92). Michelangelo's wet nurse was the wife of a stonecutter in Settignano, and to her he attributed his later calling in life. Alas, these artists' works no longer adorn their native town, but Settignano is worth a visit simply to breathe its fresh air, walk its tiny streets, and sit in its small **piazza** with an aperitivo.

GETTING HERE AND AROUND

To get to the village, take Bus 10 from the station at Santa Maria Novella or at Piazza San Marco, all the way to the end of the line, the *capolinea.* It will put you in the middle of Settignano's piazzetta.

EXPLORING

Oratorio della Vannella. A 20-minute walk through scenic countryside from Settignano's piazzetta leads to the Oratorio della Vannella. The exterior, dating from 1719–21, is unremarkable, but the fresco of the *Madonna and Child Enthroned* (circa 1470), attributed to a young Sandro Botticelli (1445–1510), is housed here. It's in sad shape but is said to work miracles. To get here, take Via Desiderio di Settignano, walk around the very modern cemetery, turn left, and then follow the narrow path lined with olive trees. The oratory is open for 6 pm Mass the last Sunday of each month; otherwise, you can call the tourist information

Gardens Around Florence

Like any well-heeled Florentine, you, too, can get away from Florence's hustle and bustle by heading for the hills. Take a break from city sightseeing to enjoy gardens and villas. Villa di Castello and Villa La Petraia, both northwest of Florence's historic center, can be explored in one trip. The Italian garden at Villa Gamberaia is an 8-km (5-mile) jaunt east of the center near Settignano. Plan for a full-day excursion, picnic lunch included, if visiting all three gardens. Though Villa Demidoff, originally a Medici country house, is in somewhat dilapidated shape, it's worth a trip to see Giambologna's *Appenino*. For a prime taste of Medici living, venture farther afield to the family's Villa Medicea in Poggio a Caiano, south of Prato (⇨ *Chapter 3, Northwest Tuscany*).

VILLA DI CASTELLO

Villa di Castello. A fortified residence in the Middle Ages, Villa di Castello was bought in 1477 by Lorenzo and Giovanni di Pierfrancesco de' Medici and significantly restructured by Cosimo I in the 16th century. The palace isn't open to the public; the gardens, however, are the main attraction.

Though the original garden design has been altered somewhat over the centuries, the allegorical theme of animals, devised by Tribolo in 1537, remains. The artificial cave, Grotta degli Animali (Animal Grotto), displays sculpted animals by Giambologna and his assistants. An Ammannati sculpture, a figure of an old man representing the Appenines, sits at the center of a pond on the terrace overlooking the garden. Two bronze sculptures by Ammannati, centerpieces of fountains studding the garden, can now be seen

indoors in Villa La Petraia. Allow about 45 minutes to visit the garden; you can easily visit Villa La Petraia from here, making for a four-hour trip in total.

To get to Villa di Castello by car, head northwest from Florence on Via Reginaldo Giuliani (also known as Via Sestese) to Castello, about 6 km (4 miles) northwest of the city center in the direction of Sesto Fiorentino; follow signs to Villa di Castello. Or take Bus 28 from the city center and tell the driver you want to get off at Villa di Castello; from the stop, walk north about ½ km (¼ mile) up the tree-lined allée from the main road. ⊠ *Via di Castello 47, Castello* 🕾 *055/454791* 🎟 *Free* ☉ *Garden: Nov.–Feb., daily 8:15–4:30; Mar., daily 8:15–5:30; Apr., May, Sept., and Oct., daily 8:15–6:30; June–Aug., daily 8:15–7:30. Closed 2nd and 3rd Mon. of month; palace closed to public.*

VILLA LA PETRAIA

Villa La Petraia. The splendidly planted gardens of Villa La Petraia sit high above the Arno with a sweeping view of Florence. The villa was built around a medieval tower and reconstructed after it was purchased by the Medici sometime after 1530. Virtually the only traces of their having lived here are the courtyard frescoes, some by Volterrano, executed between 1636 and 1648.

The garden and the vast park behind the palace suggest a splendid contrast between formal and natural landscapes. Allow 60 to 90 minutes to explore the park and gardens, plus 30 minutes for the guided tour of the so-called museum, the villa interior. This property is best visited after the Villa di Castello.

CLOSE UP

Gardens Around Florence

To get here by car, follow directions to Villa di Castello, but take the right off Via Reginaldo Giuliani, following the sign for Villa La Petraia. You can walk from Villa di Castello to Villa La Petraia in about 15 minutes; turn left beyond the gate of Villa di Castello and continue straight along Via di Castello and the imposing Villa Corsini; take Via della Petraia uphill to the entrance. ⊠ *Via della Petraia 40, Località Castello* ☏ *055/451208* 🎫 *Free* 🕙 *Nov.–Feb., daily 8:15–4:30; Mar.–May, Sept., and Oct., daily 8:15–6:30; June–Aug., daily 8:15–7:30. Closed 2nd and 3rd Mon. of month.*

VILLA GAMBERAIA

Villa Gamberaia. Villa Gamberaia, near the village of Settignano on the eastern outskirts of Florence, was the rather modest 15th-century country home of Matteo di Domenico Gamberelli, the father of noted Renaissance sculptors Bernardo, Antonio, and Matteo Rossellino. In the early 1600s the villa passed into the hands of the wealthy Capponi family. They spared no expense in rebuilding it and, more important, creating its garden, one of the finest near Florence. Studded with statues and fountains, the garden suffered damage during World War II, but has been restored according to the original 17th-century design. This excursion takes about 1½ hours, allowing 45 minutes to visit the garden. Parts of the villa are open by appointment.

To get here by car, head east on Via Aretina, an extension of Via Gioberti, which is picked up at Piazza Beccaria; follow the sign to the turnoff to the north to Villa Gamberaia, about 8 km (5 miles) from the center. To go by bus, take Bus 10 to Settignano. From Settignano's main Piazza Tommaseo, walk east on Via di San Romano; the second lane on the right is Via del Rossellino, which leads southeast to the entrance of Villa Gamberaia. The walk from the piazza takes about 10 minutes. ⊠ *Via del Rossellino 72, near Settignano* ☏ *055/697205* 🎫 *€10* 🕙 *Garden: Apr.–Oct., daily 9–6; Nov.–Mar., daily 9–4.*

VILLA DEMIDOFF

Villa Demidoff. Francesco I de' Medici commissioned the multitalented Bernardo Buontalenti in 1568 to build a villa and a grandiose park to accompany it. The park, particularly the colossal and whimsical sculpture of the *Fontana dell'Appennino* (*Fountain of the Appenines*), executed by Giambologna in 1579–89, is worth the price of admission alone. Besides providing a nice excursion from Florence, the villa is an excellent picnic spot.

To get here by car, head north from Florence on the SR65 toward Pratolino and follow signs to the villa. Or take Bus 25 from Piazza San Marco and get off at Pratolino. ⊠ *Località Pratolino, Vaglia* ☏ *055/409427* 🎫 *Free* 🕙 *May–Sept., Thurs.–Sun. 10–7:30.*

office in Florence (☎ *055/2340444*) to open the doors. ⊠ *Via Desiderio da Settignano 56/b* ⊕ *www.oratoriovannella.it.*

WHERE TO EAT AND STAY

For expanded hotel reviews, visit Fodors.com.

$ ✕ **Osvaldo.** If you're making the trip to Settignano, this is a great dining
TUSCAN option (get off Bus 10 at the stop called Ponte a Mensola). The small, unassuming family-run trattoria is situated along a street and a tiny stream; if you sit outside (there are no views, alas), you might hear the trickle of the stream. The food is terrific, and though it is described as *cucina casalinga* (home cooking), only the portions are home-style. Service is prompt and courteous. ⊠ *Via G. D'Annunzio 51/r* ☎ *055/603972* ⊗ *Closed Wed. No lunch Tues.*

$$ ☶ **Fattoria di Maiano.** In the foothills between Florence and Fiesole are these lovely apartments, which sleep 4 to 11 people and rent by the week. **Pros:** great way to have a country experience with the city nearby. **Cons:** requires a week's stay during high season (December–January 12, April–September). ⊠ *Via Benedetto da Maiano 11* ☎ *055/599600* ⊕ *www.fattoriadimaiano.com* ⊰ *8 apartments* ♨ *In-room: no a/c, kitchen. In-hotel: restaurant, some pets allowed* ❖ *No meals.*

Pisa, Lucca, and Northwest Tuscany

WORD OF MOUTH

"[In Pisa] you'll spend time at the [Leaning Tower] for sure, of course. Whatever you do otherwise, take a walk along the Arno River too, maybe at dusk when you can see the sun setting over the river."

—Andrew

WELCOME TO NORTHWEST TUSCANY

TOP REASONS TO GO

★ **Leaning Tower of Pisa:** It may be touristy, but now that you can once again climb to the top, it's touristy fun.

★ **Olive-oil tasting in and around Lucca:** Italian olive oil is justifiably world famous, and cognoscenti insist that the best is found here.

★ **Cappella Maggiore, Duomo, Prato:** Filippo Lippi's solemn frescoes depicting scenes from the lives of John the Baptist and Saint Stephen positively glow.

★ **Bagni di Lucca:** This sleepy little town attracted the English Romantics, among others, who were drawn to its salubrious waters and air.

★ **Tomb of Ilaria del Carretto, Duomo, Lucca:** Check out this moving sculpture by Jacopo della Quercia commemorating a young woman who died in childbirth.

LIGURIA

GARFAGNANA

Vernazza
Riomaggiore
CINQUE TERRE
Portovenere

La Spezia

Castelnuovo

Carrara
Massa
Barga

Old city, Pisa

Forte dei Marmi
Lido di Camaire
Viareggio

Lucca

Pisa

Cascina

Mare Tirreno

Collesalvetti

Livorno

Castiglioncello

Cecina

1 Towns west of Florence. At industrial centers from the Middle Ages such as Prato and Pistoia you can relax far from Florence's throngs and savor fine food and some art gems. Fragrant white truffles adorn many a restaurant menu in San Miniato.

2 Pisa. Thanks to an engineering mistake, the name Pisa is recognized the world over. The Leaning Tower, the baptistery, the Camposanto, and the cathedral make an impressive foursome on the Piazza del Duomo.

3 Lucca. This laid-back yet elegant town is surrounded by tree-bedecked 16th-century ramparts that are now a delightful promenade.

4 The Garfagnana. Sports enthusiasts and nature addicts flock to Abetone to ski in winter and refresh themselves with cool, mountain air in summer.

5 The Northwest Coast. Experience Italian beach culture at Forte dei Marmi, a crowded and expensive place to see and be seen. Farther west, it's a worthwhile side trip out of Tuscany to visit the coastal villages of the Cinque Terre.

Lucca

TUSCANY
UMBRIA

EMILLA-
ROMAGNA

Abetone
12
4
12
San
Marcello
Bagni
di Lucca
66
Pistoia
Pescia
Montecatini
64
A1
325
Borgo
San Lorenzo
EMILLA-
ROMAGNA
67
65
Prato
65
A11
1
Mt
Albano
Florence
67
Vinci
Arno River
Montelupo
A1
Mt
Pisano
Fucecchio
Empoli
Impruneta
CHIANTI
San
Miniato
Castelfiorentino
222
67
Pontedera
2
429
Greve
Certaldo
Poggibonsi
Volterra
68
0   10 mi
0   10 km
68
1
Piombino
Golfo
di Follónica

GETTING ORIENTED

The landscape west of Florence is flat and generally unremarkable, but when you reach the coast there are beautiful sandy beaches on the Tyrrhenian Sea—and the almost surreal charm of Pisa's Piazza del Duomo, with the Leaning Tower as the star attraction. Heading north, lush hills and olive trees dot the countryside around Lucca, and the elevation climbs as you enter the Garfagnana and its Alpi Apuane—the Apuane Alps.

Montecatini

Updated
by Patricia
Rucidlo

LUCCA AND PISA ARE THE MOST-VISITED CITIES of northwest Tuscany, and with good reason: Lucca has a charming historic center set within its 16th-century walls, and Pisa is home to what may be the most famous tower in the world. Both cities are due west of Florence; the landscape along the way isn't Tuscany's finest, but it has several smaller cities with low-key appeal: good restaurants, a few noteworthy sights, and a taste of Italian life away from the main tourism centers.

Farther north the setting gets more impressive. Craggy, often snow-capped mountains rise above sparsely populated valleys, accessed by narrow winding roads. This is the Garfagnana, Tuscany's most mountainous territory, cut through by the majestic Alpi Apuane (Apuane Alps). The steep terrain rolls down into pine-forested hills and eventually meets the wide, sandy beaches of the Ligurian Sea. Along this stretch, known as the Versilian Coast, are the resort towns of Viareggio and Forte dei Marmi, both of which pack in Italian and other European beachgoers in the summer. Farther west, a hop over the border from Tuscany into Liguria brings you to the Cinque Terre—five tiny, cliff-hugging seaside villages that have become one of Italy's most popular destinations. Due to a drastic mud slide in October 2011, two of the towns—Monterosso al Mare and Vernazza—were washed out and were accessible only by sea. At press time, residents hoped to have both towns up and running by March 2012.

PLANNING

BEACH KNOW-HOW

You may not think of Tuscany as a beach destination, but its long coastline is popular with Italian vacationers. From June through August the resort towns of Viareggio, Forte dei Marmi, and Marina di Massa are packed with beachgoers. Bagni (bathhouses) open, and the sands fill with colorful umbrellas and beach chairs; you can rent your own for about €20 a day and upward.

MAKING THE MOST OF YOUR TIME

The majority of first-time visitors to Tuscany start out by exploring Florence, and then are lured south by the Chianti district and Siena. Heading west instead is an appealing alternative. **Pisa** is the main attraction, and it certainly isn't short on tourists. If that's all you want (or have time) to see here, you're probably best off doing it as a day trip from Florence. If you want to stick around for a while, consider making **Lucca** your base. It's a tremendously appealing town, with fine food and an easygoing atmosphere.

From Lucca you can discover the rest of the area on day trips. The **Garfagnana** has gorgeous mountain peaks and excellent hiking opportunities (as well as skiing in winter). You can follow a day in the mountains with a day along the coast, at the resort towns along the Ligurian Sea and the **Cinque Terre.**

GETTING HERE AND AROUND

BUS TRAVEL

Many of the cities in the region do have bus stations, but service is often sporadic or complicated; it's easier to take the train to Pisa, Prato, Pistoia, Lucca, Montecatini Terme, Livorno, and Empoli, where service is regular and trains run frequently. San Miniato and environs are best reached by car, as service is limited.

It's possible to take a bus from Pistoia or Florence to get to Abetone. A car is necessary to see Carrara and the rest of the Versilian Coast, because bus service is sporadic. For the Cinque Terre, the Lazzi bus service will get you to La Spezia, and then you can take the train to Riomaggiore.

There are three primary bus lines.

COPIT. This bus service connects Empoli, Montelupo, Florence, Prato, and Pistoia; it also has Florence–Abetone service. ☎ *0573/3630 in Pistoia ⊕ www.copitspa.it.*

Lazzi. This bus service connects Florence, Pisa, Lucca, Pescia, Pistoia, and Montecatini. ☎ *055/363041 in Florence ⊕ www.lazzi.it.*

SITA. This bus service connects Florence and Empoli. ☎ *055/47821 in Florence ⊕ www.sitabus.it.*

CAR TRAVEL

The best way to explore the region is by car—and part of the fun is stopping to take in the scenery. In the northern part of the region, towns are spread out and driving the winding mountain roads adds to your travel time.

The A1 autostrada connects Florence to Prato; for Pistoia, Montecatini, and Lucca, follow signs for Firenze Nord, which connects to the A11. For Empoli, Pisa, and hill towns west, take the Strada Grande Communicazione Firenze-Pisa-Livorno, commonly known as the Fi-Pi-Li and sometimes indicated on signage as S.G.C. Firenze-Pisa-Livorno, from Scandicci, just outside Florence. (Note that the Fi-Pi-Li is notorious for its frequent delays due to accidents and construction.) The A12 will take you from near Pisa along the Versilian Coast to La Spezia, entryway to the Cinque Terre. The Cinque Terre itself is impractical for car travel because of the narrow roads and lack of parking (although better access and parking are available at the northern and southern towns of Monterosso al Mare and Riomaggiore); from La Spezia you can take the train, which is the main means of access to the area.

TRAIN TRAVEL

Two main train lines run from Florence's Santa Maria Novella station into northwest Tuscany—one traveling through Prato, Pistoia, Montecatini, and Lucca; the other through Empoli and Pisa. The two lines meet up on the coast with a line that runs through Livorno, Viareggio, and La Spezia.

Trains are a viable option if you're going to any of these cities. For the rest of northwest Tuscany, train connections are extremely limited or nonexistent. To get to the Cinque Terre, you can take a train to La Spezia and then pick up a local train to any of the five towns.

HOTELS

Excluding the beach resort towns, lodging is generally a better deal here than in much of the rest of Tuscany; some real bargains can be found in off-the-beaten-path towns. Consider staying at an *agriturismo*, a farm or vineyard with guest accommodations, which can range from rustic to stately. Many area hotel restaurants serve excellent food, and meal plans are usually available as supplements to your room rate. In summer, when Florence is hot and crowded, it's not a bad plan to base yourself in one of the surrounding towns and use the train to make day trips into the city.

DINING AND LODGING PRICE CATEGORIES (IN EUROS)				
	¢	$	$$	$$$	$$$$
Restaurants	under €15	€15–€25	€25–€35	€35–€45	over €45
Hotels	under €70	€70–€110	€110–€160	€160–€220	over €220

Restaurant prices are for a first course (*primo*), second course (*secondo*), and dessert (*dolce*). Hotel prices are for two people in a standard double room in high season, including tax and service.

ALONG THE ARNO FROM FLORENCE TO PISA

Off the beaten path in Empoli, San Miniato, and the neighboring hill towns are fine examples of art—especially in Empoli and Carmignano—and stirring views. The terrific restaurants in this area are often less expensive than those in the larger surrounding cities, and this is also a good place to find local handmade products—ceramics in Montelupo, glass and leather in the Empoli–Vinci area.

MONTELUPO

30 km (19 miles) southwest of Florence, 6 km (4 miles) east of Empoli.

This small town, which straddles the Arno, and its surrounding villages have been producing ceramics for centuries. A ceramics museum proudly displays the work of the past, but the finest tribute to the tradition is the fact that top-quality ceramics are still hand made in the region. Montelupo's *centro storico* (historic center) is filled with shops selling the finished product.

GETTING HERE

Train service does run from Florence's Santa Maria Novella to Montelupo, but it's sporadic. It's an easy drive on the Fi-Pi-Li highway.

VISITOR INFORMATION

Montelupo tourism office ✉ *Piazza Vittorio Veneto 8-10* ☎ *0571/51352* ⊕ *www.museomontelupo.it.*

EXPLORING

Museo della Ceramica (*Museum of Archaeology and Ceramics*). The Museo della Ceramica has some 3,000 pieces of majolica, a type of glazed pottery made in this region since the early 14th century. The museum is beautifully lighted; objects dating from the early 14th century to the late 18th century are well labeled and arranged, and provide a good overview of the region's ceramics-making history. There's also an interesting display of the coats of arms of important Renaissance families such as the Medici and Strozzi. ⌂ *Piazza Vittorio Veneto 10* ☎*0571/51087* ⌂*€5, combination ticket €8 (includes Museo Leonardiano in Vinci and Collegiata di Sant'Andrea in Empoli)* ⊙ *Tues.–Sun. 10–6.*

3

WHERE TO EAT

$ × **Osteria BoNanni.** A short drive from Montelupo, this osteria is well
TUSCAN worth the detour—if you don't drive right past it by mistake. Its plain exterior—and interior, for that matter—belies the glories coming from the kitchen; the menu depends heavily upon seasonal ingredients, and it's a blessed event if you arrive during porcini season. Locals come to eat large portions of grilled meats and to swill the local wine. The osteria has been in the hands of the BoNanni family since it opened in 1920, and ebullient service contributes to the sheer enjoyment of the meal. ⌂ *Via Turbone 9* ☎ *0571/913477* ⊙ *Closed Mon. No lunch Sun.*

FESTIVAL

Festa della Ceramica. Every June, Montelupo hosts the weeklong Festa della Ceramica, a ceramics festival that includes exhibitions of local and international art, demonstrations of techniques new and ancient, street theater and music—and, of course, sales of ceramics from around the world. Additional information about the ceramics festival is available from the Montelupo Fiorentino tourist office. ☎ *0571/518993, 0571/51352 tourist office.*

SHOPPING

Many of the pieces for sale at Montelupo's ceramics shops follow traditional styles, but some artists bring modern inspiration to their wheels. Note that not all of the stores will ship items home for you.

Ceramica ND Dolfi. This ceramics-making compound, located 3 km (2 miles) from Montelupo on the road heading east toward Florence, has been in the family for three generations. It consists of a sun-drenched *spazio aziendale* (selling floor), a factory workshop, the family residence, and a yard where terra-cotta planters are displayed. The ceramics, all priced reasonably given the high-quality handcrafted work, include large vases, plates suitable for hanging, and brightly colored serving pieces for the table. ⌂ *Via Toscoromagnola 1, Località Antinoro* ☎ *0571/51264* ⊙ *Daily 9–8.*

Le Ceramiche del Borgo. This shop sells the work of Eugenio Taccini, which includes bowls, platters, tiles, and plates. The store's proprietor (and artist's daughter), Lea Taccini, speaks English. ⌂ *XX Settembre 30, Empoli* ☎ *0571/518856* ⊙ *Daily 9–1 and 4–8.*

Maioliche Dolfi Otello. Many serious ceramics lovers think that Maioliche Dolfi Otello produces the region's finest work. The shop, in the same building as the factory, is a couple of miles outside Montelupo, down the SS67 highway in the direction of Florence. In addition to fine platters, vases, and pitchers, the shop produces devotional ceramics by hand in the style of the della Robbia. You can often watch the artisans at work. ⊠ *Via Toscoromagnola Nord 20/b, Località Camaioni* ☎ *0571/910105* ⊕ *www.otellodolfi.it* ⊗ *Weekdays 8–noon and 1:30–6:30.*

EMPOLI

33 km (21 miles) west of Florence, 50 km (31 miles) east of Pisa.

Empoli, roughly halfway between Florence and Pisa, is a small town with a long history. References to the city first appear in documents from the 800s. By the late 12th century it was under the control of Florence. It was here in 1260, after the Battle of Montaperti, that Farinata degli Uberti, leader of the Ghibellines, decided not to burn Florence to the ground. Dante immortalized this decision in Canto X of his *Inferno*.

Now Empoli is a sleepy little town a quick train ride from Florence. If you're traveling in summer, when Florence is at its hottest and most crowded, you might consider staying here and hopping on the train for day trips into the city. But don't overlook the sights of Empoli itself—they're worth seeing.

GETTING HERE

Empoli is an easy 20-minute train ride from Florence's Santa Maria Novella station. If you're driving, take the Fi-Pi-Li—and head out armed with patience. The road is regularly under construction, and there are often delays due to accidents. Lazzi provides bus service from Florence to Empoli.

VISITOR INFORMATION

Empoli tourism office ⊠ *Piazza Farinata degli Uberti 3* ☎ *0571/757729* ⊕ *www.terredelrinascimento.it.*

EXPLORING

★ **Collegiata di Sant'Andrea.** This jewel of a museum is filled with terra-cotta sculptures from the della Robbia school, including one by Andrea della Robbia. There's also a magnificent 15th-century fresco pietà by Masolino (circa 1383–1440), as well as a small work by Fra Filippo Lippi (1406–69) and a wonderful tabernacle attributed to Francesco Botticini (circa 1446–97) and Antonio Rossellino (1427–79). ⊠ *Just off Piazza Farinata degli Uberti* ☎ *0571/76284* 🎫 *€3, combination ticket €8 (includes Museo Leonardiano in Vinci and Museo della Ceramica in Montelupo)* ⊗ *Tues.–Sun. 9–noon and 2–7.*

NEED A BREAK? **Vinegar.** This bar near the train station sells all sorts of *panini* (sandwiches) as well as coffee and *aperitivi* (cocktails). It's a great spot to grab a sandwich before hopping on the bus to Vinci. ⊠ *Piazza della Vittoria 36–37* ☎ *0571/74630.*

Santo Stefano. Originally founded by Augustinians in the 11th century, the church of Santo Stefano can be visited only by requesting a tour in

Cities West of Florence

0   7.5 mi

0   7.5 km

Marches

Tuscany   Umbria

the Collegiata di Sant'Andrea. It's worth the walk around the corner and down the street to see the *sinopie* (preparatory drawings) by Masolino depicting scenes from the *Legend of the True Cross.* He left without actually frescoing them; it may be that the Augustinian friars were late in making payment. ✉ *Via de' Neri* 📞 *0571/76284* 🎟 *Free with admission to the Collegiata* ⏱ *Tues.–Sun. 9–noon and 2–7.*

San Michele in Pontorme. A short but not very scenic walk from the center of town brings you to the little church of San Michele in Pontorme, chiefly notable for the gorgeous *St. John the Baptist* and *St. Michael the Archangel,* two works dating from about 1519 by native son Jacopo Carrucci (1494–1556), better known as Pontormo. ✉ *Piazza San Michele* 📞 *No phone* 🎟 *Free* ⏱ *Ring bell for sacristan; no set hrs, but most consistently open in morning.*

OFF THE
BEATEN
PATH
Villa Medicea. On the night of July 15, 1576, Isabella de' Medici, daughter of the all-powerful Cosimo I, grand duke of Tuscany, was murdered by her husband in the Villa Medicea in the town of Cerreto Guidi for "reasons of honor"—that is, she was suspected of adultery. These days, although the villa's formal garden is in somewhat imperfect condition, the vast halls and chambers within remain majestic. Copies of portraits of various Medici, including Isabella, cover the walls. The villa sits atop the highest point in Cerreto Guidi, encircled by two narrow streets

Going Local at Festivals

A great way to get a feel for the region and its people is to attend a local *sagra* (festival). During the summer there's one taking place nearly every weekend in some small town or village, usually with a food theme, such as a *sagra dei funghi* (mushroom festival) or *sagra della zuppa* (soup festival). Held at night, the events dish out plenty to eat and drink, and there's usually dancing, sometimes with live music. Old-school ballroom moves are the norm; you're likely to see couples fox-trotting or doing the tango.

These are village affairs, with few people speaking English. There are no numbers to call for information. The festivals are advertised only by crudely printed signs on the side of the road. Attending a sagra is a unique opportunity to experience small-town Italian culture.

where the daily business of the town goes on. As you stand on the wide, flat front lawn, high above the streets of the town, with the villa behind you and terraced hillsides of olive groves and vineyards stretching into the distance, you can imagine what it was like to be a Medici. To see the villa, ring the bell for the custodian. ⊠ *8 km (5 miles) west of Empoli, Cerreto Guidi* ☎ *0571/55707* 🎫 *Free* ⊘ *Daily 8:30–6:30. Closed 2nd and 3rd Mon. of each month.*

WHERE TO EAT

$$
ITALIAN

✕ **Il Galeone.** This relaxed and friendly place is known for its fish, but the meat dishes are just as good. Pale-pink walls and pink tablecloths play off the gray-and-white tile floors. Give the *moscardini con fagioli e rucola* (baby squid gently cooked with cannellini beans, diced tomatoes, and olive oil, served on a bed of arugula) a try; the *spiedini di seppioline e gamberoni* (kebabs of squid with shrimp) are terrific, too. Pizza is also served here. ⊠ *Via Curtatone e Montanara 67* ☎ *0571/72826* ⊘ *Closed Sun. and Aug.*

VINCI

10 km (6 miles) north of Empoli, 45 km (28 miles) west of Florence.

The small hill town from which Leonardo da Vinci derived his name is a short drive or bus ride north of Empoli. At the church of Santa Croce, near the town square, you can see the baptismal font in which Leonardo was baptized. But if you want to see the house where he was born, you'll have to travel to Anchiano, 3 km (2 miles) north of Vinci. Though it's somewhat of a tourist trap, a trip to Vinci is worth the effort for the views alone.

GETTING HERE

To get to Vinci via public transportation, take the train to Empoli, then catch a Lazzi bus to Vinci.

VISITOR INFORMATION

Vinci tourism office ⊠ *Via delle Torre 11* ☎ *0571/568012* ⊕ *www. terredelrinascimento.it.*

EXPLORING

Museo Leonardiano. Atop the castle belonging to the Guidi family in the historic center of Vinci, Museo Leonardiano has replicas of many of Leonardo's machines and gadgets. The stunning country views most likely influenced the artist, as some of his painted backgrounds suggest the hills of Vinci. ⊠ *Via della Torre 2* ☎ *0571/933251* ✉ *€7, €8 combination ticket (includes Collegiata di Sant'Andrea in Empoli and Museo della Ceramica in Montelupo)* ☉ *Daily 9:30–7.*

OFF THE BEATEN PATH

Casa Natale di Leonardo. No one knows the precise location of Leonardo da Vinci's birthplace, but this typical 15th-century Tuscan house is in the general vicinity and probably shares much in common with the house where he was born. It's in Anchiano, 3 km (2 miles) from Vinci, and can be reached easily on foot or by car. It has a primitive interior—it hasn't been gussied up for tourists. Note the printed inventory of Leonardo's library. His tastes in literature were wide-ranging, from the ancients to contemporary (15th-century) authors. At press time, the house was undergoing restoration and was closed to the public. ⊠ *Località Anchiano* ☎ *0571/56519* ✉ *Free* ☉ *Mar.–Oct., daily 9:30–7; Nov.–Feb., daily 9:30–6.*

WHERE TO STAY

For expanded hotel reviews, visit Fodors.com.

$ ☷ **Il Fondaccio.** The Falzari family operates this moderately priced agriturismo overlooking the hills near Vinci. **Pros:** central location; good for kids; dog-friendly. **Cons:** one-week stay required. ⊠ *Via del Fondaccio 19* ☎ *0571/559511* ⊕ *www.fondaccio.it* ⇆ *5 apartments* ♿ *In-room: no a/c, kitchen, no TV, Wi-Fi. In-hotel: pool, laundry facilities, some pets allowed* ▭ *No credit cards* ⦿ *No meals.*

SAN MINIATO

20 km (12 miles) southwest of Vinci, 43 km (27 miles) west of Florence.

San Miniato has a history dating to Etruscan and Roman times; today it's a tiny, pristine hill town of narrow streets lined with austere 13th- to 17th-century facades, some covering buildings that are centuries older. The Holy Roman Empire had very strong ties here—the local castle was built in 962 under the aegis of Otto I (912–973). Eventually the town, with its Ghibelline (pro-imperial) sympathies, passed into the hands of the Florentines. San Miniato's artistic treasures are limited by Tuscan standards, but the town's prettiness makes a visit worthwhile. On three weekends in November an annual truffle festival adds to San Miniato's allure; it's well worth visiting if you're in the area. The food stalls teem with fantastic local stuff, while restaurants are crammed with locals and visitors chowing down on truffled things.

GETTING HERE

The easiest way to get to San Miniato is by car via the Fi-Pi-Li. The San Miniato train station is far from the centro storico.

VISITOR INFORMATION

San Miniato tourism office ⊠ *Piazza del Popolo 3* ☎ *0571/418739* ⊕ *www. sanminiatopromozione.it.*

EXPLORING

Convento di San Francesco (*Convent and Church of St. Francis*). In 1211 Saint Francis founded the Convento di San Francesco, which contains two cloisters and an ornate wooden choir. For a dose of monastic living, you can stay overnight (€39 for a double room). ⊠ *Piazza San Francesco* ☎ *0571/43051* ⊒ *Free* ⊙ *Daily 9–noon and 3–7 (or ring bell).*

Convento e Chiesa di Santi Jacopo e Lucia (*Convent and Church of Sts. Jacob and Lucia*). This place of worship is also known as the church of San Domenico, which refers to the fact that the Dominicans took over the church in the 14th century. Most of the interior suffers from too much baroque, but there is a lovely sculpted tomb by Bernardo Rossellino for Giovanni Chellini, a doctor who died in 1461. You'll find it on the right-hand nave close to the high altar. ⊠ *Piazza del Popolo* ☎ *0571/418739* ⊙ *Daily 8:30–noon and 3:30–6.*

NEED A BREAK?

Bar Cantini. This social hub for San Miniatans serves wonderful panini that are made with bread baked on-site. There is also pizza by the slice, tasty *granita* (flavored ice), and homemade ice cream. ⊠ *Via Conti 1* ☎ *0571/43030.*

Duomo. The only thing remarkable about San Miniato's Duomo, set in a pretty piazza, is its 13th-century facade, which has been restored. The interior is largely uninteresting, though there's a poignant plaque commemorating the 55 citizens who were killed in this church in July 1944 by German occupying forces. (The Taviani brothers' 1982 movie, *The Night of San Lorenzo,* was about this tragedy.) ⊠ *Piazza del Castello* ☎ *No phone* ⊙ *Daily 8–12:30 and 3–6:30.*

Museo Diocesano. Although the Museo Diocesano is small, the modest collection incorporates a number of subtle and pleasant local works of art. Note the rather odd *Crucifixion* by Fra Filippo Lippi, Verrocchio's (1435–88) *Il Redentore,* and the small but exquisite *Education of the Virgin* by Tiepolo (1696–1770). ⊠ *Piazza del Castello* ☎ *0571/406700* ⊒ *€2.50* ⊙ *Apr.–Oct., weekends 10–1 and 2–6; Nov.–Mar., Tues.– Sun. 11–5.*

Torre di Federico II. Dating from the time of Frederick II (1194–1250), the Torre di Federico II was destroyed during World War II. A point of civic pride for San Miniatans and visible for miles, the tower was rebuilt and reopened in 1958. The hapless, ill-fated Pier della Vigna, chancellor and minister to Frederick II, leaped to his death from the tower, earning a mention in Dante's *Inferno*. The hill on which the tower stands—a surprisingly large oval of green grass—is one of the loveliest places in the area to have a picnic, enjoy the 360-degree view, and perhaps join local children in a pickup game of *calcio* (soccer). ⊠ *Piazza la Torre*

🕾 *0571/42745* 🖃 *€2.50* 🕘 *Apr.–Oct., Tues.–Sun. 11–6; Nov.–Mar., Tues.–Sun. 11–5.*

WHERE TO EAT AND STAY

For expanded hotel reviews, visit Fodors.com.

$$$ ✕ **Il Convio.** A short drive down a steep, serpentine road from San Min-
TUSCAN iato brings you to this rustic country *ristorante* with sponged walls, stenciled decorations, and checkered tablecloths. The main courses are mostly Tuscan classics, such as *bistecca fiorentina* (a generous cut of grilled steak). White truffles, the local specialty, are showcased—you can get them with pasta, *crespelle* (thin pancakes filled with ricotta), tripe, eggs, beef fillet, and even with a postprandial truffled grappa. All this good fare pairs marvelously with their fine selection of local, lesser-known wines. If truffles don't float your boat, there are untruffled things on the menu and, at night, they fire up the pizza oven. 🖂 *Via San Maiano 2* 🕾 *0571/408114* 🕘 *Closed Wed.*

¢ 🏠 **Convento di San Francesco.** For a complete change of pace, you can stay in this 13th-century convent in the company of five Franciscan friars. **Pros:** great price; tranquillity. **Cons:** rooms are rather spartan; most of staff speaks only Italian. 🖂 *Piazza San Francesco* 🕾 *0571/43051* 🛏 *30 rooms* ⚲ *In-room: no a/c, no TV. In-hotel: some age restrictions* ▬ *No credit cards* 🍽 *No meals.*

PISA

If you can get beyond the kitsch of the stalls hawking cheap souvenirs around the Leaning Tower, you'll find that Pisa has much to offer. Its treasures aren't as abundant as those of Florence, to which it is inevitably compared, but the cathedral-baptistery-tower complex of Piazza del Duomo, known collectively as the Campo dei Miracoli (Field of Miracles), is among the most dramatic settings in Italy.

Pisa may have been inhabited as early as the Bronze Age. It was certainly populated by the Etruscans and, in turn, became part of the Roman Empire. In the early Middle Ages it flourished as an economic power-house—along with Amalfi, Genoa, and Venice, it was one of the four maritime republics. The city's economic and political power ebbed in the early 15th century as it fell under Florence's domination, though it enjoyed a brief resurgence under Cosimo I in the mid-16th century. Pisa sustained heavy damage during World War II, but the Duomo and Tower were spared, along with some other grand Romanesque structures.

GETTING HERE

Pisa is an easy hour's train ride from Florence. By car it's a straight shot on the Fi-Pi-Li autostrada. The Pisa–Lucca train runs frequently and takes about 30 minutes.

VISITOR INFORMATION

Pisa tourism office 🖂 *Piazza Vittorio Emanuele II* 🕾 *050/42291* ⊕ *www.pisaturismo.it.*

EXPLORING PISA

Pisa, like many Italian cities, is best explored on foot, and most of what you'll want to see is within walking distance. The views along the Arno River are particularly grand and shouldn't be missed—there's a feeling of spaciousness that isn't found along the Arno in Florence.

As you set out, note that there are various combination-ticket options for sights on the Piazza del Duomo.

TOP ATTRACTIONS

Battistero. This lovely Gothic baptistery, which stands across from the Duomo's facade, is best known for the pulpit carved by Nicola Pisano (circa 1220–84; father of Giovanni Pisano) in 1260. Ask one of the ticket takers if he'll sing for you inside; the acoustics are remarkable. ⊠ *Piazza del Duomo* ☎ *050/835011* ⊕ *www.opapisa.it* 🎟 *€5, discounts available if bought in combination with tickets for other monuments* ⊙ *Nov.–Feb., daily 10–5; Mar., daily 9–6; Apr.–Sept., daily 8–8; Oct., daily 9–7.*

Duomo. Pisa's cathedral brilliantly utilizes the horizontal marble-stripe motif (borrowed from Moorish architecture) that became common to Tuscan cathedrals. It is famous for the Romanesque panels on the transept door facing the tower that depict scenes from the life of Christ.

The beautifully carved 14th-century pulpit is by Giovanni Pisano (son of Nicola). ⊠ *Piazza del Duomo* ☎ *050835011* ⊕ *www.opapisa.it* 🎫 *€5* ☉ *Nov.–Feb., daily 10–12:45 and 2–5; Mar., daily 10–6; Apr.–Sept., daily 10–8; Oct., daily 10–7.*

Fodor's Choice **Leaning Tower (Torre Pendente).** Legend holds that Galileo conducted an
★ experiment on the nature of gravity by dropping metal balls from the top of the 187-foot-high Leaning Tower of Pisa. Historians, however, say this legend has no basis in fact—which isn't quite to say that it's false. Work on this tower, built as a campanile (bell tower) for the Duomo, started in 1173: the lopsided settling began when construction reached the third story. The tower's architects attempted to compensate through such methods as making the remaining floors slightly taller on the leaning side, but the extra weight only made the problem worse. The settling continued, and by the late 20th century it had accelerated to such a point that many feared the tower would simply topple over, despite all efforts to prop it up. The structure has since been firmly anchored to the earth. The final phase to restore the tower to its original tilt of 300 years ago was launched in early 2000 and finished two years later. The last phase removed some 100 tons of earth from beneath the foundation. Reservations, which are essential, can be made online or by calling the Museo dell'Opera del Duomo; it's also possible to arrive at the ticket office and book for the same day. Note that children under eight years of age are not allowed to climb. ⊠ *Piazza del Duomo* ☎ *050/835011* ⊕ *www.opapisa.it* 🎫 *€17* ☉ *Dec. and Jan., daily 10–4:30; Nov. and Feb., daily 9:30–5:30; Mar., daily 9–5:30; Apr.–Sept., daily 8:30–8; Oct., daily 9–7.*

WORTH NOTING

Camposanto. According to legend, the cemetery—a walled structure on the western side of the Campo dei Miracoli—is filled with earth that returning Crusaders brought back from the Holy Land. Contained within are numerous frescoes, notably *The Drunkenness of Noah*, by Renaissance artist Benozzo Gozzoli (1422–97), presently under restoration; and the disturbing *Triumph of Death* (14th century; artist uncertain), whose subject matter shows what was on people's minds in a century that saw the ravages of the Black Death. ⊠ *Piazza del Duomo* ☎ *050/835011* ⊕ *www.opapisa.it* 🎫 *€5, discounts available if bought in combination with tickets for other monuments* ☉ *Nov.–Feb., daily 10–5; Mar., daily 9–6; Apr.–Sept., daily 8–8; Oct., daily 9–7.*

Museo delle Sinopie. The well-arranged museum on the south side of the Piazza del Duomo holds the *sinopie* (preparatory drawings) for the Camposanto frescoes. Though the exhibits are mostly of interest to specialists, some didactic audiovisual material provides a good introduction to the whole religious complex. ⊠ *Piazza del Duomo* ☎ *050/835011* ⊕ *www.opapisa.it* 🎫 *€5, discounts available if bought in combination with tickets for other monuments* ☉ *Nov.–Feb., daily 10–5; Mar., daily 9–6; Apr.–Sept., daily 8–8; Oct., daily 9–7.*

Museo dell'Opera del Duomo. At the southeast corner of the sprawling Campo dei Miracoli, this museum holds a wealth of medieval sculptures and the ancient Roman sarcophagi that inspired Nicola Pisano's figures.

✉ *Piazza del Duomo* ☎ *050/835011* ⊕ *www.opapisa.it* 🖃 *€5, discounts available if bought in combination with tickets for other monuments* ⊙ *Nov.–Feb., daily 10–5; Mar., daily 9–6; Apr.–Sept., daily 8–8; Oct., daily 9–7.*

Museo Nazionale di San Matteo. On the north bank of the Arno, this museum contains some incisive examples of local Romanesque and Gothic art. ✉ *Lungarno Mediceo* ☎ *050/541865* 🖃 *€5* ⊙ *Tues.–Sat. 9–7, holidays 9–2.*

Piazza dei Cavalieri. The piazza, with its fine Renaissance **Palazzo dei Cavalieri, Palazzo dell'Orologio,** and Chiesa di **Santo Stefano dei Cavalieri,** was laid out by Giorgio Vasari in about 1560. The square was the seat of the Ordine dei Cavalieri di San Stefano (Order of the Knights of St. Stephen), a military and religious institution meant to defend the coast from possible invasion by the Turks. Also in this square is the prestigious **Scuola Normale Superiore,** founded by Napoléon in 1810 on the French model. Here graduate students pursue doctorates in literature, philosophy, mathematics, and science. In front of the school is a large statue of Ferdinando I de' Medici dating from 1596. On the extreme left is the tower where the hapless Ugolino della Gherardesca (died 1289) was imprisoned with his two sons and two grandsons; legend holds that he ate them. Dante immortalized him in Canto XXXIII of his *Inferno.* Duck into the **Church of Santo Stefano** (if you're lucky enough to find it open) and check out Bronzino's splendid *Nativity of Christ* (1564–65).

Santa Maria della Spina. Originally an oratory dating from the 13th century, this gem of a church has been restored several times, most recently in 1996–98, owing to flood damage. It's a delicate, tiny church, and a fine example of Tuscan Gothic architecture. ✉ *Lungarno Gambacorti* ☎ *No phone* 🖃 *€2.50* ⊙ *Apr.–Oct., Tues.–Fri. 10–1:15 and 2:30–5:45; Nov.–Mar., Tues.–Sun. 10–1 and 3–6.*

OFF THE BEATEN PATH

La Certosa di Pisa. A *certosa* is a monastery whose monks belong to the strict Carthusian order. This vast and sprawling complex, begun in 1366, was suppressed by Napoléon in the early 1800s, and then again in 1866. Most of the art and architecture you see dates from the 17th and 18th centuries. The Carthusians returned here, only to leave it permanently in 1969. Also within it is the **Museo di Storia Naturale e del Territorio.** This museum of natural history contains fossils, 24 whale skeletons that serve to trace the mammal's development over the millennia, and some exhibits of local minerals. ✉ *10 km (6 miles) east of Pisa via road north of Arno, through Mezzana and then toward Calci and Montemagno* ☎ *050/938430* 🖃 *€4* ⊙ *Tues.–Sat. 8:30–6:30, Sun. 8:30–12:30, with tours on half hr.*

San Piero a Grado. This 11th-century basilica, located 8 km (5 miles) southwest of Pisa along the Arno, was built over the remains of two earlier churches. According to legend, it was here that Peter the Apostle stepped off the boat in AD 42—his first step on Italian soil. (It would have made more sense for him to land on the Adriatic Coast, as he was coming from Antioch.) The structure is a lovely example of Romanesque architecture, and it's not without its quirks: it has two apses, one at each end. On the walls are some crumbling, but still vibrant, frescoes dating from the 12th and 13th centuries. Thirty-one of these frescoes depict scenes from the lives of Saints Peter and Paul, an uncommon subject in Tuscan wall painting. ⊠ *Via Vecchia di Marina, San Piero a* 🕿 *050/960065* ⊘ *Daily 8–7.*

WHERE TO EAT

$$ ✕**Beny.** Apricot walls hung with etchings of Pisa make this small, single-
ITALIAN room restaurant warmly romantic. Husband and wife Damiano and
★ Sandra Lazzerini have been running the place for two decades, and it shows in their obvious enthusiasm while talking about the menu and daily specials. Fish is a specialty here: the *ripieno di polpa di pesce a pan grattato con salsa di seppie e pomodoro* (fish-stuffed ravioli with tomato-octopus sauce) delights. Seasonal ingredients are key throughout the menu; Sandra works wonders with *tartufi estivi* (summer truffles), artichokes, and market fish of the day. ⊠ *Piazza Gambacorti 22* 🕿 *050/25067* ⊘ *Closed Sun. and 2 wks in mid-Aug. No lunch Sat.*

$$ ✕**La Pergoletta.** On an old town street named for its beautiful towers,
TUSCAN this small, simple restaurant is in one such tower itself. There's also a shady garden for outdoor dining. Emma Forte, the proprietor and chef, cooks such Tuscan classics as *minestra di farro* (spelt soup) and choice interpretations of *grigliata* (grilled beef, veal, or lamb). Her sense of whimsy accounts for some of the non-Italian ingredients, such as ginger, that find their way into her dishes. Parents with small children may be pleased to find that there's a children's menu, and couples looking for a romantic spot could find no better place in Pisa. ⊠ *Via delle Belle Torri 40* 🕿 *050/542458* ⊘ *Closed Mon. and 1 wk in Aug. No lunch Sat.*

$$ ✕**Osteria dei Cavalieri.** This charming white-wall restaurant, a few steps
ITALIAN from Piazza dei Cavalieri, is reason enough to come to Pisa. They can
★ do it all here—serve up exquisitely grilled fish dishes, please vegetarians, and prepare *tagliata* (thin slivers of rare beef) for meat lovers. Three set menus, from the sea, garden, and earth, are available, or you can order à la carte. For dinner there's an early seating (around 7:30) and a later one (around 9); opt for the later one if you want time to linger over your meal. ⊠ *Via San Frediano 16* 🕿 *050/580858* 📖 *Reservations essential* ⊘ *Closed Sun., 2 wks in Aug., and Dec. 29–Jan. 7. No lunch Sat.*

¢ ✕**Trattoria la Faggiola.** It's only seconds away from the Leaning Tower,
ITALIAN which probably explains the "No Pizza" sign written in big, bold letters on the blackboard outside. Inside, another blackboard lists two or three *primi* and *secondi*. The amiable Carlo Silvestrini presides over this little eatery, and he cares if you don't clean your plate. That's not a problem though, because everything's good, from the *pasta pasticciata con speck e carciofi* (oven-baked penne with cured ham and artichokes) to

the finishing touch of *castagnaccio con crema di ricotta* (a chestnut flan topped with ricotta cream). ⊠ *Via della Faggiola 1, Pisa* ☎ *050/556179* ⌂ *Reservations essential* ▬ *No credit cards.*

WHERE TO STAY

For expanded hotel reviews, visit Fodors.com.

$ ★ ⊞ **Fattoria di Migliarino.** Martino Salviati and his wife Giovanna have turned their working *fattoria* (farm)—on which they raise soybeans, corn, and sugar beets—into an inn. **Pros:** near Pisa airport, a good choice for a tranquil last night in Italy. **Cons:** mandatory one-week apartment stay during high season. ⊠ *Via dei Pini 289, 10 km (6 miles) northwest of Pisa, Migliarino* ☎ *050/803046, 335/6608411 mobile* ⊕ *www.fattoriadimigliarino.it* ⌁ *10 rooms in B&B, 13 apartments* ⌂ *In-room: no a/c, kitchen, no TV, Wi-Fi. In-hotel: pool* ⦿ *Breakfast.*

$$$$ ⊞ **Hotel Relais dell'Orologio.** What used to be a private family palace is now an intimate hotel. **Pros:** location—in the center of town, but on a quiet side street. **Cons:** breakfast costs extra. ⊠ *Via della Faggiola 12/14, off Campo dei Miracoli, Santa Maria* ☎ *050/830361* ⊕ *www. hotelrelaisorologio.com* ⌁ *16 rooms, 5 suites* ⌂ *In-room: safe, Wi-Fi. In-hotel: restaurant, bar, parking, some pets allowed* ⦿ *No meals.*

$$ ⊞ **Royal Victoria.** In a pleasant palazzo facing the Arno, a 10-minute walk from the Campo dei Miracoli, this comfortably furnished hotel has been in the Piegaja family since 1837. **Pros:** friendly staff; free use of a Lancia that seats five—a great vehicle for tooling around Pisa. **Cons:** rooms vary significantly in size; all are a little worn. ⊠ *Lungarno Pacinotti 12* ☎ *050/940111* ⊕ *www.royalvictoria.it* ⌁ *48 rooms, 40 with bath* ⌂ *In-room: no a/c, Wi-Fi. In-hotel: parking, some pets allowed* ⦿ *Breakfast.*

NIGHTLIFE AND THE ARTS

Luminaria. Pisa at its best during the Luminaria feast day, on June 16. The day honors Saint Ranieri, the city's patron saint. Palaces along the Arno are lighted with white lights, and there are plenty of fireworks.

Fondazione Teatro di Pisa. Pisa has a lively performing-arts scene, most of which happens at the 19th-century Teatro Verdi. Music and dance performances are presented from September through May. Contact Fondazione Teatro di Pisa for schedules and information. ⊠ *Via Palestro 40, Lungarni* ☎ *050/941111* ⊕ *www.teatrodipisa.pi.it.*

THE ROAD FROM FLORENCE TO LUCCA

The cities along the route between Florence and Lucca are primarily industrial—and they've been that way for a long time. Prato has been producing textiles since the Middle Ages; Renaissance art lovers should pay a visit to the Duomo, with its magnificent Filippo Lippi frescoes. Farther northwest, Pistoia's historic center abounds with art treasures. If you're looking for a spa treatment, or if you want to experience a bit of kitsch, Italian style, visit Montecatini Terme, where the clock seems to have stopped sometime in the 1950s.

PRATO

19 km (12 miles) northwest of Florence, 60 km (37 miles) east of Lucca.

The wool industry in this city, one of the world's largest producers of cloth, was famous throughout Europe as early as the 13th century. Business was further stimulated in the late 14th century by a local cloth merchant, Francesco di Marco Datini, who built his business, according to one of his surviving ledgers, "In the name of God and of profit." One thing that distinguishes Prato from other Italian towns of its size is the presence of modern public art—most notably Henry Moore's mammoth, marble *Square Form with Cut* in Piazza San Marco. ■TIP➔ Most of Prato's major museums are closed Tuesday.

GETTING HERE
Prato is a quick train ride from Florence. By car it's a 45-minute trip on the A11/E76 toll road.

VISITOR INFORMATION
Prato tourism office ✉ *Piazza del Duomo 8* ☎ *0574/24112* ⊕ *www. pratoturismo.it.*

EXPLORING
Duomo. Prato's Romanesque Duomo, reconstructed from 1211, is famous for its **Pergamo del Sacro Cingolo** (Chapel of the Holy Girdle), to the left of the entrance, which enshrines the sash of the Virgin Mary. It is said that the girdle was given to the apostle Thomas by the Virgin Mary when she miraculously appeared after her Assumption into heaven. The Duomo also contains 15th-century frescoes by Prato's most famous son, Fra Filippo Lippi. His scenes from the life of Saint Stephen are on the left wall of the **Cappella Maggiore** (Main Chapel); those from the life of John the Baptist are on the right. ✉ *Piazza del Duomo* ☎ *0574/26234* ⊕ *www.diocesiprato.it* 💲*€3 to visit Cappella Maggiore* ☉ *Daily 10–1 and 3–5:30.*

NEED A BREAK?

Antonio Mattei. Prato's *biscotti* (literally "twice-cooked" cookies) have an extra-dense texture, lending themselves to submersion in your caffè or vin santo. The best biscotti in town are at Antonio Mattei. Their *brutti buoni* (ugly but good) almond-laced cookies are especially delicious. ✉ *Via Ricasoli 20/22* ☎ *0574/25756* ⊕ *www.antoniomattei.it.*

Museo dell'Opera del Duomo. A sculpture by Donatello (circa 1386–1466) that originally adorned the Duomo's exterior pulpit is now on display in the Museo dell'Opera del Duomo. The museum also includes such 15th-century gems as Fra Filippo Lippi's *Madonna and Child*, Giovanni Bellini's (circa 1432–1516) *Christ on the Cross*, and Caravaggio's (1571–1610) *Christ Crowned with Thorns*. ✉ *Piazza del Duomo 49* ☎ *0574/29339* ⊕ *www.diocesiparti.it* 💲*€5, combination ticket €8 (includes Museo di Pittura Murale and il Castello)* ☉ *Mon. and Wed.– Sat. 10–1 and 3–5:30, Sun. 10–1.*

Museo di Pittura Murale (*Museum of Mural Painting*). The permanent collection in the Museo di Pittura Murale contains frescoes and altarpieces (removed from sites in and around Prato) by artists such as Filippo

Lippi, Agnolo Gaddi, Nicolo Gerini, and Il Volterrano, among others. ✉ *Piazza San Domenico 8* ☎ *0574/440501* 💶 *€5, combination ticket €8 (includes Museo dell'Opera del Duomo and il Castello)* 🕐 *Mon., Wed.–Fri., and Sun. 9–1; Sat. 9–1 and 3–6.*

Centro per l'Arte Contemporanea Luigi Pecci (*Luigi Pecci Center of Contemporary Art*). This museum contains works of artists from around the world completed after 1965. The exhibitions constantly change, and often feature debut presentations. ✉ *Viale della Repubblica 277* ☎ *0574/5317* ⊕ *www.centropecci.it* 💶 *€4* 🕐 *Wed.–Mon. 10–6:30.*

Museo del Tessuto (*Textile Museum*). Preserved in this museum is what made Prato a Renaissance economic powerhouse. The collection includes clothing, fabric fragments, and the machines used to make them, all dating from the 14th to the 20th century. Check out the 15th-century fabrics with pomegranate prints, a virtuoso display of Renaissance textile wizardry. The well-designed museum (objects are clearly labeled in English) is within the medieval walls of the city in the old Cimatoria, a 19th-century factory that finished raw fabrics. The temporary exhibitions are usually noteworthy; check with the Prato tourist office to see what's on display when you visit. ✉ *Via Santa Chiara 24* ☎ *0574/611503* ⊕ *www.museodeltessuto.it* 💶 *€4, free Sun.* 🕐 *Daily 10–6.*

Santa Maria delle Carceri. The church of Santa Maria delle Carceri was built by Giuliano Sangallo in the 1490s, and is a landmark of Renaissance architecture. ✉ *Piazza Santa Maria delle Carceri, off Via Cairoli and southeast of the cathedral* ☎ *0574/27933* 🕐 *Daily 7–noon and 4–7.*

Castello (*Castle*). The formidable Castello, near Santa Maria delle Carceri, is an impressive sight. The (Sicilian) Holy Roman Emperor Frederick II (1194–1250) built the seat of his authority in Tuscany in this somewhat unlikely spot. Frederick's castles were designed to echo imperial Rome, and the many columns, lions, and porticoes testify to his ambition. This is the only castle he built outside of Sicily and Puglia in southern Italy. ✉ *Piazza Santa Maria delle Carceri* ☎ *0574/38207* 💶 *€2.50, combination ticket €8 (includes Museo dell'Opera del Duomo and Museo di Pittura Murale)* 🕐 *Wed.–Mon. 9:30–1 and 3–7.*

Poggio a Caiano. For a look at gracious country living Renaissance style, take a detour to the Medici villa in Poggio a Caiano. Lorenzo "il Magnifico" (1449–92) commissioned Giuliano da Sangallo (circa 1445–1516) to redo the villa, which was lavished with frescoes by important Renaissance painters such as Pontormo (1494–1556), Franciabigio (1482–1525), and Andrea del Sarto (1486–1531). You can walk around the austerely ornamented grounds while waiting for one of the hourly villa tours, which start on the half hour. The guides do not speak, but follow you around the place. ✉ *Piazza dei Medici 14, 7 km (4½ miles) south of Prato (follow signs)* ☎ *055/877012* 💶 *Free* 🕐 *Sept. and Oct., daily 8:15–5:30; Nov.–Feb., daily 8:15–3:30; Mar., daily 8:15–4:30; Apr. and May, daily 8:15–5:30; June–Aug., daily 8:15–6:30.*

Carmignano. Pontormo's *Visitation* is in this small village a short drive from Poggio a Caiano. The Franciscan church of **San Michele**, dedicated in 1211, houses the work. The painting dates from 1527–30, and it may well be Pontormo's masterpiece. The luminous colors, flowing drapery, and steady gaze shared between the Virgin and Saint Elizabeth are breathtaking. The church's small cloister, shaded by olive trees, is always open, and offers a quiet place to sit. ✉ *15 km (9 miles) south of Prato, through Poggio a Caiano, up Mt. Albano* 🕾 *055/8712046* 🕙 *Oct.–Apr., daily 7:30–5; May–Sept., daily 7:30–6.*

OFF THE BEATEN PATH

Villa Medicea La Ferdinanda di Artimino. In the small town of **Artimino**, next door to Carmignano, is the Villa Medicea La Ferdinanda di Artimino. Built by Ferdinando I de' Medici (1549–1609) in the 1590s, it was originally used as a hunting lodge. Though it's closed to the public (except for special occasions or by prior arrangement), it's simply a stunning villa to look at. ✉ *11 km (7 miles) south of Prato (head east from Carmignano or south from Poggio a Caiano, up Mt. Albano)* 🕾 *055/875141.*

WHERE TO EAT

$$
TUSCAN
★

✕ **Baghino.** In the heart of the historic center, Baghino is the best restaurant in town. It's been serving since 1870, capably run by five generations of the Pacetti family (daughters Guja and Silvia are presently in charge). Part of the building dates to the 15th century, when it was a convent; later it was the seat of the Freemasons. The food lives up to the building's colorful history. Do not miss the *sedano ripieno alla pratese* (stuffed celery), in which celery is pressed, stuffed with a minced veal and mortadella filling, coated in flour and egg, and fried in olive oil. A tasty ragù crowns the dish. Another house specialty is the *filetto al pepe verde* (beef fillet in a creamy green peppercorn sauce). The wine list boasts local favorites, which are among the best in Tuscany. ✉ *Via dell'Accademia 9* 🕾 *0574/27920* 🕙 *Closed Aug. No lunch Mon. No dinner Sun.*

$$
TUSCAN
★

✕ **Da Delfina.** Delfina Cioni began cooking many years ago for hungry hunters in the town of Artimino, 20 km (12 miles) south of Prato; now her son Carlo maintains the culinary legacy. Dishes celebrate Tuscan food, with an emphasis on fresh local ingredients. Secondi such as *coniglio con olive e pignoli* (rabbit sautéed with olives and pine nuts—the house specialty) are a real treat. The seasonal menu is complemented by a fine wine list, and service is gracious. From the restaurant's four comfortably rustic rooms (and outside terrace when it's warm) you have a glorious view of the Tuscan countryside, including a Medici villa. ✉ *Via della Chiesa 1, Artimino* 🕾 *055/8718074* 🗫 *Reservations essential* ▭ *No credit cards* 🕙 *Closed Mon. and 3 wks in Aug. No lunch Tues. No dinner Sun.*

¢
TUSCAN

✕ **La Vecchia Cucina di Soldano.** This place could be mistaken for a grandmother's kitchen: it's completely unpretentious, with red-and-white-checked tablecloths and a waitstaff who treat you like an old friend. The restaurant teems with locals who appreciate fine dining at rock-bottom prices. Typical Tuscan specialties are on hand, including a superb *tagliolini sui fagioli* (thin noodles with beans). ✉ *Via Pomeria 23* 🕾 *0574/34665* ▭ *No credit cards* 🕙 *Closed Sun.*

$
TUSCAN

✕ **Osteria da i'Peruzzi.** If you've just visited the Medici Villa at Poggio a Caiano, wander down the street to this intimate restaurant, the rooms of which date to the 16th century. Here you'll find hearty, wonderful food, a great wine list, and lovely staff. The osteria's version of *peposo,* a local specialty, is a small masterpiece: a beef stew, laced with black pepper and a little bit of red wine, served on creamy polenta. The chef has an equally deft touch with vegetables; the *carciofi al tegame con olive nere* contains gently stewed artichokes, their flavor sharpened by the addition of black olives. Biscotti di Prato (the twice-baked cookie) dipped in vin santo (a sweet dessert wine) provides a fitting conclusion. ⊠ *Via Cancellieri 29, Poggio a Caiano* ☎ *055/8798692* ⊘ *Closed Mon.*

WHERE TO STAY
For expanded hotel reviews, visit Fodors.com.

$$ ⊡ **Hotel Paggeria Medicea.** Ferdinando I loved to hunt, and so erected his villa to accommodate this whim. **Pros:** peace and tranquillity; spectacular views. **Cons:** a car is essential. ⊠ *Viale Papa Giovanni XXIII 1* ☎ *055/875141* ⊕ *www.artimino.com* ⮌ *37 rooms* ⚬ *In-room: safe, Internet, Wi-Fi. In-hotel: bar, pool, parking, some pets allowed.*

PISTOIA

18 km (11 miles) northwest of Prato, 43 km (27 miles) east of Lucca, 37 km (23 miles) northwest of Florence.

Founded in the 2nd century BC as a support post for Roman troops, Pistoia grew over the centuries into an important trading center. In the Middle Ages it was troubled by civic strife and eventually fell to the Florentines, who imposed a pro-Guelf government in 1267; it lost its last vestiges of independence to Florence in 1329.

Reconstructed after heavy bombing during World War II, it has preserved some fine Romanesque architecture. Modern-day Pistoia's major industries include the manufacture of rail vehicles (including the cars for Washington, D.C.'s Metro) and tree and plant nurseries, which flourish on the alluvial plain around the city.

GETTING HERE
From Florence or Lucca, Pistoia is an easy train ride; trains run frequently. By car, take the A11/E76.

VISITOR INFORMATION
Pistoia tourism office ⊠ *Palazzo dei Vescovi* ☎ *0573/21622* ⊕ *www.pistoia. turismo.toscana.it.*

EXPLORING
Duomo. The Romanesque Duomo, the Cattedrale di San Zeno, dates from as early as the 5th century. It houses a magnificent silver altar dedicated to Saint James. The two half-figures on the left are by Filippo Brunelleschi (1377–1446), the first Renaissance architect (and designer of Florence's magnificent Duomo cupola). The octagonal **Battistero,** with green-and-white-stripe marble cladding, dates from the middle of the 14th century. Three of its eight sides have doorways; the main door facing the piazza is crowned with a rose window. Note the lovely little lantern crowning the top of the building. ⊠ *Piazza del Duomo* ☎ *0573/25095* ⊡ *Free; access to altarpiece €2* ⊘ *Church: Oct.–Apr., Mon.–Sat. 8–12:30 and 3:30–7, Sun. 8–1 and 3:30–7; May–Sept., daily*

8–1 and 3:30–7. Altar: Mon.–Sat. 10–12:30 and 3–5:30, Sun. 8–9:30, 11–11:30, and 4–5:30.

Museo Civico. The Palazzo del Comune, begun around 1295, houses the Museo Civico, containing works by local artists from the 13th to 19th century. ⊠ *Piazza del Duomo 1* ☎ *0573/371296* 🖭 *€3.50, combination ticket €6.50 (includes Palazzo Rospigliosi and Fondazione Marino Marini)* ⊙ *Apr.–Oct., Tues.–Sun. 10–6; Nov.–Mar., Tues.–Sun. 10–5.*

Musei dell'Antico Palazzo dei Vescovi (*Old Bishop's Palace*). At the end of the 11th century, the bishop of Pistoia began construction on this palace. One thousand years later, it houses several collections including the **Museo della Cattedrale di San Zeno**, which contains spectacular treasures from Pistoia's cathedral—including ornate pieces in gold, rings with jewels the size of small eggs, and solemn, powerful statuary. Below, however, is the **Percorso Archeologico**—Roman, medieval, and Etruscan archaeological sites uncovered during a 1970s renovation. The warren of corridors and caves below and the plain, spare rooms above both show off their treasures with simple elegance. Also in the complex is the **Museo Tattile**, which allows visitors to touch various local buildings built to scale. A guide accompanies you while you wander, and wandering days and times are limited. ⊠ *Piazza del Duomo* ☎ *0573/369272* 🖭 *€4* ⊙ *Tues., Thurs., and Fri. 10, 11:30, and 3.*

Ospedale del Ceppo. Founded in the 13th century and still a functioning hospital, the Ospedale del Ceppo has a facade with a superb early-16th-century exterior terra-cotta frieze. It was begun by Giovanni della Robbia (1469–1529) and completed by the workshop of Santi and Benedetto Buglioni between 1526 and 1528. Don't miss the 17th-century graffiti on the columns outside. ⊠ *Piazza Giovanni XIII, down Via Pacini from Piazza del Duomo* ⊙ *Closed to public.*

Sant'Andrea. In the 12th-century church of Sant'Andrea, the fine pulpit by Giovanni Pisano (circa 1250–1314) depicts scenes from the life of Christ in a series of high-relief, richly sculpted marble panels. ⊠ *Piazzetta Sant'Andrea, Via Sant'Andrea* ☎ *0573/21912* ⊙ *Daily 7:30–12:30 and 3:30–6.*

Palazzo Rospigliosi. The 16th-century mannerist-style Palazzo Rospigliosi houses the **Museo Rospigliosi** and the **Museo Diocesano,** with a collection of mostly 16th- and 17th-century works. The Museo Rospigliosi contains a room referred to as Pope Clement IX's (1600–69) apartment, although there's no evidence that the Pistoian native, born Giulio Rospigliosi, actually stayed there. The Museo Diocesano has liturgical objects and furnishings from the diocese of Pistoia. Many date from the 13th, 14th, and 15th centuries. ⊠ *Via Ripa del Sale 3* ☎ *0573/28740* 🖭 *€3.50, combination ticket €6.50 (includes both museums and Museo Civico and Fondazione Marino Marini)* ⊙ *Tues.–Sat. 10–1 and 3–6.*

Fondazione Marino Marini. Lest you think that Tuscany produced only Renaissance artists, the Fondazione Marino Marini presents many works from its namesake modern native Pistoian (1901–80). Sculpture, etchings, paintings, engravings, and mixed media have all been installed in the elegantly renovated 14th-century Convento del Tau. ⊠ *Corso Silvano Fedi 30* ☎ *0573/30285* 🖭 *€3.50, combination ticket*

€6.50 (includes Palazzo Rospigliosi and Museo Civico) ☉ Oct.–Mar., Mon.–Sat. 10–5; Apr.–Sept., Mon.–Sat. 10–6.

San Giovanni Fuorcivitas. An architectural gem in green-and-white marble, the medieval church of San Giovanni Fuorcivitas holds a *Visitation* by Luca della Robbia (1400–82), a painting attributed to Taddeo Gaddi, and a holy-water font that may have been made by Fra Guglielmo around 1270. ⊠ *Via Cavour* ☎ *0573/24784* ☉ *Daily 7:30–noon and 5–6:30.*

Giardino Zoologico. A 20-minute drive out of town brings you to the Giardino Zoologico, a small zoo laid out to accommodate the wiles of both animals and children. ⊠ *Via Pieve a Celle 160/a, take Bus 29 from train station* ☎ *0573/911219* 🎟 *€12.50* ☉ *Oct.–Mar., daily 9–5; Apr.–Sept., daily 9–7.*

WHERE TO EAT

$ ╳ **La Botte Gaia.** Jazz plays softly in the background as patrons sip wine
WINE BAR at rustic tables in rooms with exposed brick-and-stone walls. In warm weather you can also dine alfresco with a splendid view of the Piazza del Duomo. Typical wine-bar fare, such as plates of cured ham and cheese, shares the menu with a surprisingly sophisticated list of daily specials. For example, you might try *insalatina con foie gras condita con vinaigrette* (foie gras with dressed greens). ⊠ *Via del Lastrone 17* ☎ *0573/365602* ⌂ *Reservations essential* ☉ *Closed Mon. and last 3 wks in Aug. No lunch Sun.*

$ ╳ **MagnoGaudio.** It bills itself as a *caffetteria/ristorante*, which means it
ITALIAN opens at 8 in the morning for coffee, serves lunch and dinner, and then closes well after dinner is over. Warm sponged colored walls and simple wooden tables and chairs provide the backdrop for some tasty fare. They're particularly big on fish here; if it's available, order the *calamari spadellati su crema di fagioli alla paprika e valeriana* (panfried squid on a creamy bean purèe spiced with paprika and garnished with delicate green leaves). Their ample portion of lasagna is cheesy and thoroughly satisfying. Service is great, and the wine list (strong on local wines) equally so. ⊠ *Via Curtatone e Montanara 12, Pistoia* ☎ *0573/26905* ⌂ *Reservations essential* ☉ *Closed 1st and 3rd Sun. of every month.*

$$ ╳ **Trattoria dell'Abbondanza.** Entering from a quiet side street, you walk
TUSCAN into a small place with cream-color walls that's busy but not noisy. Run by husband and wife team Patrizio (affectionately known by all as "Iccio") and Rosella Meuci, the trattoria serves traditional dishes like *minestra di farro* (a hearty soup made with farro) and *maccheroni all'anatra* (pasta in a duck sauce). For seconds, the house specialties of *baccalà alla Livornese* (salt cod in a tomato sauce) and *fritto di pollo con verdure* (fried chicken with vegetables) are standouts. *Torta rustica,* a cake of cornmeal and cream, makes a fine dessert. ⊠ *Via dell'Abbondanza 10/14, off Via degli Orafi* ☎ *0573/368037* ☉ *Closed Wed. No lunch Thurs.*

Pistoia's medieval skyline

NIGHTLIFE AND THE ARTS

★ **Pistoia Blues.** In mid-July Pistoia Blues brings international blues artists and rock-and-rollers to town for performances in the main square. ☎ 0573/994659 ⊕ www.pistoiablues.com.

La Giostra dell'Orso (*Bear Joust*). On July 25, La Giostra dell'Orso celebrates Saint James, Pistoia's patron saint. During the staged event three knights from each section of the city fight a "bear" (actually a target shaped like a bear that they strike, on horseback). The visitor center has more information on the event.

MONTECATINI TERME

15 km (9 miles) west of Pistoia, 49 km (30 miles) west of Florence, 29 km (18 miles) northeast of Lucca.

Immortalized in Fellini's film *8½*, Montecatini Terme is the home of Italy's premier *terme* (spas). Known for their curative powers—and, at least once upon a time, for their great popularity among the wealthy— the mineral springs flow from five sources and are taken for a variety of ailments, including liver and skin disorders. Those "taking the cure" report each morning to one of the town's *stabilimenti termali* (thermal establishments) to drink their prescribed cupful of water. Afterward, guests can enjoy a leisurely breakfast, read the newspaper, recline and listen to music, or walk in the parks that surround these grand old spas.

Montecatini Terme's wealth of art nouveau buildings date to the town's most active period of development at the beginning of the 20th century. Like most other well-heeled resort towns, Montecatini attracts the leisured traveler, convention-eer, and senior citizen on a group tour; it's trimmed with a measure of neon and glitz; aside from tak-ing the waters and people-watching in Piazza del Popolo, there's not a whole lot to do here. There are, however, plenty of places to stay, making the town a good base from which to explore the region.

GETTING HERE

Montecatini Terme is one of the stops on the Florence–Lucca train line, and getting to the centro storico is an easy walk from the station. The A11/E76 will get you here by car.

VISITOR INFORMATION

Montecatini Terme tourism office ✉ *Viale Verdi 66–68* ☎ *0572/772244* ⊕ *www.pistoia.turismo.toscana.it.*

Terme di Montecatini. The umbrella group Terme di Montecatini has infor-mation on the town's nine thermal spas. ✉ *Viale Verdi 43* ☎ *0572/78474* ⊕ *www.termemontecatini.it.*

EXPLORING

Excelsior. For traditional beauty treatments, the Excelsior offers mani-cures, facials, and massage therapies with mud, algae, and oils. ✉ *Viale Verdi 61* ☎ *0572/778518 for appointments.*

Terme Tettuccio. The most attractive art nouveau structure in town, Terme Tettuccio, has lovely colonnades. Here fountains set up on marble coun-ters dispense mineral water, bucolic scenes painted on tiles decorate walls, and an orchestra plays under a frescoed dome. ✉ *Viale Verdi 71* ☎ *0572/778501* 💶 *€14* ⊗ *Mar.–Oct., daily 8–noon and 3–5:30.*

Piazza del Popolo. The town's main square teems with cafés and bars. It's an excellent spot for people-watching; in the evening and on weekends it seems like everyone is out walking, seeing, and being seen.

Santa Maria Assunta. Piazza del Popolo offers a view of the basilica of Santa Maria Assunta. The church and bell tower, completed in 1962, have bold geometric lines that are a little incongruous among its more ornate neighbors. ✉ *Piazza del Popolo* ☎ *No phone* ⊗ *Daily 8–noon and 3–5:30.*

NEED A BREAK?

Bargilli. *Cialde,* a local specialty, are circular wafers made with flour, sugar, eggs, and almonds from Puglia. The Bargilli family has been serv-ing them with their terrific ice cream since 1936. Try them at Bargilli, the family's shop and probably the best *gelateria* in town. ✉ *Viale Grocco 2* ☎ *0572/79459.*

Montecatini Alto. The older town, Montecatini Alto, sits atop a hill nearby, and is reached by a funicular from Viale Diaz. Though there isn't much to do once you get up there, the medieval square is lined with restaurants and bars, the air is crisp, and the views of the Nievole, the valley below, are gorgeous.

WHERE TO STAY

For expanded hotel reviews, visit Fodors.com.

$$ ☷ **Grand Hotel Croce di Malta.** Taste and sophistication have been the calling cards of this hotel since 1911. **Pros:** good location; attentive staff. **Cons:** attracts many tour groups. ⊠ *Viale IV Novembre 18* ☎ *0572/9201* ⊕ *www.crocedimalta.com* ⤳ *122 rooms, 22 suites* ⌂ *In-room: Internet, Wi-Fi. In-hotel: restaurant, bar, pool, gym, parking, some pets allowed* ⦿ *Breakfast.*

LUCCA

Ramparts built in the 16th and 17th centuries enclose a charming fortress town filled with churches (99 of them), terra-cotta–roofed buildings, and narrow cobblestone streets, along which local ladies maneuver bikes to do their daily shopping. Here Caesar, Pompey, and Crassus agreed to rule Rome as a triumvirate in 56 BC; Lucca was later the first Tuscan town to accept Christianity. The town still has a mind of its own, and when most of Tuscany was voting communist as a matter of course, Lucca's citizens rarely followed suit. The famous composer Giacomo Puccini (1858–1924) was born here; he is celebrated during the summer Opera Theater and Music Festival of Lucca. The ramparts circling the centro storico are the perfect place to stroll, bicycle, or just admire the view.

GETTING HERE

You can reach Lucca easily by train from Florence; the historic center is a short walk from the station. If you're driving, take the A11/E76.

VISITOR INFORMATION

Lucca tourism office ⊠ *Piazza Santa Maria* ☎ *0583/91991* ⊕ *www. luccaturismo.it.*

EXPLORING LUCCA

Traffic (including motorbikes) is restricted in the walled historic center of Lucca. Walking is the best, most enjoyable way to get around. Or you can rent a bicycle; getting around on bike is easy, as the center is quite flat.

TOP ATTRACTIONS

★ **Duomo.** The blind arches on the cathedral's facade are a fine example of the rigorously ordered Pisan Romanesque style, in this case happily enlivened by an extremely varied collection of small, carved columns. Take a closer look at the decoration of the facade and that of the portico below; they make this one of the most entertaining church exteriors in Tuscany. The Gothic interior contains a moving Byzantine crucifix—called the Volto Santo, or Holy Face—brought here, according to legend, in the 8th century (though it probably dates from between the 11th and early 13th century). The masterpiece of the Sienese sculptor Jacopo della Quercia (circa 1371–1438) is the marble *Tomb of Ilaria del Carretto* (1407–08). ⊠ *Piazza del Duomo* ☎ *0583/490530* ⊕ *www. museocattedralelucca.it* ⤳ *€2* ⊘ *Duomo: Nov. 2–Mar. 14, weekdays*

9:30–4:45, Sat. 9:30–6:45, Sun. 9:30–10:45 and noon–5; Mar. 15–Nov. 1, weekdays 9:30–5:45, Sat. 9–6:45, Sun. 9:30–10:45 and noon–6.

NEED A
BREAK?

Stella Polare. Stella Polare bills itself as a "classic bar and bistrot." In this case, that means expertly mixed cocktails, wines by the glass, and light meals at lunch and dinner. Because it's on Piazza Napoleone (the city's largest and prettiest square), it's a great spot for people-watching. On weekends Stella offers an English breakfast, which means bacon and eggs. ✉ *Via Vittorio Veneto 21* ☎ *0583/496332.*

3

★ **Passeggiata delle Mura.** Any time of day when the weather is clement, you can find the citizens of Lucca cycling, jogging, strolling, or kicking a soccer ball in this green, beautiful, and very large park—neither inside nor outside the city but rather right on the ring of ramparts that defines Lucca. Sunlight streams through two rows of tall plane trees to dapple the *passeggiata delle mura* (walk on the walls), which is 4 (2½ miles) in length. Ten bulwarks are topped with lawns, many with picnic tables and some with play equipment for children. Be aware at all times of where the edge is—there are no railings, and the drop to the ground outside the city is a precipitous 40 feet.

Piazza dell'Anfiteatro Romano. Here's where the ancient Roman amphitheater once stood; some of the medieval buildings built over the amphitheater retain its original oval shape and brick arches. ✉ *Off Via Fillungo, near north side of old town.*

San Frediano. The church of San Frediano, just steps from the Anfiteatro, has a 14th-century mosaic decorating its facade, and contains works by Jacopo della Quercia (circa 1371–1438) and Matteo Civitali (1436–1501), as well as the lace-clad mummy of Saint Zita (circa 1218–78), the patron saint of household servants. ✉ *Piazza San Frediano* ☎ *No phone* ⏱ *Mon.–Sat. 8:30–noon and 3–5, Sun. 10:30–5.*

San Michele in Foro. The facade here is even more fanciful than that of the Duomo. Its upper levels have nothing but air behind them (after the front of the church was built, there were no funds to raise the nave), and the winged Archangel Michael, who stands at the very top, seems precariously poised for flight. The facade, heavily restored in the 19th century, displays busts of 19th-century Italian patriots such as Garibaldi and Cavour. Check out the superb Filippino Lippi (1457/58–1504) panel painting of Saints Jerome, Sebastian, Rocco, and Helen in the right transept. ✉ *Piazza San Michele* ☎ *No phone* ⏱ *Nov.–Mar., daily 9–noon and 3–5; Apr.–Oct., daily 9–noon and 3–6.*

⏱ **Torre Guinigi.** The tower of the medieval Palazzo Guinigi contains one of the city's most curious sights: a grove of ilex trees has grown at the top of the tower, and their roots have pushed their way into the room below. From the top you have a magnificent view of the city and the surrounding countryside. (Only the tower is open to the public, not the palazzo.) ✉ *Palazzo Guinigi, Via Sant'Andrea* ☎ *0583/48524* 🎟 *€3.50* ⏱ *Mar. and Apr., daily 9:30–6:30; May–Sept., daily 9–7:30; Oct.–Feb., daily 10:30–4:30.*

Lucca

WORTH NOTING

Museo della Cattedrale. The cathedral museum exhibits many items too precious to be in the church, most notably the finely worked golden decorations of the Volto Santo, the Byzantine crucifix that remains in the Duomo. ⊠ *Piazza Antelmi-nelli* ☎ *0583/490530* ⊕ *www.museocattedralelucca.it* ✐ *€4, combination ticket €6 (includes tomb in Duomo and Ss. Giovanni e Reparata)* ◷ *Mid-Mar.–mid-Nov., daily 10–6; mid-Nov.–mid-Mar., weekdays 10–2, weekends 10–5.*

Museo Nazionale di Palazzo Mansi. Highlights here include the lovely *Portrait of a Youth* by Pontormo; portraits of the Medici painted by Bronzino (1503–72); and paintings by Tintoretto, Vasari, and others. ⊠ *Palazzo Mansi, Via Galli Tassi 43, near west walls of old city* ☎ *0583/55570* ✐ *€4, combination ticket €6.50 (includes Museo Nazionale di Villa Guinigi)* ◷ *Tues.–Sat. 8:30–7, Sun. 8:30–1:30.*

Museo Nazionale di Villa Guinigi. On the eastern end of the historic center, this museum has an extensive collection of local Romanesque and Renaissance art. The museum represents an overview of Lucca's artistic traditions from Etruscan times until the 17th century, housed in the former 15th-century villa of the Guinigi family. ⊠ *Villa Guinigi, Via della Quarquonia* ☎ *0583/496033* ✐ *€4, combination ticket €6.50 (includes Museo Nazionale di Palazzo Mansi)* ◷ *Tues.–Sat. 9–7, Sun. 9–2.*

Palazzo Pfanner. Here you can rest your feet and let time pass, surrounded by a harmonious arrangement of sun, shade, blooming plants, water, and mysterious statuary. The palazzo's well-kept formal garden, which abuts the city walls, centers on a large fountain and pool. Allegorical statues line pebbled paths that radiate outward. The palazzo, built in the 17th century, was purchased in the 19th century by the Pfanners, a family of Swiss brewers. The family, which eventually gave the town a mayor, still lives here. ⊠ *Via degli Asili 33* ☎ *0583/954029* ⊕ *www.palazzopfanner.it* ✐ *Garden €4, palazzo €4, garden and palazzo €5.50* ◷ *Apr.–Oct., daily 10–6; mid-Nov.–Feb., by appointment only.*

Ss. Giovanni e Reparata. The baptistery of this church is lovely enough, but the unusual element here is an archaeological site, discovered in 1969, where five layers of Luccan history were uncovered. As you walk the paths and catwalks suspended above the delicate sites in the grottoes under the church, you move from one era to another—from the 2nd-century-BC site of a Roman temple through the 5th, 8th, 9th, and 11th centuries. After leaving the underground sights, the 12th-century church feels almost modern. ⊠ *Piazza San Giovanni* ☎ *0583/490530* ⊕ *www.museocattedralelucca.it* ✐ *Baptistery and archaeological site €2.50, combination ticket €6 (includes tomb in Duomo and Museo della Cattedrale)* ◷ *Mid-Mar.–mid-Nov., daily 10–6; mid-Nov.–mid-Mar., weekdays 10–2, weekends 10–5.*

NEED A BREAK?

Gelateria Veneta. Gelateria Veneta makes outstanding gelato, sorbet, and ices (some sugar-free). They prepare their confections three times a day, using the same recipes with which the Brothers Arnoldo opened the place in 1927. The pièces de résistance are frozen fruits stuffed with creamy filling: don't miss the apricot sorbet–filled apricot. Note that they close up shop in October and reopen around Easter. ⊠ *Via V. Veneto 74* ☎ *0583/467037.*

Torre delle Ore (*Tower of the Hours*). The highest spot in Lucca is the top of this tower, which had its first mechanical clock in 1390. It's since contained several clocks over the centuries; the current timepiece was installed in 1754. The reward for climbing 207 steps to the top is a panoramic view of the town. ⊠ *Via Fillungo at Via dell'Arancio* ☎ *0583/316846* ⊠ *€3.50* ⊗ *Mar.–Nov., daily 9–7.*

OFF THE BEATEN PATH

Villa Reale. Eight kilometers (5 miles) north of Lucca in Marlia, this villa was once the home of Napoléon's sister, Princess Elisa. Restored by the Counts Pecci-Blunt, the estate is celebrated for its spectacular gardens, laid out in the 16th century and redone in the middle of the 17th. Gardening buffs adore the legendary *teatro di verdura*, a theater carved out of hedges and topiaries; concerts are occasionally held here. During the summer, concerts are held in the gardens of other famous Lucca villas as well. Contact the Lucca tourist office (☎ *0583/91991*) for details. ⊠ *North of Lucca along river Serchio, in direction of Barga and Bagni di Lucca, Marlia* ☎ *0583/30108* ⊠ *€7* ⊗ *Guided visits: Mar.–Nov., Tues.–Sun. at 10, 11, noon, 3, 4, and 5.*

WHERE TO EAT

$$
TUSCAN
Fodor'sChoice
★

✕**Buca di Sant'Antonio.** The staying power of Buca di Sant'Antonio— it's been around since 1782—is the result of superlative Tuscan food brought to the table by waitstaff that doesn't miss a beat. The menu includes the simple but blissful, like *tortelli lucchesi al sugo* (meat-stuffed pasta with a tomato-and-meat sauce), and more daring dishes such as roast *capretto* (kid) with herbs. A white-wall interior hung with copper pots and brass musical instruments creates a classy but comfortable dining space. ⊠ *Via della Cervia 3* ☎ *0583/55881* ⊗ *Closed Mon., 1 wk in Jan., and 1 wk in July. No dinner Sun.*

$$
WINE BAR

✕**i Santi.** This intimate little wine bar, just outside the Piazza dell'Anfiteatro, is the perfect place to have a light meal and a fine glass of wine. The extensive wine list is strong on local varietals, as well as on foreign (French) selections. The *carpaccio di manzo affumicato* (thin slices of smoked beef served with celery and a young cheese) is a standout, as is just about everything else on the menu. Specials always include a pasta of the day. Great attention is given to sourcing top-quality local, seasonal ingredients. ⊠ *Via dell'Anfiteatro 29/a* ☎ *0583/496124* ⊗ *Closed Wed.*

$$
TUSCAN

✕**Il Giglio.** Just off Piazza Napoleone, this restaurant has quiet, late-19th-century charm and classic cuisine. It's a place for all seasons, with a big fireplace for chilly weather and an outdoor terrace in summer. If mushrooms are in season, try the *tacchonni con funghi,* a homemade pasta with mushrooms and a local herb called *nepitella*. A local favorite during winter is the *coniglio con olive* (rabbit stew with olives). ✉ *Piazza del Giglio 2* ☎ *0583/494508* ⊘ *Closed Wed. and 15 days in Nov. No dinner Tues.*

$$$ ✕**La Mora.** Detour to this former stagecoach station, now a gracious,
TUSCAN rustic country inn 9 km (5½ miles) north of Lucca, for local specialties—from minestra di farro to homemade *tacconi* (a thin, short, wide pasta) with rabbit sauce and lamb from the nearby Garfagnana mountains. You might be tempted by the varied *crostini* (toasted bread) and delicious desserts. ✉ *Via Ludovica 1748, Ponte a Moriano* ☎ *0583/406402* ⊘ *Closed Wed., Jan. 1–15, and June 15–30.*

$ ✕**La Pecora Nera.** This lively, gaily colored little trattoria (the name
ITALIAN means "black sheep") with a high-vaulted ceiling is staffed by *giovani disabili* (both mentally challenged and learning-disabled young people), who wait tables under the supervision of a non-disabled companion. The food's terrific, from the made-in-house *tordelli lucchesi* (meatstuffed tortelli sauced with a fragrant meat ragù) to the tasty crostata. Great care is taken with sourcing, when possible, local organic ingredients, and such care translates into a lovely meal. ✉ *Piazza San Francesco 4* ☎ *0583/469738* ⊕ *www.lapecoraneralucca.it.*

$ ✕**Trattoria da Leo.** A few short turns away from the facade of San
ITALIAN Michele, this noisy, informal, traditional trattoria delivers *cucina alla casalinga* (home cooking) in the best sense. Try the typical minestra di farro to start or just go straight to *secondi piatti* (entrées); in addition to the usual roast meats, there's excellent chicken with olives and a good cold dish of boiled meats served with a sauce of parsley and pine nuts. Save some room for a dessert, such as the rich, sweet, fig-and-walnut torte or the lemon sorbet brilliantly dotted with bits of sage, which tastes almost like mint, and is indescribably delicious. ✉ *Via Tegrimi 1, at corner of Via degli Asili* ☎ *0583/492236* ▭ *No credit cards* ⊘ *Closed Sun. Nov.–Mar. No lunch Sun.*

WHERE TO STAY

For expanded hotel reviews, visit Fodors.com.

$$ ▥**Albergo San Martino.** Down a narrow street facing a quiet, sunsprinkled *piazzale* (small square) stands this small hotel. **Pros:** comfortable bed; great breakfast. **Cons:** it can seem a little removed from things. ✉ *Via della Dogana 9* ☎ *0583/469181* ⊕ *www.albergosanmartino.it* ➥ *6 rooms, 2 suites* ⌂ *In-room: Wi-Fi* ⦿ *No meals.*

$$ ▥**Alla Corte degli Angeli.** This charming hotel with a friendly staff is right off the main shopping drag, Via Fillungo. **Pros:** many rooms are connecting, making them good for families. **Cons:** some rooms have tubs but no showers. ✉ *Via degli Angeli 23* ☎ *0583/469204* ⊕ *www. allacortedegliangeli.com* ➥ *12 rooms* ⌂ *In-room: Wi-Fi. In-hotel: bar, business center, parking, some pets allowed* ⦿ *Breakfast.*

$$$ ▥**Hotel Ilaria.** The former stables of the Villa Bottini have been transformed into a modern hotel within the historic center. **Pros:** a Fodor's reader sums it up as a "nice, modern small hotel"; free bicycles. **Cons:** though in the city center, it's a little removed from main attractions.

✉ *Via del Fosso 26* ✆ *0583/47615* ⊕ *www.hotelilaria.com* → *36 rooms, 5 suites* ♧ *In-room: safe, Wi-Fi. In-hotel: bar, business center, parking, some pets allowed* ➏ *Breakfast.*

$$ ⑓ **La Luna.** On a quiet, airy courtyard close to the Piazza del Mercato, this hotel, run by the Barbieri family for more than four decades, occupies two renovated wings of an old building. **Pros:** professional staff; the annex has wheelchair-accessible rooms. **Cons:** some rooms feel dated. ✉ *Corte Compagni 12, at Via Fillungo* ✆ *0583/493634* ⊕ *www.hotellaluna.com* → *27 rooms, 2 suites* ♧ *In-room: safe. In-hotel: bar, parking* ☉ *Closed Jan. 7–31* ➏ *No meals.*

$$$ ⑓ **Locanda l'Elisa.** When Napoléon's sister, Elisa Baciocchi, arrived in Lucca to preside over it as a princess, she came with an entourage. **Pros:** multilingual staff; top-notch restaurant. **Cons:** a car is essential. ✉ *Via Nuova per Pisa 1952, Massa Pisana* ✆ *0583/379737* ⊕ *www.locandalelisa.it* → *3 rooms, 7 suites* ♧ *In-room: safe, Internet. In-hotel: restaurant, bar, pool, business center, parking* ☉ *Closed Jan. 7–Feb. 11* ➏ *No meals.*

$$ ⑓ **Palazzo Alexander.** This small, elegant boutique hotel is on a quiet
★ side street a short walk from San Michele in Foro. **Pros:** intimate feel; gracious staff; bacon and eggs included in the buffet breakfast. **Cons:** some Fodor's readers complain of too-thin walls. ✉ *Via S. Giustina 48* ✆ *0583/583571* ⊕ *www.palazzoalexander.it* → *9 rooms, 3 suites, 1 apartment* ♧ *In-room: safe, Wi-Fi. In-hotel: bar, business center, parking* ➏ *Breakfast.*

$ ⑓ **Piccolo Hotel Puccini.** Steps away from the busy square and church of San Michele, this little hotel is quiet and calm—and a great deal. **Pros:** cheery, English-speaking staff. **Cons:** breakfast costs extra; some rooms are on the dark side. ✉ *Via di Poggio 9* ✆ *0583/55421* ⊕ *www.hotelpuccini.com* → *14 rooms* ♧ *In-room: no a/c, safe, Wi-Fi. In-hotel: bar, some pets allowed* ➏ *No meals.*

NIGHTLIFE AND THE ARTS

Opera Theater and Music Festival of Lucca. Sponsored by the Opera Theater of Lucca and the music college of the University of Cincinnati, the Opera Theater and Music Festival of Lucca, runs from mid-June to mid-July; performances are staged in open-air venues. Call the Lucca tourist office or the Opera Theater of Lucca (✆ *0583/46531*) for information.

Estate Musicale Lucchese. Throughout the summer there are jazz, pop, and rock concerts in conjunction with the Estate Musicale Lucchese music festival. It happens in the large, beautiful Piazza Napoleone.

Lucca Tourist Office. Schedule and ticket information for many local events, including the Opera Theater and Estate Musicale Lucchese festivals, is available at the Lucca Tourist Office. ✉ *Piazza Santa Maria 35, San Michele* ✆ *0583/91991.*

Teatro del Giglio. From September through April you can see operas, plays, and concerts staged at the Teatro del Giglio. ✉ *Piazza del Giglio, Duomo* ✆ *0583/46531* ⊕ *www.teatrodelgiglio.it.*

Lucca Comics and Games. During the first weekend of November, the city's piazzas are filled with tents featuring exhibitions and games, and the streets are invaded with comic-book fans and gamesters for Lucca Comics and Games. During the last week of October, and continuing through the Comics festival, a *mostra mercato* (market show) takes place as well. ☎ *0583/48522* ⊕ *www.luccacomicsandgames.com.*

SPORTS AND THE OUTDOORS

A good way to spend the afternoon is to go biking around the large path atop the city's ramparts. There are two good spots right next to each other where you can rent bikes. The prices are about the same (about €12.50 for the day and €2.50 per hour for city bikes) and they are centrally located, just beside the town wall.

Berutto Cicli. The vendors at Berutto Cicli, which sell bikes near the Piazza dell'Anfiteatro, are friendly and speak English. ⊠ *Via dei Gaspari Alcide 83/r, Anfiteatro* ☎ *0583/517073.*

Poli Antonio Biciclette. This is the best option for bicycle rental on the east side. ⊠ *Piazza Santa Maria 42, Lucca East* ☎ *0583/493787.*

SHOPPING

CHOCOLATE
Caniparoli. Chocolate lovers will be pleased with the selection at Caniparoli, a small, stylish shop specializing in artisanal chocolates. They are so serious about their sweets that they do not make them from June to August, because of the heat. ⊠ *Via San Paolino 96* ☎ *0583/53456.*

CLOTHING
Benetton Stock Outlet. Bargain hunters won't want to miss Benetton Stock Outlet, with its brightly colored garments at reduced prices. ⊠ *Via Mordini 17/19, Anfiteatro* ☎ *0583/464533.*

Mode Mignon. Come here for one-stop high-end designer shopping, including Prada, Miu-Miu, Gucci, Dolce e Gabbana, Jil Sander, and Tod's—among others. ⊠ *Piazza Bernardini 1-2-3* ☎ *0583/491217.*

★ **My Walit.** Brightly colored wallets, purses, and other lovely leather accessories are on offer here at affordable prices. ⊠ *Piazza Anfiteatro 40* ☎ *0583/051578.*

FOOD
Lucca is known for its farro, an ancient barleylike grain that has found its way into regional specialties such as *zuppa* (or *minestra*) *di farro* (farro soup). It's available in food shops all over the city. Lucca is most famous for its olive oil, however, which is exported throughout the world. Look for extra-virgin oil whose label clearly indicates that it is entirely from Tuscany or, better yet, entirely from a local *fattoria*, or farm. *Olio nuovo* (new oil) is available for a few weeks in November, when the olive-picking season begins. This new oil is strong-flavored and peppery—great for drizzling on soup, pasta, and bread—and it's also nearly impossible to find in North America. Wine from small Lucca producers is also difficult to find abroad.

Antica Bottega di Prospero. Stop by this shop for top-quality local products, including farro, dried porcini mushrooms, olive oil, and wine. ⊠ *Via San Lucia 13* ☎ *No phone.*

Enoteca Vanni. A huge selection of wines, as well as an ancient cellar, make this a place worth stopping at. For the cost of the wine only, tastings can be organized through the shopkeepers and are held in the cellar. ⊠ *Piazza del Salvatore 7* ☎ *0583/491902* ⊕ *www.enotecavanni.com.*

Massei Ugo. This small shop offers great wine prices and assorted local delicacies. The store's owner, Ugo Massei, doesn't speak English, but he's friendly and helpful. ⊠ *Via S. Andrea 19* ☎ *0583/467656.*

MARKETS

antiques market. On the third weekend of the month there's an antiques market in Piazza San Martino. Vendors unveil their wares around 8:30, and start packing up around dusk. There's something for everyone, including old-fashioned glassware, ancient coins, and furniture—some antique, some just old. Check out the 19th-century tools and collections of fascist memorabilia.

bookstalls. Looking for old prints? Old postcards? Old comic books? Just behind the church of San Giusto (off Via Beccheria, which runs for about two blocks between Piazza Napoleone and Piazza San Michele) are bookstalls that open their cupboard doors on clement days (including Sunday), from about 10 to 7. You may discover anything from hand-tinted prints of orchids to back issues of *Uomo Ragno* (Spiderman looks and acts just the same even when he's speaking Italian).

PASTRIES

Pasticceria Pinelli. For a broad selection of scrumptious pastries, visit this favorite haunt of Lucca's senior citizens, who frequently stop in after Sunday Mass. ⊠ *Via Beccheria 28* ☎ *0583/496119.*

Pasticceria Taddeucci. A particularly delicious version of *buccellato*—the sweet, anise-flavor bread with raisins that is a Luccan specialty—is baked at Pasticceria Taddeucci. ⊠ *Piazza San Michele 34* ☎ *0583/494933.*

THE GARFAGNANA

In the heart of the Alpi Apuane, the Garfagnana is one of the most visually stunning regions in Tuscany. Roads wind around precipitous, jagged peaks and through old stone villages. Cool mountain air tempers even the sultriest summer. Most of the major cities and towns are found along the Serchio, Italy's third-largest river, which runs north–south. The Val di Lima (Lima Valley), formed by the Lima River, has for centuries been known for its curative thermal waters and its lush chestnut groves.

As you plan your travels through the area, keep in mind that you'll encounter winding two-lane mountain roads—driving 16 km (10 miles) may take longer than you'd expect. Pass through in October, though, and you'll be rewarded with bursts of yellow and splashes of red as the leaves change color.

SAN MARCELLO PISTOIESE

33 km (21 miles) northwest of Pistoia, 66 km (41 miles) northwest of Florence.

This small town—small, but still the largest in the area—bustles in summer and winter (when it's one of Tuscany's few ski destinations), but calms down in spring and fall. It's set amid spectacular scenery; you can drive across a dramatic suspension bridge over the Lima River.

GETTING HERE
By car, you're likely to approach San Marcello Pistoiese from Pistoia; take the SS435 to the SS66, which takes you right into town (follow the signs). COPIT provides frequent bus service as well. There is no train service.

VISITOR INFORMATION
San Marcello Pistoiese ⊠ *Piazza del Duomo, Pistoia* ☎ *0573/21622* ⊕ *www.turismo.pistoia.it.*

EXPLORING
Pieve di San Marcello. This church dates from the 12th century, though the interior was redone in the 18th century and most of the art inside is from that period. ⊠ *Piazza Arcangeli* ☎ *No phone* 🎫 *Free* ⊙ *Daily 9–1 and 3–6.*

SPORTS AND THE OUTDOORS
Nonsolovolo. You can rent mountain bikes and equipment for paragliding from Nonsolovolo. The website is in Italian only. ⊠ *Via XXIV Maggio 10, Lizzano Pistoiese* ☎ *0573/677700* ⊕ *www.nonsolovolo.it.*

ABETONE

20 km (12 miles) northwest of San Marcello Pistoiese, 53 km (33 miles) northwest of Pistoia, 86 km (53 miles) northwest of Florence.

Abetone is one of the most-visited vacation spots in the Apennine Mountains, where Tuscans, Emilia-Romagnans, and others come to ski. Set above two valleys, the resort town is on the edge of a lush and ancient forest of more than 9,000 acres. The numerous ski trails are mostly for beginners and intermediate skiers (the entire area has only two expert slopes). Summer is the time to trek or mountain bike in and around the beautiful hills and mountains.

GETTING HERE
By car from Pistoia, take the SS435/SR436 and follow signs for Abetone-Modena. You'll exit onto the SS66/SR66; continue for some 30 km (18 miles) to the SS12, which will take you into Abetone. COPIT buses run to Abetone, but there is no train service.

VISITOR INFORMATION
San Marcello Pistoiese tourism office ⊠ *Piazza del Duomo, Pistoia* ☎ *0573/630145* ⊕ *www.turismo.provincia.pistoia.it.*

WHERE TO EAT AND STAY

For expanded hotel reviews, visit Fodors.com.

$ ✕ **La Capannina.** Duccio Ugolini is in the kitchen, and his wife Miriam
ITALIAN Manni runs this large, one-room trattoria, which has a grand view of
beautiful woods and ski slopes. In the middle of the room is a fireplace, which casts a lovely glow in cooler months. Local ingredients
like mushrooms and chestnuts take center stage here. The chef has a
deft touch with mushrooms; his *insalatina di porcini e grana* (salad of
raw, shaved porcini and cheese) is delicate; his *flan di finferli e crema di
tartufo* (an eggy dish with fine, thin mushrooms), sublime. Sommeliers
abound in the couple's extended family, and it shows in the exquisite
wine list. ⊠ *Via Brennero 256* ☎ *0573/60562* ☉ *Closed Mon. and 2 wks
in May and Oct.*

$$ ✕ **La Locanda dello Yeti.** Stop at this restful osteria after a day on the
ITALIAN slopes or a trek through the forest. The specialty of the house is mush-
rooms—on *crostini* (toasted bread), polenta, or pasta. Mushrooms also
garnish the fine grilled meats, most of which are significant cuts of beef.
They also do a fine *lombatina di capriolo* (a venison T-bone steak). The
local house wine is refreshing. ⊠ *Via Brennero 324* ☎ *0573/606974*
🍽 *Reservations essential* ☉ *Closed Tues., 20 days in June, and 10 days
in Sept.*

$ ⊞ **Hotel Bellavista.** Originally a 19th-century villa belonging to Marchesa Guendalina Strozzi—her ancestors were powerful bankers in Renaissance Florence—this is now a contemporary inn. **Pros:** you can ski from hotel to chairlift. **Cons:** attracts a younger; sometimes rowdy crowd. ⊠ *Via Brennero 383* ☎ *0573/60028* ⊕ *www.bellavista-abetone.it* ⤴ *40 rooms, 2 suites* ⚐ *In-room: no a/c, safe. In-hotel: restaurant, bar* ⊗ *Closed May, Oct., and Nov.* ⦿ *Breakfast.*

WORD OF MOUTH

"If you are going to be in Lucca then you should definitely plan on touring the Garfagnana area. It is beautiful, unspoiled, not heavily trafficked and lots of trees."
—janelp

3

SKIING

Consorzio Impianti. This group manages the ski facilities in Abetone and has information on the Multipass, as well as maps, directions, and area information. ⊠ *Via Brennero 429* ☎ *0573/60557.*

F. Ballantini. Rental skis are available at this shop. ⊠ *Via Brennero 615* ☎ *0573/60482.*

Pistoiese ski area. The area has 37 ski slopes, amounting to about 50 km (31 miles) of ski surface, all accessible through the purchase of a single Multipass. You can check the Abetone section of the Pistoiese ski area website for details on the Multipass. ⊕ *www.lamontagnapistoiese.it.*

EN ROUTE
San Pellegrino in Alpe. Stop at the San Pellegrino in Alpe monastery en route from Abetone to Castelnuovo di Garfagnana to see the staggering view and the large wooden cross. Story has it that a 9th-century Scot, Pellegrino ("Little Pilgrim") by name, came to this spot to repent. ⊠ *Via del Voltone 14, Off SR12, 16 km (10 miles) northeast of Castelnuovo di Garfagnana, 28 km (17 miles) northwest of Abetone, San Pellegrino in Alpe* ☎ *0583/649072* ⦿ *Free* ⊗ *Tues.–Sat. 9:30–12:30, Sun. 9:30–12:30 and 2–5.*

BAGNI DI LUCCA

36 km (22 miles) southwest of Abetone, 27 km (17 miles) north of Lucca, 101 km (63 miles) northwest of Florence.

Pretty Bagni di Lucca was a fashionable spa town in the early 19th century—in part because of its thermal waters. The Romantic poet Percy Bysshe Shelley (1792–1822) installed his family here during the summer of 1818. He wrote to a friend in July of that year that the waters here were exceedingly refreshing: "My custom is to undress and sit on the rocks, reading Herodotus, until perspiration has subsided, and then to leap from the edge of the rock into this fountain." In 1853, Robert and Elizabeth Browning spent the summer in a house on the main square. Its heyday behind it, the town is now a quiet, charming place where elegant thermal spas still soothe on temperate summer days.

GETTING HERE

By car from Florence, take the A11 and exit at Capannori. Take the SS439 in the direction of Lucca. From Lucca, take the SS12/Via del Brennero. This leads to the SP18, which takes you directly into Bagni di Lucca. Lazzi bus lines also operate from Lucca and Florence. Trains run nearly every hour from Lucca and take about 25 minutes.

VISITOR INFORMATION

Bagni di Lucca tourism office ⊠ *Via Umberto I 139* ☎ *0583/805754* ⊕ *www. prolocobagnidilucca.it.*

OFF THE BEATEN PATH

Centro Termale Bagni di Lucca. Here, you'll find two natural steam-room caves, as well as spa services such as mud baths, massage, hydrotherapy, and facials. ⊠ *Piazza San Martino 11* ☎ *0583/87221* ⊕ *www. termebagnidilucca.it* 🎫 *€12 for thermal pool weekdays, €15 weekends; spa services vary* ⊙ *Daily 9–6.*

Il Ponte della Maddalena (*The Magdalen's Bridge*). Il Ponte della Maddalena is, oddly, also known as the Devil's Bridge. Commissioned in all likelihood by Matilde di Canossa (1046–1115), it was restructured by the petty despot Castruccio Castracani in the early 14th century. It's worth the climb to the middle—the bridge is narrow, steep, and pedestrians-only—to check out the view. Despite 1836 flood damage and early-20th-century alterations, it seems little changed from the Middle Ages. If you're heading north along the Serchio from Lucca to Bagni di Lucca, you will see the bridge on your left.

WHERE TO EAT

$

TUSCAN

★

✕ **Osteria i Macelli.** Honest Tuscan cooking prevails at this simple trattoria next to a large parking lot. No matter that there's no view: the terrific food and pleasing service—all of it served in a typical Tuscan dining room with high timbered ceilings—make a stop here well worth the detour. Locals swear by the *affettati misti* (sliced cured meats), which include the stellar *biroldo* (cured pork from nearby Garfagnana). The *ravioli di castagne* (ravioli stuffed with chestnut puree, sauced with radicchio and pancetta bits) should not be missed. ⊠ *Piazza i Macelli, Borgo a Mozzano, 21 km (13 miles) north of Lucca on the SS12* ☎ *0583/88700* ⊙ *Closed Jan. 1–15 and Sept. 1–15.*

BARGA

17 km (11 miles) northwest of Bagni di Lucca, 111 km (69 miles) northwest of Florence.

Barga is a lovely little hill town with a finely preserved medieval core. It produced textiles—particularly silk—during the Renaissance and wool in the 18th century. You won't find textiles here today; now the emphasis is on tourism. Here the African-American troops known as the Buffalo Soldiers, are remembered by the locals for their bravery in defending this mountainous area during World War II.

Walking around Barga is not for the faint of heart: it's one steep uphill after another to get to the tiny centro storico, and more steps to get to Piazza del Duomo.

GETTING HERE

By car from Lucca, take the SS12/Via del Brennero directly to Barga. Though there is train service to Barga, the station is far away from the centro storico. The only bus option is the small CLAP line (⊠ *Via*

Roma 7 ☎ *0583/723050)*, which runs between here and Castelnuovo di Garfagnana.

VISITOR INFORMATION

Barga tourism office ✉ *Via di Mezzo 45* ☎ *0583/72471* ⊕ *www.comune.barga. lu.it.*

EXPLORING

Duomo. Dedicated to Saint Christopher, the Duomo is a Romanesque cathedral, made from elegant limestone (quarried from nearby caves), which saw four separate building campaigns. The first began in the 9th century, and it was only finished in the 15th. Inside, the intricately carved pulpit, one of the finest examples of mid-12th-century Tuscan sculpture, commands center stage. The view from the Duomo is incredible: Tuscan mountains have never looked so good. ✉ *Via del Duomo* ☎ *No phone* ⊗ *Daily 9–7.*

OFF THE BEATEN PATH

Grotta del Vento. About 14 km (9 miles) southwest of Barga, after following a winding road flanked by both sheer cliffs and fantastic views, you come to Tuscany's Cave of the Wind. As the result of a steady internal temperature of 10.7°C (about 51°F), the wind is sucked into the cave in winter and blown out in summer. It has a long cavern with stalactites, stalagmites, "bottomless" pits, and subterranean streams. One-, two-, and three-hour guided tours of the cave are given. (The one-hour tour is offered only from November through March.) ✉ *SP 39, west at Galliciano, Fornovolasco* ☎ *0583/722024* ⊕ *www.grottadelvento.com* ✑ *€9 for 1 hr, €14 for 2 hrs, €20 for 3 hrs* ⊗ *Daily 10–6.*

WHERE TO STAY

For expanded hotel reviews, visit Fodors.com.

$$ ⊞ **Il Ciocco.** A huge resort and convention center, Il Ciocco has its own soccer stadium, basketball court, and equestrian center. **Pros:** a great place for kids. **Cons:** public spaces are characterless. ✉ *Off SP7, 7 km (4½ miles) north of Barga, Castelvecchio Pascoli* ☎ *0583/7191* ⊕ *www. ciocco.it* ⤳ *220 rooms, 15 suites, 56 apartments, 12 chalets* ⬧ *In-room: no a/c, kitchen, Wi-Fi. In-hotel: restaurant, pool, tennis court, gym, children's programs, business center, some pets allowed* ⦿ *Breakfast.*

NIGHTLIFE AND THE ARTS

Opera Barga. From mid-July to mid-August, the stony streets of Barga come alive as opera fans come to Opera Barga. This highly regarded opera festival takes place at the **Teatro dell'Accademia dei Differenti** (Theater of the Academy of the Different). The Opera Barga began in 1967 as a workshop for young singers and musicians. Now it stages lesser-known baroque operas, as well as contemporary works. Check their website for current information. ✉ *Teatro dell'Accademia dei Differenti, Piazza Angelio 4* ⊕ *www.giornaledibarganews.com.*

Barga Jazz. Listen to the newest music during Barga Jazz, a jazz orchestra competition (in July and August). The scores presented each year are selected by a special committee, and a winner is selected by an international jury. ✉ *Teatro dell'Accademia dei Differenti, Piazza Angelio 4* ⊕ *www.giornaledibarganews.com.*

CASTELNUOVO DI GARFAGNANA

13 km (8 miles) northwest of Barga, 47 km (27 miles) north of Lucca, 121 km (75 miles) northwest of Florence.

Castelnuovo di Garfagnana might be the best base for exploring the Garfagnana, because it's central with respect to the other towns. During the Renaissance the town's fortunes were frequently tied to those of the powerful Este family of Ferrara. It's now a bustling town with a lovely historic center.

GETTING HERE

By car from Lucca, take the SS12/Via del Brennero, follow signs to Borgo a Mozzano; then take the SS445, which leads directly into town.

CLAP buses. Buses run between Castelnuovo di Garfagnana and Barga. You can purchase tickets at Paolini, the tobacconist's shop in Piazza della Repubblica. ⊠ *Piazza della Repubblica.*

There is no train service.

VISITOR INFORMATION

Castelnuovo di Garfagnana tourism office ⊠ *Piazza della Erbe* ☏ *0583/641007* ⊕ *www.castelnuovogarfagnana.org.*

EXPLORING

La Rocca (*The Fortress*). Dating from the 13th century, *La Rocca* (The Fortress) has a plaque commemorating writer Ludovico Ariosto's brief tenure here as commissar general for the Este. Ariosto (1474–1533) wrote the epic poem *Orlando Furioso* (1516), among other works. You can only see the impressive walls and great entryway of the fort from the outside—at press time, entry into La Rocca was not allowed. ⊠ *Piazza Umberto.*

Duomo. Dedicated to Saint Peter, the Duomo was begun in the 11th century and was reconstructed in the early 1500s. Inside is a crucifix dating from the 14th to 15th century. There's also an early-16th-century terra-cotta attributed to the school of the della Robbia. ⊠ *Piazza del Duomo* ☏ *0583/62170* ⊙ *Daily 9–7.*

Parco Naturale delle Alpi Apuane. Preserved ancient forests and barren rocky peaks create dramatic scenery in the Parco Naturale delle Alpi Apuane (Natural Park of the Apuane Alps), a national park that encompasses several towns. Its highest peak, Monte Pisanino, rises more than 6,000 feet, and towers over an artificial lake, Lago di Vagli, which covers the submerged village of Fabbricca. The tiny stone villages of Vagli di Sotto and Vagli di Sopra sit alongside the lake. Plan on a half or full day of hiking in the park. Remember to wear comfortable sports shoes or hiking boots and bring plenty of drinking water. A two-lane winding road through the park (SP13) connects Castelnuovo di Garfagnana to the sea. To get to Vagli di Sotto and Vagli di Sopra, go north of Castelnuovo di Garfagnana on SR445 to Poggio and then turn west on SP50. ☎ *0583/644478* ⊕ *www.parcapuane.toscana.it* 🖃 *Free.*

WHERE TO EAT

$$ ✕ **Giaccò.** A beautiful ride along winding, tree-lined mountain roads
TUSCAN brings you to this little gem in the middle of nowhere. A simple interior provides the perfect backdrop for Tuscan classics. Start with the antipasto della casa, a delightful mix of sliced, cured meats, truffled polenta, and an exquisite farro salad. The grill takes center stage here, and all the usual fare's on hand; the bistecca fiorentina is particularly good. The wine list isn't exceptional, but there are some well-priced bottles that pair nicely with the food. ⊠ *Via Provinciale di Arni 2* ☎ *0583/667048* ⊙ *Closed Tues. and 3 wks in Nov.*

$ ✕ **Osteria Vecchio Mulino.** "The old mill" has an antique marble serv-
TUSCAN ing counter filled with free nibbles and two large wooden tables in a room lined with wine bottles. The enthusiastic host, Andrea Bertucci, proudly touts local products on his simple menu, which usually consists of superior cheese and affettati misti (mixed sliced cured meats). Traditional local dishes with farro grain, polenta, pecorino cheese, and salami round out the selections. Finish your meal with their famous *caffè al vetro con miele di castagno* (coffee in a glass with chestnut honey). This osteria is open from 7:30 am to 8 pm in the warmer months, and from 11 to 8 in winter. ⊠ *Via Vittorio Emanuele 12* ☎ *0583/62192* ⊕ *www. ilvecchiomulino.com* ⊙ *Closed Mon. and 3 wks in Oct. or Jan.*

SPORTS AND THE OUTDOORS

HIKING AND **Centro Accoglienza Parco.** Stop here for help you with hiking information,
CLIMBING particularly for the Parco Naturale delle Alpi Apuane. ⊠ *Piazza Erbe 1* ☎ *0583/644242* ✍ *garfagnana@tin.it.*

Club Alpino Italiano (*Italian Alpine Club*). For detailed maps and information about trekking in the mountains surrounding Castelnuovo di Garfagnana, contact the Club Alpino Italiano. ⊠ *Via Vittorio Emanuele* ☎ *0583/65577* ⊕ *www.cai.it.*

THE NORTHWEST COAST

Livorno has been a port town since the 16th century, and continues to host countless cruise and cargo ships from around the world. It has a gritty, lively feel. Heading up the coast you'll pass lots of beaches (both sandy and rocky, but none all that inviting) until you hit the popular destinations of Viareggio and swank, expensive Forte dei Marmi. The air gets clearer if you head up the hills toward Carrara, a lively, beautiful, rarely visited town.

On the Ligurian coast west of Tuscany are the five seaside villages that make up the Cinque Terre. They're a hugely popular side trip for visitors to northwest Tuscany.

LIVORNO

24 km (15 miles) south of Pisa, 187 km (116 miles) west of Florence.

Livorno is a gritty city with a long and interesting history. In the early Middle Ages it alternately belonged to Pisa and Genoa. In 1421 Florence, seeking access to the sea, bought it. Cosimo I (1519–74) started construction of the harbor in 1571, putting Livorno on the map. After Ferdinando I de' Medici (1549–1609) proclaimed Livorno a free city, it became a haven for people suffering from religious persecution; Roman Catholics from England and Jews and Moors from Spain and Portugal, among others, settled here. The *Quattro Mori* (Four Moors), also known as the Monument to Ferdinando I, commemorates this. (The statue of Ferdinand I dates from 1595, the bronze Moors by Pietro Tacca from the 1620s.)

In the following centuries, and particularly in the 18th, Livorno boomed as a port. In the 19th century the town drew a host of famous Britons passing through on their grand tours. Its prominence continued up to World War II, when it was heavily bombed. Much of the town's architecture, therefore, postdates the war, and it's somewhat difficult to imagine what it might have looked liked before. Livorno has recovered from the war, however, as it's become a huge point of departure for container ships, as well as the only spot in Tuscany for cruise ships to dock for the day.

Most of Livorno's artistic treasures date from the 17th century and aren't all that interesting unless you dote on obscure baroque artists. Livorno's most famous native artist, Amedeo Modigliani (1884–1920), was of much more recent vintage. Sadly, there's no notable work by him in his hometown.

There may not be much in the way of art, but it's still worth strolling around the city. The **Mercato Nuovo**, which has been around since 1894, sells all sorts of fruits, vegetables, grains, meat, and fish. Outdoor markets nearby are also chock-full of local color. The presence of Camp Darby, an American military base just outside of town, accounts for the availability of many American products.

If you have time, Livorno is worth a stop for lunch or dinner at the least.

GETTING HERE

Livorno is easily reached by rail; trains from Florence run hourly. By car it's about an hour west of Florence on the Fi-Pi-Li.

VISITOR INFORMATION

Livorno tourism office ✉ *Piazza Cavour 6* ☎ *0586/204611* ⊕ *www. costadeglietruschi.it.*

WHERE TO EAT

$ ✕ **Cantina Nardi.** It's only open for lunch, and it's well off the beaten path
ITALIAN (even if it is in the center of Livorno's shopping district). But getting here is worth the trouble: this tiny place, lined with bottles of wine, has a small menu that changes daily, a superb wine list, and gregarious staff. Their *baccalà alla livornese* (deep-fried salt cod served with chickpeas)

is succulently crisp; soups, such as ribollita, are very soothing. ✉ *Via Cambini 6/8* ☎ *0586/808006* ✆ *Closed Sun. No dinner.*

$$
SEAFOOD

✕**Osteria del Mare.** Husband and wife Claudio and Marila run this fish restaurant across the (busy) street from the docks. The decor's nothing to write home about (paneled walls with framed prints and navigational coats of arms), but it doesn't much matter once you get into the essentials of tucking into the food. Order the fish of the day, and the waiter will bring the fish to the table for approval; then order it cooked *all'isolana* (baked whole with tomatoes and potatoes). Marila has created a one-of-a-kind dessert, a cross between a cheesecake and a semifreddo. It's heavenly, especially when sauced with either a chocolate, caramel, or strawberry concoction. Polite service and an affable wine list make eating here a pleasure. ✉ *Borgo Cappuccini 5, Livorno* ☎ *0586/881027.*

VIAREGGIO

8 km (5 miles) south of Pietrasanta, 25 km (15 miles) northwest of Lucca, 97 km (60 miles) northwest of Florence.

Tobias Smollett (1721–71), the English novelist, wrote in the 1760s that Viareggio was "a kind of sea-port on the Mediterranean. . . . The roads are indifferent and the accommodation is execrable." Much has changed here since Smollett's time. For one, this beach town becomes very crowded in summer, so accommodations are plentiful. It can also be loud and brassy at the height of the season, though there's peace and quiet in the autumn and early spring.

Viareggio has numerous buildings decorated in the 1920s Liberty style, characterized by colorful wood and some with ornate exterior decoration. Locals and tourists alike stroll along the town's wide seaside promenade lined with bars, cafés, and some very fine restaurants. If you can't make it to Venice for *Carnevale* (Carnival), come here, where the festivities are in some ways more fun than in Venice. The city is packed with revelers from all over Tuscany, taking part in the riot of colorful parades with giant floats. Book lodging far in advance, and be aware that hotels charge top prices during Carnevale.

GETTING HERE

Trains run frequently from Florence on the Lucca line. By car from Lucca, take the A11 and follow the signs for Viareggio. Exit at Massarosa and take the SS439 to the SP5, which goes into the center of town.

VISITOR INFORMATION

Viareggio tourism office ✉ *Info Point, train station* ☎ *0584/46382* ⊕ *www. comune.viareggio.lu.it.*

WHERE TO EAT AND STAY

For expanded hotel reviews, visit Fodors.com.

$$$
TUSCAN

✕**Pino Ristorante.** Locals swear by this unpretentious trattoria a couple of blocks away from the beach. The Artizzu family has been serving specialties from the sea since 1979 in their small eatery with yellow-sponged walls. The menu notes that the availability of various dishes changes due to conditions at sea: you get the idea that what you're eating just came off the boat (and you are). The house specialty is the pricey but divine *aragosta alla catalana con verdure* (Mediterranean lobster with steamed and raw vegetables). The *spiedino di sogliola* (sole kebab) arrives with silken mashed potatoes topped with bottarga (a smoked tuna product); the unoily, crunchy fritto misto (mixed fish fry) is a joy. If you can't decide, order the tasting menu, which gives you a little bit of a lot of the menu. Patrizia makes all the desserts; remember to leave room for them.

☒ *Via Matteotti 18* ☎ *0584/961356* ☉ *Closed Wed.*

$$$$ ✕ **Romano.** The Franceschini family has been running this swank sea-
SEAFOOD food eatery since the 1970s. Ebullient host Romano Franceschini is
★ justifiably proud of the food produced by his wife and daughter, Franca and Cristina; son Roberto, an accomplished sommelier, presides over the floor. Don't miss the *fantasia di pesce crudo* (fantasy of raw fish), which arrives at the table with an aroma redolent of the sea, and follow up with any of the marvelous fish seconds. Or you can leave everything in the Franceschinis' hands and order the tasting menu (€95 without wine). ☒ *Via Mazzini 122* ☎ *0584/31382* ☖ *Reservations essential* ☉ *Closed Mon. and Jan. No lunch Tues. in July and Aug.*

$$$$ ⌂ **Hotel Plaza e de Russie.** Opened in 1871, this was Viareggio's first hotel, playing host to those on the Grand Tour. **Pros:** proximity to beach; excellent restaurant. **Cons:** some rooms facing street can get street noise. ☒ *Piazza d'Azeglio 1* ☎ *0584/31714* ⊕ *www.plazaederussie.com* ⇗ *50 rooms, 3 suites* ☖ *In-room: safe, Internet. In-hotel: restaurant, bar, business center, parking, some pets allowed* ⍾ *Breakfast.*

NIGHTLIFE AND THE ARTS

Carnevale. For four Sundays and Shrove Tuesday preceding Lent, this little seaside town produces its world-famous Carnevale, with intricate floats, or *carri,* representing Italy's most influential celebrities and politicians and sometimes the famous and infamous from around the world. Started in the late 1800s, the Viareggio Carnevale differs from the carnival held in Venice because of its parades of huge and fantastical floats. Traditionally, they were put together by Viareggio's shipbuilders, and in the beginning the masked celebrants were civil and political protesters, and the floats were, and often still are, used as a vehicle to lampoon popular figures of the day. Other events—music, parties, and art displays—also take place during Carnevale. The crowds are huge, with many attending in costume. ☎ *0584/962568* ⊕ *www.viareggio. ilcarnevale.com.*

SPORTS AND THE OUTDOORS

Club Nautico Versilia. Sailors who wish to tour the coastal waters should contact Club Nautico Versilia for assistance with maps, port and docking information, charter and craft-rental resources, and information

Outrageous is the rule at Viareggio's Carnevale festivities.

about craft repair and refueling. ⊠ *Piazza Artiglio* ☎ *0584/31444* ⊕ *www.cnv-viareggio.it.*

FORTE DEI MARMI

8 km (5 miles) south of Massa, 37 km (27 miles) northwest of Lucca, 106 km (66 miles) northwest of Florence.

Forte dei Marmi is a playground for wealthy Italians and equally well-heeled tourists. Its wide, sandy beaches—strands are 6 km (4 miles) long—have the Alpi Apuane as a dramatic backdrop. The town was, from Roman times, the port for marble quarried in Carrara. In the 1920s the Agnelli family (of Fiat fame) began summering here, and other tycoons followed suit. It remains the East Hamptons of Italy; everyone seems to be dripping in gold, and prices are very, very high. In winter the town's population is about 7,000; in summer, it swells to about 150,000, most of those folks staying in their own private villas.

GETTING HERE

By car from Florence, take the A11, following signs for Viareggio. From there, take the A12/E80 following signs for Genova. Exit at Versilia, and take the SP70 directly into town. Arriving by train isn't a good option; the station is far from the center of town, and the taxi ride in is expensive.

VISITOR INFORMATION

Forte dei Marmi tourism office ⊠ *Via A. Franceschi 8b* ☎ *0584/80091* ⊕ *www. comune.forte-dei-marmi.lucca.it.*

WHERE TO EAT AND STAY

For expanded hotel reviews, visit Fodors.com.

$$$
ITALIAN
✕**Bagno Annetta.** Although Bagno Annetta is an ultra-exclusive beach club (you have to be an exceedingly wealthy person to join), its restaurant on the beach is open to the public. A handful of tables, surrounded by well-trimmed high hedges, sit underneath a large umbrella. The menu (with no prices on it) features specialties from the sea. The *tartare di tonno e ricciola* (tuna and amberjack tartare) comes with thinly sliced apples and a drizzle of balsamic vinegar; the *spaghetti alle arselle* (spaghetti with a minced clam sauce) should not be missed. Another standout is the delicious and expensive mixed grill with scampi the size of small lobsters. For something more modest, try one of the terrific wood-fired thin-crust pizzas. ✉ *Via Achille Franceschi 23* ☎ *0584/89314* ⌚ *Reservations essential* ⊗ *Closed Sept.–Easter.*

$$$$
SEAFOOD
✕**Lorenzo.** The affable Lorenzo Viani has presided here for more than 30 years, and his restaurant still draws a well-heeled, sophisticated crowd. Start with the chilled raw oysters before moving on to seafood pasta, sea bass with chopped tomatoes, or a fish tartare. Or request the *menu degustazione* (tasting menu) and let chef Gioacchino Pontrelli prepare the freshest items of the day. You can also choose vegetarian and *terra* (meat) tasting menus. ✉ *Via Carducci 61* ☎ *0584/874030* ⌚ *Reservations essential* ⊗ *Closed mid-Dec.–Jan. and Mon. No lunch July and Aug.*

$$$$
SEAFOOD
✕**Osteria del Mare.** If you want to have a terrific dinner without breaking the bank (at least by Forte dei Marmi standards), have a meal at this lively beachfront (though there are no water views) trattoria. Outdoor seating and candlelit tables provide a romantic setting, and the rosemary and olive-oil foccacina, hot from the wood-burning oven, whet the appetite. The menu offers a little of everything, including oysters on the half shell, and a lovely local specialty, *la vaporata di mare:* in this case, steamed squid and other fishes served on a bed of local, organic lettuce. The *pizziauoli* (the guys who make pizza) also know their stuff, and are a perfect option if you want to keep the bill low. Though the atmosphere is decidedly casual, this osteria boasts a fantastic sommelier named Sokol—a rarity in osterie. ✉ *Via Franceschi 4* ☎ *0584/83661* ⌚ *Reservations essential* ⊗ *Closed Thurs.*

$$$$
★
🛏**Byron.** The pale yellow exterior only hints at the elegance inside the hotel created by joining two Liberty villas from 1899 and 1902. **Pros:** cutting-edge chef Andrea Mattei at the hotel restaurant; golf and tennis privileges; sunny staff. **Cons:** one-week minimum stay. ✉ *Viale Morin 46* ☎ *0584/787052* ⊕ *www.hotelbyron.net* ⤴ *29 rooms, 3 suites* ⌂ *In-room: kitchen, Wi-Fi. In-hotel: restaurant, bar, pool, business center* ⊗ *Closed Oct.–Easter* ⦿*Multiple meal plans.*

$$$$
🛏**Hotel Ritz.** The Biagi family lovingly restored this 1920s beaux arts villa, and opened it to the public in 1980. **Pros:** multilingual staff; award-winning barman Lorenzo mixing drinks in the hotel bar; the Beemousine (a free pick-up and drop-off service for points in town), the hotel's very own Mercedes to take you or pick you up at at the airport. **Cons:** beach costs extra (you have to join a beach club); sea-view rooms can pick up some street noise. ✉ *Via Flavio Gioia 2* ☎ *0584/787531*

⊕ *www.ritzfortedeimarmi.com* ⟲ *32 rooms* ⚘ *In-room: safe, Wi-Fi. In-hotel: restaurant, bar, pool, business center* ¡Ỗ¡ *Multiple meal plans.*

NIGHTLIFE AND THE ARTS

Almarosa Art Music and Bar. After a day at the beach, the place to see and be seen is Almarosa Art Music and Bar. The clientele during high season frequently includes Italian soccer players and young, good-looking celebrities and politicians. ⊠ *Viale Morin 89/a* ☎ *0584/82503.*

Almarosa Friends by Didi's. Next door to Almarosa Art Music and Bar, this bar serves aperitivi and various fish carpacci and plates of pasta. ⊠ *Viale Morin 91* ☎ *0584/787166.*

SPORTS AND THE OUTDOORS

BIKING **Claudio Maggi Cicli.** This shop has been selling bicycle equipment and renting bikes since 1906. From May through September it's open daily 8 to 1 and 3 to 8; from October through April it's closed Wednesday and Sunday. ⊠ *Viale Morin 85* ☎ *0584/89529* ⊕ *www.ciclimaggi.it.*

Maggi-Coppa. Right on the beach, Maggi-Coppa rents bicycles and keeps late hours: 8 am to midnight daily from May through August, 8 to 8 daily the rest of the year. ⊠ *Via A. Franceschi 4/d* ☎ *0584/83528.*

HIKING AND CLIMBING **Forte dei Marmi Club Alpino Italiano.** This group can provide information on area hiking, spelunking, and rock climbing, and about guided tours. ⊠ *Via Buonarroti 47* ☎ *0584/89808* ⊕ *www.caifortedeimarmi.it.*

SCUBA DIVING **Associazione Subacquei Versilia.** For information about the best places to scuba dive on the Versilian and Ligurian coasts, contact the Associazione Subacquei Versilia. ⊠ *Via S. Allende 38* ☎ *0584/82070.*

CARRARA

45 km (28 miles) southeast of Riomaggiore, 126 km (79 miles) northwest of Florence.

Carrara, from which the famous white marble takes its name, lies in a beautiful valley midway up a spectacular mountain in the Apuane Alps. The surrounding peaks are free of foliage and white as snow, even in summer, because they are full of marble stone. Marble has been quarried in the area for the past 2,000 years. The art historian Giorgio Vasari (1511–74) recorded that Michelangelo came to Carrara with two apprentices to quarry the marble for the never-completed tomb of Julius II (1443–1513). According to Vasari, Michelangelo spent eight months among the rocks conceiving fantastical ideas for future works.

GETTING HERE

By car, take the A11, following signs for Lucca, then at Viareggio take the A12. Trains run frequently from Florence, but a change of trains is almost always required, and the Carrara station is not centrally located. Coming from Lucca, you usually have to change trains at Viareggio.

VISITOR INFORMATION

Carrara tourism office ⊠ *Lungomare A. Vespucci 24, Marina di Massa* ☎ *0585/240063* ⊕ *www.aptmassacarrara.it.*

EXPLORING

Museo del Marmo (*Marble Museum*). Carrara's history as a marble-producing center is well documented in the Museo del Marmo, beginning with early works from the 2nd century. Exhibits detail the working of marble, from quarrying and transporting it to sculpting it. ⊠ *Viale XX Settembre 85* ☎ *0585/845746* 🔄 *€4.50* ⊙ *Mon.–Sat. 10–1 and 1:30–5:30.*

Marble quarries. The area around Carrara has a lot of still-active quarries—more than 100 at last count. Most of them are not open to the public for safety reasons. However, it is possible to tour specific marble caves. The Carrara tourism office, 7 km (4½ miles) away in Marina di Massa, has details about which areas you can visit. ⊠ *Carrara tourism office:, Lungomare A. Vespucci 24, Marina di Massa* ☎ *0585/240063.*

Duomo. Work began on the Duomo in the 11th century and continued into the 14th. The cathedral, dedicated to Saint Andrew, is the first church of the Middle Ages constructed entirely of marble. Most of it comes from the area (the white, light blue-gray, black, and red). The tremendous facade is a fascinating blend of Pisan Romanesque and Gothic influences. Note the human figures and animals on Corinthian capitals. ⊠ *Piazza del Duomo* ☎ *No phone* ⊙ *Daily 9–7.*

San Francesco. The lovely baroque church of San Francesco is a study in understated elegance. It dates from the 1620s to 1660s, and even though it was built during the peak years of the baroque, the only excess can be found in the twisting marble columns embellishing the altars. ⊠ *Piazza XXVII Aprile* ☎ *No phone* ⊙ *Daily 9–7.*

Accademia di Belle Arti. During the 19th and 20th centuries Carrara became a hotbed for anarchism, and during World War II it put up fierce resistance to the Nazis. The town is still lively thanks to its art institute. The Accademia di Belle Arti, founded by Maria Teresa Cybo Malaspina d'Este in 1769, draws studio art students from all over Italy. This may explain why there are many good bars and cafés in many of the town's squares.

WHERE TO EAT AND STAY

For expanded hotel reviews, visit Fodors.com.

$$
TUSCAN

✕ **Ristorante Venanzio.** *Lardo di colonnata*, treated pork fat, is a gastronomic specialty in Italy, and there's no place better to try it than the place from which it hails. From the center of Carrara, the restaurant is a 15-minute drive up winding roads cut through marble-filled mountains. Chef Alessio Lucchetti works wonders in the kitchen; if you're undecided on where to start, the €40 tasting menu with four courses is a great deal. The succulent primi are also impressive, such as the house specialty *ravioli di carne ed erbette di montagne* (mixed meat and lardo ravioli with a simple tomato ragù). Most of the secondi feature the local product; the *coniglio farcito con mandorle e verdure* (stuffed rabbit with almonds and Savoy cabbage) is a heavenly marriage between rabbit and pork. Do save room for dessert: they do terrific semifreddi here. ⊠ *Piazza Palestro 3, Colonnata Carrara, 2 km (1 mile) from Carrara* ☎ *0585/758033* ⊙ *Closed Thurs. No dinner Sun.*

$ ⬚ **Hotel Carrara.** Although this quiet hotel isn't actually in Carrara, it is right across the street from the Avenza-Carrara train station. **Pros:** proximity to train station. **Cons:** rooms are somewhat utilitarian. ⊠ *Via Petacchi 21, 4 km (2½ miles) southeast of Carrara, Avenza* ☎ *0585/857616* ⊕ *www.hotelcarrara.it* ⇝ *32 rooms* ♿ *In-room: safe, Wi-Fi. In-hotel: restaurant, business center, some pets allowed* ⑴ *Breakfast.*

THE CINQUE TERRE

FIVE REMOTE VILLAGES MAKE ONE MUST-SEE DESTINATION

"Charming" and "breathtaking" are adjectives that get a workout when you're traveling in Italy, but it's rare that both apply to a single location. The Cinque Terre is such a place, and this combination of characteristics goes a long way toward explaining its tremendous appeal.

The area is made up of five tiny villages (Cinque Terre literally means "Five Lands") clinging to the cliffs along a gorgeous stretch of the Ligurian coast. The terrain is so steep that for centuries footpaths were the only way to get from place to place. It just so happens that these paths provide beautiful views of the rocky coast tumbling into the sea, as well as access to secluded beaches and grottoes.

Backpackers "discovered" the Cinque Terre in the 1970s, and its popularity has been growing ever since. Despite summer crowds, much of the original appeal is intact. Each town has maintained its own distinct charm, and views from the trails in between are as breathtaking as ever.

Monterosso

Corniglia

Terracing around Corniglia

HIKING THE CINQUE TERRE

Mount Malpertuso

Mount Castello

Monterosso—Vernazza Trail
The most demanding portion of the trail. Often narrow, with significant climbs and descents, particularly near Vernazza. Your labors are rewarded with the Trail No. 2's best views.

Mount Gaginara

Le Stalle

Trail No 8a

(Red Trail)

Drignana

Vernazza—Corniglia Trail
Ups and downs interspersed with olive groves and terraced vineyards.

38

Trail No 1

370

Madonna di Soviore

51

Santuario del Reggio

1hr

Santuario Bernardino

1 hr 30min

Trail No 89

Trail No 8

S. Bernardo
Trail No 8

Trail No 7

1hr

Trail No 2 (Blue Trail)
3 km/2 mi—2 hrs

3 km/2 mi—1 hr 30 min

Guvano Beach

Vernazza

Palma Pt

del Frate Island

Molinara Pt

Monterosso al Mare

0 —————— 1 mi

0 —————— 1 km

Monterosso
The most resort-like of the villages, with the largest beach.

Vernazza
Pretty and visitor-friendly. The best spot for lingering in a café and watching waves crash against the shore.

FERRY TO LEVANTO

THE CLASSIC HIKE

Hiking is the most popular way to experience the Cinque Terre, and Trail No. 2, the Sentiero Azzurro (Blue Trail), is the most traveled path. To cover the entire trail is a full day: it's approximately 13 km (8 mi) in length, takes you to all five villages, and requires about five hours, not including stops, to complete. The best approach is to start at the eastern-most town of Riomaggiore and warm up your legs on the easiest segment of the trail. As you work your way west, the hike gets progressively more demanding. For a less strenuous experience, you can choose to skip a leg or two and take the ferry (which provides its own beautiful views) or the inland train running between the towns instead.

Manarola · Along Trail No.2 · Via dell'Amore

Corniglia–Manarola Trail
Runs through the hills near Manarola, descends to rocky beach near Corniglia.

Manarola–Riomaggiore Trail
Known as the Via dell'Amore (Lovers' Lane). A wide, paved, flat path with fine views.

KEY

····················	*Major footpaths*
- - - - - - -	*Sanctuary footpaths*
- - - - - - -	*Connecting footpaths*
45min	*Hiking times*
☦	*Sanctuaries*

Trail No 1 (Red Trail)

Mount Cuna

Mount Capri

Mount Galera

Mount Grosso

Trail No 6

Trail No 7a

Trail No 6d

1hr 30min

Madonna della Salute
1hr

Volastra

Trail No 02

3 km/2 mi–1 hr
Trail No 2 (Blue Trail)

Spiaggione di Corniglia

51

370

Madonna di Montenero
☦ 45min

Trail No 3

370

TO LA SPEZIA

Corniglia

Luogo Pt

Ligurian Sea

Manarola

Buonfiglio Pt

Via dell' Amore

30min

Riomaggiore

Torre Guardiola

C di M Nero

Trail No 2 (Blue Trail)

Corniglia
Perched on a cliff 500 ft. above the sea, reached by a switchback path (or by shuttle bus).

Manarola
The most photogenic of the villages, best seen from the cemetery a few minutes up the path toward Corniglia.

Riomaggiore
Cliff-clinging buildings are almost as striking as those in Manarola. Stairs to the left of the train station entrance cross over the tracks and lead to the trailhead.

BEYOND TRAIL NO.2

Trail No. 2 is just one of a network of trails crisscrossing the hills. If you're a dedicated hiker, spend a few nights and try some of the other routes. Trail No. 1, the Sentiero Rosso (Red Trail), climbs from Portovenere (east of Riomaggiore) and returns to the sea at Levanto (west of Monterosso al Mare). To hike its length takes from 9 to 12 hours; the ridge-top trail provides spectacular views from high above the villages, each of which can be reached via a steep path. Other shorter trails go from the villages up into the hills, some leading to religious sanctuaries. Trail No. 9, for example, starts from the old section of Monterosso and ends at the Madonna di Soviore Sanctuary.

UPDATE: THE OCTOBER 2011 FLOODS

When Mother Nature rages, the end results can be shocking. On October 25th 2011, two of the Cinque Terre's most picturesque towns—Vernazza and Monterossa—were devastated by a freak storm. More than 20 inches of rain lead to torrential flooding and devastating mudslides that, in less than three hours, transformed these pastel-hued, picture-perfect beauties into disaster areas.

"Monterosso does not exist anymore," Mayor Angelo Betta declared. By the next morning, much of Vernazza's population had been evacuated by boat and the famed walking trails of the Cinque Terre were declared off-limits. Vernazza's seaside harbor—an image that has graced innumerable travel posters—had been transformed into a sea of caked mud. During the storm, downpours caused landslides that filled the canals that run under Monterosso's streets. In Vernazza, streets became rivers. Luckily, at 2:45 pm, a "pause" of 15 minutes occurred in Vernazza, giving many people the chance to escape to higher ground—just before a second wave of mud arrived. The final toll: four dead and over 100 million euro of damages.

Thanks to aid groups like Save Vernazza, things are slowly getting back to normal. Many businesses are now operational, the canals have been restructured, the trails are being restored, and Vernazza hopes to finish reconstructing its famous harbor in time for the summer season of 2012.

Although she may have unleashed much of the disaster, Mother Nature was not entirely to blame. Since tourism has long marginalized farming—the former mainstay of the coastal economy—many stone walls used to strengthen all the terraced hillsides decayed. When these stones washed away, Vernazzo's mayor Vincenzo Resasco said to the *New York Times*, "We've recovered enough to build a second wall of China." Today, along with the towns, those walls are being rebuilt to save the Cinque Terre from nature's wrath in the future.

PRECAUTIONS

If you're hitting the trails, you'll want to carry water with you, wear sturdy shoes (hiking boots are best), and have a hat and sunscreen handy. ⚠ Check weather reports before you start out; especially in late fall and winter, thunderstorms can send townspeople running for cover and make the shelterless trails slippery and dangerous. Rain in October and November can cause landslides and close the trails. Note that the lesser-used trails aren't as well maintained as Trail No. 2. If you're undertaking the full Trail No. 1 hike, bring something to snack on as well as your water bottle.

ADMISSION

Entrance tickets for use of the trails are available at ticket booths located at the start of each section of Trail No. 2, and at information offices in the Levanto, Monterosso, Vernazza, Corniglia, Manarola, Riomaggiore, and La Spezia train stations.

A one-day pass costs €5, which includes a trail map and a general information leaflet. A one-day Cinque Terre Card costs €4, €12 for the weekend. The card combines park entrance fees with unlimited daily use of the regional train between villages.

Working Cinque Terre's vertical vineyards

GETTING HERE AND AROUND

The local train on the Genoa–La Spezia line stops at each of the Cinque Terre, and runs approximately every 30 minutes. Tickets for each leg of the journey (€1.80–2) are available at the five train stations. In Corniglia, the only one of the Cinque Terre that isn't at sea level, a shuttle service (€1) is provided for those who don't wish to climb (or descend) 300-plus steps that link the train station with the cliff-top town.

Along the Cinque Terre coast two ferry lines operate. From June to September, Golfo Paradiso runs from Genoa and Camogli to Monterosso al Mare and Vernazza. The smaller, but more frequent, Golfo dei Poeti stops at each village from Lerici (east of Riomaggiore) to Monterosso, with the exception of Corniglia, four times a day. A one-day ticket costs €22.

WHEN TO GO

The ideal times to see the Cinque Terre are September and May, when the weather is mild and the summer tourist season isn't in full swing.

SWIMMING & BEACHES

Each town has something that passes for a beach, but there are only two options where you'll find both sand and decent swimming. The more accessible is in Monterosso, opposite the train station; it's equipped with chairs, umbrellas, and snack bars. The other is the secluded, swimwear-optional Guvano Beach, between Corniglia and Vernazza. To reach it from the Corniglia train station, bypass the steps leading up to the village, instead following signs to an abandoned train tunnel. Ring a bell at the tunnel's entrance, and the gate will automatically open; after a dimly lit 10-minute walk, you'll emerge at the beach. Both beaches have a nominal admission fee.

Monterosso al Mare

THE TOWNS

Riomaggiore

At the eastern end of the Cinque Terre, Riomaggiore is built into a river gorge (thus the name, which means "river major") and is easily accessible from La Spezia by train or car. It has a tiny harbor protected by large slabs of alabaster and marble, which serve as as tanning beds for sunbathers, as well as being the site of several outdoor cafés with fine views. According to legend, settlement of Riomaggiore dates far back to the 8th century, when Greek religious refugees came here to escape persecution by the Byzantine emperor.

Manarola

The enchanting pastel houses of Manarola spill down a steep hill overlooking a spectacular turquoise swimming cove and a bustling harbor. The whole town is built on black rock. Above the town, ancient terraces still protect abundant vineyards and olive trees. This village is the center of the wine and olive oil production of the region, and its streets are lined with shops selling local products.

Corniglia

The buildings, narrow lanes, and stairways of Corniglia are strung together amid vineyards high on the cliffs; on a clear day views of the entire coastal strip are excellent. The high perch and lack of harbor make this farming community the most remote of the Cinque Terre. On a pretty pastel square sits the 14th-century church of **San Pietro.** The rose window of marble imported from Carrara is impressive, particularly considering the work required to get it here. ⊠ *Main Sq.* ☎ *0187/3235582* ⊘ *Wed. 4–6, Sun. 10–noon.*

Vernazza

With its narrow streets and small squares, Vernazza is arguably the most charming of the five towns. Because it has the best access to the sea, it became wealthier than its neighbors—as evidenced by the elaborate arcades, loggias, and marblework. The village's pink, slate-roof houses and colorful squares contrast with the remains of the medieval fort and castle, including two towers, in the old town. The Romans first inhabited this rocky spit of land in the 1st century.

Today Vernazza has a fairly lively social scene. It's a great place to refuel with a hearty seafood lunch or linger in a café between links of the hike on Trail No. 2.

Monterosso al Mare

Beautiful beaches, rugged cliffs, crystal-clear turquoise waters, and plentiful small hotels and restaurants make Monterosso al Mare, the largest of the Cinque Terre villages (population 1,730), the busiest in midsummer. The village center bustles high on a hillside. Below, connected by stone steps, are the port and seaside promenade, where there are boats for hire. The medieval tower, Aurora, on the hills of the Cappuccini, separates the ancient part of the village from the more modern part. The village is encircled by hills covered with vineyards and olive groves, and by a forest of scrubby bushes and small trees.

Monterosso has the most festivals of the five villages, starting with the Lemon Feast on the Saturday preceding Ascension Sunday, followed by the Flower Festival of Corpus Christi, celebrated yearly on the second Sunday after Pentecost. During the afternoon, the streets and alleyways of the *centro storico* (historic center) are decorated with thousands of colorful flower petals set in beautiful designs that the evening procession passes over. Finally, the Salted Anchovy and Olive Oil Festival takes place each year during the second weekend of September.

Thursday, the **market** attracts mingled crowds of tourists and villagers from along the coast to shop for everything from pots and pans and underwear to fruits, vegetables, and fish. Often a few stands sell local art and crafts as well as olive oil and wine. ⊠ *Old town center* ⊙ *Thurs. 8–1.*

The **Chiesa di San Francesco,** was built in the 12th century in the Ligurian Gothic style. Its distinctive black stripes and marble rose window make it one of the most photographed sites in the Cinque Terre. ⊠ *Piazza Garibaldi* ☎ *No phone* ✐ *Free* ⊙ *Daily 9–1 and 4–7.*

Main Square, Vernazza

WHERE TO EAT AND STAY

From June through September, reservations are essential if you plan to stay in a hotel or B&B here. *Affitacamere* (rooms for rent in private homes) are a more modest alternative, often indicated by a simple sign on the front door. At agencies in Riomaggiore and Monterosso you can book officially licensed affitacamere. Rooms run the gamut; arrive early for a good selection.

Riomaggiore

$$$ ✕ **La Lanterna.** Chalkboards in front of this small trattoria by the harbor list the day's selection of fresh fish; the set-up seems modest, but this is arguably the finest restaurant in the Cinque Terre. During winter, Chef Massimo teaches at the Culinary Academy in Switzerland; he always returns with new ideas for his menu. When available, their *cozze ripiene* (stuffed mussels) shouldn't be missed. Other offerings may be a touch exotic, such sting ray with Ligurian herbs. ⊠ *Via San Giacomo 10* ☎ *0187/920589* ⊘ *Closed Jan. and 2 wks in Nov.*

Manarola

$ ☎ **Ca' d'Andrean.** If you want to stay in one of the less crowded Cinque Terre offerings, this tiny, simple hotel is one of your best options. White-tile floors cool off the rooms, some of which have balconies. In summer, breakfast, an optional extra at €6 per person, is served in a flower garden. ⊠ *Via Discovolo 101* ☎ *0187/920040* ⊕ *www.cadandrean. it* ⌨ *10 rooms* ⌂ *no a/c, bar* ⊘ *Closed mid-Nov.–mid-Dec.*

Corniglia

$–$$ ☎ **Cecio.** On the outskirts of Corniglia, many of the spotless rooms at the family-run Cecio have spectacular views of the town. The same memorable vista can be enjoyed from the hotel's restaurant, which serves inexpensive and well-prepared local seafood dishes. Try the delicious lasagna with pesto sauce as a first course. ⊠ *Via Serra 58, toward Vernazza* ☎ *0187/812043* ⌨ *12 rooms* ⌂ *In-room: no a/c, no TV (some). In-hotel: restaurant* ❙◯❙ *Breakfast.*

Vernazza

$$$ ✕ **Ristorante Belforte.** High above the sea in one of Vernazza's remaining stone towers is this unique restaurant serving typical Cinque Terre dishes. The prices are high, but it's worth it. People come from all over Liguria for Bel Forte's famous stuffed mussels and insalata di polpo (octopus salad). The setting is magnificent. ⊠ *Via Guidoni 42* ☎ *0187/812222* ⊘ *Closed Tues. and Nov.–Easter.*

DID YOU KNOW?

Tina Manarola is the best spot for purchasing the wine and olive oil produced in the Cinque Terre.

$$$ ✕ **Gambero Rosso.** Relax on Vernazza's main square at this fine trattoria looking out at a church. Enjoy such delectable dishes as shrimp salad, vegetable torte, and squid-ink risotto. The creamy pesto, served atop spaghetti, is some of the best in the area. End your meal with Cinque Terre's own *sciacchetrà,* a dessert wine served with semisweet biscotti. Don't drink it out of the glass—dip the biscotti in the wine instead. ✉ *Piazza Marconi 7* ☎ *0187/812265* ☉ *Closed Mon., Jan., and Feb.*

$$$ ⛱ **La Malà.** A cut above other lodging options in the Cinque Terre, this family-run B&B has only four rooms, and they fill up quickly. The rooms are small but well equipped, with flat screen TVs, a/c, marble showers, and comfortable bedding. Two of the rooms have sea views; the other two face the port of Vernazza. There's a shared terrace literally suspended over the Mediterranean. Book early! ✉ *Giovanni Battista 29* ☎ *334/2875718* ⊕ *www.lamala.it* ↝ *4 rooms* ⚡ *In-room: a/c* ☉ *Closed Jan. 10–Mar.* ⦿ *Breakfast.*

Monterosso al Mare

★ $$$ ✕ **Miki.** Specialties here are anything involving seafood. The *insalata di mare* (seafood salad), with squid and fish, is more than tasty; so are the grilled fish and any pasta with seafood. Miki has a beautiful little garden in the back, perfect for lunch on a sunny day. ✉ *Via Fegina 104* ☎ *0187/817608* ☉ *Closed Nov. and Dec., and Tues. Sept.–July.*

$ ✕ **Enoteca Internazionale.** Located on the main street in centro, this wine bar offers a large variety of vintages, both local from farther afield, plus delicious light fare; its umbrella-covered patio is a perfect spot to recuperate after a day of hiking. The owner, Susanna, is a certified sommelier who's always forthcoming with helpful suggestions on local wines. ✉ *Via Roma 62* ☎ *0187/817278* ☉ *Closed Tues. and Jan–Mar.*

$$ ⛱ **Il Giardino Incantato.** This small B&B in the historic center of Monterosso oozes comfort and Old-World charm. The building dates back to the 16th century and still maintains its wood-beam ceiling and stone walls. Each room has been impeccably restored with modern amenities. Breakfast is served either in your room (on request) or in the lovely private garden under the lemon trees. The owner, Maria Pia, goes out of her way to make you feel at home and whips up a fabulous frittata for breakfast. ✉ *Via Mazzini 18* ☎ *0185/818315* ⊕ *www.ilgiardinoincantato.net* ↝ *3 rooms, 1 junior suite* ⦿ *Breakfast.*

$$$ ⛱ **Porto Roca.** The Cinque Terre's only "high-end" hotel is perched on the famous terraced cliffs, hovering over the magnificent sea below, and thankfully removed from the crowds. The hotel has an old-fashioned feel but the large balconies and panoramic views make it all worth it. There is also a nice restaurant serving very good Ligurian cuisine. Avoid the back rooms as they are dark and have no view. Pros: unobstructed sea views; tranquil position. Cons: some of the rooms could use updating; back-facing rooms can be a bit dark. ✉ *Via Carrone 1* ☎ *0187/817502* ⊕ *www. portoroca.it* ↝ *40 rooms* ⚡ *In-room: a/c (some). In-hotel: restaurant, bar, spa* ⦿ *Breakfast.*

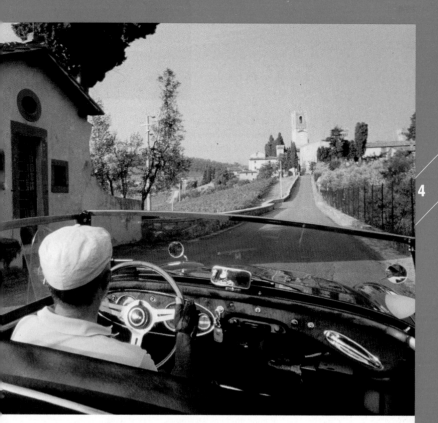

Chianti, Siena, and Central Tuscany

WORD OF MOUTH

"Siena (or Sienna? . . . potato/patatoe). . . . However it's spelled it IS a charming hill town, with emphasis on HILLY, so be sure to have good walking shoes. . . . The bus really is the better option for convenience [traveling to Siena]. The train station for Siena is a couple miles outside the city walls. Additionally San Gimignano is another town well worth day-tripping via bus." —JBX

WELCOME TO CENTRAL TUSCANY

TOP REASONS TO GO

★ **Wine tasting in Chianti:** Sample the fruits of the region's many vineyards at either the wineries or the wine bars found in just about every town.

★ **The Piazza del Campo, Siena:** Sip a cappuccino or enjoy some gelato as you take in this spectacular shell-shaped piazza.

★ **San Gimignano:** Grab a spot at sunset on the steps of the Collegiata as flocks of swallows swoop in and out of the famous medieval towers.

★ **Buying alabaster in Volterra:** Watch the carving of this softly luminous milk-white stone at the shops belonging to local craftspeople.

★ **Cheering the Palio in Siena:** Vie for a spot among thousands to salute the winners of this race, which takes over Siena's main square twice each year.

1 Chianti. The heart of Italy's most famous wine region is dotted with appealing towns. The largest, Greve, comes alive with a bustling local market in its town square every Saturday, while Radda sits on a hilltop in classic Tuscan style, ringed by a 14th-century walkway. Cutting through the region is the Strada Chiantigiana, one of Italy's great drives.

2 Siena. Throughout the Middle Ages Siena competed with Florence for regional supremacy. Today it remains one of Italy's most enchanting medieval towns, with an exceptional Gothic cathedral and a main square, il Campo, that has an almost magical charm.

3 Monteriggioni and Colle di Val d'Elsa. These two sleepy hill towns are pleasing, laid-back stops on the road between Siena and San Gimignano.

4 San Gimignano. From miles away you can spot San Gimignano's soaring medieval "skyscrapers"— towers that were once the ultimate status symbols of the aristocracy.

San Gimignano

5 **Volterra.** Etruscan artifacts and Roman ruins are highlights of this city set in a rugged moonscape of a valley.

GETTING ORIENTED

Undulating hills blanketed with vineyards, groves of silver-green olive trees, and enchanting towns perched on hilltops are the essence of central Tuscany. Siena, with its extraordinary piazza and magnificent cathedral, anchors the southern end of the region. Cypress-lined roads wind their way west to San Gimignano and Volterra, and north through the Chianti district.

Piazza del Campo, Siena

Updated
by Peter
Blackman

COUNTRY ROADS WIND AROUND CYPRESS trees on hilltops that often appear to catch and hold onto the clouds. Planted vineyards, fields, and orchards turn those curving hills into a patchwork of colors and textures that have inspired artists and delighted travelers for centuries. Sitting majestically in the midst of all this natural splendor is Siena, longtime rival of Florence and one of Italy's best-preserved medieval cities. Other hilltop towns will beckon you as well: San Gimignano, with its lofty towers; the ancient city of Volterra, once capital of a flourishing Etruscan state; and myriad charming villages dotting the rolling hills of Chianti.

The rolling hills are the region's most famous geographic feature, and you can expect to do a lot of winding up and down on the beautifully panoramic roads that link the area's hill towns. The narrow medieval streets of these old town centers are mostly closed to traffic. Park outside the city walls and walk in. Keep in mind that roads often lack shoulders in these parts, and that gas stations are rarely open Sunday.

Siena fills to the brim in the weeks surrounding the running of the Palio on July 2 and August 16, when prices, crowds, and commotion are at their highest. Between May and late September hotels and restaurants throughout the region fill up and foreign license plates and rental cars cram the roads. There's a reason for the crush: summer is a glorious time to be driving in the hills and sitting on terraces. If you want fewer crowds, try visiting during spring or fall. Spring can be especially spectacular, with blooming poppy fields, bursts of yellow broom, and wild irises growing by the side of the road. Fall is somewhat more soothing, when all those colors typically associated with Tuscany—burnt sienna, warm ocher, mossy forest greens—predominate.

In the winter months you may have towns mostly to yourself, although the choices for hotels and restaurants can be a bit more limited than when the season is in full swing. From November through mid-March it's fairly difficult to find a room in San Gimignano and Volterra: plan accordingly.

PLANNING

MAKING THE MOST OF YOUR TIME

Central Tuscany has an enticing landscape, one that invites you to follow its meandering roads to see where they might lead. Perhaps you'll come to a farmhouse selling splendid olive oil or one of the superb wines produced in the region; or perhaps you'll arrive at a medieval *pieve* (country church), an art-filled abbey, a *castello* (castle), or a restaurant where a flower-bedecked terrace looks out on a spectacular panorama.

Whatever road you take, **Siena,** Italy's most enchanting medieval city, is the one stop that's mandatory. The perfectly preserved *centro storico*, with its medieval palaces, is a delight to walk around; vehicle traffic is banned. Once in the region, however, there are plenty of other places to explore: **San Gimignano** is known as the "medieval Manhattan" because of its enormous towers, built by rival families, that still stand today. Like Siena, it benefited from commerce and trade along the pilgrimage

The classic rolling hills of central Tuscany

routes, as the wonderful art in its churches and museums attests. With additional time, consider venturing farther afield to **Volterra,** with a stop in **Colle di Val d'Elsa** along the way.

GETTING HERE AND AROUND

BICYCLE TRAVEL

In spring, summer, and fall, cyclists are as much a part of the landscape as the cypress trees. Many are on weeklong tours, but it's also possible to rent bikes or to join afternoon or day tours.

I Bike Italy. I Bike Italy leads one-day rides through the Chianti countryside. ⊠ *Via dei Lamberti 1, Florence* ☏ *055/0123994* ⊕ *www.ibikeitaly. com.*

Marco Ramuzzi. Marco Ramuzzi rents bikes by the day or week from his shop in Greve, and organizes tours in the surrounding area. ⊠ *Via Stecchi 23, Greve in Chianti* ☏ *055/853037* ⊕ *www.ramuzzi.com.*

BUS TRAVEL

Buses are a reliable but time-consuming means of getting around the region because they often stop in every town.

Tra-In covers much of the territory south of Florence, and the province of Siena. ☏ *0577/204225 Siena ticket office* ⊕ *www.trainspa.it.*

SENA provides regular daily three-hour service between Siena and Rome. ☏ *0861/1991900.*

SITA has regular service between Florence and Siena (one hour) as well as to numerous towns in Chianti. ☏ *0577/204246, 800/373760 toll-free in Italy* ⊕ *www.sitabus.it.*

CPT has infrequent buses between Volterra and Colle di Val d'Elsa, and also connects Volterra with the nearest train station in Saline. ☎ *050/505511* ⊕ *www.cpt.pisa.it.*

CAR TRAVEL

The best way to discover central Tuscany is by car, as its beauty often reveals itself along the road less traveled. The Certosa exit from the A1 highway (the Autostrada del Sole, running between Rome and Florence) provides direct access to the area. The Florence–Siena Superstrada (no number) is a four-lane, divided road with exits onto smaller country roads. The Via Cassia (SR2) winds its way south from Florence to Siena, along the western edge of the Chianti region. The superstrada is more direct, but much less scenic, than the SR2, and it can have a lot of traffic, especially on Sunday evenings. The Strada Chiantigiana (SR222) cuts through Chianti, east of the superstrada, in a curvaceous path past vineyards and countryside.

From Poggibonsi, a modern town to the west of the superstrada, you can quickly reach San Gimignano and then take the SR68 toward Volterra. The SR68 continues westward to join the Via Aurelia (SR1), linking Pisa with Rome.

TRAIN TRAVEL

Traveling between Florence and Siena by train is quick and convenient; trains make the 80-minute trip several times a day, with a change in Empoli sometimes required. Train service also runs between Siena and Chiusi–Chianciano Terme, where you can make Rome–Florence connections. Siena's train station is 2 km (1 mile) north of the centro storico, but cabs and city buses are readily available.

Other train service within the region is limited. For instance, the nearest station to Volterra is at Saline di Volterra, 10 km (6 miles) to the west. From Siena, trains run north to Poggibonsi and southeast to Sinalunga. Trains run from Chiusi-Chianciano Terme to Siena (one hour) with stops in Montepulciano Scalo, Sinalunga, and Asciano. There are no trains to San Gimignano, Monteriggioni, or the Chianti wine region.

Ferrovie dello Stato. You can check the website of the state railway, the Ferrovie dello Stato, for information. You can also get information and tickets at most travel agencies. ☎ *892021 toll-free within Italy* ⊕ *www. trenitalia.com.*

HOTELS

Siena, San Gimignano, and Volterra are among the most-visited towns in Tuscany, so there's no lack of choice for hotels across the price ranges. You can often stay right on the main square. The best accommodations, however, are often a couple of miles outside town. If you're staying a week, you have enough time to rent an *agriturismo (working farm)* apartment. Stock up your refrigerator with local groceries and wines, go for hikes in the hills, and take leisurely day trips to the main towns of the region.

DINING AND LODGING PRICE CATEGORIES (IN EUROS)					
	¢	$	$$	$$$	$$$$
Restaurants	under €15	€15–€25	€25–€35	€35–€45	over €45
Hotels	under €70	€70–€110	€110–€160	€160–€220	over €220

Restaurant prices are for a first course (*primo*), second course (*secondo*), and dessert (*dolce*). Hotel prices are for two people in a standard double room in high season, including tax and service.

VISITOR INFORMATION

The tourist information office in Greve is an excellent source for general information about the Chianti wine region and its hilltop towns. In Siena the centrally located tourist office, in Piazza del Campo, has information about Siena and its province. Both offices book hotel rooms for a nominal fee. Offices in smaller towns can also be a good place to check if you need last-minute accommodations.

Tourist bureaus in larger towns are typically open from 8:30 to 1 and 3:30 to 6 or 7; bureaus in villages are generally open from Easter until early November, but usually remain closed Saturday afternoon and Sunday.

CHIANTI

This is the heartland: both sides of the Strada Chiantigiana, or SR222, are embraced by glorious panoramic views of vineyards, olive groves, and castle towers. Traveling south from Florence, you first reach the aptly named one-street-town of Strada in Chianti. Farther south, the number of vineyards on either side of the road dramatically increases—as do the signs inviting you in for a free tasting of wine. Beyond Strada lies Greve in Chianti, completely surrounded by wineries and filled with wineshops. There's art to be had as well: Passignano, west of Greve, has an abbey that shelters a 15th-century *Last Supper* by Domenico and Davide Ghirlandaio. Farther still, along the Strada Chiantigiana, are Panzano and Castellina in Chianti, both hill towns. It's from near Panzano and Castellina that branch roads head to the other main towns of eastern Chianti: Radda in Chianti, Gaiole in Chianti, and Castelnuovo Berardenga.

The Strada Chiantigiana gets crowded during the high season, but no one is in a hurry. The slow pace gives you time to soak up the beautiful scenery.

GREVE IN CHIANTI

40 km (25 miles) north of Siena, 28 km (17½ miles) south of Florence.

If there is a capital of Chianti, it is Greve, a friendly market town with no shortage of cafés, *enoteche* (wine bars), and crafts shops lining its streets.

CENTRAL TUSCANY, PAST AND PRESENT

It may be hard to imagine that much of central Tuscany was once the battleground of warring Sienese and Florentine armies, but until Florence finally defeated Siena in 1555, the enchanting walled cities of this gentle area were strategic-defensive outposts in a series of seemingly never-ending wars.

Since the 1960s many British and northern Europeans have relocated here: they've been drawn to the unhurried life, balmy climate, and old villages. They've bought and restored farmhouses, many given up by the young heirs who decided not to continue life on the farm and instead found work in cities. There are so many Britons, in fact, that the area has been nicknamed Chiantishire. But don't let this be a deterrent to a visit: the whole area still proudly exerts its strongly Tuscan character.

GETTING HERE

Driving from Florence or Siena, Greve is easily reached via the Strada Chiantigiana (SR222). SITA buses travel frequently between Florence and Greve. Tra-In and SITA buses connect Siena and Greve, but a direct trip is virtually impossible. There is no train service to Greve.

VISITOR INFORMATION

Greve in Chianti tourism office ⊠ *Piazza Matteotti 11* ☎ *055/8546299.*

EXPLORING

Piazza Matteotti. Greve's gently sloping and asymmetrical central piazza is surrounded by an attractive arcade with shops of all kinds. In the center stands a statue of the discoverer of New York harbor, Giovanni da Verrazano (circa 1480–1527). Check out the lively market held here on Saturday morning.

Montefioralle. A tiny hilltop hamlet, about 2 km (1 mile) west of Greve in Chianti, Montefioralle is the ancestral home of Amerigo Vespucci (1454–1512), the mapmaker, navigator, and explorer who named America. (His niece Simonetta may have been the inspiration for Sandro Botticelli's *Birth of Venus,* painted sometime in the 1480s.)

Chiesa di San Donato a Lamole. The tiny village of Lamole contains this Romanesque church that was greatly modified in 1860; the only remnant of its earlier incarnation can be found in its simple facade. Inside is a 14th-century altarpiece, as well as a curious side chapel on the right that is decorated with rather garish 20th-century religious works. From Greve in Chianti, drive south on SR222 for about 1 km (½ mile); take a left and follow signs for Lamole. It's about 10 km (6 miles) southeast of Greve. ⊠ *Località Lamole in Chianti 1* ☎ *055/8547000* ☉ *Daily 9–12:30 and 4–6:30.*

WHERE TO EAT

¢ ✕ **Da Padellina.** Locals don't flock to this restaurant on the outskirts
TUSCAN of Strada in Chianti for the art on the walls, some of it questionable, most of it kitsch, but for the *bistecca fiorentina* (Florentine beefsteak). As big as a breadboard and served rare, one of these justly renowned steaks is enough to feed a family of four, with doggy bags willingly

provided if required! First courses are typical, desserts are standard, but the wine list is a varied and extensive surprise. Outdoor seating on the upstairs terrace provides great views of the surrounding countryside. ✉ *Via Corso del Popolo 54, 10 km (6 miles) north of Greve, Località Strada in Chianti* ☎ *055/858388* ⊕ *www.ristorantedapadellina.com* ⊘ *Closed Tues.*

¢ ✕ **Enoteca Fuoripiazza.** Detour off Greve's flower-strewn main square for food that relies heavily on local ingredients (like cheese and salami produced nearby). The lengthy wine list provides a bewildering array of choices to pair with *affettati misti* (a plate of cured meats) or one of their primi—the *pici* (a thick, short noodle) is deftly prepared here. All the dishes are made with great care. ✉ *Via I Maggio, Greve in Chianti* ☎ *055/8546313* ⊘ *Closed Mon.*

TUSCAN

¢ ✕ **Il Caminetto.** The pasta is all homemade at this small, cozy country restaurant; the *gnocchi ripieno ai funghi porcini* (potato dumplings stuffed with porcini mushrooms) are a real treat. There's a terrace for summer dining under the shade of lime trees. ✉ *Via della Montagnola 52, 11 km (7 miles) north of Greve, Località Strada in Chianti* ☎ *055/8588909* ⊘ *Closed Tues. No lunch Mon.–Sat.*

TUSCAN

¢ ✕ **Locanda il Gallo.** Terrific thin-crust pizzas come out of the wood-burning oven here, but the menu also includes Tuscan favorites, such as Florentine beefsteak and pasta with mushrooms or truffles. The large, informal, country dining rooms have stone walls and wood-beam ceilings, and there's a veranda for dining outside in summer. The restaurant is about 4 km (2½ miles) north of Greve in Chianti. ✉ *Via Lando Conti 18, Località Chiocchio* ☎ *055/8572266* ⊕ *www.locandailgallo.it* ⊘ *Closed Tues. and Nov.–Mar.*

TUSCAN

$ ✕ **Ristoro di Lamole.** Although off the beaten path, this place is worth the effort to find—up a winding road lined with olive trees and vineyards. The view from the outdoor terrace is divine, as is the simple, exquisitely prepared Tuscan cuisine. Start with the bruschetta drizzled with olive oil or the sublime *verdure sott'olio* (marinated vegetables) before moving on to any of the fine secondi. The kitchen has a way with *coniglio* (rabbit); don't pass it up if it's on the menu. ✉ *Via di Lamole 6, Località Lamole in Chianti* ☎ *055/8547050* ⊕ *www.ristorodilamole.it* ⊘ *Closed Wed. and Nov.–Apr.*

TUSCAN
★

WHERE TO STAY

For expanded hotel reviews, visit Fodors.com.

$ ⊞ **Albergo del Chianti.** At a corner of the Piazza Matteotti, this ideally situated hotel has rooms with views of the town square or out over the tile rooftops toward the surrounding hills. **Pros:** central location; best value in Greve. **Cons:** rooms facing the piazza can be noisy; small bathrooms. ✉ *Piazza Matteotti 86* ☎ *055/853763* ⊕ *www.albergodelchianti.it* ⤴ *16 rooms* ⌂ *In-hotel: restaurant, bar, pool* ⊘ *Closed Jan.* ⎮⊙⎮ *Breakfast.*

$$ ⊞ **Castello Vicchiomaggio.** Stay in a fortified castle built more than a millennium ago (and rebuilt during the Renaissance). **Pros:** spacious rooms; spectacular views; very helpful staff. **Cons:** some rooms lack air-conditioning; you need a car to get around. ✉ *Via Vicchiomaggio 4,*

Località Vicchiomaggio ☎ *055/854079* ⊕ *www.vicchiomaggio.it* 🔀 *7 rooms, 8 apartments, 1 house* ⚐ *In-room: a/c, safe, kitchen, Wi-Fi. In-hotel: restaurant, pool.*

$$$$

Fodor's Choice

★

🏨 **Villa Bordoni.** David and Catherine Gardner, Scottish expats, have transformed a ramshackle 16th-century villa into a stunning little hotel nestled in the hills above Greve. **Pros:** splendidly isolated; beautiful decor; wonderful hosts. **Cons:** on a long and bumpy dirt road; need a car to get around. ⊠ *Via San Cresci 31/32, Località Mezzuola* ☎ *055/8547453* ⊕ *www.villabordoni.com* 🔀 *8 rooms, 3 suites* ⚐ *In-room: safe, Wi-Fi. In-hotel: restaurant, pool, parking* ⊙ *Closed 3 wks in Jan. and Feb.* ⦿*Breakfast.*

$$

Fodor's Choice

★

🏨 **Villa Il Poggiale.** Renaissance gardens, beautiful rooms with high ceilings and elegant furnishings, a panoramic pool, and expert staff are just a few of the things that make a stay at this 16th-century villa memorable. **Pros:** beautiful gardens and panoramic setting; elegant historical building; exceptionally professional staff. **Cons:** a little isolated, making private transportation necessary; some rooms face a country road and may be noisy during the day. ⊠ *Via Empolese 69, 20 km (12 miles) northwest of Greve, San Casciano Val di Pesa* ☎ *055/828311* ⊕ *www.villailpoggiale.it* 🔀 *20 rooms, 4 suites* ⚐ *In-room: Wi-Fi. In-hotel: restaurant, bar, pool, tennis court* ⊙ *Closed Nov.–Easter* ⦿*Breakfast.*

$$$

🏨 **Villa Vignamaggio.** Reputed to be the birthplace of the woman made famous by Leonardo da Vinci's *Mona Lisa*, and used as the setting of Kenneth Branagh's 1993 film, *Much Ado About Nothing*, Villa Vignamaggio has origins in the 14th century. **Pros:** unbeatable views; informative wine tastings. **Cons:** no elevator to third floor; private transportation required. ⊠ *Via Petriolo 5, Località Vicchiomaggio* ☎ *055/854661* ⊕ *www.vignamaggio.com* 🔀 *9 rooms, 16 suites, 13 apartments, 2 cottages* ⚐ *In-room: kitchen. In-hotel: restaurant, pool, tennis court, business center, some pets allowed* ⊙ *Closed mid-Nov.–mid-Mar.* ⦿*Breakfast.*

PASSIGNANO

8 km (5 miles) south of Mercatale, 29 km (18 miles) south of Florence.

Other than its Romanesque abbey and the few houses clustered around it, there is very little to actually see in this tiny hamlet. But the panoramic setting and the beautiful natural surroundings do make a short side-trip recommendable.

GETTING HERE

By car, take the Tavernelle exit from the Florence–Siena Superstrada. Direct bus or train service is not available.

EXPLORING

Badia a Passignano (*Abbey of Passignano*). One of the finest and best-preserved works of art in Italy is in the dining hall of the towering 11th-century Abbey of Passignano: a stunningly massive, 21-foot-wide *Last Supper* (1476) by Domenico and Davide Ghirlandaio. The monastery's church of San Michele Arcangelo has a 13th-century sculpture of Saint

EATING WELL IN CENTRAL TUSCANY

Chianti restaurants serve Tuscan dishes similar to those in Florence, but they also have local specialties, such as pasta creations made with *pici* (a long, thick, hand-rolled spaghetti). You'll find other pasta dishes, like *pappardelle alla lepre* (a long, flat type of pasta noodle with hare sauce), and soups, such as *pappa al pomodoro* (a thick tomato soup) and *ribollita* (Tuscan bread soup), on most menus.

Panzanella, a salad of tomato, basil, bread, and onion, is a common first course on summer menus. Many recipes are from the *nonna* (grandmother) of the restaurant's owner, handed down through time but never written down.

The so-called *tonno del Chianti* (Chianti tuna) is really a dish of tender flakes of rabbit meat that look and, believe it or not, taste like tuna—it's actually delicious. Pecorino, a soft sheep's-milk cheese, makes it onto many menus in pasta dishes and appetizers.

The Sienese often add a subtle flair of extra herbs and garlic to their rendition of traditional Tuscan fare. Antipasti (usually made of the simplest ingredients) are extremely satisfying.

A typical starter might be a plate of excellent locally cured meats, such as those made from *cinta senese*, a species of domestic pig rescued from near extinction. *Verdure sott'olio* (marinated vegetables) are usually artichokes, red peppers, carrots, celery, cauliflower, olives, and capers marinated in olive oil. Second courses are traditionally game meats, and *piccione* (pigeon), served either roasted or stuffed and baked, is commonly on the menu.

After your meal, try some delicious amber-color *vin santo*, a sweet dessert wine with *cantuccini* (hard almond cookies), which are dunked once or twice in the glass. It's made from choice white Trebbiano Toscano or Malvasia del Chianti grapes and is aged in small, partially filled oak barrels. Other favorite Sienese sweets include *ricciarelli*, succulent almond-flavor cookies.

Excellent extra-virgin olive oil is produced throughout the region, and the best way to taste it is in the form of a *fettunta* (oily slice), a thick slice of toasted Tuscan bread rubbed with garlic, sprinkled with salt, and dripping with olive oil. Asking for a plate or bowl to sample olive oil with bread before a meal is a dead giveaway that you're a tourist—it's the invention of American restaurateurs.

Michael slaying the dragon. At this writing, the abbey was closed for restoration, but even if you can't get in to see the *Last Supper*, it's still worth the drive to walk on the beautiful hillsides. ⊠ *Via Passignano 20* ☎ *055/8071622.*

WHERE TO EAT

¢ ✕ **La Cantinetta di Rignana.** On Sunday afternoons this old-fashioned

ITALIAN trattoria is teeming with lively Italian families. Grilled meats are the

★ specialty of the house. If you have room for dessert, the kitchen whips up a mean tiramisu. Enjoy the farmhouse feel of the dining room, or choose a shady table in the garden overlooking the vineyards. The

Continued on page 211

GRAPE ESCAPES
THE PLEASURES OF TUSCAN WINE

The vineyards stretching across the landscape of Tuscany may look like cinematic backdrops, but in fact they're working farms, and they produce some of Italy's best wines. No matter whether you're a wine novice or a connoisseur, there's great pleasure to be had from exploring this lush terrain, visiting the vineyards, and uncorking a bottle for yourself.

GETTING TO KNOW TUSCAN WINE

Most of the wine produced in Tuscany is red (though there are some notable whites as well), and most Tuscan reds are made primarily from one type of grape, sangiovese. That doesn't mean, however, that all wines here are the same. God (in this case Bacchus) is in the details: differences in climate, soil, and methods of production result in wines with several distinct personalities.

Chianti

Chianti is the most famous name in Tuscan wine, but what exactly the name means is a little tricky. It once identified wines produced in the region extending from just south of Florence to just north of Siena. In the mid-20th century, the official Chianti zone was expanded to include a large portion of central Tuscany. That area is divided into eight subregions. **Chianti Classico** is the name given to the original zone, which makes up 17,000 of the 42,000 acres of Chianti-producing vineyards.

WINE REGIONS OF CENTRAL TUSCANY

Classico wines, which bear the *gallo nero* (black rooster) logo on their labels, are the most highly regarded Chiantis (with **Rùfina** running second), but that doesn't mean Classicos are always superior. All Chiantis are strictly regulated (they must be a minimum 75% to 80% sangiovese, with other varieties blended in to add nuance), and they share a strong, woodsy character that's well suited to Tuscan food. It's a good strategy to drink the local product—**Colli Senesi Chianti** when in Siena, for example. The most noticeable, and costly, difference comes when a Chianti is from *riserva* (reserve) stock, meaning it's been aged for at least two years.

DOC & DOCG The designations "DOC" and "DOCG"—Denominazione di Origine Controllata (e Garantita)—mean a wine comes from an established region and adheres to rigorous standards of production. Ironically, the esteemed Super Tuscans are labeled *vini da tavola* (table wines), the least prestigious designation, because they don't use traditional grape blends.

Brunello di Montalcino

The area surrounding the hill town of Montalcino, to the south of Siena, is drier and warmer than the Chianti regions, and it produces the most powerful of the sangiovese-based wines. Regulations stipulate that Brunello di Montalcino be made entirely from sangiovese grapes (no blending) and aged at least four years. **Rosso di Montalcino** is a younger, less complex, less expensive Brunello.

The Super Tuscans

Beginning in the 1970s, some winemakers, chafing at the regulations imposed on established Tuscan wine varieties, began blending and aging wines in innovative ways. Thus were born the so-called Super Tuscans. These pricey, French oak–aged wines are admired for their high quality, led by such star performers as **Sassicaia**, from the Maremma region, and **Tignanello**, produced at the Tenuta Marchesi Antinori near Badia a Passignano. Purists, however, lament the loss of local identity resulting from the Super Tuscans' use of nonnative grape varieties such as cabernet sauvignon and merlot.

Vino Nobile di Montepulciano

East of Montalcino is Montepulciano, the town at the heart of the third, and smallest, of Tuscany's top wine districts.

Blending regulations aren't as strict for Vino Nobile as for Chianti and Brunello, and as a result it has a wider range of characteristics. Broadly speaking, though, Vino Nobile is a cross between Chianti and Brunello—less acidic than the former and softer than the latter. It also has a less pricey sibling, **Rosso di Montepulciano**.

The Whites

Most whites from Tuscany are made from **trebbiano** grapes, which produce a wine that's light and refreshing but not particularly aromatic or flavorful—it may hit the spot on a hot afternoon, but it doesn't excite connoisseurs.

Golden-hewed **Vernaccia di San Gimignano** is a local variety with more limited production but greater personality—it's the star of Tuscan whites. Winemakers have also brought chardonnay and sauvignon grapes to the region, resulting in wines that, like some Super Tuscans, are pleasant to drink but short on local character.

TOURING & TASTING IN TUSCAN WINE COUNTRY

Strade del Vino di Toscana

Tuscany has visitor-friendly wineries, but the way you go about visiting is a bit different here from what it is in California or France. Many wineries welcome drop-ins for a tasting, but for a tour you usually need to make an appointment a few days in advance. There are several approaches you can take, depending on how much time you have and how serious you are about wine:

PLAN 1: FULL IMMERSION. Make an appointment to tour one of the top wineries (see our recommendations on the next page), and you'll get the complete experience: half a day of strolling through vineyards, talking grape varieties, and tasting wine, often accompanied by food. Groups are small; in spring and fall, it may be just you and the winemaker. The cost is usually €10 to €15 per person, but can go up to €40 if a meal is included. Remember to specify a tour in English.

PLAN 2: SEMI-ORGANIZED. If you want to spend a few hours going from vineyard to vineyard, make your first stop one of the local tourist information offices—they're great resources for maps, tasting itineraries, and personalized advice about where to visit. The offices in **Greve**, **Montalcino**, and **Montepulciano** are the best equipped. **Enoteche** (for more about them, turn the page) can also be good places to pick up tips about where to go for tastings.

PLAN 3: SPONTANEOUS. Along Tuscany's country roads you'll see signs for wineries offering **vendita diretta** (direct sales) and **degustazioni** (tastings). For a taste of the local product with some atmosphere thrown in, a spontaneous visit is a perfectly viable approach. You may wind up in a simple shop or an elaborate tasting room; either way, there's a fair chance you'll sample something good. Expect a small fee for a three-glass tasting.

THE PICK OF THE VINEYARDS

Within the Chianti Classico region, these wineries should be at the top of your to-visit list, whether you're dropping in for a taste or making a full tour. (Tours require reservations unless otherwise indicated.)

Badia a Coltibuono
(✉ Gaiole in Chianti ☎ 0577/749498 ⊕ www.coltibuono.com). Along with an extensive prelunch tour and tasting, there are shorter afternoon tours, no reservation required, starting on the hour from 2 to 5. (See "Radda in Chianti" in this chapter.)

Castello di Fonterutoli
(✉ Castellina in Chianti ☎ 0577/73571 ⊕ www.fonterutoli.it). Hour-long tours include a walk through the neighboring village.

Castello di Volpaia
(✉ Radda in Chianti ☎ 0577/738066 ⊕ www.volpaia.com). The castle is part of the tiny town of Volpaia, perched above Radda.

Castello di Verrazzano
(✉ Via S. Martino in Valle 12, Greve in Chianti ☎ 055/854243 ⊕ www.verrazzano.com). Tours here take you down to the cellars, through the gardens, and into the woods in search of wild boar.

Villa Vignamaggio
(✉ Via Petriolo 5, Greve in Chianti ☎ 055/854661 ⊕ www.vignamaggio.com). Along with a wine tour, you can spend the night at this villa where Mona Lisa is believed to have been born. (See "Where to Stay" under "Greve in Chianti" in this chapter.)

Rocca delle Màcie
(✉ Località Le Macìe 45, Castellina in Chianti ☎ 0577/732236 ⊕ www.roccadellemacie.com). A full lunch or dinner can be incorporated into your tasting here.

Castello di Brolio
(✉ Gaiole in Chianti ☎ 0577/730220 ⊕ www.ricasoli.it). One of Tuscany's most impressive castles also has a centuries-old winemaking tradition. (See "Radda in Chianti" in this chapter.)

REMEMBER ⚠

Always have a designated driver when you're touring and tasting. Vineyards are usually located off narrow, curving roads. Full sobriety is a must behind the wheel.

4

IN FOCUS GRAPE ESCAPES

MORE TUSCAN WINE RESOURCES

Enoteche: Wine Shops

The word *enoteca* in Italian can mean "wine store," "wine bar," or both. In any event, *enoteche* (the plural, pronounced "ay-no-*tek*-ay") are excellent places to sample and buy Tuscan wines, and they're also good sources of information about local wineries. There are scores to choose from. These are a few of the best:

Enoteca Italiana, Siena (Fortezza Medicea, Viale Maccari ☎ 0577/288497 ⊕ www. enoteca-italiana.it). The only one of its kind, this *enoteca* represents all the producers of DOC and DOCG wines in Italy and stocks over 400 labels. Wine by the glass and snacks are available.

Enoteca Osticcio, Montalcino (✉ Via Matteotti 23 ☎ 0577/848271 ⊕ www. osticcio.com). There are more than one thousand labels in stock. With one of the best views in Montalcino, it is also a very pleasant place to sit and meditate over a glass of Brunello.

Enoteca del Gallo Nero, Greve in Chianti (✉ Piazzetta S. Croce 8 ☎ 055/853297). This is one of the best stocked *enoteche* in the Chianti region.

La Dolce Vita, Montepulciano (Via di Voltaia nel Corso 80/82 ☎ 0578/757872). An elegantly restored monastery is home to the excellent enoteca in the upper part of Montepulciano, which has a wide selction of wines by the glass.

Wine on the Web

Tuscan wine country is well represented on the Internet. A good place for an overview is ⊕ www.terreditoscana.regione. toscana.it. (Click on "Le Strade del Vino"; the page that opens next will give you the option of choosing an English-language version.) This site shows 14 *strade del vino* (wine roads) that have been mapped out by consortiums representing major wine districts (unfortunately, Chianti Classico isn't included), along with recommended itineraries. You'll also find links to the consortium Web sites, where you can dig up more detailed information on touring. The Chianti Classico consortium's site is ⊕ www.chianticlassico.com. The Vino Nobile di Montepulciano site is ⊕ www.vinonobiledimontepulciano.it, and Brunello di Montalcino is ⊕ www. consorziobrunellodimontalcino.it. All have English versions.

restaurant is 4 km (2 miles) west of Passignano. ✉ *Via di Rignana 15, 4, Località Rignana* ☎ *055/852601* ⊕ *www.lacantinettadirignana. it* ⌕ *Reservations essential* ⊗ *Closed Tues.*

\$\$ **ITALIAN** **★**
✕ **Osteria di Passignano.** In an ancient wine cellar owned by the Antinori family—who also happen to own much of what you see in these parts—is a sophisticated restaurant ably run by chef Marcello Crini and his attentive staff. The menu changes seasonally; traditional Tuscan cuisine is given a delightful twist through the use of unexpected herbs. Particularly tantalizing is the *filetto di vitello alle spezie* (spiced veal fillet), served with roast tomatoes and beans flavored with sage. The extensive wine list includes local vintages as well as numerous international labels. Daylong cooking courses are also available. ✉ *Via Passignano 33* ☎ *055/8071278* ⊕ *www.osteriadipassignano.com* ⊗ *Closed Sun., 3 wks in Jan., and 1 wk in Aug.*

¢ **TUSCAN**
✕ **Ristoro L'Antica Scuderia.** Across the street from the abbey and run by the same family for more than 30 years, this once simple eatery in what were once the monk's stables has undergone a complete face-lift. The interior is decorated along modern-elegant lines, and the menu, while thoroughly based on traditional cuisine, is filled with creative interpretations. The *tagliolini al tartuffo* (pasta with truffles) is delicious, the *tagliata al rosmarino* (grilled sliced beef with rosemary) excellent, and the wine list superb. Pizza is also available, but only at dinner time. Shaded, outdoor seating on the restaurant's stepped terrace provides a pleasant setting for dinner on a warm summer's evening. ✉ *Via di Passignao 17* ☎ *055/80716233* ⊕ *www.ristorolanticascuderia.com* ⊗ *Closed Tues.*

PANZANO

7 km (4½ miles) south of Greve in Chianti, 36 km (22 miles) south of Florence.

The magnificent views of the valleys of the Pesa and Greve rivers easily make Panzano one of the prettiest stops in Chianti. The triangular Piazza Bucciarelli is the heart of the new town. A short stroll along Via Giovanni da Verrazzano brings you up to the old town, Panzano Alto, which is still partly surrounded by medieval walls. The town's 13th-century castle is now almost completely absorbed by later buildings (its central tower is now a private home).

GETTING HERE

From Florence or Siena, Panzano is easily reached by car along the Strada Chiantigiana (SR222). SITA buses travel frequently between Florence and Panzano. From Siena, the journey by bus is extremely difficult because SITA and Tra-In do not coordinate their schedules. There is no train service to Panzano.

EXPLORING

Santa Maria Assunta. Situated next to the castle in the upper part of town, this church was completely rebuilt in the 19th century. In the small chapel to the right of the nave is an Annunciation attributed to Michele di Ridolfo del Ghirlandaio (1503–77). ✉ *Via Castellana 6* ⊗ *Daily 7–noon and 4–6.*

San Leolino. Ancient even by Chianti standards, this hilltop church probably dates from the 10th century, but was completely rebuilt in the Romanesque style sometime in the 13th century. It has a 14th-century cloister worth seeing. The 16th-century terra-cotta tabernacles are attributed to Giovanni della Robbia, and there's also a remarkable triptych (attributed to the Master of Panzano) that was executed sometime in the mid-14th century. Open days and hours are unpredictable; check with the tourist office in Greve in Chianti for the latest. ⊠ *Località San Leolino, 3 km (2 miles) south of Panzano* ☎ *055/8546299.*

WHERE TO EAT

¢ ✕ **Dario +.** Local butcher and restaurateur, Dario Cecchini, has extended
INTERNATIONAL his empire of meat to include this space located directly above his butcher's shop. Here, you'll find only two items on the menu: the *Dario +*, a half-pound burger in a crisp crumb crust served with roast potatoes and onions; and the *Welcome*, four different dishes of beef and pork served with fresh garden vegetables. Both are a nice change from the more standard options found at restaurants throughout Chianti. Outdoor seating is available in summer, but get here early—it's enormously popular. Enter from the public parking area behind the restaurant. ⊠ *Via XX Luglio 11, Panzano* ☎ *055/852176* ⊕ *www.dariocecchini. com* ⚐ *Reservations not accepted* ⊗ *Closed Sun.*

¢ ✕ **Enoteca Baldi.** Sample the local *vino* while satisfying your appetite
WINE BAR with simply prepared and presented bruschetta, soups, and pastas. In summer a few tables are set in the shade under the trees in the town's main square. ⊠ *Piazza Bucciarelli 26* ☎ *055/852843.*

$ ✕ **Montagliari.** This ancient stone farmhouse is the place to go for very
TUSCAN tasty Tuscan food. Enjoy your meal in the courtyard, or, when the temperature drops, the main dining room with a farm-style fireplace. The *peposo* (beef stew laced with black pepper) is particularly piquant; the *papardelle al cinghiale* (flat noodles with a wild boar sauce) delightfully fragrant. The wine list, particularly strong on local varieties, includes the farm's own Chianti Classico. ⊠ *Via Montagliari 29* ☎ *055/852014* ⊕ *www.montagliari.it* ⚐ *Reservations essential* ⊗ *Closed Mon. and early Jan.–late Feb.*

¢ ✕ **Solociccia.** "Abandon all hope, ye who enter here," announces the
TUSCAN menu, "you're in the hands of a butcher." Indeed you are, for this restaurant is the creation of Dario Cecchini, Panzano's local merchant of meat. Served at communal tables, the set meal (€30) consists of no less than six meat courses, chosen at Dario's discretion. They are accompanied by seasonal vegetables, white beans with olive oil, and focaccia bread. Though Cecchini emphasizes that steak is never on the menu, this lively, crowded place is definitely not for vegetarians. The entrance is on Via XX Luglio. ⊠ *Via Chiantigiana 5* ☎ *055/852727* ⊕ *www.solociccia. it* ⚐ *Reservations essential* ⊗ *Closed Mon.–Wed. No dinner Sun.*

WHERE TO STAY

For expanded hotel reviews, visit Fodors.com.

$$$$ ⊡ **Villa Le Barone.** Once the home of the Viviani della Robbia fam-
Fodor's Choice ily, this 16th-century villa in a grove of ancient cypress trees retains
★ many aspects of a private country dwelling. **Pros:** beautiful location;

wonderful restaurant; great base for exploring the region. **Cons:** rooms vary in size; 20-minute walk to nearest town. ✉ *Via San Leolino 19* ☎ *055/852621* ⊕ *www.villalebarone.com* ⤳ *28 rooms* ⚒ *In-room: no TV. In-hotel: restaurant, bar, pool, tennis court* ☾ *Closed Nov.–Easter* ⍾⦿⍾ *Breakfast.*

$$ 🏨 **Villa Sangiovese.** On the town's main square, this simple, well-run hotel has rooms that look out to the hillside or face the piazza. **Pros:** immaculate rooms; pool area great for kids; great location for exploring Chianti. **Cons:** front rooms can be noisy; lots of stairs. ✉ *Piazza Bucciarelli 5* ☎ *055/852461* ⊕ *www.villasangiovese.it* ⤳ *19 rooms* ⚒ *In-room: a/c, no TV. In-hotel: restaurant, pool* ☾ *Closed mid-Dec.– mid-Mar. Restaurant closed Wed.* ⍾⦿⍾ *Breakfast.*

SHOPPING

★ **Antica Macelleria Cecchini.** This just might be the world's most dramatic butcher shop. Here, amid classical music and lively conversation, owner Dario Cecchini holds court: while quoting Dante, he serves samples of his very fine *sushi di Chianina* (raw slices of Chianina beef gently salted and peppered). He has researched recipes from the 15th century, and sells pâtés and herb concoctions found nowhere else. Serious food enthusiasts should not miss the place. ✉ *Via XX Luglio 5* ☎ *055/852020.*

CASTELLINA IN CHIANTI

13 km (8 miles) south of Panzano, 59 km (35 miles) south of Florence, 22 km (14 miles) north of Siena.

Castellina in Chianti—or simply Castellina—is on a ridge above three valleys: the Val di Pesa, Val d'Arbia, and Val d'Elsa. No matter what direction you turn, the panorama is bucolic. The strong 15th-century medieval walls and fortified town gate give a hint of the history of this village, which was an outpost during the continuing wars between Florence and Siena. In the main square, the Piazza del Comune, there's a 15th-century palace and a 15th-century fort constructed around a 13th-century tower. It now serves as the town hall.

GETTING HERE

As with all the towns along the Strada Chiantigiana (SR222), Castellina is an easy drive from either Siena or Florence. From Siena, Castellina is well served by the local Tra-In bus company. However, only one bus a day travels here from Florence. The closest train station is at Castellina Scalo, some 15 km (9 miles) away.

VISITOR INFORMATION

Castellina in Chianti tourism office ✉ *Piazza del Comune 1* ☎ *0577/741392.*

NEED A BREAK?

L'Antica Delizia. Treat yourself to one of the terrifically fragrant ice creams at this *gelateria* just outside the town center. The fruit flavors—*fragola* (strawberry), *melone* (cantaloupe), and *limone* (lemon)—are all home-made and particularly good. ✉ *Via Fiorentina 4* ☎ *0577/741337.*

WHERE TO EAT

$$ ✕**Albergaccio.** The fact that the dining room can seat only 35 guests
TUSCAN makes a meal here an intimate experience. The ever-changing menu
mixes traditional and creative dishes. In late September and October
zuppa di funghi e castagne (mushroom and chestnut soup) is a treat;
grilled meats and seafood are on the list throughout the year. There's
also an excellent wine list. When the weather is warm, make sure you
dine on the terrace. ⊠ *Via Fiorentina 25* ☎ *0577/741042* ⊕ *www.
albergacciocast.com* ⌂ *Reservations essential* ⊟ *No credit cards*
⊘ *Closed Sun. No lunch Wed. and Thurs.*

$ ✕**Osteria alla Piazza.** Relax amid vineyards on a countryside terrace with
ITALIAN one of Chianti's most spectacular views of the vineyards in the valley
of the River Pesa. Enjoy the sophisticated menu: the *girasole ai quattro
sapori,* a giant vegetable-filled ravioli flavored with fresh tomato sauce
and a few drops of cream, arrives at the table looking much like a *gira-
sole* (sunflower). For pistachio fans, the *raviolo con pistacchi di Bronte,
ragù e nocciole* (pistachio ravioli with meat sauce and hazelnuts) is a
must. And certainly, try any of the delicious desserts. It's in La Piazza, 15
km (8 miles) north of Castellina. ⊠ *Località La Piazza* ☎ *0577/733580*
⊕ *www.osteriaallapiazza.com* ⌂ *Reservations essential* ⊘ *Closed Mon.
and Jan. and Feb.; closed weekdays Mar., Nov., and Dec.*

¢ ✕**Ristorante Le Tre Porte.** Grilled meat dishes are the specialty at this
TUSCAN popular restaurant, with a Florentine beefsteak (served very rare) tak-
ing pride of place. Paired with grilled fresh porcini mushrooms when in
season (in spring and fall), it's a particularly heady dish. The panoramic
terrace is a good choice for dining in summer. Inside, the upper floor
offers an umistakably Tuscan setting, while the downstairs is more
modern and intimate. Reservations are essential in July and August.
⊠ *Via Trento e Trieste 4* ☎ *0577/741163* ⊘ *Closed Tues.*

¢ ✕**Sotto Le Volte.** As the name suggests, you'll find this small restaurant
TUSCAN under the arches of Castellina's medieval walkway. The restaurant has
vaulted ceilings, which make for a particularly romantic setting. The
menu is short and emminently Tuscan, with typical soups and pasta
dishes. The *costolette di agnello alle erbe* (herbed lamb chops) are espe-
cially tasty. ⊠ *Via delle Volte 14–16, Castellina in Chianti* ☎ *0577/
056530* ⊟ *No credit cards* ⊘ *Closed Wed.*

WHERE TO STAY
For expanded hotel reviews, visit Fodors.com.

$$ 🏨 **Hotel Belvedere di San Leonino.** Stroll around the wonderful gardens on
this restored country estate dating from the 14th century. **Pros:** great
family atmosphere; lovely old house; central location. **Cons:** stairs to
climb; need a car to get around. ⊠ *Località San Leonino* ☎ *0577/740887*
⊕ *www.hotelsanleonino.com* ⌂ *28 rooms* ⌂ *In-room: no a/c, safe. In-
hotel: restaurant, pool* ⊘ *Closed mid-Nov.–mid-Apr.* ⦿ *Breakfast.*

$$ 🏨 **Hotel Salivolpi.** The family that owns this farmhouse took special care
not to change too much when they began accepting guests: faded family
photos, mementos of long-past journeys, and bric-a-brac of all kinds
decorate the common areas. **Pros:** tranquil location; 10-minute walk to
nearest town. **Cons:** some stairs to climb; no air-conditioning in some

rooms. ✉ *Via Fiorentina 89* ☏ *0577/740484* ⊕ *www.hotelsalivolpi.com* ⇆ *19 rooms* ⚬ *In-room: a/c, Wi-Fi. In-hotel: pool* ❍| *Breakfast.*

$$ ✈ **Locanda Le Piazze.** This old farmhouse has been transformed into a marvelous hotel in the midst of vineyards. **Pros:** pastoral setting; fun cooking classes; luxurious bathrooms. **Cons:** no air-conditioning; need a car to get around. ✉ *Località Le Piazze 41* ☏ *0577/743190* ⊕ *www. locandalepiazze.it* ⇆ *20 rooms* ⚬ *In-room: no a/c, Wi-Fi. In-hotel: restaurant, bar, pool* ☉ *Closed Nov.–Apr.* ❍| *Breakfast.*

$$ ✈ **Palazzo Squarcialupi.** In the center of Castellina, this 15th-century palace is an especially tranquil and well-positioned place to stay. **Pros:** great location; elegant public spaces. **Cons:** on a street with no car access; across from a busy restaurant. ✉ *Via Ferruccio 22* ☏ *0577/741186* ⊕ *www.palazzosquarcialupi.com* ⇆ *17 rooms* ⚬ *In-room: Wi-Fi. In-hotel: bar, pool, some pets allowed* ☉ *Closed Nov.–Mar.* ❍| *Breakfast.*

Fodor's Choice ★

SHOPPING

Castellina is a small town, with most of its shops located either along Via Ferruccio or on the Piazza del Comune. But don't miss the specialty stores hidden away on Via delle Volte, which runs inside the eastern medieval walls of the town—you can reach it from either end of Via Ferruccio.

Bottega Antichità. Antiquario Mario Cappelletti carries interesting prints and reproductions of well-known Renaissance artworks. ✉ *Via Ferruccio 39* ☏ *0577/740980.*

Laboratorio di Ceramica. Lucia Volentieri has a delightful selection of delicately hand-painted ceramics in her studio/shop. ✉ *Via Trento e Trieste 24* ☏ *0577/741133* ⊕ *www.luciavolontieri.com.*

Le Volte Enoteca. On Castellina's main street, Aleandro and his daughter Roberta stock an ample and well-chosen supply of local wines produced by small estates. On request, they can also organize visits to nearby wineries. ✉ *Via Ferruccio 12* ☏ *0577/741314* ⊕ *www.enotecalevolte.com.*

RADDA IN CHIANTI

10 km (6 miles) east of Castellina in Chianti, 55 km (34 miles) south of Florence.

Radda in Chianti sits on a ridge stretching between the Val di Pesa and Val d'Arbia. It is easily reached by following the SR429 from Castellina. It's another one of those tiny villages with steep streets for strolling; follow the signs that point you toward the *camminamento medioevale*, a covered 14th-century walkway that circles part of the city inside the walls.

GETTING HERE

Radda can be reached by car from either Siena or Florence along the SR222 (Strada Chiantigiana), and from the A1 highway. Three Tra-In buses make their way from Siena to Radda. One morning SITA bus travels from Florence to Radda. There is no train service convenient to Radda.

VISITOR INFORMATION

Radda in Chianti tourism office ✉ *Piazza Castello 6* ☏ *0577/738494.*

EXPLORING

Palazzo del Podestà. Radda's town hall (aka Palazzo Comunale), in the middle of town, was built in the second half of the 14th century and has served the same function ever since. Fifty-one coats of arms (the largest is the Medici's) are imbedded in the facade, representing the past governors of the town, but unless you have official business, the building is closed to the public. ⊠ *Piazza Ferrucci 1.*

Volpaia. This tiny town, with a population of roughly 50, is perched on a hill 10 km (6 miles) north of Radda. During the wars between Florence and Siena it served as a key castle and military outpost, but lost its importance when the Florentines defeated Siena in 1555. Approximately three-quarters of the town are now given over to the production of wine and olive oil.

Castello di Volpaia. At this small enoteca on Piazza della Torre you can sample and purchase the fine wines, olive oil, and flavored vinegars made by Castello di Volpaia. Booked in advance, tours in English of the winery and olive press are also available. ⊠ *Piazza della Cisterna 1* ☎ *0577/738066.*

WHERE TO EAT AND STAY

For expanded hotel reviews, visit Fodors.com.

¢ ✕ **Osteria Le Panzanelle.** Silvia Bonechi's experience in the kitchen—with the help of a few precious recipes handed down from her grandmother—is one of the reasons for the success of this small restaurant. The other is the front-room hospitality of Nada Michelassi. These two *panzanelle* (women from Panzano) serve a short menu of tasty and authentic dishes at what the locals refer to as *il prezzo giusto* (the right price). Both the *pappa al pomodoro* (tomato soup) and the *peposo* (peppery beef stew) are exceptional. Whether you are eating inside or under large umbrellas on the terrace near a tiny stream, the experience is always congenial. "The best food we had in Tuscany," writes one user of fodors.com. Reservations are essential in July and August. ⊠ *Località Lucarelli 29, 8 km (5 miles) northwest of Radda on the road to Panzano* ☎ *0577/733511* ⊕ *www.osteria.lepanzanelle.it* ☉ *Closed Mon. and Jan. and Feb.*

TUSCAN
Fodor's Choice
★

$$$$ 🏨 **Il Borgo di Vescine.** At this former Etruscan settlement a series of low-slung medieval stone buildings with barrel-tile roofs are connected by cobbled paths and punctuated by cypress trees. **Pros:** set in a lovely park; cozy public rooms. **Cons:** long walk to nearest town; isolated location. ⊠ *Località Vescine, 5 km (3 miles) west of Radda in Chianti* ☎ *0577/741144* ⊕ *www.vescine.it* 🛏 *19 rooms, 7 suites* ⚲ *In-hotel: pool, tennis court, some pets allowed* ☉ *Closed Nov.–Apr., except at Christmas* ⧖ *Breakfast.*

$ 🏨 **La Bottega di Giovannino.** The name is actually that of the wine bar run by Giovannino Bernardoni and his children Monica and David, who also rent out rooms in the house next door. **Pros:** great location in the center of town; close to restaurants and shops; super value. **Cons:** some rooms are small; some bathrooms are down the hall; basic decor.

Tuscany in its autumn gold

⌂ *Via Roma 6–8* ☎ *0577/738056* ⊕ *www.labottegadigiovannino.it* ⤳ *9 rooms, 1 apartment* ⚐ *In-room: no a/c, kitchen. In-hotel: bar* ❑ *No meals.*

$$$ ▦ **La Locanda.** At an altitude of more than 1,800 feet, this converted farmhouse is probably the loftiest luxury inn in Chianti. **Pros:** idyllic setting; panoramic views; wonderful hosts. **Cons:** on a very rough gravel access road; isolated location; need a car to get around. ⌂ *Località Montanino di Volpaia, off Via della Volpaia, 13 km (8 miles) northwest of Radda* ☎ *0577/738833* ⊕ *www.lalocanda.it* ⤳ *6 rooms, 1 suite* ⚐ *In-room: no a/c. In-hotel: pool* ⊘ *Closed Nov.–Mar.* ❑ *Breakfast.*

$$ ▦ **Palazzo San Niccolò.** Conveniently located in the center of Radda, this 19th-century town palace has been converted into an elegant hotel. **Pros:** central location; friendly service. **Cons:** some rooms face a main street; room sizes vary. ⌂ *Via Roma 16, Radda in Chianti* ☎ *0577/735666* ⊕ *www.hotelsannicolo.com* ⤳ *17 rooms, 1 suite* ⚐ *In-room: a/c, safe. In-hotel: bar, parking, some pets allowed* ⊘ *Closed Nov.–Mar.* ❑ *Breakfast.*

$$$$ ▦ **Relais Fattoria Vignale.** On the outside, it's a plain manor house with an annex across the street. **Pros:** intimate public spaces; excellent restaurant; helpful and friendly staff. **Cons:** north-facing rooms blocked by tall cypress trees; single rooms are small; annex across a busy road. ⌂ *Via Pianigiani 9* ☎ *0577/738300 hotel, 0577/738094 restaurant* ⊕ *www.vignale.it* ⤳ *37 rooms, 5 suites* ⚐ *In-room: safe. In-hotel: restaurant, bar, pool* ⊘ *Closed Nov.–Mar. 15* ❑ *Breakfast.*

SHOPPING

Ceramiche Rampini. With a shop also in Florence, this kiln and painting studio, 5 km (3 miles) south of Radda in Chianti, produces exquisite (and expensive) hand-painted ceramic objects, including plates, bowls, and candlesticks. The firm ships anywhere in the world and keeps its customers' information on file. If you break a plate or want to buy more, they'll know exactly what your pattern is. ⊠ *Casa Beretone, Località Beretone di Vistarenni* ☎ *0577/738043* ⊕ *www.rampiniceramics.com.*

Tecno-Casa. Locals come here to buy their nuts, bolts, and small tools, but visitors will also find a surprisingly varied assortment of traditional Italian household items, including coffeemakers and cups, wine decanters, and decorative bottle stoppers. ⊠ *Via Roma 20/22* ☎ *0577/738613.*

La Bottega delle Fantasie. Colorful pillows and carefully crafted linens in sun-drenched Tuscan hues are the speciality of this centrally located shop. ⊠ *Via Roma 47* ☎ *0577/738978.*

GAIOLE IN CHIANTI

9 km (5½ miles) southeast of Radda in Chianti, 69 km (43 miles) south of Florence.

A market town since 1200, Gaiole is now a central destination for touring southern Chianti. A stream runs through its center, and flowers adorn many of its window boxes. The surrounding area is dotted with castles perched on hilltops (the better to see the approaching enemy): they were of great strategic importance during the Renaissance, and still make dazzling lookout points.

GETTING HERE

To get here by car from the A1, take the Montevarchi exit and follow signs for Gaiole on the SR408. Gaiole is relatively well connected to Siena by Tra-In buses. Gaiole cannot be reached by train.

EXPLORING

Castello di Meleto. It's a pretty drive up winding and curving roads to this 13th-century fortress. Attached is an 18th-century villa; more importantly, there's a wineshop that serves tastes of the locally produced wine as well as honeys and jams. It's worth touring the castle if you want to get a sense of how 18th-century aristocrats lived; if that doesn't interest you, proceed directly to the enoteca for a tasting. Six apartments clustered near the castle are available for rent. ⊠ *Località Meleto, 5 km (3 miles) south of Gaiole* ☎ *0577/749217 castle, 0577/749129 enoteca* ⊕ *www.castellomeleto.it* ⊡ *€10* ☉ *Tours: Mon. 3 and 4:30; Tues.–Sat. 11:30, 3, and 4:30; Sun. 11:30, 4, and 5. Wineshop: mid-Mar–mid-Nov., daily 11:30–4:30.*

★ **Castello di Brolio.** If you have time for only one castle in Tuscany, this is it. At the end of the 12th century, when Florence conquered southern Chianti, Brolio became Florence's southernmost outpost, and it was often said, "When Brolio growls, all Siena trembles." Brolio was built about AD 1000 and owned by the monks of the Badia Fiorentina; the "new" owners, the Ricasoli family, have been in possession since 1141. Bettino Ricasoli (1809–80), the so-called Iron Baron, was one of the founders of modern Italy, and is said to have invented the original formula for Chianti wine. Brolio, one of Chianti's best-known labels, is still justifiably famous. Its cellars may be toured by appointment. The grounds are worth visiting, even though the 19th-century manor house is not open to the public. A small museum, where the Ricasoli Collection is housed in a 12th-century tower, displays objects that relate the long history of the family and the origins of Chianti wine. There are two apartments here available for rent by the week. ⊠ *Località Brolio, 2 km (1 mile) southeast of Gaiole* ☎ *0577/730280* ⊕ *www.ricasoli.it* 🎟 *€5 gardens, €8 gardens and museum, €10 guided tours* ⊙ *Last 2 wks Mar., weekdays 10–6:30, weekends 11–6:30; Apr.–Oct., daily 10–7; last entrance 1 hr before closing time. Guided tours, Wed. and Fri.–Mon. at 10:30, daily at 3, and Mon. and Fri. at 5; must be booked in advance.*

Vertine. Dating back to the 10th century, this walled town is oval in shape and has a tall watchtower guarding the entrance gate. A walk along the still unspoiled streets gives you a glimpse of life in a Tuscan hill town as it once was, and the views of the undulating countryside from the occasional opening in the walls are simply spectacular. ⊠ *Località Vertine, 2 km (1 mile) west of Gaiole.*

Badia a Coltibuono (Abbey of the Good Harvest) (*Abbey of the Good Harvest*). North of Gaiole a turnoff leads to this Romanesque abbey that has been owned by Lorenza de' Medici's family for more than a century and a half (the family isn't closely related to the Renaissance-era Medici). Wine has been produced here since the abbey was founded by Vallombrosan monks in the 11th century. Today the family continues the tradition, making Chianti Classico and other wines, along with cold-pressed olive oil and various flavored vinegars and floral honeys. A small church with campanile is surrounded by 2,000 acres of oak, fir, and chestnut woods threaded with walking paths—open to all—that pass two small lakes. Though the abbey itself, built between the 11th and 18th century, serves as the family's home, parts are open for tours (in English, German, or Italian). Visit the jasmine-draped main courtyard, the inner cloister with its antique well, the musty old aging cellars, and the Renaissance-style garden redolent of lavender, lemons, and roses. In the shop, **L'Osteria,** you can taste wine and honey, as well as pick up other items like homemade beeswax hand lotion in little ceramic dishes. The Badia is closed on public holidays. ⊠ *Località Badia a Coltibuono, 4 km (2½ miles) north of Gaiole* ☎ *0577/74481 for tours, 0577/749479 for shop* ⊕ *www.coltibuono.com* 🎟 *Abbey €5* ⊙ *Tours: Easter–Oct., weekdays at 2, 3, 4, and 5; shop: Mar.–mid-Jan., daily 9–1 and 2–7.*

WHERE TO EAT

$
ITALIAN

× **Badia a Coltibuono.** Outside the walls of Badia a Coltibuono is the abbey's pleasant restaurant, with seating on a terrace or in soft-yellow rooms divided by ancient brick arches. The *crema di peperoni e patate* (a creamless red pepper and potato soup) arrives at the table accompanied by homegrown olive oil; the *costata di manzo nostrano* (locally raised T-bone steak) for two, is particularly flavorfull. It all pairs marvelously with the abbey's own wines. Between 2:30 and 7:30 you can order from a bistro menu that has sandwiches, salads, and desserts. ⊠ *Località Badia a Coltibuono, 4 km (2½ miles) north of Gaiole* ☎ *0577/749031* ⊗ *Closed Mon. and Nov.–Feb.*

¢
ITALIAN

× **La Grotta della Rana.** A perfect stop for lunch while exploring the region's wineries, this trattoria offers *cucina casalinga* (home cooking) that can be eaten in the dining room or on a lovely outdoor patio. (If you time dinner right, you might get to watch a memorable sunset.) Outstanding primi include *maccheroni alla nonna* (macaroni with asparagus in a light cream sauce dotted with truffle oil). The *misto alla griglia* (mixed grilled meats) includes succulent pork. Also notable is the *filetto al pepe verde* (Chianina beef in a creamy green-peppercorn sauce). ⊠ *Località San Sano 8 km (5 miles) south of Gaiole* ☎ *0577/746020* ⊗ *Closed Wed. and Feb.–mid-Mar.*

¢
ITALIAN
★

× **Lo Sfizio di Bianchi.** A pleasant restaurant with outdoor seating on Gaiole's main square, this spot is as popular with the locals as it is with travelers. The menu, presented on small blackboards, has the occasional unexpected item, like the plate of perfectly grilled vegetables that is listed as an antipasto but almost makes a meal in itself. The kitchen also makes its own delicious pastries and ice cream, so skipping dessert is difficult. Reservations are essential on weekends. ⊠ *Via Ricasoli 44/46* ☎ *0577/749501* ⊕ *www.losfiziodibianchi.it* ⊗ *Closed Tues. No dinner Mon.*

WHERE TO STAY

For expanded hotel reviews, visit Fodors.com.

$$$
Fodor's Choice
★

⌂ **Borgo Argenina.** Elena Nappa, a former interior designer, is now the consummate hostess at this centuries-old villa. **Pros:** homemade buffet breakfasts; off-the-beaten-path feel. **Cons:** no pool; need a car to get around. ⊠ *Località Borgo Argenina, 15 km (9 miles) south of Gaiole* ☎ *0577/747117* ⊕ *www.borgoargenina.it* ⟿ *5 rooms, 2 suites, 3 houses* ⌂ *In-room: no a/c. In-hotel: parking* ⊗ *Closed mid-Nov.–mid-Mar.* ⊙| *Breakfast.*

$$$$
★

⌂ **Castello di Spaltenna.** This rustic yet elegant lodging includes a former convent (dating to the 1300s) and a Romanesque church. **Pros:** romantic setting; excellent restaurant; discreet and professional service. **Cons:** some rooms are reached via narrow stairways; some rooms look over the interior courtyard. ⊠ *Pieve di Spaltenna 13* ☎ *0577/749483* ⊕ *www.spaltenna.it* ⟿ *32 rooms, 5 suites, 2 apartments* ⌂ *In-room: Wi-Fi. In-hotel: restaurant, bar, pool, tennis court* ⊗ *Closed early Jan.–mid-Mar.* ⊙| *Breakfast.*

$$

⌂ **Hotel Residence San Sano.** An open-hearth fireplace and hand-hewn stone porticoes hark back to a time when this was a 13th-century fortress. **Pros:** good base for exploring Chianti; great family atmosphere;

warm and friendly hosts. **Cons:** need a car to get around; furnishings, in true Tuscan style, are very plain. ⊠ *Località San Sano 21, 10 km (6 miles) south of Gaiole* ☎ *0577/746130* ⊕ *www.sansanohotel.it* ⥽ *16 rooms* ⌂ *In-room: safe, Wi-Fi. In-hotel: restaurant, pool, laundry facilities, some pets allowed* ⊙ *Closed Jan. and Feb.* ⦿ *Breakfast.*

CASTELNUOVO BERARDENGA

20 km (12 miles) southeast of Gaiole in Chianti, 90 km (56 miles) southeast of Florence, 23 km (14 miles) east of Siena.

The southernmost village in Chianti has a compact center with hilly, curving streets. A plethora of piazzas invite wandering.

GETTING HERE
Castelnuovo is easily reached by car from Siena via the SS73. Tra-In buses run infrequently from Siena. Castelnuovo's train station, Castelnuovo Berardenga Scalo, is 8 km (5 miles) away.

VISITOR INFORMATION
Castelnuovo Berardenga tourism office ⊠ *Via Garibaldi 12* ☎ *0577/351335.*

EXPLORING
Villa Chigi. Peek at the gardens of Villa Chigi, a 19th-century villa built on the site of a 14th-century castle (actually the "new castle" from which Castelnuovo got its name). The villa is closed to the public, but its manicured gardens are open Sunday and holidays. ⊠ *Via Berardenga 20* ☎ *No phone* ⊠ *Free* ⊙ *Apr.–Sept., Sun. 10–8; Oct.–Mar., Sun. 10–5.*

San Giusto e San Clemente. Built in the 1840s on a Greek-cross plan, this neoclassical church contains a Madonna and Child with angels by an anonymous 15th-century master. Also inside is the *Holy Family with St. Catherine of Siena*, attributed to Arcangelo Salimbeni (1530/40–79). ⊠ *Piazza Matteotti 4* ☎ *No phone* ⊙ *Daily 7:30–7.*

San Gusmè. The oldest and most interesting of the hilltop medieval towns that surround Castelnuovo Berardenga, this village still retains its early 1400s layout, with arched passageways, gates topped with coats of arms, narrow squares, and steep streets. You can walk through the entire village in 20 minutes, but in those 20 minutes you may feel as if you have stepped back in time some 600 years. ⊠ *SR484 5 km (3 miles) north of Castelnuovo Berardenga.*

WHERE TO STAY
For expanded hotel reviews, visit Fodors.com.

$$$$ ⊞ **Borgo San Felice.** Spread across five buildings, this elegant lodging used to be a small medieval town. **Pros:** beautiful buildings; romantic setting; heated pool. **Cons:** service is sometimes lax; need a car to get around. ⊠ *Località San Felice, 8 km (5 miles) northwest of Castelnuovo Berardenga* ☎ *0577/3964* ⊕ *www.borgosanfelice.com* ⥽ *28 rooms, 15 suites* ⌂ *In-room: safe, Wi-Fi. In-hotel: restaurant, bar, pool, tennis court, gym, business center, some pets allowed* ⊙ *Closed Nov.–Mar.* ⦿ *Breakfast.*

Siena's frenetic Palio

SIENA

With its narrow streets and steep alleys, a stunning Gothic Duomo, a bounty of early Renaissance art, and the glorious Palazzo Pubblico overlooking its magnificent Campo, Siena is often described as Italy's best-preserved medieval city. It is also remarkably modern: many shops sell cutting-edge clothes by up-and-coming designers. Make a point of catching the *passeggiata* (evening stroll), when the locals throng the Via di Città, Banchi di Sopra, and Banchi di Sotto, the city's three main streets.

Sienese mythology holds that the city shares common ancestry with Rome: the legendary founder, Senius, was said to be the son of Remus, the twin brother of Rome's founder, Romulus. The city emblem—a she-wolf and suckling twins—promulgates the claim. Archaeological evidence suggests there were prehistoric as well as Etruscan settlements here, which undoubtedly made way for Saena Julia, the Roman town established by Augustus in the 1st century BC.

Siena rose to prominence as an essential stop on that most important of medieval roads, the Via Francigena (or Via Romea), prospering from the yearly flow of thousands of Christian pilgrims coming south to Rome from northern Europe. Siena developed a banking system—one of Europe's oldest banks, the Monte dei Paschi, is still very much in business—and dominated the wool trade, thereby establishing itself as a rival to Florence. The two towns became regional powers and bitter enemies, each taking a different side in the struggle that divided the peninsula between the Guelphs (loyal to the Pope) and Ghibellines (loyal to the Holy Roman Emperor). Siena aligned itself with the latter.

Victory over Florence in 1260 at Montaperti marked the beginning of Siena's golden age. Even though the Florentines avenged the loss nine years later, Siena continued to prosper. During the following decades Siena erected its greatest buildings (including the Duomo); established a model city government presided over by the Council of Nine; and became a great art, textile, and trade center. All of these achievements came together in the decoration of the Sala della Pace in Palazzo Pubblico. It makes you wonder what greatness the city might have gone on to achieve had its fortunes been different, but in 1348 a plague decimated the population, brought an end to the Council of Nine, and left Siena economically weak and vulnerable. Siena succumbed to Florentine rule in the mid-16th century, when a yearlong siege virtually eliminated the native population. Ironically, it was precisely this decline that, along with the steadfast pride of the Sienese, prevented further development, to which we owe the city's marvelous medieval condition today.

But although much looks as it did in the early 14th century, Siena is no museum. Walk through the streets and you can see that the medieval *contrade,* 17 neighborhoods into which the city has been historically divided, are a vibrant part of modern life. You may see symbols of the *contrada*—Tartuca (turtle), Oca (goose), Istrice (porcupine), Torre (tower)—emblazoned on banners and engraved on building walls. The Sienese still strongly identify themselves by the contrada where they were born and raised; loyalty and rivalry run deep. At no time is this more visible than during the centuries-old Palio, a twice-yearly horse race held in the Piazza del Campo, but you need not visit during the wild festival to come to know the rich culture and enchanting pleasures of Siena; those are evident at every step.

GETTING HERE

From Florence, the quickest way to Siena is via the Florence–Siena Superstrada. Otherwise, take the Via Cassia (SR2), for a scenic route. Coming from Rome, leave the A1 at Valdichiana, and follow the Siena–Bettole Superstrada. SITA provides excellent bus service between Florence and Siena. Because buses are direct and speedy, they are preferable to the train, which sometimes involves a change in Empoli.

VISITOR INFORMATION

Siena tourism office ✉ *Piazza del Campo 56* ☎ *0577/280551* ⊕ *www.comune. siena.it.*

EXPLORING SIENA

If you come by car, you're better off leaving it in one of the parking lots around the perimeter of town. Driving is difficult or impossible in most parts of the city center. Practically unchanged since medieval times, Siena is laid out in a "Y" over the slopes of several hills, dividing the city into *terzi* (thirds). Although the most interesting sites are in a fairly compact area around the Campo at the center of town, be sure to leave some time to wander into the narrow streets that rise and fall steeply from the main thoroughfares, giving yourself at least two days to really explore the town. At the top on the list of things to see is the Piazza del Campo, considered by many to be the finest public square in Italy. The Palazzo Pubblico sits at the lower end of the square, and is well worth a visit. The Duomo is a must-see, as is the nearby Cripta.

Tra-In. City buses run frequently within and around Siena, including the centro storico. Tickets cost €1 and should be bought in advance at tobacconists or newsstands. Routes are marked with signposts. ☎ *0577/204225* ⊕ *www.trainspa.it.*

TIMING It's a joy to walk in Siena—hills notwithstanding—as it's a rare opportunity to stroll through a medieval city rather than just a town. (There is quite a lot to explore, in contrast to tiny hill towns that can be crossed in minutes.) The walk can be done in as little as a day, with minimal stops at the sights. But stay longer and take time to tour the church building and museums, and to enjoy the streetscapes themselves. Several of the sites have reduced hours Sunday afternoon and Monday.

TOP ATTRACTIONS

Fodor's Choice **Cripta.** After it had lain unseen for possibly 700 years, a crypt was redis-
★ covered under the grand *pavimento* (floor) of the Duomo during routine excavation work and was opened to the public in 2003. An unknown master executed the breathtaking frescoes here sometime between 1270

and 1280; they retain their original colors and pack an emotional punch even with sporadic damage. The *Deposition/Lamentation* gives strong evidence that the Sienese school could paint emotion just as well as the Florentine school—and did it some 20 years before Giotto. Guided tours in English take place more or less every half hour and are limited to no more than 35 persons. ☒ *Piazza del Duomo, entrance on the right side of the cathedral, Città* ☎ *0577/286300* ☒ *€6; €10 combined ticket includes the Duomo, Battistero, and Museo dell'Opera Metropolitana* ☉ *Mar.–mid-June and mid-Sept.–Oct., daily 9:30–7:30; mid-June–mid-Sept., daily 9:30–8; Nov.–Feb., daily 10–5.*

Fodor'sChoice
★

Duomo. Siena's cathedral is beyond question one of the finest Gothic churches in Italy. The multicolored marbles and painted decoration are typical of the Italian approach to Gothic architecture—lighter and much less austere than the French. The amazingly detailed facade has few rivals in the region, although it's quite similar to the Duomo in Orvieto. It was completed in two brief phases at the end of the 13th and 14th centuries. The statues and decorative work were designed by Nicola Pisano and his son Giovanni, although most of what we see today are copies, the originals having been removed to the nearby Museo dell'Opera Metropolitana. The gold mosaics are 18th-century restorations. The Campanile (no entry) is among central Italy's finest, the number of windows increasing with each level, a beautiful and ingenious way of reducing the weight of the structure as it climbs to the heavens.

The Duomo's interior, with its black-and-white striping throughout and finely coffered and gilded dome, is simply striking. Step in and look back up at Duccio's (circa 1255–1319) panels of stained glass that fill the circular window. Finished in 1288, it's the oldest example of stained glass in Italy. The Duomo is most famous for its unique and magnificent inlaid-marble floors, which took almost 200 years to complete; more than 40 artists contributed to the work, made up of 56 separate compositions depicting biblical scenes, allegories, religious symbols, and civic emblems. The floors are covered for most of the year for conservation purposes, but are unveiled during September and October. The Duomo's carousel pulpit, also much appreciated, was carved by Nicola Pisano (circa 1220–84) around 1265; the *Life of Christ* is depicted on the rostrum frieze. In striking contrast to all the Gothic decoration in the nave are the magnificent Renaissance frescoes in the **Biblioteca Piccolomini**, off the left aisle. Painted by Pinturicchio (circa 1454–1513) and completed in 1509, they depict events from the life of native son Aeneas Sylvius Piccolomini (1405–64), who became Pope Pius II in 1458. The frescoes are in excellent condition, and have a freshness rarely seen in work so old.

The Duomo is grand, but the medieval Sienese people had even bigger plans. They wanted to enlarge the building by using the existing church as a transept for a new church, with a new nave running toward the southeast, to make what would be the largest church in the world. But only the side wall and part of the new facade were completed when the Black Death struck in 1348, decimating Siena's population. The city fell into decline, funds dried up, and the plans were never carried out. (The dream of building the biggest church was actually doomed to failure from the start—subsequent attempts to get the project going revealed that the foundation was insufficient to bear the weight of the proposed structure.) The beginnings of the new nave, extending from the right side of the Duomo, were left unfinished, perhaps as a testament to unfulfilled dreams, and ultimately enclosed to house the adjacent **Museo dell'Opera Metropolitana.** The **Cripta** was discovered during routine preservation work on the church and has been opened to the public. ✉ *Piazza del Duomo, Città* ☎ *0577/286300* 🎫 *€3 Nov.–Aug.; €6 Sept. and Oct.; €10 combined ticket includes the Cripta, Battistero, and Museo dell'Opera Metropolitana* ⊙ *Mar.–mid-June, Mon.–Sat. 10:30–7:30, Sun. 1:30–6; mid-June–mid-Sept., Mon.–Sat. 10:30–8, Sun. 1:30–6; mid-Sept.–Oct., Mon.–Sat. 10:30–7:30, Sun. 1:30–6; Nov.– Feb., Mon.–Sat. 10:30–6:30, Sun. 1:30–5:30.*

Fodor'sChoice
★
Museo dell'Opera Metropolitana. Part of the unfinished nave of what was to have been a new cathedral, the museum contains the Duomo's treasury and some of the original decoration from its facade and interior. The first room on the ground floor displays weather-beaten 13th-century sculptures by Giovanni Pisano (circa 1245–1318) that were brought inside for protection and replaced by copies, as was a tondo of the *Madonna and Child* (now attributed to Donatello) that once hung on the door to the south transept. The masterpiece is unquestionably Duccio's *Maestà*, one side with 26 panels depicting episodes from the Passion, the other side with a *Madonna and Child Enthroned*. Painted between 1308 and 1311 as the altarpiece for the Duomo (where it remained until 1505), its realistic elements, such as the lively depiction of the Christ child and the treatment of interior space, proved an enormous influence on later painters. The second floor is divided between the treasury, with a crucifix by Giovanni Pisano and several statues and busts of biblical characters and classical philosophers, and La Sala della Madonna degli Occhi Grossi (the Room of the Madonna with the Big Eyes), named after the namesake painting it displays by the Maestro di Tressa, who painted in the early 13th century. The work originally decorated the Duomo's high altar, before being displaced by Duccio's *Maestà*. There is a fine view from the tower inside the museum. ✉ *Piazza del Duomo 8, Città* ☎ *0577/286300* 🎫 *€6; €10 combined ticket includes the Duomo, Cripta, and Battistero* ⊙ *Mar.–mid-June, daily 9:30–7:30; mid-June–mid-Sept., daily 9:30–8; mid-Sept.–Oct., daily 9:30–7:30; Nov.–Feb., daily 10–5.*

★
Pinacoteca Nazionale. The superb collection of five centuries of local painting in Siena's national picture gallery can easily convince you that the Renaissance was by no means just a Florentine thing—Siena was arguably just as important a center of art and innovation as its rival to the north, especially in the mid-13th century. Accordingly, the most interesting section of the collection, chronologically arranged, has several important "firsts." Room 1 contains a painting of the *Stories of the True Cross* (1215) by the so-called Master of Tressa, the earliest identified work by a painter of the Sienese school, and is followed in Room 2 by late-13th-century artist Guido da Siena's *Stories from the*

Life of Christ, one of the first paintings ever made on canvas (earlier painters used wood panels). Rooms 3 and 4 are dedicated to Duccio, a student of Cimabue (circa 1240–1302) and considered to be the last of the proto-Renaissance painters. Ambrogio Lorenzetti's landscapes in Room 8 are the first truly secular paintings in Western art. Among later works in the rooms on the floor above, keep an eye out for the preparatory sketches used by Domenico Beccafumi (1486–1551) for the 35 etched marble panels he made for the floor of the Duomo. ⊠ *Via San Pietro 29, Città* ☎ *0577/286143* ⌫*€4* ⊙ *Tues.–Sat. 8:15–7:15, Sun. and Mon. 9–1; last entrance ½ hr before closing.*

★ **Spedale di Santa Maria della Scala.** For more than a thousand years, this complex across from the Duomo was home to Siena's hospital, but now it serves as a museum to display some terrific frescoes and other Sienese Renaissance treasures. Restored 15th-century frescoes in the Sala del Pellegrinaio (once the emergency room) tell the history of the hospital, which was created to give refuge to passing pilgrims and to those in need, and to distribute charity to the poor. Incorporated into the complex is the church of the Santissima Annunziata, with a celebrated *Risen Christ* by Vecchietta (also known as Lorenzo di Pietro, circa 1412–80). Down in the dark Cappella di Santa Caterina della Notte is where Saint Catherine went to pray at night. The subterranean archaeological museum contained within the *ospedale* (hospital) is worth seeing even if you're not particularly taken with Etruscan objects: the interior design is sheer brilliance—it's beautifully lighted, eerily quiet, and an oasis of cool on hot summer days. The displays—including the *bucchero* (dark, reddish clay) ceramics, Roman coins, and tomb furnishings—are clearly marked and can serve as a good introduction to the history of regional excavations. Don't miss della Quercia's original sculpted reliefs from the Fonte Gaia. Although the fountain has been faithfully copied for the Campo, there's something incomparably beautiful about the real thing. ⊠ *Piazza del Duomo 1, Città* ☎ *0577/534511* ⌫*€6* ⊙ *Mid-Mar.–mid-Oct., daily 10:30–6:30; mid-Oct.–mid-Mar., daily 10:30–4:30; ticket office closes 1 hr before closing.*

WORTH NOTING

Battistero. The Duomo's 14th-century Gothic Baptistery was built to prop up the apse of the cathedral. There are frescoes throughout, but the highlight is a large bronze 15th-century baptismal font designed by Jacopo della Quercia (1374–1438). It's adorned with bas-reliefs by various artists, including two by Renaissance masters: the *Baptism of Christ* by Lorenzo Ghiberti (1378–1455) and the *Feast of Herod* by Donatello. ⊠ *Piazza San Giovanni* ☎ *0577/286300* ⌫*€3; €10 combined ticket includes the Duomo, Cripta, and Museo dell'Opera del Duomo* ⊙ *Mar.–mid-June, daily 9:30–7:30; mid-June–mid-Sept., daily 9:30–8; mid-Sept.–Oct., daily 9:30–7:30; Nov.–Feb., daily 10–5.*

Casa di Santa Caterina. Caterina Benincasa was born here in 1347, and although she took the veil of the Dominican Tertiary order at age eight, she remained here, devoting her life to the sick and poor in the aftermath of the devastating plague of 1348. She had divine visions and received the stigmata, but is most famous for her words and her argumentative

Continued on page 232

Climbing the 400 narrow steps of the **Torre del Mangia** rewards you with unparalleled views of Siena's rooftops and the countryside beyond.

The **Palazzo Pubblico**, Siena's town hall since the 14th century.

Something about the fan-shaped, sloping design of **Il Campo** encourages people to sit and relax (except during the Palio, when they stand and scream). The communal atmosphere here is unlike that of any other Italian piazza.

PIAZZA DEL CAMPO

Fodor'sChoice ★

9 The fan-shaped **Piazza del Campo**, known simply as il Campo (The Field), is one of the finest squares in Italy. Constructed toward the end of the 12th century on a market area unclaimed by any contrada, it's still the heart of town. The bricks of the Campo are patterned in nine different sections—representing each member of the medieval Government of Nine. At the top of the Campo is a copy of the **Fonte Gaia**, decorated in the early 15th century by Siena's greatest sculptor, Jacopo della Quercia, with 13 sculpted reliefs of biblical events and virtues. Those lining the rectangular fountain are 19th-century copies; the originals are in the Spedale di Santa Maria della Scala. On Palio horse race days (July 2 and August 16), the Campo and all its surrounding buildings are packed with cheering, frenzied locals and tourists craning their necks to take it all in.

10 The Gothic **Palazzo Pubblico**, the focal point of the Piazza del Campo, has served as Siena's town hall since the 1300s. It now also contains the **Museo Civico**, with walls covered in early Renaissance frescoes. The nine governors of Siena once met in the Sala della Pace, famous for Ambrogio Lorenzetti's frescoes called *Allegories of Good and Bad Government,* painted in the late 1330s to demonstrate the dangers of tyranny. The good government side depicts utopia, showing first the virtuous ruling council surrounded by angels and then scenes of a perfectly running city and countryside. Conversely, the bad government fresco tells a tale straight out of Dante. The evil ruler and his advisers have horns and fondle strange animals, and the town scene depicts the seven mortal sins in action. Interestingly, the bad government fresco is severely damaged, and the good government fresco is in terrific condition. The **Torre del Mangia,** the palazzo's famous bell tower, is named after one of its first bell ringers, Giovanni di Duccio (called Mangiaguadagni, or earnings eater). The climb up to the top is long and steep, but the view makes it worth every step. ⊠ *Piazza del Campo 1, Città* ☏ *0577/41169* ✎ *Museo €7, Torre €6, combined ticket €10* ☺ *Museo Nov.–Mar. 15, daily 10–6:30; Mar. 16–Oct., daily 10–7. Torre Nov.–Mar. 15, daily 10–4; Mar. 16–Oct., daily 10–7.*

THE PALIO

The three laps around a makeshift racetrack in Piazza del Campo are over in less than two minutes, but the spirit of Siena's Palio—a horse race held every July 2 and August 16—lives all year long.

The Palio is contested between Siena's contrade, the 17 neighborhoods that have divided the city since the Middle Ages. Loyalties are fiercely felt. At any time of year you'll see on the streets contrada symbols—Tartuca (turtle), Oca (goose), Istrice (porcupine), Torre (tower)—emblazoned on banners and engraved on building walls. At Palio time, simmering rivalries come to a boil.

It's been that way since at least August 16, 1310, the date of the first recorded running of the Palio. At that time, and for centuries to follow, the race went through the streets of the city. The additional July 2 running was instituted in 1649; soon thereafter the location was moved to the Campo and the current system for selecting the race entrants established. Ten of the contrade are chosen at random to run in the July Palio. The August race is then contested between the 7 contrade left out in July, plus 3 of the 10 July participants, again chosen at random. Although the races are in theory of equal importance, Sienese will tell you that it's better to win the second and have bragging rights for the rest of the year.

The race itself has a raw and arbitrary character—it's no Kentucky Derby. There's barely room for the 10 horses on the makeshift Campo course, so falls and collisions are inevitable. Horses are chosen at random three days before the race, and jockeys (who ride bareback) are mercenaries hired from surrounding towns. Almost no tactic is considered too underhanded. Bribery, secret plots, and betrayal are commonplace—so much so that the word for "jockey," *fantino*, has come to mean "untrustworthy" in Siena. There have been incidents of drugging (the horses) and kidnapping (the jockeys); only sabotaging a horse's reins remains taboo.

Above: The tension of the starting line. Top left: The frenzy of the race. Bottom left: A solemn flag bearer follows in the footsteps of his ancestors.

| AQUILA | BRUCO | CHIOCCIOLA |

17 MEDIEVAL CONTRADE

Festivities kick off three days prior to the Palio, with the selection and blessing of the horses, trial runs, ceremonial banquets, betting, and late-night celebrations. Residents don their contrada's colors and march through the streets in medieval costumes. The Campo is transformed into a racetrack lined with a thick layer of sand. On race day, each horse is brought to the church of the contrada for which it will run, where it's blessed and told, "Go little horse and return a winner." The Campo fills through the afternoon, with spectators crowding into every available space until bells ring and the piazza is sealed off. Processions of flag wavers in traditional dress march to the beat of tambourines and drums and the roar of the crowds. The *palio* itself—a banner for which the race is named, dedicated to the Virgin Mary—makes an appearance, followed by the horses and their jockeys.

The race begins when one horse, chosen to ride up from behind the rest of the field, crosses the starting line. There are always false starts, adding to the frenzied mood. Once underway, the race is over in a matter of minutes. The victorious rider is carried off through the streets of the winning contrada (where in the past tradition dictated he was entitled to the local girl of his choice), while winning and losing sides use television replay to analyze the race from every possible angle. The winning contrada will celebrate into the night, at long tables piled high with food and drink. The champion horse is guest of honor.

Reserved seating in the stands is sold out months in advance of the races; contact the Siena Tourist Office (✉ Piazza del Campo 56 ☎ 0577/280551) to find out about availability, and ask your hotel if it can procure you a seat. The entire area in the center is free and unreserved, but you need to show up early in order to get a prime spot against the barriers.

CIVETTA	DRAGO
GIRAFFA	ISTRICE
LEOCORNO	LUPA
NICCHIO	OCA
ONDA	PANTERA
SELVA	TARTUCA
TORRE	VALDIMONTONE

skills. Her letters—many of which are preserved in the Biblioteca Comunale—were dictated because she did not know how to write. She is credited with convincing Pope Gregory XI (1329–78) to return the papacy to Rome after 70 years in Avignon and French domination, ending the Western Schism. Caterina died in Rome in 1380 and was canonized in 1461. A few

years later the city purchased the family house and turned it into a shrine, one of the first examples of its kind in Italy. The rooms of the house, including her cell and the kitchen, were converted into a series of chapels and oratories and decorated by noteworthy artists over the following centuries with scenes from Caterina's life. In 1939 she was made a patron saint of Italy, along with Saint Francis of Assisi. In 1970 she was elevated to Doctor of the Church, the highest possible honor in Christendom. She has been named a patron saint of Europe but, strangely enough, never of her hometown. ⊠ *Costa di Sant'Antonio 6, Camollìa* ☎ *0577/288175* ☐ *Free* ☉ *Daily 9:30–7.*

Enoteca Italiana. The bastions of the Fortezza Medici are home to a fantastically well-stocked wine bar and shop. It serves wines by the glass and various small dishes. Take some time to peruse the labels that are on the shelves (the wines of more than 400 wineries are stocked here). On Friday evenings in winter there's also a piano bar. ⊠ *Fortezza Medicea, Piazza Libertà 1, Camollìa* ☎ *0577/228811* ☉ *Mon.–Sat. noon–1 am.*

San Domenico. Although the Duomo is celebrated as a triumph of 13th-century Gothic architecture, this church, built at about the same time, turned out to be an oversize, hulking brick box that never merited a finishing coat in marble, let alone a graceful facade. Named for the founder of the Dominican order, the church is now more closely associated with Saint Catherine of Siena. Just to the right of the entrance is the chapel in which she received the stigmata. On the wall is the only known contemporary portrait of the saint, made in the late 14th century by Andrea Vanni (circa 1332–1414). Farther down is the famous **Cappella di Santa Caterina,** the church's official shrine. Catherine, or bits and pieces of her, was literally spread all over the country—a foot is in Venice, most of her body is in Rome, and only her head (kept in a reliquary on the chapel's altar) and her right thumb are here. She was revered throughout the country long before she was officially named a patron saint of Italy in 1939. On either side of the chapel are well-known frescoes by Sodoma (aka Giovanni Antonio Bazzi, 1477–1549) of *St. Catherine in Ecstasy.* Don't miss the view of the Duomo and town center from the apse-side terrace. ⊠ *Via Camporegio 2, Camollìa* ☎ *0577/280893* ⊕ *www.basilicacateriniana.com* ☉ *May–Oct., daily 7 am–7 pm; Nov.–Apr., daily 9–6.*

Sinagoga. Down a small street around the corner from Il Campo, this synagogue is worth a visit simply to view the two sobering plaques that adorn its facade. One commemorates June 28, 1799, when 13 Jews

Ricciarelli, delicate almond cookies native to Siena

were taken from their homes by a fanatic mob and burned in the square. The other memorializes the Sienese Jews who were deported during World War II. Guided tours in English are available by arrangement. ⊠ *Vicolo delle Scotte 14, San Martino* ☎ *055/2346654* 🎫 *€4* ⊗ *Apr., May, Sept., and Oct., Thurs. and Sun. 10–5.*

WHERE TO EAT

¢ ✕ **Hosteria il Carroccio.** Angle for one of the few seats here to have an
ITALIAN intimate meal and to try dishes both creative and deliciously simple. The *palline di pecorino con lardo e salsa di pere* (pecorino cheese balls wrapped with pork fat and briefly grilled), for instance, are sublime. So, too, are the amply portioned primi—the *pici* (a local pasta specialty resembling a thick spaghetti) is especially good. Sit at tables outside in summer. ⊠ *Via Casato di Sotto 32, Città* ☎ *0577/41165* ⊗ *Closed Wed., 2 wks in Jan., and 2 wks in July.*

$ ✕ **Le Logge.** Bright flowers provide a dash of color at this classic Tuscan
TUSCAN dining room, and stenciled designs on the ceilings add some whimsy. The wooden cupboards (now filled with wine bottles) lining the walls recall its past as a turn-of-the-19th-century grocery store. The menu, with four or five *primi* (first courses) and *secondi* (second courses), changes regularly, but almost always includes their classic *malfatti all'osteria* (ricotta and spinach dumplings in a cream sauce). Desserts such as *coni con mousse al cioccolato e gelato allo zafferano* (two diminutive ice-cream cones with chocolate mousse and saffron ice cream) provide an inventive ending to the meal. When not vying for one of the outdoor tables, make sure to ask for one in the main downstairs room. ⊠ *Via*

del Porrione 33, San Martino ☎ 0577/48013 ⊕ www.osterialelogge.it 🍴 Reservations essential ⊘ Closed Sun. and 3 wks in Jan.

¢ ✗**Osteria Castelvecchio.** On the daily menu you're likely to find both
TUSCAN Sienese standards, such as spaghetti *saporiti con gli aromi* (with tomatoes and herbs), as well as more offbeat selections like *bocconcini di
pollo alla mediterranea* (tender chicken cooked in a robust tomato-
and-olive sauce). Husband-and-wife team Simone Romi and Sabrina
Fabi are committed to including *piatti di verdura* (vegetarian dishes)
among the choices, and they've put together a great wine list. A tasting
menu allows you to sample just about all the daily specials. The little
restaurant with high vaulted ceilings is in the oldest part of town. ⊠ *Via
Castelvecchio 65, Città* ☎ 0577/49586 ⊘ *Closed Tues.*

¢ ✗**Osteria Il Grattacielo.** Wiped out from too much sightseeing? Con-
TUSCAN sider a meal at this hole-in-the-wall restaurant where locals congregate for a simple lunch over a glass of wine. There's a collection of
verdure sott'olio (marinated vegetables), a wide selection of *affettati
misti* (cured meats), and various types of frittatas. All off this can be
washed down with the cheap, yet eminently drinkable, house red. A
couple of bench tables provide outdoor seating in summer. Don't be
put off by the absence of a written menu. All the food is displayed at
the counter, so you can point if you need to. ⊠ *Via Pontani 8, Camollìa*
☎ 0577/289326 ▭ *No credit cards* ⊘ *Closed Sun.*

¢ ✗**Trattoria Papei.** The menu hasn't changed for years, and why should it?
TUSCAN The *pici al cardinale* (handmade spaghetti with a duck and bacon sauce)
★ is wonderful, and all the other typically Sienese dishes are equally delicious. Grilled meats are the true speciality; the *bistecca di vitello* (grilled
veal steak) is melt-in-your-mouth wonderful. Tucked away behind the
Palazzo Pubblico in a square that serves as a parking lot for most of
the day, the restaurant's location isn't great, but the food is. Thanks to
portable heaters, there is outdoor seating all year-round. ⊠ *Piazza del
Mercato 6, Città* ☎ 0577/280894 ⊘ *Closed Mon.*

WHERE TO STAY

For expanded hotel reviews, visit Fodors.com.

$$ 🏨 **Antica Torre.** The cordial Landolfo family has carefully evoked a pri-
vate home with their eight guest rooms inside a restored 16th-century
tower. **Pros:** near the town center; charming atmosphere. **Cons:** narrow
stairway up to the rooms; low ceilings; cramped bathrooms. ⊠ *Via
Fieravecchia 7, San Martino* ☎ 0577/222255 ⊕ www.anticatorresiena.
it ⤴ 8 rooms ⅙ In-room: no a/c, Wi-Fi ⑩ Breakfast.

$$$$ 🏨 **Certosa di Maggiano.** A 14th-century monastery has been converted
into this upscale country hotel. **Pros:** elegant service; luxurious rooms.
Cons: some find the atmosphere too formal; located outside town. ⊠ *Si-
ena Sud exit off Superstrada, Strada di Certosa 82, ½ km (¼ mile) east
of Siena* ☎ 0577/288180 ⊕ www.certosadimaggiano.com ⤴ 9 rooms,
8 suites ⅙ In-room: Wi-Fi. In-hotel: restaurant, pool, tennis court, gym
⑩ Some meals.*

$$ 🏨 **Chiusarelli.** Caryatids stud the grounds of this well-kept neoclassical
villa; a small garden invites reading. **Pros:** near the main bus terminal;

spacious rooms; quiet garden. **Cons:** on a busy street; bland furnishings. ⊠ *Viale Curtatone 15, Camollìa* ☎ *0577/280562* ⊕ *www.chiusarelli. com* ⟿ *48 rooms, 1 suite* ♿ *In-room: safe, Wi-Fi. In-hotel: restaurant, bar, parking, some pets allowed* ❍ *Breakfast.*

$$$$ 🏨 **Grand Hotel Continental.** Pope Alexander VII of the famed Sienese Chigi family gave this palace to his niece as a wedding present in 1600; through the centuries it has been a private family home as well as a grand hotel. **Pros:** luxurious accommodations; great location on the main drag; first-rate concierge. **Cons:** sometimes stuffy atmosphere; rooms show signs of wear. ⊠ *Banchi di Sopra 85, Camollìa* ☎ *0577/56011* ⊕ *www.royaldemeure.com* ⟿ *40 rooms, 11 suites* ♿ *In-room: safe, Wi-Fi. In-hotel: restaurant, bar, business center, parking, some pets allowed* ❍ *Breakfast.*

$$$ 🏨 **Hotel Santa Caterina.** Manager Lorenza Capannelli and her fine staff
★ are welcoming, hospitable, enthusiastic, and go out of their way to ensure a fine stay. **Pros:** friendly staff; a short walk to center of town; breakfast in the garden. **Cons:** on a busy intersection; outside city walls. ⊠ *Via Piccolomini 7, San Martino* ☎ *0577/221105* ⊕ *www.hscsiena.it* ⟿ *22 rooms* ♿ *In-room: Internet. In-hotel: parking, some pets allowed* ❍ *Breakfast.*

$$$ 🏨 **Palazzo Ravizza.** This romantic palazzo exudes a sense of genteel
★ shabbiness. **Pros:** 10-minute walk to the center of town; pleasant garden with a view beyond the city walls; professional staff. **Cons:** not all rooms have views; some rooms are a little cramped. ⊠ *Pian dei Mantellini 34, Città* ☎ *0577/280462* ⊕ *www.palazzoravizza.it* ⟿ *38 rooms, 4 suites* ♿ *In-room: safe, Wi-Fi. In-hotel: bar, parking, some pets allowed* ❍ *Breakfast.*

NIGHTLIFE AND THE ARTS

THE ARTS

Settimane Musicali Senesi festival. Performances by local and national classical musicians take place during a series of concerts held in churches and courtyards during the Settimane Musicali Senesi festival in mid-July. ⊕ *www.chigiana.it.*

Estate Musicale Chigiana. Master classes and workshops held by internationally famous musicians result in top-notch performances in Siena between July and September. Age-old venues such as the Accademia Musicale Chigiana, the Spedale di Santa Maria della Scala, the church of Sant'Agostino, and Piazza Duomo are used for these exceptional concerts. It is best to book well in advance as tickets are usually in high demand. ⊠ *Accademia Musicale Chigiana, Via di Città 89, Città* ☎ *0577/22091* ⊕ *www.chigiana.it.*

NIGHTLIFE

Caffè del Corso. Join the locals for *aperitivi* (apertifs) at this very popular bar, where aspiring artists and savvy students hobnob until 3 am. ⊠ *Banchi di Sopra 25, Camollìa* ☎ *0577/226656.*

Sapordivino. This wine bar at the Grand Hotel Continental has live piano music most evenings. A well-stocked liquor collection includes a well-thought-out list of whiskeys. ⊠ *Banchi di Sopra 85, Città* ☎ *0577/56011.*

SPORTS AND THE OUTDOORS

Palio. Siena's thrilling horse race takes place every year on July 2 and August 16. Three laps around the track in the Piazza del Campo earn the victor the *palio* (a hand-painted banner, unique to each event), and the respect or scorn of the remaining 16 contrade. Tickets usually sell out months in advance; call the Siena tourist office for more information. Note that some hotels reserve a number of tickets for guests. It's also possible you might luck out and get an unclaimed seat or two. The standing-room center of the piazza is free to all on a first-come, first-served basis, until just moments before the start. If you opt for this option, beware of the summer heat, and take water with you. The entry of the horses into the starting gate can sometimes be a lengthy process—they are easily spooked and it can take up to several hours to get things ready—all-in-all, you might be better off finding a comfortable seat in front of a TV. ⊠ *Siena tourist office, Piazza del Campo 56, Città* ☎ *0577/280551.*

SHOPPING

Siena is known for a delectable variety of cakes and cookies with recipes dating to medieval times. Some Sienese sweets are *cavallucci* (sweet spice biscuits), *panforte* (a traditional Christmas delicacy, literally "strong bread," with honey, hazelnuts, almonds, and spices), *ricciarelli* (almond-paste cookies), and *castagnaccio* (a baked Tuscan flat cake made in fall and winter from a batter of chestnut flour topped with pine nuts and rosemary).

ARTS AND CRAFTS

Antiche Dimore. Embroidered linens, curtains, and sheets made by Sienese artisans are among the housewares sold at this store run by Debora Loreni. ⊠ *Via di Città 115, Città* ☎ *0577/45337.*

Bottega dell'Arte. If you've always wanted a 14th- or 15th-century painting to hang on your wall, but the cost of acquiring one is prohibitive, consider purchasing one of the superb copies at this shop made by Chiara or her brother Michelangelo Casoni. Their work in tempera and in gold leaf is of the highest quality. ⊠ *Via Stalloreggi 47, Città* ☎ *0577/40755.*

Fioretta Bacci. Wool, mohair, silk, linen, and cotton are woven on-site, and turned into sweaters and jackets in the colors of the rainbow. ⊠ *Via San Pietro 7, Città* ☎ *0577/282200* ⊕ *www.fiorettabacci.it.*

Siena Ricama. Siena has been famous for centuries for its fine embroidery work, and Bruna Brizza continues the tradition in her tiny shop. Hand stitching, usually on simple white and cream-color linen, adorns lamp shades, tablecloths, and other housewares. ⊠ *Via di Città 61, Città* ☎ *0577/288339.*

Vetrate Artistiche Toscane. Stained-glass artists create and sell contemporary secular and religious works here. If you want to learn the technique, they also offer workshops and apprenticeship programs. ⊠ *Via della Galluzza 5, Camollìa* ☎ *0577/48033* ⊕ *www.glassisland.com.*

FOOD AND DRINK

Antico Pizzicheria. There has been a *salumeria* (delicatessen) here since 1889. The cheeses, cured meats, and made-to-order panini are top-notch. ⊠ *Via di Città 93–95, Città* ☎ *0577/289164.*

Enoteca Italiana. Italy's only state-sponsored enoteca has a vast selection of wines from all parts of the country. Housed in the fortress that the Florentines built to dominate Siena after they conquered the town in 1555, it's a must for any lover of Italian wines. ⊠ *Fortezza Medicea 1, Camollìa* ☎ *0577/228832* ☉ *Mon.–Sat., noon–1 am.*

La Bottega dei Sapori Antichi. Bruno De Miccoli stocks an impressive array of verdure sott'olio, local wines, and dried herbs in his food and wine bar. ⊠ *Via delle Terme 39–41, Camollìa* ☎ *0577/285501.*

Nannini. Locals flock to this central café to quaff a cappuccino and pick up panforte (the chocolate panforte is a real treat) and ricciarelli to go. ⊠ *Banchi di Sopra 24, Camollìa* ☎ *0577/236009.*

MONTERIGGIONI AND COLLE DI VAL D'ELSA

From Siena the Via Cassia (SR2) heading north passes through two pretty towns, Monteriggioni and Colle di Val d'Elsa. Both are well worth visiting: Monteriggioni, for its spectacularly well-preserved ring of medieval walls, and Colle di Val d'Elsa for the elegance of its 15th-century upper town.

MONTERIGGIONI

19 km (12 miles) northwest of Siena, 55 km (34 miles) south of Florence.

Tiny Monteriggioni makes a nice stop on the way north to Colle di Val d'Elsa, San Gimignano, or Volterra. It's hard to imagine that this little town surrounded by poppy fields was ever anything but sleepy, but in the 13th century Monteriggioni served as Siena's northernmost defense against impending Florentine invasion. (It's likely that the residents of the town spent many a sleepless night.) The town's formidable walls are in good condition, although the 14 square towers are not as tall as in Dante's (1265–1321) time, when the poet likened them to giants guarding the horrifying central pit of hell. The town empties of day-trippers at sundown, and this hamlet becomes very tranquil.

GETTING HERE

You can reach Monteriggioni by car on either the SR2 or the Florence–Siena Superstrada. Buses run frequently to and from Siena. The closest train station to Monteriggioni with frequent service to and from Siena is in Castellina Scalo. You will then have to reach Monteriggioni on foot—it's a 4-km (2½-mile) walk.

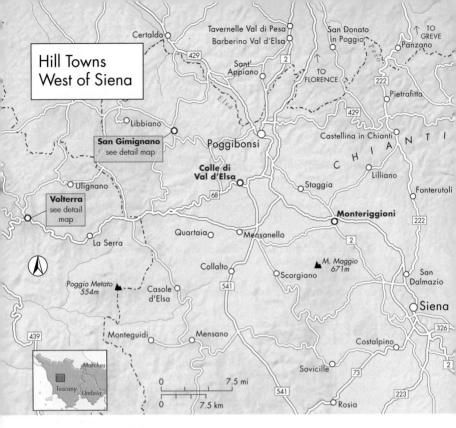

Hill Towns
West of Siena

VISITOR INFORMATION
Monteriggioni tourism office ✉ *Piazza Roma 23, Monteriggioni*
☎ *0577/304834.*

WHERE TO EAT AND STAY

For expanded hotel reviews, visit Fodors.com.

$ ✗ **Il Pozzo.** Famous for its preparation of a 16th-century recipe of *cing-*
TUSCAN   *hiale al cioccolato* (wild boar stewed in chocolate sauce), this restaurant
is a popular spot. Tamer specialties include a range of homemade fresh
pastas, *filetto alla boscaiola* (fillet of beef with porcini mushrooms), *pic-*
cione ripieno (stuffed squab), and a long list of homey desserts. ✉ *Piazza*
Roma 2 ☎ *0577/304127* ⊕ *www.ilpozzo.net* ☽ *Closed Mon., last 3 wks*
in Jan.–mid-Feb. No dinner Sun.

$$$ ⛫ **Borgo San Luigi.** This 17th-century villa lined with lavender bushes
and cypress trees sits just outside Monteriggioni. **Pros:** good base for
exploring Siena; some rooms have kitchens; excellent gym and pool.
Cons: somewhat isolated; few restaurants are within walking distance.
✉ *Strada della Cerretta 7, 4 km (2½ miles) southwest of Monterig-*
gioni, Località San Luigi Strove ☎ *0577/301055* ⊕ *www.borgosanluigi.*
it ⤳ *54 rooms, 10 apartments* ⌂ *In-room: safe, kitchen. In-hotel: res-*
taurant, bar, pool, tennis court, gym, business center, some pets allowed
⛶⦿ *Breakfast.*

$$$$ ⊞ **Hotel Monteriggioni.** A sense of freshness comes from the terra-cotta floors, high wood-beamed ceilings, and soothing whitewashed walls in the hotel's guest rooms. **Pros:** great location inside town walls; well-appointed rooms; peaceful setting. **Cons:** no views beyond the walls; no nightlife to speak of. ⊠ *Via I Maggio 4* ☎ *0577/305009* ⊕ *www.hotelmonteriggioni.net* ⮐ *12 rooms* ⚒ *In-room: safe, Wi-Fi. In-hotel: restaurant, pool, some pets allowed* ⊘ *Closed Jan. 9–Feb. 28* ⦿ *Breakfast.*

WORD OF MOUTH

"What Tuscany has to offer is beautiful vistas and winding roads that take you to small towns and villages—like Monteriggioni. We found it on the way to Siena from Florence. It was a charming walled village. When we got home, we found out that Dante described the well in the center of the piazza as the entrance to hell in his *Divine Comedy*." —tony

COLLE DI VAL D'ELSA

12 km (7 miles) west of Monteriggioni, 25 km (16 miles) northwest of Siena, 51 km (32 miles) south of Florence.

Most people pass through on their way to and from popular tourist destinations Volterra and San Gimignano—a shame, since Colle di Val d'Elsa has a lot to offer. It's another town on the Via Francigena that benefited from trade along the pilgrimage route to Rome. Colle got an extra boost in the late 16th century when it was given a bishopric, probably related to an increase in trade when nearby San Gimignano was cut off from the well-traveled road. The town is arranged on two levels, and from the 12th century onward the flat lower portion was given over to a flourishing papermaking industry; today the area is mostly modern, and efforts have shifted toward the production of fine glass and crystal.

Make your way from the newer lower town (Colle Bassa) to the prettier, upper part of town (Colle Alta); the best views of the valley are to be had from Viale della Rimembranza, the road that loops around the western end of town, past the church of San Francesco. The early-16th-century Porta Nuova was inserted into the preexisting medieval walls, just as several handsome Renaissance palazzos were placed into the medieval neighborhood to create what is now called the Borgo. The Via Campana, the main road, passes through the facade of the surreal Palazzo Campana, an otherwise unfinished building that serves as a door connecting the two parts of the upper town. Via delle Volte, named for the vaulted arches that cover it, leads straight to Piazza del Duomo. There is a convenient parking lot off the SS68, with stairs leading up the hill. Buses arrive at Piazza Arnolfo, named after the town's favorite son, Arnolfo di Cambio (circa 1245–1302), the early-Renaissance architect who designed Florence's Duomo and Palazzo Vecchio (but sadly nothing here).

GETTING HERE

You can reach Colle di Val d'Elsa by car on either the SR2 from Siena or the Florence–Siena Superstrada. Bus service to and from Siena and Florence is frequent.

VISITOR INFORMATION

Colle di Val d'Elsa Tourism Office ⊠ *Via Campana 43* ☎ *0577/922791.*

EXPLORING

Chiesa di Santa Caterina. Visit this 15th-century church to view the excellent stained-glass window in the apse, executed by Sebastiano Mainardi (circa 1460–1513), as well as a haunting *Pietà* created by local artist Zacchia Zacchi (1473–1544). ⊠ *Via Campana 35* ☎ *0577/920647* ☉ *Daily 8–noon and 3–6.*

Duomo. Several reconstructions have left little to admire of the once-Romanesque Duomo. Inside is the **Cappella del Santo Chiodo** (Chapel of the Holy Nail), built in the 15th century to hold a nail allegedly from the cross upon which Christ was crucified. (Perhaps it inspired the locals to go into the nail-making business, which became another of the town's flourishing industries.) ⊠ *Piazza del Duomo, on Via del Castello* ☎ *No phone* ☉ *Daily 8–noon and 4–6.*

Museo Civico e d'Arte Sacra. The museum of sacred art displays religious relics as well as triptychs from the Sienese and Florentine schools dating from the 14th and 15th centuries. It also contains the town's tribute to Arnolfo di Cambio, with photos of the buildings he designed for other towns. Down Via del Castello, at No. 63, is the house-tower where Arnolfo was born in 1245. (It's not open to the public.) Note that despite the posted opening times, winter hours are highly variable. ⊠ *Via del Castello 31* ☎ *0577/923888* 🎫 *€6, includes the Museo Archeologico and the Museo del Cristallo* ☉ *Apr.–Oct., Tues.–Sun. 10:30–12:30 and 4:30–7:30; Nov.–Mar., weekends 10:30–noon and 3:30–6:30.*

WHERE TO EAT

¢

TUSCAN

✕ **L'Angolo di Sapia.** A short and simple set menu that changes with the seasons is one of the reasons to eat here. The other is the sweeping view from the terrace of the countryside below. You might want to start with the *piatto misto* (mixed plate, which in this case includes a slice of vegetable tart and mozzarella and tomatoes) and then continue with one of the house specialties like the *topini della torre* (gnocchi in a vibrant saffron sauce). Every evening there's a cocktail hour with an ample free buffet. ⊠ *Via del Castello 4* ☎ *0577/921453* ☉ *No lunch. Closed Mon.–Wed. and Oct.–Apr.*

$

TUSCAN

✕ **L'Antica Trattoria.** Residents of Colle di Val d'Elsa hold this trattoria in high esteem, even though it's a little overpriced. Tuscan classics fill the large menu, which concentrates on game, particularly pheasant, pigeon, and quail. Some of the pastas, such as *tortelli di sedano in purea di fagioli* (stuffed pasta with creamy celery and topped with a light bean puree) differ from the usual fare. The decor is simple; in warmer months outdoor seating on a square is a possibility. The service is first-rate. ⊠ *Piazza Arnolfo di Cambio 23* ☎ *0577/923747* 🍴 *Reservations essential* ☉ *Closed Tues. and last wk in Aug.*

¢

TUSCAN

✕ **Molino il Moro.** The early-12th-century grain mill, now a romantic restaurant, is perched over a rushing river. The chef concocts sophisticated spins on traditional dishes, such as the divine *filetto di coniglio in crosta con purè di pruge* (rabbit loin with a prune puree). The wine list is short but sweet, the service note-perfect. ⊠ *Via della Ruota 2* ☎ *0577/920862* ⊕ *www.molinoilmoro.it* ⊙ *Closed Mon. No lunch Tues.*

$$$ ╳ **Ristorante Arnolfo.** Food lovers should not miss Arnolfo, one of Tus-
ITALIAN cany's most highly regarded restaurants. Chef Gaetano Trovato sets
Fodor's Choice high standards of creativity; his dishes daringly ride the line between
★ innovation and tradition, almost always with spectacular results. The
menu changes frequently but you are always sure to find fish and lots of
fresh vegetables in summer. You're in for a treat if the specials include
carrè di agnello al vino rosso e sella alle olive (rack of lamb in a red
wine sauce and lamb saddle with olives). ⊠ *Piazza XX Settembre 52*
☎ *0577/920549* ⊕ *www.arnolfo.com* ⊙ *Closed Tues. and Wed., last wk
in Jan. and Feb., and last wk in Aug.*

WHERE TO STAY

For expanded hotel reviews, visit Fodors.com.

$$$$ ⊡ **La Suvera.** Pope Julius II once owned this luxurious estate in the valley
★ of the River Elsa. **Pros:** luxurious accommodations; historic setting; far
from the madding crowd. **Cons:** out-of-the-way location; showing its
age; some bristle at the extremely formal service. ⊠ *Off SS541 15 km (9
miles) south of Colle di Val d'Elsa, Pievescola* ☎ *0577/960300* ⊕ *www.
lasuvera.it* ⊅ *36 rooms, 12 suites* ⌂ *In-room: safe, Wi-Fi. In-hotel: res-
taurant, bar, pool, tennis court, business center, some age restrictions*
⊙ *Closed Nov.–Easter* ¶⊙¶ *Breakfast.*

$$ ⊡ **Palazzo San Lorenzo.** Occupying a 17th-century palace in the historic center of Colle, this hotel boasts rooms that exude warmth and
comfort, with light-color wooden floors, soothingly tinted fabrics, and
large bright windows. **Pros:** central location; spotless; extremely well
maintained. **Cons:** caters to business groups; some of the public spaces
feel rather sterile. ⊠ *Via Gracco del Secco 113, Colle di Val d'Elsa*
☎ *0577/923675* ⊕ *www.palazzosanlorenzo.it* ⊅ *43 rooms, 6 suite, 6
apartments* ⌂ *In-room: a/c, safe, Wi-Fi. In-hotel: restaurant, gym, spa,
business center, parking, some pets allowed* ¶⊙¶ *Breakfast.*

SHOPPING

Cristalleria Ceramica Artistica. The crystal displayed here runs the gamut
from conventional to inspired: particularly gorgeous are the opaque-
glass vases, which look as if they've just been dug up, intact, from
Etruscan tombs. ⊠ *Via di Campiglia 146* ☎ *0577/959666.*

La Moleria Gelli. Art meets contemporary design in the glass objects here.
The slanted champagne flutes are a marvel of engineering, as are the
wine carafes, shaped like a child's top, that perfectly balance and gently
spin. ⊠ *Via delle Romite 26* ☎ *0577/920163.*

SAN GIMIGNANO

Fodor's Choice *14 km (9 miles) northwest of Colle di Val d'Elsa, 38 km (24 miles)*
★ *northwest of Siena, 54 km (34 miles) southwest of Florence.*

When you're on a hilltop surrounded by soaring medieval towers sil-
houetted against the sky, it's difficult not to fall under the spell of San
Gimignano. Its tall walls and narrow streets are typical of Tuscan hill

towns, but it's the medieval "skyscrapers" that set the town apart from its neighbors. Today 14 towers remain, but at the height of the Guelph–Ghibelline conflict there was a forest of more than 70, and it was possible to cross the town by rooftop rather than by road. The towers were built partly for defensive purposes—they were a safe refuge and useful for pouring boiling oil on attacking enemies—and partly for bolstering the egos of their owners, who competed with deadly seriousness to build the highest tower in town.

The relative proximity of San Gimignano, arguably Tuscany's best-preserved medieval hill town, to Siena and Florence also makes it one of Italy's most-visited ones. But the traffic is hardly a new thing; the Etruscans were encamped here, and the Romans made it an outpost. With the yearly flow of pilgrims to and from Rome in the Middle Ages, the town—then known as Castel di Selva—became a prosperous market center. When locals prayed to a martyred bishop from Modena for relief from invading barbarians, relief they got, and in gratitude they rechristened the town in his honor as San Gimignano. Devastated by the Black Death of 1348, the town subsequently fell under Florentine control. Things got going again in the Renaissance, with some of the best and brightest painters in the area—Ghirlandaio (1449–94), Benozzo Gozzoli (1420–97), and Pinturicchio (circa 1454–1513)—coming to work, but soon after, the main road was moved, cutting San Gimignano off from the main trade route and sending it into decline.

Today San Gimignano isn't much more than a gentrified walled city, touristy but still very much worth exploring because, despite the profusion of cheesy souvenir shops lining the main drag, there's some serious Renaissance art to be seen here. Tour groups arrive early and clog the wine-tasting rooms—San Gimignano is famous for its light white Vernaccia—and art galleries for much of the day, but most sights stay open through late afternoon, when all the tour groups have long since departed.

GETTING HERE

You can reach San Gimignano by car from the Florence–Siena Superstrada. Exit at Poggibonsi Nord and follow signs for San Gimignano. Although it involves changing buses in Poggibonsi, getting to San Gimignano by bus from Florence is a relatively straightforward affair. SITA operates the service between Siena or Florence and Poggibonsi. From Siena, Tra-In offers direct service to San Gimignano several times daily. You cannot reach San Gimignano by train.

VISITOR INFORMATION

San Gimignano tourism office ✉ *Piazza Duomo 1* ☏ *0577/940008* ⊕ *www.sangimignano.com.*

EXPLORING SAN GIMIGNANO

The center of San Gimignano is closed to traffic. If you arrive by car, there are parking lots next to the Parco della Rimembranza, near Porta San Giovanni, the main pedestrian entrance into town. Buses from Florence and Siena all stop at Porta San Giovanni. Follow Via San Giovanni a short way to the center of town. Souvenir shops lining the way leave no doubt about the lifeblood of the town, but better things lie ahead. Pass under Arco dei Becci, a leftover from the city's Etruscan walls, to Piazza della Cisterna, a square named for the cistern at its center. The Piazza del Duomo, where you'll find the Museo Civico, lies just beyond the two towers built by the Ardinghelli family. Continue along Via San Matteo and turn right just before Porta San Matteo to reach Sant'Agostino.

TIMING You can see all of San Gimignano's main sights in a single day. But, if you arrive in the morning and leave in the afternoon, you miss the town at its best. From 9 to 5 tourists on jaunts from Florence and Siena swarm San Gimignano's streets, filling the shops and museums. In the evening, when all the day-trippers have departed, the town is transformed. Reclaiming its serenity, San Gimignano takes on a magically medieval air that, if you can possibly stay the night in or near town, is not to be missed.

TOP ATTRACTIONS

Collegiata. The town's main church is not officially a *duomo* (cathedral), because San Gimignano has no bishop. But behind the simple facade of the Romanesque Collegiata lies a treasure trove of fine frescoes, covering nearly every part of the interior. Bartolo di Fredi's 14th-century fresco cycle of Old Testament scenes extends along one wall. Their distinctly medieval feel, with misshapen bodies, buckets of spurting blood, and lack of perspective, contrasts with the much more reserved scenes from the *Life of Christ* (attributed to 14th-century artist Lippo Memmi), painted on the opposite wall just 14 years later. Taddeo di Bartolo's otherworldly *Last Judgment* (late 14th century), with its distorted and suffering nudes, reveals the great influence of Dante's horrifying imagery in *The Inferno* and was surely an inspiration for later painters. Proof that the town had more than one protector, Benozzo Gozzoli's arrow-riddled *St. Sebastian* was commissioned in gratitude after the locals prayed to the saint for relief from plague. The Renaissance **Cappella di Santa Fina** is decorated with a fresco cycle by Domenico Ghirlandaio illustrating the life of Saint Fina. A small girl who suffered from a terminal disease, Fina repented for her sins—among them having accepted an orange from a boy—and in penance lived out the rest of her short life on a wooden board, tormented by rats. The scenes depict the arrival of Saint Gregory, who appeared to assure her that death was near; the flowers that miraculously grew from the wooden plank; and the miracles that accompanied her funeral, including the healing of her nurse's paralyzed hand and the restoration of a blind choirboy's vision. ⊠ *Piazza Pecori 2* ☎ *0577/940316* 💶 *€3; €5.50 includes the Museo d'Arte Sacra* ⊙ *Apr.–Oct., weekdays 9:30–7:10, Sat. 9:30–5:10, Sun. 12:30–5:10; Nov. 1–15, Dec. 1–Jan. 15, and Feb. 1–Mar., Mon.–Sat. 9:30–4:40, Sun. 12:30–5:10. Closed Nov. 16–30 and Jan. 16–31.*

★ **Museo Civico.** The impressive civic museum occupies what was the "new" Palazzo del Popolo; the Torre Grossa is adjacent. Dante visited San Gimignano for only one day as a Guelph ambassador from Florence to ask the locals to join the Florentines in supporting the pope—just long enough to get the main council chamber, which now holds a 14th-century *Maestà* by Lippo Memmi, named after him. Off the stairway is a small room containing the racy frescoes by Memmo di Filippuccio (active 1288–1324), depicting the courtship, shared bath, and wedding of a young, androgynous-looking couple. That the space could have been a private room for the commune's chief magistrate may have something to do with the work's highly charged eroticism.

Upstairs, paintings by famous Renaissance artists Pinturicchio (*Madonna Enthroned*), and Benozzo Gozzoli (*Madonna and Child*), and two large *tondi* (circular paintings) by Filippino Lippi (circa 1457–1504) attest to the importance and wealth of San Gimignano. Also worth seeing are Taddeo di Bartolo's *Life of San Gimignano*, with the saint holding a model of the town as it once appeared; Lorenzo di Niccolò's gruesome martyrdom scene in the *Life of St. Bartholomew* (1401); and scenes from the *Life of St. Fina* on a tabernacle that was designed to hold her head. Admission includes the steep climb to the top of the Torre Grossa, which on a clear day has spectacular views. ⊠ *Piazza Duomo 2* ☎ *0577/990312* 💶 *€5* ⊙ *Jan., daily 10:30–5:30; Feb., Mar., and Oct.–Dec., daily 10–5:30; Apr.–Sept., daily 9:30–7.*

NEED A
BREAK?
Enoteca Gustavo. There's no shortage of places to try Vernaccia di San Gimignano, the justifiably famous white wine with which San Gimignano would be singularly associated—if it weren't for all those towers. At this wine bar, run by energetic Maristella Becucci, you can buy a glass of Vernaccia di San Gimignano and sit down with a cheese plate or with one of the fine crostini. ⊠ *Via San Matteo 29* ☎ *0577/940057*.

★ **Sant'Agostino.** Make a beeline for Benozzo Gozzoli's superlative 15th-century fresco cycle depicting scenes from the life of Saint Augustine. The saint's work was essential to the early development of church doctrine. As thoroughly discussed in his autobiographical *Confessions* (an acute dialogue with God), Augustine, like many saints, sinned considerably in his youth before finding God. But unlike the lives of other saints, where the story continues through a litany of deprivations, penitence, and often martyrdom, Augustine's life and work focused on philosophy and the reconciliation of faith and thought. Benozzo's 17 scenes on the choir wall depict Augustine as a man who traveled and taught extensively in the 4th and 5th centuries. The 15th-century altarpiece by Piero del Pollaiolo (1443–96) depicts *The Coronation of the Virgin* and the various protectors of the city. On your way out of Sant'Agostino, stop in at the **Cappella di San Bartolo,** with a sumptuously elaborate tomb by Benedetto da Maiano (1442–97). ⊠ *Piazza Sant'Agostino 10* ☎ *0577/907012* ☎ *Free* ☉ *Apr.–Oct., daily 7–noon and 3–7; Nov., Dec., and Mar., daily 7–noon and 3–6; Jan. and Feb., Mon. 3–6, Tues.–Sun. 10–noon and 3–6.*

WORTH NOTING

Museo d'Arte Sacra. Even with all the decoration in the Collegiata, the fine collection of various religious articles in the church museum, across the pretty courtyard, is still worth a look. The highlight is a *Madonna and Child* by Bartolo di Fredi. Other pieces include several busts, wooden statues of Christ, the Virgin Mary, and the angel Gabriel, and several illuminated songbooks. ⊠ *Piazza Pecori 4* ☎ *0577/940316* ☎ *€2.50; €5.50 includes the Collegiata* ☉ *Apr.–Oct., weekdays 9:30–7:10, Sat. 9:30–5:10, Sun. 12:30–5:10; Nov. 1–15, Dec. 1–Jan. 15, Feb., and Mar., Mon.–Sat. 9:30–4:40, Sun. 12:30–4:40. Closed Nov. 16–30 and Jan. 16–31.*

Palazzo del Podestà. Across the piazza from the Collegiata is the "old" town hall built in 1239. Its tower was erected by the municipality in 1255 to settle the raging "my-tower-is-bigger-than-your-tower" contest—as you can see, a solution that just didn't last long. The palace is closed to visitors. ⊠ *Piazza Duomo.*

Rocca di Montestaffoli. If you want to see more of that quintessential Tuscan landscape, walk up to the Rocca di Montestaffoli, which sits at the highest point in San Gimignano. Built after the Florentine conquest to keep an eye on the town, and dismantled a few centuries later, it's now a public garden. ⊠ *Off Porta Quercecchio* ☎ *No phone* ☎ *Free* ☉ *Daily dawn–dusk.*

WHERE TO EAT

¢ ✕**La Mangiatoia.** Multicolor ging-
TUSCAN ham tablecloths provide an interesting juxtaposition with rib-vaulted
ceilings dating from the 13th century. The lighthearted touch might
be explained by the influence of chef
Susi Cuomo, who has been presiding over the kitchen for more than
20 years. The menu is seasonal—in
autumn, don't miss her *sacottino di
pecorino al tartufo* (little packages
of pasta stuffed with pecorino and
seasoned with truffles). In summer, eat lighter fare on the intimate,
flower-bedecked terrace in the back. ⊠ *Via Mainardi 5* ☎ *0577/941528*
⊕ *www.ristorantelamangiatoia.it* ☉ *Closed Tues., 3 wks in Nov., and
1 wk in Jan.*

> **WORD OF MOUTH**

"It's nice to arrive in San Gimignano after the bus tours leave
for the day. Make sure you take
a walk around the walls of the
town…it's lovely in the morning. There's a path to follow and
the views are jaw dropping."
—CRAZY4TRAVEL

4

¢ ✕**Osteria del Carcere.** Though it calls itself an *osteria* (a tavern), this
WINE BAR place much more resembles a wine bar, with a bill of fare that includes
several different types of pâtés and a short list of seasonal soups and salads. The sampler of goat cheeses, which can be paired with local wines,
should not be missed. Operatic arias play softly in the background, and
service is courteous. ⊠ *Via del Castello 13* ☎ *0577/941905* ▭ *No credit
cards* ☉ *Closed Wed. and early Jan.–Mar. No lunch Thurs.*

WHERE TO STAY

For expanded hotel reviews, visit Fodors.com.

$ ⊞ **Bel Soggiorno.** If you're looking for a place within the town walls,
this is a fine choice. **Pros:** inside the ancient walls of San Gimignano;
magnificent views; some rooms have small terraces facing the countryside. **Cons:** plain decor; somber public spaces. ⊠ *Via San Giovanni 91*
☎ *0577/940375* ⊕ *www.hotelbelsoggiorno.it* ⇱ *21 rooms* ⇱ *In-hotel:
parking* ☉ *Closed late Nov.–late Dec.* ⍩ *Breakfast.*

$$$$ ⊞ **La Collegiata.** After serving as a Franciscan convent and then the residence of the noble Strozzi family, the Collegiata has been converted into
a fine hotel, with no expense spared in the process. **Pros:** gorgeous views
from terrace; elegant rooms in main building. **Cons:** long walk into
town; service can be impersonal; some rooms are dimly lighted. ⊠ *Località Strada 27, 1 km (½ mile) north of San Gimignano town center*
☎ *0577/943201* ⊕ *www.lacollegiata.it* ⇱ *20 rooms, 1 suite* ⇱ *In-room:
safe, Internet. In-hotel: restaurant, bar, pool, business center, parking,
some pets allowed* ☉ *Closed Nov.–Mar.* ⍩ *Breakfast.*

$ ⊞ **Pescille.** A rambling farmhouse has been transformed into a hand-
some hotel with understated contemporary furniture in the bedrooms
and country-classic motifs such as farm implements hanging on the
walls in the bar. **Pros:** splendid views; quiet atmosphere; 10-minute
walk to town. **Cons:** furnishings a bit austere; there's an elevator for
luggage but not for guests. ⊠ *Località Pescille, 4 km (2½ miles) south
of San Gimignano* ☎ *0577/940186* ⊕ *www.pescille.it* ⇱ *38 rooms, 12*

suites ⚫ *In-room: Wi-Fi. In-hotel: bar, pool, tennis court, gym, business center, parking* ⊘ *Closed Nov.–Mar.* ⦿*Breakfast.*

$$ 🔟**Torraccia di Chiusi.** A perfect retreat for families, this tranquil hilltop *agriturismo* (farm stay) with is own restaurant and extensive grounds is just 5 km (3 miles) from the hubbub of San Gimignano. **Pros:** tranquil haven close to San Gimignano; great walking possibilities; family-run hospitality. **Cons:** 30 minutes from the nearest town on a windy gravel road; need a car to get here. ✉ *Località Montauto, San Gimignano* 📞*0577/941972* ⊕ *www.torracciadichiusi.com* 🛏 *8 rooms, 3 apartments* ⚫ *In-room: no a/c, kitchen. In-hotel: restaurant, pool, some pets allowed* ⦿*Breakfast.*

NIGHTLIFE AND THE ARTS

Carnevale. San Gimignano is one of the few small towns in the area that make a big deal out of carnival festivities, with locals dressing up in colorful costumes and marching through the streets from 3:30 to 6:30 on the four Sundays preceding Shrove Tuesday.

Estate San Gimignanese. If you visit in summer, check with the tourist office about concerts and performances related to San Gimignano's arts festival, one of Tuscany's oldest. It's held mid-June to August each year. ✉ *Piazza Duomo 1* 📞 *0577/940008* ⊕ *www.sangimignano.com.*

SHOPPING

Antica Latteria di Maurizio e Tiziana. Maurizio and Tiziana's shop has an arresting array of cheeses, and perhaps the best array of verdure sott'olio in town. They also make top-notch panini. ✉ *Via San Matteo 19* 📞 *0577/941952.*

Mercato. As everywhere else, the town brightens on *mercato* (open-air market) mornings, every Thursday and Saturday, in Piazza del Duomo. It's the place to pick up fresh fruits and other snacks.

VOLTERRA

30 km (18 miles) southwest of San Gimignano.

As you approach the town through bleak, rugged terrain, you can see that not all Tuscan hill towns rise above rolling green fields. Volterra stands mightily over Le Balze, a stunning series of gullied hills and valleys formed by erosion that has slowly eaten away at the foundation of the town—now considerably smaller than it was during its Etruscan glory days 25 centuries ago. The town began as the northernmost city of the 12 that made up the Etruscan League, and excavations in the 18th century revealed a bounty of relics, which are on exhibit at the impressively overstocked Museo Etrusco Guarnacci. The Romans and later the Florentines laid siege to the town to secure its supply of minerals and stones, particularly alabaster, which is still worked into handicrafts on sale in many of the shops around town.

GETTING HERE

By car, the best route from San Gimignano follows the SP1 south to Castel San Gimignano and then the SS68 all the way to Volterra. Coming from the west, take the SS1, a coastal road to Cecina, then follow

Volterra

0   100 yards
0   100 meters

the SS68 to Volterra. Either way, there's a long, winding climb at the end of your trip. Traveling to Volterra by bus or train is complicated; avoid it if possible, especially if you have lots of luggage. From Florence or Siena the journey is best made by bus and involves a change in Colle di Val d'Elsa. From Rome or Pisa, it is best to take the train to Cecina and then take a bus to Volterra or a train to the Volterra-Saline station. The latter is 10 km (6 miles) from town.

VISITOR INFORMATION
Volterra tourism office ✉ *Piazza dei Priori 20* ☎ *0588/87257* ⊕ *www. volterratur.it.*

EXPLORING VOLTERRA

Driving in the old town is forbidden. There are several parking lots around the perimeter of the city walls, the most convenient of which is the underground parking lot at Piazza Martiri della Libertà. Begin your exploration of Volterra from Piazza Martiri della Libertà and take Via Marchesi to Piazza dei Priori. It's lined with an impressive collection of medieval buildings, including the imposing Palazzo dei Priori, the seat of city government for more than seven centuries. Across the piazza is the Palazzo Pretorio topped by the Torre del Porcellino, named after the sculpted little boar mounted at the upper window. Walk down Via Turazza along the side of the Duomo to the triangular Piazza San Giovanni, and head out the left corner of the piazza to steal a look at the ancient Porta all'Arco Etrusco.

TIMING Allow at least three hours to see the town. Off-season, it's best to make an early start in order to have time in the museums before they close. The whole town can easily be seen in a day, although its distance from everything else makes it a good stopover as well.

TOP ATTRACTIONS

Duomo. Behind the textbook 13th-century Pisan–Romanesque facade is proof that Volterra counted for something during the Renaissance, when many important Tuscan artists came to decorate the church. Three-dimensional stucco portraits of local saints are on the gold, red, and blue ceiling (1580) designed by Francesco Capriani, including Saint Linus, the successor to Saint Peter as pope and claimed by the Volterrans to have been born here. The highlight of the Duomo is the brightly painted 13th-century wooden life-size *Deposition* in the chapel of the same name. The unusual Cappella dell'Addolorata (Chapel of the Grieved) has two terra-cotta Nativity scenes; the depiction of the arrival of the Magi has a background fresco by Benozzo Gozzoli. The 16th-century pulpit in the middle of the nave is lined with fine 14th-century sculpted panels, attributed to a member of the Pisano family. Across from the Duomo in the center of the piazza is the **Battistero,** with stripes that match the Duomo. Evidently this baptistery got a lot of use, as the small marble baptismal font carved by Andrea Sansovino in 1502 was moved to the wall to the right of the entrance in the mid-18th century to make room for a much larger one. ⊠ *Piazza San Giovanni* ☏ *0588/88524* ⊘ *Daily 7–7.*

Museo Etrusco Guarnacci. An extraordinarily large and unique collection of Etruscan relics is made all the more interesting by clear explanations in English. The bulk of the collection is comprised of roughly 700 carved funerary urns: the oldest, dating from the 7th century BC, were made from tufa (volcanic rock); a handful are made of terra-cotta; and the vast majority—from the 3rd to 1st century BC—are from alabaster. The urns are grouped by subject and taken together form a fascinating testimony about Etruscan life and death. Some illustrate domestic scenes, others the funeral procession of the deceased. Greek gods and mythology, adopted by the Etruscans, also figure prominently. The sculpted figures on many of the covers may have been made in the image of the deceased, reclining and often holding the cup of life overturned. Particularly well known is *Gli Sposi* (*Husband and Wife*), a haunting, elderly duo in terra-cotta. Also on display are Attic vases, bucchero ceramics, jewelry, and household items. ⊠ *Via Don Minzoni 15* ☏ *0588/86347* ▣ *€8; €10 including the Museo Diocesano di Arte Sacra and the Pinacoteca* ⊘ *Mid-Mar.–early Nov., daily 9–6:45; early Nov.–mid-Mar., daily 9–1:15.*

Pinacoteca. One of Volterra's best-looking Renaissance buildings contains an impressive collection of Tuscan paintings arranged chronologically on two floors. Head straight for Room 12, with Luca Signorelli's (circa 1445–1523) *Madonna and Child with Saints* and Rosso Fiorentino's *Deposition*. Both are masterpieces, and though painted just 30 years apart, they serve to illustrate the shift in style from the early-16th-century Renaissance ideals to full-blown mannerism: the balance of Signorelli's composition becomes purposefully skewed in Fiorentino's painting, where the colors go from vivid but realistic to emotively bright. Other impor-

tant paintings in the small museum include Ghirlandaio's *Apotheosis of Christ with Saints* and a polyptych of the *Madonna and Saints* by Taddeo di Bartolo, which once hung in the Palazzo dei Priori. ⊠ *Via dei Sarti 1* ☎ *0588/87580* 🔗 *€6; €8 including the Museo Etrusco Guarnacci and the Museo Diocesano di Arte Sacra* ⊗ *Mid-Mar.–early Nov., daily 9–7; early Nov.–mid-Mar., daily 8:30–1:45.*

Porta all'Arco Etrusco. Even if a good portion of the arch was rebuilt by the Romans, the three dark, weather-beaten, 3rd-century BC heads carved in basaltic rock (thought to represent Etruscan gods) still face outward, greeting those who enter. A plaque recalls the efforts of the locals who saved the arch from destruction by filling it with stones during the German withdrawal at the end of World War II.

Teatro Romano. Just outside the walls past Porta Fiorentina are the ruins of the 1st-century BC Roman theater, one of the best-preserved in Italy, with adjacent remains of the Roman *terme* (baths). You can enjoy an excellent bird's-eye view of the theater from Via Lungo le Mura. ⊠ *Viale Francesco Ferrucci* ☎ *No phone* 🔗 *€3.50* ⊗ *Mar.–May and Sept.–Nov., daily 10–1 and 2–4; June–Aug., daily 10–6:45; Dec.–Feb., weekends 10–1 and 2–4.*

WORTH NOTING

Museo Diocesano di Arte Sacra. The religious-art collection housed in the Bishop's Palace was collected from local churches, and includes an unusual reliquary by Antonio Pollaiolo with the head of Saint Octavian in silver resting on four golden lions. There's also a fine terra-cotta bust of Saint Linus by Andrea della Robbia (1435–1525/28). Two paintings are noteworthy: Rosso Fiorentino's (1495–1540) *Madonna di Villamagna* and Daniele da Volterra's (1509–66) *Madonna di Ulignano*, named for the village churches in which they were originally placed. ⊠ *Palazzo Vescovile, Via Roma 13* ☎ *0588/86290* 🔗 *€10, includes admission to Museo Etrusco Guarnacci and Pinacoteca* ⊗ *Mid-Mar.– early Nov., daily 9–1 and 3–6; early Nov.–mid-Mar., daily 9–1.*

Palazzo dei Priori. Tuscany's first town hall was built between 1208 and 1254, with a no-nonsense facade, fortresslike crenellations, and a five-sided tower. Such fortifications were commonplace at the time; these served as a model for other similar structures throughout the region, including Florence's Palazzo Vecchio. The Florentine medallions that adorn the facade here were added after the Florentines conquered Volterra. The town leaders still meet on the first floor in the Sala del Consiglio; the room is open to the public and has a mid-14th-century fresco of the *Annunciation.* ⊠ *Piazza dei Priori* ☎ *0588/87257* ⌑ *€1.50* ⊙ *Mid-Mar.–Oct., daily 10:30–5:30; Nov.–mid-Mar., weekends 10–5.*

San Francesco. Look inside the church for the celebrated early-15th-century frescoes of the *Legend of the True Cross* by a local artist. It traces the history of the wood used to make the cross upon which Christ was crucified. From Piazza San Giovanni, take Via Franceschini (which becomes Via San Lino) to the church. ⊠ *Piazza Inghirami, off Via San Lino* ☎ *No phone* ⊙ *Daily 8–noon and 3–6.*

LE BALZE

Walk along Via San Lino, through Porta San Francesco, and out Borgo Santo Stefano into Le Balze—a desolate, undulating landscape of yellow earth drawn into crags and gullies as if worn down by a desert torrent long past. This area was originally part of the Etruscan town (called Vlathri; as usual, the current name is closer to the Roman name, Volaterrae), as evidenced by walls that extend 1 km (½ mile) toward the old Porta Menseri. Toward the end of the road, on the right, is the church of San Giusto (with terra-cotta statues of the town's patron saints). The church was built to replace an earlier church under which the earth had eroded. The haunting landscape is thought to be the result of rainwater collecting and wearing down the soil substructure. The bus for Borgo San Giusto, leaving from Piazza Martiri, goes through Le Balze (about 10 runs per day).

WHERE TO EAT

¢ ✗ **Da Badò.** This is the best place in town to eat traditional food elbow-to-elbow with the locals. Da Badò is family-run, with Lucia in the kitchen and her sons Giacomo and Michele waiting tables. Lucia likes to concentrate on just a few dishes, so it won't take long to decide between the standards, all prepared with a sure hand: *zuppa alla volterrana* (a soup made with vegetables and bread), *pappardelle alla lepre* (wide fettuccine with rabbit sauce), and a stew of either rabbit or wild boar. A slice of homemade almond tart is a must. ⊠ *Borgo San Lazzaro 9* ☎ *0588/86477* ⊕ *www.trattoriadabado.com* ⊙ *Closed Wed.*

TUSCAN

¢ ✗ **Il Sacco Fiorentino.** Start with the *antipasti del Sacco Fiorentino*—a medley of sautéed chicken liver, porcini mushrooms, and polenta drizzled with balsamic vinegar. The meal just gets better when you move on to the *tagliatelle del Sacco Fiorentino,* a riot of curried spaghetti with chicken and roasted red peppers. The wine list is a marvel, as it's long and very well priced. White walls, tile floors, and red tablecloths create an understated tone that is unremarkable, but once the food starts arriving, it's easy to forgive the lack of decoration. ⊠ *Piazza XX Settembre 18* ☎ *0588/88537* ⊙ *Closed Wed.*

TUSCAN
★

Volterra's Porta all'Arco Etrusco

WHERE TO STAY

For expanded hotel reviews, visit Fodors.com.

$ **Etruria.** Giuseppina and Lisa, who run this simple yet tastefully decorated hotel, go out of their way to make your visit memorable. **Pros:** great central location; friendly staff; tranquil garden. **Cons:** some rooms can be noisy during the day; no air-conditioning; bathrooms old-fashioned and small. ✉ *Via Matteotti 32* ☎ *0588/87377* ⊕ *www.albergoetruria.it* ↗ *21 rooms* ⌂ *In-room: no a/c, Wi-Fi.*

$ **San Lino.** Within the town's medieval walls, this convent-turned-hotel has wood-beam ceilings, graceful archways, and terra-cotta floors in public spaces. **Pros:** steps away from center of town; friendly and helpful staff; convenient parking. **Cons:** rooms facing the street can be noisy; breakfast is adequate, but nothing to write home about. ✉ *Via San Lino 26* ☎ *0588/85250* ⊕ *www.hotelsanlino.com* ↗ *43 rooms* ⌂ *In-room: Wi-Fi. In-hotel: bar, pool, parking, some pets allowed* ☉ *Closed Nov. and Jan.–Feb.* ☉|*Breakfast.*

FESTIVALS

Astiludio festival. On the first Sunday in September the Astiludio festival celebrates a flag-throwing tradition that dates to 1406. Performances and processions are part of the activities.

SHOPPING

Anna Maria Molesini. A large loom dominates this tiny workshop/showroom where scarves, shawls, throws, and jackets are woven. Anna Maria's work, mostly in mohair, is done in lively hues. ⊠ *Via Gramsci 45* ☎ *0588/88411.*

Camillo Rossi. At Camillo Rossi you can watch the artisans create household items in alabaster, and then buy their wares. ⊠ *Via Lungo le Mura del Mandorlo 7* ☎ *0588/86133.*

Cooperativa Artieri Alabastro. The two large showrooms here are housed in medieval buildings and contain a large number of alabaster objects for sale, including bookends, ashtrays, and boxes. ⊠ *Piazza dei Priori 5* ☎ *0588/87590.*

Galleria Agostiniane. In a former medieval monastery, Galleria Agostiniane displays alabaster objects in all shapes and sizes. There's also a video demonstrating how the mineral is quarried and shaped. ⊠ *Piazza XX Settembre 3* ☎ *0588/86868.*

Mercato (*market*). Volterra's market is held on Saturday morning from November to April in Piazza dei Priori, and on Viale Ferrucci (just outside the city walls) from May through October. On hand are a selection of fresh fruits and vegetables, as well as vendors selling everything from corkscrews to *intimi* (underwear).

Arezzo, Cortona, and Eastern Tuscany

WORD OF MOUTH

"I love Arezzo . . . it is just a great town rich with attractions: Food, shops, atmosphere, an active evening passeggiata, and some exquisite art and architecture, and even ancient history. [But] if you are coming in at any time during the monthly antiques fair (the first Sunday of the month and the preceding Saturday) traffic driving into town will be brutal." —tuscanlifeedit

WELCOME TO EASTERN TUSCANY

TOP REASONS TO GO

★ **Driving through the Parco Nazionale Casentino:** The vistas along the winding road of this park in the Casentino will not disappoint.

★ **Piero della Francesca's True Cross frescoes:** If your holy grail is great Renaissance art, seek out these 12 silently enigmatic scenes in Arezzo's Basilica di San Francesco.

★ **Santa Maria al Calcinaio:** The interior of this Cortona church is much like that of Florence's Duomo, and it's a prime example of Renaissance architecture.

★ **Shopping for jewelry in Arezzo:** Gold has been part of Arezzo's economy since Etruscan times, and today the town is well known worldwide for jewelry design.

1 Arezzo. Tuscany's third-largest city feels a touch more cosmopolitan than the neighboring hill towns—meaning among other things that it has the best shopping in the region. The real draw, though, is the Basilica di San Francesco, adorned with frescoes by Piero della Francesca.

2 Cortona. This ancient stone town, made famous by the book *Under the Tuscan Sun*, sits high above the perfectly flat Valdichiana valley, offering great views of beautiful countryside.

3 Sansepolcro. Lovers of Renaissance painting make pilgrimages to out-of-the-way Sansepolcro, birthplace of Piero della Francesca. He often worked in, or near, his hometown, finding inspiration for the landscapes in his often enigmatic paintings.

4 **The Casentino.** A short distance north of Arezzo, the Casentino region is highlighted by the Parco Nazionale Casentino—a drive through the park reveals one gorgeous view after another. Dante, exiled here from Florence, recorded his love of the countryside in *The Divine Comedy*.

GETTING ORIENTED

The hill towns of Arezzo and Cortona are the main attractions of eastern Tuscany; despite their appeal, this part of the region gets less tourist traffic than its neighbors to the west. You'll truly escape the crowds if you venture north to the Casentino, which is backwoods Tuscany—tiny towns and abbeys are sprinkled through beautiful forestland, some of which is set aside as a national park.

Updated
by Peter
Blackman

CLOSER TO ITALY'S RUGGED APENNINES than any other part of the region, eastern Tuscany hides its secrets in the deep valleys of the upper Arno and Tiber rivers, and among mountains covered with thick forests of chestnut, fir, and beech: it was here, at La Verna, that Saint Francis founded a sanctuary and received the signs of Christ's wounds, and here that Michelangelo first saw the light of day. One of Tuscany's finest "off-the-beaten-path" experiences, Parco Nazionale Casentino, is also here, with beautiful mountain scenery that has been maintained and safeguarded by monks for eight centuries. This part of Tuscany invites visitors who seek a more contemplative approach to travel, away from the madding crowd.

PLANNING

MAKING THE MOST OF YOUR TIME

The lovely hill towns of **Arezzo** and **Cortona** serve as introductions to the region. They carry on age-old local traditions—each September Arezzo's beautiful Romanesque and Gothic churches are enlivened by the Giostra del Saracino, a costumed medieval pageant. Since ancient times, Arezzo has been home to important artists: from the Etruscan potters who produced those fiery-red vessels to the poet Petrarch and the writer, architect, and painter Giorgio Vasari. Cortona, magnificently situated, with olive groves and vineyards creeping up to its walls, commands sweeping views over Lago Trasimeno and the plain of the Valdichiana. The delightful medieval streets are a pleasure to wander, and the town has two fine galleries and a scattering of churches that are worth a visit.

Plan on spending a good four days to tour the area. Arezzo and Cortona each merit a full day, and if you stay in the vicinity you'll have a good base from which to explore the countryside. Both towns are close to the A1 (Autostrada del Sole) and are on main train lines.

GETTING HERE AND AROUND

BUS TRAVEL

SITA. Bus service between Florence and Arezzo is provided three times daily by SITA, which also offers a regular service between Arezzo and Cortona, as well as service between Arezzo, Monterchi, and Sansepolcro. ☎ *055/47821 in Florence, 0575/74361 in Sansepolcro, 800/373760 toll-free in Italy ⊕ www.sitabus.it.*

Baschetti. The bus company Baschetti provides service between Arezzo, Monterchi, and Sansepolcro. ☎ *0575/749816 in Sansepolcro ⊕ www. baschetti.it.*

Etruria Mobilità. All bus service in the province of Arezzo is coodinated by Etruria Mobilità, a cooperative of seven different transport companies, including SITA and Baschetti; it's the best source for information about bus service to outlying towns in the region. ☎ *0575/39881 in Arezzo ⊕ www.etruriamobilita.it.*

CAR TRAVEL

The best way to travel within the region, making it possible to explore tiny hill towns and country restaurants, is by car. The roads are better north–south than east–west, so allow time for excessively winding roads when heading east or west. Sometimes it's faster to go a little out of your way and get on one of the bigger north–south routes.

The A1 (Autostrada del Sole), which runs from Florence to Rome, passes close to Arezzo. Cortona is just off the highway linking Perugia to the A1, and Sansepolcro can be reached from Arezzo on the SR73, with Monterchi a short 3-km (2-mile) detour along the way.

Though Arezzo is the third-largest city in Tuscany (after Florence and Pisa), the old town is pretty small, and is on a low hill almost completely closed to traffic. Look for parking along the roads that circle the lower part of town, near the train station, and walk into town from there.

In Cortona, the city center is completely closed to traffic and the few parking areas sprinkled outside the city walls don't make it easy to park. The majority of Cortona's streets are very steep. Fortunately, most of the main sights are grouped near the Duomo in the lower part of town, but if you want to visit the upper town, be prepared for a stiff climb.

For visits to the mountainous National Park of the Casentino and the smaller towns and villages farther to the east, such as Sansepolcro and Monterchi, a rental car is almost a necessity: bus schedules can be difficult to plan around, and train service is either infrequent or nonexistent. All make for rewarding day trips, though a fair part of your time will be spent on winding, beautiful, country roads. If you want time to explore, plan to stay the night.

TRAIN TRAVEL

Ferrovia dello Stato. The national railway service, Ferrovia dello Stato, has frequent trains between Florence and Arezzo. A regular service links Arezzo with Cortona, and with Poppi and the Casentino. ☎ *892021 in Italy* ⊕ *www.trenitalia.com.*

HOTELS

A visit to Tuscany is a trip to the country. There are good hotels in Arezzo and Cortona, but for a classic experience stay in one of the rural accommodations—often converted villas, sometimes working farms or vineyards (known as *agriturismi*).

DINING AND LODGING PRICE CATEGORIES (IN EUROS)				
¢	$	$$	$$$	$$$$
Restaurants	under €15	€15–€25	€25–€35	€35–€45	over €45
Hotels	under €70	€70–€110	€110–€160	€160–€220	over €220

Restaurant prices are for a first course (*primo*), second course (*secondo*), and dessert (*dolce*). Hotel prices are for two people in a standard double room in high season, including tax and service.

AREZZO

Arezzo is today best known for the magnificent Piero della Francesca frescoes in the church of San Francesco. It's also the birthplace of the poet Petrarch (1304–74), the Renaissance artist and art historian Giorgio Vasari, and Guido d'Arezzo (aka Guido Monaco), the inventor of musical notation. Arezzo dates from pre-Etruscan times, when around 1000 BC the first settlers—who continue to puzzle scholars today—erected a cluster of huts. Arezzo thrived as an Etruscan capital from the 7th to the 4th century BC, and was one of the most important cities in the Etruscans' anti-Roman 12-city federation, resisting Rome's rule to the last.

The city eventually fell and in turn flourished under the Romans. In 1248 Guglielmino degli Ubertini, a member of the powerful Ghibelline family, was elected bishop of Arezzo. This sent the city headlong into the enduring conflict between the Ghibellines (pro-emperor) and the Guelphs (pro-pope). In 1289 Florentine Guelphs defeated Arezzo in a famous battle at Campaldino. Among the Florentine soldiers was Dante Alighieri (1265–1321), who often referred to Arezzo in his *Divine Comedy*. Guelph–Ghibelline wars continued to plague Arezzo until the end of the 14th century, when Arezzo lost its independence to Florence.

GETTING HERE

Arezzo is easily reached by car from the A1 (Autostrada del Sole), the main highway running between Florence and Rome. Direct trains connect Arezzo with Rome (2½ hours) and Florence (1 hour). Direct bus service is available from Florence, but not from Rome.

VISITOR INFORMATION

Arezzo tourism office ✉ *Piazza della Libertà, 1* ☎ *0575/401905* ⊕ *www.apt. arezzo.it.*

EXPLORING AREZZO

Sitting on a low hill in a wide plain, Arezzo, especially the clock tower of its Duomo, is visible from afar. Surrounding the older town is an extensive area of urban and industrial sprawl, but once you begin to walk along the narrow, gently climbing pedestrian streets inside the walls, all sense of the surrounding confusion disappears. As you climb, the standard stores of the lower town are gradually replaced by the exclusive antiques and jewelry shops for which Arezzo is famous, and the anonymous modern buildings of the new town give way to elegant Renaissance town palaces, fine Romanesque and Gothic churches, and the charming medieval squares of the upper town—all of which is crowned, quite naturally, by the Duomo itself.

TOP ATTRACTIONS

Fodor's Choice
★

Basilica di San Francesco. The famous Piero della Francesca frescoes depicting *The Legend of the True Cross* (1452–66) were executed on the three walls of the Capella Bacci, the main apse of this 14th-century church. What Sir Kenneth Clark called "the most perfect morning light in all Renaissance painting" may be seen in the lowest section of the right wall, where the troops of Emperor Maxentius flee before the sign of the cross. The view of the frescoes from the nave of the church is limited, but a much closer look is available from the Capella Bacci. The ticket office for the latter is located directly in front of the main entrance, down steps in the lower church. Reservations are recommended June–September. ✉ *Piazza San Francesco* ☎ *0575/352727*

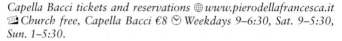

Capella Bacci tickets and reservations ⊕ *www.pierodellafrancesca.it* ✉ *Church free, Capella Bacci €8* ⊙ *Weekdays 9–6:30, Sat. 9–5:30, Sun. 1–5:30.*

Duomo. Arezzo's medieval cathedral at the top of the hill contains an eye-level fresco of a tender *Magdalene* by Piero della Francesca (1420–92); look for it in the north aisle next to the large marble tomb near the organ. Construction of the Duomo began in 1278, but twice came to a halt, and the church wasn't completed until 1510. The facade, designed by Arezzo's Dante Viviani, was added later (1901–14). ✉ *Piazza del Duomo 1* ☎ *0575/23991* ⊙ *Daily 6:30–12:30 and 3–6:30.*

Piazza Grande. With its irregular shape and sloping brick pavement, framed by buildings of assorted centuries, Arezzo's central piazza echoes Siena's Piazza del Campo. Though not quite so magnificent, it's lively enough during the outdoor antiques fair the first Sunday of the month and when the **Giostra del Saracino** (Saracen Joust), featuring medieval costumes and competition, is held here on the first Sunday of September.

Santa Maria della Pieve (*Church of Saint Mary of the Parish*). The curving, tiered apse on Piazza Grande belongs to a fine Romanesque church that was originally Paleo-Christian, built on the remains of an old Roman temple. It was redone in Romanesque style in the 12th century. The facade dates from the early 13th century, but it includes granite columns from the Roman period. Interior frescoes by Piero della Francesca, Lorenzo Ghiberti (1378–1455), and Pietro Lorenzetti (circa 1290–1348) were sadly lost in the 16th, 17th, and 18th centuries. To the left of the altar there is a 16th-century episcopal throne by Vasari. ⊠ *Corso Italia 7* ☎ *0575/22629* ☉ *May–Sept., daily 8–1 and 3–7; Oct.– Apr., daily 8–noon and 3–6.*

WORTH NOTING

Anfiteatro Romano. Periodic excavations since 1950 have brought to light segments of Arezzo's Roman amphitheater, which was probably built during the early 2nd century AD. The entire perimeter has been exposed, and you can see some of the entrance passages and the structures that supported the amphitheater's central arena. ⊠ *Via Margaritone 10* ☎ *0575/20882* ☜ *Free* ☉ *Daily 8:30–7:30.*

NEED A BREAK?

Caffè dei Costanti. Outdoor seating on Arezzo's main pedestrian square and a tasty range of chef's salads (named after the waitresses that serve here) make this a very pleasant spot for a light lunch during a tour of town. In continuous operation since 1886, it's the oldest café in Arezzo, and the charming Old World interior served as backdrop to scenes in Roberto Benigni's 1997 film, *Life is Beautiful.* If you're here in the early evening, the dei Costanti serves up an ample buffet of snacks to accompany predinner aperitifs. ⊠ *Piazza San Francesco 19, Arezzo* ☎ *0575/1824075.*

Casa di Giorgio Vasari. Giorgio Vasari (1511–74), the region's leading mannerist artist, architect, and art historian, designed and decorated this house after he bought it in 1540. He ended up not spending much time here, since he and his wife moved to Florence in 1554. Today the building houses archives on Vasari, and underwhelming works by the artist and his peers are on view. In the first room, which Vasari called the "Triumph of Virtue Room," a richly ornamented wooden ceiling shows Virtue combating Envy and Fortune in a central octagon. Frescoes on the walls depict, among other things, Extravagance, Charity, the Fire of Troy, and a panorama of a Rome cow field. ⊠ *Via XX Settembre 55* ☎ *0575/409040* ☜ *€2* ☉ *Mon. and Wed.–Sat. 9–7, Sun. 9–1.*

Museo Archeologico. The Archaeological Museum in the **Convento di San Bernardo,** just outside the **Anfiteatro Romano,** exhibits a fine collection of Etruscan bronzes. ⊠ *Via Margaritone 10* ☎ *0575/20882* ☜ *€4* ☉ *Daily 8:30–7.*

San Domenico. Inside the northern city walls, this church was begun by Dominican friars in 1275 and completed in the 14th century. The walls were once completely frescoed and decorated with niches and chapels. Very little remains of the original works: a famous 13th-century crucifix by Cimabue (circa 1240–1302), frescoes by Spinello Aretino (1350–1410), and some 14th- and 15th-century paintings. ⊠ *Piazza San Domenico, 7* ☎ *0575/23255* ☉ *Daily 8–7.*

WHERE TO EAT

$ ╳**I Tre Bicchieri.** Providing a welcome change to ubiquitous Tuscan fare,
SEAFOOD the food here is prepared with an inspired flair more typical of southern
Italian cuisine. Chef Luigi Casotti hails from Amalfi and this shows
through in his fine adaptations of dishes more commonly served near
the Bay of Naples. The *raviolone farcito con gamberi rossi di Sicilia
e tonno* (a large raviolo stufffed with Sicilian prawns and tuna served
with a sauce of tomatoes, capers, and olives) and the *filetto di Branzino
in panuria di erbe* (breaded fillet of sea bass) are particularly delicious.
⊠ *Piazzetta Sopra i Ponti 3–5, Arezzo* ☎ *0575/26557.*

¢ ╳**La Torre di Gnicche.** Wine lovers shouldn't miss this wine bar/eatery
ITALIAN with more than 700 labels on the list, just off Piazza Grande. Seasonal
dishes of traditional fare, such as *acquacotta del casentino* (porcini
mushroom soup) and *baccalà in umido* (salt-cod stew), are served in
the simply decorated, vaulted dining room. You can accompany your
meal with one, or more, of the almost 30 wines that are available by the
glass. Limited outdoor seating is available in warm weather. ⊠ *Piaggia
San Martino 8* ☎ *0575/352035* ⊕ *www.latorredignicche.it* ☉ *Closed
Wed., Jan., and 2 wks in July.*

WHERE TO STAY

For expanded hotel reviews, visit Fodors.com.

$$$$ ⊞**Calcione Country and Castle.** The elegant Marchesa Olivella Lotter-
★ inghi della Stufa has turned her six-centuries-old family estate (circa
1483) into a top-notch agriturismo. **Pros:** houses can sleep up to 17;
large swimming pools; quiet, beautiful, remote setting. **Cons:** private
transportation is a must: nearest village is 8 km (5 miles) away; some
complain about insects in summer; no air-conditioning. ⊠ *Calcione, 26
km (15 miles) southwest of Arezzo, Lucignano* ☎ *0575/837100* ⊕ *www.
calcione.com* ⇄ *2 houses, 1 cottage, 6 apartments* ⚿ *In-room: no a/c,
kitchen, no TV, Wi-Fi. In-hotel: pool, tennis court, laundry facilities,
some pets allowed* ▭ *No credit cards* ☉ *Closed Sept.–Mar.* ¶⊙¶ *No meals.*

$$ ⊞**Castello di Gargonza.** Enchantment reigns at this tiny 13th-century
countryside hamlet, part of the fiefdom of the aristocratic Floren-
tine Guicciardini. **Pros:** romantic, one-of-a-kind accommodation in a
medieval castle; peaceful, isolated setting. **Cons:** standard rooms are
extremely basic; a little out of the way for exploring the region; private
transportation is a necessity. ⊠ *SR73 28 km (17 miles) southwest of
Arezzo, Località Gargonza, Monte San Savino* ☎ *0575/847021* ⊕ *www.
gargonza.it* ⇄ *37 rooms, 8 apartments* ⚿ *In-room: a/c, kitchen, no TV.
In-hotel: restaurant, bar, pool, business center* ☉ *Closed last 3 wks in
Jan. and Feb.* ¶⊙¶ *Breakfast.*

$$$$ ⊞**Il Borro.** The location has been described as "heaven on earth," and a
stay at Salvatore Ferragamo's estate, just outside the village of San Gius-
tino Valdarno, 20 km (12 miles) northwest of Arezzo, is sure to bring
similar descriptions to mind. **Pros:** superlative service; great location
for exploring eastern Tuscany; unique setting and atmosphere. **Cons:**
off the beaten track making private transport a must; not all suites have

DID YOU KNOW?

Arezzo's Piazza Grande is the site of a major antiques fair on the first weekend of every month, as well as a medieval joust on the last Saturday of June and the first Sunday in September.

country views; ultra-modern spa facility seems out of place. ⊠ *Località Il Borro* ☎ *055/977053* ⊕ *www.ilborro.com* ⊅ *16 suites, 3 villas, 7 farmhouses, 4 apartments* ⚲ *In-room: safe, kitchen, Wi-Fi. In-hotel: restaurant, bar, pool, tennis court, gym, spa, laundry facilities, parking, some pets allowed* ⦿ *Breakfast.*

SHOPPING

Ever since Etruscan goldsmiths set up their shops here more than 2,000 years ago, Arezzo has been famous for its jewelry. Today the town lays claim to being one of the world's capitals of jewelry design and manufacture, and you can find an impressive display of big-time baubles in the town center's shops. Arezzo is also famous, at least in Italy, for its antiques dealers.

ANTIQUES

The first weekend of every month, between 8:30 and 5:30 each day, a colorful flea market selling antiques and not-so-antiques takes place in the town's main square, **Piazza Grande**.

Grace Gallery. Look for antique jewelry, furniture, and paintings at this gallery. ⊠ *Via Cavour 30* ☎ *0575/354963.*

La Belle Epoque. Specialties here include period clothing, antique lace, and embroidered linens. ⊠ *Piazza San Francesco 18* ☎ *0575/355495.*

CORTONA

Cortona is called "Mother of Troy and Grandmother of Rome" in popular speech, and so may be one of Italy's oldest towns. Tradition claims it was founded by Dardanus, the founder of Troy (after whom the Dardanelles are named). He was fighting a local tribe, so the story goes, when he lost his helmet (*corythos* in Greek) on Cortona's hill. In time a town grew up that took its name (Corito) from the missing headgear. By the 4th century BC the Etruscans had built the first set of town walls, the cyclopean traces of which can still be seen in the 3-km (2-mile) sweep of the present fortifications. As a member of the Etruscans' 12-city league, Cortona became one of the federation's leading northern cities. The area's important consular road, the Via Cassia, passed the foot of Cortona's hill, maintaining the town's importance under the Romans. Medieval fortunes waned, however, as the plain below reverted to marsh. After holding out against such neighbors as Perugia, Arezzo, and Siena, the *commune* was captured by King Ladislas of Naples in 1409 and sold to the Florentines two years later.

GETTING HERE

Cortona is easily reached by car from the A1 (Autostrada del Sole): take the Valdichiana exit toward Perugia, then follow signs for Cortona. Regular bus service, provided by Etruria Mobilità, is available between Arezzo and Cortona (one hour). Train service to Cortona is made inconvenient by the location of the train station, in the valley 3 km (2 miles) steeply below the town itself. From there, you have to rely on bus or taxi service to get up to Cortona.

5

EXPLORING CORTONA

Brought into the limelight by Frances Mayes's book *Under the Tuscan Sun* and a subsequent movie, Cortona is no longer the destination of just a few specialist art historians, and of those seeking reprieve from busier tourist venues. The main street, Via Nazionale, is now lined with souvenir shops and thronged with people during the summer. Though the main sights of Cortona certainly make braving the crowds worthwhile, much of the town's very considerable charm still lies in its maze of quiet and narrow backstreets. It's here that you will see laundry hanging from high windows and children playing, and catch the delightful smell of slowly simmering pasta sauce wafting on the breeze. Wander off the beaten track and you won't be disappointed.

TOP ATTRACTIONS

Duomo. Cortona's cathedral stands on an edge of the city, next to what's left of the Etruscan and medieval walls running from Porta Santa Maria to Porta Colonia. It was built on the site of an old Romanesque church, but the present Renaissance church was begun in 1480 and finished in 1507. An arcade along the outside wall was erected in the 16th century. The interior is a mixture of Renaissance and baroque styles featuring an exquisite 1664 baroque tabernacle on the high altar by Francesco Mazzuoli. ⊠ *Piazza Duomo 1* ☎ *0575/62830* ⊙ *Daily 10–12:30 and 3–5.*

Museo Diocesano. Housed in part of the original cathedral structure, this nine-room museum houses an impressive number of large, splendid paintings by native son Luca Signorelli (1445–1523), as well as a beautiful *Annunciation* by Fra Angelico (1387/1400–1455), which is a delightful surprise in this small town. The former oratory of the Compagnia del Gesù, reached by descending the 1633 staircase opposite the Duomo, is part of the museum. The church was built between 1498 and 1505 and restructured by Giorgio Vasari in 1543. Frescoes depicting sacrifices from the Old Testament by Doceno (1508–56), based on designs by Vasari, line the walls. ⊠ *Piazza Duomo 1* ☎ *0575/62830* ⊡ *€5, €13 in combination with the Museo dell'Accademia Etrusca* ⊙ *Apr.–Oct., daily 10–7; Nov.–Mar., Tues.–Sun. 10–5.*

★ **Santa Maria al Calcinaio.** Legend has it that the image of the Madonna appeared on a wall of a medieval *calcinaio* (lime pit used for curing leather), the site on which the church was then built between 1485 and 1513. The linear gray-and-white interior recalls Florence's Duomo. Sienese architect Francesco di Giorgio (1439–1502) most likely designed the sanctuary: the church is a terrific example of Renaissance architectural principles. ⊠ *Località Il Calcinaio 227, 3 km (2 miles) southeast of Cortona's center* ☎ *0575/604830* ⊙ *Mon.–Sat. 3:30–6, Sun. 10–12:30.*

WORTH NOTING

Palazzo Casali. Built originally by the Casali family, who lived here until 1409, this palace combines 13th- to 17th-century architectural styles. Today it is home to the Accademia Etrusca, with an extensive library; **La Biblioteca Comunale;** and the **Museo dell'Accademia Etrusca e della Città di Cortona (aka MAEC).** An eclectic mix of Egyptian objects, Etruscan and Roman bronzes and statuettes, and paintings is on display in the museum. Perhaps the most famous piece is the Tabula Cortonensis, an Etruscan contract written on bronze that was found in 1922 but dates back to the 2nd century BC. In the basement, sections of the Etruscan and Roman buildings that form the foundations of the palace have been exposed. Look for work by Renaissance artists such as Luca Signorelli and Pinturicchio (circa 1454–1513). From May through September, guided tours are available in English with prior arrangement. Accompanied visits, but only with Italian guides, to the Etruscan tombs on the slopes below Cortona may also be booked. ⊠ *Piazza Signorelli 9* ☎ *0575/637235* ⊡ *Museo €10, €13 in combination with the Museo Diocesano, Biblioteca free* ⊙ *Apr.–Oct., daily 10–7; Nov.–Mar., Tues.–Sun. 10–5.*

San Domenico. Inside this rather anonymous-looking 14th-century church, just outside Cortona's walls, is an altarpiece depicting the Coronation of the Virgin against a sparkling gold background by Lorenzo di Niccolò Gerini (active late 14th–early 15th century). Among the other works is a Madonna and Child by Luca Signorelli. ⊠ *Largo Beato Angelico 1* ☏ *0575/603217* ☉ *Daily 9–6.*

NEED A BREAK?

Caffe degli Artisti. If you need a break from sightseeing, this is a pleasant place to stop for a cappuccino, sandwiches at lunchtime, or the array of appetizers set out during the cocktail hour. In the summer months a few outdoor tables are set up directly on Via Nazionale, Cortona's main pedestrian street, and provide a great perch for those who love to people-watch. ⊠ *Via Nazionale 18* ☏ *0575/601237.*

San Francesco. In the mid-13th century, this Gothic-style church was built on the site of Etruscan and Roman baths. It's closed for reconstruction at this writing, but it contains frescoes dating from 1382, a big crucifix by Giuseppe Piamontini of Florence, and the Relic of Santa Croce, a vestige from the True Cross given to Brother Elia when he served as an envoy for Federico II in Constantinople. The church has a beautiful organ, built in 1466 and fortunately only partially damaged during World War II. ⊠ *Via Berrettini 4* ☏ *0575/603205* ☉ *Daily 9–7.*

San Niccolò. A small, cypress-lined courtyard and porch stand in front of the delightful San Niccolò, a Renaissance church. On the main altar is a fresco by Luca Signorelli, the *Deposition of Christ,* painted around 1510. On the left wall is another fresco by Signorelli of the Madonna and Child, which was plastered over in 1768 and rediscovered in 1847. To visit the church, ring the custodian's doorbell on the left-hand side of the building. ⊠ *Via S. Niccolò* ☏ *0575/604591* ✉ *A minimum donation of €1 is requested* ☉ *Daily 9–noon and 3–5.*

Santa Margherita. The large 1897 basilica was constructed over the foundation of a 13th-century church dedicated to the same saint. What makes the 10-minute uphill walk worthwhile is the richly decorated interior. The body of the 13th-century Saint Margherita—clothed but with skull and bare feet clearly visible—is displayed in a case on the main altar. ⊠ *Piazzale Santa Margherita 1* ☏ *0575/603116* ☉ *Daily 8–noon and 3–6.*

WHERE TO EAT AND STAY

For expanded hotel reviews, visit Fodors.com.

¢ TUSCAN ★ ✕ **Osteria del Teatro.** Photographs from theatrical productions spanning many years line the walls of this tavern off Cortona's large Piazza del Teatro. The food is simply delicious—try the *filetto al lardo di colonnata e prugne* (beef cooked with bacon and prunes); service is warm and friendly. ⊠ *Via Maffei 2* ☏ *0575/630556* ⊕ *www.osteria-del-teatro.it* ☉ *Closed Wed. and 2 wks in Nov. and in Feb.*

$$$$ ★ **Il Falconiere.** Accommodation options here include rooms in an 18th-century villa, suites in the *chiesetta* (chapel, or little church), or, for more seclusion, Le Vigne del Falco suites at the far end of the property.

Piazza Signorelli, Cortona

Pros: attractive setting in the valley beneath Cortona; excellent service; elegant, but relaxed. **Cons:** a car is a must; some find rooms in main villa a little noisy. ⊠ *Località San Martino 370, 3 km (2 miles) north of Cortona* ☎ *0575/612679* ⊕ *www.ilfalconiere.com* ⬎ *13 rooms, 7 suites* ⟳ *In-room: safe, Internet. In-hotel: restaurant, bar, pool, spa, business center, parking, some pets allowed* ⊙ *No lunch in restaurant Tues. Nov.–Mar. Hotel closed last 3 wks in Jan.–mid-Feb.* ❙◯❙ *Breakfast.*

SHOPPING

Il Cocciaio. For nice ceramics, with many pieces depicting the brilliant sunflowers that blanket local fields, check here. ⊠ *Via Nazionale 54* ☎ *0575/604405.*

SANSEPOLCRO AND THE CASENTINO

Sansepolcro, as far east as you can go in Tuscany without entering either Umbria or the Marches, sits in the Valtiberina, the upper valley of the Tiber River. Once a provincial Roman town, and then a busier medieval city, Sansepolcro has now developed an extremely unappealing urban sprawl that almost completely masks its real treasures. Pass the 'burbs, enter the ancient walls, and you'll find narrow pedestrian streets, Romanesque and Gothic churches, elegant Renaissance palazzi (the Florentines conquered Sansepolcro in 1441), and charming city squares. All roads in Sansepolcro eventually lead to the small Museo Civico, where works by Piero della Francesca, the town's most famous artist, adorn the walls—a must-visit for any lover of Italian Renaissance art.

The sparsely populated region of the Casentino—defined as the upper valley of the Arno, the Val d'Arno, which originates here as a spring on Mt. Falterona—contains enough castles, Romanesque parish churches, and unspoiled villages to keep you happily exploring for days. But the jewels in its crown are contained within the Parco Nazionale Casentino, an 89,000-acre preserve of great beauty. The heart of the park, on an Apennine ridge between the Arno and the Tiber, straddling Tuscany and Emilia-Romagna, is the antique forest tended as a religious duty for eight centuries by the monks of the Abbazia Camaldoli, designers of the world's first forestry code. Every year they have planted 4,000–5,000 saplings, resulting in large tracts of early-growth forest. Although they began by maintaining the mix of silver firs and beeches, eventually they planted only firs, creating vast, majestic stands of the deep green trees whose 150-foot, straight black trunks were once floated down the Arno to be used for the tallest masts of warships.

SANSEPOLCRO

40 km (25 miles) northeast of Arezzo.

Originally called *Borgo San Sepolcro* (City of the Holy Sepulchre), this sprawling, largely agricultural town takes its name from relics brought here from the Holy Land by two pilgrims in the 10th century. Today, inside a circle of 15th-century walls, the gridlike street plan hints at the town's even more ancient Roman origins. Known, foremost, as the birthplace of Piero della Francesca—several of his paintings are displayed in the town's Civic Museum—the old center of Sansepolcro retains a distinctly medieval air, with narrow streets lined with medieval churches and 15th-century palaces.

GETTING HERE

Traveling to Sansepolcro by either car or bus from Arezzo will be much preferred over the journey by train, which can take up to four hours. By car, follow the SS73; if traveling by bus (one hour), check with Etruria Mobilità for the schedule, though service is infrequent.

VISITOR INFORMATION

Sansepolcro tourism office ✉ *Via Matteotti 8* ☎ *0575/740536* ⊕ *www.apt. arezzo.it.*

EXPLORING

Museo Civico. Piero della Francesca is the star at this small provincial museum. Three—possibly four—of his works are on display: the reassembled altarpiece of the *Misericordia* (1445–62) and frescoes depicting the *Resurrection* (circa 1460), *Saint Julian,* and the disputed *Saint Louis of Toulouse,* which is possibly the work of a close follower of the artist. Other works of interest are those by Santi di Tito (1536–1603), also from Sansepolcro, and Pontormo's *San Quintino* (1517–18). ✉ *Via Aggiunti 65* ☎ *0575/732218* 🖂 *€6* ⊙ *June 15–Sept. 15, daily 9:30–1:30 and 2:30–7; Sept. 16–June 14, daily 9:30–1 and 2:30–6.*

OFF THE
BEATEN
PATH

Monterchi. This sleepy town, sitting on a small knoll about 15 km (9 miles) south of Sansepolcro, would probably attract little attention if it were not for the fact that Piero della Francesca stopped here to paint one of his greatest masterpieces in the 1450s. And not surprisingly, Monterchi's **Museo "Madonna del Parto"** displays only one painting, Piero's *Madonna del Parto* (circa 1455), a fresco depicting the expectant Virgin flanked by two angels. Originally painted for the small chapel of Santa Maria a Momentana in Monterchi's cemetery, the work was restored in 1992–93 and moved, shortly thereafter, into the museum. The iconography of the image is extremely rare and, emphasized by its static atmosphere and studied symmetry, the fresco achieves an extraordinary sense of enigmatic and monumental spirituality. ⊠ *Via Reglia 1* ☎ *0575/70713* 🖃 *€3.50; pregnant women are admitted free of charge* ☙ *Apr.–Oct., Tues.–Sun. 9–1 and 2–7; Nov.–Mar., Tues.–Sun. 9–1 and 2–5.*

WHERE TO EAT

¢ ✕ **Taverna Toscana.** An exceptionally fresh and tasty *panzanella* (Tuscan

TUSCAN bread salad) might start off your meal at this deliciously authentic trattoria in the center of Sansepolcro. Follow it with a homemade pasta, accompanied by a glass of house wine, a Banfi Cabernet Sauvignon from Montalcino, and you can't go wrong. A complimentary glass of *vin santo* is offered with your choice of dessert. ⊠ *Via Luca Pacioli 50/a* ☎ *0575/742017* ⊕ *www.tavernatoscana.it* ☙ *Closed Tues.*

PARCO NAZIONALE CASENTINO

★ *Pratovecchio: 55 km (34 miles) north of Arezzo, 50 km (31 miles) east of Florence.*

GETTING HERE

You'll need a car to explore this area: getting here by bus, though surprisingly easier from Florence than it is from Arezzo, is a complicated and time-consuming process; it's impossible by train.

VISITOR INFORMATION

Park information office. In addition to this office, there are branch offices at Camaldoli (⊠ *Località Camaldoli 19* ☎ *0575/556130*) and Chiusi della Verna (⊠ *Viale S. Francesco 1* ☎ *0575/532098*). ⊠ *Guido Brocchi 7* ☎ *0575/50301* ⊕ *www.parcoforestecasentinesi.it.*

EXPLORING

Parco Nazionale Casentino. A drive through the park, especially on the very winding 34-km (21-mile) road between the Monastero di Camaldoli and Santuario della Verna, passing through the lovely abbey town of Badia Prataglia, reveals one satisfying vista after another, from walls of firs to velvety pillows of pastureland where sheep or white cattle graze. In autumn the beeches add a mass of red-brown to the palette, and in spring torrents of bright golden broom pour off the hillsides with an unforgettable profusion and fragrance. Walking the forests—which also include sycamore, lime, maple, ash, elm, oak, hornbeam, and chestnut trees and abundant brooks and impressive waterfalls—is the best way to see some of the wilder creatures, from deer and mouflon (wild sheep imported from Sardinia starting in 1872) to eagles and many other birds, as well as 1,000 species of flora, including many rare and endangered plants and an orchid found nowhere else. The **Grande Escursione Apenninica** (GEA) hiking route, which is accessible from both the Monastero di Camaldoli and the Sanutario della Verna, runs along a winding ridge. The park organizes theme walks in summer and provides English-speaking guides anytime with advance notice. ☎ *0575/50301* ⊕ *www.parcoforestecasentinesi.it.*

WHERE TO STAY

For expanded hotel reviews, visit Fodors.com.

$$ ᵀⁱ **Fattoria di Celli.** Set on a gentle rise in the countryside outside the castle town of Poppi, this former *fattoria*—a dormitory housing farm workers—is a tranquil place with lawns punctuated by flowers and modern sculptures, play areas for children, and picnic tables placed to take advantage of mountain views. **Pros:** great for kids; peaceful and beautiful location. **Cons:** no air-conditioning; 5 km (3 miles) to nearest town—a car is a must; simple, rustic accommodations. ✉ *Località Celli, Poppi* ☎ *0575/500294* ⊕ *www.fattoriedicelli.it* ↪ *15 apartments* ⚐ *In-room: no a/c, kitchen, no TV. In-hotel: pool, tennis court, laundry facilities, some pets allowed* ⊘ *Closed Nov.–Mar.* ⦿ *No meals.*

MONASTERO DI CAMALDOLI

20 km (12 miles) northeast of Pratovecchio, 55 km (34 miles) north of Arezzo.

GETTING HERE

As with the Casentino National Park in general, the only practical way to reach the monastery is by car: take SP71 to Serravalle, then follow the signs. Bus service is infrequent and the schedule is tortuous; train service is nonexistent.

EXPLORING

Monastero di Camaldoli. In 1012 Saint Romualdo, scion of a noble Ravenna family, came upon the forests of the Casentino and found their remoteness, their beauty, and their silence conducive to religious contemplation. He stayed and founded a hermitage, Monastero Camaldoli (named for Count Maldoli, who donated the land), which became the seat of a new, reformed Benedictine order. Four centuries after the order's founding by Saint Benedict, Romualdo felt it had become too permissive. An important requirement of the order was preserving its ascetic atmosphere: "If the hermits are to be true devotees of solitude, they must take the greatest care of the woods." When the flow of pilgrims began to threaten that solitude, Romualdo had a monastery and hospital built 1 km (½ mile) down the mountain to create some distance. Today the hermitage, **Sacro Eremo di Camaldoli**—where the monks live in complete silence in 20 separate little cottages, each with its own walled garden—can be seen through gates, and the church and original cell of Romualdo, the model for all the others, can be visited. The church, rebuilt in the 13th century and transformed in the 18th to its present appearance, strikes an odd note in connection with such an austere order and the simplicity of the hermits' cells, because it's done up in gaudy baroque style, complete with gilt cherubs and a frescoed vault. Its most appealing artwork is the glazed terra-cotta relief *Madonna and Child with Saints* (including a large figure of Romualdo and a medallion depicting his fight with the devil) by Andrea della Robbia.

Within the monastery half a mile away is a church (repeatedly restructured) containing 14th-century frescoes by Spinello Aretino, seven 16th-century panel paintings by Giorgio Vasari, and a quietly lovely monastic choir. The choir has 18th-century walnut stalls, more Vasari paintings, and a serene fresco (by Santi Pacini) of Saint Romualdo instructing his white-robed disciples. In a hospital built for sick villagers in 1046 is the 1543 **Antica Farmacia** (Old Pharmacy), with original carved walnut cabinets. Here you can buy herbal teas and infusions, liqueurs, honey products, and toiletries made by the monks from centuries-old recipes as part of their daily routine balancing prayer, work, and study (the monastery is entirely self-supporting). In the back room is an exhibit of the early pharmacy's alembics, mortars, and other equipment with which the monks made herbs into medicines. You can attend short spiritual retreats organized by the monks throughout the year: contact the *foresteria* (visitors lodge) for details. ☒ *Località Camaldoli, Poppi* ☏ *0575/556021 Monastero, 0575/556013 Foresteria* ⊕ *www.camaldoli.it* ☑ *Free* ☉ *Daily 6:30–12:30 and 3–7.*

SANTUARIO DELLA VERNA

34 km (21 miles) southeast of Monastero di Camaldoli and of Pratovecchio.

GETTING HERE

The only practical way to reach the sanctuary is by car—it's 21 km (13 miles) east of Bibbiena on SP208. There is no direct bus service, and train service is nonexistent.

EXPLORING

Santuario della Verna. A few hills away from the Monastero di Camaldoli, dramatically perched on a sheer-walled rock surrounded by firs and beeches, is La Verna, founded by Saint Francis of Assisi in 1214. Ten years later, after a 40-day fast, Saint Francis had a vision of Christ crucified, and when it was over, Francis had received the stigmata, the signs of Christ's wounds, on his hands, feet, and chest. A stone in the floor of the 1263 Chapel of the Stigmata marks the spot. A covered corridor through which the monks pass, chanting in a solemn procession each afternoon at 3 on the way to Mass, is lined with simple frescoes of the *Life of St. Francis* by a late 17th-century Franciscan artist. The true artistic treasures of the place, though, are 15 della Robbia glazed terra-cottas. Most, like a heartbreakingly beautiful Annunciation, are in the 14th- to 15th-century basilica, which has a 5,000-pipe organ that sings out joyously at masses.

Several chapels, each with its own story, can be visited, and some natural and spiritual wonders can also be seen. A walkway along the 230-foot-high cliff leads to an indentation where the rock is said to have miraculously melted away to protect Saint Francis when the devil tried to push him off the edge. Most touching is the enormous Sasso Spicco (Projecting Rock), detached on three sides and surrounded with mossy rocks and trees, where Saint Francis meditated. You can also view the Letto di San Francesco (Saint Francis's Bed), a slab of rock in a cold, damp cave with an iron grate on which he prayed, did penance, and sometimes slept. A 40-minute walk through the woods to the top of Mt. Penna passes some religious sites and ends in panoramic views of the Arno Valley, but those from the wide, cliff-edge terrace are equally impressive, including the tower of the castle in Poppi, the Prato Magno (great meadow), and the olive groves and vineyards on the lower slopes. Santuario della Verna's foresteria also has simple but comfortable rooms with or without bath. A restaurant ($) with basic fare is open to the public, and a shop sells souvenirs and the handiwork of the monks.

As you leave La Verna, be glad you needn't do it as Edith Wharton (1862–1937) did on a 1912 visit during a drive across the Casentino. As she wrote, her car "had to be let down on ropes to a point about ¾ mile below the monastery, Cook [her chauffeur] steering down the vertical descent, and twenty men hanging on to a funa [rope] that, thank the Lord, didn't break." ⊠ *21 km (13 miles) east of Bibbiena on the Sp 208* ☎ *0575/5341* ⊕ *www.santuariolaverna.org* ☽ *Apr.–Oct., daily 6:30 am–9:30 pm; Nov.–Mar. daily 6:30 am–7:30 pm.*

OFF THE
BEATEN
PATH

Caprese Michelangelo. Some 10 km (6 miles) south of La Verna on SR54 is the small hilltop town where Michelangelo Buonarroti, sculptor, painter, architect, and poet, was born on March 6, 1475. Opened in 1964 to honor the 400th anniversary of Michelangelo's death, **Museo Michelangelo** displays photographs, plaster casts, and documents relating to the artist's work. ⊠ *Via Capoluogo 3* ☎ *0575/793912* 🖰 *€5* ☽ *Apr. and May, Mon.–Sat. 11–6, Sun. 11–7; June, July, and Sept., Mon.–Sat. 10–7, Sun. 9:30–7:30; Aug., daily 9:30–7:30; Oct., Mon.–Sat. 10:30–5:30, Sun. 10:30–6:30; Nov.–Mar., Mon.–Sat. 11–5, Sun. 11–6.* During two weekends in mid-October, Caprese Michelangelo's very lively **Sagra della Castagna** (*Chestnut Festival*) takes place. Among the many other chestnut-based delights that feature in the fair, the freshly made *castagnaccia* (a typically Tuscan dessert made with chestnut flour, pine nuts, and rosemary) is a must-try. ⊠ *Tourist office, Via Capoluogo 46* ☎ *0575/793760* ⊕ *www.capresemichelangelo.net.*

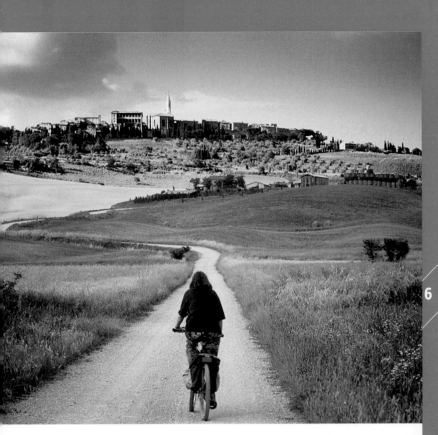

Southern Tuscany

WORD OF MOUTH

"The best times of day to see the Val d'Orcia are in the early morning or late afternoon. When the shadows are long, the cypress trees and umbrella pines look more pronounced as they 'dance up the hill' (my wife's term)."

—StuDudley

WELCOME TO SOUTHERN TUSCANY

TOP REASONS TO GO

★ **Pienza's urban renewal:** A 15th-century makeover turned this otherwise unpretentious village into a model Renaissance town.

★ **Saturnia's hot water:** The gods themselves reportedly had a hand in creating the springs at this world-famous spa town.

★ **Napoléon's home in exile:** The island of Elba, where the French leader was once imprisoned, is the prettiest island in the Tuscan archipelago.

★ **Wine tastings in Montepulciano:** This gorgeous town also happens to be the home of one of Italy's finest wines—Vino Nobile di Montepulciano.

★ **A stroll through Abbazia di Sant'Antimo:** This 12th-century Romanesque abbey shows French, Lombard, and even Spanish influences.

1 Val d'Orcia. In the area surrounding this lush valley you'll find some of southern Tuscany's most attractive towns. Montalcino and Montepulciano are famed for their wine, Pienza for its urban planning and its pecorino cheese.

2 Le Crete. South of Siena, the stark clay landscape and unassuming towns are interrupted by Abbazia di Monte Oliveto Maggiore, the most-visited abbey in Tuscany.

3 The Maremma. Tuscany's deep south may not conform to your expectations for the region; it's best known for its cattle ranches and its coastline. "Discovering" the Maremma has become popular with off-the-beaten-path travelers, though you hardly have to rough it here—you'll find exceptional food and wine, and the spa town of Saturnia is all about indulgence.

TUSCANY

UMBRIA

GETTING ORIENTED

Southeast of Siena, not far from the Umbrian border, the towns of Montepulciano, Montalcino, and Pienza are Tuscan classics—perched on hills, constructed during the Middle Ages and the Renaissance, and saturated with fine wine. Venture farther south and you encounter Tuscany with a rougher edge: the Maremma region is populated by cowboys, and a good portion of the landscape remains wild. But you won't forget you're in Italy here; the wine is still excellent, and some locals store their supply in Etruscan tombs.

6

4 Elba and the Surrounding Islands. It's a short hop from the coast to the islands of the Tuscan archipelago. Several of them—most notably Elba—have long been vacation getaways.

Updated
by Peter
Blackman

AS DIVERSE AS ITALY ITSELF, southern Tuscany ranges from the green knolls of the Val d'Orcia to the sandy beaches at Punta Ala. It contains the wildest parts of Tuscany—the Maremma, once a malaria-ridden swampland where the *butteri,* Italy's cowboys, rounded up their cattle, now a peaceful woodland fringed with beaches; Monte Amiata, a scruffy mountain landscape where goats gnaw at clumps of brown grass among scattered rocks; and the still-wild islands of the Tuscan archipelago. Some of Tuscany's best-kept secrets lie here in the south, among them the Abbazia di San Galgano, which is open to the sky, and the cool mountain enclaves of Monte Amiata. This is Etruscan country, where the necropolis near Sovana hints at a rich and somewhat mysterious pre-Roman civilization.

Apart from the occasional rocky promontory, the coast of southern Tuscany is virtually one long stretch of fine-sand beach. Private beach areas are common near the resort towns south of Livorno and just north of Monte Argentario, where there are chairs and umbrellas for rent, shower facilities, and bars. Along the rest of the coast, the beaches are public. They're particularly pleasant in the nature reserve at Monti dell'Uccellina and along the sandbars that connect Monte Argentario to the mainland. On the islands, rocky shores predominate, although Elba has sandy beaches on its southern side.

You can visit the whole region in about five days. Keep in mind that southern Tuscany isn't well served by trains, so if you aren't renting a car you'll have to plan around sometimes difficult bus schedules, and the going will be slow. The A1 (Autostrada del Sole), which runs from Florence to Rome, passes near the Val d'Orcia. SS1 (the Via Aurelia) follows the western coastline for much of the way, before jutting inland at Grosseto.

PLANNING

MAKING THE MOST OF YOUR TIME

The towns in southern Tuscany are fairly close together, so it's possible to pick one of them as your base and take day trips to almost everywhere else in the region. **Pienza,** in the middle of the **Val d'Orcia,** makes an excellent place to begin your trip. Other good choices include **Montepulciano** and **Montalcino.** From any of these it's only a short drive to all the other towns in the Val d'Orcia, as well as the famous abbeys in and around **Le Crete.**

If your main reason for visiting this region is a dip in the hot springs, you should stay in **Saturnia** or one of the surrounding villages. (Because so many people go there for a soak, Saturnia has the most luxurious lodgings.)

If your destination is the Tuscan archipelago, you'd do best to choose one island, as there is no ferry service between them. **Elba** is more famous, but it's hard to find a place to lay your towel in the summer months. **Giglio** has less-crowded beaches, and a few accessible on foot or by boat that you might have to yourself.

GETTING HERE AND AROUND
BUS TRAVEL

Although tortuous roads and circuitous routes make bus travel in southern Tuscany slow, it's a reliable way to get around if you don't have a car. Schedules are always changing, so plan your trip carefully with the aid of local tourist offices. (They're more likely to have an English-speaking staff than are bus stations.) The major bus stations for the region are in Siena and Grosseto, but most towns have bus service even if they don't have actual bus stations.

SITA. This bus company provides regular rapid service between Florence and Siena. ☎ *0577/204225 in Siena, 800/570530 toll-free in Italy* ⊕ *www.sitabus.it.*

Tra-In. Bus service throughout the province of Siena is provided by Tra-In. ☎ *0577/204111* ⊕ *www.trainspa.it.*

RAMA. Based in Grosseto, this company provides bus service through the Maremma region. ☎ *199/848787* ⊕ *www.griforama.it.*

ATL. On Elba, ATL provides bus service around the island. ☎ *0565/914392.*

CAR TRAVEL

The area is easily reached by car on the A1 highway (Autostrada del Sole), which runs between Rome and Florence—take the Chiusi–Chianciano Terme exit for Montepulciano, Pienza, and San Quirico Val d'Orcia. From Florence the fastest route to southern Tuscany is via the Florence–Siena Superstrada and then the Via Cassia (SR2) from Siena for Buonconvento and Montalcino. There is also a good road (SR223) linking Siena and Grosseto, for outings to the Parco Naturale della Maremma and Monte Argentario.

From Genoa or the northern Tuscan coast, follow the coastal highway (A12) to reach Livorno and its ferry service to Capraia. For direct ferry service to Elba, continue south on the SS1 (the Via Aurelia) to reach Piombino. Past Piombino, the SS1 passes Grosseto, the Parco Naturale della Maremma, and Monte Argentario, before continuing south toward Rome.

TRAIN TRAVEL

Train service within this region is slow; in many cases buses are quicker. Trains run from Chiusi–Chianciano Terme to Siena (one hour) with stops in Montepulciano and Asciano.

Ferrovie dello Stato. You can check the website of the state railway for train schedules, or stop in any travel agency— many speak English and will book and print train tickets for you. ☎ *892021 toll-free within Italy* ⊕ *www.trenitalia.com.*

HOTELS

Southern Tuscany is a great place to enjoy the *agriturismo* (agrotourism) lifestyle: if you have a week to stay in one of these rural farmhouses, pick someplace central, such as Pienza, and explore the region from that base. It may be so relaxing and the food so good that you might have trouble wandering away.

You will also find many hotels in this region: modern affairs in cities, surfside beach resorts, and timeworn villas.

DINING AND LODGING PRICE CATEGORIES (IN EUROS)				
¢	$	$$	$$$	$$$$
Restaurants	under €15	€15–€25	€25–€35	€35–€45	over €45
Hotels	under €70	€70–€110	€110–€160	€160–€220	over €220

Restaurant prices are for a first course (*primo*), second course (*secondo*), and dessert (*dolce*). Hotel prices are for two people in a standard double room in high season, including tax and service.

VAL D'ORCIA

The Val d'Orcia (Orcia Valley) is a sumptuous green valley with breathtaking views of the Orcia River, which runs through it. The area's long-standing agricultural tradition has left it utterly undeveloped, and so the vistas here are classic Tuscany—rolling hills topped by villages, wide plains, swaths of blooming fields punctuated by vineyards and olive groves. Picture-perfect Pienza, medieval San Quirico d'Orcia, and Bagno Vignoni are great photo-op stops; amateur archaeologists will enjoy pondering Chiusi's painted Etruscan tombs; and Chianciano Terme's thermal baths can provide a sybaritic treat during your stay. Hills near Montalcino border the valley in the west, and it's in that hilltop town that Siena chose to make a last desperate stand against the invading Florentines. Not to be missed is the superbly positioned Abbazia di Sant'Antimo to the south. Montepulciano, filled with town palaces and Renaissance churches—and fortified by some great red wine—is at the valley's boundary in the east.

CHIUSI

40 km (25 miles) south of Cortona, 84 km (50 miles) southeast of Siena, 126 km (78 miles) southeast of Florence.

Chiusi was once one of the most powerful of the ancient cities of the Etruscan League, and it's now a valuable source of information about that archaic civilization. Fifth-century BC tombs found in the nearby hills have provided archaeologists with a wealth of artifacts. On the route of the ancient Via Cassia, Chiusi became a major Roman center and an important communication hub that linked Rome with the agriculturally rich Chiana Valley to the east, with Siena to the northwest, and to other major cities in central and northern Italy. When the Chiana Valley became a malaria-ridden swamp during the Middle Ages, Chiusi's importance declined, and it was not until the Medici devised a scheme to drain the valley (with plans supplied by Leonardo da Vinci) in the early 15th century that the town began to reestablish itself.

Val d'Orcia
and the Crete

Siena

Armaiolo

Monte San Savino

LE CRETE

Monteroni d'Arbia   Asciano

Montecontieri   Sinalunga   Bettolle

Suvignano

Abbazia di Monte Oliveto Maggiore

Montelifre

Torrita

Fontazzi

San Giovanni d'Asso   Montisi

Buonconvento

Montefollónico

Acquaviva

Montepulciano

Torrenieri

Pienza

Montalcino

San Quirico d'Orcia

Chianciano Terme

Bagno Vignoni

Chiusi

Sant' Angelo in Colle

Castiglione

Res. Nat. Lucciola Bella

Res. Nat. Pietraprociana

Abbazia di Sant'Antimo

Sarteano

Lago di Chiusi

Seggiano

TO ROMA

Tuscany   Marches   Umbria

0   5 mi

0   5 km

GETTING HERE

Chiusi is easily reached by car on the A1 highway (Autostrada del Sole), which runs between Rome and Florence. Tra-In buses link Chiusi with Siena, but train service is faster and more frequent. Chiusi is on a main rail line between Florence and Rome, and can be reached from either city.

VISITOR INFORMATION

Chiusi tourism office ✉ Via Porsena 79 ☎ 0578/227667 ⊕ www.prolocochiusi.it.

EXPLORING

Museo Nazionale Etrusco. Most of the artifacts found during the excavations of Chiusi's Etruscan sites are now on display in this small but expertly laid out museum. Relics include elegant Etruscan and Greek vases, carved Etruscan tomb chests, and a number of the strange canopic jars with anthropomorphic shapes that are particular to this area. The tombs themselves can be seen by arrangement with the museum; visits are accompanied by a member of the museum staff. These underground burial chambers are still evocative of ancient life, particularly in the Tomba della Scimmia (Tomb of the Monkey), where well-preserved frescoes depict scenes from ordinary life 2,500 years ago. The Tomba del Leone (Tomb of the Lion) and Tomba della Pellegrina (Tomb of the

Pilgrim) are open by appointment during museum hours. ⊠ *Via Porsenna 93* ☏ *0578/20177* 🖾 *Museum €4, with tombs €6* ⊙ *Museum: daily 9–8 (last entrance 7:30). Tomba della Scimmia: by appointment Apr.–Oct., Tues., Thurs., and Sat. at 11 and 4; Nov.–Mar., Tues., Thurs., and Sat. at 11 and 2:30.*

WHERE TO STAY

For expanded hotel reviews, visit Fodors.com.

$$$$ 🍴 **La Frateria di Padre Eligio.** It's not an overstatement to say that this
★ former convent, founded in 1212 by Saint Francis himself, remains a
spiritual place. **Pros:** contemplative surroundings; excellent restaurant;
small and intimate inn. **Cons:** no air-conditioning; off-the-beaten-path
location; need a car to get around. ⊠ *Via San Francesco, 10 km (6 miles)
southwest of Chiusi, Cetona* ☏ *0578/238261* ⊕ *www.lafrateria.it* ⤳ *5
rooms, 2 suites* 🍴 *In-room: no a/c, no TV. In-hotel: restaurant* ⊙ *Closed
early Jan.–mid-Feb. Restaurant closed Tues.*

CHIANCIANO TERME

*11 km (7 miles) northwest of Chiusi, 73 km (44 miles) southeast of
Siena.*

People from around the world come to the *città del fegato sano* (city
of the healthy liver) to experience the curative waters. The area's innumerable mineral-water springs are reputed to restore and maintain the
health of the skin, among other things. This is nothing new; as early
as the 5th century BC Chianciano Terme was the site of a temple to
Apollo the Healer. It's no secret, either—the Terme di Chianciano spa
alone claims to draw 120,000 visitors a year, and Italian state health
insurance covers visits to the baths and springs for qualified patients.
But you can test the waters yourself at a number of springs. If you're not
here for the waters, probably the most interesting part of Chianciano
is the old town, which lies to the north. The modern town, stretching
along a hillside to the south, is a series of hotels, shops, and restaurants
catering to spa aficionados.

GETTING HERE

From Rome or Florence, Chiusi is easily reached by car on the A1 highway (Autostrada del Sole). Tra-In buses link Chianciano with Siena.
The closest train station to Chianciano Terme is in Chiusi, about 15
km (9 miles) away.

VISITOR INFORMATION

Chianciano Terme tourism office ⊠ *Piazza Italia 67* ☏ *0578/671122* ⊕ *www.
chianciano.com.*

EXPLORING

Terme di Chianciano. This organization represents three spas in Chianciano: Acqua Santa, Acqua Fucoli, and Acqua Sillene, where mud baths
are also available. The Terme website lists the varied spa treatments
available. Perhaps to offset the clinical coldness of the actual treatment
centers, each spa is surrounded by a large park filled with trees, flower
gardens, and reflecting pools. There are facilities for such light sporting
activities as tennis and boccie, and dance floors are available for musical

events on summer evenings. The all-important water is served up at long counters, where the spa staff is always ready to refill your glass. Be warned: The mineral water can have a cleansing effect on your system that may come on suddenly.

Acqua Santa. The water at Acqua Santa, taken as a drinking cure, is known for curing liver and digestive ailments and for detoxifying in general. ⊠ *Piazza Martiri Perugini* ☎ *0578/68411* 🕾 *Jan.–May, Nov., and Dec., €7.50; June–Sept., €9.50; entrance includes Acqua Fucoli spa until noon* ☉ *Daily 8–noon.*

Acqua Fucoli. The waters here are usually taken as a drinking cure for all manner of intestinal disorders. ⊠ *Viale G. Bacelli* ☎ *0578/68430* 🕾 *Morning €9.50, entrance fee includes Acqua Santa spa; afternoon €5.50* ☉ *Apr. 16–Oct. 16, daily 8–7:30.*

Acqua Sillene. The steamy-hot waters at Acqua Sillene are used for private mineral and mud tub baths. The spa has nonaquatic activities including tennis, boccie, and miniature golf (all for additional fees). ⊠ *Piazza Marconi* ☎ *0578/68551* 🕾 *Varies according to treatments chosen* ☉ *Daily 8–noon and 4–7:30* ⊠ *Via delle Rose 12* ☎ *0578/68111* ⊕ *www.termechianciano.it.*

Terme Sant'Elena. The waters here are said to help with kidney and urinary-tract ailments and all manner of digestive disorders; there are boccie courts and a pretty park to stroll in while you sip. On summer afternoons you can dance to live orchestra music in the park. ⊠ *Viale dell Libertà 112* ☎ *0578/31141* ⊕ *www.acquasantelena.it* 🕾 *Mid-Apr.–May and last 2 wks in Oct., €6; June–mid-Oct, €7.50* ☉ *Mid.-Apr.–Oct., weekdays 8–noon and 4:30–7:30, Sat. 9–noon.*

Chianciano. This walled medieval town, 3 km (2 miles) northeast of Chianciano Terme, is best known for its proximity to the spa town; nevertheless, the well-preserved old town is appealing.

Museo Civico Archeologico. This museum contains a good collection of Etruscan and Roman sculpture and pottery excavated from around the area. ⊠ *Via Dante 80, Chianciano* ☎ *0578/30471* ⊕ *www. museoetrusco.it* 🕾 *€5* ☉ *Apr.–Oct., daily 10–1 and 4–7; Nov.–Mar., weekends 10–1 and 4–7 .*

Sarteano. To the southeast of Chianciano, 10 km (6 miles) along SP19, lies this relatively unspoiled village that dates from the 12th and 13th centuries. The town's narrow streets, which wind slowly up toward an imposing fortress, now privately owned, make for very pleasant strolling.

San Martino in Foro. Don't miss this small church, which houses a striking Annunciation by the important Sienese painter Domenico Beccafumi (1486–1551). ⊠ *Piazza San Martino* ☎ *No phone* ☉ *Daily 9–12:30 and 4–7:30 .*

Cetona. Follow SP19 past Sarteano and continue on SP21 to reach this delightful village. Time may seem to have stopped as you walk along the quiet, narrow, medieval lanes and back alleys. Peer through the locked gate for a glimpse of the privately owned castle, and take in splendid views of olive orchards, cypress groves, and the quiet wooded slopes of Mt. Cetona from the town's terraced streets. ✉ *20 km (12 miles) southeast of Chianciano Terme.*

MONTEPULCIANO

10 km (6 miles) northeast of Chianciano Terme, 65 km (40 miles) southeast of Siena, 114 km (70 miles) southeast of Florence.

Perched on a hilltop, Montepulciano is made up of a pyramid of red-brick buildings set within a circle of cypress trees. At an altitude of almost 2,000 feet, it is cool in summer and chilled in winter by biting winds sweeping down its spiraling streets. The town has an unusually harmonious look, the result of the work of three architects: Antonio Sangallo "il Vecchio" (circa 1455–1534), Vignola (1507–73), and Michelozzo (1396–1472). The group endowed it with fine palaces and churches in an attempt to impose Renaissance architectural ideals on an ancient Tuscan hill town.

GETTING HERE

From Rome or Florence, take the Chiusi–Chianciano exit from the A1 highway (Autostrada del Sole). From Siena, take the SR2 south to San Quirico and then the SP146 to Montepulciano. Tra-In offers bus service from Siena to Montepulciano several times a day. Montepulciano's train station is in Montepulciano Stazione, 10 km (6 miles) away.

VISITOR INFORMATION

Montepulciano tourism office ✉ *Piazza Don Minzoni 1* ☎ *0578/757341* ⊕ *www.prolocomontepulciano.it.*

EXPLORING

★ **Piazza Grande.** Filled with handsome buildings, the Piazza Grande is Montepulciano's pièce de résistance.

Duomo. On the Piazza Grande the unfinished facade of Montepulciano's cathedral doesn't measure up to the beauty of its neighboring palaces. On the inside, however, its Renaissance roots shine through. The high altar has a splendid triptych painted in 1401 by Taddeo di Bartolo (ca. 1362–1422), and you can see fragments of the tomb of Bartolomeo Aragazzi, secretary to Pope Martin V, which was sculpted by Michelozzo between 1427 and 1436. ✉ *Piazza Grande* ☎ *0578/757341* ⊙ *Daily 9–12:30.*

Palazzo Comunale. Montepulciano's town hall dates to the late 13th century, though it was restructured in the 14th century and again in the mid-15th century. Michelozzo oversaw this last phase, using the Palazzo Vecchio in Florence as his inspiration. From the tower, a commanding view of Siena, Mt. Amiata (the highest point in Tuscany), and Lake Trasimeno (the largest lake on the Italian peninsula) can be enjoyed on a clear day. ✉ *Piazza Grande 1* ☎ *0578/757341* ⊿ *Free* ⊙ *Daily 8–1.*

Summer in Valle d'Orcia

Sant'Agostino. Michelozzo had a hand in creating the beautiful travertine facade on the church of Sant'Agostino, which was built in 1285 and renovated in the early 1400s. He also sculpted the terra-cotta relief of the Madonna and Child above the entrance. ⊠ *Piazzale Pasquino da Montepulciano 6* ☎ *0578/757341* ⊙ *Daily 9–12:30 and 3:30–7:30.*

★ **San Biagio.** Designed by Antonio da Sangallo il Vecchio, and considered his masterpiece, this church sits on the hillside below the town walls and is a model of High Renaissance architectural perfection. Inside the church is a painting of the Madonna. According to legend, the painting was the only thing remaining in an abandoned church that two young girls entered on April 23, 1518. The two girls saw the eyes of the Madonna moving, and that same afternoon so did a farmer and a cow, who knelt down in front of the painting. In 1963 the image was proclaimed the Madonna del Buon Viaggio (Madonna of the Good Journey), the protector of tourists in Italy. ⊠ *Via di San Biagio* ☎ *0578/757164* ⊙ *Daily 9–12:30 and 3:30–7:30.*

WHERE TO EAT

$ ✕ **La Grotta.** You might be tempted to pass right by the innocuous
TUSCAN entrance across the street from San Biagio, but you'd miss some fan-
★ tastic food. Try the *tagliolini con carciofi e rigatino* (thin noodles with artichokes and bacon) or *tagliatelle di grano saraceno con asparagi e zucchine* (flat, buckwheat-flour noodles with asparagus and zucchini). Wash it down with the local wine, which just happens to be one of Italy's finest—Vino Nobile di Montepulciano. The desserts, such as an extravagantly rich triple-chocolate flan, are prepared with particular flair. ⊠ *Via di San Biagio 15* ☎ *0578/757479* ⊙ *Closed Wed. and Jan. and Feb.*

¢ ✗ **Osteria del Conte.** As high in Montepulciano as you can get, just behind
TUSCAN the Duomo, this small and intimate restaurant is expertly run by the
mother-and-son team of Lorena and Paolo Brachi. Passionate about the
food they prepare, both have a flair for the region's traditional dishes—
the *pici all'aglione* (handmade spaghetti with garlic sauce) and the *filetto
ai funghi porcini* (steak with porcini mushrooms) are mouthwateringly
good. The wine list, though limited in range, presents a decent selection
of wines from both Montepulciano and Montalcino. For a change from
the usual Tuscan meat dishes, fresh fish is served on Friday. Outdoor
seating is limited. ⊠ *Via di San Donato 19* ☎ *0578/756062* ⊕ *www.
osteriadelconte.it* ⌸ *Reservations essential* ☾ *Closed Wed.*

WHERE TO STAY
For expanded hotel reviews, visit Fodors.com.

$ ⊞ **La Terrazza.** On a quiet street in the upper part of town, these unpre-
tentious lodgings are given sparkle by the welcoming and friendly service of the owners, Roberto and Vittoria Giardinelli. **Pros:** friendly
family atmosphere; quiet central location. **Cons:** no air-conditioning;
no service at night. ⊠ *Via del Piè al Sasso 16* ☎ *0578/757440* ⊕ *www.
laterrazzadimontepulciano.it* ⇗ *12 rooms* ⌂ *In-room: no a/c, kitchen,
Wi-Fi. In-hotel: parking* ⍟ *Breakfast.*

$$$$ ⊞ **Podere Dionora.** From the moment you arrive at this secluded inn,
★ which sits serenely on an estate of manicured lawns, private woodlands,
and vineyards, you know that you have found something special. **Pros:**
secluded setting; great views; attentive service. **Cons:** long walk to the
nearest town; need a car to get around. ⊠ *Via Vicinale di Poggiano
9, 3 km (2 miles) east of Montepulciano town center* ☎ *0578/717496*
⊕ *www.dionora.it* ⇗ *6 rooms* ⌂ *In-room: safe. In-hotel: pool* ☾ *Closed
mid-Dec.–mid-Feb.* ⍟ *Breakfast.*

$$ ⊞ **San Biagio.** A five-minute walk from the church of the same name,
★ this family-run inn makes a great base for exploring Montepulciano and
the surrounding countryside. **Pros:** heated indoor pool; family-friendly
atmosphere. **Cons:** some rooms face a busy road; lots of tour groups.
⊠ *Via San Bartolomeo 2* ☎ *0578/717233* ⊕ *www.albergosanbiagio.it*
⇗ *27 rooms* ⌂ *In-hotel: restaurant, pool, parking* ⍟ *Breakfast.*

NIGHTLIFE AND THE ARTS
Cantiere Internazionale d'Arte. This festival of art, music, and theater
takes place in a variety of venues during July and August, ending with
a dramatic stage production in the Piazza Grande. ⊠ *Via del Teatro 4*
☎ *0578/758473.*

PIENZA

★ *12 km (7 miles) west of Montepulciano, 52 km (31 miles) southeast of
Siena, 120 km (72 miles) southeast of Florence.*

Pienza owes its appearance to Pope Pius II (1405–64), who had grand
plans to transform his hometown of Corsignano—its former name—
into a compact model Renaissance town. The man entrusted with the
transformation was Bernardo Rossellino (1409–64), a protégé of the

great Renaissance architectural theorist Leon Battista Alberti (1404–72). His mandate was to create a cathedral, a papal palace, and a town hall that adhered to the vainglorious pope's principles. Gothic and Renaissance styles were fused, and the buildings were decorated with Sienese paintings. The net result was a project that expressed Renaissance ideals of art, architecture, and civilized good living in a single scheme: it stands as an exquisite example of the architectural canons that Alberti formulated in the early Renaissance and that were utilized by later architects, including Michelangelo, in designing many of Italy's finest buildings and piazzas. Today the cool nobility of Pienza's center seems almost surreal in this otherwise unpretentious village, known locally for *pienzino*, a smooth sheep's-milk pecorino cheese.

GETTING HERE

From Siena, drive south along the SR2 to San Quirico d'Orcia and then take the SP146. The trip should take just over an hour. Tra-In shuttles passengers between Siena and Pienza. There is no train service to Pienza.

VISITOR INFORMATION

Pienza tourism office ⊠ *Piazza Dante 18* ☎ *0578/749071* ⊕ *www.pienza.info.*

EXPLORING

Palazzo Piccolomini. In 1459 Pius II commissioned Rossellino to design the perfect palazzo for his papal court. The architect took Florence's Palazzo Rucellai by Alberti as a model and designed this 100-room palace. Three sides of the building fit perfectly into the urban plan around it, while the fourth, looking over the valley, has a lovely loggia uniting it with the gardens in back. Guided tours departing every 30 minutes take you to visit the papal apartments, including a beautiful library, the Sala delle Armi (with an impressive weapons collection), and the music room, with its extravagant wooden ceiling forming four letter Ps, for Pope, Pius, Piccolomini, and Pienza. The last tour departs 30 minutes before closing. ⊠ *Piazza Pio II* ☎ *0578/748392* ⊕ *www. palazzopiccolominipienza.it* ⊠ €7 ⊙ *Mid-Mar.–mid-Oct., Tues.–Sun. 10–6:30; mid-Oct.–mid-Mar., Tues.–Sun. 10–4:30.*

Duomo. This 15th-century cathedral was built by the architect Rossellino under the influence of Alberti. The travertine facade is divided in three parts, with Renaissance arches under the pope's coat of arms encircled by a wreath of fruit. Inside, the cathedral is simple but richly decorated with Sienese paintings. The building's perfection didn't last long—the first cracks appeared immediately after the building was completed, and its foundations have shifted slightly ever since as rain erodes the hillside behind. You can see this effect if you look closely at the base of the first column as you enter the church and compare it with the last. ⊠ *Piazza Pio II* ☎ *0578/749071* ⊙ *Tues.–Sun. 10–1 and 3–7.*

Museo Diocesano. This museum sits to the left of Pienza's Duomo. It's small but has a few interesting papal treasures and rich Flemish tapestries. The most precious piece is a rare mantle woven in gold with pearls and embroidered religious scenes that belonged to Pope Pius II. ⊠ *Corso Il Rossellino 30* ☎ *0578/749071* ⊠ €4 ⊙ *mid-Mar.–Oct., Wed.–Mon. 10–1 and 3–7; Nov.–mid-Mar., weekends 10–1 and 3–7.*

Sant'Anna in Camprena. Part of the acclaimed 1996 film *The English Patient* was filmed at this former Benedictine monastery where you can view frescoes by Sodoma (1477–1549) in the dining hall and in the room where the eponymous patient lay in bed. It's best reached by car or bicycle, as public transportation isn't available. For the world-weary, extremely plain rooms are available in the austere silence of the monastery. Double rooms with private bathroom and breakfast are €80 per night; those without private bathroom are €65. To get here from Pienza, take the road to San Quirico for 1 km (½ mile), then turn right at the sign for the monastery. ✉ *Località Sant'Anna in Camprena 5* 🕾 *0578/748037 or 338/4079284* ⊕ *www.camprena.it* ⊗ *Weekends 9–6.*

WORD OF MOUTH

"We rented an apartment in the Pienza area—arguably the most scenic area of Tuscany. From our apartment, we were able to explore the surrounding hill villages, the St. Antimo Abby, and also do a little hiking and biking. Just realize that maps can be deceiving—getting from one village to another can take a lot more time than it appears due to the narrow, twisting roads."
—zootsi

6

WHERE TO EAT AND STAY

For expanded hotel reviews, visit Fodors.com.

¢   ✕**La Chiocciola.** Take the few minutes to walk from the old town for
TUSCAN   typical Pienza fare, including homemade *pici* (thick, short spaghetti) with hare or wild-boar sauce. The restaurant's version of *formaggio in forno* (baked cheese) with assorted accompaniments such as fresh porcini mushrooms is reason enough to venture here. ✉ *Viale Mencatelli 2* 🕾 *0578/748683* ⊕ *www.trattorialachiocciola.it* ⊗ *Closed Wed. and 10 days in Feb.*

¢   ✕**Osteria Sette di Vino.** Tasty dishes based on the region's cheeses are the
TUSCAN   specialty at this simple and inexpensive *osteria* (tavern). Try versions of pici or the starter of radicchio baked quickly to brown the edges. The local pecorino cheese appears often on the menu—the pecorino *grigliata con pancetta* (grilled with cured bacon) is divine. Can't decide? Try the pecorino tasting menu. Osteria Sette di Vino is on a quiet, pleasant square in the center of Pienza. ✉ *Piazza di Spagna 1* 🕾 *0578/749092* ⊟ *No credit cards* ⊗ *Closed Wed., July 1–15, and Nov.*

$ ⌸**Agriturismo Cerreto.** Built a short distance from Pienza in the 18th
★   and 19th centuries, this grouping of farm buildings, now a small hotel, sits on a hilltop surrounded by open fields and woodland. **Pros:** peaceful country setting; great for families and small groups; good base for exploring the Val d'Orcia. **Cons:** private transportation a must; closest restaurants and town 5 km (3 miles) away. ✉ *Strada Provinciale per Sant'Anna in Camprena, 5 km (3 miles) north of Pienza, Pienza* 🕾 *0578/749121* ⊕ *www.agriturismocerreto.com* ⟿*7 rooms* ⌂ *In-room: no a/c, kitchen, Wi-Fi. In-hotel: pool, laundry facilities, some pets allowed* ⍟*Breakfast.*

SAN QUIRICO D'ORCIA

9½ km (5½ miles) southwest of Pienza, 43 km (26 miles) southeast of Siena, 111 km (67 miles) southeast of Florence.

San Quirico d'Orcia, on the modern Via Cassia (SR2) south from Siena toward Rome, has almost-intact 15th-century walls topped with 14 turrets. The pleasantly crumbling appearance of the town recalls days of yore. It's well suited for a stop to enjoy a gelato or a meal and to see its Romanesque church.

GETTING HERE

From Siena, San Quirico d'Orcia is an hour-long drive on the SR2. Tra-In provides buses from Siena to San Quirico. There is no train service to San Quirico.

VISITOR INFORMATION

San Quirico d'Orcia tourism office ✉ *Piazza Chigi 2* ☎ *0577/897211* ⊕ *www.comunesanquirico.it.*

EXPLORING

Collegiata. The 13th-century Collegiata church has three majestic portals, one possibly the work of Giovanni Pisano (circa 1245/48–1318). Behind the high altar are some fine examples of inlaid woodwork by Antonio Barilli (1482–1502). In the floor of the right aisle, look for the tomb slab of Henry of Nassau, a pilgrim knight who died here in 1451. ✉ *Piazza Chigi* ☎ *No phone* ☉ *Daily 8:30–12:30.*

Palazzo Chigi. Near the Collegiata stands this splendid town palace, named after the family to whom the Medici bestowed San Quirico in 1667. Small art exhibitions are occasionally displayed in the palace courtyard, and the tourist office is here. The rest of the building is closed to the public. ✉ *Piazza Chigi 2.*

Horti Leonini. Against the walls of San Quirico d'Orcia, these Italian-style gardens retain merely a shimmer of their past opulence. They were planted in 1581 by Diomede Leoni—hence the name of the park. In the center there's a 17th-century statue of Cosimo III, one of the last of the Medici dukes of Tuscany. ✉ *Off Piazza della Libertà.*

WHERE TO EAT AND STAY

For expanded hotel reviews, visit Fodors.com.

¢ ✕ **Trattoria al Vecchio Forno.** A meal here is always special. Don't miss the
TUSCAN dishes accented with porcini mushrooms, such as the excellent mushroom soup. You might also try pici with tomato or boar sauce, and roast boar and game. The menu is rounded out by a varied wine selection. There's a nice garden out back. ✉ *Via Piazzola 8* ☎ *0577/897380* ☉ *Closed Feb.*

$$ ⊡ **Palazzo del Capitano.** The guest rooms at this 14th-century palace are named for signs of the zodiac, but the astrological reference stops at the painted symbol on the door. **Pros:** central location; elegant furnishings; secluded garden. **Cons:** rooms are on the small side; some street noise; getting here by car is difficult. ✉ *Via Poliziano 18* ☎ *0577/899028 or 0577/899421* ⊕ *www.palazzodelcapitano.com* ⤴ *14 rooms, 8 suites* ⌂ *In-room: safe, Wi-Fi. In-hotel: restaurant, bar, pool, spa* ⑂⊙⊣ *Breakfast.*

BAGNO VIGNONI

5 km (3 miles) south of San Quirico d'Orcia, 48 km (29 miles) southeast of Siena, 116 km (70 miles) southeast of Florence.

Bagno Vignoni has been famous since Roman times for the mildly sulfurous waters that come bubbling up into the large rectangular pool that forms the town's main square, Piazza delle Sorgenti (Square of the Springs). Medieval pilgrims and modern hikers alike have soothed their tired feet in the pleasantly warm water that flows through open channels on its way to the River Orcia. Of particular interest are the ruins of an 18th-century bathhouse on the edge of town and the Chapel of Saint Catherine, who, it seems, came here often.

GETTING HERE

Bagno Vignoni is off the SR2, about an hour from Siena. Tra-In provides bus service from Siena to Bagno Vignoni. There is no train station nearby.

VISITOR INFORMATION

Bagno Vignoni tourism office ⊠ *Località Bagno Vignoni 2* ☎ *0577/888975* ⊕ *www.comunesanquirico.it.*

EXPLORING

Piscina Val di Sole. Bagno Vignoni's public hot-spring pool provides warm-water relaxation for more than just your feet. Stand under the waterfall to massage and soothe weary shoulder muscles. Though the facility remains open, there's no swimming permitted between 1 and 2:30 from April to September. The last admission is one hour before closing. ⊠ *Via Ara Urcea 43* ☎ *0577/887112* ⊕ *www.piscinavaldisole. it* ⊠ *€15* ☉ *Jan.–Mar., daily 10–5; Apr.–Sept., daily 9:30–6; Oct.–Dec., daily 10–5.*

OFF THE BEATEN PATH | **Vignoni Alto.** A steep gravel road leads north out of Bagno Vignoni for 2 km (1 mile) to the town's upper village, a tiny grouping of buildings huddled at the base of a 13th-century tower. The tower, now a private home, was built to watch over the Via Francigena. A spectacular view of the entire Val d'Orcia opens up from the eastern gate.

WHERE TO EAT

¢ × TUSCAN ★ | **Bottega di Cacio.** Lots of shaded outdoor seating makes this a pleasant place for lunch on a warm day. Pecorino cheese, spicy salami, and grilled vegetables *sott'olio* (preserved in olive oil) are served cafeteria-style. And, if you want something even spicier, the stuffed hot peppers are delicious. There is a good selection of wine, but the choice of desserts is limited and they don't serve coffee. ⊠ *Piazza del Moretto 31* ☎ *0577/887477* ⊟ *No credit cards* ☉ *Closed Thurs.*

MONTALCINO

19 km (12 miles) northeast of Bagno Vignoni, 41 km (25½ miles) south of Siena, 109 km (68 miles) south of Florence.

Tiny Montalcino, with its commanding view from high on a hill, can claim an Etruscan past. It saw a fair number of travelers, as it was directly on the road from Siena to Rome. During the early Middle Ages it enjoyed a brief period of autonomy before falling under the orbit of Siena in 1201. Now Montalcino's greatest claim to fame is that it produces Brunello di Montalcino, one of Italy's most esteemed reds. Driving to the town, you pass through the Brunello vineyards. You can sample the excellent but expensive red in wine cellars in town or visit a nearby winery, such as Fattoria dei Barbi, for a guided tour and tasting; you must call ahead for reservations.

GETTING HERE

By car, follow the SR2 south from Siena, then follow the SP45 to Montalcino. Several Tra-In buses travel between Siena and Montalcino daily, making a tightly scheduled day trip possible. There is no train service available.

VISITOR INFORMATION

Montalcino tourism office ⊠ *Costa del Municipio 1* ☎ *0577/849331* ⊕ *www. prolocomontalcino.it.*

EXPLORING

La Fortezza. Providing refuge for the last remnants of the Sienese army during the Florentine conquest of 1555, the battlements of this 14th-century fortress are still in excellent condition. Climb up the narrow, spiral steps for the 360-degree view of most of southern Tuscany. There's also an enoteca for tasting wines on-site. ⊠ *Piazzale Fortezza* ☎ *0577/849211* ⊠ *€3* ⊙ *Nov.–Mar., Tues.–Sun. 9–6; Apr.–Oct., daily 9–8.*

Museo Civico e Diocesano d'Arte Sacra. This fine museum is housed in a building that once belonged to 13th-century Augustinian monks. The ticket booth is in the glorious refurbished cloister, and the sacred art collection, gathered from churches throughout the region, is displayed on two floors in former monastic quarters. Though the art here might be called "B-list," a fine altarpiece by Bartolo di Fredi (circa 1330–1410), the *Coronation of the Virgin,* makes dazzling use of gold. In addition, there's a striking 12th-century crucifix that originally adorned the high altar of the church of Sant'Antimo. Also on hand are many wood sculptures, a typical medium in these parts during the Renaissance. ⊠ *Via Ricasoli 31* ☎ *0577/846014* ⊠ *€8* ⊙ *Jan.–Mar., Tues.–Sun. 10–1 and 2–4; Apr.–Dec., Tues.–Sun. 10–6.*

Fattoria dei Barbi. The cellars of this venerable winery date from the 17th century and hold almost 200 oak wine barrels. Some of Italy's most famous wines are produced here, including an excellent range of Brunellos, a fine Rosso di Montalcino, and the estate's special Super Tuscan brands: Brusco dei Barbi and Bruscone dei Barbi. Olive oil, salami, and pecorino cheese are made at the winery's organic farm. Guided tours of the cellars are followed by wine tastings, during which you can also sample the other products. ⊠ *Località Podernovi 1* ☎ *0577/841111* ⊕ *www.fattoriadeibarbi.it* ⊠ *€5* ⊙ *Tours weekdays at noon and 3.*

WHERE TO EAT AND STAY

For expanded hotel reviews, visit Fodors.com.

¢ ╳ **Enoteca Osteria Osticcio.** Tullio and Francesca Scrivano have beautifully
WINE BAR remodeled this restaurant and wineshop. Upon entering, you descend

a staircase to a tasting room filled with rustic wooden tables. Adjacent is a small dining area with a splendid view of the hills far below, and outside is a lovely little terrace perfect for sampling Brunello di Montalcino when the weather is warm. The menu is light and pairs nicely with the wines, which are the main draw. The *acciughe sotto pesto* (anchovies with pesto) is a particularly fine treat. ⊠ *Via Matteotti 23* ☏ *0577/848271* ⊕ *www.osticcio.it* ⊘ *Closed Sun. No dinner.*

$ ✕**Fattoria dei Barbi.** Set among the vineyards that produce excellent
TUSCAN Brunello—as well as its younger cousin, Rosso di Montalcino—is this rustic taverna with a large stone fireplace. The estate farm produces many of the ingredients used in such traditional specialties as *stracotto nel brunello* (braised beef cooked with beans in Brunello wine). This eatery is a few minutes south of Montalcino, in the direction of Sant'Antimo. ⊠ *Podere Podernuovo 170* ☏ *0577/847117* ⊕ *www.fattoriadeibarbi.it* ⚘ *Reservations essential* ⊘ *Closed Wed. and mid-Jan.–mid-Feb.*

¢ ✕**Il Grappolo Blu.** Any one of this restaurant's *piatti tipici* (typical plates)
ITALIAN is worth trying: the local specialty, *pici all'aglione* (thick, long noodles served with sautéed cherry tomatoes and many cloves of garlic), is done particularly well. The chef also has a deft touch with vegetables; if there's fennel on the menu, make sure to try it. The interior, with white walls and an odd collection of prints, doesn't leave much of an impression, but the service is warm and friendly. ⊠ *Scale di Via Moglio 1* ☏ *0577/847150* ⚘ *Reservations essential* ⊘ *Closed Fri.*

$$$$ ⊡**Castiglion del Bosco.** This estate, one of the largest still in private hands in Tuscany, was purchased by Massimo Ferragamo at the beginning of this century and meticulously converted into a second-to-none resort. **Pros:** extremely secluded; exclusive and tranquil location; top-notch service; breathtaking scenery. **Cons:** well off the beaten track, the nearest town is 12 km (7 miles) away; private transportation required. ⊠ *Località Castiglion del Bosco, Montalcino* ☏ *0577/1913111* ⊕ *www. castigliondelbosco.com* ↵ *23 suites, 9 villas* ⚐ *In-room: safe, Wi-Fi. In-hotel: restaurant, bar, golf course, pool, tennis court, gym, spa, children's programs, some pets allowed* ⊠ *Breakfast.*

$ ⊡**La Crociona.** A quiet and serene family-owned farm, La Crociona is in the middle of a small vineyard with glorious views. **Pros:** peaceful location; great for families; friendly atmosphere. **Cons:** no air-conditioning; need a car to get around. ⊠ *Località La Croce 15* ☏ *0577/848007* ⊕ *www.lacrociona.com* ↵ *11 apartments* ⚐ *In-room: no a/c, kitchen. In-hotel: pool, laundry facilities, business center* ⊠ *No meals.*

ABBAZIA DI SANT'ANTIMO

10 km (6 miles) south of Montalcino, 51 km (32 miles) south of Siena, 119 km (74 miles) south of Florence.

GETTING HERE

Abbazia di Sant'Antimo is a 15-minute drive from Montalcino. Tra-In bus service is extremely limited. The abbey cannot be reached by train.

6

EXPLORING

Fodor's Choice ★ **Abbazia di Sant'Antimo.** It's well worth your while to visit this 12th-century Romanesque abbey, as it's a gem of pale stone in the silvery green of an olive grove. The exterior and interior sculpture is outstanding, particularly the nave capitals, a combination of French,

Lombard, and even Spanish influences. The sacristy (seldom open) forms part of the primitive Carolingian church (founded in AD 781), its entrance flanked by 9th-century pilasters. The small vaulted crypt dates from the same period. Above the nave runs a *matroneum* (women's gallery), an unusual feature once used to separate the congregation. Equally unusual is the ambulatory, for which the three radiating chapels were almost certainly copied from a French model. Stay to hear the canonical hours celebrated in Gregorian chant. On the drive that leads up toward Castelnuovo dell'Abate is a small shop that sells souvenirs and has washrooms. A 2½-hour hiking trail (signed as #2) leads to the abbey from Montalcino. Starting near Montalcino's small cemetery, the trail heads south through woods, along a ridge road to the tiny hamlet of Villa a Tolli, and then downhill to Sant'Antimo. ⊠ *Castelnuovo dell'Abate* ☎ *0577/835659* ⊕ *www.antimo.it* ⊗ *Daily 6 am–9 pm.*

LE CRETE

Van Gogh never saw the area south of Siena known as Le Crete (*creta* means "clay" in Italian), but in the bare, moonstone-color clay hills around Asciano—the rolling wheat fields, the warm light, the dramatic gullies and ravines cut by centuries of erosion—he would have perhaps found worthy subjects, as these landscapes seem carved into the earth much like the furrows of paint layer his canvases.

BUONCONVENTO

27 km (17 miles) southeast of Siena, 80 km (50 miles) south of Florence.

Buonconvento dates back to the 12th century, though it was surrounded by defensive walls in the later middle ages. Though the name means "happy place" in Latin, it was here that Holy Roman Emperor Henry VII died in 1313, cutting short his ill-fated attempt to establish imperial rule in Italy.

GETTING HERE

By car, Buonconvento is a 30-minute drive south from Siena on the SR2. Tra-In buses travel daily between Siena and Buonconvento several times a day, making a carefully scheduled day trip quite possible. A train connects Siena with Buonconvento, Monte Amiato Scalo, Asciano, and Arbia.

VISITOR INFORMATION

Buonconvento tourism office ⊠ *Piazzale Garibaldi 1* ☎ *0577/807181.*

Continued on page 303

SIMPLY PERFECT
The Basic Goodness of Tuscan Food

THE CUISINE OF TUSCANY ISN'T COM-PLICATED. In fact, every dish follows the same basic recipe:

■ Begin with fresh, high-quality ingredients, preferably produced within walking distance of the kitchen.

■ Prepare them using techniques that have been refined over centuries, ideally by members of the chef's family.

■ Serve the finished dish unpretentiously ("plate" is not a verb here), accompanied by a glass of good local wine.

The recipe looks simple, but executing it is not so easy. Some of the staples of "fine dining" that chefs elsewhere depend upon are pointedly missing.

There's nothing exotic: it would violate the "walking distance" principle of fresh, local ingredients. There's nothing ostentatious: showiness would distract from the basic beauty of the food. And innovation is looked on with a skeptical eye: if a new recipe or a new technique were really so good, surely someone in the preceding ten generations would have already thought of it.

The result is a cuisine that's inextricably tied to the place where it's made. There may now be Tuscan restaurants all over the globe, but you can still only eat genuine Tuscan food in Tuscany. It's home cooking that's worth traveling halfway around the world to taste.

EXPLORING THE TUSCAN MENU

Menu Basics

A meal in Tuscany (and elsewhere in Italy) traditionally consists of five courses, and every menu you encounter will be organized along this five-course plan:

First up is the **antipasto** (appetizer), often consisting of cured meats or marinated vegetables. Next to appear is the **primo**, usually pasta or soup, and after that the **secondo**, a meat or fish course with, perhaps, a **contorno** (vegetable dish) on the side. A simple **dolce** (dessert) rounds out the meal.

This, you've probably noticed, is a lot of food. Italians have noticed as well—a full, five-course meal is an indulgence usually reserved for special occasions. Instead, restaurant meals are a mix-and-match affair: you might order a primo and a secondo, or an antipasto and a primo, or a secondo and a contorno.

■ TIP→ The crucial rule of restaurant dining is that you should **order at least two courses.** It's a common mistake for tourists to order only a secondo, thinking they're getting a "main course" complete with side dishes. What they wind up with is one lonely piece of meat.

After you've eaten at a couple of restaurants, you may feel you're experiencing déjà vu: many of the same dishes are served almost everywhere. This is a by-product of the devotion to local, traditional cuisine, and part of the pleasure of dining in Tuscany is seeing how preparations vary from region to region and restaurant to restaurant.

What follows is a rundown, course by course, of classic dishes. The ones highlighted as "quintessential" are the epitome of Tuscan cooking. They shouldn't be missed.

Clockwise from bottom left: A well-worn menu; preparing *ribollita*; a typical food shop.

ANTIPASTI: APPETIZERS

The quintessential antipasto

Affettati misti

The name, roughly translated, means "mixed cold cuts," and it's something Tuscans do exceptionally well. The platter of cured meats is sure to include ***prosciutto crudo*** (ham, cut paper thin) and ***salame*** (dry sausage, prepared in dozens of ways, some spicy, some sweet). The most distinctly Tuscan *affettati* are made from ***cinta senese*** (a once nearly extinct pig found only in the heart of the region) and ***cinghiale*** (wild boar, which roam all of central Italy). You can eat these delicious slices unadorned or layered on a piece of bread.

From left: A typical affettati misti plate; two butchers; artichokes cured in olive oil

Other classics

Crostini

Toasted slices of bread with toppings—most commonly *fegatini* (chicken liver pâté), though other meat and vegetable concoctions also appear

Verdure sott'olio

Peppers, carrots, artichokes, and other vegetables cured in olive oil

Lardo di Colonnata

Not to be confused with lard (rendered fat), *lardo* is pig back fat that's seasoned with herbs, soaked in brine, and cured for months. Sliced thin and served over bread, it's a melt-in-your-mouth delicacy.

A WELL-OILED CUISINE

Olive oil is far and away the most important ingredient in Tuscan kitchens: it's a condiment, a cooking oil, a marinade, a salad dressing, a bread topping—one way or another, it makes its way into every meal.

The oil from Tuscany is frequently lauded as the best in the world. Open a bottle and you'll immediately know why: the aroma reaches out and grabs you. Like wine connoisseurs, oil lovers struggle for words to describe the experience—"spicy," "fruity," "herby," "redolent of artichokes"—but the sensual character of Tuscan oils defies description.

Which area in Tuscany produces the best oil is the subject of a never-ending debate. Sample as you go and decide for yourself—or simply enjoy the fact that there is no right answer. It's all good.

PRIMI: FIRST COURSES

The quintessential primo
Ribollita

A vegetable soup thickened with cannellini beans and stale bread—a classic example of how Tuscans make great things from humble ingredients. *Cavolo nero* (black cabbage, sometimes called Tuscan kale in the U.S.) is another key element—it gives the flavor a little kick. Upon serving, the soup is "christened" with a generous swirl of olive oil. In southern Tuscany, ribollita sometimes comes with chopped red onions on the side.

Other classics

Panzanella
A summer salad made of bread, tomatoes, basil, cucumbers, and olive oil

Pappa al pomodoro
Pureed tomato soup, thickened with bread

Zuppa alla frantoiana
Another bean, bread, and vegetable soup, this time run through a food mill

Pappardelle col sugo di cinghiale
Fresh pasta cut in wide strips with wild boar sauce

Ravioli di ricotta e spinaci
Spinach and cheese ravioli

Local specialties
(and the town or region where they're found)

Pici all'aglione
Hand-rolled pasta with garlic sauce (Siena and Montalcino)

Linguine alla granseola
Linguine with stone crab (a staple on Elba)

Minestra al farro
Soup made with *farro*, a barley-like grain (Lucca and the Garfagnana)

Ignudi
"Naked" ravioli-spinach and cheese dumplings minus the pasta (Florence and Chianti)

Crespelle
Crepe-like pancakes, stuffed with spinach and cheese and topped with a bechamel sauce (Florence)

Polenta di castagne
Chestnut polenta (the Garfagnana)

Acquacotta
"Cooked water"—thick vegetable soup (a specialty of the Maremma)

Tordelli di carne al ragù
Meat-stuffed tortelli pasta with a meat sauce (Lucca, where they prefer the spelling with a "d")

SECONDI: SECOND COURSES

The quintessential secondo
Bistecca alla fiorentina

You can get grilled steak everywhere from Texas to Tokyo, but in Tuscany they've found a way to make it their own. *Bistecca alla fiorentina* is an extra-thick T-bone that comes from ox-like Chianina cattle, a carefully nurtured Tuscan breed. It's seasoned with salt, pepper, and olive oil, and always served rare; cooking it longer is considered a travesty. Maybe it's the high quality of the beef, maybe it's the wonderful oil—whatever the reason, *bistecca alla fiorentina* truly is exceptional.

Other classics

Arista di maiale
Roast pork with sage and rosemary

Calamari all'inzimino
Squid and spinach stew

Tagliata di manzo
Thin slices of roasted beef, drizzled with oil

Fritto di pollo e coniglio
Fried chicken and rabbit

Salsiccia e fagioli
Pork sausage with beans

Local specialties

Frittura di paranza
Mixed fish fry (found all along the coast, but best in Livorno)

Piccione
Pigeon—it can be roasted, stuffed, or baked (southern Chianti)

Baccalà con ceci
Salt cod with chickpeas (much beloved by the Livornesi)

Peposo
A peppery beef stew (Impruneta)

Trippa alla fiorentina
Tripe stewed in a tomato sauce (Florence)

Ricotta cheese, Vitereta, Tuscany

A TASTE OF THE TYPICAL

While "typical" can be a disparaging term in English, its Italian equivalent, *"tipico,"* is high praise. Whether you're talking about a type of cheese, a variety of wine, or a particular cut of pasta, *"tipico"* indicates something that's traditional to the location where you find it. Which means it's been perfected over the course of centuries. And that means, whatever it is, you won't get it better anywhere else.

CONTORNI: VEGETABLES

The quintessential contorno
Fagioli all'olio

Tuscans are known among fellow Italians as *"mangiafagioli"* (bean eaters), and with good reason. White cannellini beans are the standard, usually boiled with fresh sage, drained, and liberally laced with olive oil. Another preparation is *fagioli all'uccelletto,* in which the beans are cooked with tomato and sage. *Fagioli al fiasco* are slow-cooked in a glass bottle.

Other classics

Virtually any fresh vegetable, either briefly boiled or sautéed in oil, possibly with a touch of garlic. Greens are especially popular—look for *cime di rape* (turnip greens) as well as *spinaci* (spinach). Other seasonal favorites are *carciofi* (artichokes), *asparagi* (asparagus) *piselli* (peas), *zucchini, peperoni* (peppers), and *fave* (fava beans).

DOLCI: DESSERTS

The quintessential dolce
Cantuccini con vin santo

These hard little almond cookies, also known as *biscotti di Prato,* are virtually inedible when dry, but dip them into sweet vin santo wine, and the result is delectable.

From left: Castagnaccio; cantucci and vin santo; buccellato

Other classics

Tuscan cuisine is not particularly noted for its desserts. Meals often end with an unadorned piece of fruit. Here and there, though, you'll find exceptions.

Local specialties

Buccellato
An anise-flavored sweet bun (Lucca)

Castagnaccio
A flat chestnut-flour cake (Lucca)

Ricciarelli
Delicate almond cookies (Siena)

Panforte
Candied fruit and nut cake (Siena)

Brigidini
Sugary wafers, best when topped with gelato (Montecatini)

EXPLORING

Museo d'Arte Sacra. Today quiet Buonconvento is worth a stop for a look at its tiny museum, a two-room picture gallery with more than its fair share of works by Tuscan artists such as Duccio and Andrea di Bartolo. The highlight is a triptych with the *Madonna and Saints Bernardino and Catherine* by Sano di Pietro. ⊠ *Via Soccini 18* ☎ *0577/807181* 🎫 *€5* ⊙ *Mar.–Oct., Tues.–Sun. 10–1 and 3–7; Nov.–Feb., Thurs. and Fri. 2–7, weekends 10–1 and 3–5.*

EN ROUTE

Murlo. If you're heading northwest to Siena, stray 9 km (5½ miles) west of the Via Cassia to Vescovado and then follow the signs 2 km (1 mile) south to this tiny fortified medieval *borgo* (village) that has been completely restored.

Antiquarium Poggio Civitate. An imposing bishop's palace holds this museum of Etruscan relics. Although there are many beautiful pieces on display, the almost complete roof and pediment from a 5th-century BC Etruscan house are especially rare. The museum is named after the nearby site from which most of the artifacts were excavated. ⊠ *Piazza della Cattedrale 4, Murlo* ☎ *0577/814099* ⊕ *www.poggiocivitate.it* 🎫 *€5* ⊙ *Mar. and Oct., Tues.–Sun. 10–1 and 3–5; Apr.–June, and Sept., Tues.–Sun. 10–1 and 3–7; July and Aug., Tues.–Sun. 10–7; Nov.–Feb., Tues.–Fri. 10–1, weekends 10–1 and 3–5 .*

6

ABBAZIA DI MONTE OLIVETO MAGGIORE

9 km (5½ miles) northeast of Buonconvento, 37 km (23 miles) south-east of Siena.

GETTING HERE

From Siena, the abbey is a 45-minute drive on the SR2 south to Buonconvento and then the SP451 to Monte Oliveto. Bus and train service are not available.

EXPLORING

★ **Abbazia di Monte Oliveto Maggiore.** Tuscany's most-visited abbey sits in an oasis of olive and cypress trees amid the harsh landscape of Le Crete. It was founded in 1313 by Giovanni Tolomei, a rich Sienese lawyer who, after miraculously regaining his lost sight, changed his name to Bernardo in homage to Saint Bernard of Clairvaux, who is sometimes credited with the creation of medieval monasticism. Bernardo then founded a monastic order dedicated to the restoration of Benedictine principles. The name of the order—the White Benedictines—refers to a vision that Bernardo had in which Jesus, Mary, and his own mother were all clad in white. The monks are sometimes also referred to as Olivetans, which is the name of the hill where the monastery was built. Famous for maintaining extreme poverty—their feast-day meal consisted of two eggs—they slept on straw mats and kept a vow of silence. Although the monks look like they are eating a little better these days and are not afraid to strike up a conversation, the monastery still operates, and most of the area is off-limits to visitors. One of Italy's most important book restoration centers is here, and the monks still produce a wide variety of traditional liqueurs (distilled from herbs that grow on the premises), which are available in the gift shop along with enough food products to fill a pantry, all produced by monks in various parts of Italy.

From the entrance gate a tree-lined lane leads down to the main group of buildings, with paths veering off to several shrines and chapels dedicated to important saints of the order. The church itself is not particularly memorable, but the exquisite choir stalls (1503–05) by Fra Giovanni da Verona are among the country's finest examples of *intarsia* (wood inlay). Forty-eight of the 125 stalls have inlaid decoration, each set up as a window or arched doorway that opens onto a space (a town, a landscape) or an object (a musical instrument, a bird), rendered in marvelous perspective. Check at the entrance for the schedule of Masses, as the monks often chant the liturgy.

In the abbey's main cloister, frescoes by Luca Signorelli and Sodoma depict scenes from the life of St. Benedict. Signorelli began the cycle by painting scenes from the saint's adult life as narrated by Saint Gregory the Great, and although his nine scenes are badly worn, the individual expressions are fittingly austere and pensive, full of serenity and religious spirit, and as individualized as those he painted in the San Brizio chapel in Orvieto's Duomo. Later Sodoma filled in the story with scenes from the saint's youth and the last years of his life. The results are also impressive, but in this case what stands out are the use of color and earthier imagery. Note the detailed landscapes, the rich costumes, the animals (similar to those Sodoma was known to keep as pets), and the scantily clad boys he apparently preferred (for this he was called "the Sodomist" and described by Vasari as "a merry and licentious man . . . of scant chastity"). ⊠ *Località Monteoliveto Maggiore 1, Chiusure, Asciano* ☎ *0577/707611* ⊕ *www.monteolivetomaggiore.it* ☒ *By donation* ☉ *Nov.–Mar., daily 9:15–noon and 3:15–5; Apr.–Oct., daily 9:15–noon and 3:15–6.*

WHERE TO EAT AND STAY

For expanded hotel reviews, visit Fodors.com.

¢   ✕ **La Torre.** You can enjoy straightforward Tuscan fare in the massive
TUSCAN tower at the abbey's entrance, or, when it's warm, on a flower-filled terrace. The *pici ai funghi* (extra-thick handmade spaghetti with mushroom sauce) or *zuppa di funghi* (mushroom soup) take the sting out of a crisp winter day, and the grilled meats are a good bet at any time of year. If you want lighter fare, there's a bar serving panini that has outdoor seating. ⊠ *Località Monteoliveto Maggiore 2, 8 km (5 miles) south of Asciano on SS451, Asciano* ☎ *0577/707022* ☉ *Closed Tues.*

$$ 🏠 **Fattoria del Colle.** Amid rolling vineyards and olive trees, this *fattoria* (farmhouse) produces fine wine and olive oil. **Pros:** great for families; beautiful location. **Cons:** no air-conditioning; no phones in rooms; 30-minute walk to nearest town. ⊠ *Località Il Colle, 12 km (7 miles) east of Abbazia di Monte Oliveto Maggiore, Trequanda* ☎ *0577/662108* ⊕ *www.cinellicolombini.it* ⤵ *2 rooms, 19 apartments, 2 villas* ⚊ *In-room: no a/c, kitchen, no TV. In-hotel: restaurant, pool, tennis court* ☉|*Breakfast.*

$$$$ 🏠 **La Chiusa.** Dania and Umberto Lucherini bought this old farmhouse in 1974 and turned it into a significant restaurant ($$$$) with emphasis on Tuscan classics. **Pros:** delightful setting; excellent restaurant; personal service. **Cons:** standard rooms are on the small side; need a car to get around. ✉ *Via della Madonnina 88, 25 km (15 miles) east of Abbazia di Monte Oliveto Maggiore, Montefollonico* 📞 *0577/669668* ⊕ *www. ristorantelachiusa.it* 🛏 *15 rooms* ♿ *In-room: no a/c, safe. In-hotel: restaurant, business center, parking, some pets allowed* ⊗ *Closed Tues. and mid-Jan.–Mar.* ⊙| *Breakfast.*

$$$$

Fodor'sChoice

★

🏠 **Locanda dell'Amorosa.** What was a self-sufficient hamlet with its own chapel in the 14th century is now a refined inn. **Pros:** romantic setting; excellent restaurant; luxurious rooms. **Cons:** standard rooms are small; need a car to get around. ✉ *Località L'Amorosa 1, 23 km (14 miles) east of Abbazia di Monte Oliveto Maggiore, Sinalunga* 📞 *0577/67721* ⊕ *www.amorosa.it* 🛏 *17 rooms, 8 suites* ♿ *In-room: safe, Wi-Fi. In-hotel: restaurant, bar, pool* ⊗ *Closed Jan. and Feb.*

ASCIANO

8 km (5 miles) north of Abbazia di Monte Oliveto Maggiore, 25 km (16 miles) southeast of Siena, 124 km (77 miles) southeast of Florence.

Founded by the Etruscans around the 5th century BC, Asciano is now a sleepy little town surrounded by 13th-century walls. The tiny centro storico (historic center) is eminently bike-friendly; any serious cyclist should consider a pit stop here.

GETTING HERE

From Siena, driving to Asciano on the SP438 takes about 40 minutes. Tra-In has limited bus service, making the train, with five or six daily departures, a better option.

VISITOR INFORMATION

Asciano tourism office ✉ *Via Amos Cassioli 2* 📞 *0577/718666* ⊕ *www. prolocoasciano.it.*

EXPLORING

Fodor'sChoice

★

Museo d'Arte Sacra e Archeologico. Palazzo Corboli, a magnificent palace dating from the 12th century, has been refurbished and houses the Museo d'Arte Sacra e Archeologico. The collection of Etruscan artifacts is worth a visit, though the real highlight is the collection of lesser-known 13th- and 14th-century paintings from the Sienese school. ✉ *Corso Matteotti 122* 📞 *0577/719524* 💶 *€5* ⊙ *Mar.–Oct., Tues.–Sat. 10–1 and 3–7:30, Sun. noon–1 and 3–8; Nov.–Feb., Fri.–Sun. 10:30–1 and 3–5:30.*

Farmacia De Munari. The basement of the local pharmacy holds the town's most important Roman artifact, a polychrome Roman mosaic from the 1st to 2nd century AD. To see the mosaic, you must ask for the keys at the tourist information office. ✉ *Corso Matteotti 80* 📞 *0577/718124* 💶 *Free* ⊙ *Weekdays 9–1 and 4–8, Sat. 9–1.*

THE MAREMMA

The wildest part of Tuscany is here in its southern heart. And it's here that you get a sense of what the region looked like before Tuscany became a must-see on the grand tour. The landscape alternates between rolling hills and tufa cliffs; hill towns abound, linked by narrow, winding roads. Saturnia—with its superior hotels, restaurants, and one-of-a-kind hot springs—makes a good base to explore and sample the best of what the south has to offer: ancient Etruscan tombs and caverns at Sovana and Sorano, the famous white wine of Pitigliano, and wild mushrooms and chestnut honey from the rugged slopes of Monte Amiata, which presides over Tuscany with views from Arezzo to the sea.

MONTE AMIATA

16 km (10 miles) south of Abbazia di Sant'Antimo, 86 km (52 miles) southeast of Siena, 156 km (94 miles) southeast of Florence.

GETTING HERE

Monte Amiata can be reached by car from Siena on the SR2 (Via Cassia). Bus service is extremely limited. There is a train station at Monte Amiata Scalo, but it is at the base of the mountain and not well served by local buses.

VISITOR INFORMATION

Monte Amiata tourism office ⊠ *Via Adua 25, Abbadia San Salvatore* ☏ *0577/775811* ⊕ *www.webamiata.it.*

EXPLORING

Monte Amiata. At 5,702 feet, this benign volcano is one of Tuscany's few ski slopes, but it's no Mont Blanc. Come in warmer months to take advantage of an abundance of hiking trails that cross wide meadows full of wildflowers and slice through groves of evergreens. Panoramic views of all of Tuscany present themselves on the winding road up to the summit. Along the way, you pass through a succession of tiny medieval towns, including Castel del Piano, Arcidosso, Santa Flora, and Piancastagnaio, where you can pick up picnic supplies and sample the chestnuts and game for which the mountain is famous.

In this region, the thousand-year-old village **Abbadia San Salvatore** is worth a stop—skip the nondescript new town and head straight to the *centro storico* to explore winding stone streets with tiny churches around every corner. The abbey for which the town was named was founded in 743; its current appearance reflects an 11th-century renovation, but the original crypt remains intact. The tourist office in town has hiking-trail maps for Monte Amiata. ⊠ *Tourist office, Via Adua 25, Abbadia San Salvatore* ☏ *0577/775811* .

In Search of Etruscan Artifacts

To fully appreciate the strangely quixotic relationship that the ancient Etruscan culture had with the tufa rock that provided the fabric of the civilization, you must visit southern Tuscany. The houses and tombs, and sometimes even the roads, were carved from this soft volcanic stone, making it impossible to think about the Etruscans without also imagining the dark sandy tufa that surrounded them.

Some of the best-preserved, and most mysterious, of all their monumental tombs are in the area of Pitigliano, Sorano, and Sovana. In the necropolis of the latter, you can actually walk on a section of Etruscan road that is almost 2,500 years old.

Chiusi should not be missed if you are interested in things Etruscan: several tombs that still retain their brightly colored decorations and a particularly fine and thoughtfully organized archaeological museum await you there.

SORANO

6

38 km (23 miles) south of Abbadia San Salvatore on Monte Amiata, 138 km (86 miles) southeast of Siena, 208 km (130 miles) southeast of Florence.

GETTING HERE

Being in the southern part of Tuscany, Sorano is most easily reached from Rome. From the A1 highway, take the Orvieto exit. There are no practical ways to arrive here by bus or train.

EXPLORING

Sorano. This town's history follows the pattern of most settlements in the area: it was an ancient Etruscan citadel, built up in the 15th century and fortified by one of the many warring families of Tuscany (in this case, the Orsini). It's the execution that sets it apart. With its tiny, twisted streets and stone houses connected by wooden stairways and ramps, Sorano looks as if it was carved from the tufa beneath it—and that's because it was. Underneath the town, visible as you approach, is a vast network of *colombari*, Etruscan-era rooms lined with hundreds of niches carved into stone walls, dating from the 1st century BC. The colombari aren't yet open to the public, but Sorano is worth a visit regardless, if only to walk its medieval alleyways and to watch old-style artisans at work. Views of the densely forested hills around town will have you reaching for your camera.

WHERE TO STAY

For expanded hotel reviews, visit Fodors.com.

$$ ⌂ **Della Fortezza.** High above Sorano, this austere-looking 11th-century Orsini castle boasts spectacular views of the town and surrounding countryside. **Pros:** rooms have great views of Sorano; romantic location. **Cons:** very basic decor; no air-conditioning in rooms. ⊠ *Piazza Cairoli 5* ☎ *0564/632010* ⊕ *www.fortezzahotel.it* ⤶ *14 rooms, 1 suite* ⌂ *In-room: no a/c, Wi-Fi. In-hotel: restaurant, bar, parking* ⏐⊚⏐ *Breakfast.*

PITIGLIANO

10 km (6 miles) south of Sorano, 147 km (92 miles) southeast of Siena, 217 km (136 miles) southeast of Florence.

From a distance, the medieval stone houses of Pitigliano look as if they melt into the cliffs upon which they are perched. Etruscan tombs, which locals use to store wine, are connected by a network of caves and tunnels. At the beginning of the 14th century the Orsini family moved its base from Sovana to the better-fortified Pitigliano. They built up the town's defenses and fortified their home, Palazzo Orsini. Later, starting in 1543, Antonio da Sangallo the Younger added to the town's fortress, building bastions and towers throughout the town and adding the aqueduct as well.

Pitigliano has become a trendy locale for Italian vacation rentals, making the town center lively in summer. Restaurants serve up good meals that, as a result of the tourist boom, have inflated prices. Bianco di Pitigliano (Pitigliano white wine) is a fresh and light, dry wine produced from the vines that thrive in the tufa soil of the area.

GETTING HERE

Pitigliano is best reached by car along the SR74 from either the Via Aurelia to the west or the A1 highway to the east. Plan on a journey of about an hour. Pitigliano cannot be reached directly by train, but bus service is available from the train station in Grosseto.

VISITOR INFORMATION

Maremma regional tourism office ⊠ *Piazza Garibaldi 12* ☎ *0564/617111* ⊕ *www.lamaremmafabene.it.*

EXPLORING

Duomo. This 18th-century baroque cathedral has a single nave with chapels and paintings on the sides. There are two altarpieces by local artist Francesco Zuccarelli (1702–88), a rococo landscape artist, favorite of George III, and one of the founders of the British Royal Academy. ⊠ *Piazza S. Gregorio 1* ☎ *0564/616090* ☽ *Daily 9–7.*

Museo di Palazzo Orsini. The palace museum has several rooms featuring paintings by Zuccarelli, who was born in Pitigliano in 1702. Other works include a Madonna carved in wood by Jacopo della Quercia (1371/74–1438), a 14th-century crucifix, and a numismatic collection. ⊠ *Piazza Fortezza Orsini 25* ☎ *0564/616074* ⊠ *€3* ☽ *Apr.–July, Tues.–Sun. 10–1 and 3–7; Aug., daily 10–7; Sept. and Oct., Tues.–Sun. 10–1 and 3–7; Nov.–Mar., Tues.–Fri. 10–1 and 3–6.*

Piccola Gerusaleme di Pitigliano. Now a museum of Jewish culture, the ghetto where Jews took refuge from 16th-century Catholic persecution was a thriving community until the beginning of World War II. Inside the precinct today are the remains of ritual bathing basins, a wine cellar, a kosher butcher shop and bakery, and the restored synagogue, where religious services are held on the Sabbath. ⊠ *Via Firenze 116* ☎ *0564/616006* ⊕ *www.lapiccolagerusalemme.it* ⊠ *€2.50* ☽ *Apr.–Sept., Sun.–Fri. 10–1:30 and 2:30–6:30; Oct.–Mar., Sun.–Fri. 10–12:30 and 3–5:30.*

The Maremma and the Tuscan Islands

KEY
Ferry Lines

Parco Nazionale dell'Arcipelago Toscano

Caprαia

Elba
Portoferrάio
Porto Azzurro

ISOLA PIANOSA

ISOLA DI MONTECRISTO

Parco Nazionale dell'Arcipelago Toscano

Parco Nazionale dell'Arcipelago Toscano

20 miles
20 kilometers

Mare Tirreno

ISOLA DI GIANNUTRI

Giglio
Giglio Porto

Monte Argentario

Porto San Stefano
Orbetello

Albinia

Manciano

Saturnia

Sovana
Sorano
Pitigliano

Monte Amiata

Castel del Piano
Paganico

Scansano

Parco Naturale della Maremma

Grosseto

Castiglione della Pescaia

Follónica

Massa Marittima

Abbazia di San Galgano

Monticiano

Montalcino

Buonconvento

Asciano

Sinalunga

Montepulciano
Pienza
Chianciano Terme

Acquapendente

Tuscania

Tarquinia

TO ROMA

Lago di Bolsema

Siena

TO PERUGIA →

TO LIVORNO

San Vincenzo

Piombino

Mincio

Ombrone

Orcia

Cecina

Cornia

Fiora

Albegna

146
2
2
312
1
74
1
223
73
441
439
398
1
326
A1
A1
2
223

WHERE TO EAT AND STAY

For expanded hotel reviews, visit Fodors.com.

¢   ✕ **Il Tufo Allegro.** The name means
TUSCAN   Happy Tufa; you would be happy, too, if you ate at this fine restaurant cut directly into the tufa rock plateau upon which old Pitigliano sits. The cuisine is local and regional: *coniglio al finocchio selvatico* (rabbit with wild fennel) is particularly tasty, and fish also figures on the menu from time to time. For the particularly hungry, there are usually several four-course, fixed-price menus to choose from. ⊠ *Vicolo della Costituzione 5* ☎ *0564/616192* ⊙ *Closed Tues. and mid-Jan.–mid-Feb. No lunch Wed. Oct.–July.*

$ 🛏 **Locanda Il Tufo Rosa.** The space for part of this tiny guesthouse has been carved out of the tufa rock beneath the aqueduct at the entrance to the old town. **Pros:** excellent location; best value in town. **Cons:** rooms are small; getting here is difficult, narrow stairways to climb. ⊠ *Piazza Petruccioli 97* ☎ *0564/617019* ⊕ *www.iltuforosa.com* 📶 *6 rooms, 1 apartment* △ *In-room: no a/c* ▤ *No credit cards* ⦿ *No meals.*

SOVANA

5 km (3 miles) north of Pitigliano, 155 km (97 miles) southeast of Siena, 225 km (141 miles) southeast of Florence.

This town of Etruscan origin was once the capital of the area in southern Tuscany dominated by the Aldobrandeschi family, whose reign was at its height in the 11th and first half of the 12th centuries. One member of the family, Hildebrand, was the 11th-century Catholic reformer Pope Gregory VII (circa 1020–85). The 13th- to 14th-century Romanesque fortress known as the Rocca Aldobrandesca is now in ruins. Via di Mezzo, with stones arranged in a fish-scale pattern, is the main street running the length of the town.

GETTING HERE

Like Sorano and Pitigliano, Sovana is best reached by car along the SR74, either from the Via Aurelia to the west or the A1 highway to the east. Sovana cannot be reached by train or bus.

EXPLORING

Duomo. Sovana extends from the Rocca Aldobrandesca at the eastern end of town to the imposing cathedral, built between the 10th and 14th century, in the west. The church, dedicated to Saints Peter and Paul, is Romanesque in style but, atypically, the main entrance is on the left-hand side of the building. ⊠ *Piazza del Duomo* ☎ *No phone* ⊙ *Daily 10–1 and 2:45–5:45.*

Piazza del Pretorio. Here, in the central town square, you'll find the 13th-century Palazzo Pretorio, which has a facade adorned with crests of Sovana's captains of justice, and the Renaissance Palazzo Bourbon dal Monte.

Santa Maria Maggiore. This little 14th-century church on the main square has frescoes from the late-15th-century Sienese Umbrian school and a ciborium dating back to the 8th century. ⊠ *Piazza del Pretorio* ☎ *No phone* ☉ *Daily 8:30–12:30 and 4–6:30.*

Etruscan necropolis. Some of Italy's best-preserved monumental rock tombs, dating from the 2nd to the 3rd century BC, are found just outside the town at the Etruscan necropolis. Some of the tombs, such as the so-called Tomba Sirena (Siren's Tomb), preserve clear signs of their original and elaborately carved decorations. Others, like the Tomba Ildebranda (Hildebrand Tomb), are spectacular evidence of the architectural complexity sometimes achieved. Don't forget to walk along the section of an Etruscan road carved directly into the tufa stone. ⊠ *1½ km (1 mile) west of town center* ☎ *0564/633099* ▤ *€5* ☉ *Daily 9–sunset.*

WHERE TO EAT

$ ╳ **La Taverna Etrusca.** Elaborately prepared Tuscan fare is served at this
TUSCAN elegant restaurant on Sovana's central square. For your first course,
Fodor'sChoice try the local specialty *zuppa di ortiche con quadratini di ricotta* (nettle
★ soup with ricotta cheese). Grilled meat and some fish dishes highlight the list of second courses. Service is prompt and highly professional. An outdoor terrace provides plenty of fresh air in the summer months. ⊠ *Piazza del Pretorio 16* ☎ *0564/616183* ☉ *Closed Wed.*

SATURNIA

25 km (15 miles) east of Sovana, 129 km (77 miles) south of Siena, 199 km (119 miles) south of Florence.

Saturnia was settled even before the Etruscan period, but nowadays it's best known not for what lies buried beneath the ground but for what comes up from it: hot, sulfurous water that supplies the town's world-famous spa. According to an oft-repeated legend, the thermal waters were created when Saturn, restless with earth's bickering mortals, threw down a thunderbolt and created a hot spring whose miraculously calming waters created peace among them. Today these magnesium-rich waters bubble forth from the clay, drawing Italians and non-Italians alike seeking relief for skin and muscular ailments as well as a bit (well, a lot) of relaxation. Unlike better-known spa centers such as Montecatini Terme, nature still has her place here.

GETTING HERE

Saturnia is a 30-minute drive from Pitigliano. Follow the SS74 to Manciano, then the SS322 to Montemerano, and then turn right onto the Strada Saturnia–La Croce. The RAMA bus company travels from Grosseto to Saturnia, but three changes make the journey particularly arduous. There is no train service to Saturnia.

EXPLORING

Cascate del Gorello (*Gorello Falls*). Outside Saturnia, the hot, sulfurous waters cascade over natural limestone shelves at the Cascate del Gorello, affording bathers a sweeping view of the open countryside. The falls are on public land and can be enjoyed 24 hours a day. They get extremely crowded—day and night—during August. ✉ *2 km (1 mile) south of Saturnia, on road to Montemerano* ☎ *No phone* 💲 *Free.*

Terme di Saturnia. The swimming pools and treatments at Terme di Saturnia spa and resort are open to the public. You might make an appointment for a thermal mud therapy or rent a lounge chair and umbrella to sit by the pools. ✉ *3 km (2 miles) east of Saturnia on road to Montemerano, after Gorello Falls* ☎ *0564/600111* ⊕ *www.termedisaturnia.it* 💲 *Full day €22, half day €17* ☉ *Apr.–Oct., daily 9:30–7; Nov.–Mar., daily 9:30–5.*

Necropoli del Puntone. Pre-Etruscan tombs at this necropolis aren't kept up well, but they're interesting simply for their age, as they're even older than Saturnia's legendary baths. ✉ *1 km (½ mile) north of Saturnia, on road to Poggio Murello, turn left and follow signs* ☎ *No phone* 💲 *Free* ☉ *Daily 24 hrs.*

WHERE TO EAT

$$$$
TUSCAN
★

✕ **Da Caino.** At this excellent restaurant in the nearby town of Montemerano, specialties include tomatoes and peppers on crisp phyllo dough, lasagna with pumpkin, ravioli *ripieni di olio extra vergine di olive* (filled with extra-virgin olive oil, capers, anchovies, and tomatoes), and such hearty dishes as *cinghiale lardolato con olive* (wild boar larded with olives). Prices are among the highest in the region; locals consider it a serious splurge. ✉ *Via della Chiesa 4, 7 km (4½ miles) south of Saturnia on road to Scansano, Montemerano* ☎ *0564/602817* ⊕ *www.dacaino.it* 🍴 *Reservations essential* ☉ *Closed Wed., Jan., and 2 wks in July. No lunch Thurs.*

$
TUSCAN

✕ **I Due Cippi–Da Michele.** Owner Michele Aniello captivates with a creative menu that emphasizes local ingredients like wild boar and duck. Try the *tortelli di castagne al seme di finocchio* (chestnut-stuffed pasta pillows with butter sauce and fennel seeds). In good weather you can enjoy your meal on a terrace overlooking the town's main square. ✉ *Piazza Vittorio Veneto 26a* ☎ *0564/601074* 🍴 *Reservations essential* ☉ *Closed Dec. 20–26, Jan. 10–25, and Tues. Oct.–June.*

WHERE TO STAY

For expanded hotel reviews, visit Fodors.com.

$$$$

🏨 **Terme di Saturnia.** Spa living might not get any more top-notch than this: roam the spa resort in a plush white bathrobe (waiting in your room) before dipping into the 37.5°C (100°F) sulfurous thermal pools. **Pros:** luxurious setting; excellent service; wide range of treatments. **Cons:** on the pricey side; aseptic atmosphere. ✉ *3 km (2 miles) east of Saturnia on road to Montemerano, past Gorello Falls* ☎ *0564/600111* ⊕ *www.termedisaturnia.it* 🛏 *124 rooms, 2 suites* 🛎 *In-room: safe, Wi-Fi. In-hotel: restaurant, bar, pool, tennis court, gym, spa, laundry facilities, some pets allowed* ⍨ *Breakfast.*

$$

🏨 **Villa Acquaviva.** An elegant villa painted antique rose appears at the end of a tree-lined driveway perched on top of a hill off the main road 1 km (½ mile) before Montemerano. **Pros:** near the hot springs; lovely views; family-friendly atmosphere. **Cons:** attendants can be hard to find during the day; need a car to get around. ✉ *Strada Scansanese 6 km (4 miles) south of Saturnia, Montemerano* ☎ *0564/602890*

Terme, Wrath of the Gods

In a country known for millennia as a hotbed of seismic activity, Tuscany seems to have gotten a lucky break. Although Campania and Sicily are famous for active volcanoes, and Umbria and the Marches stand on notoriously shaky ground, Tuscany's underground activity makes itself known in the form of steamy and sulfurous hot springs that have earned the region a name as a spa-goer's paradise.

Tuscany is dotted throughout with small *terme* (thermal baths), where hot waters flow from natural springs deep under the earth's surface. Since the time of the Etruscans, these hot springs have been valued for their curative properties. The Romans attributed the springs' origins to divine thunderbolts that split the earth open and let flow the miraculous waters. Regardless of their origin, their appeal endures, as the presence of thousands of people taking the waters in the Maremma attests.

Each of the springs has different curative properties, attributable to the various concentrations of minerals and gases that individual water flows pick up on their way to the surface. Carbon dioxide, for example, is said to strengthen the immune system, and sulfur, its characteristic rotten-egg smell notwithstanding, is said to relieve pain and aid in relaxation.

Although customs and conventions vary between spas, you generally pay an admission fee to swim in baths that range from hot natural lakes and waterfalls (with accompanying mud) to giant limestone swimming pools filled with cloudy, bright blue, steaming water. Larger establishments have treatments that can range from mineral mud baths to steam inhalations.

Believers swear that Tuscany's hot springs have a positive effect on everything from skin disorders to back pain to liver function to stress. Whatever your opinion, a good soak in a Tuscan spring is a relaxing way to take a break, and as far as geological phenomena go, it beats an earthquake or a volcanic eruption any day.

A few of the region's spas, notably the world-famous Montecatini Terme (⇨ *See Chapter 3*), are well known outside Tuscany. For the most part, however, the local establishments that run the springs are not well publicized, which can mean a more local flavor, lower prices, and fewer crowds: Terme di Bagni di Lucca is near Lucca; Terme di Chianciano is near Chiusi; Bagno Vignoni is just south of San Quirico d'Orcia; and Terme di Saturnia is not too far from Grosseto.

Local tourist offices have the most up-to-date information on smaller springs, many of which are open for only part of the year.

6

⊕ *www.relaisvillaacquaviva.com* ⌁ *23 rooms, 2 suites* ⌂ *In-room: safe. In-hotel: restaurant, bar, pool, tennis court, some pets allowed* ¶⊙¶ *Breakfast.*

$$ ⊞ **Villa Clodia.** Situated in the oldest part of town, the villa has splendid
★ views over the nearby hills and the steamy clouds coming from the hot springs. **Pros:** excellent location on edge of town; great views; cozy environment. **Cons:** some rooms are small; need a car to get around. ⊠ *Via Italia 43* ☎ *0564/601212* ⊕ *www.hotelvillaclodia.com* ⌁ *8 rooms,*

2 *suites* ♿ *In-room: safe. In-hotel:*
pool, spa, parking ⊘ *Closed Dec.*
☉|*Breakfast.*

Grosseto. The largest town in southern Tuscany, Grosseto is the capital of the Maremma. First recorded in the 9th century as a *castellum* (castle) built to defend a bridge and a port on the nearby River Ombrone, the town is now a thriving agricultural center. Badly damaged during World War II, it has been largely rebuilt since the 1950s, but a small *centro storico* (historic center), protected by defensive walls that follow a hexagonal plan, is worth a short visit on your way to the coast.

PARCO NATURALE DELLA MAREMMA

10 km (6 miles) south of Grosseto, 88 km (55 miles) southwest of Siena,
156 km (97 miles) south of Florence.

GETTING HERE

The park is best reached by car from the Via Aurelia (SS1), which runs between Rome and Pisa. Local bus service connects the park with the train station in nearby Grosseto.

VISITOR INFORMATION

Parco Naturale della Maremma tourism office ⊠ *Via del Bersgliere 7/9,*
Alberese ☎ *0564/407098* ⊕ *www.parco-maremma.it.*

EXPLORING

Parco Naturale della Maremma. The well-kept nature preserve at **Monti dell'Uccellina** is an oasis of green hills sloping down to small, secluded beaches on protected coastline. Wild goats and rabbits, foxes and wild boars, as well as horses and a domesticated long-horned white ox unique to this region, make their home among miles of sea pines, rosemary plants, and juniper bushes. The park also has scattered Etruscan and Roman ruins and a medieval abbey, the **Abbazia di San Rabano.** Enter from the south at Talamone (turn right 1 km [½ mile] before town) or from Alberese, both reachable from the SS1 (Via Aurelia). Daily limits restrict the number of cars that can enter, so in summer it's best to either reserve ahead or to leave your car in Alberese and use the regular bus service; contact the park's information office for bookings, and to secure English-language guides. ⊠ *Via Bersagliere 7, Alberese* ☎ *0564/407098* 🎫 *€3–€8* ⊘ *Daily 9–1 hr before sunset.*

MONTE ARGENTARIO

Porto Santo Stefano 60 km (37 miles) southwest of Saturnia, 118 km (74 miles) southwest of Siena, 186 km (116 miles) southwest of Florence.

Connected to the mainland only by two thin strips of land and a causeway, Monte Argentario feels like an island. The north and south isthmuses, La Giannella and La Feniglia, have long sandy beaches popular with families, but otherwise the terrain is rugged, dotted with luxurious vacation houses. There are beautiful views from the panoramic mountain road encircling the promontory, and a drive here is a romantic sunset excursion. The mountain itself rises 2,096 feet above the sea, and it's ringed with rocky beaches and sheer cliffs that afford breathtaking views of the coast.

GETTING HERE

The Monte Argentario peninsula lies just off the SS1 (Via Aurelia), which connects Rome and Pisa. It's a two-hour drive from either city. Intercity buses are not a viable option. The closest train station is in Orbetello Scalo, with local bus service available to both Porto Ercole and Porto Santo Stefano.

VISITOR INFORMATION

Monte Argentario tourism office ✉ *Via Sant'Andrea, Porto Santo Stefano* ☎ *0564/814208* ⊕ *www.monteargentario.it.*

EXPLORING

Porto Santo Stefano. On the north side, busy and colorful Porto Santo Stefano is Monte Argentario's main center, with markets, hotels, restaurants, and ferry service to Giglio and Giannutri, two of the Tuscan islands.

Porto Ercole. On the southeastern side of Monte Argentario, this small port town is the haunt of the rich and famous, with top-notch hotels and restaurants perched on the cliffs.

WHERE TO EAT

$ ╳ **Gambero Rosso.** Right on the waterfront at Porto Ercole, this classic Italian restaurant offers simple preparations of locally caught fresh fish. Try the antipasto *sorpresa del Gambero* (surprise of the house), an ever-changing array of six, sometimes seven, different fish dishes (fried, chilled, or baked, for example). The chef lets his imagination run wild, and it's only to the benefit of the happy diners. It's even better if you enjoy it on the terrace with a view. ✉ *Lungomare Andrea Doria 62, Porto Ercole* ☎ *0564/832650* ⌨ *Reservations essential* ☉ *Closed Wed. and mid-Nov.–mid-Jan.*

ITALIAN

$ ╳ **La Fontanina di San Pietro.** Grapevines climbing up a trellis, cherry trees in the countryside overlooking the port—the scene here is romantic. Dine on scampi with zucchini and spaghetti *allo scoglio* (with fresh clams and mussels in a light tomato sauce), while enjoying a fruity white from the well-matched wine list. The catch of the day can be prepared a number of ways, and is priced by weight; the *pesce spada* (swordfish) is terrific. ✉ *Località San Pietro, Porto Santo Stefano* ☎ *0564/825261* ⊕ *www.lafontanina.com* ☉ *Closed Wed. and Jan.*

ITALIAN

A field of sunflowers in the Maremma

WHERE TO STAY

For expanded hotel reviews, visit Fodors.com.

$$ 🏨 **Hotel Don Pedro.** The private beach more than makes up for the lack of a pool at this hotel in Porto Ercole. **Pros:** panoramic views of port; private beach; family-friendly atmosphere. **Cons:** not all rooms have sea views; uninspired decor. ⊠ *Via Panoramica 7, Porto Ercole* 🕾 *0564/833914* ⊕ *www.hoteldonpedro.it* ⤵ *60 rooms* ⌂ *In-hotel: restaurant, bar, beach, business center* ⊗ *Closed Nov.–Easter* ⓞⓛ *No meals.*

$$$$ 🏨 **Il Pellicano.** Worldly cares are softly washed away by the comforts of the rooms (some damask linens, tapestry-like canopies, marble highboys), the superlative attentiveness of the staff, and the hotel's magnificent garden setting. **Pros:** spectacular setting and gardens; superlative service; excellent dining options. **Cons:** isolated location; on a long dirt road; beach is rocky. ⊠ *Località Lo Sbarcatello, 5 km (3 miles) west of Porto Ercole* 🕾 *0564/858111* ⊕ *www.pellicanohotel.com* ⤵ *40 rooms, 10 suites* ⌂ *In-room: safe, Wi-Fi. In-hotel: restaurant, pool, tennis court, gym, spa, business center, parking, some pets allowed* ⊗ *Closed Nov.–Mar.* ⓞⓛ *Breakfast.*

MASSA MARITTIMA

111 km (69 miles) southeast of Livorno, 48 km (30 miles) east of Piombino, 66 km (42 miles) southwest of Siena, 132 km (82 miles) southwest of Florence.

Massa Marittima is a charming medieval hill town with a rich mining and industrial heritage—pyrite, iron, and copper were found in these parts. After a centuries-long slump (most of the minerals having been depleted), the town is now popular simply for its old streets.

GETTING HERE

From Siena, the easiest way to reach Massa Marittima is to take the SP73bis, then the SP441. Bus service from Siena, provided by Tra-In, is not timed to make day trips feasible. Massa Marittima cannot be reached by train.

VISITOR INFORMATION

Massa Marittima tourism office ⊠ *Via Todini 3/5* ☎ *0566/902756* ⊕ *www. altamaremmaturismo.it.*

EXPLORING

Duomo. The central Piazza Garibaldi, dating from the 13th to the early 14th century, contains this Romanesque cathedral, with sculptures of the life of patron saint Cerbone above the door. ⊠ *Via Giroduomo 6* ☎ *0566/902237* ⊙ *Daily 8–noon and 3–6.*

Museo Archeologico. The 13th-century Palazzo Pretorio, on Piazza Garibaldi, is home to this fascinating museum with plenty of Etruscan artifacts. A number of displays reconstruct the nature of daily life for the Etruscans who once inhabited the hills in this area. ⊠ *Piazza Garibaldi 1* ☎ *0566/902289* ☞ *€3* ⊙ *Apr.–mid-July, Tues.–Sun. 10–12:30 and 3:30–7; mid-July–end Aug., Tues.–Sun. 10–12:30 and 4–8; end Aug.–Oct., Tues.–Sun. 10–12:30 and 3:30–7; Nov.–Mar., Tues.–Sun. 10–12:30 and 3–5.*

Museo di Arte Sacra. In the converted convent church of San Pietro all'Orto, this museum houses a large number of medieval paintings and sculptures gathered from churches in and around Massa Marittima. Perhaps the most important piece, Ambrogio Lorenzetti's early-14th-century *Maestà*, was discovered in the storage room of the church in 1866. ⊠ *Corso Diaz 37* ☎ *0566/901954* ☞ *€5* ⊙ *Apr.–Oct., Tues.–Sun. 10–1 and 3–6; Nov.–Mar., Tues.–Sun. 11–1 and 3–5.*

Museo Arte e Storia della Miniera (*Museum of the Art and History of Mining*). This museum, in the upper part of town, shows how dependent Massa Marittima has been since Etruscan times on the mining of copper, lead, and silver. Exhibits trace the history of the local mining industry. Across the street, you can even visit a real mine. ⊠ *Palazzetto delle Armi, Piazza Matteotti* ☎ *0566/902289* ☞ *Museum €1.50; museum and mine €5* ⊙ *Museum: Apr.–mid-July, Tues.–Sun. 3–5:30; mid-July–Aug., Tues.–Sun. 10:30–1 and 3–5:30; Sept.–Mar. by appointment for groups. Mine visits: Apr.–Oct., Tues.–Sun. at 10, 11, noon, 12:45, 3:30, 4:30, 5, and 5:45; Nov.–Mar. at 10, 11, noon, 12:45, 3, 4, and 4:30.*

Torre del Candeliere (*Tower of the Candlemaker*). Built to both defend and control their new possession after the Sienese conquered Massa Marittima in 1335, the **Fortezza dei Senesi** crowns the upper part of town. Just inside the imposing Sienese gate is the so-called Tower of the Candle Holder, a massive bastion that is connected to the outer walls by the **Arco Senese,** a high arched bridge. A visit to the tower gives access to the arch and to the upper city walls, where commanding views open before you. ⊠ *Piazza Matteotti, Piazza Matteotti* ☎ *0566/902289*

€2.50 ⊘ *Apr.–mid-July, Tues.–Sun. 3–5:30; mid-July–Aug., daily 10:30–1 and 3–5:30; Sept.–Mar., by appointment for groups.*

Antico Frantoio. On a small street, inside the walls of the **Fortezza dei Senesi,** you'll find this ancient olive press. Mules harnessed to the heavy stone wheel pulled it around, and as it rolled, the olives on the flat surface were crushed by its weight, extracting the precious oil—the same technique is used today (minus the mules). At press time, the mill was closed for restoration. ⊠ *Via Populonia 18* ☎ *0566/902289* €1.50 ⊘ *Apr.–mid-July, Tues.–Sun. 10:30–1; mid-July–Aug., Tues.– Sun. 10:30–1 and 3:30-6; Sept.–Oct., Tues.–Sun. 10:30–1; Nov.–Mar. by appointment for groups.*

WHERE TO STAY

For expanded hotel reviews, visit Fodors.com.

$$ 🛏 **Rifugio Prategiano.** Horseback trail rides through Tuscany's cowboy country are an integral part of the experience at this family-run country inn. **Pros:** great for families with children; plenty of outdoor sports activities; peaceful setting. **Cons:** very simple furnishings; no air-conditioning in rooms; need a car to get around. ⊠ *Via dei Platani 3b, Località Prategiano 17 km (11 miles) west of Abbazia San Galgano, Montieri* ☎ *0566/997700* ⊕ *www.prategiano.com* ⤴ *24 rooms* ☐ *In-room: no a/c. In-hotel: restaurant, pool, tennis court, some pets allowed* ⊘ *Closed Nov.–mid-Mar.* ⊮ *Breakfast.*

NIGHTLIFE AND THE ARTS

Balestro del Girifalco (*Falcon Crossbow Contest*). On the fourth Sunday of May, and again on the second Sunday in August, Massa Marittima's three traditional neighborhood groups dress in medieval costumes, parade through the town, and compete in a game to shoot down a toy falcon.

ABBAZIA DI SAN GALGANO

32 km (20 miles) northeast of Massa Marittima, 33 km (20 miles) southwest of Siena, 87 km (54 miles) south of Florence.

GETTING HERE

You'll need a car to get here, as bus and train service is not available. From Siena, follow the SP73bis, then take the SP441 south.

EXPLORING

★ **Abbazia di San Galgano.** Time has had its way with this Gothic cathedral without a rooftop, a hauntingly beautiful sight well worth a detour. The church was built in the 13th century by Cistercian monks, who designed it after churches built by their order in France. But starting in the 15th century it fell into ruin, declining gradually over centuries. Grass has grown through the floor, and the roof and windows are gone. What's left of its facade and walls makes a grandiose and desolate picture. In July and August the scene is enlivened by evening concerts arranged by the Accademia Musicale Chigiana in Siena. Contact the tourist information office at the abbey for details.

Chiesetta di Monte Siepi. Behind the church of San Galgano, a short climb brings you to this charming little chapel with frescoes by painter Ambrogio Lorenzetti (documented 1319–48), and a sword in a stone. Legend has it that Galgano, a medieval warrior and bon vivant, was struck by a revelation on this spot in which an angel told him to give up his fighting and frivolous ways forever. As a token of his conversion, he plunged his sword into the rock, where it still remains today. ⊠ *Above Abbazia di San Galgano* ☎ *No phone* ⊠ *Free* ☉ *Daily 9–sunset* ⊠ *Off SP441* ☎ *0577/756738 for tourist office* ⊕ *www.prolocochiusdino.it* ☎ *€2* ☉ *Apr.–Oct., daily 9–8; Nov.–Mar., daily 9–6.*

ELBA AND THE SURROUNDING ISLANDS

The Tuscan archipelago is a wide semicircle of islands that traces a path, in the crystal-clear sea, between Livorno and Monte Argentario. All of the larger islands in the group can be reached by ferry service from the mainland, whereas the smaller islands, like the charmingly named Formiche di Grosseto (Ants of Grosseto) and the Formica di Montecristo (Ant of Montecristo), can only be reached by private boat. The largest, and most famous, of the islands is Elba, with several large towns and its own airport. Equally popular as a summer destination is Giglio. Other islands, like Capraia, Pianosa, and Montecristo, more closely guard their natural beauty, offering visitors few or no hotels or restaurants. The peak season is in July and August—book your ferry journey well in advance.

GIGLIO

60 km (36 miles) south of Massa Marittima, 90 km (55 miles) south of Siena, 145 km (87 miles) south of Florence.

GETTING HERE

To get to Giglio, take one of the Toremar car ferries that run between Porto Santo Stefano on the Monte Argentario peninsula and Giglio Porto. The trip, which costs €6.30 for passengers and €30 for cars, takes about an hour.

VISITOR INFORMATION

Giglio tourism office ⊠ *Via Provinciale 9, Giglio Porto* ☎ *0564/809400* ⊕ *www.isoladelgiglio.it.*

EXPLORING

Isola del Giglio. This rocky, romantic isle, whose name translates to "Island of the Lily," is an hour by ferry from Porto Santo Stefano— but a world away from the mainland's hustle and bustle. The island's three towns—**Giglio Porto,** the charming harbor where the ferry arrives; **Giglio Castello,** a walled village at Giglio's highest point; and **Giglio Campese,** a modern town on the west side of the island—are connected by one long, meandering road. But to really explore Giglio you need a good pair of hiking boots. A network of rugged trails climbs up the steep hills through clusters of wild rosemary and tiny daffodils, and once you leave town, chances are your only company will be the goats who thrive on Giglio's sunbaked hills.

The island's main attraction, however, is at sea level—a sparkling array of lush coves and tiny beaches, most accessible only on foot or by boat. With the exception of Giglio Campese, where the sandy beach is as popular in summer as any mainland resort, most of the little island's coastline is untouched, leaving plenty of room for peaceful sunning for those willing to go off the beaten path.

WHERE TO STAY

For expanded hotel reviews, visit Fodors.com.

$$ ⛱ **Hotel Arenella.** Sitting above the sea, this isolated hotel has a private rocky beach reachable by a steep 60-foot descent. **Pros:** magnificent views; peaceful location; shuttle service to the port. **Cons:** long walk to nearest restaurants; modern decor geared to a business clientele. ✉ *Via Arenella 5, Giglio Porto* ☎ *0564/809340* ⊕ *www.hotelarenella. com* ⤴ *26 rooms* ⌂ *In-room: Internet. In-hotel: beach, business center* ☾ *Closed Nov.–Easter* ⫮ *Some meals.*

$$$$ ⛱ **Pardini's Hermitage.** This ultraprivate hotel is free from noise except
★ for the lapping of waves on the rocks. **Pros:** pure pampering; spectacular views; homey accommodations. **Cons:** isolation makes the hotel a poor base from which to tour the island; no air-conditioning. ✉ *Località Cala degli Alberi, Giglio Porto* ☎ *0564/809034* ⊕ *www.hermit.it* ⤴ *12 rooms* ⌂ *In-room: no a/c, no TV, Wi-Fi. In-hotel: restaurant, beach, some pets allowed* ☾ *Closed Oct.–Mar.* ⫮ *All meals.*

SPORTS AND THE OUTDOORS

HIKING For day-trippers, the best hike is the 1,350-foot ascent from Giglio Porto to Giglio Castello. It's a 4-km (2½-mile) trek that takes about an hour and affords marvelous views of the island's east coast. Frequent bus service to and from Castello allows the option of walking just one way. The rest of the island's trails are reasonably well marked. Pick up maps at the tourist office in Giglio Porto.

WATER **Boatmen.** Rent motorboats for exploring the island's innumerable coves
SPORTS at this kiosk on the waterfront. Look for signs reading *noleggio barche* (boat rentals) near the ferry dock. ✉ *On port, Via Umberto I, Giglio Porto* ☎ *347/0547755* ⊕ *www.boatmen.it.*

Spiaggia Arenella. You can charter your own snorkeling or beach excursion and let someone else do the driving through Marco Bartoletti and his son Andrea. You'll find them at the Arenella beach. ✉ *Località Arenella, 2½ km (1 mile) north of Giglio Porto* ☎ *336/535054 Marco, 348/7078990 Andrea.*

ELBA

40 km (24 miles) southwest of Massa Marittima, 80 km (48 miles) southwest of Siena, 120 km (72 miles) southwest of Florence.

Elba is the Tuscan archipelago's largest island, but it resembles nearby verdant Corsica more than it does its rocky Italian sisters, thanks to a network of underground springs that keep it lush and green. It's this combination of semitropical vegetation and dramatic mountain

GETTING HERE AND AROUND: THE ISLANDS

Passenger and car ferries link the Tuscan islands with the mainland.

Moby Lines. From Piombino, this company provides one-hour ferry service to Portoferraio on Elba. ⊠ *Piazzale Premuda, Nuova Stazione Marittima, Piombino* ☎ *0565/221212* ⊕ *www.mobylines.it.*

Toremar. This ferry service provides transportation between Piombino and Elba's main ports as well as to the smaller islands: from Livorno to Capraia; from Piombino to Pianosa; and from Porto Santo Stefano to Giglio. ⊠ *Piazzale Premuda 13, Nuova Stazione Marittima, Piombino* ☎ *0565/31100* ⊕ *www.toremar.it.*

Prices can differ drastically, so comparison shop before buying your tickets. Reserve your seat ahead of time in the peak-season months of July and August.

Baby Rent. On Elba there are numerous places to rent bikes, scooters, motorcycles, or cars: here you can choose, all of the above as well as dune buggies and convertibles. ⊠ *Piazza Marinai d'Italia 9, Portoferraio* ☎ *0565/918883.*

Chiappi. Honda and Yamaha scooters as well as campers, cars, and boats can be rented here. ⊠ *Calata Italia 30, Elba, Portoferraio* ☎ *0565/916779.*

scenery—unusual in the Mediterranean—that has made Elba so prized for so long, and the island's uniqueness continues to draw boatloads of visitors throughout the warm months. A car is very useful for getting around the island, but public buses stop at most towns several times a day; the tourist office has timetables.

GETTING HERE

Torremar car ferries make the one-hour trip between Portoferraio and Piombino on the mainland. The cost is €7.10 for passengers, €36 for cars.

VISITOR INFORMATION

For information about the flora and fauna to be found on Elba, as well as throughout the Tuscan archipelago, contact the Parco Nazionale dell'Arcipelago Toscano. The tourism office also has detailed walking and hiking maps.

Elba tourism office ⊠ *Viale Elba 4, Portoferraio* ☎ *0565/914671* ⊕ *www.aptelba.it.*

Parco Nazionale dell'Arcipelago Toscano tourism office. For information about the flora and fauna to be found on Elba, as well as throughout the Tuscan archipelago, contact the park board. ⊠ *Via Guerrazzi Francesco 1, Portoferraio* ☎ *0565/919411* ⊕ *www.islepark.it.*

EXPLORING

Portoferraio. The lively port town, where Victor Hugo (1802–85) spent his boyhood, makes a good base for visiting Elba. Head right when you get off the ferry to get to the centro storico, fortified in the 16th century by the Medici grand duke Cosimo I (1519–74). Most of the pretty, multicolor buildings that line the old harbor date from the 18th and 19th centuries when the boats in the port were full of mineral exports rather than tourists.

Museo Archeologico. Exhibits at this museum reconstruct the island's ancient history through a display of Etruscan and Roman artifacts recovered from shipwrecks. ⊠ *Località Linguella, Calata Buccari, Portoferraio* ☎ *0565/937111* ⊠ *€2* ⊙ *June 15–Sept. 15, daily 9:30–2:30 and 5–midnight; Sept. 16–June 14, Thurs. 10:30–1:30 and 4–8.*

Palazzina dei Mulini. During Napoléon's famous exile on Elba in 1814–15, he built this residence out of two windmills. It still contains furniture from the period and Napoléon's impressive library, with the more than 2,000 volumes that he brought here from France. ⊠ *Piazzale Napoleone 1, Portoferraio* ☎ *0565/915846* ⊠ *€7, €13 with admission to Villa San Martino* ⊙ *Mon. and Wed.–Sat. 9–7, Sun. 9–1.*

Villa San Martino. A couple of miles outside Portoferraio, this splendid villa was Napoléon's summer home during his 10-month exile on Elba. Temporary exhibitions are held in a gallery attached to the main building. The Egyptian Room, decorated with idealized scenes of the Egyptian campaign, may have provided Napoléon the consolation of glories past. The villa's classical facade was added by a Russian prince, Anatolia Demidoff, after he bought the house in 1852. ⊠ *Località San Martino* ☎ *0565/914688* ⊠ *€7, €13 with admission to Palazzina dei Mulini* ⊙ *Tues.–Sat. 9–7 and Sun. 9–1.*

Marina di Campo. On the south side of Elba, this small town with a long sandy beach and protected cove is a classic summer vacationer's spot. The laid-back marina is full of bars, boutiques, and restaurants.

Porto Azzurro. The waters of the port at Elba's eastern end are noticeably *azzurro* (sky-blue). It's worth a stop for a walk and a gelato along the rows of yachts harbored here.

Rio Marina. Elba's quietest town is an old-fashioned port on the northeastern edge of the island. Here you'll find a pebble beach, an old mine, a leafy public park, and ferry service to Piombino.

Monte Capanne. The highest point on Elba, Monte Capanna is crossed by a twisting road that provides magnificent vistas at every turn; the tiny towns of **Poggio** and **Marciana** have enchanting little piazzas full of flowers and trees. You can hike to the top of the mountain, or take an unusual open-basket cable car from just above Poggio.

Montecristo. The most famous prisoner of the island, about 50 km (30 miles) south of Elba, was fictional: Alexandre Dumas's legendary count. Today the island is a well-protected nature preserve with wild Montecristo goats and vipers, peregrine falcons, and rare Corsican seagulls who make their home amid rosemary bushes and stunted pine trees. Scientific-research teams are given priority for permission to land on the island, and an annual quota of 1,000 visitors strictly limits even their number.

Corpo Forestale. Montecristo is monitored by the National Forestry Service. Contact them for access permits to the island. ⊠ *Via Bicocchi 2, Follonica* ☎ *0566/40019* ⊕ *www.corpoforestale.it* .

A cove on Elba

WHERE TO EAT

¢ ✕ **Il Cantuccio.** This small, simple eatery is a standout in the touristy
ITALIAN Marina di Campo. Shady outdoor tables on a backstreet keep diners
★ cool on warm nights. If the long menu seems daunting, focus on the
list of specials, which often includes such local delicacies as spaghetti
alle uova di pesce (with sea-bream caviar). The staff is friendly and well
informed, particularly about wine. ⊠ *Via Largo Garibaldi 6, Marina di
Campo* ☎ *0565/976775* ⊕ *www.ristoranteilcantuccio.eu.*

¢ ✕ **Il Mare.** Homemade pastas and fresh seafood are served here with a
ITALIAN dash of style. The young chef puts a creative spin on the classics, coming
★ up with such delights as homemade vegetable gnocchi with scampi in a
butter-and-saffron sauce. The *semifreddi* (literally, "half cold"; frozen
desserts made with ice cream and eggs) are particularly good. Just a few
steps from Rio Marina's pretty port, this is an easy stop on your way
to or from the ferry. ⊠ *Via del Pozzo 16, Rio Marina* ☎ *0565/962117.*

$ ✕ **La Canocchia.** In the center of Rio Marina sits this breezy restaurant.
ITALIAN Seafood takes center stage: specialties include ravioli *scampi e asparagi o calamari* (stuffed with large shrimp or squid, in light asparagus
sauce) and saffron-perfumed catches of the day. The *frittura di paranza*
(mixed fried fish) is crisp and light, and the *involtini di pesce spada*
(swordfish rolls) melt in your mouth. Book ahead in summer, as it
can get very crowded. ⊠ *Via Palestro 3, Rio Marina* ☎ *0565/962432*
⊕ *www.lacanocchia.com* ⌖ *Reservations essential* ☉ *Closed Mon. and
Nov.–mid-Feb.*

$ ✕ **Trattoria da Lido.** Come here for commendable *gnocchetti di pesce*
ITALIAN (bite-size potato-and-fish dumplings) with a white cream sauce and
fresh *pesce all'elbana* (whitefish baked with vegetables and potatoes).

The bustling, casual trattoria is in the old center of Portoferraio, at the beginning of the road to the old Medici walls. ✉ *Salita del Falcone 2, Portoferraio* ☎ *0565/914650* ⊘ *Closed mid-Dec.–mid-Feb.*

WHERE TO STAY

For expanded hotel reviews, visit Fodors.com.

$$$$ ⊡ **Hermitage.** You have private access to a white sandy beach at this hotel on a private bay. **Pros:** wide range of sports equipment; several good restaurants; on a private beach and bay. **Cons:** half-board is mandatory in high season; can get very crowded. ✉ *Strada della Biodola 1, 8 km (5 miles) west of Portoferraio, Portoferraio* ☎ *0565/9740* ⊕ *www.hotelhermitage.it* ⤳ *114 rooms, 16 suites* ⚲ *In-hotel: restaurant, bar, golf course, pool, tennis court, business center, some pets allowed* ⊘ *Closed Oct.–Mar.*

$ ⊡ **Hotel Riva del Sole.** A short walk from the center of lively Marina di ★ Campo, this bright, pleasant hotel caters to a loyal Italian and German clientele. **Pros:** caters to families with children; the beach is steps away; very close to town center. **Cons:** standard rooms lack balconies and are small; not all rooms have sea views. ✉ *Viale degli Eroi 11, Marina di Campo* ☎ *0565/976316* ⊕ *www.hotel-rivadelsole.com* ⤳ *60 rooms* ⚲ *In-room: safe. In-hotel: restaurant, bar, parking* ⊘ *Closed Nov.–Apr.* ⦿ *Breakfast.*

$$$ ⊡ **Rio sul Mare.** Convenient to Rio Marina's charming town center and gravel beach, this comfortable hotel has pretty sea views. **Pros:** close to town center; very attractive sea views from all rooms. **Cons:** not all rooms have air-conditioning; the nearby beach is rocky. ✉ *Via Palestro 31, Rio Marina* ☎ *0565/924225* ⊕ *www.hotelriomarina.com* ⤳ *35 rooms* ⚲ *In-room: no a/c. In-hotel: restaurant, beach, parking, some pets allowed* ⊘ *Closed Nov.–Mar.* ⦿ *Breakfast.*

SPORTS AND THE OUTDOORS

BEACHES Elba's most celebrated beaches are the sandy stretches at **Biodola, Procchio,** and **Marina di Campo,** but the entire island—and particularly the westernmost section, encircling Monte Capanne—is ringed with beautiful coastline. Indeed, it seems every sleepy town has its own perfect tiny beach. Try **Cavoli** and **Fetovaia** anytime but July and August, when the car-accessible beaches on the island are packed (there are also some accessible only by boat, such as the black-sand beach of **Punta Nera**).

WATER **Subnow.** Contact this group of experienced divers for information on SPORTS diving excursions in the waters of Elba's National Marine Park. ✉ *Via della Foce 89, Località La Foce, Marina di Campo* ☎ *0565/979051* ⊕ *www.subnow.it.*

Spaziomare. If you are hoping to rent a motorboat for a half or full day, this is the place. Sailboats to rent by the week are also available. ⊠ *Via Vittorio Veneto 13, Porto Azzurro* ☎ *0565/95112 or 348/6017862* ⊕ *www.spaziomare.it.*

Il Viottolo. Adventurous types can rent sea kayaks and mountain bikes from this tour operator, or participate in three-day guided excursions on land or by sea. ⊠ *Via Fucini 279, Marina di Campo* ☎ *0565/978005* ⊕ *www.ilviottolo.it.*

CAPRAIA

60 km (35 miles) west of Massa Marittima, 90 km (55 miles) west of Siena, 110 km (66 miles) southwest of Florence.

GETTING HERE
Car ferry service from Livorno is provided by Toremar. The trip takes 2½ hours.

VISITOR INFORMATION
Capraia tourism office ⊠ *Via Assunzione 72* ☎ *0586/905138.*

EXPLORING
Capraia. Only a handful of people actually live on the island of Capraia, which is frequented mainly by sailors. It's a rocky and hilly unspoiled national park, with only one sandy beach, **Cala della Mortola,** on the northern end of the island; the rest of the coast is a succession of cliffs and deep green coves with pretty rock formations. The 2½-hour ferry trip departs from Livorno and pulls in at the town of **Capraia Isola,** dominated by the Fortezza di San Giorgio up above. Nearby, an archway leads to an area that was once a prison.

SPORTS AND THE OUTDOORS
Capraia Diving Service. Capraia's clear waters and undersea life draw raves from scuba divers. Alessandro Pettarin's diving service has scuba-diving equipment and boats for rent. ⊠ *Via Assunzione 100/B, Capraia Isola* ☎ *0586/905137* ⊕ *www.capraiadiving.it.*

6

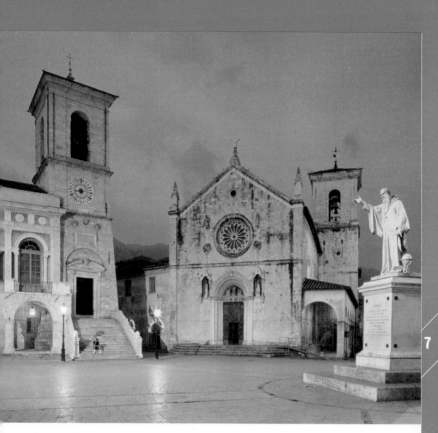

Umbria and the Marches

WORD OF MOUTH

"It was pure bliss to have two weeks in Umbria. The drives were out of this world. . . . We also enjoyed hiking the roads and market trails through olive groves at the end of our 'street.' We could have hiked all the way to Spoleto!"

—uhoh_busted

WELCOME TO UMBRIA AND THE MARCHES

TOP REASONS TO GO

★ **Palazzo Ducale, Urbino:** A visit here reveals more about the ideals of the Renaissance than a shelf of history books.

★ **Assisi, shrine to Saint Francis:** Recharge your soul in this rose-color hill town with a visit to the gentle saint's majestic basilica, adorned with great frescoes.

★ **Spoleto, Umbria's musical Mecca:** Crowds may descend and prices ascend here during summer's Festival dei Due Mondi, but Spoleto's hushed charm enchants year-round.

★ **Tantalizing truffles:** Are Umbria's celebrated "black diamonds" coveted for their pungent flavor, their rarity, or their power in the realm of romance?

★ **Orvieto's Duomo:** Arresting visions of heaven and hell on the facade and brilliant frescoes within make this Gothic cathedral a dazzler.

1 Perugia. Umbria's largest town is easily reached from Rome, Siena, or Florence. Home to some of Perugino's great frescoes and a hilltop *centro storico* (historic center), it's also favored by chocolate lovers, who celebrate their passion at October's Eurochocolate Festival.

2 Assisi. The city of Saint Francis is a major pilgrimage site, crowned by one of Italy's greatest churches. Despite the throngs of visitors, it still maintains its medieval hill-town character.

3 Northern Umbria. The quiet towns lying around Perugia include **Deruta**, which produces exceptional ceramics. A trip through the rugged terrain of northeast Umbria takes you to **Gubbio**, where from the Piazza della Signoria you can admire magnificent views of the countryside below.

4 Spoleto. Though it's known to the world for its annual performing-arts festival, Spoleto offers much more than Puccini in its Piazza del Duomo. There are Filippo Lippi frescoes in the cathedral, a massive castle towering over the town, and a bridge across the neighboring valley that's an engineering marvel.

5 **Southern Umbria.** Of central Italy's many hill towns, none has a more impressive setting than **Orvieto**, perched on a plateau 1,000 feet above the surrounding valley. Its cathedral ranks with Assisi's as the most spectacular in Umbria. Between Spoleto and Orvieto there's a collection of quiet, laid-back towns, including the jewel of the area, **Todi.**

GETTING ORIENTED

Central Italy doesn't begin and end with Tuscany; the pastoral, hilly provinces of Umbria and the Marches pick up where the more famous neighbor leaves off. Divided by the Apennine range, both regions are studded with Renaissance-era villages and fortresses—a landscape hallowed by Saint Francis and immortalized in the works of native son Raphael.

6 **The Marches.** East of Umbria, the steep, twisting roads of this region lead to well-preserved medieval towns before settling down to the sandy beaches of the Adriatic. The main attraction is **Urbino**, the best surviving example of the ideal Renaissance city.

EATING AND DRINKING WELL IN UMBRIA AND THE MARCHES

Central Italy is mountainous, and its food is hearty and straightforward, with a stick-to-the-ribs quality that sees hardworking farmers and artisans through a long day's work and helps them make the steep climb home at night.

In restaurants here, as in much of Italy, you're rewarded for seeking out the local cuisines, and you'll often find better and cheaper food if you're willing to stray a few hundred yards from the main sights. Spoleto is noted for its good food and service, probably a result of high expectations from the international arts crowd. For gourmets, however, it's hard to beat Spello, which has both excellent restaurants and first-rate wine merchants.

A rule of thumb for eating well throughout Umbria is to order what's in season; the trick is to stroll through local markets to see what's for sale. A number of restaurants in the region offer *degustazione* (tasting) menus, which give you a chance to try different local specialties without breaking the bank.

TASTY TRUFFLES

More truffles are found in Umbria than anywhere else in Italy. Spoleto and Norcia are prime territory for the *tartufo nero* (reddish-black interior and fine white veins), pictured below right, prized for its extravagant flavor and intense aroma.

The mild summer truffle, *scorzone estivo* (black outside and beige inside), is in season from May through December. The *scorzone autunnale* (burnt brown color and visible veins inside) is found from October through December. Truffles can be shaved into omelets or over pasta, pounded into sauces, or chopped and mixed with oil.

OLIVE OIL

Nearly everywhere you look in Umbria, olive trees grace the hillsides. The soil of the Apennines allows the olives to ripen slowly, guaranteeing low acidity, a cardinal virtue of fine oil. Look for restaurants that proudly display their own oil, often a sign that they care about their food.

Umbria's finest oil is found in Trevi, where the local product is intensely green and fruity. You can sample it in the town's wine bars, which often do double duty, offering olive-oil tastings.

PORK PRODUCTS

Much of traditional Umbrian cuisine revolves around pork. It can be cooked in wood-fire stoves, sometimes basted with a rich sauce made from innards and red wine. The roasted pork known as *porchetta*, pictured at left, is grilled on a spit and flavored with fennel and herbs, leaving a crisp outer sheen.

The art of pork processing has been handed down through generations in Norcia, so much so that charcuterie producers throughout Italy are often known as *norcini*. Don't miss *prosciutto di Norcia*, which is aged for two years.

LENTILS AND SOUPS

The town of Castelluccio di Norcia is particularly known for its lentils and its *farro* (an ancient grain used by the Romans, similar to wheat), and a variety of beans used in soups. Throughout

Umbria, look for *imbrecciata*, a soup of beans and grains, delicately flavored with local herbs. Other ingredients that find their way into thick Umbrian soups are wild beet, sorrel, mushrooms, spelt, chickpeas, and the elusive, fragrant saffron, grown in nearby Cascia.

WINE

Sagrantino grapes are the star in Umbria's most notable red wines. For centuries they've been used in Sagrantino *passito*, a semisweet wine made by leaving the grapes to dry for a period after picking in order to intensify their sugar content. In recent decades, the *secco* (dry) Sagrantino has occupied the front stage. Both passito and secco have a deep red-ruby color, with a full body and rich flavor.

In the past few years the phenomenon of the *enoteca* (wineshop and wine bar) has taken off, making it easier to arrange wine tastings. Many also let you sample different olive oils on toasted bread, known as *bruschetta*. Some wine information centers, such as La Strada del Sagrantino in the town of Montefalco, will help set up appointments for tastings.

7

Updated
by Jonathan
Willcocks

BIRTHPLACE OF SAINTS AND HOME TO some of the country's greatest artistic treasures, central Italy is a collection of misty green valleys and picture-perfect hill towns laden with centuries of history.

Umbria and the Marches are the Italian countryside as you've imagined it: verdant farmland, steep hillsides topped with medieval fortresses, and winding country roads. No single town here has the extravagant wealth of art and architecture of Florence, Rome, or Venice, but this works in your favor: small jewels of towns feel knowable, not overwhelming. And the cultural cupboard is far from bare. Orvieto's cathedral and Assisi's basilica are two of the most important sights in Italy, while Perugia, Todi, Gubbio, and Spoleto are rich in art and architecture.

East of Umbria, the Marches (Le Marche to Italians) stretch between the Apennines and the Adriatic Sea. It's a region of great turreted castles on high peaks defending passes and roads—a testament to the centuries of battle that have taken place here. Rising majestically in Urbino is a splendid palace, built by Federico da Montefeltro, where the humanistic ideals of the Renaissance came to their fullest flower, while the town of Ascoli Piceno can lay claim to one of the most beautiful squares in Italy. Virtually every small town in the region has a castle, church, or museum worth a visit—but even without them, you'd still be compelled to stop for the interesting streets, panoramic views, and natural beauty.

PLANNING

MAKING THE MOST OF YOUR TIME

Umbria is a nicely compact collection of character-rich hill towns; you can settle in one, then explore the others, as well as the countryside and forest in between, on day trips.

Perugia, Umbria's largest and most lively city, is a logical choice for your base, particularly if you're arriving from the north. If you want something a little quieter, virtually any other town in the region will suit your purposes; even Assisi, which overflows with bus tours during the day, is delightfully quiet in the evening and early morning. Spoleto and Orvieto are the most developed towns to the south, but they're still of modest proportions.

If you have the time to venture farther afield, consider trips to Gubbio, northeast of Perugia, and Urbino, in the Marches. Both are worth the time it takes to reach them, and both make for pleasant overnight stays. In southern Umbria, Valnerina and the Piano Grande are out-of-the-way spots with the region's best hiking.

FESTIVALS

Festival dei Due Mondi. Each summer Umbria hosts one of Italy's biggest arts festivals: Spoleto's Festival dei Due Mondi, the Festival of the Two Worlds. Starting out as a classical music festival, it has now evolved into one of Italy's brightest gatherings of arts aficionados. Running from late June through early July, it features modern and classical music, theater, dance, and opera. In recent years there have also been a number of small cinema producers and their films. ⊕ *www.festivaldispoleto.com.*

Umbria Jazz Festival. Perugia is hopping for 10 days in July, when famous names in contemporary music perform at the Umbria Jazz Festival ⊕ *www.umbriajazz.com.*

If you want to attend either event, you should make arrangements in advance. And if you don't want to attend, you should plan to avoid the cities during festival time, when hotel rooms and restaurant tables are at a premium. A similar caveat applies for Assisi during religious festivals at Christmas, Easter, the feast of Saint Francis (October 4), and Calendimaggio (May 1), when pilgrims arrive en masse.

Eurochocolate Festival. If you've got a sweet tooth and you're visiting in fall, head to Perugia for the Eurochocolate Festival in the third week of October. ⊕ *www.eurochocolate.perugia.it.*

GETTING HERE AND AROUND
BUS TRAVEL
Perugia's bus station is in Piazza Partigiani, which you can reach by taking the escalators from the town center.

Sulga Line. Perugia is served by the Sulga Line, which has daily departures to Rome's Stazione Tiburtina and to Florence's Piazza Adua. ☎ *075/5009641* ⊕ *www.sulga.it.*

Bucci. Connections between Rome, Spoleto, and the Marches are provided by the bus company Bucci. ☎ *800/664332* ⊕ *www.adriabus.eu.*

Local bus services between all the major and minor towns of Umbria are good. Some of the routes in rural areas are designed to serve as many places as possible and are, therefore, quite roundabout and slow. Schedules change often, so consult with local tourist offices before setting out.

CAR TRAVEL
On the western edge of the region is the Umbrian section of the Autostrada del Sole (A1), Italy's principal north–south highway. It links Florence and Rome with Orvieto and passes near Todi and Terni. The S3 intersects with A1 and leads on to Assisi and Urbino. The Adriatica superhighway (A14) runs north–south along the coast, linking the Marches to Bologna and Venice.

The steep hills and deep valleys that make Umbria and the Marches so idyllic also make for challenging driving. Fortunately, the area has an excellent, modern road network, but be prepared for tortuous mountain roads if your explorations take you off the beaten track. Central Umbria is served by a major highway, the S75bis, which passes along the shore of Lake Trasimeno and ends in Perugia. Assisi is served by the modern highway S75; the S75 connects to the S3 and S3bis, which cover the heart of the region. Major inland routes connect coastal A14 to large towns in the Marches, but inland secondary roads in mountain areas can be winding and narrow. Always carry a good map, a flashlight, and, if possible, a cell phone in case of a breakdown.

TRAIN TRAVEL
Several direct daily trains run by the Italian state railway, **Ferrovia dello Stato** (☎ *892021 toll-free in Italy* ⊕ *www.trenitalia.com*), link Florence and Rome with Perugia and Assisi, and local service to the same area is available from Terontola (on the Rome–Florence line) and from Foligno

(on the Rome–Ancona line). Intercity trains between Rome and Florence make stops in Orvieto, and the main Rome–Ancona line passes through Narni, Terni, Spoleto, and Foligno.

Within Umbria, a small, privately owned railway operated by **Ferrovia Centrale Umbra** (☎ *024/73000541*) runs from Città di Castello in the north to Terni in the south via Perugia. Note: train service isn't available to either Gubbio or Urbino.

HOTELS

Virtually every older town, no matter how small, has some kind of hotel. A trend, particularly around Gubbio, Orvieto, and Todi, is to convert old villas, farms, and monasteries into first-class hotels. The natural splendor of the countryside more than compensates for the distance from town—provided you have a car. Hotels in town tend to be simpler than their country cousins, with a few notable exceptions in Spoleto, Gubbio, and Perugia.

Hotel reviews have been condensed for this book. Please go to Fodors. com for expanded reviews of each property.

WHAT IT COSTS (IN EUROS)					
	¢	$	$$	$$$	$$$$
Restaurants	under €20	€20–€30	€30–€45	€45–€65	over €65
Hotels	under €75	€75–€125	€125–€200	€200–€300	over €300

Restaurant prices are for a first course (*primo*), second course (*secondo*), and dessert (*dolce*). Hotel prices are for two people in a standard double room in high season, including tax and service.

VISITOR INFORMATION

Umbria's regional tourism office. Umbria's regional tourism office is in Perugia. The staff is well informed about the area and can give you a wide selection of leaflets and maps to assist you during your trip. It's open Monday to Saturday 9 to 6:30. ⊠ *Piazza Matteotti 18, Perugia* ☎ *075/5736458* ⊕ *www.regioneumbria.eu.*

PERUGIA

Perugia is a majestic, handsome, wealthy city, and with its trendy boutiques, refined cafés, and grandiose architecture, it doesn't try to hide its affluence. A student population of more than 30,000 means that the city is abuzz with activity throughout the year. Umbria Jazz, one of the region's most important music festivals, attracts music lovers from around the world every July, and Eurochocolate, the international chocolate festival, is an irresistible draw for anyone with a sweet tooth each October.

GETTING HERE

The best approach to the city is by train. The area around the station doesn't attest to the rest of Perugia's elegance, but buses running from the station to Piazza d'Italia, the heart of the old town, are frequent. If you're in a hurry, take the minimetro, a one-line subway, to Stazione

KEY

P Parking

Escalator

Perugia

7

della Cupa. If you're driving to Perugia and your hotel doesn't have parking facilities, leave your car in one of the lots close to the center. Electronic displays indicate the location of lots and the number of spaces free. If you park in the Piazza Partigiani, take the escalators that pass through the fascinating subterranean excavations of the Roman foundations of the city and lead to the town center.

EXPLORING PERUGIA

Thanks to Perugia's hilltop position, the medieval city remains almost completely intact. It's the best-preserved hill town of its size, and few other places in Italy better illustrate the model of the self-contained city-state that so shaped the course of Italian history.

TOP ATTRACTIONS

★ **Collegio del Cambio** (*Bankers' Guild Hall*). These elaborate rooms, on the ground floor of the **Palazzo dei Priori,** served as the meeting hall and chapel of the guild of bankers and money-changers. Most of the frescoes were completed by the most important Perugian painter of the Renaissance, Pietro Vannucci, better known as Perugino. He included a remarkably honest self-portrait on one of the pilasters. The iconography includes common religious themes, such as the Nativity and the Transfiguration seen on the end walls. On the left wall are female figures representing the virtues, beneath them the heroes and sages of antiquity. On the right wall are figures presumed to have been painted in part by Perugino's most famous pupil, Raphael. (His hand, experts say, is most apparent in the figure of Fortitude.) The *cappella* (chapel) of San Giovanni Battista has frescoes painted by Giannicola di Paolo, another student of Perugino's. ⊠ *Corso Vannucci 25* ☎ *075/5728599* 🖭 *€4.50, €5.50 with Collegio della Mercanzia* ☉ *Mon.–Sat. 9–1 and 2:30–5:30, Sun. 9–1.*

Corso Vannucci. A string of elegantly connected *palazzi* (palaces) expresses the artistic nature of this city center, the heart of which is concentrated along Corso Vannucci. Stately and broad, this pedestrians-only street runs from Piazza d'Italia to Piazza IV Novembre. Along the way, the entrances to many of Perugia's side streets might tempt you to wander off and explore. But don't stray too far as evening falls, when Corso Vannucci fills with Perugians out for their evening *passeggiata*, a pleasant predinner stroll that may include a pause for an aperitif at one of the many bars that line the street.

Fodor'sChoice ★ **Galleria Nazionale dell'Umbria.** The region's most comprehensive art gallery is housed on the fourth floor of the **Palazzo dei Priori.** Enhanced by skillfully lighted displays and computers that allow you to focus on the works' details and background information, the collection includes work by native artists—most notably Pintoricchio (1454–1513) and Perugino (circa 1450–1523)—and others of the Umbrian and Tuscan schools, among them Gentile da Fabriano (1370–1427), Duccio (circa 1255–1318), Fra Angelico (1387–1455), Fiorenzo di Lorenzo (1445–1525), and Piero della Francesca (1420–92). In addition to paintings, the gallery has frescoes, sculptures, and some superb examples of crucifixes from the 13th and 14th centuries. Some rooms are dedicated to Perugia itself, showing how the medieval city evolved. ⊠ *Corso Vannucci 19, Piazza IV Novembre* ☎ *075/5721009* ⊕ *www.gallerianazionaleumbria. it* 🖭 *€6.50* ☉ *Tues.–Sun. 8:30–7:30; last admission ½ hr before closing.*

★ **Palazzo dei Priori** (*Palace of Priors*). A series of elegant connected buildings, the palazzo serves as Perugia's city hall and houses three of the city's museums. The buildings string along Corso Vannucci and wrap around the Piazza IV Novembre, where the original entrance is located. The steps here lead to the **Sala dei Notari** (Notaries' Hall). Other entrances lead to the **Galleria Nazionale dell'Umbria**, the **Collegio del Cambio**, and the **Collegio della Mercanzia**. The Sala dei Notari, which dates back to the 13th century and was the original meeting place of the town merchants, had become the seat of the notaries by the second half of the 15th century. Wood beams and an interesting array of frescoes attributed to Maestro di Farneto embellish the room. Coats of arms and crests line the back and right lateral walls; you can spot some famous figures from Aesop's *Fables* on the left wall. The palazzo facade is adorned with symbols of Perugia's pride and past power: the griffin is the city symbol, and the lion denotes Perugia's allegiance to the Guelph (or papal) cause. ⊠ *Piazza IV Novembre, 25* 🖭 *Free* ☉ *June– Sept., Tues.–Sun. 9–1 and 3–7.*

UMBRIA THROUGH THE AGES

The earliest inhabitants of Umbria, the Umbri, were thought by the Romans to be the most ancient inhabitants of Italy. Little is known about them; with the coming of Etruscan culture the tribe fled into the mountains in the eastern portion of the region. The Etruscans, who founded some of the great cities of Umbria, were in turn supplanted by the Romans. Unlike Tuscany and other regions of central Italy, Umbria had few powerful medieval families to exert control over the cities in the Middle Ages—its proximity to Rome ensured that it would always be more or less under papal domination.

In the center of the country, Umbria has for much of its history been a battlefield where armies from north and south clashed. Hannibal destroyed a Roman army on the shores of Lake Trasimeno, and the bloody course of the interminable Guelph–Ghibelline conflict of the Middle Ages was played out here. Dante considered Umbria the most violent place in Italy. Trophies of war still decorate the Palazzo dei Priori in Perugia, and the little town of Gubbio continues a warlike rivalry begun in the Middle Ages—every year it challenges the Tuscan town of Sansepolcro to a crossbow tournament. Today the bowmen shoot at targets, but neither side has forgotten that 500 years ago they were shooting at each other. In spite of—or perhaps because of—this bloodshed, Umbria has produced more than its share of Christian saints. The most famous is Saint Francis, the decidedly pacifist saint whose life shaped the Church of his time. His great shrine at Assisi is visited by hundreds of thousands of pilgrims each year. Saint Clare, his devoted follower, was Umbria-born, as were Saint Benedict, Saint Rita of Cascia, and the patron saint of lovers, Saint Valentine.

Rocca Paolina. A labyrinth of little streets, alleys, and arches, this underground city was originally part of a fortress. It was built at the behest of Pope Paul III between 1540 and 1543 to confirm papal dominion over the city. Parts of it were destroyed after the end of papal rule, but much still remains. Begin your visit by taking the escalators from Piazza Italia and Via Masi. In summer this is the coolest place in the city. ⊠ *Piazza Italia* 🎟 *€3.50* ⏲ *Tues.–Sun. 10–1 and 4–7:30.*

WORTH NOTING
Duomo. Severe yet mystical, the Duomo, also called the Cathedral of San Lorenzo, is most famous for being the home of the wedding ring of the Virgin Mary, stolen by the Perugians in 1488 from the nearby town of Chiusi. The ring, kept high up in a red-curtained vault in the chapel immediately to the left of the entrance, is kept under lock—15 locks, to be precise—and key most of the year. It's shown to the public on July 30 (the day it was brought to Perugia) and the second-to-last Sunday in January (Mary's wedding anniversary). The cathedral itself dates from the Middle Ages, and has many additions from the 15th and 16th centuries. The most visually interesting element is the altar to the Madonna of Grace; an elegant fresco on a column at the right of the entrance of the altar depicts *La Madonna delle Grazie* and is

surrounded by prayer benches decorated with handwritten notes to the Holy Mother. Around the column are small amulets—symbols of gratitude from those whose prayers were answered. There are also elaborately carved choir stalls, executed by Giovanni Battista Bastone in 1520. The altarpiece (1484), an early masterpiece by Luca Signorelli (circa 1441–1523), shows the Madonna with Saint John the Baptist, Saint Onophrius, and Saint Lawrence. Sections of the church may be closed to visitors during

religious services. The **Museo Capitolare** displays a large array of precious objects associated with the cathedral, including vestments, vessels, and manuscripts. Outside the Duomo is the elaborate **Fontana Maggiore,** which dates from 1278. It's adorned with zodiac figures and symbols of the seven arts. ⊠ *Piazza IV Novembre* ☎ *075/5724853* 🖼 *Museum €3.50* ☉ *Duomo: Mon.–Sat. 7–12:30 and 4–6:30, Sun. 8–12:30 and 4–6:30. Museum: daily 10–1 and 2:30–5:30; last admission ½ hr before closing.*

Museo Archeologico Nazionale. The museum, next to the imposing church of San Domenico, contains an excellent collection of Etruscan artifacts from throughout the region. Perugia was a flourishing Etruscan city long before it fell under Roman domination in 310 BC. Little else remains of Perugia's mysterious ancestors, although the Arco di Augusto, in Piazza Fortebraccio, the northern entrance to the city, is of Etruscan origin. ⊠ *Piazza G. Bruno 10* ☎ *075/5727141* ⊕ *www.archeopg.arti. beniculturali.it* 🖼 *€4* ☉ *Mon. 2:30–7:30, Tues.–Sun. 8:30–7:30.*

WHERE TO EAT

¢   ✕ **Antica Trattoria San Lorenzo.** Brick vaults are not the only distinguishing
UMBRIAN   feature of this small restaurant next to the Duomo, as both the food and the service are outstanding. Particular attention is paid to adapting traditional Umbrian cuisine to the modern palate. There's also a nice variety of seafood dishes on the menu. The *trenette alla farina di noce con pesce di mare* (flat noodles made with walnut flour topped with fresh fish) is a real treat. ⊠ *Piazza Danti 19-A* ☎ *075/5721956* ⊕ *www. anticatrattoriasanlorenzo.com* ☉ *Closed Sun.*

¢   ✕ **Dal Mi' Cocco.** A great favorite with Perugia's university students, this
UMBRIAN   place is fun, crowded, and inexpensive. You may find yourself seated
★   at a long table with other diners, but some language help from your neighbors could come in handy—the menu is in pure Perugian dialect. The fixed-price meals change with the season, and each day of the week brings some new creation *dal cocco* (from the "coconut," or head) of the chef. ⊠ *Corso Garibaldi 12* ☎ *075/5732511* 🍴 *Reservations essential* ▭ *No credit cards* ☉ *Closed late July–mid-Aug.*

¢ ✕**Il Falchetto.** Exceptional food at reasonable prices makes this Peru-
UMBRIAN gia's best bargain. Service is smart but relaxed in the two medieval
dining rooms that put the chef on view. The house specialty is *falchetti*
(homemade gnocchi with spinach and ricotta cheese). ⊠ *Via Bartolo 20*
☏ *075/5731775* ☉ *Closed Mon. and last 2 wks in Jan.*

¢ ✕**La Rosetta.** The restaurant, in the hotel of the same name, is a peace-
ITALIAN ful, elegant spot. In winter you dine inside under medieval vaults; in
summer, in the cool courtyard. The food is simple but reliable, and
flawlessly served. The restaurant caters to travelers seeking to get away
from the bustle of central Perugia. The delightful courtyard is 10 meters
off the Corso Vannucci. ⊠ *Piazza d'Italia 19* ☏ *075/5720841* ⌕ *Reservations essential.*

¢ ✕**La Taverna.** Medieval steps lead to a rustic two-story restaurant where
UMBRIAN wine bottles and artful clutter decorate the walls. Good choices from
the regional menu include *caramelle al gorgonzola* (pasta rolls filled
with red cabbage and mozzarella and topped with a Gorgonzola sauce)
and grilled meat dishes, such as the *medaglioni di vitello al tartuffo*
(grilled veal with truffles). ⊠ *Via delle Streghe 8, off Corso Vannucci*
☏ *075/5724128* ☉ *Closed Mon.*

WHERE TO STAY

For expanded hotel reviews, visit Fodors.com.

$ 🛏**Borgo Laurice.** The friendly and laid-back owners will pamper you at
this small *agriturismo* (farm stay) in the valley near Torgiano. **Pros:** laid-
back country atmosphere; good views from balconies. **Cons:** slightly
difficult to find; outside Perugia. ⊠ *Via del'Aratro 59, San Martino in
Campo* ☏ *075/6099222* ⊕ *www.borgolaurice.it* ⇥ *2 apartments* ⌕ *In-
room: no a/c, kitchen. In-hotel: pool, parking.*

$$ 🛏**Castello dell'Oscano.** A splendid neo-Gothic castle, a late-19th-century
villa, and a converted farmhouse hidden in the tranquil hills north of
Perugia offer a wide range of accommodations. **Pros:** quiet elegance;
fine gardens; Umbrian wine list. **Cons:** distant from Perugia; not easy
to find. ⊠ *Strada della Forcella 32, Cenerente* ☏ *075/584371* ⊕ *www.
oscano.it* ⇥ *24 rooms, 8 suites, 13 apartments* ⌕ *In-room: no a/c, Inter-
net. In-hotel: restaurant, bar, pool, gym* ⎟○⎟ *Breakfast.*

$$ 🛏**Hotel Fortuna.** The elegant decor in the large rooms of this friendly
hotel complements the frescoes, which date from the 1700s. **Pros:**
central but quiet; cozy atmosphere. **Cons:** some small rooms; no restaurant. ⊠ *Via Bonazzi 19, Corso Vannucci* ☏ *075/5722845* ⊕ *www.
hotelfortunaperugia.com* ⇥ *51 rooms* ⌕ *In-room: a/c. In-hotel: restaurant, bar, parking* ⎟○⎟ *Breakfast.*

$ 🛏**Locanda della Posta.** In the city's old district, this lodging is in an
18th-century palazzo. **Pros:** some fine views; central position. **Cons:**
uninspiring lobby; some small rooms; no restaurant. ⊠ *Corso Vannucci
97* ☏ *075/5728925* ⇥ *38 rooms, 1 suite* ⌕ *In-room: a/c. In-hotel: bar,
parking* ⎟○⎟ *Breakfast.*

$$ 🛏**Posta dei Donini.** In the center of a small village between Perugia and
Torgiano, this hotel is known for privacy and exclusivity. **Pros:** plush
atmosphere; extensive gardens. **Cons:** outside Perugia; uninteresting

7

village. ⊠ *Via Deruta 43, San Martino in Campo* ☎ *075/609132* ⊕ *www.postadonini.it* ↪ *33 rooms* ⚘ *In-room: a/c, Wi-Fi. In-hotel: restaurant, bar, pool, parking.*

$$ ⊡ **Tre Vaselle.** Four stone buildings, linked underground, make up this hotel in the center of Torgiano. **Pros:** perfect for visiting Torgiano wine area and Deruta; friendly staff. **Cons:** somewhat far from Perugia; uninspiring village. ⊠ *Via Garibaldi 48, Torgiano* ☎ *075/9880447* ⊕ *www.3vaselle.it* ↪ *47 rooms* ⚘ *In-room: a/c, Wi-Fi. In-hotel: restaurant, pool, gym, spa.*

NIGHTLIFE AND THE ARTS

With its large student population, the city has plenty to offer in the way of bars and clubs. The best ones are around the city center, off Corso Vanucci. *Viva Perugia* is a good source of information about nightlife. The monthly, sold at newsstands, has a section in English.

MUSIC FESTIVALS
Summer sees two music festivals in Perugia.

Umbria Jazz. This hugely popular festival is held for 10 days in July; tickets are available starting at the end of April. ☎ *075/5732432* ⊕ *www.umbriajazz.com.*

Sagra Musicale Umbra. Held from mid-August to mid-September, the Sagra Musicale Umbra celebrates sacred music. ☎ *075/5721374* ⊕ *www.perugiamusicaclassica.com.*

SHOPPING

Take a stroll down any of Perugia's main streets, including Corso Vannucci, Via dei Priori, Via Oberdan, and Via Sant'Ercolano, and you'll see many well-known designer boutiques and specialty shops.

The most typical thing to buy in Perugia is some Perugina chocolate, which you can find almost anywhere. The best-known chocolates made by Perugina are the chocolate-and-hazelnut-filled nibbles called Baci (literally, "kisses"). They're wrapped in silver paper that includes a sliver of paper, like the fortune in a fortune cookie, with multilingual romantic sentiments or sayings.

ASSISI

The small town of Assisi is one of the Christian world's most important pilgrimage sites and home of the Basilica di San Francesco—built to honor Saint Francis (1182–1226) and erected in swift order after his death. The peace and serenity of the town is a welcome respite after the hustle and bustle of some of Italy's major cities.

Like most other towns in the region, Assisi began as an Umbri settlement in the 7th century BC and was conquered by the Romans 400 years later. The town was Christianized by Saint Rufino, its patron saint, in the 3rd century, but it's the spirit of Saint Francis, a patron saint of Italy and founder of the Franciscan monastic order, that's felt throughout its narrow medieval streets. The famous 13th-century basilica was decorated by the greatest artists of the period.

GETTING HERE

Assisi lies on the Terontola–Foligno rail line, with almost hourly connections to Perugia and direct trains to Rome and Florence several times a day. The Stazione Centrale is 4 km (2½ miles) from town, with a bus service about every half hour. Assisi is easily reached from the A1 Motorway (Rome–Florence) and the S75b highway. The walled town is closed to traffic, so cars must be left in the parking lots at Porta San Pietro, near Porta Nuova, or beneath Piazza Matteotti. Pay your parking fee at the *cassa* (ticket booth) before you return to your car to get a ticket to insert in the machine that will allow you to exit. It's a short but sometimes steep walk into the center of town; frequent minibuses (buy tickets from a newsstand or tobacco shop near where you park your car) make the rounds for weary pilgrims.

VISITOR INFORMATION

Assisi tourism office ✉ *Piazza del Commune 22* ☎ *075/8138680* ⊕ *www.regioneumbria.eu.*

EXPLORING ASSISI

Assisi is pristinely medieval in architecture and appearance, owing in large part to relative neglect from the 16th century until 1926, when the celebration of the 700th anniversary of Saint Francis's death brought more than 2 million visitors. Since then, pilgrims have flocked here in droves, and today several million arrive each year to pay homage. But not even the constant flood of visitors to this town of just 3,000 residents can spoil the singular beauty of this significant religious center, the home of some of the Western tradition's most important works of art. The hill on which Assisi sits rises dramatically from the flat plain, and the town is dominated by a medieval castle at the very top.

Even though Assisi is sometimes besieged by busloads of sightseers who clamor to visit the famous basilica, it's difficult not to be charmed by the tranquillity of the town and its medieval architecture. Once you've seen the basilica, stroll through the town's narrow winding streets to see beautiful vistas of the nearby hills and valleys peeking through openings between the buildings.

TOP ATTRACTIONS

Basilica di Santa Chiara. The lovely, wide piazza in front of this church is reason enough to visit. The red-and-white-striped facade of the church frames the piazza's panoramic view over the Umbrian plains. Santa Chiara is dedicated to Saint Clare, one of the earliest and most fervent of Saint Francis's followers and the founder of the order of the Poor Ladies—or Poor Clares—which was based on the Franciscan monastic order. The church contains Clare's body, and in the **Cappella del Crocifisso** (on the right) is the cross that spoke to Saint Francis. A heavily veiled nun of the Poor Clares order is usually stationed before the cross in adoration of the image. ✉ *Piazza Santa Chiara* ☎ *075/812282*

Assisi

**Basilica di
San Francesco**
see feature in
this chapter

**Rocca
Maggiore**

**Anfiteatro
Romano**

TO
EREMO DELLE
CARCERI

**Porto
Nuova**

TO
SAN DAMIANO →

TO SANTA MARIA
DEGLI ANGELI

TO TRAIN STATION

Basilica di
Santa Chiara **3**

Cattedrale di
San Rufino **2**

Santa Maria
Sopra Minerva **1**

KEY

||||| Steps

0   200 yards

0   200 meters

⊙ *Nov.–mid-Mar., daily 6:30–noon and 2–6; mid-Mar.–Oct., daily 6:30–noon and 2–7.*

Cattedrale di San Rufino. Saint Francis and Saint Clare were among those baptized in Assisi's Cattedrale, which was the principal church in town until the 12th century. The baptismal font has since been redecorated, but it's possible to see the crypt of Saint Rufino, the bishop who brought Christianity to

Assisi and was martyred on August 11, 238 (or 236 by some accounts). Admission to the crypt includes the small **Museo Capitolare,** with its detached frescoes and artifacts. ⊠ *Piazza San Rufino* 🕾 *075/5812283* ⊕ *www.sistemamuseo.it* 🖾 *Crypt and Museo Capitolare €2.50* ⊙ *Cathedral: daily 7–noon and 2–6. Crypt and Museum: mid-Mar.–mid-Oct., daily 10–1 and 3–6; mid-Oct.–mid-Mar., daily 10–1 and 2:30–6.*

WORTH NOTING

Santa Maria Sopra Minerva. Dating from the time of the Emperor Augustus (27 BC–AD 14), this structure was originally dedicated to the Roman goddess of wisdom, in later times used as a monastery and prison before being converted into a church in the 16th century. The expectations raised by the perfect classical facade are not met by the interior, which was subjected to a thorough baroque transformation in the 17th century. ⊠ *Piazza del Comune* 🕾 *075/812268* ⊙ *Daily 7:15 am–8 pm.*

OFF THE BEATEN PATH

Eremo delle Carceri. About 4 km (2½ miles) east of Assisi is a monastery set in a dense wood against Monte Subasio. The "Hermitage of Prisons" was the place where Saint Francis and his followers went to "imprison" themselves in prayer. The only site in Assisi that remains essentially unchanged since Saint Francis's time, the church and monastery are the kinds of tranquil places that Saint Francis would have appreciated. The walk out from town is very pleasant, and many trails lead from here across the wooded hillside of Monte Subasio (now a protected forest), with beautiful vistas across the Umbrian countryside. True to their Franciscan heritage, the friars here are entirely dependent on alms from visitors. ⊠ *Via Santuario delle Carceri 4 km (2½ miles) east of Assisi* 🕾 *075/812301* ⊕ *www.eremocarceri.it* 🖾 *Donations accepted* ⊙ *Nov.–Mar., daily 6:30–6; Apr.–Oct., daily 6:30 am–7 pm.*

WHERE TO EAT

Assisi isn't a late-night town, so don't plan on any midnight snacks. What you can count on is the ubiquitous *stringozzi* (thick spaghetti), as well as the local specialty *piccione all'assisana* (roasted pigeon with olives and liver). The locals eat *torta al testo* (a dense flatbread, often stuffed with vegetables or cheese) with their meals.

¢ ✕ **Buca di San Francesco.** In summer, dine in a cool green garden; in
UMBRIAN winter, under the low brick arches of the restaurant's cozy cellars. The
unique settings and the first-rate fare make this central restaurant Assisi's busiest. Try homemade spaghetti *alla buca,* served with a roasted
mushroom sauce. ⊠ *Via Eugenio Brizi 1* ☎ *075/812204* ⊘ *Closed Mon.
and 10 days late July.*

¢ ✕ **La Pallotta.** At this homey, family-run trattoria with a crackling fire-
UMBRIAN place and stone walls, the women do the cooking and the men serve
Fodor's Choice the food. Try the *stringozzi alla pallotta* (thick spaghetti with a pesto
★ of olives and mushrooms). Connected to the restaurant is an inn whose
eight rooms have firm beds and some views across the rooftops of town.
Hotel guests get a discount if they dine here. ⊠ *Vicolo della Volta Pinta
3* ☎ *075/812649* ⊘ *Closed Tues. and 2 wks in Jan. or Feb.*

¢ ✕ **Osteria Piazzetta dell'Erba.** Hip service and sophisticated presentations
UMBRIAN attract locals to this trattoria. The owners carefully select wine at local
★ vineyards, buy it in bulk, and then bottle it themselves, resulting in
high quality and reasonable prices. Choose from the wide selection
of appetizers, including smoked goose breast, and from four or five
types of pasta, plus various salads and a good selection of *torta al testo*
(dense flatbread stuffed with vegetables or cheese). For dessert, try the
homemade biscuits, which you dunk in sweet wine. Outdoor seating
is available. ⊠ *Via San Gabriele dell'Addolorata 15b* ☎ *075/815352*
⊘ *Closed Mon. and a few wks in Jan. or Feb.*

$ ✕ **San Francesco.** An excellent view of the Basilica di San Francesco is the
UMBRIAN primary reason to come here. Locals consider this the best restaurant in
town, where creative Umbrian dishes are made with aromatic locally
grown herbs. The seasonal menu might include gnocchi topped with a
sauce of wild herbs and *oca stufata di finocchio selvaggio* (goose stuffed
with wild fennel). Appetizers and desserts are especially good. ⊠ *Via
di San Francesco 52* ☎ *075/812329* ⊘ *Closed Wed. and July 15–30.*

WHERE TO STAY

Advance reservations are essential at Assisi's hotels between Easter and
October and over Christmas. Latecomers are often forced to stay in
the modern town of Santa Maria degli Angeli, 8 km (5 miles) away.
As a last-minute option, you can always inquire at restaurants to see if
they're renting out rooms.

Until the early 1980s, pilgrim hostels outnumbered ordinary hotels in
Assisi, and they present an intriguing and economical alternative to
conventional lodgings. They're usually called *conventi* or *ostelli* ("convents" or "hostels") because they're run by convents, churches, or other
Catholic organizations. Rooms are spartan but peaceful. Check with
the tourist office for a list.

For expanded hotel reviews, visit Fodors.com.

$$ 🏨 **Castello di Petrata.** Built as a fortress in the 14th century, the Castello
Fodor's Choice di Petrata rightfully dominates the area, with Monte Subasio, Assisi,
★ and the distant hills and valleys of Perugia all in view. **Pros:** great views
of Assisi hills, gardens, and walks. **Cons:** slightly isolated; far from
Assisi town center. ⊠ *Via Petrata 25, Località Petrata* ☎ *075/815451*

Continued on page 349

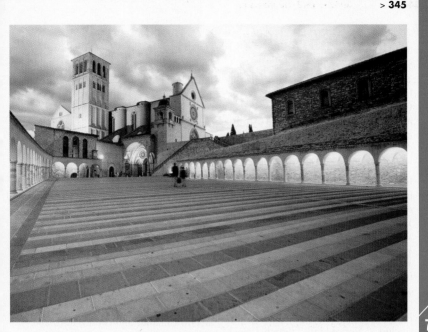

ASSISI'S BASILICA DI SAN FRANCESCO

The legacy of St. Francis, founder of the Franciscan monastic order, pervades Assisi. Each year the town hosts several million pilgrims, but the steady flow of visitors does nothing to diminish the singular beauty of one of Italy's most important religious centers. The pilgrims' ultimate destination is the massive Basilica di San Francesco, which sits halfway up Assisi's hill, supported by graceful arches.

The basilica is not one church but two. The Romanesque **Lower Church** came first; construction began in 1228, just two years after St. Francis's death, and was completed within a few years. The low ceilings and candlelit interior make an appropriately solemn setting for St. Francis's tomb, found in the crypt below the main altar. The Gothic **Upper Church**, built only half a century later, sits on top of the lower one, and is strikingly different, with soaring arches and tall stained-glass windows (the first in Italy). Inside, both churches are covered floor to ceiling with some of Europe's finest frescoes: the Lower Church is dim and full of candlelit shadows, and the Upper Church is bright and airy.

VISITING THE BASILICA

THE LOWER CHURCH

The most evocative way to experience the basilica is to begin with the dark Lower Church. As you enter, give your eyes a moment to adjust. Keep in mind that the artists at work here were conscious of the shadowy environment—they knew this was how their frescoes would be seen.

In the first chapel to the left, a superb fresco cycle by Simone Martini depicts scenes from the life of St. Martin. As you approach the main altar, the vaulting above you is decorated with the *Three Virtues of St. Francis* (poverty, chastity, and obedience) and *St. Francis's Triumph*, frescoes attributed to Giotto's followers. In the transept to your left, Pietro Lorenzetti's *Madonna and Child with St. Francis and St. John* sparkles when the sun hits it. Notice Mary's thumb; legend has it Jesus is asking which saint to bless, and Mary is pointing to Francis. Across the way in the right transept, Cimabue's *Madonna Enthroned Among Angels and St. Francis* is a famous portrait of the saint. Surrounding the portrait are painted scenes from the childhood of Christ, done by the assistants of Giotto.

Nearby is a painting of the crucifixion attributed to Giotto himself.

You reach the crypt via stairs midway along the nave—on the crypt's altar, a stone coffin holds the saint's body. Steps up from the transepts lead to the cloister, where there's a gift shop, and the treasury, which contains holy objects.

THE UPPER CHURCH

The St. Francis fresco cycle is the highlight of the Upper Church. (See facing page.) Also worth special note is the 16th-century choir, with its remarkably delicate inlaid wood. When a 1997 earthquake rocked the basilica, the St. Francis cycle sustained little damage, but portions of the ceiling above the entrance and altar collapsed, reducing their frescoes (attributed to Cimabue and Giotto) to rubble. The painstaking restoration is ongoing. ⚠ The dress code is strictly enforced—no bare shoulders or bare knees. Piazza di San Francesco, 075/819001, Lower Church Easter–Oct., Mon.–Sat. 6 AM–6:45 PM, Sun. 6:30 AM–7:15 PM; Nov.–Easter, daily 6:30–6. Upper Church Easter–Oct., Mon.–Sat. 8:30–6:45, Sun. 8:30–7:15; Nov.–Easter, daily 8:30–6.

FRANCIS, ITALY'S PATRON SAINT

DREGANDO ASPETTERO CHE TORNI

St. Francis was born in Assisi in 1181, the son of a noblewoman and a well-to-do merchant. His troubled youth included a year in prison. He planned a military career, but after a long illness Francis heard the voice of God, renounced his father's wealth, and began a life of austerity. His mystical embrace of poverty, asceticism, and the beauty of man and nature struck a responsive chord in the medieval mind; he quickly attracted a vast number of followers. Francis was the first saint to receive the stigmata (wounds in his hands, feet, and side corresponding to those of Christ on the cross). He died on October 4, 1226, in the Porziuncola, the secluded chapel in the woods where he had first preached the virtue of poverty to his disciples. St. Francis was declared patron saint of Italy in 1939, and today the Franciscans make up the largest of the Catholic orders.

THE UPPER CHURCH'S ST. FRANCIS FRESCO CYCLE

The 28 frescoes in the Upper Church depicting the life of St. Francis are the most admired works in the entire basilica. They're also the subject of one of art history's biggest controversies. For centuries they thought to be by Giotto (1267-1337), the great early Renaissance innovator, but inconsistencies in style, both within this series and in comparison to later Giotto works, have thrown their origin into question. Some scholars now say Giotto was the brains behind the cycle, but that assistants helped with the execution; others claim he couldn't have been involved at all.

Two things are certain. First, the style is revolutionary—which argues for Giotto's involvement. The tangible weight of the figures, the emotion they show, and the use of perspective all look familiar to modern eyes, but in the art of the time there was nothing like it. Second, these images have played a major part in shaping how the world sees St. Francis. In that respect, who painted them hardly matters.

Starting in the transept, the frescoes circle the church, showing events in the saint's life (and afterlife). Some of the best are grouped near the church's entrance—look for the nativity at Greccio, the miracle of the spring, the death of the knight at Celano, and, most famously, the sermon to the birds.

The St. Francis fresco cycle
1. Homage of a simple man
2. Giving cloak to a poor man
3. Dream of the palace
4. Hearing the voice of God
5. Rejection of worldly goods
6. Dream of Innocent III
7. Confirmation of the rules
8. Vision of flaming chariot
9. Vision of celestial thrones
10. Chasing devils from Arezzo
11. Before the sultan
12. Ecstasy of St. Francis
13. Nativity at Greccio
14. Miracle of the spring
15. Sermon to the birds
16. Death of knight at Celano
17. Preaching to Honorius III
18. Apparition at Arles
19. Receiving the stigmata
20. Death of St. Francis
21. Apparition before Bishop Guido and Fra Agostino
22. Verification of the stigmata
23. Mourning of St. Clare
24. Canonization
25. Apparition before Gregory IX
26. Healing of a devotee
27. Confession of a woman
28. Repentant heretic freed

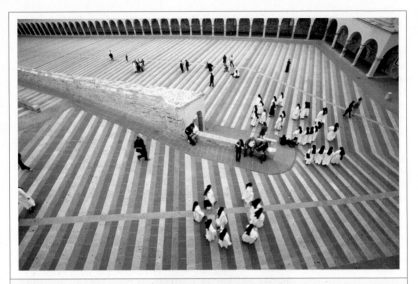

FODOR'S FIRST PERSON

Sister Marcellina,
Order of St. Bridget

Sister Marcellina of the Order of St. Bridget talks about her life in Assisi, where she and 11 other sisters live in a convent and guesthouse on the outskirts of the town:

"Before coming to Assisi, I lived in various countries. I've lived in India, and in England, and been to Holland, to Sweden, and to Finland, as well as lived in Rome. But Assisi is the place that I would never want to change for any other. I don't know, I think there is something very special about this place. I've been here 13 years now, and each year I pray that I won't be sent somewhere else. I'm very happy here.

"I like the atmosphere of Assisi, it's very friendly, and of course with St. Francis and St. Claire, but especially St. Francis, there is a simplicity to life that I like very much. Even though I'm in the Order of St. Bridget, living here I feel very much a part of Franciscan spirituality. There is also a very strong ecumenical feeling to Assisi and this is very nice. There are over 60 different religious communities, with people from all over the world. And even though they come from different religious backgrounds they still feel a part of Assisi. Living here, you don't see the people of Assisi, you see people who have come from all over the world.

"There is something you feel when you come to Assisi, something you feel in your heart that makes you want to come back. And people do return! They feel the peacefulness and tranquility. Not that there aren't other aspects, like the commercialism—but these things happen. People return for the simplicity of this place. People feel attracted to Assisi. There's always something that people feel when they come here—even the hard-hearted ones!"

Asked if she thinks Assisi is changing, Sister Marcellina answers, with laughter in her voice, "When they wanted to make all the changes in the year 2000, the Jubilee Year, our Lord said, 'I must stop everything.' They had lots of projects to build new accommodations to house the people coming for the Jubilee Year, but the Lord said, 'No!'"

⊕ *www.castellopetrata.com* ⤳ *16 rooms, 7 suites* ⛄ *In-room: no a/c, Internet. In-hotel: restaurant, bar, pool, some pets allowed* ⊙ *Closed Jan.–Mar.* ⦿ *Breakfast.*

$$ ⛉ **Hotel Subasio.** The converted monastery close to the Basilica di San Francesco is well past its prime, when guests included celebrities like Marlene Dietrich and Charlie Chaplin. **Pros:** perfect location; views of the Assisi plain. **Cons:** lobby a bit drab; some small rooms; service can be spotty. ⊠ *Via Frate Elia 2* ☏ *075/812206* ⊕ *www.hotelsubasio. com* ⤳ *54 rooms, 8 suites* ⛄ *In-room: no a/c. In-hotel: restaurant, bar, parking* ⦿ *Breakfast.*

$ ⛉ **Hotel Umbra.** A 16th-century town house is the setting for this charming hotel near Piazza del Comune. **Pros:** friendly welcome; pleasant small garden. **Cons:** difficult parking; some small rooms. ⊠ *Via degli Archi 6* ☏ *075/812240* ⊕ *www.hotelumbra.it* ⤳ *25 rooms* ⛄ *In-room: a/c. In-hotel: restaurant, bar* ⊙ *Closed Dec. and Jan.* ⦿ *Breakfast.*

$$ ⛉ **San Francesco.** You can't beat the location—the roof terrace and some of the rooms look out onto the Basilica di San Francesco, which is opposite the hotel. **Pros:** excellent location; great views. **Cons:** simple rooms; sometimes noisy in peak season. ⊠ *Via San Francesco 48* ☏ *075/812281* ⊕ *www.hotelsanfrancescoassisi.it* ⤳ *44 rooms* ⛄ *In-room: a/c, Internet. In-hotel: restaurant, bar, some pets allowed* ⦿ *Breakfast.*

NORTHERN UMBRIA

To the north of Perugia, placid, walled Gubbio watches over green countryside, true to its nickname, City of Silence—except for its fast and furious festivals in May, as lively today as when they began more than 800 years ago. To the south, along the Tiber River valley, are the towns of Deruta and Torgiano, best known for their hand-painted ceramics and wine—as locals say, go to Deruta to buy a pitcher and to Torgiano to fill it.

GUBBIO

35 km (22 miles) southeast of Città di Castello, 39 km (24 miles) northeast of Perugia, 92 km (57 miles) east of Arezzo.

There's something otherworldly about this jewel of a medieval town tucked away in a mountainous corner of Umbria. Even at the height of summer, the cool serenity and quiet of Gubbio's streets remain intact. The town is perched on the slopes of Monte Ingino, meaning the streets are dramatically steep. Gubbio's relatively isolated position has kept it free of hordes of high-season visitors, and most of the year the city lives up to its Italian nickname, *La Città del Silenzio* (City of Silence). Parking in the central Piazza dei Quaranta Martiri—named for 40 hostages murdered by the Nazis in 1944—is easy and secure, and it's wise to leave your car in the piazza and explore the narrow streets on foot.

At Christmas, kitsch is king. From December 7 to January 10, colored lights are strung down the mountainside in a shape resembling an evergreen, the world's largest Christmas tree.

GETTING HERE

The closest train station is Fossato di Vico, about 20 km (12 miles) from Gubbio. Ten daily buses connect the train station with the city, a 30-minute trip. If you're driving from Perugia, take the SS298, which rises steeply up toward the Gubbio hills. The trip will take you one hour. There are also 10 buses a day that leave from Perugia's Piazza Partigiani, the main Perugia bus terminal.

VISITOR INFORMATION

Gubbio tourism office ⊠ *Piazza Odersi 6* ☎ *075/9220693.*

EXPLORING

Duomo. On a narrow street on the highest tier of the town, the Duomo dates from the 13th century, with some baroque additions—in particular, a lavishly decorated bishop's chapel. ⊠ *Via Ducale* ⊙ *Daily 8–12:45 and 3–7.*

★ **Palazzo dei Consoli.** Gubbio's striking Piazza Grande is dominated by the medieval Palazzo dei Consoli, attributed to a local architect known as Gattapone, who is still much admired by today's residents. Studies have suggested that the palazzo was in fact the work of another architect, Angelo da Orvieto. In the Middle Ages the Parliament of Gubbio assembled in this palace, which has become a symbol of the town.

The Palazzo dei Consoli houses a museum, famous chiefly for the Tavole Eugubine, seven bronze tablets written in the ancient Umbrian language, employing Etruscan and Latin characters and providing the best key to understanding this obscure tongue. Also in the museum is a fascinating miscellany of rare coins and earthenware pots. The museum has exhilarating views over Gubbio's roofscape and beyond from the lofty loggia. For a

few days at the beginning of May, the palace also displays the famous *ceri*, the ceremonial wooden pillars at the center of Gubbio's annual festivities. ⊠ *Piazza Grande* ☎ *075/9274298* ⊕ *www.comune.gubbio.pg.it* ⊡ *€5* ⊙ *Apr.–Oct., daily 10–1 and 3–6; Nov.–Mar., daily 10–1 and 2–5.*

Palazzo Ducale. This scaled-down copy of the Palazzo Ducale in Urbino (Gubbio was once the possession of that city's ruling family, the Montefeltro) contains a small museum and a courtyard. Some of the public rooms offer magnificent views. ⊠ *Via Ducale* ☎ *075/9275872* ⊡ *€5* ⊙ *Tues.–Sun. 9–7:30.*

Funicular. Just outside the city walls at the eastern end of town is a funicular that provides a bracing ride to the top of Monte Ingino. (It's definitely not for those who suffer from vertigo.) ⊠ *Follow Corso Garibaldi or Via XX Settembre to end* ⊡ *€4, €5 round-trip* ⊙ *Sept.–June, daily 10–1:15 and 2:30–6; July and Aug., daily 9–7:30.*

Basilica di Sant'Ubaldo. At the top of Monte Ingino is the Basilica di Sant'Ubaldo, repository of Gubbio's famous ceri—three 16-foot-tall pillars crowned with statues of Saints Ubaldo, George, and Anthony. The pillars are transported to the Palazzo dei Consoli on the first Sunday of May, in preparation for the Festa dei Ceri. ⊠ *Monte Ingino* ☎ *075/9273872* ⊙ *Daily 8:30–noon and 4–7.*

WHERE TO EAT

¢ ✕ **Grotta dell'Angelo.** The rustic trattoria sits in the lower part of the old
UMBRIAN town near the main square. The menu features simple local specialties, including *capocollo* (a type of salami), *stringozzi* (thick spaghetti), and lasagna *tartufata* (with truffles). The few outdoor tables are in high demand in summer. The restaurant also offers a few small, basically furnished guest rooms, which should be booked in advance. ⊠ *Via Gioia 47* ☎ *075/9273438* ⌂ *Reservations essential* ⊙ *Closed Tues. and Jan. 7–Feb. 7.*

$ ✕ **Taverna del Lupo.** One of the city's most famous taverns, this popular
UMBRIAN place gets hectic on weekends and during the high season. Lasagna
Fodor'sChoice made in the Gubbian fashion, with ham and truffles, is an unusual
★ indulgence, and the *suprema di faraono* (guinea fowl in a delicately spiced sauce) is a specialty. The restaurant has two fine wine cellars and an extensive wine list. Save room for the excellent desserts. ⊠ *Via Ansidei 21* ☎ *075/9274368* ⊙ *Closed Mon. Oct.–June.*

¢ ✕ **Ulisse e Letizia.** The building dates to the 1300s, and its original stone-and-wood structure has been kept intact. (In the 1400s the space housed an important ceramics factory.) The menu, with seasonal changes, includes traditional but creative fare: tagliatelle *al tartuffo* (in a truffle sauce), *gnochetti al finocchio selvatico* (potato dumplings with wild fennel), and *raviolini di faro con asparagi* (tiny ravioli with spelt and asparagus). ⊠ *Via Mastro Giorgio 2* ☎ *075/9221970* ⊘ *Closed Mon.*

WHERE TO STAY

For expanded hotel reviews, visit Fodors.com.

$ ⬚ **Hotel Bosone Palace.** A former palace is now home to this elegant hotel. **Pros:** friendly welcome; excellent location. **Cons:** some noise in tourist season; simple lobby. ⊠ *Via XX Settembre 22* ☎ *075/9220688* ⊕ *www.bosonepalace-gubbio.com* ⌁ *28 rooms, 2 suites* ⬠ *In-room: no a/c. In-hotel: restaurant, bar* ⊘ *Closed 3 wks in Jan.* ⦿*Breakfast.*

DERUTA

7 km (4½ miles) south of Torgiano, 19 km (11 miles) southeast of Perugia.

This 14th-century medieval hill town is most famous for its ceramics. A drive through the countryside to visit the ceramics workshops is a good way to spend a morning, but be sure to stop in the town itself.

GETTING HERE

From Perugia follow the directions for Rome and the E45 highway; Deruta has its own exits. There are also trains from the smaller St. Anna train station in Perugia. Take the train in the direction of Terni, and get off at Deruta.

VISITOR INFORMATION

Deruta tourism office ⊠ *Piazza dei Consoli 4* ☎ *075/9711559.*

EXPLORING

Museo Regionale della Ceramica (*Regional Ceramics Museum*). The notable sights in Deruta include the Museo Regionale della Ceramica, part of which extends into the adjacent 14th-century former convent of San Francesco. Half the museum tells the history of ceramics, with panels in Italian and English explaining artistic techniques and production processes. The museum also holds the country's largest collection of modern Italian ceramics—nearly 8,000 pieces are on display. The most notable are the Renaissance vessels using the *lustro* technique, which originated in Arab and Middle Eastern cultures some 500 years before coming into use in Italy in the late 1400s. Lustro, as the name sounds, gives the ceramics a rich finish, which is accomplished with the use of crushed precious materials such as gold and silver. ⊠ *Largo San Francesco* ☎ *075/9711000* ⊕ *www.museoceramicaderuta.it* ⬠*€5* ⊘ *Daily 10:30–1 and 2:30–5.*

SHOPPING

Deruta is home to more than 70 ceramics shops. They offer a range of ceramics, including extra pieces from commissions for well-known British and North American tableware manufacturers. If you ask, most owners will take you to see where they actually throw, bake, and paint their wares. A drive along Via Tiberina Nord takes you past one shop after another.

SPELLO

12 km (7 miles) southeast of Assisi, 33 km (21 miles) north of Spoleto.

Spello is a gastronomic paradise, especially compared to Assisi. Only a few minutes from Assisi by car or train, this hilltop town at the edge of Monte Subasio makes an excellent strategic and culinary base for exploring nearby towns. Its hotels are well appointed and its restaurants serve some of the best cuisine and wines in the region—sophisticated in variety and of excellent quality. Spello's art scene includes first-rate frescoes by Pinturicchio and Perugino and contemporary artists who can be observed at work in studios around town. If antiquity is your passion, the town also has some intriguing Roman ruins. And the warm, rosy-beige tones of the local *pietra rossa* stone on the buildings brighten even cloudy days.

GETTING HERE

Spello is an easy half-hour drive from Perugia. From the E45 highway, take the exit toward Assisi and Foligno. Merge onto the SS75 and take the Spello exit. There are also regular trains on the Perugia–Assisi line. Spello is 1 km (½ mile) from the train station, and buses run every 30 minutes for Porta Consolare. From Porta Consolare continue up the steep main street that begins as Via Consolare and changes names several times as it crosses the little town, following the original Roman road. As it curves around, notice the winding medieval alleyways to the right and the more uniform Roman-era blocks to the left.

VISITOR INFORMATION

Spello tourism office ⊠ *Piazza Matteotti 3* ☎ *0742/301009* ⊕ *www.prospello.it* ⊙ *Daily 9:30–12:30 and 3:30–5.*

EXPLORING

Santa Maria Maggiore. The basilica of Santa Maria Maggiore has vivid frescoes by Pinturicchio in the Cappella Baglioni (1501). Striking in their rich colors, finely dressed figures, and complex symbolism, the *Nativity, Christ Among the Doctors* (on the far left side is a portrait of Troilo Baglioni, the prior who commissioned the work), and the *Annunciation* (look for Pinturicchio's self-portrait in the Virgin's room) are among Pinturicchio's finest works. They were painted after the artist had already won great acclaim for his work in the Palazzi Vaticani in Rome for Borgia Pope Alexander VI. Two pillars on either side of the apse are decorated with frescoes by Perugino (circa 1450–1523), the other great Umbrian artist of the 16th century. ⊠ *Piazza Matteotti 18* ☎ *0742/301792* ⊙ *Daily 9–12:30 and 3–7.*

WHERE TO EAT AND STAY

For expanded hotel reviews, visit Fodors.com.

$ ╳ **Il Molino.** Almost a destination in itself, this former mill is one of the region's best restaurants. The types of olive oil used in the dishes and the names of the local farmers who grew the produce are noted on the menu. Appetizers are varied, and often highlight foods found only here,

UMBRIAN

Fodor's Choice

★

like the *risina,* a tiny white bean. Pasta sauces can vary from exquisitely rich to extremely delicate. The meat is first-rate, either elaborately prepared or grilled and topped with a signature sauce. The service is attentive, and the wine list has plenty of local and Italian options, including the pungent Sagrantino di Montefalco and fresh Orvieto whites. If you want something with a bit more depth, go for one of the Montepulciano wines, or even a Brunello di Montalcino, one of Italy's greatest reds. Outside seating lets you soak up the passing street scene; inside is a series of impressive 14th-century arches. ⊠ *Piazza Matteotti 6/7* ☎ *0742/301021* ⊙ *Closed Tues.*

$$ ⬚ **Hotel Palazzo Bocci.** Quiet and elegant, this hotel is on Spello's main
★ street. **Pros:** central location; splendid views of the valley. **Cons:** noisy in summer months; not all rooms have views. ⊠ *Via Cavour 17* ☎ *0742/301021* ⊕ *www.palazzobocci.com* ⌁ *23 rooms* ⛉ *In-room: a/c, Wi-Fi. In-hotel: restaurant, bar* ⦿| *Breakfast.*

$ ⬚ **La Bastiglia.** This cozy hotel is in a former grain mill, but polished
★ wood planks and handwoven rugs have replaced the rustic flooring. **Pros:** lovely terrace restaurant; cozy rooms; fine views. **Cons:** some shared balconies; breakfast is underwhelming; no elevator. ⊠ *Via Salnitraria 15* ☎ *0742/651277* ⊕ *www.labastiglia.com* ⌁ *31 rooms, 2 suites* ⛉ *In-room: a/c. In-hotel: restaurant, bar, pool* ⊙ *Closed early Jan.–early Feb.* ⦿| *Breakfast.*

MONTEFALCO

6 km (4 miles) southeast of Bevagna, 34 km (21 miles) south of Assisi.

Nicknamed the "balcony over Umbria" for its high vantage point over the valley that runs from Perugia to Spoleto, Montefalco began as an important Roman settlement situated on the Via Flaminia. The town owes its current name—which means "Falcon's Mount"—to Emperor Frederick II (1194–1250). Obviously a greater fan of falconry than Roman architecture, he destroyed the ancient town, which was then called Coccorone, in 1249, and built in its place what would later become Montefalco. Aside from a few fragments incorporated in a private house just off Borgo Garibaldi, no traces remain of the old Roman center. However, Montefalco has more than its fair share of interesting art and architecture and is well worth the drive up the hill.

GETTING HERE

If you're driving from Perugia, take the E45 toward Rome. Take the Foligno exit, then merge onto the SP445 and follow it into Montefalco. The drive takes around 50 minutes. The nearest train station is in Foligno, about 7 km (4½ miles) away. From there you can take a taxi or a bus into Montefalco.

VISITOR INFORMATION

Montefalco tourism office ⊠ *Piazza del Comune, 17* ☎ *0742/378490* ⊕ *www. stradadelsagrantino.it.*

La Strada del Sagrantino. The staff at this tourist office in the piazza will advise you on selecting a wine, direct you to nearby enoteche for tastings, and give you free maps with which to find your way around the

Sagrantino Road and some remarkable wine territory. They can also book you a room in a hotel or hillside apartment, or at an agriturismo or vineyard (some of the wine producers, including Antonelli, have *casale*, or small apartments, near the vineyards that are usually rented by the week, but in low season are often available for a weekend). ⊠ *Piazza del Comune 17* ☎ *0742/378490* ⊕ *www.stradadelsagrantino.it.*

WHERE TO EAT AND STAY

For expanded hotel reviews, visit Fodors.com.

Montefalco is a good stop for sustenance: here you need go no farther than the main square to find a restaurant or bar with a hot meal, and most establishments—both simple and sophisticated—offer a splendid combination of history and small-town hospitality.

¢ ✕ **L'Alchemista.** "The Alchemist" is an apt name, as the chef's transfor-
ITALIAN mations are magical. Try the *fiore molle della Valnerina*, baked saffron cheese, bacon, and zucchini—served only here. In summer, cold dishes to try are *panzanella*, a local vegetable salad mixed with bread, or the barley salad tossed with vegetables. The *farro* (spelt) soup made with Sagrantino wine is a local specialty. The desserts are delicious: all are made on the premises and not too sweet. ⊠ *Piazza del Comune 14* ☎ *0742/378558* ☉ *Closed Tues. and Jan.–Mar.*

$$ ⌂ **Villa Pambuffetti.** If you want to be pampered in the refined atmosphere
Fodor'sChoice of a private villa, this is the spot. **Pros:** peaceful gardens; refined fur-
★ nishings. **Cons:** outside the town center; can get crowded on weekends. ⊠ *Viale della Vittoria 20* ☎ *0742/379417* ⊕ *www.villapambuffetti.com* ⟿ *15 rooms, 3 suites* ⌂ *In-room: a/c. In-hotel: restaurant, bar, pool* ⦿ *Breakfast.*

SPOLETO

For most of the year, Spoleto is one more in a pleasant succession of sleepy hill towns, resting regally atop a mountain. But for three weeks every summer the town shifts into high gear for a turn in the international spotlight during the Festival dei Due Mondi (Festival of Two Worlds), an extravaganza of theater, opera, music, painting, and sculpture. As the world's top artists vie for honors, throngs of art aficionados vie for hotel rooms. If you plan to spend the night in Spoleto during the festival, make sure you have confirmed reservations, or you may find yourself scrambling at sunset.

Spoleto has plenty to lure you during the rest of the year as well: the final frescoes of Filippo Lippi; beautiful piazzas and streets with Roman and medieval attractions; and superb natural surroundings with rolling hills and a dramatic gorge. Spoleto makes a good base for exploring all of southern Umbria, as Assisi, Orvieto, and the towns in between are all within easy reach.

GETTING HERE

Spoleto is an hour's drive from Perugia. From the E45 highway, take the exit toward Assisi and Foligno, then merge onto the SS75 until you reach the Foligno Est exit. Merge onto the SS3, which leads to Spoleto.

CLOSE UP

The Sagrantino Story

Sagrantino grapes have been used for the production of red wine for centuries. The wine began centuries ago as Sagrantino *passito,* a semisweet version in which the grapes are left to dry for a period after picking to intensify the sugar content. One theory traces the origin of Sagrantino back to ancient Rome in the works of Pliny the Elder, the author of the *Natural History,* who referred to the Itriola grape that some researchers think may be Sagrantino. Others believe that in medieval times Franciscan friars returned from Asia Minor with the grape. ("Sagrantino" perhaps derives from *sacramenti,* the religious ceremony in which the wine was used.)

The passito is still produced today, and is preferred by some. But the big change in Sagrantino wine production came in the past decades, when Sagrantino *secco* (dry) came onto the market. Both passito and secco have a deep ruby-red color that tends toward garnet highlights, with a full body and rich flavor.

For the dry wines, producers not to be missed are Terre di Capitani, Antonelli, Perticaia, and Caprai. Try those labels for the passito as well, in addition to Ruggeri and Scacciadiavoli. Terre di Capitani is complex, and has vegetable and mineral tones that join tastes of wild berries, cherries, and chocolate—this winemaker hand-pampers

his grapes and it shows. Antonelli is elegant, refined, and rich. The Ruggeri passito is one of the best, so don't be put off by its homespun label. Caprai is bold and rich in taste, and has the largest market share, including a high percentage exported to the United States. Perticaia has a full, rounded taste.

Some wineries are small and not equipped to receive visitors.

There you can pick up a map of the wine route and set up appointments, book accommodations, and then visit local enoteche. At the enoteche, ask the sommelier to guide you to some smaller producers you'll have difficulty finding elsewhere.

Centro Agro-Alimentare dell'Umbria. Sagrantino di Montefalco is celebrated twice yearly in the town of Montefalco, during September's Festa Della Vendemmia (Grape or Harvest Festival) and spring's Settimana Enologica (Wine Week), during which area grape farmers turn out for a parade through the streets and a tasting of past years' labors in the Piazza del Comune. Details can be obtained from the Centro Agro-Alimentare dell'Umbria or the Strada del Sagrantino (⇨ *above*). ☎ *075/56811* ⊕ *www.umbriadoc.com.*

Salute!

There are regular trains on the Perugia–Foligno line. From the train station it's a 15-minute uphill walk to the center, so you'll probably want to take a taxi.

VISITOR INFORMATION

Spoleto tourism office ⊠ *Piazza della Libertà 7* ☎ *0743/238921* ⊕ *www. regioneumbria.eu.*

EXPLORING SPOLETO

The walled city is set on a slanting hillside, with the most interesting sections clustered toward the upper portion. Parking options inside the walls include Piazza Campello (just below the Rocca) on the southeast end, Via del Trivio to the north, and Piazza San Domenico on the west end. You can also park at Piazza della Vittoria farther north, just outside the walls. There are also several well-marked lots near the train station. If you arrive by train, you can walk 1 km (½ mile) from the station to the entrance to the lower town. Regular bus connections are every 15 to 30 minutes. You can also use the *trenino,* as locals call the shuttle service, from the train station to Piazza della Libertà, near the upper part of the old town, where you'll find the tourist office.

Like most other towns with narrow, winding streets, Spoleto is best explored on foot. Bear in mind that much of the city is on a steep slope, so there are lots of stairs and steep inclines. The well-worn stones can be slippery even when dry; wear rubber-sole shoes for good traction. Several pedestrian walkways cut across Corso Mazzini, which zigzags up the hill. A €12 combination ticket purchased at the tourist office allows you entry to all the town's museums and galleries.

TOP ATTRACTIONS

★ **Duomo.** The cathedral's 12th-century Romanesque facade received a Renaissance face-lift with the addition of a loggia in a rosy pink stone. A stunning contrast in styles, the Duomo is one of the finest cathedrals in the region. The eight rose windows are especially dazzling in the late afternoon sun. Look under the largest rose window and you see two figures that appear to be holding up the structure; in the corners of the square surrounding the window, the four Evangelists are sculpted. Inside, the original tile floor dates from an earlier church that was destroyed by Frederick I (circa 1123–90).

Above the church's entrance is Bernini's bust of Pope Urban VIII (1568–1644), who had the rest of the church redecorated in 17th-century baroque; fortunately he didn't touch the 15th-century frescoes painted in the apse by Fra Filippo Lippi (circa 1406–69) between 1466 and 1469. These immaculately restored masterpieces—the *Annunciation, Nativity,* and *Dormition*—tell the story of the life of the Virgin. The *Coronation of the Virgin,* adorning the half dome, is the literal and figurative high point. Portraits of Lippi and his assistants are on the right side of the central panel. The Florentine artist priest "whose colors expressed God's voice" (the words inscribed on his tomb) died shortly after completing the work. His tomb, which you can see in the right transept (note the artist's brushes and tools), was designed by his son, Filippino Lippi (circa 1457–1504).

Another fresco cycle, including work by Pinturicchio, is in the Cappella Eroli, off the right aisle. Note the grotesques in the ornamentation, then very much in vogue with the rediscovery of ancient Roman paintings. The bounty of Umbria is displayed in vivid colors in the abundance of leaves, fruits, and vegetables that adorn the center seams of the cross vault. In the left nave, not far from the entrance, is the well-restored 12th-century crucifix by Alberto Sozio, the earliest known example of this kind of work, with a painting on parchment attached to a wood cross. To the right of the presbytery is the Cappella della Santissima Icona (Chapel of the Most Holy Icon), which contains a small Byzantine painting of a Madonna given to the town by Frederick Barbarossa as a peace offering in 1185, following his destruction of the cathedral and town three decades earlier. ✉ *Piazza del Duomo* ☎ *0743/44307* ⊘ *Apr.–Oct., daily 8:30–12:30 and 3:30–6:30; Nov.–Mar., daily 8:30–12:30 and 3:30–5.*

★ **Ponte delle Torri** (*Bridge of the Towers*). Standing massive and graceful through the deep gorge that separates Spoleto from Monteluco, this 14th-century bridge is one of Umbria's most photographed monuments, and justifiably so. Built over the foundations of a Roman-era aqueduct, it soars 262 feet above the forested gorge—higher than the dome of St. Peter's in Rome. Sweeping views over the valley and a pleasant sense of vertigo make a walk across the bridge a must, particularly on a starry night. ✉ *Via del Ponte.*

WORTH NOTING

Casa Romana. Spoleto became a Roman colony in the 3rd century BC, but the best excavated remains date from the 1st century AD. Excavated in the late 9th century, the Casa Romana was not a typical Roman residence. According to an inscription, it belonged to Vespasia Polla, the mother of Emperor Vespasian (one of the builders of the Colosseum and perhaps better known by the Romans for taxing them to install public toilets, later called "Vespasians"). The rooms, arranged around a large central atrium built over an *impluvium* (rain cistern), are decorated with black-and-white geometric mosaics. ⊠ *Palazzo del Municipio, Via Visiale 9* ☎ *0743/234250* 💶 *€2.50, €6 combination ticket (includes Pinacoteca Comunale and Galleria d'Arte Moderna* ⊘ *Wed.–Mon. 11–5; closed last wk Dec.*

La Rocca. Built in the mid-14th century for Cardinal Egidio Albornoz, this massive fortress served as a seat for the local pontifical governors, a tangible sign of the restoration of the Church's power in the area when the pope was ruling from Avignon. Several popes spent time here, and one of them, Alexander VI, in 1499 sent his capable teenage daughter Lucrezia Borgia (1480–1519) to serve as governor for three months. The Gubbio-born architect Gattapone (14th century) used the ruins of a Roman acropolis as a foundation and took materials from many Roman-era sites, including the Teatro Romano. La Rocca's plan is long and rectangular, with six towers and two grand courtyards, an upper loggia, and inside some grand reception rooms. In the largest tower, Torre Maestà, you can visit an apartment with some interesting frescoes. A small shuttle bus gives you that last boost up the hill from the ticket booth to the entrance of the fortress. If you phone in advance, you may be able to secure an English-speaking guide. ⊠ *Via del Ponte* ☎ *0743/223055* 💶 *€6* ⊘ *Tues.–Sun. 9–5.*

Teatro Romano. The Romans who had colonized the city in 241 BC constructed this small theater in the 1st century AD; for centuries afterward it was used as a quarry for building materials. The most intact portion is the hallway that passes under the *cavea* (stands). The rest was heavily restored in the early 1950s and serves as a venue for Spoleto's Festival dei Due Mondi. The theater was the site of a gruesome episode in Spoleto's history: during the medieval struggle between Guelph (papal) and Ghibelline (imperial) forces, Spoleto took the side of the Holy Roman Emperor. Afterward, 400 Guelph supporters were massacred in the theater, their bodies burned in an enormous pyre. In the end, the Guelphs were triumphant, and Spoleto was incorporated into the states of the Church in 1354. Through a door in the west portico of the adjoining building is the **Museo Archeologico,** with assorted artifacts found in excavations primarily around Spoleto and Norcia. The collection contains Bronze Age and Iron Age artifacts from Umbrian and pre-Roman eras. Another section contains black-glaze vases from the Hellenistic period excavated from the necropolis of Saint Scolastica in Norcia. The highlight is the stone tablet inscribed on both sides with the Lex Spoletina (Spoleto Law). Dating from 315 BC, this legal document prohibited the desecration of the woods on the slopes of nearby Monteluco. ⊠ *Piazza della Libertà* ☎ *0743/223277* 💶 *€4* ⊘ *Daily 8:30–7:30.*

7

WHERE TO EAT

$ ✕ **Apollinare.** Low wooden ceilings and flickering candlelight make this
UMBRIAN monastery from the 10th and 11th centuries Spoleto's most romantic
spot. The kitchen serves sophisticated, innovative variations on local
dishes. Sauces of cherry tomatoes, mint, and a touch of red pepper, or
of porcini mushrooms, top the long, slender *strangozzi*. The *caramella*
(light puff-pastry cylinders filled with local cheese and served with a
creamy Parmesan sauce) is popular. In warm weather you can dine
under a canopy on the piazza across from the archaeological museum.
⊠ *Via Sant'Agata 14* ☎ *0743/223256* ⊗ *Closed Tues.*

¢ ✕ **Il Tartufo.** As the name indicates, dishes prepared with truffles are the
UMBRIAN specialty here—don't miss the risotto al tartufo. But there are also dishes
not perfumed with this expensive delicacy. Incorporating the ruins of
a Roman villa, the restaurant's decor is rustic on the ground floor and
more modern upstairs. In summer, tables appear outdoors and the traditional fare is spiced up to appeal to the cosmopolitan crowd attending
(or performing in) the Festival dei Due Mondi. ⊠ *Piazza Garibaldi 24*
☎ *0743/40236* ⌂ *Reservations essential* ⊗ *Closed Mon. and last 2 wks
in July. No dinner Sun.*

¢ ✕ **Osteria del Trivio.** At this friendly trattoria everything is made on the
UMBRIAN premises. The menu changes daily, depending on what's in season.
Dishes might include stuffed artichokes, pasta with local mushrooms,
or chicken with artichokes. For dessert, try the homemade biscotti,
made for dunking in sweet wine. There's a printed menu, but the owner
can explain the dishes in a number of languages. A complete meal from
appetizer to dessert with house wine is likely to cost no more than €25.
⊠ *Via del Trivio 16* ☎ *0743/44349* ⊗ *Closed Tues.*

¢ ✕ **Ristorante Panciolle.** In the heart of Spoleto's medieval quarter, this
UMBRIAN restaurant has one of the most appealing settings you could wish for: a
★ small garden filled with lemon trees. Dishes change throughout the year,
and may include pastas served with asparagus or mushrooms, as well
as grilled meats. More expensive dishes prepared with fresh truffles are
also available in season. ⊠ *Via Duomo 3/5* ☎ *0743/45677* ⌂ *Reservations essential* ⊗ *Closed Wed.*

WHERE TO STAY

For expanded hotel reviews, visit Fodors.com.

$$ ⊡ **Cavaliere Palace Hotel.** An arched passageway off one of the city's busy
★ shopping streets leads to an elegant world through a quiet courtyard.
Pros: quiet elegance; central position. **Cons:** finding parking can be a
problem; crowded in summer. ⊠ *Corso Garibaldi 49* ☎ *0743/220350*
⊕ *www.hotelcavaliere.eu* ⤵ *29 rooms, 2 suites* ⌂ *In-room: a/c. In-hotel:
restaurant, bar* ⦿| *Breakfast.*

$ ⊡ **Hotel Clitunno.** A renovated 18th-century building in the center of
town houses this pleasant hotel. **Pros:** friendly staff; good restaurant.
Cons: difficult to find a parking space; some small rooms. ⊠ *Piazza
Sordini 6* ☎ *0743/223340* ⊕ *www.hotelclitunno.com* ⤵ *45 rooms* ⌂ *In-
room: a/c. In-hotel: restaurant, bar* ⦿| *Breakfast.*

A Taste of Truffles

Umbria is rich with truffles—more are found here than anywhere else in Italy—and those not consumed fresh are processed into pastes or flavored oils. The primary truffle areas are around the tiny town of Norcia, which holds a truffle festival every February, and near Spoleto, where signs warn against unlicensed truffle hunting at the base of the Ponte delle Torri.

Although grown locally, the rare delicacy can cost a small fortune, up to $200 for a quarter pound—fortunately, a little goes a long way. At such a price there's great competition among the nearly 10,000 registered truffle hunters in the province, who use specially trained dogs to sniff them out among the roots of several types of trees, including oak and ilex. Despite a few incidents involving inferior tubers imported from China, you can be reasonably assured that the truffle shaved onto your pasta has been unearthed locally. Don't pass up the opportunity to try this delectable treat. The intense aroma of a dish perfumed with truffles is unmistakable and the flavor memorable.

$$ ⊞ **Hotel San Luca.** The elegant San Luca is one of Spoleto's finest hotels,
Fodor's Choice thanks to its commendable attention to detail, such as the hand-
★ painted friezes that decorate the walls of the spacious guest rooms
and the generous selection of up-to-date magazines for your reading
pleasure. **Pros:** very helpful staff; peaceful location. **Cons:** outside the
town center; a long walk to the main sights. ⊠ *Via Interna delle Mura
19* ☎ *0743/223399* ⊕ *www.hotelsanluca.com* ⟿ *33 rooms, 2 suites*
⌂ *In-room: a/c, Internet. In-hotel: restaurant, business center, parking*
⊦⊙⊦ Breakfast.

THE ARTS

Fodor's Choice **Festival dei Due Mondi** (*Festival of Two Worlds*). In 1958, composer
★ Gian Carlo Menotti chose Spoleto for the first Festival dei Due Mondi,
a gathering of artists, performers, and musicians intending to bring
together the "new" and "old" worlds of America and Europe. (A cor-
responding festival in South Carolina is no longer connected to this
festival.) The annual event, held in late June and early July, is one of the
most important cultural happenings in Europe, attracting big names in
all branches of the arts, particularly music, opera, and theater. ⊠ *Piazza
del Comune 1* ☎ *0743/221689* ⊕ *www.festivaldispoleto.com.*

SOUTHERN UMBRIA

Orvieto, built on a tufa mount, produces one of Italy's favorite white
wines and has one of the country's greatest cathedrals and most com-
pelling fresco cycles. Nearby Narni and Todi are pleasant medieval
hill towns. The former stands over a steep gorge, its Roman pedigree
evident in dark alleyways and winding streets; the latter is a fairy-tale
village with incomparable views and one of Italy's most perfect piazzas.

TODI

34 km (22 miles) south of Perugia, 34 km (22 miles) east of Orvieto.

As you stand on Piazza del Popolo, looking out onto the Tiber Valley below, it's easy to see why Todi is often described as Umbria's prettiest hill town. Legend has it that the town was founded by the Umbri, who followed an eagle who had stolen a tablecloth. They liked this lofty perch so much that they settled here for good. The eagle is now perched on the insignia of the medieval palaces in the main piazza.

GETTING HERE

Todi is best reached by car, as the town's two train stations are way down the hill and connected to the center by infrequent bus service. From Perugia, follow the E45 toward Rome. Take the Todi/Orvieto exit, then follow the SS79bis into Todi. The drive takes around 40 minutes.

VISITOR INFORMATION

Todi tourism office ⊠ *Piazza del Popolo 38* ☎ *075/8942526* ⊕ *www. regioneumbria.eu.*

EXPLORING

Piazza del Popolo. Built above the Roman Forum, Piazza del Popolo is Todi's high point, a model of spatial harmony with stunning views onto the surrounding countryside. In the best medieval tradition, the square was conceived to house both the temporal and the spiritual centers of power.

Duomo. On one end of the Piazza del Popolo is the 12th-century Romanesque-Gothic Duomo, which was built over the site of a Roman temple. The simple facade is enlivened by a finely carved rose window. Look up at that window as you step inside and you'll notice its peculiarity: each "petal" of the rose has a cherub's face in the stained glass. Take a close look at the capitals of the double columns with pilasters: perched between the acanthus leaves are charming medieval sculptures of saints—Peter with his keys, George and the dragon, and so on. You can see the rich brown tones of the wooden choir near the altar, but unless you have binoculars or request special permission in advance, you can't get close enough to see all the exquisite detail in this Renaissance masterpiece of woodworking (1521–30). The severe, solid mass of the Duomo is mirrored by the Palazzo dei Priori (1595–97) across the way. ⊠ *Piazza del Popolo* ☎ *075/8943041* ☉ *Daily 8–1 and 3–6.*

WHERE TO EAT AND STAY

For expanded hotel reviews, visit Fodors.com.

¢ ✕ **Ristorante Umbria.** Todi's most popular restaurant for more than
UMBRIAN four decades, the Umbria is reliable for its sturdy country food and its wonderful view from the terrace. Since it has only 16 tables outside, make sure you reserve ahead. In winter, try legume soup, homemade pasta with truffles, or *palombaccio alla ghiotta* (roasted squab). Steaks, accompanied by a rich dark-brown wine sauce, are good as well. ⊠ *Via San Bonaventura 13* ☎ *075/8942737* ☉ *Closed Tues.*

$ ▦ **San Lorenzo 3.** Surrounded by antique furniture, paintings, and period knickknacks, you get a sense of a place more in tune with the 19th than the 21st century. **Pros:** delightful Old World atmosphere; excellent central location. **Cons:** few modern amenities; basic furnishings; some shared bathrooms. ⊠ *Via San Lorenzo 3* ☎ *075/8944555* ⊕ *www.sanlorenzo3.it* ⤶ *6 rooms, 3 with bath* ♿ *In-room: no a/c, no TV* ▤ *No credit cards* ☉ *Closed Jan. and Feb.* ⏐◯⏐ *Breakfast.*

ORVIETO

30 km (19 miles) southwest of Todi, 81 km (51 miles) west of Spoleto.

Carved out of an enormous plateau of volcanic rock high above a green valley, Orvieto has natural defenses that made the high walls seen in many Umbrian towns unnecessary. The Etruscans were the first to settle here, digging a honeycombed network of more than 1,200 wells and storage caves out of the soft stone. The Romans attacked, sacked, and destroyed the city in 283 BC; since then, it has grown up out of the rock into an enchanting maze of alleys and squares. Orvieto was solidly Guelph in the Middle Ages, and for several hundred years popes sought refuge in the city, at times needing protection from their enemies, at times seeking respite from the summer heat of Rome.

When painting his frescoes inside the Duomo, Luca Signorelli asked that part of his contract be paid in Orvietan wine, and he was neither the first nor the last to appreciate the region's popular white. In past times the caves carved underneath the town were used to ferment the Trebbiano grapes used in making Orvieto Classico; now local wine production has moved out to more traditional vineyards, but you can still while away the afternoon in tastings at any number of shops in town.

GETTING HERE

Orvieto is well connected by train to Rome, Florence, and Perugia. It's also adjacent to the A1 Superstrada that runs between Florence and Rome. Parking areas in the upper town tend to be crowded. A better idea is to follow the signs for the Porta Orvetiana parking lot, then take the funicular that carries people up the hill.

VISITOR INFORMATION

Orvieto tourism office ⊠ *Piazza del Duomo 24* ☏ *0763/341772* ⊕ *www. regioneumbria.eu.*

A *Carta Orvieto Unica* (single ticket) is expensive but a great deal if you want to visit everything; for €18 you get admission to the three major sights in town—Cappella di San Brizio (at the Duomo), Museo Claudio Faina, and Orvieto Underground *(see below)*—along with entry to the Torre del Moro; with views of Orvieto, plus a combination bus-funicular pass or five hours of free parking.

EXPLORING

Fodor's Choice ★ **Duomo.** Orvieto's Duomo is, quite simply, stunning. The church was built to commemorate the Miracle at Bolsena. In 1263 a young priest who questioned the miracle of transubstantiation (in which the Communion bread and wine become the flesh and blood of Christ) was saying mass at nearby Lago di Bolsena. His doubts were put to rest, however, when a wafer he had just blessed suddenly started to drip blood, staining the linen covering the altar. The cloth and the host were taken to the pope, who proclaimed a miracle and a year later provided for a new religious holiday—the Feast of Corpus Domini. Thirty years later, construction began on a *duomo* to celebrate the miracle and house the stained altar cloth.

It's thought that Arnolfo di Cambio (circa 1245–1302), the famous builder of the Duomo in Florence, was given the initial commission for the Duomo, but the project was soon taken over by Lorenzo Maitani (circa 1275–1330), who consolidated the structure and designed the monumental facade. Maitani also made the bas-relief panels between the doorways, which graphically tell the story of the Creation (on the left) and the Last Judgment (on the right). The lower registers, now protected by Plexiglas, succeed in conveying the horrors of hell as few other works of art manage to do, an effect made all the more powerful by the worn gray marble. Above, gold mosaics are framed by finely detailed Gothic decoration.

Inside, the cathedral is rather vast and empty; the major works are in the transepts. To the left is the **Cappella del Corporale,** where the square linen cloth (*corporale*) is kept in a golden reliquary that's modeled on the cathedral and inlaid with enamel scenes of the miracle. The cloth is removed for public viewing on Easter and on Corpus Domini (the ninth Sunday after Easter). In the right transept is the **Cappella di San Brizio,** or Cappella Nuova. In this chapel is one of Italy's greatest fresco cycles, notable for its influence on Michelangelo's *Last Judgment,* as well as for the extraordinary beauty of the figuration. In these works, a few by Fra Angelico and the majority by Luca Signorelli, the damned fall to hell, demons breathe fire and blood, and Christians are martyred. Some scenes are heavily influenced by the imagery in Dante's (1265–1321) *Divine Comedy.* ⊠ *Piazza del Duomo* ☏ *0763/342477* ✉ *Cappella Nuova €4* ☺ *Mar–Oct., daily 9:30–7:30; Nov.–Feb., daily 9:30–1 and 2:30–5.*

★ **Museo Archeologico Claudio Faina.** This superb private collection, beautifully arranged and presented, goes far beyond the usual museum offerings of a scattering of local remains. The collection is particularly rich in Greek- and Etruscan-era pottery, from large Attic amphorae (6th– 4th century BC) to Attic black- and red-figure pieces to Etruscan *bucchero* (dark-reddish clay) vases. Other interesting pieces in the collection include a 6th-century sarcophagus and a substantial display of Roman-era coins. ⊠ *Piazza del Duomo 29* ☏ *0763/341511* ⊕ *www.museofaina. it* ✉ *€4.50* ☺ *Apr.–Sept., daily 10–5; Oct.–Mar., Tues.–Sun. 9:30–6.*

Orvieto Underground. More than just about any other town, Orvieto has grown from its own foundations—if one were to remove from present-day Orvieto all the building materials that were dug up from below, there would hardly be a building left standing. The Etruscans, the Romans, and those who followed dug into the tufa (the same soft volcanic rock from which catacombs were made), and over the centuries created more than 1,000 separate cisterns, caves, secret passages, storage areas, and production areas for wine and olive oil. Some of the tufa removed was used as building blocks for the city that exists today, and some was partly ground into *pozzolana,* which was made into mortar. The most thorough **Orvieto Underground tour** (*Orvieto tourism office,* ⊠ *Piazza del Duomo 24* ☏ *0763/341772*) is run daily at 11, 12:15, 4, and 5:15. (In February tours are given only on weekends.) Admission for the hour-long English tour is €6.

Pozzo della Cava. If you're short on time but still want a look at what it was like in the cisterns and caves beneath the city, head for the Pozzo della Cava, an Etruscan well for spring water. It's open Tuesday through Friday from 9 to 8, and costs €3. ⊠ *Via della Cava 28* ☏ *0763/342373.*

WHERE TO EAT
The streets around the Duomo are lined with all types of bars and restaurants where you can eat simple or elaborate food and try wines by the glass.

¢ ✕ **Il Giglio D'Oro.** A great view of the Duomo is coupled with superb
UMBRIAN food. Eggplant is transformed into an elegant custard with black truffles
Fodor's Choice in the *sformatino di melenzane con vellutata al tartuffo nero.* Pastas,
★ like *ombrichelli al pesto umbro,* are traditional, but perhaps with a

7

new twist like fresh coriander leaves instead of the usual basil. Lamb roasted in a crust of bread is delicately seasoned with a tomato cream sauce. The wine cellar includes some rare vintages. ⊠ *Piazza Duomo 8* ☎ *0763/341903* ⊗ *Closed Wed.*

¢ ✕ **Le Grotte del Funaro.** If you can't do the official hour-long tour of Underground Orvieto, dine here instead, inside tufa caves under central Orvieto, where the two windows have splendid views of the hilly countryside during the day. The traditional Umbrian food is reliably good, with simple grilled meats and vegetables and pizzas. Oddly, the food is outclassed by an extensive wine list, with top local and Italian labels and quite a few rare vintages. ⊠ *Via Ripa Serancia 41* ☎ *0763/343276* ⌂ *Reservations essential* ⊗ *Closed 1 wk in July.*

UMBRIAN

¢ ✕ **Trattoria La Grotta.** The owner has been in this location for more than 20 years, and locals are still fond of him. He has attracted a steady American clientele without losing his touch with homemade pasta, perhaps with a duck or wild-boar sauce. Roast lamb, veal, and pork are all good, and the desserts are homemade. Franco knows the local wines well and has a carefully selected list, including some from smaller but excellent wineries, so ask about them. ⊠ *Via Luca Signorelli 5* ☎ *0763/341348* ⊗ *Closed Tues.*

UMBRIAN ★

WHERE TO STAY
For expanded hotel reviews, visit Fodors.com.

$$ 🏨 **Hotel Palazzo Piccolomini.** This hotel is often preferred by local winemakers and other professionals for its updated look with inviting lobby areas and a convenient location near the church of San Giovanni. **Pros:** peaceful atmosphere; efficient staff; good location. **Cons:** unattractive building; slightly overpriced. ⊠ *Piazza Ranieri 36* ☎ *0763/341743* ⊕ *www.hotelpiccolomini.it* ⤢ *28 rooms, 3 suites* ⌂ *In-room: Internet. In-hotel: bar, parking* ⦿ *Breakfast.*

NARNI

13 km (8 miles) southwest of Terni, 46 km (29 miles) southeast of Orvieto.

Once a bustling and important town at a major crossroads on the Via Flaminia, Narni is now a quiet backwater with only the occasional tourist invading its hilltop streets. Modern development is kept out of sight in the new town of Narni Scalo, below. This means that you'll find the older neighborhood safely preserved behind, and in the case of Narni's subterranean Roman ruins, beneath, the town's sturdy walls.

GETTING HERE
From Perugia, take the E45 highway toward Rome. Merge onto the SS675, then take the exit to San Gemini and follow signs for Narni Scalo. The drive takes around 1½ hours. There are also regular trains from Perugia.

VISITOR INFORMATION
Terni tourism office. Stop here for information about Narni and a number of other smaller towns. ⊠ *Via Cassian Bon 4, Terni* ☎ *0744/423047* ⊕ *www.regioneumbria.eu.*

CLOSE UP

Hiking the Umbrian Hills

Magnificent scenery makes the heart of Italy excellent walking, hiking, and mountaineering country. In Umbria, the area around Spoleto is particularly good; several pleasant, easy, and well-signed trails begin at the far end of the Ponte alle Torri bridge over Monteluco. From Cannara, an easy half-hour walk leads to the fields of Pian d'Arca, the site of Saint Francis's sermon to the birds. For slightly more arduous walks, you can follow the saint's path, uphill from Assisi to the Eremo delle Carceri, and then continue along the trails that crisscross Monte Subasio. At 4,250 feet, the Subasio's treeless summit affords views of Assisi, Perugia, far-off Gubbio, and the distant mountain ranges of Abruzzo.

For even more challenging hiking, the northern reaches of the Valnerina are exceptional; the mountains around Norcia should not be missed. Throughout Umbria and the Marches, you'll find that most recognized walking and hiking trails are marked with the distinctive red-and-white blazes of the Club Alpino Italiano. Tourist offices are a good source for walking and climbing itineraries to suit all ages and levels of ability, while bookstores, *tabacchi* (tobacconists), and *edicole* (newsstands) often have maps and hiking guides that detail the best routes in their area. Depending on the length and location of your walk, it can be important that you have comfortable walking shoes or boots, appropriate attire, and plenty of water to drink.

7

EXPLORING

Roman Aqueduct. You can take a unique tour of Narni's underground Roman aqueduct—the only one open to the public in all of Italy—but it's not for the claustrophobic. Contact Narni Sotterranea at least 10 days ahead to book a visit. ✉ *Narni Sotterranea, Via San Bernardo 12* ☎ *0744/722292* ⊕ *www.narnisotterranea.it* 🎫 *€20* ☼ *Apr.–Oct., weekends by appointment.*

WHERE TO EAT

¢ ✕ **Il Cavallino.** Run by the third generation of the Bussetti family, this
UMBRIAN trattoria is south of Narni on the Via Flaminia. The most dependable menu selections are the grilled meats. Rabbit roasted with rosemary and sage and juicy grilled T-bone steaks are house favorites; in winter, phone ahead to request the wild pigeon. The wine list has a limited selection of dependable local varieties. ✉ *Via Flaminia Romana 220, 3 km (2 miles) south of center* ☎ *0744/761020* ☼ *Closed Tues. and Dec. 20–26.*

VALNERINA

Terni is 13 km (8 miles) northeast of Narni, 27 km (17 miles) southeast of Spoleto.

The Valnerina (the valley of the River Nera, to the east of Spoleto) is the most beautiful of central Italy's many well-kept secrets. The twisting roads that serve the rugged landscape are poor, but the drive is well worth the effort for its forgotten medieval villages and dramatic mountain scenery.

GETTING HERE

You can head into the area from Terni on the S209, or on the SP395bis north of Spoleto, which links the Via Flaminia (S3) with the middle reaches of the Nera Valley through a tunnel.

VISITOR INFORMATION

Terni tourism office ✉ *Via Cassian Bon 4, Terni* ☎ *0744/423047* ⊕ *www. regioneumbria.eu.*

EXPLORING

Cascata delle Marmore. The road east of Terni (SS Valnerina) leads 10 km (6 miles) to the Cascata delle Marmore (Waterfalls of Marmore), which, at 541 feet, are the highest in Europe. A canal was dug by the Romans in the 3rd century BC to prevent flooding in the nearby agricultural plains. Nowadays the waters are often diverted to provide hydroelectric power for Terni, reducing the roaring falls to an unimpressive trickle, so check with the information office at the falls (there's a timetable on their website) or with Terni's tourist office before heading here. On summer evenings, when the falls are in full spate, the cascading water is floodlighted to striking effect. The falls are usually at their most energetic at midday and at around 4 pm. This is a good place for hiking, except in December and January, when most trails may be closed. ✉ *SP79 10 km (6 miles) east of Terni* ☎ *0744/62982* ⊕ *www. marmorefalls.it* 🎟 *€8* ⊙ *May, weekends noon–1 and 4–5; June–Aug., daily 11am–10 pm; mid-Mar.–Apr. and Sept., weekends noon–9; Jan.– mid-Mar., weekends noon–4.*

Norcia. The birthplace of Saint Benedict, Norcia is best known for its Umbrian pork and truffles. Norcia exports truffles to France and hosts a truffle festival, the Sagra del Tartufo, every February. The surrounding mountains provide spectacular hiking. ✉ *67 km (42 miles) northeast of Terni.*

Piano Grande. A mountain plain 25 km (15 miles) to the northeast of the valley, Piano Grande is a hang glider's paradise and a wonderful place for a picnic or to fly a kite. It's also nationally famous for the quality of the lentils grown here, which are a traditional part of every Italian New Year's feast.

THE MARCHES

An excursion from Umbria into the Marches region allows you to see a part of Italy rarely visited by foreigners. Not as wealthy as Tuscany or Umbria, the Marches has a diverse landscape of mountains and beaches, and marvelous views. Like that of neighbors to the west, the patchwork of rolling hills of Le Marche (as it's known in Italian) is stitched with grapevines and olive trees, bearing luscious wine and olive oil.

Traveling here isn't as easy as in Umbria or Tuscany. Beyond the narrow coastal plain and away from major towns, the roads are steep and twisting. An efficient bus service connects the coastal town of Pesaro to Urbino. Train travel in the region is slow, however, and stops are limited—although you can reach Ascoli Piceno by rail.

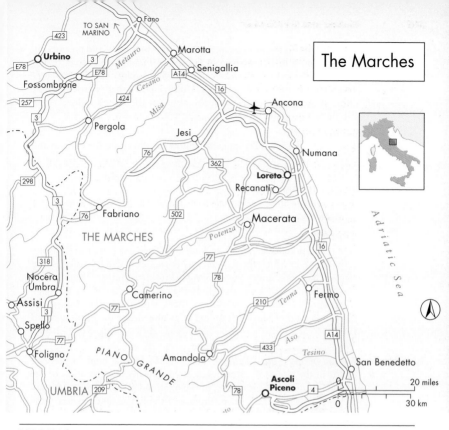

The Marches

URBINO

75 km (47 miles) north of Gubbio, 116 km (72 miles) northeast of Perugia, 230 km (143 miles) east of Florence.

Majestic Urbino, atop a steep hill with a skyline of towers and domes, is something of a surprise to come upon. Although quite remote, it was once a center of learning and culture almost without rival in Western Europe. The town looks much as it did in the glory days of the 15th century: a cluster of warm brick and pale stone buildings, all topped with russet-color tile roofs. The focal point is the immense and beautiful Palazzo Ducale.

The city is home to the small but prestigious Università di Urbino—one of the oldest in the world—and the streets are usually filled with students. Urbino is very much a college town, with the usual array of bookshops, bars, and coffeehouses. In summer the Italian student population is replaced by foreigners who come to study Italian language and arts at several prestigious private fine-arts academies.

Urbino's fame rests on the reputation of three of its native sons: Duke Federico da Montefeltro (1422–82), the enlightened warrior-patron who built the Palazzo Ducale; Raffaello Sanzio (1483–1520), or

Raphael, one of the most influential painters in history and an embodiment of the spirit of the Renaissance; and the architect Donato Bramante (1444–1514), who translated the philosophy of the Renaissance into buildings of grace and beauty. Unfortunately there's little work by either Bramante or Raphael in the city, but the duke's influence can still be felt strongly.

GETTING HERE

Take the SS3bis from Perugia, and follow the directions for Gubbio and Cesena. Exit at Umbertide and take the SS219, then the SS452, and at Calmazzo, the SS73bis to Urbino.

VISITOR INFORMATION

Urbino tourism office ⊠ *Piazza de Rinascimento 1* ☎ *0722/2613* ⊕ *www. comune.urbino.ps.it.*

EXPLORING

Casa Natale di Raffaello (*House of Raphael*). The Casa Natale di Raffaello is the house in which the painter was born and where he took his first steps in painting, under the direction of his artist father. There's some debate about the fresco of the Madonna here; some say it's by Raphael, whereas others attribute it to the father—with Raphael's mother and the young painter himself standing in as models for the Madonna and Child. ⊠ *Via Raffaello 57* ☎ *0722/320105* ▱ *€3* ☉ *Mon.–Sat. 9–2, Sun. 10–1.*

Fodor's Choice
★
Palazzo Ducale (*Ducal Palace*). The Palazzo Ducale holds a place of honor in the city. If the Renaissance was, ideally, a celebration of the nobility of man and his works, of the light and purity of the soul, then there's no place in Italy, the birthplace of the Renaissance, where these tenets are better illustrated. From the moment you enter the peaceful courtyard, you know you're in a place of grace and beauty, the harmony of the building reflecting the high ideals of the time. Today the palace houses the **Galleria Nazionale delle Marche** (National Museum of the Marches), with a superb collection of paintings, sculpture, and other objets d'art. Some works were originally the possessions of the Montefeltro family; others were brought here from churches and palaces throughout the region. Masterworks in the collection include Paolo Uccello's *Profanation of the Host,* Titian's *Resurrection* and *Last Supper,* and Piero della Francesca's *Madonna of Senigallia.* But the gallery's highlight is Piero's enigmatic work long known as *The Flagellation of Christ.* Much has been written about this painting, and few experts agree on its meaning. Legend had it that the figures in the foreground represent a murdered member of the Montefeltro family (the barefoot young man) and his two killers. However, Sir John Pope-Hennessy—the preeminent scholar of Italian Renaissance art—argues that they represent the arcane subject of the vision of Saint Lawrence. Academic debates notwithstanding, the experts agree that the work is one of the painter's masterpieces. Piero himself thought so: it's one of the few works he signed (on the lowest step supporting the throne). ⊠ *Piazza Duca Federico* ☎ *0722/322625* ⊕ *www.comune.urbino.ps.it* ▱ *€5* ☉ *Mon. 8:30–2, Tues.–Sun. 8:30–7:15; ticket office closes at 6.*

WHERE TO EAT AND STAY

For expanded hotel reviews, visit Fodors.com.

¢ ✕ **Angolo Divino.** At this *osteria* (informal restaurant) in the center of
ITALIAN Urbino, tradition reigns supreme: the menu is written in local dialect, flanked by Italian and English translations. Dishes range from
the deliciously simple *spaghetti col pane grattugiato* (spaghetti with
bread crumbs) to the temptingly rich *filetto al tartufo* (beef fillet with
truffles). ⊠ *Via S. Andrea 14* ☎ *0722/327559* ☉ *Closed Mon. and mid-
Oct.–mid-Nov. No dinner Sun.*

¢ ✕ **La Vecchia Fornarina.** Locals often crowd this small, two-room trattoria
ITALIAN near the Piazza della Repubblica. The specialty is meaty country fare,
such as *coniglio* (rabbit) and *vitello alle noci* (veal cooked with walnuts)
or *ai porcini* (with mushrooms). There's also a good selection of pasta
dishes. ⊠ *Via Mazzini 14* ☎ *0722/320007* ⌦ *Reservations essential.*

$$ 🛏 **Hotel Bonconte.** This classic hotel dating from the beginning of the
20th century is just inside the city walls and close to the Palazzo Ducale.
Pros: some nice views; away from the bustle. **Cons:** slightly overpriced;
service is sleepy. ⊠ *Via delle Mura 28* ☎ *0722/2463* ⊕ *www.viphotels.
it* ⌐ *23 rooms, 2 suites* ⌂ *In-room: a/c, Internet. In-hotel: bar* 🍴 *No
meals.*

LORETO

*31 km (19 miles) south of Ancona, 118 km (73 miles) southeast of
Urbino.*

There's a strong Renaissance feel about this hilltop town, which is home
to one of the most important religious sites in Europe, the Sanctuario
della Santa Casa (House of the Virgin Mary). Bramante and Sanso-
vino gave the church its Renaissance look, although many other artists
helped create its special atmosphere. Today the town revolves around
the religious calendar; if you can be here on December 10, you will wit-
ness the Feast of the Translation of the Holy House, when huge bonfires
are lighted to celebrate the miraculous arrival of the house in 1294.

GETTING HERE

If you're driving from Perugia, take the SS318 and then the SS76 high-
way to Fabriano and then on to Chiaravalle, where it merges with the
A14 autostrada. The drive takes around 2½ hours. Trains also go to
Loreto, but the station is about a mile outside the town center. Regular
buses leave from the station to the center.

VISITOR INFORMATION

Loreto tourism office ⊠ *Via Solari 3* ☎ *071/970276* ⊕ *www.turismo.marche.it.*

EXPLORING

★ **Basilica della Santa Casa.** Loreto is famous for one of the best-loved
shrines in the world, that of the **Santuario della Santa Casa** (House of
the Virgin Mary), within the Basilica della Santa Casa. Legend has it
that angels moved the house from Nazareth, where the Virgin Mary
was living at the time of the Annunciation, to this hilltop in 1295. The
reason for this sudden and divinely inspired move was that Nazareth
had fallen into the hands of Muslim invaders, whom the angelic hosts

viewed as unsuitable keepers of this important shrine. Excavations made at the behest of the Catholic Church have shown that the house did once stand elsewhere and was brought to the hilltop—by either crusaders or a family named Angeli—around the time the angels (*angeli*) are said to have done the job.

The house itself consists of three rough stone walls contained within an elaborate marble tabernacle. Built around this centerpiece is the giant basilica of the Holy House, which dominates the town. Millions of visitors come to the site every year (particularly at Easter and on the December 10 Feast of the Holy House), and the little town of Loreto can become uncomfortably crowded with pilgrims. Many great Italian architects, including Bramante, Antonio da Sangallo the Younger (1483–1546), Giuliano da Sangallo (circa 1445–1516), and Sansovino (1467–1529), contributed to the design of the basilica. It was begun in the Gothic style in 1468 and continued in Renaissance style through the late Renaissance. The bell tower is by Luigi Vanvitelli (1700–73). Inside the church are a great many mediocre 19th- and 20th-century paintings but also some fine works by Renaissance masters such as Luca Signorelli and Melozzo da Forlì (1438–94).

If you're a nervous air traveler, you can take comfort in the fact that the Holy Virgin of Loreto is the patron saint of air travelers and that Pope John Paul II composed a prayer for a safe flight—available here in a half dozen languages. ⊠ *Piazza della Madonna* ☎ *071/970104* ⊕ *www. santuarioloreto.it* ☉ *Apr.–Sept., daily 6 am–8 pm; Oct.–Mar., daily 6:15 am–7:30 pm. Santuario della Santa Casa closed daily 12:30–2:30.*

ASCOLI PICENO

88 km (55 miles) south of Loreto, 105 km (65 miles) south of Ancona.

Ascoli Piceno sits in a valley ringed by steep hills and cut by the Tronto River. In Roman times it was one of central Italy's best-known market towns, and today, with almost 60,000 residents, it's a major fruit and olive producer, making it one of the most important towns in the region. Despite growth during the Middle Ages and at other times, the streets in the town center continue to reflect the grid pattern of the ancient Roman city. You'll even find the word *rua*, from the Latin *ruga*, used for "street" instead of the Italian *via*. Now largely closed to traffic, the city center is great to explore on foot.

GETTING HERE

From Perugia take the SS75 to Foligno, then merge onto the SS3 to Norcia. From here take the SS4 to Ascoli Piceno. There are also trains, but the journey would be quite long, taking you from Perugia to Ancona before changing for Ascoli Piceno.

VISITOR INFORMATION

Ascoli Piceno tourism office ⊠ *Piazza Aringo 7* ☎ *0736/253045* ⊕ *www. comune.ascolipiceno.it.*

EXPLORING

★ **Piazza del Popolo.** The heart of the town is the majestic Piazza del Popolo, dominated by the Gothic church of **San Francesco** and the **Palazzo del Popolo,** a 13th-century town hall that contains a graceful Renaissance courtyard. The square itself functions as the living room of the entire city. At dusk each evening the piazza is packed with people strolling and exchanging news and gossip—the sweetly antiquated ritual called the *passeggiata,* performed all over the country.

WHERE TO EAT AND STAY

For expanded hotel reviews, visit Fodors.com.

¢ ✕ **Ristorante Tornasacco.** You won't find nouvelle cuisine here, at one
ITALIAN of Ascoli Piceno's oldest restaurants. The owners pride themselves on
★ meaty local specialties such as *olive ascolane* (olives stuffed with minced meat, breaded and deep-fried), *maccheroncini alla contadina* (home-made short pasta in a lamb, pork, and veal sauce), and *bistecca di toro* (bull steak). ⊠ *Piazza del Popolo 36* ☎ *0736/254151* ⊙ *Closed Fri., July 15–31, and Dec. 23–28.*

¢ ⊞ **Il Pennile.** Look for this modern, family-run hotel in a quiet resi-dential area outside the old city center, amid a grove of olive trees. **Pros:** peaceful; a good budget option. **Cons:** distance from town center; basic rooms. ⊠ *Via G. Spalvieri* ☎ *0736/41645* ⊕ *www.hotelpennile. it* ⇨ *33 rooms* ⚒ *In-room: a/c, Internet. In-hotel: bar, gym, business center* ⊙⊦ *Breakfast.*

7

UNDERSTANDING
FLORENCE AND TUSCANY

VOCABULARY

ITALIAN VOCABULARY

	ENGLISH	ITALIAN	PRONUNCIATION
BASICS			
	Yes/no	Sí/No	see/no
	Please	Per favore	pear fa-**vo**-ray
	Yes, please	Sí grazie	see **grah**-tsee-ay
	Thank you	Grazie	**grah**-tsee-ay
	You're welcome	Prego	**pray**-go
	Excuse me, sorry	Scusi	**skoo**-zee
	Sorry!	Mi dispiace!	mee dis-spee-**ah**-chay
	Good morning/ afternoon	Buongiorno	bwohn-**jor**-no
	Good evening	Buona sera	**bwoh**-na **say**-ra
	Good-bye	Arrivederci	a-ree-vah-**dare**-chee
	Mr. (Sir)	Signore	see-**nyo**-ray
	Mrs. (Ma'am)	Signora	see-**nyo**-ra
	Miss	Signorina	see-nyo-**ree**-na
	Pleased to meet you	Piacere	pee-ah-**chair**-ray
	How are you?	Come sta?	**ko**-may **stah**
	Very well, thanks	Bene, grazie	**ben**-ay **grah**-tsee-ay
	Hello (phone)	Pronto?	**proan**-to
NUMBERS			
	one	uno	**oo**-no
	two	due	**doo**-ay
	three	tre	Tray
	four	quattro	**kwah**-tro
	five	cinque	**cheen**-kway
	six	sei	Say
	seven	sette	**set**-ay
	eight	otto	**oh**-to
	nine	nove	**no**-vay
	ten	dieci	dee-**eh**-chee
	twenty	venti	**vain**-tee

ENGLISH	ITALIAN	PRONUNCIATION
thirty	trenta	**train**-ta
forty	quaranta	kwa-**rahn**-ta
fifty	cinquanta	cheen-**kwahn**-ta
sixty	sessanta	seh-**sahn**-ta
seventy	settanta	seh-**tahn**-ta
eighty	ottanta	o-**tahn**-ta
ninety	novanta	no-**vahn**-ta
one hundred	cento	**chen**-to
one thousand	mille	**mee**-lay
ten thousand	diecimila	dee-eh-chee-**mee**-la

USEFUL PHRASES

Do you speak English?	Parla inglese?	**par**-la een-**glay**-zay
I don't speak Italian	Non parlo italiano	non **par**-lo ee-tal-**yah**-no
I don't understand	Non capisco	non ka-**peess**-ko
Can you please repeat?	Può ripetere?	pwo ree-**pet**-ay-ray
Slowly!	Lentamente!	**len**-ta-men-tay
I don't know	Non lo so	non lo **so**
I'm American	Sono americano(a)	**so**-no a-may-ree-**kah**-no(a)
I'm British	Sono inglese	so-no een-**glay**-zay
What's your name?	Come si chiama?	**ko**-may see kee-**ah**-ma
My name is . . .	Mi chiamo . . .	mee kee-**ah**-mo
What time is it?	Che ore sono?	kay **o**-ray **so**-no
How?	Come?	**ko**-may
When?	Quando?	**kwan**-doe
Yesterday/today/tomorrow	Ieri/oggi/domani	**yer**-ee/**o**-jee/do-**mah**-nee
This morning/	Stamattina/Oggi	sta-ma-**tee**-na/**o**-jee
afternoon	pomeriggio	po-mer-**ee**-jo

ENGLISH	ITALIAN	PRONUNCIATION
Tonight	Stasera	sta-**ser**-a
What?	Che cosa?	kay **ko**-za
Why?	Perché?	pear-**kay**
Who?	Chi?	Kee
Where is . . .	Dov'è . . .	doe-**veh**
the bus stop?	la fermata dell'autobus?	la fer-**mah**-tadel ow-toe-**booss**
the train station?	la stazione?	la sta-tsee-**oh**-nay
the subway	la metropolitana?	la may-tro-po-lee-**tah**-na
the terminal?	il terminale?	eel ter-mee-**nah**-lay
the post office?	l'ufficio postale?	loo-**fee**-cho po-**stah**-lay
the bank?	la banca?	la **bahn**-ka
the . . . hotel?	l'hotel . . .?	lo-**tel**
the store?	il negozio?	eel nay-**go**-tsee-o
the cashier?	la cassa?	la **kah**-sa
the . . . museum?	il museo . . .?	eel moo-**zay**-o
the hospital?	l'ospedale?	lo-spay-**dah**-lay
the elevator?	l'ascensore?	la-shen-**so**-ray
the restrooms?	Dov'è il bagno?	do-**vay** eel **bahn**-yo
Here/there	Qui/là	kwee/la
Left/right	A sinistra/a destra	a see-**neess**-tra/a **des**-tra
Straight ahead	Avanti dritto	a-**vahn**-tee **dree**-to
Is it near/far?	È vicino/lontano?	ay vee-**chee**-no/ lon-**tah**-no
I'd like . . .	Vorrei . . .	vo-**ray**
a room	una camera	**oo**-na **kah**-may-ra
the key	la chiave	la kee-**ah**-vay
a newspaper	un giornale	oon jor-**nah**-lay
a stamp	un francobollo	oon frahn-ko-**bo**-lo
I'd like to buy . . .	Vorrei comprare . . .	vo-**ray** kom-**prah**-ray

ENGLISH	ITALIAN	PRONUNCIATION
How much is it?	Quanto costa?	kwahn-toe coast-a
It's expensive/ cheap	È caro/economico	ay car-o/ ay-ko-no-mee-ko
A little/a lot	Poco/tanto	po-ko/tahn-to
More/less	Più/meno	pee-oo/may-no
Enough/too (much)	Abbastanza/troppo	a-bas-tahn-sa/tro-po
I am sick	Sto male	sto mah-lay
Call a doctor	Chiama un dottore	kee-ah-mah oondoe-toe-ray
Help!	Aiuto!	a-yoo-toe
Stop!	Alt!	ahlt
Fire!	Al fuoco!	ahl fwo-ko
Caution/Look out!	Attenzione!	a-ten-syon-ay

DINING OUT

A bottle of . . .	Una bottiglia di . . .	oo-na bo-tee-lee-ahdee
A cup of . . .	Una tazza di . . .	oo-na tah-tsa dee
A glass of . . .	Un bicchiere di . . .	oon bee-key-air-ay dee
Bill/check	Il conto	eel cone-toe
Bread	Il pane	eel pah-nay
Breakfast	La prima colazione	la pree-ma ko-la-tsee-oh-nay
Cocktail/aperitif	L'aperitivo	la-pay-ree-tee-vo
Dinner	La cena	la chen-a
Fixed price menu	Menù a prezzo	may-noo a pret-so fee-so
Fork	La forchetta	la for-ket-a
I am diabetic	Ho il diabete	o eel dee-a-bay-tay
I am vegetarian	Sono vegetariano/a	so-no vay-jay-ta-ree-ah-no/a
I'd like . . .	Vorrei . . .	vo-ray
I'd like to order	Vorrei ordinare	vo-ray or-dee-nah-ray
Is service included?	Il servizio è incluso?	eel ser-vee-tzee-o ay een-kloo-zo

ENGLISH	ITALIAN	PRONUNCIATION
It's good/bad	È buono/cattivo	ay **bwo**-no/ka-**tee**-vo
It's hot/cold	È caldo/freddo	ay **kahl**-doe/**fred**-o
Knife	Il coltello	eel kol-**tel**-o
Lunch	Il pranzo	eel **prahnt**-so
Menu	Il menù	eel may-**noo**
Napkin	Il tovagliolo	eel toe-va-lee-**oh**-lo
Please give me . . .	Mi dia . . .	mee **dee**-a
Salt	Il sale	eel **sah**-lay
Spoon	Il cucchiaio	eel koo-kee-**ah**-yo
Sugar	Lo zucchero	lo **tsoo**-ker-o
Waiter/Waitress	Cameriere/ cameriera	ka-mare-**yer**-ay/ ka-mare-**yer**-a
Wine list	La lista dei vini	la **lee**-sta **day**-ee **vee**-nee

Travel Smart Florence and Tuscany

GETTING HERE AND AROUND

■ AIR TRAVEL

If you want to fly into Florence from the United States, you'll have to make connections in any number of major European cities (like Paris, Frankfurt, or London). Delta Airlines has a (seasonal) nonstop flight from New York's JFK to Pisa's Galileo Galilei. Florence is one hour away by train, and the train stops at the airport.

Airline Security Issues Transportation Security Administration ⊕ *www.tsa.gov.*

AIRPORTS

The major gateways to Italy include Rome's Aeroporto Leonardo da Vinci (airport code FCO), better known as Fiumicino, and Milan's Aeroporto Malpensa (MIL). Flights to Florence make connections at Fiumicino and Malpensa.

Florence is served by Aeroporto A. Vespucci (FLR), also called Peretola, and by Aeroporto Galileo Galilei (PSA), which is about a mile outside the center of Pisa and about one hour from Florence.

Perugia is served by Aeroporto S. Egidio (PEG), a small airport that receives connecting flights from Milan's Malpensa airport and London's Stansted airport.

Italy's airports have restaurants and snack bars and Internet or Wi-Fi access. Each airport has at least one nearby hotel—the city centers of Florence and Pisa are only 15 minutes away by taxi, so if you encounter a long delay, spend it in town.

Airports in Italy have been ramping up security measures, which include random baggage inspections and the presence of bomb-sniffing dogs.

Airport Information Aeroporto A. Vespucci (*FLR, usually called Peretola*). ☎ *055/30615* ⊕ *www.aeroporto.firenze.it.* **Aeroporto Galileo Galilei** (*PSA*). ☎ *050/849300* ⊕ *www. pisa-airport.com.* **Aeroporto Leonardo da Vinci** (*FCO, more commonly known as Fiumicino*). ☎ *06/65951* ⊕ *www.adr.it.* **Aeroporto**

Malpensa (*MIL*). ☎ *02/74852200* ⊕ *www.sea-aeroportimilano.it.* **Aeroporto S. Egidio** (*PEG*). ☎ *075/592141* ⊕ *www.airport.umbria.it.*

■**TIP→** Ask the local tourist board about hotel and local transportation packages that include tickets to major museum exhibits or other special events.

GROUND TRANSPORTATION

It takes about 20 minutes to get from **Aeroporto A. Vespucci** into Florence. Taxis are readily available, charging between €23 and €25, with a €1 surcharge for each bag and a €3 surcharge for nighttime trips. Outside the main terminal to the right is a bus stop where the SITA bus leaves every 30 minutes, making its final stop at the main Florence train station (Santa Maria Novella)—a ticket costs €5.

Taxis from **Aeroporto Galileo Galilei** to central Pisa cost about €15. Train service runs from the airport to the Central Pisa train station (€1.20); from there you can make connections to trains reaching all parts of Tuscany and Umbria. A train ride from Pisa to Florence takes just over an hour (€5.90). You can also reach Florence from the Pisa airport by taxi (€180) or by bus—the Terravision service runs from the Pisa airport to the train station in Florence (70 minutes; one-way €10, round-trip €16).

The train from **Aeroporto Leonardo da Vinci** stops at five stations in Rome and takes one hour (cost: €14) to get to the city. A taxi from the airport to the central train station costs about €60.

Metered taxis are available outside both Arrivals and Departures areas of **Aeroporto Malpensa.** The journey time to central Milan is around 50 minutes; the taxi fare is €75–€90. The Malpensa Shuttle departs every half hour from the train station at Milano Centrale; it's €7 one way and takes about an hour.

FLIGHTS

TO FLORENCE, TUSCANY, AND UMBRIA

Air travel to Italy is frequent and virtually problem-free. Sometimes, however, airport- or airline-related union strikes may cause delays. These delays are usually reported in advance. Alitalia, Italy's national flag carrier, has the most nonstop flights to Rome and Milan. Frequent flights are available from the United States aboard Lufthansa, Air France, United, US Airways, Delta, and Continental; these stop once in Europe before they or their code-sharing partners continue on to Florence or Pisa.

WITHIN ITALY

Alitalia—in addition to other major European airlines and smaller, privately run companies such as Ryanair, Meridiana, and Air One—has an extensive network of flights within Italy. Ask your domestic or Italian travel agent about discounts.

Information **Air One** ☎ 06/2222 in Rome, 800/650055 elsewhere in Italy ⊕ www. flyairone.it. **Alitalia** ☎ 800/223–5730 in U.S., 06/2222 in Rome, 800/650055 elsewhere in Italy ⊕ www.alitalia.it. **American Airlines** ☎ 800/433–7300 ⊕ www.aa.com. **Continental Airlines** ☎ 800/231–0856 for U.S reservations, 06/60053030 in Rome ⊕ www.continental. com. **Delta Airlines** ☎ 800/221–1212 for U.S. reservations ⊕ www.delta.com. **Meridiana** ☎ 0789/52600 in Italy ⊕ www.meridiana.it. **Ryanair** ☎ 44/871 246 002 England ⊕ www. ryanair.com. **United Airlines** ☎ 800/864–8331 for U.S. reservations, 800/538–2929 for international reservations ⊕ www.united.com. **US Airways** ☎ 800/428–4322 for U.S. and Canada reservations, ⊕ www.usairways.com.

■ BOAT AND FERRY TRAVEL

Ferries (*traghetti*) connect the mainland with the Tuscan islands, including Elba, Capraia, Pianosa, Giglio, and Giannutri. Hydrofoil (*aliscafo*) service goes to many destinations; it is generally twice as fast as the ferries—and double the price. All ferry service is considerably more frequent in summer.

Passenger and car ferries serve Elba. If you're traveling in July or August, try to make reservations at least a month in advance. Two ferry lines operate along the coast of Cinque Terre: Golfo Paradiso, which operates from June to September from Genoa and Camogli to the Cinque Terre villages of Monterosso al Mare and Vernazza; and the smaller, but more frequent, Golfo dei Poeti, which stops at each village (from Portovenere to Riomaggiore, except for Corniglia) four times a day.

The easiest place to find schedules and fare information for Tuscany ferry service is on each company's website. If you are already in the area, local tourist information offices, tourist agencies, and the ticket offices at the port will have printed schedules. Most ferry operators accept credit cards or cash, but no traveler's checks (the Toremar and Moby Lines ferry companies definitely do not accept traveler's checks).

Information **Golfo Paradiso** ☎ 0185/772091 ⊕ www.golfoparadiso.it. **Golfo dei Poeti** ☎ 0187/732987 ⊕ www. navigazionegolfodeipoeti.it. **Moby Lines** ☎ 199/303040 ⊕ www.mobylines.it. **Toremar** ☎ 199/117723 ⊕ www.toremar.it.

■ BUS TRAVEL

Italy's bus network is extensive, but because of its low cost and convenience train travel is usually a more attractive option. Bus schedules are often drawn up with commuters and students in mind, and service may be sporadic on weekends. That said, regional bus companies often provide the only means (not including car travel) of getting to out-of-the-way places. Even when this isn't the case, buses can be faster and more direct than local trains, so it's a good idea to compare bus and train schedules.

CLASSES

Both public and private buses offer only one class of service. Cleanliness and comfort levels are high on private buses, which have plenty of legroom and comfortable seats, but no toilets.

CUTTING COSTS

Public bus lines offer student and monthly passes. Private lines offer one-, three-, and six-month passes. Children under 3 feet in height ride free if they're traveling with an adult and don't require their own seat. Infant car seats are permitted on private bus lines. Bassinets are not made available by the bus companies.

DISCOUNT PASSES

None of the cities in Tuscany and Umbria are big enough to make the various discount bus pass schemes that appear and disappear with regularity worth the trouble. Most weeklong tourists to Florence, the largest city, will ride the city buses no more than four times at a cost of €1.20 per ticket. There is a 24-hour pass (€5) and a three-day pass (€12). A monthlong pass is available for €35. Students staying for a semester in Florence may wish to look into an ATAF Student Pass, a monthlong pass costing €23. Passes are available at the central bus station located at the side of the train station, and may be renewed at newsstands. See ⊕ *www.ataf. net* for information.

ATAF has an arrangement with Firenze City SightSeeing, a red open-top sightseeing bus in Florence. For €22 (€11 for children under 15) you can ride both it and all of the city buses for a 24-hour period, hopping on and off at your whim. Pisa also has a City SightSeeing hop-on/off tour bus which runs from April to November (€15 adults/€7 children).

In Perugia the public bus system is operated by APM, with the fare of €1 for a 70-minute ticket.

FARES AND SCHEDULES

You may purchase tickets for city buses with cash at newsstands or tobacco shops. The Florence public bus service ATAF allows customers to buy tickets, with a surcharge, in cash (€2), on the bus from the driver—exact fare is necessary, as no change is given. You must validate the bus ticket in the machine on the bus. For the private lines, tickets may be purchased with cash at the bus station or at travel agencies bearing the bus line's logo. Be sure to validate the ticket either at the bus station or on the bus as soon as you board. Bus schedules for private lines may be obtained online or at the bus station; city bus schedules for Florence (ATAF) are available online at ⊕ *www.ataf.net*.

PAYING

Credit cards and traveler's checks are generally not accepted for private-line bus tickets (some travel agencies may accept them), and public bus tickets purchased at newsstands and tobacco shops must be paid for in cash.

RESERVATIONS

Public bus lines do not issue reservations. For some private bus line direct routes (i.e., during commute hours) reservations are required.

Bus Information APM Perugia
☎ 075/506781 ⊕ www.umbriamobilita.it. **ATAF**
✉ Stazione Centrale di Santa Maria Novella
☎ 055/5650642 ⊕ www.ataf.net. **Firenze**
City SightSeeing ⊕ www.city-sightseeing.
com. **Lazzi Eurolines** ✉ Via Mercadante 2
☎ 055/363041 ⊕ www.lazzi.it. **SITA** ✉ Via
Santa Caterina da Siena 17/r ☎ 055/47821
⊕ www.sita-on-line.it.

▍ CAR TRAVEL

Tuscany and Umbria have an extensive network of *autostrade* (toll highways), complemented by equally well-maintained but free *superstrade* (expressways). The ticket you are issued upon entering an autostrada must be returned when you exit and pay the toll; on some shorter autostrade, mainly connecting highways, the toll is paid upon entering. Viacards, debit payment cards on sale at many autostrada locations (€25 at tollbooths), make paying tolls easier and faster by avoiding the hunt for change to pay the toll. Pass through the Viacard lane at tollbooths, slipping the card into the designated slot.

A *raccordo* is a ring road surrounding a city. *Strade regionale* and *strade provinciale* (regional and provincial highways, denoted by *S, SS, SR,* or *SP* numbers) are usually two-lane roads, as are all secondary roads; directions and turnoffs on toll roads and expressways are frequent and clear; secondary roads aren't always clearly marked. Be prepared for fast and impatient fellow drivers.

GASOLINE

Gas stations are located at frequent intervals along the main highways and autostrade. In case you run out of gas along the toll roads or the main free *superstrade,* emergency telephones are provided. To find the phone, look on the pavement at the shoulder of the highway where painted arrows and the term "SOS" point in the direction of the nearest phone.

Gas stations on autostrade are usually open 24 hours. Gas stations in towns and cities are usually located on the periphery; they're rarely found in the city center. These stations are generally open Monday through Saturday 7–7 with a break at lunchtime.

Many stations have automatic self-service pumps that accept only bills of €5, €10, €20, and €50 and don't give change; if you want a receipt (*ricevuta*), you have to push a button before starting the process. Full-service stations or those with an attendant take both cash and credit cards. It's not customary to tip the attendant when full service is provided.

As of this writing, gas (*benzina*) costs about €1.60 a liter. It's available in unleaded (*verde*) and superunleaded (*super*). Many rental cars in Italy take only diesel (*gasolio*), which costs less per liter; ask about the fuel type before you leave the rental office.

PARKING

Parking is at a premium in most towns and cities, but especially in the *centri storici* (historic centers), which are filled with narrow streets and restricted circulation zones. It's advisable to leave your car only in guarded parking areas. In Florence such indoor parking costs €23–€30 for 12–24 hours; outside attended parking costs about €10–€20. Parking in an area signposted "zona disco" (disk zone), usually found only in small towns, is allowed for limited periods (from 30 minutes to two hours or more—the limit is posted); if you don't have the cardboard disk (located in the glove box of your rental car) to show what time you parked, you can use a piece of paper. The *parcometro,* the Italian version of metered parking in which you put coins into a machine for a stamped ticket that you leave on the dashboard, has been introduced in most large towns and cities.

Parking regulations are strictly enforced both in the cities and small towns. Fines run as high as €70 (more for taking a space designated for people with disabilities), and towing (or tire clamps) is a possible penalty in Florence. Car-rental companies may use your credit card to be reimbursed for any fines you incur during your rental period. In Tuscany and Umbria vandalism and theft of cars are rare. Nevertheless, don't leave luggage or valuables in your car, especially in cities and large towns where thieves target rental cars.

ROAD CONDITIONS

Driving on the back roads of Tuscany and Umbria isn't difficult as long as you're on the alert for bicycles, scooters, and passing cars. In addition, street and road signs are often missing or placed in awkward spots, so a good map and patience are essential. Be aware that some maps may not use the *SR* or *SP* (*stradale regionale* and *stradale provinciale*) highway designations, which took the place of the old *SS* designations in 2004. They may use the old *SS* designation or no numbering at all. Autostrade are well maintained, as are most interregional highways. The condition of provincial (county) roads varies, but road maintenance at this level is generally good in Italy. In many small hill towns the streets are winding and extremely narrow; consider parking at the edge of town and exploring on foot.

Most autostrade have two lanes in both directions; the left lane is used only for passing. Italians drive fast and are impatient with those who don't, so tailgating is the norm here; the only way to avoid it is to get out of the way.

ROAD MAPS

Michelin and Touring Club Italia, which has shops in major Italian cities, both produce good road maps. The Michelin website (⊕ *www.viamichelin.com*) is a good source of driving instructions and maps. Do note their highly optimistic travel times. You can also get free street maps for most Tuscan and Umbrian towns at local information offices.

RULES OF THE ROAD

Driving is on the right. Regulations largely resemble those in the United States, except that the police have the power to levy on-the-spot fines. In some Italian towns the use of the horn is forbidden in certain, if not all, areas; a large sign, "zona di silenzio" (silent zone), indicates where this is the case. Speed limits are 130 kph (80 mph) on autostrade and 100 kph (60 mph) on state and provincial roads, unless otherwise marked. Enforcement of speed limits varies from region to region. If you are driving on superstrade, pay particular attention to the gray machines that appear periodically along the road. They snap photos if you're exceeding the speed limit, and the rental-car company will eventually catch up with you to pay the fine. Stiff penalties include high fines and suspension of driving privileges. Penalties for driving after drinking are heavy, too, including license suspension and the additional possibility of six months' imprisonment. The legal maximum blood-alcohol level is 0.05.

Right turns on red lights are forbidden. Headlights are required to be on day and night while driving on all roads (large or small) outside of municipalities. Seat belts are required for adults, and infant and children's car seats are compulsory for babies and toddlers.

CAR RENTAL

When you reserve a car, ask about cancellation penalties, taxes, drop-off charges (if you're planning to pick up the car in one city and leave it in another), and surcharges (for being under or over a certain age, for additional drivers, or for driving across state or country borders or beyond a specific distance from your point of rental). All these things can add substantially to your costs. Request child car seats and extras, such as GPS, when you book. Rates are sometimes—but not always—better if you book in advance or reserve through a rental agency's website. There are other reasons to book ahead, though: for popular destinations, during busy times of the year, or to ensure that you get certain types of cars (vans, SUVs, exotic sports cars).

■TIP➔ Make sure that a confirmed reservation guarantees you a car. Agencies sometimes overbook, particularly for busy weekends and holiday periods.

Florence, Tuscany, and Umbria have an intricate network of autostrade routes, good highways, and secondary roads, making renting a car a better but expensive alternative (because of high gas prices and freeway tolls) to public transportation. A rental car can be a good investment for carefree countryside rambles, offering time to explore more remote towns.

Having a car in major cities, however, often leads to parking and traffic headaches, plus the additional expense of garage and parking fees. In major cities, such as Florence, Siena, and Perugia, there are restricted zones for cars. These areas are monitored by cameras. If you drive to your hotel in the city center of these cities, inquire at the front desk of your hotel as to whether your rental car's license tag number must be submitted by the hotel to the police or traffic authority. Failure to do this may result in a large fine being levied on your car-rental company and passed on to you.

Major car-rental companies offer Ford-type cars (such as the Ford Fusion) and Fiats in various sizes and in good condition, all with air-conditioning. The local rental companies provide good service, and depending on the time of year, they may have greater availability than the well-known international companies. Because most Italian cars have standard transmissions, automatics are more expensive and must be reserved well in advance. Mileage is usually unlimited, although certain offers limit included mileage to 150 km (93 miles) a day, after which you must pay for additional miles.

Most major U.S. car-rental companies have offices or affiliates in Italy, but the rates are generally better if you make a reservation from abroad rather than from within Italy. Each company's rental prices are uniform throughout Italy, so you won't save money by, for example, picking up a vehicle from a city rental office rather than from an airport location.

In Italy a U.S. driver's license is acceptable to rent a car, but you might also want to consider getting an International Driver's Permit (IDP). Italy, by law at least, requires non-Europeans to carry an IDP along with their domestic license because the IDP states in Italian (and a dozen other languages) that your license is valid. In practice, it depends on the police officer who pulls you over whether you will be penalized for not carrying the IDP.

In Italy you must be 18 years old to drive a car. Most rental companies will not rent to someone under age 21; refuse to rent any car larger than an economy or sub-compact car to anyone under age 23; and further require customers under age 23 to pay by credit card. Additional drivers must be identified in the contract and must meet age requirements. There may be an additional daily fee for more than one driver. Upon rental, all companies require credit cards as a warranty; to rent

bigger cars (2,000 cc or more), you must often show two credit cards. There are no special restrictions on senior-citizen drivers. Book car seats, required for children under age three, in advance. The cost is generally about €36 for the duration of the rental.

Hiring a car with a driver can come in handy, particularly if you plan to do some wine tasting. Ask at your hotel for recommended drivers, or inquire at the local tourist-information office. Typically, drivers are paid by the day, and are usually rewarded with a tip of about 15% on completion of the journey.

CAR-RENTAL INSURANCE

Italy requires car-rental companies to include Collision Damage Waiver (CDW) coverage in quoted rates. Ask your rental company about other coverage when you reserve the car and/or pick it up.

Everyone who rents a car wonders whether the insurance that the rental companies offer is worth the expense. No one has a simple answer. It all depends on how much regular insurance you have, how comfortable you are with risk, and whether or not money is an issue.

▌ TRAIN TRAVEL

The fastest trains on the Ferrovie dello Stato (FS), the Italian State Railways, are the Eurostar trains, operating on several main lines, including Rome–Milan via Florence and Bologna. A new high-speed Eurostar called Alta Velocita runs between Milan and Naples, stopping in Florence. Seat reservations are mandatory on Eurostar trains. Some Eurostar trains (the ETR 460 trains) have little aisle and luggage space (though there is a space near the door where you can put large bags). To avoid having to squeeze through narrow aisles, board only at your car (look for the number on the reservation ticket and match it to the number on the exterior of the car; it's usually on the door). The next-fastest trains are the Intercity (IC) trains, for which you pay a supplemental fee and seat reservations may be required (which is always advisable, especially during high season). *Interregionale* trains usually make more stops and are a little slower. *Regionale* and *locale* trains are the slowest and the most unpleasant—most cars are covered in graffiti, dirty, crowded, and geared to commuters. When train workers go on strike (which is often), the regionali trains are the ones that stop running.

There is refreshment service on all long-distance trains, with mobile carts and a cafeteria or dining car. Tap water on trains is not drinkable.

Traveling overnight can be efficient but it's not inexpensive (compared to the cost of a hotel room), but never leave your belongings unattended (even for a minute) and make sure the door of your compartment is locked.

Train service between Milan, Florence, Rome, and Naples is frequent throughout the day. For the most part, trains stick to the schedule, although delays may occur during peak tourist season. Train strikes of various kinds are also frequent, so it's a good idea to make sure the train you want to take is in fact running.

The train from Rome to Florence takes 90 minutes; Rome to Perugia takes 2½ hours; Milan to Florence takes about 3 hours (it's another 2 hours by train from Florence to Perugia).

CLASSES

Many Italian trains have first and second classes, but regional trains frequently don't have first class. On interregional trains the higher first-class fare gets you little more than a clean doily on the headrest of your seat, but on long-distance trains you get wider seats, more legroom, and better ventilation and lighting. At peak travel times first-class train travel is worth the difference. One advantage of traveling first class is that the cars are almost always uncrowded—or, at the very least, less crowded than the second-class compartments. A first-class ticket, in Italian, is *prima classe*; second is *seconda*

classe. Remember always to make seat reservations in advance, for either class on Eurostar or Intercity (IC) trains.

CUTTING COSTS

If you're traveling only in Tuscany and Umbria, rail passes won't save you money. If Italy is your only destination in Europe, consider purchasing a Eurail Italy Pass, which allows a limited number of travel days within one month. Four days of travel cost €208 (first class) or €169 (second class); for further details, access Eurail's website. Note that you must purchase your Eurail Italy Pass before arriving in Italy.

Don't assume that a rail pass guarantees a seat on the trains you wish to ride; you need to reserve seats ahead even if you use a rail pass. There's a nominal fee (usually €5) for the reservation.

Information and Passes Eurail Italy Pass ☎ 800/6228600 ⊕ www.eurail.com/eurail-countries-italy. RailPass ☎ No phone ⊕ www. railpass.com.

FARES AND SCHEDULES

You can buy train tickets for nearby destinations (within a 200-km [124-mile] range) at newsstands or tobacconists (usually only those inside the station) and at ticket machines in stations, as well as at the ticket windows at the station or at travel agencies in town. Tickets are good for two months after the date of issue, but right before departure you must validate tickets in the yellow machines in the departure area. Once stamped, tickets are valid for 6 hours on distances of less than 200 km (124 miles) or for 24 hours on longer distances. If you wish to stop along the way and your final destination is more than 200 km [124 miles] away, you can stamp the ticket a second time before it expires so as to extend its validity to a maximum of 48 hours from the time it was first stamped. If you forget to stamp your ticket in the machine, or you didn't make it to the station in time to buy the ticket, you must seek out a conductor. Don't wait for the conductor to find out that you're without a valid ticket (unless the train is overcrowded and walking becomes impossible), as he or she might charge you a hefty fine. However, you often can avoid getting fined if you immediately write the time, date, and name of the departure station on the back of the ticket and sign it—essentially "validating" it and making it unusable for another trip.

Kilometric tickets—tickets priced according to kilometer amounts instead of specific destinations—are sold at newsstands and can be a great time-saver if the line at the official ticket booth is too long. Note, however, that you may have to round up amounts, and therefore pay more for your trip than if you purchased a destination-specific ticket. (For example, it's only 70 km [43 miles] from Florence to Pisa, but if the ticket amounts only come in 20-km [12-mile] denominations, you'd have to pay for an extra 10 km [6 miles].)

PAYING
You can pay for destination-specific train tickets in cash or with any major credit card such as American Express, Diners Club, MasterCard, and Visa. Newsstands only accept cash for kilometric tickets.

RESERVATIONS
Trains can be very crowded; it is always a good idea to make a reservation. In summer it's fairly common to stand for a good part of the journey, especially if you are coming off a cruise ship and heading to Florence. On the fast, direct Eurostar trains reservations are mandatory. To avoid long lines at station windows, buy tickets and make seat reservations up to two months in advance at travel agencies in Italy displaying the FS emblem or from a travel agent or website (⊕ *www.railpass. com*) before you leave home. Tickets can be purchased at the last minute, but seat reservations can be made only at agencies (or the train station) up until about three hours before the train departs from its city of origin. For trains that require a reservation (all Eurostar and some Intercity), you may be able to get a seat assignment

just before boarding the train; look for the conductor on the platform, but do this only as a last resort. If you plan on traveling around August 15, make sure to book your tickets well in advance. Italians make a mass exodus to the sea or mountains, and sardinelike conditions prevail in many cases.

Train Information Trenitalia ☎ *892021 in Italy (fee charged)* ⊕ *www.trenitalia.com.*

ESSENTIALS

■ ACCOMMODATIONS

Florence, Tuscany, and Umbria have a varied and abundant number of hotels, B&Bs, *agriturismi* (farm stays), and rental properties. In both the cities and the country you can find very sophisticated, luxurious palaces and villas as well as rustic farmhouses and small hotels.

Throughout the region you'll find historic properties, such as 600-year-old palazzi and former monasteries, which have been restored as luxurious hotels while retaining their original mystique. On the other hand, modern Italian design has swept the world, and many boutique hotels in historic buildings have favored chic modern interior design. Increasingly, the famed Tuscan and Umbrian wineries are creating rooms and apartments for three-day to weeklong stays. Tuscan and Umbrian establishments are generally run with pride and are very clean. Although Italy has a star system for rating hotels, it is based on amenities provided and is not a definitive indication of an establishment's quality.

Most hotels and other lodgings require credit-card details before they will confirm your reservation. If you don't feel comfortable emailing this information, ask if you can fax it (some places even prefer faxes). However you book, get confirmation in writing and have a copy of it handy when you check in.

Be sure you understand the hotel's cancellation policy. Some places allow you to cancel without any kind of penalty—even if you prepaid to secure a discounted rate—if you cancel at least 24 hours in advance. Others require you to cancel a week in advance or penalize you the cost of one night. Small inns and B&Bs are most likely to require you to cancel far in advance.

Some hotels allow children under a certain age to stay in their parents' room at no extra charge, but others charge for them as extra adults; find out the cutoff age for discounts.

APARTMENT AND HOUSE RENTALS

Italy gave birth to the Slow Food movement, and it appears to be at the start of the Slow Travel phenomenon also. More and more, travelers are turning away from the three-countries-in-two-weeks style of touring and choosing to spend a week in one city or a month in the countryside.

Often the most economical way to spend time in one place is to rent an apartment, a farmhouse, or a villa, even if you're traveling alone or with one other person.

These are readily available in Tuscany and Umbria. Most are owned by individuals and managed by rental agents who advertise available properties on the Internet. Many properties are represented by more than one rental agent and thus the same property is frequently renamed ("Chianti Bella Vista" and "Tuscan Sun Home" and "Casa Toscana Sole" are all names of the same farmhouse) on various online rental sites. The rental agent may meet you at the property for the initial check-in, or the owner may be present, with the rental agent only handling the online reservation and financial arrangements.

Things to inquire about when renting an apartment in a city or town include: the type of neighborhood (ask about street noise, safety, and general ambience), the availability of an elevator or the number of stairs you'll have to climb, the available furnishings (including pots and pans and linens), where the nearest grocery store is, and the cost of utilities (included in the rental cost or not?). Inquiries about countryside properties should include all of that information plus an idea of how isolated the property is—do you have to drive for 45 minutes to reach the nearest town?

BED-AND-BREAKFASTS

You can find cozy B&Bs in Florence, Perugia, Assisi, and Siena, as well as in more rural areas. In towns and villages B&Bs tend to be personal, homey, simple, and clean. In the Tuscan countryside you can find private villas that offer B&B accommodations; many are very upscale.

Reservation Services Bed & Breakfast. com ☎ *512/322-2710 or 800/462-2632* ⊕ *www.bedandbreakfast.com.* **BnB Finder.com** ☎ *888/469-6663* ⊕ *www.bnbfinder.com.*

CONVENTS AND MONASTERIES

Throughout Tuscany and Umbria tourists looking for lodging at a reasonable price seek out convents, monasteries, and religious houses. Religious orders usually charge €30–€60 per person per night for rooms that are clean, comfortable, and convenient. Most have private bathrooms; spacious lounge areas and secluded gardens or terraces are standard features. A Continental breakfast ordinarily comes with the room. Sometimes, for an extra fee, family-style lunches and dinners are available.

Be aware of three issues when considering a convent or monastery stay: most have a curfew of 11 pm or midnight; you need to book in advance, because they fill up quickly; and your best means of booking is usually email or fax—the person answering the phone may not speak English. For a list of convents in most cities in Tuscany and Umbria, go to ⊕ *www. hospites.it.*

Religious Guest Houses in Florence Casa Santo Nome di Gesù ⊠ *Piazza del Carmine 21* ☎ *055/213856 or 055/281835* ⊕ *www.fmmfirenze.it.* **Istituto Gould/ Foresteria Valdese di Firenze** ⊠ *Via dei Serragli 49* ☎ *055/212576 or 055/280274* ✉ *foresteriafirenze@diaconiavaldese.org* ⊕ *www.istitutogould.it/foresteria.* **Istituto Oblate Dell'Assunzione** ⊠ *Borgo Pitti 15* ☎ *055/2480582 or 055/2346291* ✉ *info@ fmmfirenze.it.*

Religious Guest Houses in Assisi Albergo Ancajani ⊠ *Via Ancajani 16* ☎ *075/815128 or 075/815129* ✉ *albergoancajani@libero. it* ⊕ *www.albergoassisi.it.* **St. Anthony Guest House** ⊠ *Via Galeazzo Alessi 10* ☎ *075/ 812542 or 075/813723* ✉ *atoneassisi@ tiscali.it.*

FARM HOLIDAYS AND AGRITOURISM

Rural accommodations in the *agriturismo* (agricultural tourism) category are increasingly popular with both Italians and visitors—you stay on a working farm or vineyard.

Accommodations vary in size and range from luxury apartments, farmhouses, and villas to very basic facilities. Agriturist has compiled *Agriturismo*, which is available only in Italian but includes more than 1,600 farms in Italy; pictures and the use of international symbols to describe facilities make the guide a good tool. Local APT tourist offices also have information.

Agencies Agriturismo.net ⊕ *www. agriturismo.net.* **Agriturist** ⊕ *www.agriturist. it.* **Italy Tourist: Farm Holiday** ⊕ *www. italytourist.it.*

HOME EXCHANGES

With a direct home exchange you stay in someone else's home while they stay in yours. Some outfits also deal with vacation homes, so you're not actually staying in someone's full-time residence, just their vacant weekend place.

Exchange Clubs Home Exchange.com. This agency charges $99.95 for a one-year online listing. ☎ *800/877-8723* ⊕ *www. homeexchange.com.* **HomeLink International.** Web-only membership costs $115 per year; $175 includes web access and two catalogs. ☎ *800/638-3841* ⊕ *www.homelink.org.*

HOSTELS

Hostels in Florence, Tuscany, and Umbria run the gamut from low-end hotels to beautiful villas. In Florence the campground and hostel near Piazzale Michelangelo has a better view of the city than any luxury hotel in town (though there's also a really nice hostel in the centro storico). Hostels in these two regions are not just for student travelers; they are good budget accommodations for couples and families.

Hostels In Italy Hostelling International—USA ☎ 301/495–1240 national office, check online for phone number of office in your state ⊕ www.hiusa.org. **Hostel World** ⊕ www.hostelworld.com.

HOTELS

Italian hotels are awarded stars (one to five) based on their facilities and services. Keep in mind, however, that these are general indications and that a charming three-star might make for a better stay than a more expensive four-star. In major cities room rates are on a par with other European capitals: five- and four-star rates can be downright extravagant. In those categories, ask for one of the better rooms, because the less desirable rooms—and there usually are some—don't give you what you're paying for. Even in some five- and four-star hotels, rooms may be very small by U.S. standards, and equally small bathrooms usually have showers rather than bathtubs. Hotels with three or more stars always have bathrooms in all rooms.

In all hotels a rate card inside the door of your room or inside the closet door tells you the maximum rate that can be legally charged for that particular room (rates in the same hotel may vary according to the location and type of room). On this card, breakfast and any other options must be listed separately. Any discrepancy between the basic room rate and that charged on your bill is cause for complaint to the manager and to the police.

High season in Italy, when rooms are at a premium, generally runs from Easter through the beginning of November, and then for two weeks at Christmastime. During low season and whenever a hotel isn't full, it's often possible to negotiate a discounted rate. Major cities have no official off-season as far as hotel rates go, but some hotels do offer substantial discounts during the slower parts of the year and on weekends. Always inquire about special rates. Major cities have hotel-reservation service booths in train stations. It's always a good idea to confirm your reservation, dates, and rate by fax or email.

Although by law breakfast is supposed to be optional, most hotels quote room rates including breakfast. When you book a room, specifically ask whether the rate includes breakfast (*colazione*). You are under no obligation to take breakfast at your hotel, but in practice most hotels expect you to do so. The trick is to "offer" guests "complimentary" breakfast and have its cost built into the rate. However, it's encouraging to note that many of the hotels we recommend provide generous buffet breakfasts instead of simple, even skimpy, "Continental" breakfasts. Remember, if the latter is the case, you can eat for less at the nearest coffee bar.

Hotels in the $$ and $ categories may charge extra for air-conditioning. In older hotels the quality of the rooms may be very uneven; if you don't like the room you're given, request another. This applies to noise, too. Front rooms may be larger or have a view, but they also may have a lot of street noise. If you're a light sleeper, request a quiet room when making reservations. Rooms in lodgings listed in this guide have a shower and/or bath, unless noted otherwise. (All hotels listed have private bath unless otherwise noted.) Remember to specify whether you care to have a bath or shower—not all rooms have both.

▮ COMMUNICATIONS

INTERNET

Getting online in Italian cities isn't difficult: public Internet stations and Internet cafés, some open 24 hours, are common, and many bars and cafés have Wi-Fi available (sometimes for a small fee). Prices differ from place to place, so check out a few spots to find the best deal. This

LOCAL DO'S AND TABOOS

Social behavior in Tuscany and Umbria tends to be more conservative and formal than in other parts of Italy.

GREETINGS

Upon meeting and leave-taking, both friends and strangers wish each other good day or good evening (*buon giorno, buona sera*); *ciao* isn't used between strangers. "Please" is *per favore*, "thank you" is *grazie*, and "you're welcome" is *prego*. When meeting, strangers will shake hands. Italians who are friends greet each other with a kiss, usually first on the left cheek, and then on the right.

SIGHTSEEING

Italy is full of churches, and many of them contain significant works of art. They are places of worship, so care should be taken to dress appropriately. Shorts, miniskirts, tank tops, spaghetti straps, and sleeveless garments are taboo in most churches; short shorts are inappropriate anywhere. When touring churches—especially in summer when it's hot and no sleeves are desirable—carry a sweater, large scarf, or a light shawl to wrap around your shoulders before entering the church, and always remember to take off your hat. Do not enter a church with food, and don't drink from your water bottle while inside. If a service is in progress, don't go inside. And if you have a cell phone, turn it off before entering.

OUT ON THE TOWN

Table manners are formal; rarely do Italians share food from their plates. Flowers, dessert (in the form of a cake or torte from a pasticceria), or a bottle of wine are appropriate hostess gifts when invited to dinner.

Wiping your bowl clean with a small piece of bread is considered a sign of appreciation, not bad manners. Spaghetti should be eaten with a fork only, although a little help from a spoon won't horrify locals the way cutting spaghetti into little pieces might. Order your espresso (Italians don't usually drink cappuccino after breakfast) after dessert, not with it. Don't ask for a doggy bag unless you really have a dog.

DOING BUSINESS

Showing up on time for business appointments is the norm and expected in Italy. There are more business lunches than business dinners, and even business lunches aren't common, as Italians view mealtimes as periods of pleasure and relaxation. Business cards are used throughout Italy, and business suits are the norm for both men and women.

LANGUAGE

One of the best ways to avoid being an Ugly American is to learn a little of the local language. You need not strive for fluency; even just mastering a few basic words and terms is bound to make chatting with the locals more rewarding.

In the main tourist cities, such as Florence, most hotels have English speakers at their reception desks, and you can always find someone who speaks at least a little English otherwise. Remember that the Italian language is pronounced exactly as it is written. You may run into a language barrier in the countryside, but a phrase book and the use of pantomime and expressive gestures will go a long way. Try to master a few phrases for daily use and familiarize yourself with the terms you'll need for deciphering signs, menus, and museum labels.

A phrase book and language-tape set can help get you started. *Fodor's Italian for Travelers* (available at bookstores everywhere) provides a terrific starting point.

isn't always readily apparent: a place might appear to have higher rates, but if it belongs to a chain, it might not charge you an initial flat fee again when you visit a branch in another city.

Some hotels have in-room modem lines, but, as with phones, using the hotel's line is relatively expensive. Always check modem rates before plugging in.

You may need an adapter for your computer for the European-style plugs. If you are traveling with a laptop, carry a spare battery and an adapter. Never plug your computer into any socket before asking about surge protection. IBM sells a tiny modem tester that plugs into a telephone jack to check whether the line is safe to use.

Contacts Cybercafes. This website lists more than 4,000 Internet cafés worldwide. ⊕ *www.cybercafes.com.*

PHONES

Telephone service in Tuscany and Umbria is efficient. Cell phones, however, are widely used by Italians, resulting in a decrease in the number of public pay phones. Calling from a hotel landline phone is almost always the most expensive option; hotels usually add huge surcharges to all calls, particularly international ones.

The country code for Italy is 39. Area codes for major cities are as follows: Florence, 055; Perugia, 075; Pisa, 050; Siena, 0577. For example, a call from New York City to Florence would be dialed as 011 + 39 + 055 + phone number.

When dialing an Italian number from abroad, do not drop the initial 0 from the local area code.

CALLING WITHIN ITALY

For all calls within Italy—local and long distance—you must dial the regional area code (*prefisso*), which begins with a 0, such as 055 for Florence. If you are calling from a public phone, you must deposit a coin or use a calling card to get a dial tone. Some of the newer public phones don't accept coins. Local calling cards are available at newsstands or tobacco shops. Rates on landline phones vary during the day; it's less expensive to call within Italy during nonworking hours (before 9 am and after 7 or 8 pm).

CALLING OUTSIDE ITALY

The country code for the United States is 1, so from most phones in Italy you will dial 001 + area code + phone number. To place international telephone calls and collect calls via an English-speaking operator-assisted service, dial 170 (available only on landline phones) or an international carrier's long-distance access code, or use an international prepaid calling card.

You can also place a direct call to the United States using your U.S. phone calling-card number, through which you automatically reach a U.S. operator and thereby avoid all language difficulties.

Access Codes AT&T USADirect ☎ *800/172–444.* **MCI Worldwide Access** ☎ *800/905–825.* **Sprint Express** ☎ *800/172–405.*

CALLING CARDS

Prepaid *carte telefoniche* (calling cards) for intra-country calls are prevalent throughout Italy and more convenient than coins. You buy the card (values vary) at post offices, tobacconists, most newsstands, and bars. Tear off the corner of the card and insert it in the slot on a public pay phone. When you dial, its value appears in the window. After you hang up, the card is returned so you can use it until its value runs out.

International phone cards offer good value, allowing you to call Europe and the United States for less than 20 European cents a minute during peak hours. Follow the directions on the back of the card. These will include revealing the identification number on the card and calling an "800" number or other free number. If you wish to use this card at a public phone, you may need a local calling card (*see above*) to activate the public phone. If you are using your hotel phone, the call should be charged as any other "800" number call.

MOBILE PHONES

If you have a multiband phone (some countries use different frequencies from those used in the United States) and your service provider uses the world-standard GSM network (as do T-Mobile, AT&T, and Verizon), you can probably use your phone abroad. Roaming fees can be steep, however: 99¢ a minute is considered reasonable. And overseas you normally pay the toll charges for incoming calls. It's almost always cheaper to send a text message than to make a call, since text messages have a very low set fee (often less than 5¢).

If you just want to make local calls, consider buying a new SIM card (note that your provider may have to unlock your phone for you to use a different SIM card) and a prepaid service plan in the destination. You'll then have a local number and can make local calls at local rates. If your trip is extensive, you could also simply buy a new cell phone in your destination, as the initial cost will be offset over time.

■TIP→ If you travel internationally frequently, save one of your old mobile phones or buy a cheap one on the Internet; ask your cell-phone company to unlock it for you, and take it with you as a travel phone, buying a new SIM card with pay-as-you-go service in each destination.

The cost of cell phones is dropping, and you can purchase a cell phone with a prepaid calling card (no monthly service plan) in Italy for around €35. Inexpensive cell phones are dual band and will not allow you to call the United States, but using an international calling card and the cell phone solves that problem in a very inexpensive manner. Most medium to large towns in Tuscany and Umbria (Florence, Siena, Lucca, Pisa, and Perugia) have stores dedicated to selling cell phones. You will need to present your passport to purchase the SIM card that goes with the phone.

Rental cell phones are available in cities and large towns. Most rental contracts require a refundable deposit that covers the cost of the cell phone (€75–€125) and then the purchase of a monthly service plan that is automatically charged to your credit card. Frequently, rental cell phones will be triple band and allow you to call the United States. Be sure to check the rate schedule before you rent a cell phone and commence calling to prevent a nasty surprise when you receive your credit-card bill two or three months later.

■TIP→ Beware of cell-phone (and PDA) thieves. Keep your phone or PDA in a secure pocket or purse. Do not lay it on the bar when you stop for an espresso. Do not zip it into the outside pocket of your backpack in crowded cities. Do not leave it in your hotel room. If you are using a phone with a monthly service plan, notify your provider immediately if it is lost or stolen.

Contacts **Cellular Abroad.** This company rents and sells GMS phones and sells SIM cards that work in many countries. ☎ 800/287–5072 ⊕ www.cellularabroad.com. **Mobal.** Rent mobiles and buy GSM phones (starting at $49) that will operate in 140 countries from Mobal. Per-call rates vary throughout the world. ⊕ www.mobalrental.com. **Planet Fone.** Cell phones are available for rent through Planet Fone, but the per-minute rates are expensive. ☎ 888/988–4777 ⊕ www.planetfone.com.

▮ CUSTOMS AND DUTIES

Travelers from the United States should experience little difficulty clearing customs at any airports in Italy.

Of goods obtained anywhere outside the EU, the allowances are (1) 200 cigarettes or 100 cigarillos (under 3 grams) or 50 cigars or 250 grams of tobacco; (2) 2 liters of still table wine or 1 liter of spirits over 22% volume; and (3) 50 milliliters of perfume and 250 milliliters of toilet water.

Of goods obtained (duty and tax paid) within another EU country, the allowances are (1) 800 cigarettes or 400 cigarillos (under 3 grams) or 200 cigars or 1 kilogram of tobacco; and (2) 90 liters of still table wine or 10 liters of spirits over 22% volume or 20 liters of spirits under 22% volume or 110 liters of beer.

There is no quarantine period in Italy, so if you want to travel with Fido, it's possible. Contact your nearest Italian consulate to find out what paperwork is needed for entry into Italy; generally, it is a certificate noting that the animal is healthy and up-do-date on its vaccinations. Keep in mind, however, that the United States has some stringent laws about reentry: pets must be free of all diseases, especially those communicable to humans, and they must be vaccinated against rabies at least 30 days before returning. This means that if you are in Italy for a short-term stay, you must find a veterinarian or have your pet vaccinated before departure. (This law does not apply to puppies less than three months old.) Pets should arrive at the point of entry with a statement, in English, attesting to this fact.

Information in Italy Dogana Sezione Viaggiatori ⊕ www.agenziadogane.it. **Ministero delle Finanze, Direzione Centrale dei Servizi Doganali, Divisione I** ⊕ www.finanze.it.

U.S. Information U.S. Customs and Border Protection ⊕ www.cbp.gov.

▌ EATING OUT

The restaurants we list are the cream of the crop in each price category.

Not too long ago, ristoranti tended to be more elegant and expensive than trattorie and osterie, which serve traditional, home-style fare in an atmosphere to match. But the distinction has blurred considerably, and an osteria in the center of town might be far fancier (and pricier) than a ristorante across the street. Although most restaurants in Tuscany and Umbria serve traditional local cuisine, you can find Asian and Middle Eastern alternatives in Florence, Perugia, and other cities (though they are often pale imitations of what you would get in other American and European cities). Menus are posted outside most restaurants (in English in tourist areas); if not, you might step inside and ask to take a look at the menu (but don't ask for a table unless you intend to stay).

Italians take their food as it is listed on the menu, seldom, if ever, making special requests such as "dressing on the side" or "hold the olive oil." If you have special dietary needs, however, make them known; they can usually be accommodated. Although mineral water makes its way to almost every table, you can order a carafe of tap water (*acqua di rubinetto* or *acqua semplice*) instead, but keep in mind that such behavior is sneered at by Italians, who deem it *brutta figura* (bad form).

The handiest and least expensive places for a quick snack between sights are bars, cafés, and pizza *al taglio* (by the slice) spots. Bars in Italy are primarily places to get a coffee and a bite to eat, rather than drinking establishments. Most have a selection of *panini* (sandwiches, often warmed up on the griddle) and sometimes you'll find the very Roman *tramezzini* (sandwiches served on triangles of white bread). In larger cities, bars also serve prepared salads, fruit salads, and cold and hot pasta dishes. Most bars offer beer and a variety of alcohol, as well as wines by the glass. A café (*caffè* in Italian) is like a bar but usually with more tables. If you place your order at the counter, ask if you can sit down: some places charge extra for table service. In self-service bars and caffè, cleaning up your table before you leave is considered good manners. Note that in some places you have to pay before you place an order and then show your *scontrino* (receipt) when you move to the counter. Pizza al taglio shops are easy to negotiate. They sell pizza by weight: just point out which kind you want and how much. Very few pizza al taglio shops have seats.

MEALS AND MEALTIMES

The Italian breakfast (*la colazione*) is typically a cappuccino and a sweet roll (usually a brioche) served at the local bar. For a larger breakfast, consider dining rooms of large hotels. For lunch Italians may eat a couple of small panini while standing at a local bar or self-serve caffè. A more substantial lunch (*il pranzo*) consists of one or two courses at a trattoria. Dinner (*la cena*) out is likely to be two or three courses at a restaurant or trattoria, or pizza and beer at a pizzeria.

Menus separate dishes into *antipasti* (starters), *primi piatti* (first courses), *secondi piatti* (second courses), *contorni* (side dishes), and *dolci* (desserts). At ristoranti, trattorie, and osterie, you're generally expected to order at least a two-course meal: a *primo* and a *secondo*; an antipasto followed by either primo or secondo; or, perhaps, a secondo and a *dolce*. Italian cuisine is still largely regional, so ask about the local specialties.

In an *enoteca* (wine bar) or pizzeria it's not inappropriate to order one dish. An enoteca menu is often limited to a selection of cheeses, cured meats, salads, and desserts; if there's a kitchen, you may also find soups, pasta, meat, and fish. Most pizzerias don't offer just pizza, but also a variety of antipasti, salads, and simple pasta dishes, as well as dolce. Pizza at a caffè is to be avoided—it's usually frozen and reheated in a microwave oven.

Breakfast is usually served 7–10:30, lunch 12:30–2, and dinner 7:30–9:30 or 10. Enoteche are open in the morning and late afternoon for a snack at the counter. Most pizzerias open at 7:30 pm and close around midnight or 1 am, or later in summer and on weekends. Most bars and caffès are open 7 am–8 or 9 pm; a few stay open until midnight or so.

Unless otherwise noted, the restaurants listed in this guide are open daily for lunch and dinner.

PAYING

Major credit cards are widely accepted in Italian eating establishments, though cash is usually the preferred, and sometimes the only means of payment—especially in small towns and rural areas. (More restaurants take Visa and MasterCard than American Express.) When you've finished your meal and are ready to go, ask for the check (*il conto*); unless it's well past closing time, no waiter will put a bill on your table until you've requested it.

Prices for goods and services in Italy include tax. The price of fish dishes is often given by weight (before cooking), so the price you see on the menu is for 100 grams of fish, not for the whole dish. (An average fish portion is about 350 grams.) Tuscan *bistecca fiorentina* is also often priced by weight (€4 for 100 grams or €40 for one kilogram [2.2 pounds]).

Most restaurants charge a separate "cover" charge per person, usually listed on the menu as *pane e coperto* (or just *coperto*); this charge is not for the service. It should be a modest charge (€1–€2.50 per person), except at the most expensive restaurants. A charge for service (*servizio*) may be included either as part of the menu prices or the total bill; if it is, tipping is unnecessary. It is customary to leave a small tip (€1–€5) in appreciation of good service when the service charge is not included in the bill. Tips are always given in cash. Whenever in doubt, ask about the servizio and pane e coperto policies upon ordering to avoid unpleasant discussions about payment later. At some places in Florence, if you pay by credit card the restaurant will automatically slap a 15% tip onto your bill, which means you should leave absolutely nothing on the table.

When you leave a dining establishment, take your meal bill or receipt with you; although not a common experience, the Italian finance (tax) police can approach you within 100 yards of the establishment at which you've eaten and ask for a receipt. If you don't have one, they can fine you and will fine the business owner for not providing the receipt. The measure is intended to prevent tax evasion; it's not necessary to show receipts when leaving Italy.

⇨ *For guidelines on tipping, see Tipping below.*

RESERVATIONS AND DRESS

Reservations are always a good idea in restaurants and trattorie, especially on weekends and holidays. We mention them only when they're essential or not accepted. Book as far ahead as you can, and reconfirm as soon when you arrive in town. (Large parties should always call ahead to check the reservations policy; and should leave a 10% tip on the table if servizio is not included.)

Unless they're eating outdoors at a seaside resort and are perfectly tanned, Italian men never wear shorts or running shoes in a restaurant—no matter how humble—or in an enoteca. If you see people in shorts, you can be 100% sure that they are for-eigners. Shorts are acceptable in pizzerias and caffès. The same "rules" apply to women's casual shorts, running shoes, plastic sandals, and clogs.

We mention dress only when men are required to wear a jacket and tie.

WINES, BEER, AND SPIRITS

The grape has been cultivated in Italy since the time of the Etruscans, and Italians justifiably take pride in their local vintages. Though almost every region produces good-quality wine, Tuscany is one of the most renowned areas. Wine in Italy is considerably less expensive than almost anywhere else, so it's often affordable to order a bottle of wine at a restaurant rather than to stick with the house wine (which, nevertheless, is probably quite good). Many bars have their own *aperitivo della casa* (house aperitif); Italians are imaginative with their mixed drinks, so you may want to try one.

You may purchase beer, wine, and spirits in any bar, grocery store, or enoteca, any day of the week. Italian and German beers

are readily available, but they can be more expensive than wine.

There's no minimum drinking age in Italy. Italian children begin drinking wine mixed with water at mealtimes when they are teens (or thereabouts). Italians are seldom seen drunk in public, and public drinking, except in a bar or eating establishment, isn't considered acceptable behavior. Bars usually close by 9 pm; hotel and restaurant bars stay open until midnight. Brewpubs and discos serve until about 2 am.

▌ ELECTRICITY

The electrical current in Italy is 220 volts, 50 cycles alternating current (AC); wall outlets take Continental-type plugs, with two round prongs.

Consider making a small investment in a universal adapter, which has several types of plugs in one lightweight, compact unit. Most laptops and mobile phone chargers are dual voltage (i.e., they operate equally well on 110 and 220 volts), so require only an adapter. These days the same is true of small appliances such as hair dryers. Always check labels and manufacturer instructions to be sure. Don't use 110-volt outlets marked "for shavers only" for high-wattage appliances such as hair-dryers.

▌ EMERGENCIES

No matter where you are in Italy, dial 113 for all emergencies, or find somebody (your concierge, a passerby) who will call for you, as not all 113 operators speak English; the Italian word to use to draw people's attention in an emergency is *aiuto* (help; pronounced "ah-YOU-toh"). *Pronto soccorso* means first aid and the emergency room of a hospital, and when said to an operator, it will get you an *ambulanza* (ambulance). If you just need a doctor, you should ask for *un medico*; most hotels can refer you to a local doctor. Don't forget to ask the doctor for *una ricevuta* (an invoice) to show your insurance company in order to get a reimbursement. Other useful Italian words to use in an emergency are *al fuoco* (fire; pronounced "ahl fuh-WOE-co") and *al ladro* (follow the thief; pronounced "ahl LAH-droh").

Italy has a national police force (*carabinieri*) as well as local police (*polizia*). Both are armed and have the power to arrest and investigate crimes. Always report the loss of your passport to either the carabinieri or the police, as well as to your embassy. Local traffic officers are known as *vigili* (though their official name is *polizia municipale*)—they are responsible for, among other things, giving out parking tickets and clamping cars, so before you even consider parking the (illegal) Italian way, make sure you are at least able to spot their white (in summer) or black uniforms. Many are women. Should you find yourself involved in a minor car accident in town, you should contact the vigili. Many police stations have English-speaking staff to deal with travelers' problems. When reporting a crime, you'll be asked to fill out and sign a report form (*una denuncia*); keep a copy for your insurance company.

A countrywide toll-free number (112) is used to call the carabinieri in case of emergency.

United States Embassies U.S. Consulate ⊠ *Via Lungarno Vespucci 38* ☎ *055/266951.* **U.S. Embassy** ⊠ *Via Vittorio Veneto 121, Rome* ☎ *06/46741* ⊕ *www.usembassy.gov.*

General Emergency Contacts Carabinieri ☎ *112.* **Emergencies** ☎ *113.*

▌ HEALTH

The most common types of illnesses are caused by contaminated food and water. In Italy tap water is safe to drink, and eating out in Italy is perfectly safe. As in any part of the world, avoid fresh vegetables and fruits that you haven't washed or peeled yourself. If you have problems, mild cases of traveler's diarrhea may respond to Imodium (known generically as loperamide) or Pepto-Bismol. Be sure to drink plenty of fluids; if you can't keep fluids down, seek medical help immediately.

▌ HOURS OF OPERATION

Business hours vary from region to region in Italy. In larger cities, such as Florence, Pisa, Lucca, Siena, and Perugia, stores and other businesses will generally be open 10–7. Many stores close 1–3:30 for a midday break, especially in small towns. More than half of the stores close Sunday and national holidays. Many businesses stay closed Monday morning but open in the afternoon. In August, many stores, restaurants, and other businesses shut down for two to four weeks for the traditional summer holiday.

HOLIDAYS

National holidays include New Year's Day; Epiphany (January 6); Easter Sunday and Monday; Liberation Day (April 25); Labor Day or May Day (May 1); Assumption of Mary, also known as Ferragosto (August 15); All Saints' Day (November 1); Immaculate Conception (December 8); Christmas Day and Boxing Day (December 25 and 26).

The feast days of patron saints are observed locally. Many businesses and shops may be closed in Florence on June 24 (St. John the Baptist).

▌ MAIL

Allow from 7 to 15 days for mail to get to the United States. Receiving mail in Italy, especially packages, can sometimes take longer than you'd think: like weeks.

Most post offices are open Monday–Saturday 9–12:30; central post offices are open weekdays 9–6:30, Saturday 9–12:30. On the last day of the month, post offices close at midday. You can buy stamps at tobacco shops as well as post offices.

An expensive express delivery, *Postacelere* (for larger letters and packages), guarantees one-day delivery to most places in Italy and three- to five-day delivery abroad.

Mail sent to the United States costs €0.85 for up to 20 grams, €1.50 for 21–50 grams, and €1.85 for 51–100 grams. Mail sent as Postacelere to the United States costs €43–€50 for up to 500 grams.

Other package services to check are Quick Pack Europe, for delivery within Europe; and EMS Express Mail Service, a global three- to five-day service for letters and packages that can be less expensive than Postacelere.

Two-day mail is generally available during the week in all major cities and at popular resorts via UPS and Federal Express. Service is reliable; a Federal Express letter to the United States costs about €35. If your hotel can't assist you, try an Internet café, many of which also offer two-day mail services using major carriers—though keep in mind, you'll pay more for this service.

SHIPPING PACKAGES

You can ship parcels via air or surface. Air takes about two weeks, and surface anywhere up to three months to most countries. If you have purchased antiques, ceramics, or other objects, ask if the vendor will do the shipping for you; in most cases, this is a possibility. If so, ask if the article will be insured against breakage. When shipping a package out of Italy, it is virtually impossible to find an overnight delivery option—the fastest delivery time is 48 to 72 hours.

▌ MONEY

As in most countries, prices vary from region to region and are a bit lower in the countryside than in cities. Umbria and the Marches offer good value for money. Admission to the Galleria degli Uffizi is €11 (surcharges for reservations and special exhibits may increase the ticket price). A movie ticket is €7.50. A daily English-language newspaper is €2.50. A taxi ride (1 km [1 mile]) costs around €9.

Prices throughout this guide are given for adults, in euros. Substantially reduced fees are sometimes available for children, students, and senior citizens from the EU; citizens of non-EU countries rarely get discounts, but be sure to inquire before you purchase your tickets, because this situation is constantly changing.

▌TIP→ Banks never have every foreign currency on hand, and it may take as long as a week to order. If you're planning to exchange funds before leaving home, don't wait until the last minute.

ATMS AND BANKS

Your own bank may charge a fee for using ATMs abroad or charge for the cost of conversion from euros to dollars. Nevertheless, you'll usually get a better rate of exchange at an ATM than you will at a currency-exchange office or even when changing money inside a bank with a teller. Extracting funds as you need them is also a safer option than carrying around a large amount of cash.

▌TIP→ PIN numbers with more than four digits are not recognized at ATMs in many countries. If yours has five or more, remember to change it before you leave. PIN numbers beginning with a 0 (zero) tend to be rejected in Italy.

Fairly common in banks in large and small towns, as well as in airports and train stations, ATMs are the easiest way to get euros in Italy. All major banks are members of Cirrus and/or Plus. You won't find an ATM (*bancomat* in Italian) in hotels or grocery stores, however. Before you leave home, memorize your PIN in numbers, not letters, because ATM keypads in Italy frequently don't show letters. Check with your bank to confirm that you have an international PIN (*codice segreto*), to find out your maximum daily withdrawal allowance, and to learn what the bank fee is for withdrawing money.

CREDIT CARDS

In Italy, Visa and MasterCard are preferred over American Express, but in tourist areas American Express is usually accepted. While increasingly common, credit cards aren't accepted at all establishments, and some places require a minimum expenditure. If you want to pay with a card in a small hotel, store, or restaurant, it's a good idea to make your intentions known early on. ■TIP→ Notify your credit-card companies of your travel plans before you leave home; the recent fraud prevention programs frequently suspend a cardholder's credit when foreign activity is detected on the card.

CURRENCY AND EXCHANGE

The euro is the main unit of currency in Italy, as well as in 16 other European countries. Under the euro system, there are eight coins: 1, 2, 5, 10, 20, and 50 *centesimi* (cents, at 100 centesimi to the euro), and 1 and 2 euros. There are seven notes: 5, 10, 20, 50, 100, 200, and 500 euros.

At press time, the exchange rate is about 75 European cents to US$1.

■TIP→ Even if a currency-exchange booth has a sign promising no commission, rest assured that there's some kind of huge, hidden fee. (Oh ... that's right. The sign didn't say no *fee*). And as for rates, you're almost always better off getting foreign currency at an ATM or exchanging money at a bank.

EXCHANGE RATES

Google does currency conversion. Just type in the amount you want to convert and an explanation of how you want it converted (e.g., "14 Swiss francs in dollars"), and then voilà. Oanda.com also allows you to print out a handy table with the current day's conversion rates. XE.com is another good currency conversion website.

Conversion sites Google ⊕ *www.google. com.* **Oanda.com** ⊕ *www.oanda.com.* **XE.com** ⊕ *www.xe.com.*

■ PACKING

If you're traveling between Easter and October, it's always good to pack with layering in mind: it can be very cool in the morning, and then heat up during the course of the day. Murderously hot weather, especially in June, July, and August, calls for breathable fabrics. If you visit in November, pack rain gear, as it seems that all the rain that didn't happen in summer happens then. Winters in most parts of Tuscany and Umbria are not particularly cold, but there are exceptions. Pack your fleece.

You can get aspirin and the like over the counter, though it's best to bring it and other possible necessities with you. It's always wise to travel with tissues, as very often public toilets are not equipped with basic necessities. If you rent a car, be particularly vigilant when making a bathroom or food break: don't leave unattended luggage in the front or back seat of the car—thieves recognize rental cars, and often target them for smash-and-grabs.

■ PASSPORTS AND VISAS

You must have a valid passport for travel to Italy. U.S. citizens who plan to travel or live in Italy or the E.U. for longer than 90 days must acquire a valid visa from the Italian consulate serving their state before leaving the United States. Plan ahead, because the process of obtaining a visa will take at least 30 days and the Italian government does not accept visa applications submitted by visa expediters. ■**TIP→** Before your trip, make two copies of your passport's data page (one for someone at home and another for you to carry separately). Or scan the page and email it to someone at home and/or yourself.

U.S. Passport Information U.S. Department of State ☏ 877/487–2778 ⊕ travel.state.gov/passport.

U.S. Passport Expediters American Passport Express ☏ 800/455–5166 or 603/559–9888 ⊕ www.americanpassport.com. **Passport Express** ☏ 800/362–8196 or 401/272–4612 ⊕ www.passportexpress.com. **Travel Document Systems** ☏ 877/874–5100 or 202/638–3800 ⊕ www.traveldocs.com.

■ RESTROOMS

Standards of cleanliness and comfort vary greatly in Tuscany and Umbria. The type of toilet might be small and low with no seat or even a porcelain hole in the floor with places for your feet. In cities, restaurants, hotel common areas, department stores, and McDonald's tend to have the cleanest restrooms. Pubs and bars rank among the worst. Gas stations also have facilities; again, the cleanliness varies greatly. Carry tissues with you wherever you go, in case there's no paper.

Pay and attendant-supervised restrooms are available in large towns and cities. (You can get a map of the pay toilets in Florence at city tourist-information offices.) Expect to pay or tip €0.60. There are restrooms in most museums and all airports and train stations; in major train stations you'll also find well-kept pay toilets for €0.60 to €0.75; in Florence, it's €1 at the main train station at Santa Maria Novella. (If you can make it out of the train station, you'll pay only €0.60 at the nearby public facilities just outside the basilica of Santa Maria Novella.) Churches, post offices, and public beaches don't have restrooms.

■ SAFETY

Don't wear an exterior money belt or a waist pack, both of which peg you as a tourist. If you carry a bag or camera, be absolutely sure it has straps; you should sling it across your body bandolier-style and adjust the height to hip level or higher. Always be astutely aware of pickpockets, especially when on city buses, when making your way through train corridors, and in busy piazzas.

Women traveling alone in Tuscany and Umbria encounter few special problems. Younger women have to put up with male attention, but it's rarely dangerous. Ignoring whistling and questions is a good way to get rid of unwanted attention; a firm *no, vai via* ("no, go away") sometimes works, too.

■**TIP→** Distribute your cash, credit cards, IDs, and other valuables between a deep front pocket, an inside jacket or vest pocket, and a hidden money pouch. Don't reach for the money pouch once you're in public.

Contact Transportation Security Administration (TSA). ⊕ www.tsa.gov.

■ TAXES

An embarkation tax of €3.72 (between Italy and EU destinations) or €8.26 (international flights) will be included as part of your airline ticket cost.

When making a purchase, ask for a V.A.T. refund form and find out whether the merchant gives refunds—not all stores do, nor are they required to. Have the form stamped like any customs form by customs officials when you leave the country or, if you're visiting several European Union countries, when you leave the EU. After you're through passport control, take the form to a refund-service counter for an on-the-spot refund (which is usually the quickest and easiest option), or mail it to the address on the form (or the envelope with it) after you arrive home. You receive the total refund stated on the form, but the processing time can be long, especially if you request a credit-card adjustment.

Global Refund is a Europe-wide service with 225,000 affiliated stores and more than 700 refund counters at major airports and border crossings. Its refund form, called a Tax Free Check, is the most common across the European continent. The service issues refunds in the form of cash, check, or credit-card adjustment.

V.A.T. Refunds Global Refund ☎ 866/706-6090 ⊕ *www.global-blue.com.*

▌ TIME

Italy is 6 hours ahead of New York (so when it's 1 pm in New York it's 7 pm in Florence). Like the rest of Europe, Italy uses the 24-hour (or "military") clock, which means that after 12 noon you continue counting forward: 13:00 is 1 pm, 23:30 is 11:30 pm.

Time Zones Timeanddate.com. This website can help you figure out the correct time anywhere in the world. ⊕ *www.timeanddate.com/worldclock.*

▌ TIPPING

The following guidelines apply in major cities; Italians tip—if they tip at all—in smaller amounts in smaller cities and towns. In restaurants in Tuscany and Umbria a service charge of 10% to 15% sometimes appears on your check. It's not necessary to tip in addition to this amount. If service is not included, leave a tip of €2 to not more than 10%. No one tips in bars in Florence.

Tip checkroom attendants 50 European cents per person and restroom attendants 50 European cents (more in expensive hotels and restaurants). Italians rarely tip taxi drivers, which is not to say that you shouldn't do it. A tip of 10%, depending on the length of the journey, is appreciated—but only if the driver is courteous and helps with your luggage. Railway and airport porters charge a fixed rate per bag.

Tip an additional 5% if the porter is especially helpful. Give a barber €1–€1.50 and a hairdresser's assistant €1.50–€4 for a shampoo or cut, depending on the type of establishment.

On sightseeing tours, tip guides about €2 per person for a half-day group tour, more if they are very good. In museums and other sights where admission is free, a contribution (€1) is expected. Service-station attendants are tipped only for special services, for example, 50 European cents for checking your tires.

In hotels, give the portiere (concierge) about 10% of his bill for services, or €2.50–€5 if he has been generally helpful. For two people in a double room, leave the chambermaid about €1 per day, or about €7 a week, in a moderately priced hotel; tip a minimum of €1 for valet or room service. Double amounts in expensive hotels. In very expensive hotels, tip doormen €1 for calling a cab and €1 for carrying bags to the check-in desk, bellhops €2–€4 for carrying your bags to the room, and €2–€3 for room service.

▌ TOURS

GUIDED TOURS

Guided tours are a good option when you don't want to do it all yourself. You travel along with a group (sometimes large, sometimes small), stay in prebooked hotels, eat with your fellow travelers (the cost of meals is sometimes included, sometimes not), and follow a schedule. But not all guided tours are an if-it's-Tuesday-this-must-be-Belgium experience. A knowledgeable guide can take you places that you might never discover on your own. Tours aren't for everyone, but they can be just the thing for trips to places where making travel arrangements are difficult or time-consuming. Whenever you book a guided tour, find out what's included and what isn't. A "land-only" tour includes all your travel (by bus, in most cases) in the destination, but not necessarily your flights to and from or even within it. Also, in most cases prices in tour brochures don't include fees and taxes. And remember that you'll be expected to tip your guide (in cash) at the end of the tour.

SPECIAL-INTEREST TOURS

ART

Abercrombie & Kent ☎ 800/554–7016 ⊕ www.abercrombiekent.com. **Context Travel** ☎ 888/467–1986 ⊕ www.contexttravel.com.

BIKING

Backroads ☎ 800/462–2848 ⊕ www.backroads.com. **Butterfield & Robinson** ☎ 866/551–9090 ⊕ www.butterfield.com. **Ciclismo Classico** ☎ 800/866–7314 ⊕ www.ciclismoclassico.com.

CULINARY

Divina Cucina ⊕ www.divinacucina.com. **Epiculinary** ☎ 888/380–9010 ⊕ www.epiculinary.com. **Faith Willinger** ⊕ www.faithwillinger.com. **Toscana Saporita** ⊕ www.toscanasaporita.it. **Tuscan Women Cook** ☎ 815/717–7295 ⊕ www.tuscanwomencook.com.

CULTURE

Context Travel ☎ 888/467–1986 ⊕ www.contexttravel.com. **Exploritas** ☎ 800/454–5768 ⊕ www.exploritas.org. **Italian Connection** ☎ 800/462–7911 ⊕ www.italian-connection.com. **Travcoa** ☎ 800/002–2005 ⊕ www.travcoa.com.

HIKING

Backroads ☎ 800/462–2848 ⊕ www.backroads.com. **Country Walkers** ☎ 800/464–9255 ⊕ www.countrywalkers.com.

SHOPPING

Take My Mother Please ☎ 323/737–2200 ⊕ www.takemymotherplease.com.

VOLUNTEER PROGRAMS

Exploritas ☎ 800/454–5768 ⊕ www.exploritas.org.

WINE

Food & Wine Trails ☎ 800/367–5348 ⊕ www.foodandwinetrails.com.

▌TRIP INSURANCE

Comprehensive trip insurance is valuable if you're booking a very expensive or complicated trip (particularly to an isolated region) or if you're booking far in advance. Comprehensive policies typically cover trip-cancellation and interruption, letting you cancel or cut your trip short because of illness, or, in some cases, acts of terrorism in your destination. Such policies might also cover evacuation and medical care. Some also cover you for trip delays because of bad weather or mechanical problems as well as for lost or delayed luggage.

Another type of coverage to consider is financial default—that is, when your trip is disrupted because a tour operator, airline, or cruise line goes out of business. Generally you must buy this when you book your trip or shortly thereafter, and it's available to you only if your operator isn't on a list of excluded companies.

Always read the fine print of your policy to make sure that you're covered for the risks that most concern you. Compare several policies to be sure you're getting the best price and range of coverage available.

Insurance Comparison Info Insure My Trip ☎ 800/487–4722 ⊕ www.insuremytrip.com. **Square Mouth** ☎ 800/240–0369 ⊕ www.squaremouth.com.

Comprehensive Insurers Access America ☎ 800/284–8300 ⊕ www.accessamerica.com. **AIG Travel Guard** ☎ 800/826–4919 ⊕ www.travelguard.com. **CSA Travel Protection** ☎ 877/243–4135 ⊕ www.csatravelprotection.com. **Travelex Insurance** ☎ 800/228–9792 ⊕ www.travelex-insurance.com. **Travel Insured International** ☎ 800/243–3174 ⊕ www.travelinsured.com.

INDEX

PHOTO CREDITS

NOTES

ABOUT

After completi... ...fending the
art history, **Pete**... ...ours in Chi-
nently in Italy... ...nner parties,
worked as a... ... our Experi-
guide, managin... ...Tuscany, and
most of his Ital...
leading a trip, y... ...y birth with
Chianti, listeni... ...1e, has been
his next journey. ... ...teaching courses in language, literature,
Tuscany, Eastern Tuscany, and Southern and translation at the university in Peru-
Tuscany chapters. gia since the early 1990s. He updated our
Umbria chapter.

Florence resident **Patricia Rucidlo** holds
master's degrees in Italian Renaissance
history and art history. When she's not
extolling the virtues of a Pontormo